THIRD EDITION

POWERFUL DESIGNS

for Professional Learning

EDITED BY LOIS BROWN EASTON

THE PROFESSIONAL LEARNING ASSOCIATION

Learning Forward
504 S. Locust St.
Oxford, OH 45056
800-727-7288
Fax: 513-523-0638
Email: office@learningforward.org
www.learningforward.org

Powerful Designs for Professional Learning
Third Edition
Edited by Lois Brown Easton

Editor: Joyce Pollard
Copy editor: Tracy Crow
Designers: Sue Chevalier and Jane Thurmond
Photo credits: Thinkstock

Printed in the United States of America
Item B587

ISBN: 978-0-9903158-1-0

Contents

CONTENTS

Online Resources

All online resources can be found at http://learningforward.org/publications/powerfuldesigns
For access, use password DesignPL315.

Preface

By Lois Brown Easton

Welcome to the third edition of the best-selling Learning Forward book *Powerful Designs for Professional Learning.* The first edition was published in 2004, and the second edition in 2008. Although this is called the third edition, in many ways, it is more like a third volume. Fifteen of the 24 designs in this version are new; the rest of the chapters have been revised. Most of the new designs and some of the designs originally in the first or second edition also incorporate some aspect of technology. The chart on the next two pages shows the changes from edition to edition.

Think of this, then, as the third volume in a series, adding a set of new designs and new takes on some of the designs presented in the first and second volumes.

First edition	Second edition	Third edition
Accessing Student Voices by Harvetta Robertson and Shirley Hord	Accessing Student Voices by Harvetta Robertson and Shirley Hord	**Accessing Student Voices** by Kathleen Cushman
Action Research by Cathy Caro-Bruce	Action Research by Cathy Caro-Bruce	**Action Research** by Cathy Caro-Bruce and Mary Klehr
Assessment as Professional Development by Jay McTighe and Marcella Emberger	Assessment as Professional Learning by Jay McTighe and Marcella Emberger	**Assessment as Professional Learning** by Jay McTighe and Marcella Emberger
Case Discussions by Carne Barnett-Clarke and Alma Ramirez	Case Discussions by Carne Barnett-Clarke and Alma Ramirez	
Classroom Walk-Throughs by Margery B. Ginsberg	Classroom Walk-Throughs by Carolyn J. Downey	**Classroom Walk-Throughs for Peers** by Carolyn J. Downey
		Coaching Principals by Kay Psencik
		Collaborative Assessment of Student Learning by Amy B. Colton and Georgea M. Langer
Critical Friends Groups by Stevi Quate	Critical Friends Groups by Stevi Quate	**Critical Friends Groups** by Stevi Quate
Curriculum Designers by Linda Hummel Fitzharris	Curriculum Design by Linda Hummel Fitzharris	**Curriculum as Professional Learning** by Eleanor Dougherty, Stacy Galiatsos, and Anne C. Lewis
Data Analysis by Victoria L. Bernhardt	Data Analysis by Victoria L. Bernhardt	**Data Analysis** by Victoria L. Bernhardt
	Dialogue by Oscar Graybill	**Dialogue** by Oscar Graybill
	Differentiated Coaching by Jane A. G. Kise	
		Digital Teacher Portfolios by David Niguidula
Immersing Teachers in Practice by Mary Ann Smith	Immersing Teachers in Practice by Mary Ann Smith	
		Instructional Coaching by Chris Bryan, Heather Clifton, and Cindy Harrison
		Instructional Rounds by Lee Teitel
Journaling by Joellen Killion	Journaling by Joellen Killion	
Lesson Study by Catherine C. Lewis	Lesson Study by Catherine C. Lewis	**Lesson Study** by Catherine C. Lewis

First edition	Second edition	Third edition
Mentoring by Pam Robbins	Mentoring by Pam Robbins	
		Online Coaching by Joellen Killion
		Online Courses by John D. Ross
		Online Protocols by Alan Dichter and Janet Mannheimer Zydney
Peer Coaching by Pam Robbins		
Portfolios for Educators by Mary E. Dietz	Portfolios for Educators by Mary E. Dietz	
		Professional Learning Communities by Lois Brown Easton
School Coaching by Patricia W. McNeil and Steven M. Klink	School Coaching by Patricia W. McNeil and Steven M. Klink	
Shadowing Students by Lois Brown Easton	Shadowing by Lois Brown Easton	**Shadowing** by Michael Soguero, Dan Condon, Colin Packard, and Lois Brown Easton
		Social Media by Lynmarie Hilt
Standards in Practice by Ruth Mitchell	Standards in Practice by Ruth Mitchell and Shana Kennedy-Salchow	
Study Groups by Carlene Murphy and Mike Murphy	Study Groups by Carlene Murphy and Mike Murphy	
		Teacher-Led Conferences by Matthew Esterman and Cameron Paterson
Training the Trainer by Joellen Killion and Cindy Harrison	Training the Trainer by Joellen Killion and Cindy Harrison	
Tuning Protocols by Lois Brown Easton	Tuning Protocols by Lois Brown Easton	
	Video by Sandi Everlove and Brian White	**Videos** by Pat Wasley
Visual Dialogue by Suzanne Bailey	Visual Dialogue by Suzanne Bailey and Lois Brown Easton	**Visual Dialogue** by Suzanne Bailey and Lois Brown Easton
		Webinars by Tom Manning

The link to the Standards for Professional Learning

Although many of the designs have changed from edition to edition, one thing has been constant. The designs were selected, in part, because they exemplified Learning Forward's Standards for Professional Learning.

The tight relationship between the standards and the designs is significant. The designs represent what the best minds in the profession about how professional learning can be effective — that is, resulting in educator changes in practice that lead to improvement of student learning.

Take a close look at the Learning Designs standard: Professional learning that increases educator effectiveness and results for all students **integrates theories, research, and models of human learning to achieve its intended outcomes.** You will find in each chapter descriptions of and references to the theories, research, and models of human learning that validate the designs.

The Learning Designs standard also promotes the **careful choice of design.** You will find two models for choosing designs in "Design: Form and Structure for Learning." In that chapter, you will also find a set of charts that will help you choose appropriate designs.

Another important aspect of the Learning Designs standard is **active engagement,** which is a given in the chapters included in this and former editions of *Powerful Designs* — we would never call a learning design powerful if it didn't result in educators' active engagement in learning.

Why has it been a bestseller?

It is no wonder that *Powerful Designs for Professional Learning* has been a bestseller. Each edition pulled together the best that was known about powerful professional learning strategies. For each design, the books followed a similar format: a narrative about the strategy in use, an overview, a rationale, concrete steps for implementation of the strategy, alternatives and essentials and — in the third version — challenges and how to address them.

The person who wanted theory and research found it. The person who craved information about how to do something got specific, implementable steps. The person who worried about getting stuck — or had gotten stuck — could revisit the alternatives, essentials, and challenges related to the design.

Many readers may find that the stories are the most important part of the chapters. The stories let the reader in on what the strategy looks like in practice. They establish a culture of use through depiction of the language and actions used by people involved in the strategy not just the facilitator but the participants.

How *Powerful Designs* has been used

The first and second editions of *Powerful Designs* were used by a myriad of professional educators. The growth of learning communities, going by various names, made it incumbent on school-based educators to figure out what to do in these communities. *Powerful Designs* filled a need by presenting a variety of designs that educators in PLCs could choose to guide their learning to improve classrooms and schools as a whole. Teachers and teacher leaders made study of the book a part of the agenda of their learning community. With data in hand, educators researched possible approaches to studying the data and implementing improvement strategies. Some chose to deepen their understanding by expanding the data they collected and using a sophisticated process for analyzing it. Others achieved a similar end through action research or lesson study. Some chose to revise curriculum and assessment processes.

Principals and assistant principals, seeking ways to shape a school culture focused on professional learning, used the book as a resource when working with faculties.

District supervisors (assistant superintendents or directors of professional learning or curriculum, for example) used the book as a resource for their interactions with school faculties. They used the book as a reference tool for professional learning designs that they could recommend. They consulted the book in terms of the roles they could play as leaders. They used the book as a guide for facilitating professional learning in schools. They also used the book to facilitate the work of cross-school or districtwide teams. In some cases, they used the book for their own and their district-level colleagues' professional learning.

State-level educators used the book as a reference tool, as well, recommending strategies to district- and school-level educators. Some used the book as an example of the kind of professional learning that policy makers should support. Others used the book as a way to develop their own and their colleagues' capacities.

Third-party providers have used the book in similar ways, often providing professional learning for constituent schools and districts based on designs in the book. Similarly, consultants have designed their services around powerful professional learning designs featured in the books.

Finally, university and college professors have used *Powerful Designs* along with the standards to introduce teachers-to-be to the kind of professional learning they should expect when they become part of the teaching force. Rather than "sit-n-git," educators have a right to expect real professional learning opportunities from the schools and districts they join.

How will you use this book?

I urge you to think of this book as three resources in one:

1. A culture-changer in terms of presenting specific portraits of how professionals should be treated in schools and districts;
2. Examples of the Learning Forward standards in action;
3. A how-to guide for 24 powerful designs.

The book is worth studying in a book study group or professional learning community. It is worth individual reading from start to finish, accompanied by dialogue either online or face-to-face, or both.

It is also a book for dipping into, skimming to see what interests you, and then digging deeply to explore these interests.

It is meant to be provocative in the sense that it provokes you to think about what you want for yourself and your colleagues in terms of professional learning. It is meant to be reassuring in the sense that it gives you specific instructions about how to implement a set of designs. Finally, it is meant to lead you to powerful learning — your own and your colleagues'.

PART I

Design: Form and Structure for Learning

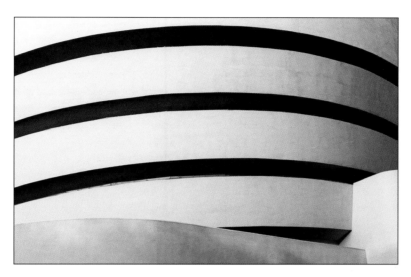

Design is one element of effective professional learning.

By Lois Brown Easton

This book is called *Powerful Designs for Professional Learning.* The word *design* has been used intentionally in the title of the book from the first edition to this third edition. The word is also the essence — along with the word *learning* — of a book I wrote for Learning Forward and Corwin Press in 2011, *Professional Learning Communities By Design: Putting the Learning Back Into PLCs.*

When I think of design, I think of Frank Lloyd Wright. His architecture was ***contextual, creative, considered,*** and ***consequential.*** Wright's architecture was contextual in terms of emanating from him, personally, and from his environment. His designs reflected his worldview — his beliefs, philosophy, perspectives, passions, and values — and his world, whether a stream in Pennsylvania or a saguaro in the desert Southwest. His designs were contextual in that they were both personal and situated.

There is no question about Frank Lloyd Wright's creativity. Visit Fallingwater to see why it was called "the best all-time work of American architecture" by the American Institute of Architects (Brewster, 2004). Walk the spiral of the Guggenheim Museum in New York City and feel awe not only for the art, but also for the architecture. Wright created wonderful wrap-around windows, stylistic stained glass panels, organic furniture that promoted particular building angles, and site locations that provided vistas from every viewpoint. He was creative in terms of the largest structures (the Johnson Wax Headquarters in Racine, Wisconsin, for example) and the smallest details (the light fixtures at Taliesin West, for example).

Wright's designs were considered in that they were thoughtful, careful, reflective, and based on the coherence of his knowledge and skills. His Usonian houses, for example, were designed for the needs of twentieth century middle-class families who would not have servants. He focused on urban design and community planning throughout his career, considering every aspect of his designs in terms of purpose, melding everything he knew with users' needs.

Wright's architecture has had consequences, not just for those who lived or worked in his structures — or still live and work in them — but also those who learned from him. His philosophy of architecture as organic, as well as his works, including over 1000 designs and more than 530 actual structures, led to a movement called The Prairie School. Architects continue to study these at Taliesin West in Scottsdale, Arizona, and around the world.

Powerful designs for professional learning require the same "4 Cs": They need to be contextual, creative, considered, and consequential. In schools, both teachers' and students' contexts, as well as the knowledge, skills, and past experiences that teachers consider as they create students' learning experiences, ensure that these experiences will be consequential. To be more specific, teachers refer to their own and their students' contexts, or their beliefs, philosophy, perspectives, passions, and values when they design learning experiences. They also fit these learning experiences to the needs of their students and school, district, state/provincial/prefectural, and, sometimes, national contexts. As they create, they bring to bear their knowledge, skills, experience, and wisdom. These learning experiences produce results, or consequences. In the case of professional learning, the consequences or results are adult learning that leads to enhanced student learning.

Models of powerful professional learning designs

The 4Cs fit nicely with two models of effective professional learning. The first is the Backmapping Model for Planning Results-Based Professional Learning, created by Joellen Killion and Patricia Roy for *Becoming a Learning School* (2009). Second is an "Anatomy of Professional Learning Designs" from *Designing Professional Learning* (2014), co-published by Learning Forward and the Australian Institute of Teaching and School Leadership. (See Online Resources D.1 and D.2.)

The Backmapping Model

The Backmapping Model for Planning Results-Based

Professional Learning (see Figure 1 on p. 5) begins and ends with students — as all professional learning should.

In this model, a learning design requires that leaders first analyze student learning needs in Step 1. In Step 2, they consider the environment of the learning. In Step 3, they develop learning needs into improvement goals and specific student outcomes. From those outcomes, they identify educator learning needs in Step 4. In Step 5, leaders study the theory, research, and models. In Steps 6 and 7, they implement the design and make changes to enhance student learning, which is the desired destination of this cycle. The cycle can be repeated as needs change.

The Anatomy

The second model sharpens the focus of Step 5 in the Backmapping Model. The second model, called The Anatomy of Professional Learning Designs (see Figure 2 on p. 5) was co-published in 2014 by Learning Forward and the Australian Institute of Teaching and School Leadership (AITSL). The purpose of the AITSL work was to investigate the key elements of effective professional learning design; more specifically, "to give greater guidance around the 'how' of professional learning construction" (p. 2). The model is built upon the following logic sequence:

Context > Educator Learning >
Implementation > Student Outcomes

While the entire logic sequence acknowledges that designs occur in a context, lead to implementation of new practices and, ultimately, result in student outcomes, the AITSL model focuses only on the "Educator Learning" ring of the logic sequence.

The researchers for this study, Lois Brown Easton and Terry Morganti-Fisher (2014), reviewed over 50 professional learning designs. They narrowed the designs to be investigated to 28 and divided them into "general" and proprietary, "name-brand" designs (see sidebar on p. 6, Final list of designs). Many professional learning designs, such as action research, professional learning communities, and lesson study have substantial general- and local-proof research to support their effectiveness. Others, especially new technology-based designs, such as Eduplanet21, Success at the Core, Learning Channel, and Teachscape, are just beginning to collect research that attests to their value.

Figure 1:
Backmapping Model for Planning Results-Based Professional Learning

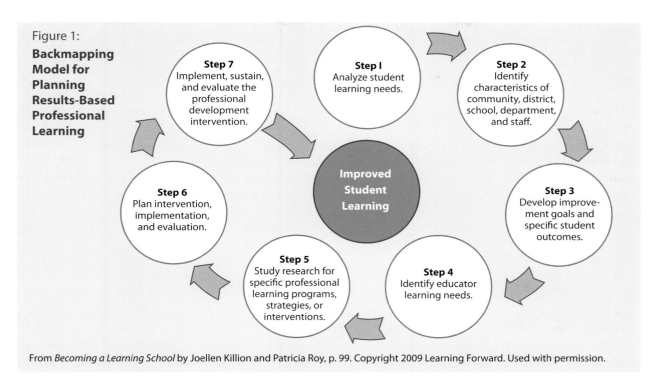

From *Becoming a Learning School* by Joellen Killion and Patricia Roy, p. 99. Copyright 2009 Learning Forward. Used with permission.

Figure 2:
The Anatomy of Professional Learning Designs

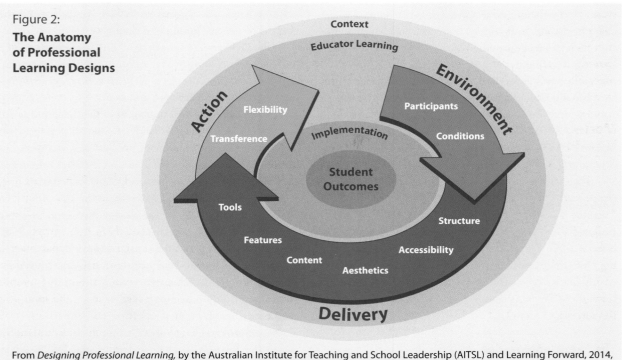

From *Designing Professional Learning,* by the Australian Institute for Teaching and School Leadership (AITSL) and Learning Forward, 2014, p. 6. Copyright 2014 Australian Institute for Teaching and School Leadership (AITSL). Used with permission.

Final list of designs	
General learning designs	**Specific, proprietary learning designs**
1. Action research	1. Collaborative Analysis of Student Learning (CASL)
2. Case discussions	2. edWeb.net
3. Coaching and online coaching	3. Eduplanet21
4. Curriculum, instruction, and assessment	4. Learning School Alliance
5. Data analysis	5. Literacy Design Collaborative
6. Dialogue and visual dialogue	6. PD 360
7. Gaming	7. Project-based learning
8. Innovation incubators	8. Project Zero & Visible Thinking
9. Lesson study	9. Success at the Core
10. Massive Open Online Courses (MOOCs)	10. Teaching Channel
11. Online courses	11. Teachscape
12. Portfolios and digital portfolios	
13. Professional learning communities	
14. Protocols and online protocols	
15. Rounds, walk-throughs, and shadowing	
16. Simulations	
17. Teacher-led conferences	

The authors scrutinized the 28 designs, teasing out the factors that made them effective according to research or to acclaim. They identified a set of elements that seemed to cut across the designs and grouped these into components. The model that emerged from their work is called The Anatomy because it is "a complex structure of internal workings, all of which affect and depend upon one another. As a structure for considering learning designs, the Anatomy can be viewed 'piece by piece' or as the whole, the 'sum of parts'" (p. 8).

The AITSL (2014) document identifies 10 key elements common to all effective professional learning designs, grouped under three broad components:

Components	Elements
Environment	• Participants • Conditions
Delivery	• Structure • Accessibility • Aesthetics • Content • Features • Tools
Action	• Transference • Flexibility

The **Environment** component focuses on the elements of *participants* and *conditions*, and roughly corresponds

to Steps 1–4 of the Backmapping Model. Having already determined purpose that is based on student and adult learning needs, educational leaders can concentrate on the context or the environment of the learners.

The **Delivery** component roughly corresponds to Step 5 of the Backmapping Model. According to this component, educators focus on the elements of *structure, accessibility, aesthetics, content features,* and *tools.*

Structure. The most pragmatic of the elements for this component, it is "concerned with the practical arrangements of learning, i.e. the amount of time it takes and decisions about location and sequence of events" (p. 10). Context and purposes for learning usually drive decisions about structure.

Accessibility. This element refers to the ease with which the learner can engage in the design. Accessible learning design is based on strategies that enable the user to participate without difficulty. Online, accessible design is seen "in a website's architecture, i.e. an intuitive layout. In face-to-face learning, accessibility may include things such as time commitment or pre-reading, convenience of location, and the way the activity is facilitated" (p. 10).

Aesthetics. This element "refers to those aspects of a learning design that elicit a sensory response from the participant. Aesthetic choices within a learning design include decisions about the visual, auditory, and physical construction of the professional learning that enable engagement with the learning" (p. 10). These may seem small considerations, but aesthetics can factor into whether participants engage or disengage with the learning.

Content. This element refers to the Knowledge, Attitudes, Behaviors, Skills, and Aspirations [KASAB] (Killion, 2008) that educators address in professional learning. "Content may be subject-area specific or related to pedagogical, personal or professional knowledge or practice. The alignment between content, purpose and context is critical" (AITSL, 2014, p. 11).

Features. These elements "are the practices associated with the delivery of, or mode of participation in, professional learning" (p. 11). Features include the following approaches:

- Face to face;
- Remote or onsite;
- Self-directed or facilitated;
- Online;
- Individual or collaborative;
- And any blended forms of these features.

Choice of features depends on the purposes of the learning, the nature of the activities, the participants' contexts, and conditions such as time and access to experts.

Tools. These elements are "instruments used to enhance knowledge transfer, deepen engagement and support understanding of content aims" (p. 11). They are generally interactive elements such as "templates, proformas or schematics, surveys, forms, questions, polls or other interactive elements," which "encourage the learner to test and apply their understanding as an active participant in the learning" (p. 11).

The third component **Action** corresponds to the sixth and seventh steps of the Backmapping Model by calling for design "aspects leading to implementation of learning, translating learning into practice" (p. 18). Such translation happens "through tailored support or an agile design that allows the learner and the design to be effective over time and in a range of contexts" (p. 18). Effective designs are likely to help learners engage in "integrated and iterative" professional learning such as "collaborative problem-solving, inquiry and research projects, peer observation, and feedback programs" (p. 18).

Transference is one element related to the action component. It "is concerned with aspects of the learning design that directly support the application of learning, in

context" (p. 18). Transference is about "the ease with which participants transfer new knowledge and understanding, implementing their learning. Transference may be expressly supported through tailored materials and resources embedded within the learning, designed as scaffolds for use in context, such as templates, guides or outlines" (p. 18).

Flexibility. This element "refers to the degree to which educators are supported to reflect on and evaluate their learning and apply it in a variety of situations and contexts over time" (p. 18). A design is flexible when it is "broad enough to provide professional learning for a variety of situations. It will support educators to link their learning to changes in the classroom or school and implement new learnings, perhaps even in a different way to what was originally intended" (p. 18).

The AITSL (2014) report features a thorough description of these components and elements as well as examples of designs for many of them. These examples are not meant to be exclusive nor perfect, but they do provide illustrations of the text. A series of questions helps professional learning leaders consider which designs would be appropriate for the following uses:

- Developing new professional learning;
- Enhancing existing professional learning; and
- Evaluating professional learning.

Criteria for gauging the effectiveness of professional learning designs

As both models suggest, the effectiveness of a professional learning design is related to its appropriateness within a particular context. What works well in one setting may work dismally in another setting. Think of this relationship as a Venn diagram:

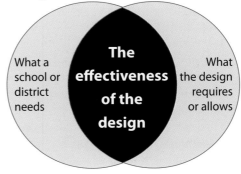

What a school or district needs — The effectiveness of the design — What the design requires or allows

Some designs cannot be altered to fit the needs of a district or school without significantly compromising the integrity of the design. However, what a design does not offer can be taken on by the school or district — as long as leaders have determined where they'll need to fill in the gaps. For example, many designs do not formally address implementation of new ideas or the problems educators may encounter during implementation; schools and districts may need to institute other designs — such as coaching or professional learning communities — to ensure that learning is implemented in the classroom. Multiple designs — essentially a *program* of professional learning — may be needed to meet the needs of a school or district.

Combining the two models and the 4 Cs creates a set of criteria for evaluating a learning design's potential for effectiveness. Here are criteria from the models, expressed as questions:

1. **Why** is professional learning needed? What are the purposes of professional learning? What consequences or outcomes are expected? What are the needs in terms of students?

2. **Who** needs to be involved in professional learning? What are the characteristics of the various communities (district, school, department, grade level, etc.) within which the adult learners function? What are the current conditions for adult learning? How well do these contexts and the conditions within them support adult learning? How could conditions within these contexts be improved to support learning related to the purposes of professional learning?

3. **How** will a selected design help the adults accomplish their purposes within their contexts? How flexible is the design? Can it be altered in terms of structure to be more effective — without compromising the integrity of the design? Can the users supplement the design where it is weak? In particular, in terms of **how** the design works,

   a. Is it accessible, whether face to face, online, or blended (affecting the **when** and **where** of design)?

   b. Is it aesthetic, that is, likely to have a positive effect on participants?

   c. Is the content the right content for the purpose, the participants, and the context?

   d. How well do the features of the design — the processes — encourage deep learning and implementation?

   e. How well do the tools help adults learn?

4. How well does the design encourage action and implementation as a result of learning? In particular, does the design include activities that help participants transfer and apply their learning? If not, how can the school, district and other entities help with transfer and application of learning?

5. How well does the design help participants evaluate their own learning and apply it in new contexts?

The designs in this book

The designs in this book have been selected because they are examples of effective design intended to improve educators' professional learning in order to improve student success. The entries are followed by descriptive symbols.

New chapters that were not in the first or second editions	NEW!
Chapters with a focus on technology	TECH
Chapters that were in the first and second editions, but have been updated, often to address uses of technology in the design	UPDATED

Accessing Student Voices – Kathleen Cushman
As a journalist who has documented student ideas on their lives and learning in books such as *Fires in the Bathroom: What Kids Can Tell Us About Motivation and Mastery* and on videos available online through WKCD (What Kids Can Do), Cushman uses plenty of student examples to describe how educators can learn from students and improve school culture. TECH NEW!

Action Research – Cathy Caro-Bruce and Mary Klehr
Caro-Bruce and Klehr describe a challenging issue that a teacher bravely takes on as an action research project. Using the classic steps for action research, she discovers what needs to be done, does it, and then reflects on and shares the results. The authors share strategies and techniques for making action research productive in today's schools. UPDATED

Assessment as Professional Learning – Jay McTighe and Marcella Embarger
McTighe and Embarger describe how professional learning occurs when educators collaboratively design and review standards-linked performance assessment tasks, including evaluation and anchoring resulting student work. They

address the effect of the Common Core State Standards (Common Core) on curriculum and assessment. TECH

Classroom Walk-Throughs for Peers – Carolyn J. Downey
Downey focuses on how peer educators can use classroom walk-throughs followed by reflective questions to help each other learn and make improvements within classrooms and schools. For Downey, the one critical aspect of walk-throughs is that reflective questions are not used to give feedback but to start productive professional conversations. UPDATED

Coaching Principals – Kay Psencik
Psencik describes how district leaders can ensure they build a successful system of support and effective, in-depth learning experiences for principals, with a focus on providing them professional coaches. She discusses coaching generally, as well as special considerations related to coaching principals. She provides strategies for embedding coaching within a principal's professional learning support. NEW!

Collaborative Analysis of Student Learning –
Amy B. Colton and Georgea M. Langer
Colton and Langer write about a process that bases school change on the analysis of student work. The process they describe is eminently doable because educators form small teams, work together to analyze and improve the learning of two or three students each, and share their work with other teams so that the whole school becomes a learning community. NEW!

Critical Friends Groups – Stevi Quate
Quate focuses on a unique form of professional learning community that has passed the test of time. Participants in critical friends groups (CFGs) focus on problems of practice and challenge each other to make substantive and significant changes in their classrooms and their schools as a whole. The deep conversations made possible through critical friend relationships benefit both adult and student learning. UPDATED

Curriculum as Professional Learning –
Eleanor Dougherty, Stacy Galiatsos, and Anne C. Lewis
Dougherty, Galiatsos, and Lewis describe how the Literacy Design Collaborative (LDC) helps educators learn together

as they create challenging assignments for use across the curriculum to promote higher levels of thinking, reading, and writing, using the Common Core State Standards as a basis for design. The online templates are a special feature of the LDC process and yield a rigorous and exciting curriculum. TECH NEW!

Data Analysis – Victoria L. Bernhardt
Bernhardt updates her classic description of how to gather and analyze four types of data. The author provides data from an example school (see Online Resources for this chapter). By analyzing another school's data, educators become learners in their own environments and are able to apply those lessons to make targeted changes that improve student learning. UPDATED

Dialogue – Oscar Graybill
Graybill argues for the benefits of face-to-face communication, especially the special form of talking called *dialogue,* in a world that is becoming increasingly face-to-machine. He describes the benefits of dialogue in terms of school culture and presents all the information a reader needs to engage with others in dialogue. UPDATED

Digital Teacher Portfolios – David Niguidula
Niguidula, an early advocate and developer of an online approach to portfolios, describes how educators collect and select artifacts and reflect on them through development of their portfolios. Through a **purposeful** process, educators find that portfolios are much more than just a collection of artifacts. TECH NEW!

Instructional Coaching – Chris Bryan, Heather Clifton, and Cindy Harrison
Bryan, Clifton, and Harrison establish the mutual learning process that goes on when two educators are engaged in a coaching relationship. Although one is coach and the other the person being coached, both learn and grow as professionals. As a result, teacher practice, student achievement, and school culture are improved. NEW!

Instructional Rounds – Lee Teitel
Teitel describes how participating in rounds benefits both visiting teams of educators and educators in the schools they

visit. His chief example is a network of superintendents, but educators from any role group or mixed role groups can participate in rounds. Teitel's focus is on the thinking that goes into a decision to engage in rounds and use of rounds for professional learning and implementation of new practice. **NEW!**

Lesson Study – Catherine C. Lewis
Lewis continues to focus her research and efforts on improving classroom learning and school culture through lesson study outside Japan, where it began and where it is not considered professional development, but simply a natural process of educators who consider themselves professionals. Her updated chapter highlights the theory and practice of lesson study, as well as recent research about its effectiveness. **UPDATED**

Online Coaching – Joellen Killion
Killion, well-known for her wide-ranging and thoughtful work related to professional learning, focuses on both words in the title: What it means to work online and what it means to coach and be coached. She understands how educators' effectiveness is paramount when working toward student success and presents theories related to coaching and strategies for making the best use of online coaching. **TECH NEW!**

Online Courses – John D. Ross
Ross focuses on the role of the developer of online courses. He zooms in on the fact that an online course must exemplify good instructional design **before** the appropriate technology is selected. He discusses the benefits of online courses, describes how to design them, and helps the reader match media to learning outcomes, even discussing appropriate marketing strategies. **TECH NEW!**

Online Protocols – Alan Dichter and Janet Mannheimer Zydney
Dichter and Zydney emphasize that the solid design principles for face-to-face protocols apply also to online protocols. They share additional principles that apply when protocols are conducted online. Finally, they also describe blended online and face-to-face protocols in detail and provide steps that educators can follow to use them. **TECH NEW!**

Professional Learning Communities – Lois Brown Easton
Easton provides some history of PLCs as well as their defining characteristics. She also summarizes the research on the impact of PLCs. She suggests a list of steps, including a variety of ways to start PLCs; how to configure them in a school; how to build solid relationships; and how important autonomy is in terms of acting on passion. **NEW!**

Shadowing – Michael Soguero, Dan Condon, Colin Packard, and Lois Brown Easton
Present and past educators from Eagle Rock School and Professional Development Center, the authors distinguish shadowing from classroom walk-throughs and rounds. They describe the steps for shadowing for a host school as well as visiting educators. **UPDATED**

Social Media – Lynmarie Hilt
Hilt shares the perspectives of both principals and teachers in her discussion of the use of social networks to forge relationships with other educators, access and share resources, and collaborate to learn. Her discussion of theory focuses on connectivism, and she provides specific steps and details that help any educator connect. **TECH NEW!**

Teacher-Led Conferences – Matthew Esterman and Cameron Paterson
Australian educators Matt Esterman and Cameron Paterson were involved in the start-up of TeachMeet Sydney based on TeachMeets in the United Kingdom and elsewhere. Esterman and Paterson describe the basics of this professional learning design known as Edcamps in the U.S. **NEW!**

Videos – Pat Wasley
Wasley, the founder of TeachingChannel and a long-time educational reformer, describes how the use of video addresses the isolation that teachers experience in their classrooms, a situation that has undesirable consequences. Wasley offers examples of the power of videos as well as steps that educators can take to ensure the use of videos deepens learning. **TECH NEW!**

Visual Dialogue – Suzanne Bailey and Lois Brown Easton
In this updated chapter, Bailey and Easton describe both the dynamic of visual dialogue and the follow-up process of gallery tours that help educators translate their collaborative

learning into system-sensitive decisions. Visual dialogue changes the nature of discourse by obliging educators to work together to craft meaning. UPDATED

Webinars – Tom Manning
Manning, associate director of e-Learning for Learning Forward, has worked with educators to design and present over 100 webinars over the last 6 years. In his chapter, he counteracts the perception that webinars are the equivalent of "one-stop workshops" with a set of principles and concrete actions for ensuring that webinars provide for effective adult learning. TECH NEW!

The reality of professional learning

Consider these models and designs as blueprints for professional learning. Just as architectural blueprints detail what a building must be like to function in a particular environment to meet specific purposes, professional learning models and designs address how educators can help all students learn and thrive in today's world. Blueprints — of both the architectural and professional learning kind — must address real world problems and needs. These problems and needs can be understood at a global as well as a local level.

A global perspective on professional learning

Welcome to this world of the "Twenty-Tens" (2010 and beyond). In all parts of our lives, we are challenged to broaden our thinking beyond our neighborhoods and towns. Our state boundaries are evaporating. Our state and national boundaries are permeable. Because of technology, we are just about as likely to converse with someone in another country as we are our neighbors. The problems faced in one country are likely to be problems for other countries as well. The dilemmas of helping educators meet the needs of all students are dilemmas faced round the world.

The Organisation for Economic Cooperation and Development (OECD), replicating a 2008–9 study of teaching and learning, published *TALIS Results: An International Perspective on Teaching and Learning* in 2014. Over 100,000 teachers in middle schools from 34 countries, including the United States, participated in the 2013–14 study. Since 2009, the OECD studies and others have tracked the conditions of teacher professional learning across the globe

(OECD, 2009; Wei et al., 2010; Jaquith et al., 2010). From that research, education decision makers can now point to several global themes related to professional learning:

- Professional learning is requisite for 21st-century teaching and learning.
- In the next decade, most countries face teacher shortages; more importantly, most countries must focus on having enough **quality** teachers in their systems.
- Self-efficacy — an important aspect of job satisfaction — is critical for attracting and keeping the best professionals in schools; professional learning contributes to feelings of self-efficacy.
- Innovation is crucial for schools and teachers especially in the 21st century, and professional learning helps individuals, schools, and systems innovate.
- What's known about effective teaching can be learned.
- What's known about what works in terms of high-quality professional learning can be implemented.
- What's known about school- and system-level conditions that privilege high-quality professional learning can be achieved.
- Standards for professional learning are valuable, whether they're embedded in teacher quality standards or stand alone.
- Every system needs an orientation toward results, both interim and, ultimately, related to student achievement.
- Evaluation systems — designed and used effectively — may be an important leverage for quality professional learning.
- Educators desperately need more professional learning, but they need high-quality and effective professional learning (Easton, 2013, p. 14).

The last theme is a wake-up call for professionals involved in professional learning. Educators around the world want more professional learning. Both TALIS studies found a number of barriers, such as

- Not having prerequisite knowledge;
- Expense;
- Lack of employer support;
- Conflict with work schedule;
- Family responsibilities;
- No incentives for participation;
- No suitable professional learning experiences (OECD, 2009).

Notice the last barrier. Teachers reported that the professional learning they participated in was **not** of high quality. It apparently did not make much of a difference in terms of their professional lives and the lives of their students. They may have been "getting" sufficient professional learning, but they needed **better** professional learning experiences.

I see educators' lack of satisfaction with what they are getting as a design problem. That's why this book is important. It's about designing the best, most effective, professional learning possible for educators around the world.

What's known about professional learning today informs the models and designs in this book. In particular educators know:

1. About adult learning preferences;
2. How the adult brain works;
3. How to address the learning-doing gap;
4. How to clearly describe what works in terms of professional learning through standards, such as Learning Forward's Standards for Professional Learning (2011);
5. About change processes in terms of how individuals and groups make or resist changes;
6. How to embrace a variety of technologies that make effective professional learning possible even when time and distance constrict participation.

Consider how each of these "knowns" shapes professional learning today.

Adult learning preferences

Many educators, behavioral psychologists, and theorists have described adult learning preferences. Jane Vella (1994) provides a comprehensive description of adult learning preferences. Here is a summary of them:

1. Needs assessment: Participation of the learners in naming what is to be learned;
2. Safety in the environment and the process;
3. A sound relationship between teacher and learner for learning and development;
4. Careful attention to sequence of content and reinforcement;
5. Praxis: Action with reflection or learning by doing;
6. Respect for learners as subjects of their own learning;
7. Cognitive, affective, and psychomotor aspects: Ideas, feelings, actions;
8. Immediacy of the learning;

9. Clear roles and role development;
10. Teamwork: Using small groups
11. Engagement of the learners in what they are learning;
12. Accountability: How do they know they know (pp. 3–4).

Think how valuable professional learning would be if it exemplified these characteristics. The designs in this book will help you create professional learning experiences that work for adult learners.

How the adult brain works

In an article for *Educational Leadership* "Revisiting Teacher Learning: Brain-Friendly Learning for Teachers," David Sousa (2009) suggests,

> The brain's biological mechanisms responsible for learning and remembering are roughly the same for learners of different ages. However, the efficiency of these mechanisms varies with the degree of development of the brain regions involved (Shaw et al., 2006). Emotional and social factors and past experiences also enter into play in terms of the brain's efficiency and an individual learner's motivation. Because these factors are more developed in adults than in children, they have greater influence over adults than they have over children. (para. 4)

Sousa shares some insights from neurology, including how social interactions cause gene expression, how neurons lead to action that mirrors what other people are doing (another argument for social learning), neuron regeneration (we never get too old to learn), age-related memory capacity that limits the effect of cramming, the ability of our neurons to hold data longer than previously thought, and the role of exercise and the arts.

Daniel Goleman's research into emotional intelligence (EQ) confirms that we remember events that have an emotion — good or bad — tied to them (Goleman, 2005). According to Sousa (2009), this means:

> How we *feel* about a learning situation often affects attention and memory more quickly than what we *think* about it.... If [a professional learning] activity captures an adult learner's interest, the mature cortex will override any negative feelings, and learning will occur. But teachers who are deeply

annoyed by mandatory attendance or who feel emotionally detached may resist learning. They can conceal their negative feelings, but they may surreptitiously turn to activities like grading papers unless the activity is engaging enough to hook into some positive emotion. (para. 8)

The physiological aspect of this emotional state is compelling:

When people feel positive about a learning situation, chemicals called endorphins and dopamine become active. Endorphins provide a feeling of euphoria. Dopamine stimulates the prefrontal cortex, keeping the individual attentive, interactive, and likely to remember what he or she experiences. Negative feelings, on the other hand, cause the hormone cortisol to enter the bloodstream. Cortisol puts the brain into survival mode; this shifts the brain's attention away from learning so it can deal with the source of stress. Instead of learning, the brain remembers the pressure and registers these kinds of situations as unpleasant. (para. 10)

Sousa (2009) challenges those who plan professional learning experiences for adults to consider several questions related to the emotions of the experience:

- Does the program offer learning experiences associated with moderate challenge, excitement, creativity, and joy so teachers will be more likely to remember what they learn and implement it in the classroom?
- Does the program speak to a problem that teachers identified rather than some outside entity? If not, can we connect this content to teachers' concerns?
- Are teachers excited about this initiative?
- Have we included opportunities for hands-on participation and activities that address a variety of learning styles?
- Will participants give leaders feedback on the program — and receive regular feedback? (para. 11)

Finally, "past experiences always affect new learning," according to Sousa (2009, para. 19). He explains:

As we learn something new, our brain transfers into working memory any long-stored items it perceives as related to the new information. These items interact with new learning to help us interpret information and extract meaning, which is part of the principle called *transfer*. (para. 19)

As a result of a professional learning experience, for example, "the brain decides whether to encode the new learning into long-term memory or let it fade away. It's an important decision because people cannot recall — let alone implement — learning that their brains have not stored" (Sousa, 2009, para. 21).

Sousa (2009) recommends that those who plan professional learning experiences consider the following actions:

- Directly connect the new initiative to job-related goals. For example, activities that show science teachers precisely how they can use new strategies to help students learn science content are more valuable than general suggestions.
- Present the topic over enough time and in enough depth so teachers gain a thorough understanding of how it relates to their work. It is foolish, for instance, to expect participants to make in-depth connections in a one-hour workshop, especially if there are no follow-up activities.
- Use instructional modalities other than "telling." Participants need to see the strategy modeled and then apply it themselves soon thereafter. When teachers actively participate in a demonstration of the primacy-recency effect, for example, they more clearly recognize that the brain remembers best the first and last items presented in a learning episode — and they are more likely to sequence instruction with this phenomenon in mind.
- Initiate action research. Conducting action research in the classroom enables teachers to personally assess the effectiveness of a new strategy, obtain validation for incorporating new strategies into their repertoire, and investigate specific problems that affect their teaching.
- Promote in-school study groups around the topic. As group members exchange new research and share in-class experiences, they can analyze why — and under what conditions — a strategy

is effective. Participating in study groups helps teachers who are reluctant to try out new ideas gain confidence. (para. 24)

The learning-doing gap

Sometimes educators confess that they learned a lot through a professional learning experience but failed to take action on their learning. They implemented no changes. Educators are not the only ones concerned about the knowing-doing gap. Len Brzozowski of the Xavier Learning Center, Xavier University, Ohio, works with business leaders and teams. He states:

> We can deliver certain concepts in a class. Heck, with 40 PowerPoint slides and a couple of readings, you can deliver a lot of content. But most of us LEARN it when we apply the content by ourselves in our own work environment. If the outcome is favorable, then we may be inclined to try it a second time, and then gradually it becomes an acquired new behavior. (Brzozowski, 2012, para. 6)

What is the solution to the learning-doing problem? For both business and education, collaboration is the answer. Collaboration takes many forms, from the casual exchange of ideas and materials to the rich interaction between a mentor and a teacher. The most effective type of collaboration in terms of closing the learning-doing gap is a tightly focused relationship in which educators are accountable to themselves and each other for making changes in the classroom or school. They have a commitment to improvement, and they enact it in an atmosphere of mutual support and responsibility.

Various types of professional learning communities, including critical friends groups, can work together to address the learning-doing gap. Members of these communities can be mutually accountable for making change. One type of collaboration is especially important for closing the gap. Though speaking about corporate change, Brzozowski (2012) remarks, "the coaching piece is the key" (para. 12).

> When we try something new and fail, our natural instinct is to go back to the old way of doing things. If a coach can help re-direct, or refocus you, thereby improving your rate of success, then you will be more encouraged to keep at it. (Brzozowski, 2012, para. 12)

This book has several chapters on different types of coaching.

Good designs — such as those in this book — naturally incorporate collaboration to assist with learning and implementation. Thus, from A to W, action researchers collaborate to make changes in their classrooms based on essential research questions, and those who design and participate in webinars pledge to try what they have learned in their own classrooms and schools.

Standards

Standards make clear what works in professional learning. Few countries have standards for professional learning, although they may have standards for educators. Two countries at least, Australia and Scotland, embed professional learning standards within their standards for effective educators.

Learning Forward developed the *Standards for Professional Learning* (2011) that includes a standard addressing learning designs: "Professional learning that increases educator effectiveness and results for all students **integrates theories, research, and models of human learning to achieve its intended outcomes**" (Learning Forward, p. 40). Educators must be involved in "selecting and constructing learning designs that facilitate their own and others' learning" (p. 41). The learning design itself must

- Address "all phases of the learning process, from knowledge and skill acquisition to application, reflection, refinement, assessment, and evaluation" (p. 41).
- Focus on important-data-based needs of both students and educators.
- Provide for the application of "learning theories, research, and models" (p. 40).
- "Promote active engagement" throughout the learning experience (p. 42). This means interaction during the learning process with the content and one another" (p. 42). It means collaboration that "respects adults as professionals and gives them significant voice and choice in shaping their own learning" and educators' constructing "personal meaning" (p. 42). Active engagement includes "discussion and dialogue, writing, demonstrations, inquiry, reflection, metacognition, co-construction of knowledge, practice with feedback, coaching, modeling, and problem-solving" (p. 42).

- Help educators move "beyond comprehension of the surface features of a new idea or practice to a more complete understanding of its purposes, critical attributes, meaning, and connection to other approaches" (pp. 41–42).
- Provide "many opportunities for educators to practice new learning with ongoing assessment, feedback, and coaching so the learning becomes fully integrated into routine behavior" (p. 41).

- "Engage adult learners in applying the processes they are expected to use" (p. 41).

This standard illustrates the criteria for adult learning and brain-based learning; it also addresses closing the learning-doing gap. However, the Learning Designs standard does not stand alone. As the following table shows, all the Learning Forward standards also connect to the issues raised in this essay, "Design: Form and Structure for Learning" (see table below).

Standards for Professional Learning	Core components of each standard
Learning Communities: Professional learning that increases educator effectiveness and results for all students occurs within learning communities committed to continuous improvement, collective responsibility, and goal alignment.	• Engage in continuous improvement; • Develop collective responsibility; and • Create alignment and accountability.
Leadership: Professional learning that increases educator effectiveness and results for all students requires skillful leaders who develop capacity, advocate, and create support systems for professional learning.	• Develop capacity for learning and leading; • Advocate for professional learning; and • Create support systems and structures.
Resources: Professional learning that increases educator effectiveness and results for all students requires prioritizing, monitoring, and coordinating resources for educator learning.	• Prioritize human, fiscal, material, technology, and time resources; • Monitor resources; and • Coordinate resources.
Data: Professional learning that increases educator effectiveness and results for all students uses a variety of sources and types of student, educator, and system data to plan, assess, and evaluate professional learning.	• Analyze student, educator, and system data; • Assess progress; and • Evaluate professional learning.
Learning Designs: Professional learning that increases educator effectiveness and results for all students integrates theories, research, and models of human learning to achieve its intended outcomes.	• Apply learning theories, research and models; • Select learning designs; and • Promote active engagement.
Implementation: Professional learning that increases educator effectiveness and results for all students applies research on change and sustains support for implementation of professional learning for long-term change.	• Apply change research; • Sustain implementation; and • Provide constructive feedback.
Outcomes: Professional learning that increases educator effectiveness and results for all students aligns its outcomes with educator performance and student curriculum standards.	• Meet performance standards; • Address learning outcomes; and • Build coherence.

From *Standards for Professional Learning,* by Learning Forward, p. 61. Copyright, 2011 by Learning Forward. Used with permission.

If you connect the Learning Designs standard to the rest of the standards, you'll find that the following must be true:

- **Learning communities** must engage in effective learning designs, and learning designs should empower learning communities.

- **Leaders** need to be learners themselves, engaging in a variety of learning designs both with other formally designated leaders and with educators in their schools and districts; learning designs must include components that enhance leadership, including teacher leadership.

- Human, fiscal, material, technology and time **resources** need to be found to support professional learning designs and, at the same time, professional learning designs need to make optimum use of these resources.

- **Data** should inform learning design throughout a continuous improvement cycle (from selection of the design, to learning, implementation, collection and analysis of new data, and evaluation of the design); the designs themselves must both be based upon and generate data that are useful for school improvement.

- **Implementation** of strategies to improve the teaching and learning experiences of everyone in a school is the target of professional learning; implementation strategies are incorporated into the design.

- **Outcomes,** both interim (changes in teacher behavior) and long-term (student achievement and well-being) are expected as a result of professional learning; professional learning designs include measurable interim and student outcomes that participants work toward.

Change processes

Several educators have described the difficulties of change. For example, Robert Marzano, Timothy Waters, and Brian McNulty (2005) described first- and second-order change. First-order change is challenging but doable. It usually requires "an extension of the past" (p. 7). However, second-order change is even more challenging because it requires "a break with the past" (p. 7). Many — even most — of all school change efforts are about second-order change, according to the characteristics that Marzano, Waters, and McNulty (2005) have identified. Robert Garmston and Bruce Wellman (1999) described these two types of changes as "tame" and "wicked" problems.

Delores Ambrose, in *Managing Complex Change*

(1987) proposed five components of change. When all are present, change can occur; when any one is missing, problems can occur. The components are ***vision, skills, incentive, resources,*** and ***action plan.*** If, for example, the vision is missing, the result may be confusion. If, however, the action plan is missing, the result may be false starts, spinning wheels, and treadmills.

One way of examining individuals and change is through Everett M. Rogers' *Diffusion of Innovations* (1982). On a normal distribution chart (sometimes called the normal curve), about 2.5% of individuals are likely to be innovators, taking a chance with something new and different. 13.5% will be early adopters; 34% will be early majority; 34% will be late majority; and 16% are laggards. Simon Sinek (2009) described the innovators and early adopters as people who are lined up outside the store on midnight to get the latest phone and laggards as people who are still bemoaning the loss of the rotary dial.

Gene Hall and Shirley Hord (2001) described how individuals go through change. They move from a stage of awareness to wanting more information, to wondering how it will affect them, to worrying about management of change. Then, they progress into thinking about the effects of change, working with others on change, and improving on the change. Hall and Hord called these stages *concerns* and codified them into the Concerns-Based Adoption Model (CBAM). They expanded on this model by looking at levels of use as well as interventions that can move an individual from one stage or level of use to another (Hall, George, & Rutherford, 1986).

In the 25th anniversary edition of *Transitions: Making Sense of Life's Changes,* William Bridges (2004) described stages of change from Ending, Losing, and Letting Go to the Neutral Zone to the New Beginning. The transitions overlap somewhat. And the Neutral Zone, although benign in name, is actually a challenging and threatening phase, although a time for great creativity.

Bruce Tuckman (1965) described how groups go through change. Community, he maintained, goes through stages: forming, storming, norming, and performing. His model is a good way to describe how teams, such as PLCs, form and progress.

Any of these models is useful for those engaged in professional learning. Indeed, any of them can serve as the basis for dialogue and discussion. These models can also reassure educators that resistance to change is natural and can be overcome. The models can ensure that educators consider how to implement change that will make a difference in schools.

Technology

Technology is one of the reasons that our lives are so interconnected around the world. Technology has affected the contents of this book, as well. Many of the designs featured in this edition are technological in nature. Although they adhere to the elements of good professional learning design, they also take advantage of new ways of learning that are possible only through technology.

Joellen Killion, Senior Advisor, Learning Forward, describes how technology enhances professional learning through the following critical attributes:

Personalization: For many learners who are frustrated with one-size-fits-all professional learning that offers little differentiation, technology allows both professional learning providers and participants to design what works best for educators;

Collaboration: Technology promotes collaboration among individuals who have common interests and needs through multiple forms of dynamic interaction;

Access: The degree to which educators can engage in high-quality professional learning influences its affects;

Efficiency: Technology can increase the efficiency of routine tasks, access to resources at the workplace, and serve as a vehicle for ongoing feedback;

Learning designs: Technology-based learning, if designed supports added practice, feedback, and support to deepen learning. (Killion, 2013, pp. 11–12)

Please note that technology does not automatically lead to professional learning. Many educators embraced early technology for student learning and were disappointed because, by itself, it did not help students do much more than they could have done without technology. Likewise, professional learning leaders today need to understand that technology alone cannot ensure educator learning. Killion (2013) cautions, for example, that technology has

limitations: misuse, disconnection from other support systems, inadequate support for learners, and limited assistance with implementation of new strategies. With consideration of the basic questions, Why? Who? What? How? When? Where? and How Much? designers can make best use of the potential of current and emerging technologies to facilitate adult and student learning.

Acting locally

Even as we think globally and learn from one other, we must still keep things local. What we do must be effective locally. This means that context is important. The charts on pages 20–28, much like those in the first and second editions of this book, help readers select appropriate learning designs for their local contexts.

WHY is the professional learning occurring? Beyond adult learning and the application of that learning, what can be accomplished with these designs? Other purposes include gathering information from external sources; creating a learning community; changing classroom and school culture; working on standards, curriculum, and assessment; focusing on pedagogy and instruction; changing policy; and developing leadership skills.

WHO should be involved as responsible leaders, participants and beneficiaries of professional learning? Roles include classroom teachers, classroom aides, building and district administrators, university/college faculty, community, parents, students, policymakers, coaches, and external technical assistance providers.

WHAT is the configuration of participants? What grouping facilitates learning among participants? Individuals? In pairs? In groups? Individuals at first and then groups?

HOW is the professional learning conducted? This question helps readers consider uses of technology (all or mostly face to face, all or mostly online, or blended) and focal point (involves looking at classrooms; involves looking at self, whole school, district, or community; involves looking at student work/students themselves).

Also, readers can consider features of the design. Is it especially useful for collaboration, problem-solving, development of a concrete product, or being experiential, modeling practice? Does it need facilitation and administrator participation or support? Does it involve coaching? Finally, how costly is the professional learning design?

WHEN does professional learning occur (assuming no less than a 1-year commitment)? Synchronously, asynchronously, or both? Is school in-session/out-of-session or a combination of in- and out-of-session? What is the duration of each session of learning? Each session is 3 hours or more; each session is 1–2 hours; each session is an hour or less; or the duration of the sessions varies? Finally, how frequently should these sessions occur? Three to six times year, at least monthly, at least weekly, daily, or varying numbers of times?

WHERE does professional learning occur? At the school site, off site, or online (anywhere or blended)?

Conclusion

This discussion has focused on design. Ann Delehant and I wrote the next essay, "Systems: The Context for Learning," to help readers create a context for use of the designs. It focuses on macro- and micro-level issues. On the macro level, the next essay describes how system leaders may support professional learning by using a design to establish school and district structures and processes for optimum success, addressing challenges, solving problems, and evaluating the impact of designs. On the micro level, the next essay presents general ideas about how to facilitate these designs. These macro and micro processes are applicable to any design in this book.

References

Ambrose, D. (1987). *Managing complex change.* Pittsburgh, PA: The Enterprise Group, Ltd.

Australian Institute for Teaching and School Leadership (AITSL). (2014). *Designing professional learning.* Melbourne, Australia: Author. Available at www.aitsl.edu.au/docs/default-source/default-document-library/designing_professional_learning_report.pdf.

Brewster, M. (2004, July 28). Frank Lloyd Wright: America's architect. *Bloomberg Businessweek.* Available at www.businessweek.com/stories/2004-07-27/frank-lloyd-wright-americas-architect.

Bridges, W. (2004). *Managing transitions: Making the most of life's changes* (Revised 25th anniversary edition). Boston, MA: Da Capo Press.

Brzozowski, L. (2012, September 23). *Bridging the learning-doing gap: Rethinking corporate learning and development.* Available at http://lenbrzozowski.wordpress.com/2012/09/23/re-thinking-corporate-learning-and-development/.

Easton, L.B. (2013, June). A global perspective: What professional learning looks like around the world. *JSD, 34*(3), 10–20.

Garmston, R., & Wellman, B. (1999). *The adaptive school: A sourcebook for developing collaborative groups.* Norwood, MA: Christopher-Gordon Publishers, Inc.

Goleman, D. (2005). *Emotional intelligence: Why it can matter more than IQ.* New York: Bantam Books.

Hall, G.E., George, A.A., & Rutherford, W.A. (1986). *Measuring stages of concern about the innovation: A manual for the use of the SoCQ questionnaire (Report No. 3032).* Austin, TX: Research and Development Center for Teacher Education, The University of Texas at Austin.

Hall, G.E. & Hord, S.M. (2001). *Implementing change: Patterns, principles, and potholes.* Upper Saddle River, NJ: Pearson.

Jaquith A., Mindich, D., Wei, R.C., & Darling-Hammond, L. (2010). *Teacher professional learning in the United States: Case studies of state policies and strategies.* Oxford, OH: NSDC.

Killion, J. & Roy, P. (2009). *Becoming a learning school.* Oxford, OH: NSDC.

Killion, J. (2013, February). Tapping technology's potential. *JSD, 34*(1), 11–12.

Learning Forward. (2011). *Standards for Professional Learning.* Oxford, OH: Author.

Marzano, R.J., Waters, T., & McNulty, B.A. (2005). *School leadership that works: From research to results.* Alexandria, VA: ASCD.

OECD. (2009). *Creating effective teaching and learning environments: First results from TALIS.* OECD Publishing. Available at www.oecd-ilibrary.org/education/creating-effective-teaching-and-learning-environments_9789264068780-en.

OECD. (2014). *TALIS 2013 Results: An international perspective on teaching and learning.* Paris: OECD Publishing. Available at http://dx.doi.org/10.1787/9789264196261-en.

Rogers, E.M. (2003). *Diffusion of innovations.* (5th ed.). New York, NY: Free Press.

Shaw, P., Greenstein, D., Lerch, I., Clasen, L., Lenroot, R., & Gotay, N. (2006). Intellectual ability and cortical development in children and adolescents. *Nature, 440*(7084), 676–679.

Sinek, S. (2009). How great leaders inspire action. [Videotape]. Available at www.ted.com/talks/simon_sinek_how_great_leaders_inspire_action.

Sousa, D. (June, 2009). Brain-friendly learning for teachers. *Educational Leadership.* 66. Available at www.ascd.org/publications/educational_leadership/summer09/vol66/num09/Brain-Friendly_Learning_for_Teachers.aspx.

Tuckman, B. (1965). Developmental sequence in small groups. *Psychological Bulletin, 63*(6), 394–99.

Vella, J. (1994). *Learning to listen, learning to teach.* San Francisco, CA: Jossey-Bass.

Wei, R.C., Darling-Hammond, L., & Adamson, F. (2010). *Professional development in the United States: Trends and challenges.* Oxford, OH: NSDC.

ONLINE RESOURCES

D.1 Backmapping model for planning results-based professional learning

D.2 The anatomy of professional learning designs

Guide to Selecting a Powerful Design

Design	**Why** is the professional learning occurring? Purposes, beyond adult learning and application of that learning, that can be accomplished with these designs.							
	Gathering data in a school	Gathering information from external sources	Creating a learning community	Changing classroom and school culture	Working on standards, curriculum, and assessment	Focusing on pedagogy and instruction	Changing policy	Developing leadership skills
Accessing Student Voices	X		X	X		X	X	
Action Research	X	X	X	X	X	X	X	
Assessment as Professional Learning			X	X	X	X		
Classroom Walk-Throughs for Peers	X		X	X	X	X		
Coaching Principals	X		X				X	X
Collaborative Analysis of Student Learning	X		X	X	X	X		
Critical Friends Groups	X		X	X	X	X		
Curriculum as Professional Learning			X	X	X	X		
Data Analysis	X	X				X	X	
Dialogue			X	X				
Digital Teacher Portfolios	X		X	X				
Instructional Coaching			X	X	X	X		
Instructional Rounds	X	X (Learning from other schools)			X	X	X	
Lesson Study	X	X	X	X	X	X		
Online Coaching	X			X	X	X		
Online Courses			X	X	X	X		
Online Protocols			X	X	X	X		
Professional Learning Communities	X	X	X	X	X	X		
Shadowing	X	X	X	X	X	X	X	
Social Media		X	X	X	X	X	X	
Teacher-Led Conferences			X	X	X	X		X
Videos				X	X	X		
Visual Dialogue	X	X	X	X	X	X	X	
Webinars				X	X	X	X	

Design	Who should be involved?									
	Responsible leaders, participants, beneficiaries of professional learning									
	Classroom teachers	Classroom aides	Building administrators	District administrators	University/ College faculty*	Community parents	Students	Policymakers	Coaches	External TA (eg BOCEs, RESCs)
Accessing Student Voices	X		X	X			X			
Action Research	X		X		X*					
Assessment as Professional Learning	X		X		X*					
Classroom Walk-Throughs for Peers	X		X							
Coaching Principals			X						X	
Collaborative Analysis of Student Learning	X									
Critical Friends Groups	X		X	X						
Curriculum as Professional Learning	X		X	X	X*					
Data Analysis	X		X	X (Data help from district office)						
Dialogue	X	X	X	X		X		X		
Digital Teacher Portfolios	X		X	X						
Instructional Coaching	X		X	X					X	
Instructional Rounds	X		X	X						
Lesson Study	X				X					
Online Coaching	X		X							X
Online Courses	X	X	X	X	X (May be developers)	X		X		
Online Protocols	X		X							
Professional Learning Communities	X	X	X	X**	X**					
Shadowing	X***	X	X***	X***	X	X	X***	X		
Social Media	X		X	X	X	X				
Teacher-Led Conferences	X (Should lead)				X (Should include teacher candidates)		X			
Videos	X		X	X	X					
Visual Dialogue	X		X	X		X			X	
Webinars	X	X	X	X		X		X		

 * In a support role e.g. providing subject-area assistance
 ** Their own PLCs
*** Can shadow and be shadowed

| Design | What is the configuration of participants? | | | |
| | Groupings that support participants' learning | | | |
	Individuals	Pairs	Groups	Individuals and groups
Accessing Student Voices	X	X (student and interviewer)	X (students and interviewer)	
Action Research	X	X	X	X (Individuals process in a group)
Assessment as Professional Learning			X	
Classroom Walk-Throughs for Peers	X	X	X	X (Individuals process in a group)
Coaching Principals		X		
Collaborative Analysis of Student Learning		X		X
Critical Friends Groups			X	
Curriculum as Professional Learning			X	X (Work in groups and then try individually)
Data Analysis			X	
Dialogue			X	
Digital Teacher Portfolios	X			X (Share portfolios)
Instructional Coaching		X		
Instructional Rounds			X	
Lesson Study			X	
Online Coaching		X		
Online Courses	X			X (May form PLCs)
Online Protocols			X	
Professional Learning Communities			X	
Shadowing		X		X (Shadow in pairs and debrief in groups)
Social Media	X			X (May form online networks)
Teacher-Led Conferences			X	
Videos				X
Visual Dialogue			X	
Webinars	X			X (May form online networks)

Design	How is professional learning conducted? (Part 1)						
	Technology			Focal point			
	Technology: All/Mostly face to face	Technology: All/Mostly online	Technology: Blended	Involves looking at classrooms	Involves looking at whole school, district, or community	Involves deep self-reflection	Involves looking at student work/Students
Accessing Student Voices			X	X	X		X
Action Research			X	X	X	X	X
Assessment as Professional Learning	X				X	X	X
Classroom Walk-Throughs for Peers	X			X		X	X
Coaching Principals	X		X		X	X	
Collaborative Analysis of Student Learning	X			X		X	X
Critical Friends Groups	X		X			X	X
Curriculum as Professional Learning			X			X	X
Data Analysis	X		X (Surveys)		X		X
Dialogue	X			X	X	X	X
Digital Teacher Portfolios			X	X		X	
Instructional Coaching	X			X	X	X	X
Instructional Rounds	X			X	X	X	X
Lesson Study	X			X		X	X
Online Coaching		X	X	X		X	X
Online Courses		X		X	X	X	X
Online Protocols			X	X	X	X	X
Professional Learning Communities	X			X	X		X
Shadowing	X			X	X	X	X
Social Media		X			X	X	X
Teacher-Led Conferences	X			X	X	X	X
Videos			X	X	X		X
Visual Dialogue	X					X	X
Webinars		X		X	X		

Design	Good for collaboration	Good for problem-solving	Results in development of a product	Is experiential	Involves modeling	Facilitator needed or helpful	Needs administrator involvement	Needs administrator support	Needs coaches
How is professional learning conducted? (Part 2)									
Features of professional learning designs									
Accessing Student Voices		X		X		X	X		
Action Research		X	X	X				X	
Assessment as Professional Learning	X		X			X		X	
Classroom Walk-Throughs for Peers	X	X		X		X	X		
Coaching Principals		X		X			X	X	X
Collaborative Analysis of Student Learning	X	X		X				X	
Critical Friends Groups	X	X		X		X		X	
Curriculum as Professional Learning	X		X			X		X	
Data Analysis	X	X	X	X		X	X		
Dialogue	X			X	X	X		X	
Digital Teacher Portfolios			X	X				X	
Instructional Coaching	X	X			X			X	X
Instructional Rounds	X	X	X	X		X	X		
Lesson Study	X	X	X	X				X	
Online Coaching		X		X	X	X			X
Online Courses			X		X	X		X	
Online Protocols	X	X				X		X	
Professional Learning Communities	X	X		X				X	
Shadowing				X				X	
Social Media				X				X	
Teacher-Led Conferences	X			X	X				
Videos		X	X		X			X	
Visual Dialogue	X	X	X	X		X	X		
Webinars			X	X	X	X		X	

Design	How is professional learning conducted? (Part 3)	
	Size of investment	
	$1000 or under per participant*	$1000 or over per participant*
Accessing Student Voices	X	
Action Research	X	
Assessment as Professional Learning		X
Classroom Walk-Throughs for Peers	X	
Coaching Principals		X
Collaborative Analysis of Student Learning	X	
Critical Friends Groups	X	
Curriculum as Professional Learning		X
Data Analysis		X
Dialogue	X	
Digital Teacher Portfolios	X	
Instructional Coaching		X
Instructional Rounds		X
Lesson Study	X	
Online Coaching		X
Online Courses		X (Course development)
Online Protocols	X	
Professional Learning Communities	X	
Shadowing	X (Travel for visitors)	
Social Media	X	
Teacher-Led Conferences	X (Zero fee for participants)	
Videos	X	
Visual Dialogue	X	
Webinars		X (Development)

* Includes substitute/stipend, materials, etc.

Design	When does professional learning occur? (Part 1) Assumes no less than a 1-year commitment					
	Synchronicity			School In/Out		
	Synchronous (people together in time and place)	Asynchronous (people not together in time and place)	Both synchronous and asynchronous	School in-session (students present)	School out-of-session (students not present)	Combination of school in- and out-of-session
Accessing Student Voices	X			X		
Action Research			X (Independent research; results processed together)			X
Assessment as Professional Learning	X					X
Classroom Walk-Throughs for Peers	X			X		
Coaching Principals	X					X
Collaborative Analysis of Student Learning	X			X		
Critical Friends Groups	X				X	
Curriculum as Professional Learning			X (Develop together; apply individually)		X	
Data Analysis			X			X
Dialogue	X				X	
Digital Teacher Portfolios			X			X
Instructional Coaching	X		X			X
Instructional Rounds	X			X		
Lesson Study	X					X
Online Coaching			X			X
Online Courses			X		X	
Online Protocols			X		X	
Professional Learning Communities	X				X	
Shadowing	X			X		
Social Media		X			X	
Teacher-Led Conferences	X				X	
Videos		X			X	
Visual Dialogue	X				X	
Webinars		X			X	

Design	When does professional learning occur? (Part 2) Assumes no less than a 1-year commitment								
	Duration				Frequency				
	Each session 3 hours or more	Each session 1–2 hours	Each session an hour or less	Varies	3–6 times/ year	At least monthly	At least weekly	Daily	Varying
Accessing Student Voices			X						X
Action Research			X		X *		X *		
Assessment as Professional Learning	X				X (Day-long meetings)				
Classroom Walk-Throughs for Peers		X			X				
Coaching Principals			X						X
Collaborative Analysis of Student Learning		X (Meetings)		X		X **		X **	
Critical Friends Groups		X			X (If full days provided)	X			
Curriculum as Professional Learning		X				X			
Data Analysis				X	X (Ongoing collection & analysis)				
Dialogue		X			X				
Digital Teacher Portfolios				X					X
Instructional Coaching				X					X
Instructional Rounds	X				X				
Lesson Study					X (Cycle)				
Online Coaching			X	X					X
Online Courses			X		X				
Online Protocols			X		X				
Professional Learning Communities		X				X			
Shadowing	X				X				X
Social Media				X					
Teacher-Led Conferences	X					X			
Videos		X				X			
Visual Dialogue	X				X				
Webinars			X		X				

* Continous research process; shared periodically
** Monthly meetings; daily application

| Design | Where does professional learning occur? | | |
| | Location | | |
	School site	Off site	Online (anywhere) or blended
Accessing Student Voices	X		
Action Research	X		
Assessment as Professional Learning	X	X (Some centralized meetings)	
Classroom Walk-Throughs for Peers	X		
Coaching Principals	X		
Collaborative Analysis of Student Learning	X		
Critical Friends Groups	X		
Curriculum as Professional Learning	X		
Data Analysis	X		X (Some online)
Dialogue	X		
Digital Teacher Portfolios	X		
Instructional Coaching	X		X (Some online)
Instructional Rounds	X	X	
Lesson Study	X		
Online Coaching	X		X
Online Courses			X
Online Protocols			X
Professional Learning Communities	X		
Shadowing	X		
Social Media			X
Teacher-Led Conferences	X	X	
Videos			X
Visual Dialogue	X	X	
Webinars			X

Systems: The Context for Learning

Professional learning designs embedded within
supportive systems lead to adult and student learning.

By Ann Delehant and Lois Brown Easton

I n the late 20th century, "sit 'n git," "spray and pray," and "drive-by" were used by educators, pejoratively, to describe traditional professional development. Some claimed that the phrase "effective professional development" was a contradiction in terms. Today,

> the very term [professional development] still trig-
> gers eye rolls, shaking heads, and heavy sighs. For
> many educators, the words summon bad memo-
> ries: the valuable instruction time that was wasted
> listening to a so-called expert who hasn't spent
> a day in a classroom, or the day-long workshop
> that was held in a half-empty, windowless hotel
> conference room filled with an endless parade of
> PowerPoint slides. (Walker, 2013, para. 2)

The term has changed in the last ten years from *professional development* to *professional learning* and, "done right [professional learning] . . . is indispensable" (Walker,

2013, para. 2). Effective professional learning is about designing comprehensive systems and facilitating adult learning to support professional practice in ways that ensure educator effectiveness and results for all students.

In the third edition of *Student Achievement Through Staff Development,* Bruce Joyce and Beverly Showers (2002) reported on their continued study of how professional learning improves teacher effectiveness and student learning. In the first edition, Joyce and Showers (1988) taught a generation of staff developers that they needed to minimize the scheduling of professional development events and maximize the design of programs and comprehensive systems in which programs are thoughtfully aligned vertically and horizontally. The results are the same in their third edition: Simple events in which a trainer presents theories do not result in successful transfer and implementation. In fact, Joyce and Showers (2002) said that, over time, there is no evidence of impact even when a trainer models the practice after presenting the theory. They report that only 5% of educators are able to transfer ideas successfully even when they are able to practice with feedback. When professional learning leaders design, plan, and implement thoughtful and comprehensive programs, however, there can be 95% fidelity of implementation that results in improved educator effectiveness and increased student achievement (p. 78).

Old-style events, such as one-time workshops, have proven to give minimal return in spite of investments of time and money, so it's foolhardy to spend even $1 on them. *Powerful Designs for Professional Learning* is filled with designs, not events, that engage learners and make efficient and effective use of the limited time available in schools for adult learning. In the previous essay, "Design: Form and Structure for Learning," you read an overview about design itself and the designs in this book. Now, you are ready to choose and use the designs. But, wait!

The designs in this book are powerful — otherwise they wouldn't be included — but they are even more powerful when embedded in a system that supports change at all levels. They are also likely to achieve maximum benefit if they are facilitated effectively. Enhance the results of using any design in this book by reading this essay, "Systems: The Context for Learning," before you begin your work. You will learn how to plan carefully for the use of these designs within a system and how to prepare the system for the changes that will result from engagement in the designs. You will also learn how to facilitate the designs that will make the most difference in your system. This essay provides information and processes at both a macro (systems) and micro level (facilitation) that will help you, a professional learning leader, make great decisions about how to implement the designs so that they impact educator and student learning.

Why systems thinking?

Imagine Lisa, a teacher in a middle school classroom. After attending a weekend conference, she has a bevy of new ideas she wants to try in her classroom. She's especially interested in a writing strategy that helps students develop fluency, but she discovers that what she wants to do takes more than one classroom period, and the strategy doesn't travel well from one day to the next. No one seems particularly interested in what she wants to do. Her colleagues are busy, and the principal has had to cancel two meetings Lisa scheduled with him to share what she learned at the conference. Most distressing to her, Lisa doesn't have anyone with whom she can solve the problem of trying to fit the strategy into the allotted time, and there's no way the school will change its schedule.

As part of the strategy, she wants to link her students to students in classrooms around the world, but the district blocks online sites that would allow her to do that. The IT department will not waive the policy. Also, the state has just instituted a new exam that doesn't ask students to engage in any prewriting at all, never mind the strategy she wants to use with students to help them become more fluent.

Resolving never to go to a conference again, she gives up on implementing the new strategy and resumes her old ways of teaching, It's just too frustrating to return to her school with new ideas.

Lisa has a systems problem.

Peter Senge and colleagues (2000) remind educators that a "system is any perceived whole whose elements 'hang together' because they continually affect each other over time" (p. 78). From Lisa's viewpoint, the system is not hanging together, at least not enough to allow her to make a change in her classroom that she thinks will significantly improve student learning. There are no supports within her school — and may even be some blockages. Similarly, there appear to be no supports within the district or the state for what she feels she needs to do to help students write better.

Schools, districts, and the states in which they operate are living systems, "always evolving," according to Senge and others (2000, p. 55). Lisa is part of the system. She participated, perhaps unknowingly, in the creation of the system of which she is a part. Being part of the system and contributing to the system's status quo, Senge notes, is not all bad. "Since we are part of the system ourselves, we are drawn to inquire more deeply, to look for ways that our own assumptions and habitual actions are integral to creating the system as it operates today" (2000, p. 55).

So, it's important to ask why Lisa attended that conference on the weekend, on her own time. Of course, she's allowed to do that — individuals can decide for themselves how to use their spare time. And, devoting her weekend to her own learning in order to help her students learn better, is an altruistic act. Perhaps her school and district do not provide professional learning otherwise. Or perhaps she's not satisfied with the learning opportunities offered by the school or district. Maybe she's just curious or wants to try something different.

Whatever the reason, consider how different the scenario might have been if it were systems oriented. First of all, Lisa and other teachers, building and district administrators, perhaps even parents and students themselves, would have made a case at the school and district levels that student writing needs to improve. They would have had data to support their case: scores from the state writing exam and examples of student work, and, perhaps, student and parent responses on a survey that indicated dissatisfaction with the writing program. The district (or schools within the district) would have made the improvement of writing a priority.

Knowing this priority, Lisa and her school colleagues might have formed a professional learning community (PLC), critical friends group, or community of practice. The district would have sanctioned regular, during-school time to meet, and the educators in Lisa's school would have decided how to make these meetings happen, perhaps through early release days every other week. School administrators not only would have supported the work in these meetings, they may also have participated in a professional learning community themselves.

Within her PLC, Lisa and her colleagues might have established goals for their own learning related to improving student writing. To meet these goals, they might have closely studied the data about writing, shared successful practices, visited other schools, or planned writing lessons together. Together, they might have determined where to focus their change, such as on helping students become more fluent through prewriting.

Perhaps other PLCs would be working on other goals related to improvement of student writing, and, several times a year, faculty meetings would be devoted to presentations of learning by each PLC. Gradually practice would begin to change schoolwide within and across PLCs.

If she worked in a coherent system, when Lisa heard about the conference, she would have shared the news with her colleagues and, with them, determined that someone from the group should attend. How lucky for the group that Lisa was able to find the time to go! When she returned

from the conference, she would have shared her ideas, and her PLC would have decided to implement some of them.

Ooops! Not so fast. Perhaps the PLC would have determined that what would benefit writing would include a change in the master schedule to allow for longer English periods. Let's go even further in this hypothetical example: When Lisa's PLC presented the need for a schedule change — based upon the entire school's dedication to improve writing — the faculty might have decided to alter the schedule for a specific time frame to see whether longer English periods made a difference in both the teaching and the learning of writing.

Perhaps when her PLC realized that the new strategy, which called for students to "talk" their ideas through with students in other countries, required online connectivity, she and her school's principal would have approached the IT department with a request to open a link for them. Since her district had set a goal to improve writing, the IT department was willing to grant her request.

The state test also appeared also to be a systems obstacle since it provided no time for students to prewrite, but the district's curriculum coordinator might have talked with the head of the assessment unit in the state department of education to see if the next draft of the state test could include some prewriting opportunities. There would be no immediate solution, but possibly a future one. It wouldn't hurt students to engage in prewriting, whether or not prewriting was part of the exam.

And, you may be asking, what about the mathematics teacher who notices a need for improving students' reading skills in mathematics? Or the art teacher who is fighting to keep art in the curriculum, or the third grade teacher who wants to teach science to her students but is afraid she doesn't know enough about science to do a good job? A system works better when it is focused, but it can have more than one focus.

There are a lot of "perhaps" in this vignette, and no system works this smoothly. Still, as Senge (1990) says, it's better to see the whole system at the beginning. Then, the pieces fit. It's harder to try "to reassemble the fragments of a broken mirror to see a true reflection" (p. 3). If educators start their improvement process with as much of a whole picture as possible, they are more likely to create an organization where people continually expand their capacity to create the results they truly desire,

> where new and expansive patterns of thinking are nurtured, where collective aspiration is set free, and where people are continually learning how to learn together. (p. 3)

Preparing systems to support change

Preparing and building a plan for professional learning within a system is similar to creating most plans. Using the conventional journalistic questions (Who? What? When? Where? Why? and How?) to build the plan, a planner starts with Why, followed by Who, then What, How, When, and Where.

Why

Clarity of purpose — the "Why" — is critical. Read any strong school or district purpose (or vision or mission) statement and you will immediately understand the reasons for professional learning: Students. School or district purposes project student success. Here are examples of some school or district purpose statements:

- Our students will use their mathematical and language literacies to engage in problem solving across the curriculum.
- Students will graduate with the will to make a difference in the world and the skills and knowledge that will help them do so.
- Graduates from XYZ High School will have active and creative minds, using knowledge and skills to build a productive future for themselves.

Data help schools and districts identify their purposes. It's important to use all available data — student achievement data (not just test scores, however), demographics, perceptions, and processes (or the learning conditions that resulted in the achievement and perceptions data) to drive the change processes. "Chapter 9: Data Analysis" in this book is an excellent resource for data collection and analysis. Author of this chapter, Victoria Bernhardt, suggests that schools and districts begin their own processes by practicing with another school's (or district's) data. In fact, as part of her chapter, she provides another school's data so that readers can practice with these data before wrestling with their own data.

Data illuminate critical needs and reveal the "pain" in the system — what worries people most. Data highlight challenges the system faces as well as assets the system can build upon. Data analysis is an exciting opportunity to discern what might drive individual, team, and system improvements.

Finding purpose is not just a cognitive process; it is also an emotional one. Educators need to surface what they have passion about, whether it's the number of drop-outs or students' lack of engagement. Passion is, in fact, moral purpose. Both objective and emotional purposes are essential for change.

The "why" of professional learning derives from school or district purposes and passions. For example, building on the school or district purposes described previously, the following professional learning purposes focus on what educators will learn and do:

School or district purposes	Professional learning purposes
Our students will use their mathematical and language literacies to engage in problem solving across the curriculum.	• Educators will help students develop mathematical and language literacies. • Educators will help students become problem solvers.
Students will graduate with the will to make a difference in the world and the skills and knowledge that will help them do so.	• Educators will help students understand their community and global responsibilities. • Educators will help students develop knowledge and skills to address community and global responsibilities.
Graduates from XYZ High School will have active and creative minds, using knowledge and skills to build a productive future for themselves.	• Across the curriculum, educators will focus on helping students develop habits of mind, including creativity. • Educators will help students apply their learning in service learning projects that benefit their school and larger communities.

Carefully designing and implementing professional learning means nothing unless there is a significant impact on student success. That is, professional learning can be judged ineffective if there is no impact on student learning. So, the most important place to begin planning and preparing to implement professional learning is with student learning. This consideration leads to analysis of what educators need to learn and do.

As educators work on the purpose for professional learning, they will want to expand their thinking to include the content of the work, expected and measureable outcomes, and a list of the deliverables that have a clear impact on student success. They may want to describe the purpose of professional learning through a SMART goal: S = specific; M = measurable; A = achievable/attainable; R = relevant; T = timely/time-bound. Here is a purpose for professional learning stated as a SMART goal:

> In order to help students apply their learning related to habits of mind, by the end of the school year, all educators will collaboratively plan, team teach, and collectively evaluate two service-learning units according to rubrics.

Setting purposes for professional learning is not a one-time event. As educators engage in professional learning related to the district's or school's purposes, they should cycle through the purpose question frequently. For example, they should ask, "How is this helping us achieve our school's purpose?" As they learn and apply their learning, they should collect data — evidence that they are or are not working toward the school's or district's purpose, as well as their own professional learning purposes. They should use a continuous process of examining evidence as a way to calibrate how successful they are in achieving purpose(s) and modify professional learning accordingly. Evidence may even point to a change in purpose, and that's good to know before the school or district goes too far down the road of change.

So far, purpose has related to school, district, and professional learning goals. Purpose is important in terms of the components of a professional learning design, too. It's important for educators engaged in a professional learning design to make sure that the purpose of each session, experience, or component advances the overall professional learning purpose and, thus, the school and district purposes. They should clearly outline what will be accomplished at each session. Some groups also find it helpful to clearly define the "nonpurpose" of the session. Stating what the team will **not** do is helpful if a group has a habit of getting distracted or rarely finishing a task.

Understanding why they are doing the work will help educators identify who will participate. After the planners of any professional learning clearly define the task, they should identify the members of the team who will commit to ensuring learning for all staff members (Delehant, 2006, pp. 8–16; Harrison, 2013).

Who

Planners need to ask two questions regarding "Who?" The first is, "Who is responsible for planning professional learning?" The second is, "Who are the right participants for each professional learning program?"

Who is responsible for planning professional learning?

The folk saying, "Thems as does the doin' does the decidin'" speaks to the first Who question. Those who will be implementing changes in their classrooms, schools, and districts as a result of professional learning need to be involved in determining exactly how the professional learning will be constructed. Gone are the days when someone "higher up" decides what teachers should be doing in terms of professional learning. Gone are the days when buy-in is needed because someone higher up has determined how to develop others and wants them to like what's happening to them.

After district education leaders have decided on the purposes of professional learning, they can ensure representation from throughout the system by having a standing committee, perhaps a Professional Learning Planning Team (PL Planning Team), that is committed to listening, reflecting, and analyzing student and staff data; establishing goals and strategies or actions to achieve them; and monitoring and adjusting along the way. Education leaders who are creating a district PL Planning Team will probably work through a superintendent or designee to invite central and school-based administrators, union/association leaders, teachers, and support staff from different grade bands, schools, and subjects. They will include those who might offer different perspectives and different levels of experience. The superintendent or designee needs to avoid hand-picking PL Planning Team members to reduce the risk of selecting only like-minded people. The process for identifying administrators, teachers, teaching assistants, and support staff needs to be transparent, fair, and open to ensure membership represents the population of educators in the district and provides divergent thinking.

Once initial Planning Team members are identified, the superintendent should ask the members to consider who might be missing. For example, some teams choose to include a partner from a local university, a business representative, a technology advisor, someone from the state department of education, or another member who would enrich the team's thinking.

District education leaders and the district-level Planning Team may encourage schools to form school-based PL Planning Teams comprised of central and school-based administrators; union/association representatives; teachers and support staff from different grades and subject areas; perhaps parents and students. School-based Planning Teams should include those with different perspectives and different levels of experience. They should be populated through the same open and fair process, and members should also ask, "Who else needs to participate in this work?"

There may be a relationship between the district-level and school-level PL Planning Teams, with representatives from school-level PL Planning Teams serving on the district-level team. Such a relationship is good for the system because it ensures communication throughout the district. But, once again, care needs to be taken in terms of who serves on these PL Planning Teams.

Usually, school-level PL Planning Teams include representation from grade levels and subject areas. Sometimes school-level PL Planning Teams are populated by representatives from smaller groups — communities of practice, PLCs, or critical friends groups. In one middle school a design team at the school level coordinated the work of various professional learning communities. Members of the design team were all volunteers, a trait which did not ensure representation, but others could join the design team at any time, as long as they agreed to serve at least three months. And, at times, all of the educators in the school met in one big professional learning community to share their work, examine data, and make future plans (Easton, 2011).

There's an upside and a downside to representation. The upside is that a design or planning team has members who will bring information to and from each constituent group, such as 4th-grade teachers or classroom aides. Taking a representative approach to PL Planning Teams at the district or school levels ensures a conduit of information and ideas.

On the downside, representation also suggests loyalty to constituent groups that might interfere with bigger, whole-school or whole-district thinking. For example, a representative of 9th-grade English teachers might maintain, "We have to teach *Romeo and Juliet* in 9th grade. We always have, and we always will, and everyone else will have to change to accommodate our curriculum because we won't." One way to address representation is to discuss the benefits and barriers of representation when setting norms for the group, a topic that is developed more thoroughly later in this essay.

Once PL Planning Team members — at the district- or school-level — are identified, they should focus on understanding the purpose (the "why") of the team's work as it relates to the district's purposes. On the basis of the district's purposes, team members should develop the purposes for their professional learning, perhaps as SMART goals, including deliverables. They should consider system effects — how the current system supports the status quo, how the system will need to change to support the innovation, and what the barriers and supports will be for change. They need to ask, "What does commitment to this goal mean in terms of how this system operates?" Throughout the planning process, PL Planning Team members should consult data that have been collected and analyzed and, perhaps, collect and analyze additional data.

Team members must establish expectations as part of their agenda. What do they expect as a result of the professional learning? What will be implemented? How will learning be different for students? What will they notice in terms of student achievement? And, by when do they anticipate that various expectations will be accomplished? At this point they're not building a strategic plan as much as describing outcomes and benchmarks as a planning team. The actual implementers of the change will need to be in charge of their own expectations and timelines, which are related, of course, to those set by the planners.

The PL Planning Team roles can vary considerably. Douglas Reeves (2006) proposed that members of a team bring to their work together a variety of assets: Visionary Leadership, Relational Leadership, Systems Leadership,

Reflective Leadership, Collaborative Leadership, Analytical Leadership, and Communicative Leadership. It might be helpful for PL Planning Team members to spend some time defining for themselves and then identifying the assets they bring to the team as well as what the team needs.

Also consider the contributions PL Planning Team members can make in a group, whether or not they have a title (such as Facilitator). Here's a list of how members can contribute to group process:

- *Initiator/Contributor.* Proposes goals, ideas, solutions; defines problems; suggests procedures.

- *Information and Opinion Seeker.* Asks for clarification and suggestions; looks for facts and feelings; solicits ideas and values of other members.

- *Information Giver.* Offers facts and relevant information or experience.

- *Opinion Giver.* States beliefs about alternatives; focuses on values rather than facts.

- *Clarifier/Elaborator.* Interprets; gives examples; defines terms; clears up confusion or ambiguity.

- *Coordinator/Summarizer.* Pulls ideas, opinions, and suggestions together; summarizes and restates; tries to draw members' activities together; offers conclusions.

- *Gatekeeper/Expediter.* Keeps communication open among all members; opens up opportunities for others to participate.

- *Harmonizer.* Tries to reduce conflict and tension; attempts to reconcile differences.

- *Encourager.* Supportive of others; praises efforts and ideas; accepts contributions. (Delehant, 2006, p. 51)

As with assets, team members should describe and discuss the types of contributions they think will be essential to the group's work. Without embarrassment, they should identify how they can best contribute to the process. If a particular type of contribution (such as harmonizer) is needed, and no one volunteers to make that contribution, the group can agree that **everyone** in the group should work together to make that contribution.

Finally, teams need to think about how members prefer to work. A good activity for identifying work preferences is

Four Corners (sometimes called Four Compass Points). See Online Resource S.1: *Directions for Four Corners.*

Groups may return as needed to discussion of assets, roles, and preferences given what's needed and how well the group is contributing to the overall effectiveness of the group. Whenever a group seems stuck, members may engage in a conversation on these aspects of group work to move forward. Also, they can consider norms, discussed later in this essay.

Even if much of the preparation, planning, and implementation of professional learning is done by staff at the district level — perhaps within the curriculum division or by staff in the director of professional learning's office — it is important that it is owned and, when possible, shared by members of the team.

Who are the right participants for each professional learning design or program of several designs?

Addressing this question requires many of the same processes described in the section on planning the professional learning program. Here is a summary of these considerations:

1. Obviously, those who are going to be directly involved in making the change should be involved in professional learning related to the change. This means administrators, teachers, teacher assistants, front office staff, etc. It may also mean students and their parents and, perhaps, other community members. Not everyone needs the same professional learning experiences, but everyone needs to know about changes being made in a school or district and have time to consider how these changes will affect them in the role(s) they play.

2. If you cannot directly involve everyone in professional learning — because the group is too big or there is not enough time allotted for the learning experiences or both — consider an Each One Teach One model. It is like training of trainers, wherein a representative of each group engages in the professional learning and then replicates it with his or her constituents. It is not enough to tell people about the professional learning; they need to engage in it, too. Faithful replication is essential here; the representatives' constituents should not get a watered-down version of the original experiences. They should be provided with all of the resources the representatives had as well as access to

expertise. Here is where online resources prove valuable.

3. Remember the cautions about representation if you go with an Each One Teach One model.

4. Consider having a design team or coordinating committee if the number of educators and others engaging in professional learning is 25 or more. Charge this smaller team with coordinating the advance notice of the innovation, the logistics of meetings, accessibility of resources, follow-up services, implementation, and evaluation of learning, including reports to the whole school or district.

5. Ensure that everyone understands "why" at a fundamental level. School-based groups may need to engage in their own data analysis to develop powerful reasons, including emotional ones, for engaging in professional learning and making change. This is not wasted time, even though it appears to duplicate what a planning committee might already have done. It is usually not enough to simply tell people that they need to do something; they must discover the reasons themselves. Return to "why" as often as needed to keep the group on track; refer to "why" for each learning experience, explaining how the experience contributes to the overall purpose of the learning.

6. Help the group understand itself through consideration of assets, contributions, and preferences.

7. Establish expectations related to those set by the planners. Be explicit this time: Exactly what do we expect to happen? How will the school culture change? How will classroom cultures change? How will teachers and other adults change? How will students change?

8. It's helpful to reference Joellen Killion's (2008) KASAB: What **K**nowledge, **A**ttitudes, **S**kills, **A**spirations, and **B**ehaviors (in terms of both students and adults) will change?

9. Also, describe evidence and sources of evidence for each expectation. Ask the question, "How will we know?" And, set timelines or general dates by which the group expects to see changes in culture and KASAB. Plan to collect data before those dates so that you know the current status of culture and KASAB for adults and students. Plan to revise your plan according to the data you collected.

In terms of both questions — Who should plan? and Who should participate? — one critical issue must be

addressed: The impact of generational attrition among the teaching workforce. According to Joan Richardson (2008), "As more and more Millennials — those born in 1978 and later — move into the teaching ranks," the last Boomers (those born between 1946 and 1964) are retiring. Richardson (2008) explains:

> Teachers beginning their careers in 2008 and for many years ahead will be strikingly different from the generations of Traditionalists, Baby Boomers, and even Gen Xers that preceded them. These generational personality differences have implications for the way beginning teachers teach, how they want to learn about improving their practice, and how they will impact the culture of the schools in which they work. (p. 1)

How and where educators from different generations learn will require differentiation and new ways of thinking.

What

In terms of professional learning, the "What" is the chosen design (or designs) based on district and school purposes and purposes for professional learning. From a systems standpoint, there are several different issues to consider when you begin to examine what needs to get done.

1. *Continue to address why you are undertaking the learning.* Make sure that what you do in terms of professional learning advances why you want to make changes. Use data to understand why and continue to use data to help you assess progress and make changes, including making changes in terms of the design you have chosen.

2. *Consider who is participating in the learning work.* Select the design(s) you want to use once you understand who will be involved in the change work. Some designs are quite sophisticated — lesson study, for example — and may be more appropriate for educators who are accustomed to professional *learning* rather than conventional *development*. Some designs deprivatize the classroom, a change that might be uncomfortable, at least initially, for some educators. Other designs, such as using video from educators outside the school, might provide an entry point into deprivatization.

3. *Consider what is already being done in terms of professional learning.* A design you are already using successfully in your school or district may be adaptable

to a new purpose. For example, you may want to continue instructional coaching in terms of a new purpose, especially if coaching has helped educators implement new practices successfully. Perhaps you already have active PLCs; you may want to continue these to address new purposes. As you keep and perhaps modify existing designs, you might also add some designs. For example, keep your effective coaching programs, but add some online courses, which will be followed by coaching, both online and face to face. If, however, a design does not seem to fit with your new "why," consider eliminating it over time.

4. *Distinguish the content you will need in terms of the design.* Use the charts in "Design: Form and Structure for Learning" to help you choose what will work best. Some designs facilitate content related to the subject areas. For example, the Learning Design Collaborative in "Chapter 8: Curriculum as Professional Learning" in this book features templates for designing units based on literacy and mathematics Common Core Standards. Some designs facilitate content related to instruction and assessment. For example, check out the chapters on assessment and instructional coaching. Other designs in the book are useful no matter what content you are addressing. For example, online protocols can be used to help educators process any change they might make in their classrooms or schools. The designs in this book were chosen because they provide strong platforms to carry the content of the work, whatever it is.

5. *Recognize that no one design may meet your purpose(s).* Think about combining several designs to meet your purpose(s). For example, consider this school purpose, which was introduced earlier in this essay:

> Students will graduate with the will to make a difference in the world and the skills and knowledge that will help them do so.

Also, consider this professional learning purpose related to the school purpose:

> Educators will help students understand their community and global responsibilities.

Here are some designs that could be used together as a professional learning program to realize both purposes:

- *Accessing student voices.* Find out what students see as their community and global responsibilities.

- *PLCs or critical friends groups.* Have educators work together in groups to learn and apply their learning.
- *Action research.* Invite members of the PLCs focusing on these purposes to start their own action research projects.
- *Dialogue.* Invite educators to explore their own ideas and ideals related to community and global responsibilities.
- *Lesson study.* Invite educators to develop, test, and debrief lessons related to community and global responsibilities.
- *Rounds and shadowing.* Arrange to participate in rounds or engage in shadowing students in schools that have made civic responsibilities a priority.
- *Social media.* Check out any number of professional learning online sites to see if there are any communities devoted to students' civic responsibilities.

How

No matter what design(s) your team is using, consider a few generic processes or ways of doing things, the "How." Consider roles, norms, active engagement, culture of continuous and reflective practice, and developing local leaders.

Roles

Among the many defined roles that people can play on a team, the following are especially important. Often, the people who play them have titles, such as "Facilitator" or "Recorder," and may be responsible for:

- *Planning and coordinating.* No matter how much work has been done at a district level through a planning or design team, local educators will need to plan and coordinate what happens at the school level. Of course, a school-level PL Planning Team or design team can continue to plan and coordinate as educators engage in professional learning, but new educators on these teams can add some diversity and augment communication channels.
- *Facilitating.* Most of the designs require a facilitator to guide the learning process. These designs are not about lecturing or sharing knowledge in traditional ways. Facilitators need to be able to guide team learning

or manage some of the details (setting up the online platform, creating the protocol for the action research or curriculum design, for example). They need to be thoroughly familiar with the design they are facilitating, perhaps having experienced it as a participant before they facilitate their own group. Here are typical facilitator roles and responsibilities:

- Facilitators can be internal or external to the team; participants may share the role (see Online Resource S.2: *The facilitator's roles and responsibilities*).
- They need to take care of logistics (see Online Resource S.3: *Logistics*).
- They may need to group people (see Online Resource S.4, *Grouping participants*).
- They need to help the group work with those who obstruct participation (see Online Resource S.5: *Working with groups*).
- Facilitators plan openings and closings (see Online Resource S.6: *Strong openings and closings*).
- They attend to the energy in the group (see Online Resource S.7: *Energizing the group*).
- They also help groups plan their next steps (see Online Resource S.8: *Defining next steps*).
- *Recording/Scribing/Archiving.* Sometimes participants working on a project, gathering data, or brainstorming ideas need someone to capture the notes. The recorder is a member of the team who agrees to record either regularly or "in the moment" based on the needs of one activity. The scribe is a partner to the recorder — the scribe captures the ideas and information publicly — usually on chart paper or on a screen so that everyone can see the ideas being generated. It's important to display the words as they are spoken (only change the words with permission). If the ideas are flowing fast, some groups will ask for a second or third scribe to assist in the data gathering. The archivist collects and organizes the group's work, inviting others to reflect on it and capturing their reflections. PLCs, for example, might participate in presentations of learning during which they share the contents of their portfolios and describe their learning.
- *Timekeeping.* The timekeeper is responsible for keeping the group focused on the task at hand. Now, most groups use timers, stopwatches and alarms on phones

or they incorporate timers right onto a slide using tools that can be found easily online at sites like www.online-stopwatch.com and www.e.ggtimer.com.

- *Process Observing.* A process observer may come from within a team but is often an invited guest. He or she remains outside the group, collecting descriptive information about the work of the group and the individuals in the group and providing feedback (to the team and to each member) so that they can reflect on the successes of the group and the opportunities for growth. A process observer generally works with a team that meets regularly.
- *Participating.* The most important role in any group is that of the engaged learner. "When participants are willing to ask questions, challenge assumptions, seek clarity and move the group forward on issues, groups are more likely to accomplish their goals" (Delehant, 2006, p. 50).

Norms

Another important process, or "how," is the creation and use of norms. Begin by developing an understanding with all team members that effective meetings and effective professional learning generally have a set of ground rules that governs individual behavior, facilitates the work of the group, and enables the group to accomplish its task. Developing norms:

1. Ensures all individuals have the opportunity to contribute in the meeting;
2. Increases team productivity and effectiveness;
3. Facilitates the achievement of goals; and
4. Expedites the development of a strong team culture.

Online Resource S.9: *Using ground rules,* contains guidelines that groups need to consider as they set norms. Online Resource S.10: *Topics for norms,* gives groups a way to develop norms. No matter what norms you set, be sure that you reference norms before the meeting: "Remember our norms? Does anyone want to change them in any way? Can we all agree to adhere to them? Do we know what to do if someone is violating the norms?" The last question is critical; the group must decide what to do if someone is violating a norm. Some groups decide that they can call for a "norm check" if someone appears to be violating a norm; the group stops to consider what to do about that violation, if anything. This is similar to inviting people to call for a "process check" when they are not sure where the meeting or learning experience is going. Other groups prefer to have anyone noticing the broken norm to have a private word with the person breaking the norm, perhaps during a break or after the meeting. Other groups want the facilitator to state that a norm is being broken and ask if that's all right with the group. Still others prefer writing a note to the person who has broken the norm, either at the time or afterward. Whatever the group decides to do becomes the norm — or accepted action — for the whole group, including the person who breaks a norm.

Finally, a group should evaluate how well it did as a group on adhering to the norms. This can be done publicly or privately at the end of the meeting. Individuals can evaluate the group as a whole or themselves individually. A "fist-to-five" can be used publicly to indicate the group's success at adhering to the norms (a fist meaning "not at all," and five fingers meaning "absolutely," with explanations required for a fist through 3 fingers, so the group can know why individuals showing those ratings did so). The group can use a Likert scale for the individual norms, with numbers shared or kept private for the facilitator to compute and share at the beginning of the next meeting ("At the last meeting, as a group we declared that we adhered to the norms at a "B+" level. Here is the norm we did not adhere to: _____.").

Active engagement

No matter what design you choose, you'll want to ensure active engagement of individuals, small groups, and large groups.

"What I hear I forget, what I see I remember, what I do I understand." This quote, which has many translations, often attributed to Confucius or Zunzi, reminds leaders that passive learners rarely develop enough understanding to ensure the transfer of the ideas into practice. One of the assumptions about the designs in this book is that learning must engage all learners to ensure the transfer of knowledge into action. All of the designs focus on deep engagement in ideas, concepts, strategies, and, ultimately, application of learning. It's impossible, for example, to access student voices or engage in instructional coaching or participate in dialogue and remain passive in the process.

Each design comes with a set of steps for a facilitator to use. Read these steps carefully when planning how to use a design because they will lead you to techniques for active engagement. Incorporate the authors' ways of involving learners. Augment these techniques whenever you can. Make sure the work is "real," not hypothetical, and create ways to integrate the ideas into practice immediately. If the ideas sit on a shelf when staff members return to their workplace, even for a week, they are likely to stay there.

Culture of continuous learning and practice

According to MaryAnn Cunningham Florez (2001) from the National Center for ESL Literacy Education:

Reflective practice is an evolving concept. In the 1930s, John Dewey defined reflection as a proactive, ongoing examination of beliefs and practices, their origins, and their impacts (Stanley, 1998). Since then, reflective practice has been influenced by various philosophical and pedagogical theories. One influence is constructivism, which views learning as an active process where learners reflect upon their current and past knowledge and experiences to generate new ideas and concepts.

A *humanistic* element of reflective practice is its concern with personal growth and its goal of liberation from values that can limit growth (Kullman, 1998). *Critical pedagogy,* espousing examination of underlying power bases and struggles, and *American pragmatism,* emphasizing active implementation, testing, and refining of ideas through experience, also shape the concepts of reflective practice, particularly in the United States (Brookfield, 1995). (para. 2)

Although she was writing about educators in adult ESL settings, Florez (2001) describes the process for all educators interested in reflection:

In reflective practice, practitioners engage in a continuous cycle of self-observation and self-evaluation in order to understand their own actions and the reactions they prompt in themselves and in learners (Brookfield, 1995; Thiel, 1999). The goal is not necessarily to address a specific problem or question defined at the outset, as in practitioner research, but to observe and refine practice in general on an ongoing basis. (para. 3)

As individuals become accustomed to reflective practice, the culture of their environment changes. Educators working in teams and schools themselves naturally take on the quest for reflection, which leads to greater student and adult learning.

Developing local leaders

In conventional professional development, as opposed to professional learning as described in this book, the leader is clearly the person presenting the content, the "sage on the stage," the guru. In this book, the leader is not the single person dispensing knowledge to everyone else. Instead, the designs in this book take an inside-out approach, by providing ways for educators themselves to learn from one other and from within the system. Such designs may be facilitated, not by "experts" from outside the system, but by teachers, vice principals, technology coaches, librarians, guidance counselors, and educators who hold many other titles. This approach provides ways for those who are usually led to become leaders themselves. It requires educators to take roles customarily left to those who are called leaders. The roles that educators play in terms of facilitating and participating in these designs help them become leaders in other ways as well.

In *Teacher Leadership That Strengthens Professional Practice*, Charlotte Danielson (2006) focuses on what teacher leaders do. What they do, of course, relates directly to their own learning and implementation of their learning with students. For example, teacher leaders demonstrate the following skills, often by facilitating or participating in professional learning:

- Using evidence and data in decision making;
- Recognizing opportunity and taking initiative;
- Mobilizing people around a common purpose;
- Marshaling resources and taking action;
- Monitoring progress and adjusting the approach as conditions change;
- Sustaining the commitment of others and anticipating negativity;
- Contributing to a learning organization (pp. 26–39).

Additionally, Danielson (2006) points out that teacher leaders have dispositions that help them lead:

- Optimism and enthusiasm;
- Open-mindedness and humility;
- Courage and willingness to take risks;
- Confidence and decisiveness;
- Tolerance for ambiguity;
- Creativity and flexibility;
- Perseverance;
- Willingness to work hard (pp. 37–40).

The designs in this book help educators develop and use these leadership skills and dispositions.

Not only will facilitators and participants in these designs change professional development to professional learning in their schools, they will also change the culture of the school so that, rather than being dependent upon others' expertise, educators will be interdependent and independent. The designs in this book invite educators to step out of the old paradigm of professional development and try something new. Each of the designs is clearly described and accessible to all. Once people begin to use them, they will clamor for more ways to learn with and from one another.

None of this means that outside expertise is unnecessary. In fact, outside expertise may be very necessary, especially when those engaged in a professional learning design realize the need for what Vygotsky (1978) calls the "knowledgeable other" (p. 86). An outsider's idea may prompt the inside work that must be done to learn. For example, educators may read or hear about an innovation and seek to learn more about it from an outside expert; however, they must then work together, from inside the school or district, to implement that idea. Thus, a professional development experience in its traditional sense should lead to professional learning experiences that result in effective application of new ideas for helping students learn. An excellent resource for understanding the role of outside expertise is Learning Forward's *Standards into Practice: External Roles* (2014).

When

Learning is no longer restricted to "seat time" in workshops. Although this evolution makes it more challenging to count hours for state and local certification and license renewal, this change in the "When" creates conditions for deeper, more reflective learning. Increasingly, professional learning is a job-embedded opportunity available to all educators. It happens online which means it can happen at different times for each participant (i.e. be asynchronous); it happens during the school day; and it happens before or after school hours.

How much time is needed for learning to take hold and show results? Some researchers claim that 80 hours or more are needed to have impact. According to Wei et al. (2009):

two separate evaluations of professional development aimed at inquiry-based science teaching found that teachers who had 80 or more hours of science-related professional development during the previous year were significantly more likely to use reform-based teacher instruction than teachers who had experienced fewer hours (Corcoran, McVay, & Riordan, 2003; Supovitz & Turner, 2000). (p. 8)

This time needs to be sustained with a focus on one innovation to allow for learning, practice, reflection, problem solving, more learning, more practice, and, finally, routine and even creative application of the innovation. Eight hours spent learning first one and then another innovation, eight hours here, eight hours there, is not a wise expenditure of time or budget.

Asynchronous online learning opportunities are both a benefit and a barrier to professional learning. It is a benefit because educators can schedule learning whenever they have free time. It is a barrier because policymakers may assume that educators do not need time embedded in their workday for professional learning. Although they may learn at home in their PJs — much as students learn in flipped classrooms — they need team time, embedded in the school day to process what they are learning with others, collaborate, implement, support each other's implementation, solve problems related to implementation, and collect and analyze results.

Addressing time means addressing the budget for professional learning. Some teams schedule "boot camps" during school vacations or summer institutes followed up by year-long support with practice, coaching, and time for reflection. Some educators may volunteer to participate in summer institutes or boot camps, but others will require a stipend for work that is beyond their contract. The budget may limit how many people can participate, and, therefore, limit the broad implementation of a new program.

Protected time for professional learning during the workday — such as late start or early release days — is a good way to go, as long as there is sufficient time (at least an hour) frequently enough (every week, if possible) for progress to be made. Other options require paying for substitutes so that teachers and staff can be released to participate in professional learning during the workday. The problem — in addition to an increased budget for substitutes — is the impact on learning when teachers are out of the classroom. Many teachers are unwilling to be away from their students, even for their own professional learning.

The issue of time becomes one of the most important questions that planners of professional learning must tackle, either at the district- or school-level. As part of its *Transforming Professional Learning Initiative* Learning Forward published the report, *Establishing Time for Professional Learning*. Teams struggling with all of the questions about how to manage the challenge of time will get many ideas from this report at http://learningforward.org/docs/default-source/commoncore/establishing-time-for-professional-learning.pdf.

Where

The transition to more job-embedded learning changes everything — and it certainly changes "where" learning happens. Learning happens in schools and in classrooms when a teacher observes a model classroom; it happens when an offsite coach viewing a lesson through Skype or similar video technology provides technical support using ear bud technology during a class; it happens when a teacher takes on a lead teacher role and facilitates a curriculum committee. It happens in lunchrooms and living rooms and it happens 1:1, in small groups and faculty meetings, and, increasingly, it happens in cross-school and cross-district networking meetings.

New technologies are changing the location of learning in an even more dramatic way. Teachers are observing classrooms across the globe and engaging in asynchronous dialogue about practice with teachers around the world. Teachers are sharing lessons and units on many Common Core sites. And, they are participating in multi-state and international learning communities with teachers.

There are no right answers to the many questions that emerge when tackling the questions of when and where professional learning happens. Teams will have to gather

ONLINE RESOURCES

S.1   Directions for Four Corners
S.2   The facilitator's roles and responsibilities
S.3   Logistics
S.4   Grouping participants
S.5   Working with groups
S.6   Strong openings and closings
S.7   Energizing the group
S.8   Defining next steps
S.9   Using ground rules
S.10   Topics for norms

data about their staff members and then use the data to plan what needs to happen face to face and what can be as successful online asynchronously. Some groups may find that a blended strategy works best.

Conclusion

The two essays in this section have looked at the macro level — a systems approach to professional learning — and a micro level — how the designs can be implemented. Surrounding a design with both system considerations and specific, nitty-gritty implementation ideas leads to results, perhaps even startling results that make a real difference in terms of student learning. Consider this section, then, as a "surround" for effective professional learning designs. Have fun and be productive as you employ the designs to change educator learning in order to improve student learning.

References

Brookfield, S. (1995). *Becoming a critically reflective teacher.* San Francisco, CA: Jossey-Bass.

Corcoran, T., McVay, S., & Riordan, K. (2003). *Getting it right: The MISE approach to professional development.* Philadelphia, PA: Consortium for Policy Research in Education.

Danielson, C. (2006). *Teacher leadership that strengthens professional practice.* Alexandria, VA: ASCD.

Delehant, A. with von Frank, V. (2006). *Making meetings work.* Thousand Oaks, CA: Corwin Press.

Easton, L.B. (Ed.). (2008). *Powerful designs for professional learning* (2nd ed.). Oxford, OH: NSDC.

Easton, L.B. (2011). *Professional learning by design: Putting the learning back into PLCs.* Thousand Oaks, CA: Corwin Press and Oxford, OH: Learning Forward.

Florez, M.C. (2001, March). *Reflective teaching practice in adult ESL settings.* Available at www.cal.org/caela/esl_resources/digests/reflect.html.

Garmston, R.J. & Wellman, B.M. (2013). *The adaptive school: A sourcebook for developing collaborative groups.* Lanham, MD: Rowman & Littlefield Publishers.

Garmston, R.J.& Zimmerman, D.P. (2013). *Lemons to lemonade: Resolving problems in meetings, workshops, and PLCs.* Thousand Oaks, CA: Corwin.

Harrison, C. (2013, November 13–14). *Presentation skills.* Session presented at the conference sponsored by Student Achievement Partners, New York, NY.

Joyce, B.R. & Showers, B. (1988). *Student achievement through staff development.* New York, NY: Longman.

Joyce, B.R. & Showers, B. (2002). *Student achievement through staff development* (3rd ed.). Alexandria, VA: ASCD.

Killion, J. (2008). *Assessing impact: Evaluating staff development* (3rd ed.). Thousand Oaks, CA: Corwin Press and Oxford, OH: NSDC.

Killion, J. (2013). *Establishing time for professional learning.* Oxford, OH: Learning Forward. Available at http://learningforward.org/docs/default-source/commoncore/establishing-time-for-professional-learning.

Kullman, J. (1998). Mentoring and the development of reflective practice: Concepts and context. *System, 26*(4), 471–484.

Learning Forward. (2014). *Standards into practice: External roles. Innovation Configuration maps for Standards for Professional Learning.* Oxford, OH: Author.

Reeves, D. (2006). *The learning leader: How to focus school improvement for better results.* Alexandria, VA: ASCD.

Richardson, J. (2008, May/June). Tune in to what the new generation of teachers can do. *Tools for Schools, 11*(4), 1.

Senge, P.M. (1990). *The fifth discipline: The art & practice of the learning organization.* New York, NY: Doubleday, Currency.

Senge, P., Cambron-McCabe, N., Lucas, T., Smith, B., Dutton, J., & Kleiner, A. (2000). *Schools that learn: A fifth discipline fieldbook for educators, parents, and everyone who cares about education.* New York, NY: Doubleday, Currency.

Stanley, C. (1998). A framework for teacher reflectivity. *TESOL Quarterly, 32*(3), 584–591.

Supovitz, J.A. & Turner, H.M. (2000). The effects of professional development on science teaching practices and classroom culture. *Journal of Research in Science Teaching, 37*, 963–980.

Thiel, T. (1999). Reflections on critical incidents. *Prospect, 14*(1), 44–52.

Vygotsky, L.S. (1978). *Mind in society: The development of higher psychological processes.* Cambridge, MA: Harvard University Press.

Walker, T. (2013, April 29). No more 'sit and get': Rebooting teacher professional development. *NEA TODAY.* Available at http://neatoday.org/2013/04/29/no-more-sit-and-get-getting-serious-about-effective-professional-development/.

Wei, R.C., Darling-Hammond, L., Andree, A., Richardson, N., & Orphanos, S. (2009). *Professional learning in the learning profession: A status report on teacher development in the United States and abroad. Technical Report.* Oxford, OH: NSDC.

PART II

CHAPTER 1

Accessing Student Voices

Listening well to youth is not just a practice but a mindset.

By Kathleen Cushman

Leila and Oscar, 11th-grade teachers in an urban high school serving a high percentage of low-income and minority students, meet every Thursday to plan so that their courses (Leila's in history, Oscar's in English) align as much as possible. This week, with the SAT tests coming up, they have set aside time to talk about the students they share — and, in particular, whether every student is headed for college.

One difference this week: They've brought a dozen students into their conversation. As everyone finds places at desks pushed into an open rectangle, Oscar starts the conversation. "How're you feeling about the test on Saturday?"

After 20 minutes of discussion, Sulimah has shared her worry that, when she times herself on practice SATs, she only gets through half of the questions. Daniela has revealed that her parents, immigrants from the Dominican Republic, do not want her to leave home to attend the university that

has been sending her information. Marco has talked about why an offer from the military recruiter seems enticing to his family but not to him.

Several of the students give a long moan of agreement after Alberto says that his father has put his foot down on the subject of taking on debt for college. "He's scared because he doesn't know enough about the whole college thing," Alberto says. "He doesn't even want me to take the SATs."

Leila, the teacher who has been taking notes all the while, looks around the circle. "It sounds like your focus here is educating your families about college," she says. "Shall we take some time for you to generate some questions?"

Leila's and Oscar's students left that meeting with a plan. It started with a protocol they had used many times in their academic courses: producing their own questions, improving those questions, and then strategizing how to use them.

In this case, the question they came up with was "What do our families need to know for us to succeed in college?"

They came up with the idea to organize an assembly in which recent graduates would come and speak with current students and their parents about the obstacles to college and the ways to overcome them. They planned to conduct a survey of their peers about the college access issues they were facing. The next day, they asked for a meeting with the guidance counselor and the principal. The next month, they analyzed the data they had gathered and prepared a presentation in both Spanish and English. Two months later, they were on the stage of a crowded auditorium, speaking to an audience of parents and peers. By turning their ideas into action, they became agents of change in their own lives, their school, and their community.

These two teachers work in a school that takes seriously its commitment to accessing student voices. For some years, its leadership has recognized that everyone wants a school that brings out the best in both young people and adults. After years of patient work, everybody can see the results in action. For example:

- Students are now routinely included in formal planning and their perspectives and ideas show up in both policy and practice.

- Classroom teachers and students participate in a mid-semester formative assessment of how they are meeting their shared responsibility for a productive learning environment.

- The curriculum includes an elective course in youth leadership offered every semester for social studies credit, and students from the higher grades act as teaching assistants.

Joaquin, the principal here for five years now, graduated from the city's public schools himself; he can remember pushing back against adults in his own youth. Now he starts every academic year by asking faculty to reflect on the moments when they began to cross the line from childhood into adulthood.

"That transition is what we're here for," he always tells his staff. "How are we going to support those growing-up moments in the life of every single student in the school?"

Joaquin began a push to make allies of students who were not recognized leaders in the school, rather than recruiting only those who fit the standard mold. He pulled together a group of young male students who often had roles in the school's disciplinary incidents. They meet in the gym's weight room every morning before school. "There's no agenda," he said. "We just lift. Pretty cool. I'm doing a lot of listening. They've got a lot to say."

He grinned. "We've started calling our group the Revolutionary Leaders. I want them to be the ones who turn that suspension rate around."

Overview

The most important partners in the mission of any school are its students. If their schools do not hear their voices, respect their perspectives, and use their energies, young people will ally themselves with some other group that does. A profound gap may then open between the adults' school and that of the kids — two cultures (or more) in an uneasy tension that invites continual repression and resistance. On the other hand, when educators trust students to help construct and shape their learning environment, they support students' growing agency and engagement.

Although this book is about designs, accessing student voices is really more of a mindset, perspective, or attitude on the part of everybody in the building. It requires practice in inviting and asking questions, listening closely, building trust and respect, and taking action with students. It requires more than just individual ideas and initiatives like those of Leila, Oscar, and Joaquin.

This chapter is based on the work of the nonprofit What Kids Can Do (WKCD), which centers on the learning of youth between the ages of 12 and 24. WKCD has documented the successful efforts of educators who integrated student voices into the most important work of their schools. Like WKCD, this chapter aims:

- To promote the habit of consulting students on matters affecting their schooling;

- To stimulate productive youth-adult discourse and action regarding their learning environment; and

- To provide mutually respectful protocols for accessing and acting on student input.

These purposes serve both the driving forces of adolescent development and the interests of the school. Adolescents have a pressing need to establish identity, agency,

History of Student Voice

Since John Dewey first advocated for democracy in education (1916), educators and youth have pressed for active participation by students in matters affecting their schooling. In 1959, the United Nations Convention on the Rights of the Child declared that those under eighteen have the right to express their opinions and to have those opinions heard and acted upon when appropriate (United Nations, 1960). The 1960s and 1970s saw the "student power" movement emerge among the youth of that politicized generation. By the turn of the 21st century, efforts to involve students more directly in school decisions had increased significantly and a new body of academic research was exploring its effects.

Largely, that research has focused on five main forms of student participation: student councils; temporary school working groups; classroom decision making; school decision making; and multiple types of decision-making environments (Mager & Nowak, 2012). Sometimes it emphasizes the importance of student voice to citizenship education (Holdsworth, 2000); indeed, a movement of democratic schools supports this purpose (Apple & Beane, 1999). In addition, many educators emphasize the fundamental part that student voice plays in school improvement as the perspectives of students provide useful insights regarding problems and their possible solutions (Cook-Sather, 2006; Levin, 2000; Yonezawa & Makeba, 2007).

and autonomy; educators have a vested interest in students' developing self-regulation in their learning. To reach these goals requires the same kind of continual professional learning that teachers need in their academic disciplines. In this case, that means regular opportunities for adults in the school to increase their expertise about accessing the voices and energies of youth.

For example, abundant research has shown the connection between student voice activities and the conditions that support cognitive development in adolescence. As young people practice planning, making decisions about, and evaluating matters that affect them and others, they strengthen the executive functions of their brains and acquire a growing sense of agency (Toshalis & Nakkula, 2012). At the same time, they are expanding their competencies in intellectual, psychological, social, emotional, and physical domains and learning to apply those skills to real-world situations (Mitra, 2009a).

Varieties of student voice

Adults in school often hold a range of attitudes and expectations when they propose to access student voice. For example, they may regard student voice as:
- Opportunities for youth to *express their perspectives,* providing data to school leaders (e.g. via surveys, focus groups, consultations, or other feedback protocols);

- Students' *formal participation,* partnership, and shared responsibility and accountability with adults in making and carrying out decisions; and
- Students' *direct leadership* in deciding, designing, and implementing change efforts, with adults as mentors, guides, and resource providers.

Toshalis and Nakkula (2013) have described this as a spectrum of student-voice-oriented activity (see Figure 1 on p. 50), most of which takes place toward the "expression" end rather than the "leadership" end (p. 195).

As the activity grows more toward partnership, activism, and leadership, it poses increasing challenges to the adult power structure. The need arises to develop capacity among both youth and adults, including providing time and resources for rich conversations about the principles, values, and practical implications of such adult-youth collaborations.

Learning to Listen

This chapter concerns itself not just with *accessing* student voice (that is, how to get students talking with adults) but *learning to listen* to students in ways that both acknowledge and promote their role as a transformative force in education. As Michael Fielding (2001) has pointed out, this involves not just the skills of respectful dialogue but also complicated issues of how adults and students regard and behave with each other in their daily encounters. In addition, organizational systems, routines, and spaces (such as the details of who meets when, where, and why) send signals to students about whether their perspectives are taken seriously.

Let's leave it to this high school student named RaShawn to describe the positive results he saw as his school began to make that process their own:

> When adults give us more responsibility than they usually would — other people might call it challenging us — they show that they trust us to accomplish it. Giving us more say in our education means that they think we're capable. They trust us to make the right decisions about our learning,

about our daily experiences at school. That would be a huge benefit to the entire student body, rather than a liability for the administration.

Rationale

Whatever adults are working on in a school, it goes better when they regard students as stakeholders and change agents. Research and on-the-ground experience make clear the rewards in key areas such as classroom behavior, school climate and culture, school restructuring, community connections, and student achievement (Fielding, 2001). Even more critical, student voice is closely linked with young learners' sense of agency, affecting their motivation and

---

Figure 1: The Spectrum of Student Voice-Oriented Activity

Students articulating their perspectives ← – – – – – – – – → **Students involved as stakeholders** ● – – – – – – – → Students directing collective activities

Students as data sources ← – – – – – – – – – – ● **Students as collaborators** ● – – – – – – – → Students as leaders of change

Expression	Consultation	Participation	Partnership	Activism	Leadership
Volunteering opinions, creating art, celebrating, complaining, praising, objecting	Being asked for their opinion, providing feedback, serving on a focus group, completing a survey	Attending meetings or events in which decisions are made, frequent inclusion when issues are framed and actions planned	Formalized role in decision making, standard operations require (not just invite) student involvement, adults are trained in how to work collaboratively with youth partners	Identifying problems, generating solutions, organizing responses, agitating and/or educating for change both in and outside of school contexts	(Co-) Planning, making decisions and accepting significant responsibility for outcomes, (co-) guiding group processes, (co-) conducting activities

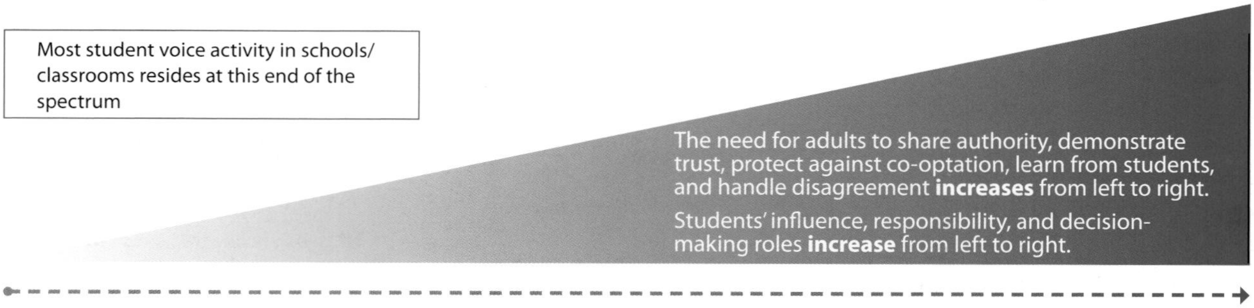

Most student voice activity in schools/classrooms resides at this end of the spectrum

The need for adults to share authority, demonstrate trust, protect against co-optation, learn from students, and handle disagreement **increases** from left to right.

Students' influence, responsibility, and decision-making roles **increase** from left to right.

From Prioritizing motivation and engagement by E. Toshalis, and M.J. Nakkula, M. J, 2013, p. 195. In *Anytime, anywhere: Student-centered learning for schools and teachers* by R.E. Wolfe, A. Steinberg, and N. Hoffman (Eds). Used with permission.

---

engagement and their growth in cognitive, behavioral, and social-emotional domains (Toshalis & Nakkula, 2012). Professional learning that focuses on accessing student voices can help educators integrate into their daily practice the engagement of students in powerful learning and purposeful action.

Some school leaders routinely access student voices so they can align policies, practices, and programs with the interests and needs of youth. Their efforts take place on a spectrum of activities along which the roles, responsibilities, and decision-making authority of students grow (Toshalis & Nakkula, 2013). For example, even the opportunity to express their views or give feedback on school or classroom decisions increases young people's sense of ownership, attachment, membership, and agency (Mitra, 2009b; Rudduck, Demetriou, & Pedder, 2003). When their involvement extends to larger issues (for example, participation in the teacher evaluation process, or action on community issues that affect the school), it has positive effects on both the effort itself and students' development as leaders (Levin, 2000; Mitra & Gross, 2009).

Youth, practitioners, and researchers alike have noted that many actions intended to bring students to the table fall flat. Their purpose and process may tokenize student voice and participation or limit their responsibility for governance. For example, a student council often primarily exists to plan social events like proms and pep rallies. Efforts grounded in a mutually respectful inquiry process regard students' experiences, perspectives, participation, and leadership as indispensable.

Steps

Students do not typically think of school in terms of design. They come to school because they have to. They come to see their friends. They know they had better come if they want to do well in life. And, if at school they find adults who acknowledge them as interesting people and help them try new things, they also come to work side by side with those adults and to learn the habits they will live by.

When educators create the conditions for that to happen, they gain an invaluable asset in the work of the school. For young people themselves, it will make all the difference in developing the crucial sense of agency that will carry them forward into a productive adult life. Both those two enormous benefits will depend on adult members of the school community listening well to students' voices, especially in the adolescent years.

What helps youth talk thoughtfully with us about their learning environments? How can schools make a habit of bringing them to the table? How can adults avoid trivializing their input? Here are six steps that What Kids Can Do found essential for accessing student voices as it documented the successful efforts of educators who integrated student voices into the most important work of their schools.

As you and your students follow these steps or develop your own and share them with others in collegial conversations, slowly but surely, you will be transforming the culture of your school.

Step 1: Bring in all kinds of students

Each school may have a different profile, but all schools have students who arrive with unique characteristics and challenges. When educators want to access student voices, they are usually tempted to go right to the ones who are already easiest to work with: high academic achievers, athletes, popular kids who speak out and stand up readily to lead.

Those students make an important contribution, for sure. But at least as much as educators need them to invest in the adult and student partnership, they need students who struggle academically. They need kids who seem alienated or apathetic. They need shy students and those who act out and get in trouble. They need students who never speak up at all.

With the exquisite social consciousness of "who's in" and "who's out," some students step up to lead their peers in ways that compromise the culture of the school, such as skipping school, fighting, or bullying. Others, marginalized by their differences, do their best to disappear. Whoever they are, whatever their individual circumstances, educators need to access the voices of them all: artistic types, computer geeks, LGBT youth, English language learners, disabled students, everyone.

Building relationships one by one will make that happen. Every student in the school must have at least one adult who knows the student very well. Whatever you do to get there — convening advisory groups, looping with the same students through two or more years, team-teaching to reduce the student load, making home visits — the goal is for all students to feel that someone is listening and that they can speak the truth. Getting to know students' personal stories — where they come from, where they live, their aspirations, dreams, challenges, and barriers — is the single most important strategy to reach that goal.

On the wall of a faculty room, staff members in one school posted a large chart bearing the name of every student in the school. With highlighter pens, staff members marked a student's name if they knew that student well. Within a week, teachers realized that many students were unknown in a meaningful way to anyone. Their next steps were clear to all. Day by day, as teachers went out of their way to seek out and make connections with "invisible" students, the weak links in this school's culture began to strengthen.

Many classroom teachers make connections with their students by giving out a simple questionnaire at the start of any course. While gathering information on their prior experience with the material, the survey also invites sharing of information, concerns, attitudes, and potential obstacles to engagement. It is an important step in building relationships in the service of learning (see Online Resource 1.1: *Student questionnaire for motivation & mastery*).

By staying aware of what students are thinking, both the positive and negative, school adults create a culture that lends itself to collaboration with youth. Ways that schools cast the net wide to engage students include:
- Advisory groups;
- Student questionnaires at the start of a course, asking about students' interests, concerns, expertise, and life outside school;
- Weekly reflective journals in academic courses, where students can write questions, concerns, and ideas;
- Connecting academic skills (e.g. survey research and statistics) with issues students care about;
- Midterm feedback from students to teachers on how a course is going;
- Drop-in hours at the principal's office;
- Monthly grade-level meetings where students can talk about issues with the principal;
- Leadership classes open to all students;
- Support for a student newspaper or website; and
- Events at which students can share their interests or expertise with an audience of peers and adults.

Step 2: Agree on a common purpose

What's the issue that brings adults and youth together? What problems do educators want to address with students as key partners? Step 1 will have brought you a steady flow of both formal and informal communication about student concerns. In addition, you as adults will have your own priorities and pressures. Some examples of issues on which adults and students have collaborated in schools:
- Attendance or lateness;
- Classroom or hallway behaviors;
- School safety (fighting, bullying, harassment, etc.);
- Student expression (speech, dress, dance, etc.);
- Transportation and parking;
- Open or closed campus policies;
- Food issues (access, quality, timing);
- Bathroom conditions;
- Community mentorships;
- Time for supported study;
- Access to health care or counseling;
- Physical plant of the school (capacity, conditions, upkeep, etc.);
- Student load of the teachers;
- Overcrowded classes;
- English-language learning issues;
- Student-led parent conferences;
- Testing policies and conditions;
- Teacher hiring and evaluation;
- Mutual mid-semester feedback on teaching and learning;
- Access to technology;
- Arts in the curriculum;
- Learning outside the school walls;
- Scope of extracurricular activities;
- Student social events;
- School fundraising; and
- District-level quality reviews.

Many factors will influence what issue you will choose as the focus of collaboration with students. Perhaps a crisis has arisen that school leadership must address immediately. Perhaps new information from students has alerted you to a condition you hope to address before it develops into a more serious problem. Perhaps your school already has set forth an improvement process that advances in stages through a number of focus areas.

Whatever the situation, school leadership has the

responsibility to select the focus that makes most sense, given your school context and goals. As Rob Evans (2001) reminds educators, focusing on everything at once will get them nowhere. Instead, as Daniel Rothstein and Luz Santana (2012) of the Right Question Institute suggest, adult leaders should:

1. Identify the target area of concern and its chief emphasis.
2. State it briefly and simply, but not as a question.
3. Not reveal their own bias or preferences.

For example, students and adults may have communicated their dissatisfaction with the lunchroom conditions at your school. How you frame the focus of your collaboration can make a big difference in the quality of student input you will get. For example,

> **Ineffective focus:** "How can we stop food fights in the lunchroom?" By beginning with their own question, adult leaders here are dominating the discourse in which they hope students will join. By revealing their own bias as to the problem, they take away an important opportunity for youth to start talking and thinking along with adults and to collaboratively generate questions that arise from the lunchroom situation.
>
> **Effective focus:** "Improving lunchroom conditions." This states the issue briefly and simply, but not as a question. It leaves to Step 3 the process of youth and adults generating questions that will lead to research and action.

If educators shut kids up, they only shut them down. But when young people see that adults consistently invite their perspectives, they begin to talk more openly and seriously with adults. Step 2 combines with Step 3 to build a framework of cooperation with those you depend on to create a positive learning environment in your school.

Step 3: Generate the right questions

The most powerful learning happens for young people and adults when they come up with their own questions and want to answer them. However, a long tradition of teachers asking the questions has atrophied that skill among students. For youth voices to make a real contribution to a school, everyone needs practice in generating questions that prompt broad and creative thinking together.

A wonderful resource for those bringing a range of voices to the complex issues schools encounter is the book *Make Just One Change* (Rothstein & Santana, 2012). Using its simple protocols, anyone — youth, adults, or a combination — can quickly learn to generate, improve, and prioritize questions in order to plan for research and action.

Through years of empowering thousands of diverse people to participate actively in school and community affairs, Rothstein and Santana (2012) developed four basic rules for generating powerful questions in less than half an hour. (Their Question Formulation Technique took so much research that it rightly bears a trademark!) The rules go like this:

1. Ask as many questions as you can.
2. Do not stop to discuss, judge, or answer any question.
3. Write down every question exactly as it is stated.
4. Change any statement into a question. (see Online Resource 1.2: *Experiencing the Question Formulation Technique*)

Why do these rules matter so much in accessing student voices? They free up young people to ask about what's really on their minds. They protect novices from judgments that could silence them. All questions receive the same respect. Yet the process insists on intellectual discipline: when a question arrives in statement form, it gets reframed right away.

By using this process to bring student voices into conversations about school, educators level the playing field. Here are some areas where this strategy has had powerful effects:

- Classroom teaching and learning, as students worked to frame their questions about important concepts. (For example, "How do we know how tall a mountain is?")
- Classroom culture, as students learned to assess what they have learned and where they will go next. (For example, "How can I demonstrate my progress in this semester?")
- School culture, as students questioned the policies that regulate them. (For example, "How does what we wear affect our learning?")
- District-level issues, as students pressed for representation in bureaucratic processes. (For example, "What role should students play in evaluating public schools?")

Once educators have agreed on clear questions about the issues that matter in classrooms and schools, they are far better equipped for the next step, coming to solutions together.

Step 4: Engage with youth in problem solving

What do we know and from what sources do we know it? What do we still need to know? How can we find out? What new questions do we have? What next steps can we try? (Lieber, 2009). As students take up a question, identify and build on what they know, test their ideas, work with evidence, and revise their views, they will be acquiring content knowledge as well as critical thinking skills.

That is one big reason that accessing student voices matters so much in schools. It aligns perfectly with the intellectual goals and academic behaviors that form the core of a good school's curriculum and instruction.

Of course, youth will inevitably have ideas that adults may not agree with.

"Something as simple as allowing kids to wear hats can make a big difference in how students feel about school," one student told What Kids Can Do. "They say wearing hats disrupts class. Other things disrupt class, like cell phones and bringing food into class, but not hats."

To some adults, remarks like this might seem like a complaint from youth intent on resisting authority. But adults can also see the hat problem as exactly the kind of problem-solving that they want to see students take up: non-routine, multi-dimensional, dynamic, and (at least partly) open-ended. To address a problem like the hat problem would require youth to develop critical thinking and executive skills like these:

- Sizing up situations;
- Examining assumptions;
- Finding information;
- Coordinating actions; and
- Knowing when to seek help.

Young people's capacity for flexibility and negotiation also grows from the give and take that results. When they offer their ideas, youth and adults will have to go back *together* to consider their options, agree on a plan, put it into action, evaluate the results, and revisit the issue for the next cycle of problem-solving.

As adults model and support that process, adolescents develop the crucial sense of agency — the initiative and capacity to act in a desired direction or toward their desired goals. Their attachment and feeling of belonging to the school community grows with every opportunity students have to act as agents of change in their own learning environment.

And as every educator knows, new problems will be presenting themselves every day. It's just part of the life of a school.

Step 5: Make student opinions public

Educators access student voices in many contexts, including quiet spaces where individual students share their experiences with their teachers and mentors. Many good things come from such one-to-one communication. However, when youth perspectives gain traction with a larger audience, students begin to see themselves even more as agents of change.

In 2006, students in a leadership class at an urban high school in Boston had an idea for a video project. They had noticed that their peers in nearby suburban schools had better teachers, more interesting classes, and a far better record of going on to college. They proposed to go into those schools and interview students and teachers to find out why — and to prompt changes at their own school. The 12-minute video they produced has now been used many hundreds of times by schools around the country as food for thought about the "opportunity gap" that low-income youth routinely experience. In a related research interview for What Kids Can Do, two young people described their perceptions as follows:

Bohb: They expect us to go far enough that we graduate, but I don't think they have too many high hopes. Like, "Oh yeah, I know he's going to go to Harvard one day, he's going to be great." I don't think they have those kinds of expectations of us.
Mekiesha: In our school, it's more or less, you finish with high school, are you going to get a job, are you going to join the military, there must be other options out there for you besides college. And that's wrong. It's wrong when your teachers are not motivating you to go on, and above.

Educators can open the door to those wider opportunities in several ways, such as encouraging students to reach out to other students, to reach out to the school community, or to report to the larger community.

Students can reach out to other students. Let the students set the parameters on what's appropriate for a public discourse. That will lead to them taking more responsibility and an even deeper discussion about rights and responsibilities.

Once students trust that they really are at the table with adults, they will make fair deals.

For example, one principal asked students to form a task force that would come up with a new dress code for their school. Students said they appreciated being part of the process of creating the rules. "Give us a chance to do away with the rules that don't make sense," one student commented, "and, believe me, we will truly honor the ones that do."

Projects that get people talking about issues that matter to students do not have to be expensive. In one school hallway display, young people took on the problem of dropouts by using poster board and markers to communicate to their peers how much they cared whether others came to school.

Students can reach out to the school community. Students at one urban high school gave a talk about college access at an assembly for parents, teachers, and other students. Read the following excerpts from interviews in which they presented their case, and ask yourself: What did it take to prepare them to stand up and speak to that group?

Student #1: For many high school students, college seems a distant dream. While 65% of white high school graduates continue on to college, only 56% of African-American. . . .

Student #2: Many low-income students decide early on that they do not have enough money for college or the skills to succeed once there.

Student #3: Sure, college costs a lot of money. But there are resources available that can make funding your college education possible. . . .

Student #4: Keeping your grades up and preparing for the SATs and ACTs is hard work, but college doesn't just guarantee you a better job. . . .

Student #5: There are a lot of hurdles on the road to a higher education. As long as you stay focused, anything is possible.

Students at Central High School in Providence, Rhode Island knew very well that their community considered Central to be a failing school. But they also knew that a lot of great things were going on in their classrooms. They decided to interview teachers and students about important questions — and then they mounted their own website to reach adults and other students in the community. It made the local paper (What Kids Can Do, 2006).

Students can report to the community. As students gain experience and confidence, they will step up and out to do action research on important community problems. San Francisco students saw school enrollment dropping because affordable housing was shrinking in their city, for example. They made a video about it and took it to the city planning board.

In San Antonio, heavy city traffic caused problems for students who used bicycles or cars to get to school. Their social studies class investigated traffic patterns and made recommendations to the city council that would allay the congestion.

As educators open their minds to students' perspectives, increasingly they will find common ground about things that matter to *both* youth *and* adults. That process can start anywhere — even just by saying "How's it going?"— and meaning it. Trusting relationships begin to form, and learning builds on both sides.

Elijah: When I look at my teachers I think about how they were as a kid, if they thought the same way that we think, what they would do about certain things like . . . I wonder like how . . . like if certain of my teachers partied or like how they were as kids, like if they were hippies back in the day or just like how they were. [laughs]. (What Kids Can Do, Inc., n.d.-a)

Elijah: The teacher, she would . . . just how she would act to us. Like she would try to be on terms with us. Like she would relate to us teenagers like, "Oh, put your phone away." Instead of like most teachers would take a student's phone. They'd be like, "Oh, put your phone away," or "Text later," or something like that. Or just you know, "Get your work done." But not sayin' it in like a manner where they're sort of abusing their authority, but where they kind of understand where you're comin' from. Like, "Oh, you can text your mom later," or something like that. (What Kids Can Do, Inc., n.d.-b)

In an interview for a What Kids Can Do research project, another student added,

Genesis: One of the common grounds is that we are, after all, teenagers. And some of them might deny, "No, I was never a child; I was never a kid."

But they were teenagers too, and we still have common problems. They might not be the same exact problem, but problems with parents, problems with friends, boyfriends, and stuff like that. We still have all those common problems. It might not be the same specific thing, but they've been through it. So we have that in common.

Variations

The previous section contained many variations on the general idea of how to access student voices. The only elements that define the integrity of the process are question generation, active listening, and collaborative action by students with adults as partners and mentors.

A rich archive of examples and resources to spark your own ideas appears in Student and Youth Voice: Asking, Listening, and Taking Action, (What Kids Can Do, n.d.-c) a special collection on the "What Kids Can Do" website (http://www.whatkidscando.org/specialcollections/student_voice/index.html).

Challenges and how to address them

Work like this isn't easy to do.

One of the hardest challenges for educators is to find the sweet spot between too much and too little adult participation. Too much adult involvement, and student voice loses its authenticity and its power to involve youth as true problem solvers and stakeholders. Too little, and student voice can become diffuse, exclusive, and ineffective.

Many adults harbor uneasy feelings that adolescents — impulsive, inexperienced, immature, resistant to authority — are too young to trust with the important things. Aren't they in school because they don't know that much?

Still, for each "Yes, but" there is a "Yes, because" that will trump those worries every time. Here are the top three:
1. Student voice is a *democracy* issue. Every country needs active citizens, so adults must give young people practice in the habits of active citizens.
2. Student voice is a *youth development* issue. Every country needs effective leaders, so adults must develop the strengths of future leaders.

3. Student voice lies at the heart of their *learning*. The science of cognition makes this very clear: unless adults listen to young people, they cannot build on what young people experience and believe.

That third reason offers adults a helpful way to shift perspective when they would rather bypass the challenge of really listening to youth.

Think back for a few moments on a time when you really learned something that mattered to you. Was it learning to drive? Mastering something on the computer? Speaking a new language? Playing a sport?

If you are human, somewhere in that experience you were grappling with questions like these:
• What am I good at?
• What do others think of me?
• What do others expect of me?
• Where do I want to go with my life?

These are the central questions of adolescent development, arising as young people ask themselves, "Who am I?" But those same questions are often on the minds of adults.

Everybody is risking something as they learn together around that table. For adults, it can feel threatening when students are given a voice in what happens at school. And for students, it can feel fake. Both adults and students need to come with open minds and open hearts, willing to work with and learn from each other.

"In the end, students do have power, I guess," 16-year old Karima said in an interview. She continued:

The problem is that we don't really know how to use it. And as soon as we start using it, acting like adults, speaking like equals, our teachers don't want us to talk to them like we're the same. As students and teachers, we need to learn how to use our power with each other respectfully, to appreciate each other.

Conclusion

To have meaningful effects in a school community, accessing student voice must:
• Be inclusive, beginning with the premise that everyone has membership;
• Be woven into the daily fabric of school (and reach far beyond afterschool clubs and "one-off" events);

- Target substantive issues;
- Involve asking and listening by all parties; and
- Lead to constructive action ("Student and youth voice: Asking, listening, and taking action," n.d., para. #3).

If young people are to be thoughtful stakeholders in improving teaching and learning, they need adult allies and mentors — and they need attentive adult listeners. Students find real value in meetings and talking without adults present. But the target here is to energize adults and youth together, in the same room, through conversations and debate.

As this chapter opened, Leila, Oscar, and Joaquin played their parts in creating that energy. When a whole school sets its sights on making the shift from "either-or" to "together," adults and students both reap the benefits.

"What matters to us more than any one question is a school that takes student voices seriously," one high school student said in a research interview. "Such a school would look a lot more cooperative. Everybody would be a role model for each other, everybody would try something new, and we'd each get to share our talents."

References

Apple, M. W. & Beane, J.A. (1999). *Democratic schools: Lessons from the chalk face.* Milton Keynes, England: Open University Press.

Cook-Sather, A. (2006). Sound, presence, and power: "Student Voice" in educational research and reform. *Curriculum Inquiry, 36*(4), 359–390.

Dewey, J. (1916). *Democracy and education: An introduction to the philosophy of education.* New York, NY: The Macmillan Company.

Evans, R. (2001). *The human side of school change.* San Francisco, CA: Jossey-Bass.

Fielding, M. (2001). Students as radical agents of change. *Journal of Educational Change, 2*(2), 123–141.

Holdsworth, R. (2000). Schools that create real roles of value for young people. *Prospects, 30*(3), 349–362.

Levin, B. (2000). Putting students at the centre in education reform. *Journal of Educational Change, 1*(2), 155–172.

Lieber, C.M. (2009). *Making learning REAL: Reaching and engaging all learners in secondary classrooms.* Cambridge, MA: Educators for Social Responsibility.

Mager, U. & Nowak, P. (2012). Effects of student participation in decision making at school. A systematic review and synthesis of empirical research. *Educational Research Review 7*(1), 38–61.

Mitra, D.L. (2009a). Strengthening student voice initiatives in high schools: An examination of the supports needed for school-based youth-adult partnerships. *Youth and Society, 40*(3), 311–335.

Mitra, D.L. (2009b). Student voice and student roles in education policy reform. In D. Plank, G. Sykes, & B. Schneider (Eds.) *AERA Handbook on Education Policy Research* (pp. 819–830). London, England: Routledge.

Mitra, D.L. & Gross, S. J. (2009, July). Increasing student voice in high school reform: Building partnerships, improving outcomes. *Educational Management Administration & Leadership, 37*(4), 522–543.

Rothstein, D. & Santana, L. (2012). *Make just one change.* Cambridge, MA: Harvard Education Press.

Rudduck, J., Demetriou, H., & Pedder, D. (2003, Spring). Student perspectives and teacher practices: The transformative potential. *McGill Journal of Education, 38*(2), 274–288.

Toshalis, E. & Nakkula, M.J. (2012). Motivation, engagement, and student voice. In the *Students at the center* series. Boston, MA: Jobs for the Future.

Toshalis, E. & Nakkula, M.J. (2013). Prioritizing motivation and engagement. In R. E. Wolfe, A. Steinberg, & N. Hoffman (Eds.), *Anytime, anywhere: Student-centered learning for schools and teachers* (pp. 171–204). Cambridge, MA: Harvard Education Press.

United Nations. (1959). *Declaration of the rights of the child, Resolution 1386. Adopted by the General Assembly of the United Nations, New York.* London, England:

> ## ONLINE RESOURCES
>
> **1.1** Student questionnaire for motivation & mastery
>
> **1.2** Experiencing the Question Formulation Technique

H.M. Stationery Office. Available at www.un.org/cyber schoolbus/humanrights/resources/child.asp.

What Kids Can Do, Inc. (Producer). (n.d.-a). *Just listen: Youth talk about learning. Imagining teachers as kid: Elijah* [Video]. Available at https://www.youtube.com/watch?v=jrVyWwh7Qlk&list=PLE7D9C40FEB05950&index=1.

What Kids Can Do, Inc. (Producer). (n.d.-b). *Just listen: Youth talk about learning. On terms with us: Elijah* [Video]. Available at https://www.youtube.com/watch?v=28-bDdBjSWI.

What Kids Can Do, Inc. (n.d.-c). *Student and youth voice: Asking, listening, and taking action.* Available at www.whatkidscando.org/specialcollections/student_voice/index.html.

What Kids Can Do, Inc. (2006). *School as subject: Four student documentaries about school equality, redesign, and college access.* Video on DVD, info@whatkidscando.org.

Yonezawa, S., & Makeba, J. (2007). Using student's voices to inform and evaluate secondary school reform. In D. Thiessen & A. Cook-Sather (Eds.), *International handbook of student experience in elementary and secondary school* (pp. 681–709). Dordrecht, The Netherlands: Springer.

CHAPTER 2

Action Research

Picture a spiral going round and round. Or a long mobile, spinning slowly in the breeze. Action research is far from a linear, formulaic, lockstep process of professional learning.

By Cathy Caro-Bruce and Mary Klehr

It's Sarah's turn to talk, and the group immediately quiets. Her question has hung out there at each meeting, creating discomfort for those who prefer that the question just go away. Despite their uneasiness, however, others want to go deeper into what she describes.

She starts, "I'm so embarrassed. I thought I was looking at a system at our school that was promoting student success and instead I found some pretty blatant racism." No one says a word. "I decided to look at the data on our rewards system to find out which kids were at which level in terms of the privileges they could receive. What I found is that all of the white students are at the top and all of the black and poor students are at the bottom. I think I need to change my question about the rewards system and its effect on student success."

Sarah hands out copies of the data she collected and describes the patterns she sees. Group members question

Sarah to encourage her to explore the situation from different perspectives, to push her to do the work on her question. They are careful not to offer solutions or solve the problem for her.

"Tell us more about the patterns your data show," says one teacher. "I'm curious if the students are aware that this dynamic is occurring," offers another. "How do you think the teachers would respond if you were to share the data with them?" asks a third. Sarah responds to the members' questions — what they are curious about, what they think she can explore to enrich her understanding of the problem. The dialogue is on its way.

As it proceeds, Sarah reflects on how her question may change. "What I really need to look at is *How can I challenge a rewards system that staff perceive positively by addressing the inequities and lack of access to opportunities for some students?*" The group grows quiet until one participant finally says,

"That is so huge. What can we do to help?"

Near the end of Sarah's time, the group facilitator asks her, "So, what's next? What steps will you take before our next meeting?" Sarah answers that she needs to collect more data to help her understand other staff members' perceptions of the rewards system. She says she will put together questions for grade-level teams and wonders if she can email the questions to the group before she conducts the interviews.

Before the group moves on to the next member, Sarah expresses her thanks and says with a huge sigh, "I am so committed to this topic, but I don't think I could do it without all of you."

Sarah's participation in a district-sponsored action research team called "Race, Class, Gender, Culture, Language, and Learning" is a powerful professional learning experience for her and her colleagues. Not only does Sarah delve deeply into studying her question, but other participants in her research group also learn about her topic and make connections to their own work along the way.

Overview

Picture a spiral going round and round. Or a long mobile, spinning slowly in the breeze. Or a rare shell whose design conveys circular motions evolving over time. Or even a Möbius Strip. These are all images of action research. Action research is an iterative form of inquiry through which participants actively engage in examining their own educational practice, systematically and carefully, using research techniques in order to impact teacher and student learning (Watts, 1985). Action research affects the researchers, the contexts in which they work, and the children they teach.

Action researchers follow steps based on good research techniques, but the process invites researchers to re-cycle through earlier phases as they construct new meaning and discover new questions based on what they find in their data, and as their instructional practice evolves. Action research is far from a linear, lockstep, formulaic process. While traditional researchers sometimes criticize the openness and flexibility of action research, its cyclical and responsive nature is what makes the process so valuable to teachers.

Rationale

Beyond some of the pragmatic learning that teachers hope to achieve, the following core principles are what drive many people to participate in this approach to professional learning:

- Action research supports teachers in identifying topics important to their teaching, examining their own work using research techniques, and exploring how to become more effective instructional leaders. In contrast to some types of professional learning that diminish teacher efficacy by viewing educators as empty receptacles to be filled with knowledge and skills, this model of professional learning puts teachers — their thinking, their questions, their desire to improve — at the center of the work. When teachers are at the center of their professional learning, they are more likely to make changes that affect student learning and improve conditions so that high quality learning occurs.

- Action research is a unique genre of research because it promotes active engagement on the part of teachers and is grounded in the real world of the classroom. It balances a classroom culture that is personal, contextual, open-ended, and ever-changing with a research culture that is analytical, structured, and systematic.

- The "action" in action research implies that, throughout the process, the researchers will reflect on their work, focus on how to be more effective, and take actions to implement improvements based on what they learn. The experience is enhanced when participants are given the opportunity to meet regularly as a research group in a safe and supportive environment away from day-to-day classroom activities.

Some reasons teachers participate in action research, and areas that show a positive impact on teacher and student learning, include the following:

- **Individual progress.** Action researchers are motivated to better understand and improve their teaching and the classroom environment. They often focus on a particular aspect of their teaching practice or context that is challenging them.

- **Student progress.** Action researchers want to know more about how to improve student learning.
- **Knowledge production.** Action research promotes producing and sharing new knowledge that benefits other educators.
- **Social change.** Action research pushes teachers to examine practices that promote or are barriers to equity and reinforces the principles of democratic decisions in schools.
- **Personal meaning.** Action research is inherently rewarding as teachers search for connections, value, and significance in their work (Zeichner, Marion, & Caro-Bruce, 1998).

Action research also supports what educators know about implementing change initiatives, schoolwide or individually. A critical component of action research is reflection. Teachers benefit students by reflecting on their practice because they question their ideas, pilot them, take part in ongoing dialogue, and look thoughtfully at their own instructional practices. Action researchers are more likely to take action on a problem or area of study because they reflect with colleagues on data from a variety of sources.

Steps

Step 1: Decide whether action research will be done with a group or individually

At any step in this process, action researchers can gain much if they meet informally, in a small group, with other action researchers in the school or district or outside the district. Throughout her participation in the process, Sarah was meeting with other action researcher colleagues in a district-sponsored class co-facilitated by a teacher and a staff developer, both experienced action researchers.

Individuals also can form a small group without any formal facilitation or class time. A monthly meeting after school may help action researchers as they share where they are in the process, ask questions of their peers, invite comments and feedback, and plan next steps for their study. Group members can even support each other by "meeting" online. Without support, researchers may get bogged down in the process and be less effective.

Step 2: Find a focus

"What's keeping you awake at night?"

"What are you curious about?"

"If you could change one thing about your practice, what would it be?"

Questions such as these are often the entry points that drive action researchers to focus on an aspect of teaching and begin to narrow their area of study. There is no right way to have a question emerge. Researchers, who may include teachers, principals, support staff, or other education stakeholders, can develop a question from broad categories such as:

- **Student outcomes:** Achievement, assessment, attitude, learning, relationships, connections to school and peers. For example, "How can I help students better assess the effectiveness of their learning strategies?"
- **Instructional practices:** Differentiated materials and strategies to meet the needs of individuals or groups of learners. For example, "How well do the instructional strategies I use in my teaching help students read for understanding in the content areas?"
- **Systems/structures:** Behavior/discipline, special education inclusion model, team structures, decision making, equitable access to all curricula, new programs and practices, strategies to improve service delivery. For example, "How do the systems we have in place in school prevent access to higher-level classes for some students?"
- **Climate:** Attitudes, relationships, safety, connection to school. For example, "How do the perceptions our students have about their safety in school impact their sense of belonging?"
- **Parents/family:** Connection to school, decision making, support to families. For example, "What are the most effective ways to communicate with our richly diverse population of parents and families?" (See sidebar on p. 62, Types of action research questions; also see Online Resource 2.1: *Starting points.*)

The action research question becomes the driving force of the work. Each researcher's question is discussed at monthly meetings, including how the question has changed over time, what data have been gathered and analyzed to answer the question, what actions a researcher is taking as a result of the findings, and what new questions are emerging.

Types of action research questions

Teacher researchers' questions fall into categories that demonstrate a range of possibilities and challenges.

To improve practice:

- How can I scaffold scientific investigations for English Language Learners to impact academic language development while maintaining scientific content? (Elementary science resource teacher)

- How can formative assessment be used in my high school mathematics classroom to improve both student and teacher understanding of learning? (High school math teacher)

- What structures can I put in place for frequent, meaningful conferences with my student teachers to ensure they are learning and growing as beginning educators? (Middle school teacher)

To better understand a particular aspect of practice:

- How does explicit instruction in and modeling of selected reading strategies affect the self-efficacy of students with learning disabilities when reading informational text? (Cross-categorical teacher)

- In what ways can I integrate technology in the early childhood setting to tap into children's funds of knowledge and increase number sense development? (Kindergarten teacher)

To better understand one's practice in general:

- How can school nurses help teachers understand and respond to the needs of students with asthma? (School nurse)

- What strategies motivate struggling children to become active participants in the classroom community and feel successful as learners? (4th–5th-grade teacher)

- How will implementing our full inclusion model affect how students perceive themselves and others as learners? (Cross-categorical teacher)

To promote greater equity:

- How can the science department and special education department heterogeneously group students with a wide variety of learning needs and make this type of grouping a successful experience for the students and staff? (Biology teacher)

- What professional learning approach can we develop to encourage more culturally responsive instruction in our school? (Teacher leader)

- How does a sense of belonging affect academic achievement? (Resource teacher)

To influence the social conditions of school:

- How can I increase staff buy-in for a schoolwide bullying and harassment prevention program? (Violence prevention coordinator)

- How can forming academic peer groups be used to reinforce positive attitudes of academic achievement in the face of negative peer pressure? (Principal intern)

- How can our school develop a decision-making structure that incorporates all staff members fairly, and what can my role be? (Librarian)

- How can I, through the development and facilitation of a peer mentorship program, foster opportunities for student leadership that support incoming 9th graders in successfully transitioning to high school? (Guidance counselor)

Teachers develop action research questions that are

- **Significant:** Focusing on teaching and learning practices that could affect students' achievement or behavior;
- **Manageable:** Can be done within the researcher's time constraints;
- **Contextual:** Embedded in the researcher's daily work;
- **Clearly stated:** Accurately conveying the focus and scope of the research;
- **Open-ended:** Generating a broad range of insights rather than trying to prove a specific point; and
- **Self-reflective:** Focusing on the actions or practice of the researcher (St. Louis Action Research Evaluation Committee, 1998).

The critical issue for researchers is how manageable the question is given the scope of the topic. The further away from the researcher — that is, the broader the focus — the more difficult it is for researchers to know if what they are studying and learning is making a difference.

Step 3: Develop an action plan

The plan will change — it should change — but this stage pushes teachers to think like researchers. It prevents researchers from impulsively giving a survey to staff members at the school, for example, when other steps need to be taken first. These questions will influence the development of a beginning action plan.

- What do I want to know? Why do I want to know this? Who can help me learn about this topic?
- What are some possible sources of data collection? Students? Staff? Parents? Team members? Administration?
- Who can review the questionnaire I develop? The interview questions I design? Who can help observe students?
- Do I want to do a literature review and find out what others have learned about this topic?

Once teachers begin to learn from their data — and as new questions, ideas, and understanding surface — the plan can be revised (see Online Resource 2.2: *Action plan*).

At this point, action researchers can meet formally or informally with their action research group to get feedback on their plans.

Step 4: Collect data

Think broadly. Think deeply. Think about multiple perspectives. Action researchers internalize these messages throughout their data collection journey.

The journey starts simply: What do you want to learn? Why do you want to learn it? When, where, and how will you collect the data? Teachers might not have a strong background in action research data collection and analysis, so incorporating the specifics of how these steps will be accomplished is essential to moving the researcher forward (see Online Resource 2.3: *Data collection and analysis*).

Action researchers use qualitative and research methods, including interviews, portfolios, surveys/questionnaires, field notes/observation records, interviews, video recordings, student work, discussions, audiotapes, and case studies. They may also include pre- and post-assessments, standardized tests, or district tests.

They collect and analyze data throughout the process. Action researchers learn about triangulation — collecting and analyzing data that originate from more than one source, at more than one point in time — to increase the validity of what they are learning. Triangulation helps researchers move from using intuition to using real information to drive decisions. Researchers also are encouraged to select data sources that will provide them with *breadth* by soliciting multiple perspectives, with *depth* by asking questions that go beyond the surface, and with *corroboration* by comparing other data sources such as student work or school practices to confirm what they are learning.

Because action researchers may fall into the trap of doing things they think they are supposed to do to make their projects legitimate research, the facilitator and group members consistently need to ask the teachers to articulate why they are working on a particular action and what they hope to learn. Staying true to the purpose of the research drives action researchers to develop a data collection process with inquiry, curiosity, and problem solving at its core.

Collecting data can become far more complicated than it initially seems, so this is a time when feedback from colleagues may prove essential. Whether meeting formally in a class or informally, action researchers can give each other feedback about their data collection processes.

Step 5: Analyze the data

Sorting through all the data they have collected can be a major task for action researchers as they synthesize what they have learned. Many action researchers enjoy the creativity in this part of the process. They develop elaborate systems using colored dots and flags, sticky paper, and highlighters. During this stage, researchers look for themes, patterns, and big ideas. They code what they see in their data and narrow down the themes into something manageable. They find sub-themes among the larger areas. They write continuously as new ideas and connections surface, and they construct meaning by bringing different sources of information together in new ways. Analyzing data involves noting how frequently certain ideas show up, as well as highlighting those powerful, interesting, and unusual bits of information that have potential to influence future thinking and directions.

This is a messy time. It is also a stimulating and heady time as the researcher brings disparate pieces together into a greater whole. (See Online Resource 2.4: *Process for analyzing data.*) As they analyze data, action researchers can turn to peers to help them see themes they may have missed or holes in their logic. Colleagues can also help celebrate the potential power of the research.

Step 6: Write about the work

While some action research programs do not emphasize writing up the process and findings, many build in this phase because the developers of action research programs understand the power of writing. Writing pushes researchers to a new level of understanding as they work to communicate what they have learned. For those who haven't written a paper in a long time, writing can challenge them. Once they have finished writing, however, teachers often describe how rewarding this aspect of the process was for them.

Writing primarily gives researchers a chance to describe the experience and synthesize what they learned. A report also allows the larger community of educators to learn from their colleagues and potentially improve their own learning environments. If teachers believe that their voices can influence policy and they have access to forums that can guide educational directions, then it is critical that they write about their findings. Action researchers simply tell the story in their reports. Components can include:

- **A description of the problem, focus area, question.** Why was it a question for the researcher?
- **A description of the context in which this study occurred.** What background information would be helpful in understanding why this question was important to study?
- **A description of actions the researcher took to learn about the topic.** What did the researcher do and why?
- **An explanation of the research methods and data collection sources used.** From where and from whom did the researcher gather data?
- **A literature review.** If the researcher did a literature review, what new information or ideas influenced the researcher's actions?

- **Data analysis.** What did the data show? What themes, patterns, and findings emerged?
- **Recommendations.** What new actions will the researcher take based on what was learned? What new questions does the researcher have?

Throughout the process, action researchers may want to share their writing with peers. If they have been meeting formally, their group facilitator may divide them into peer editing groups for focused feedback. If they have been meeting informally, action researchers can ask the group to listen and respond to parts of their writing, or pair up to get and give feedback. Sharing their writing with partners or the larger action research group often helps build action researchers' confidence to take their voices and their work to the larger educational community.

Action researchers can publish their learning online in a blog or by linking others to it through social media.

Step 7: Plan For future action

The "action" in action research is central to this professional learning model. Based on their findings, researchers determine what they will do differently in their classrooms or what might happen differently on their teams or in their schools. Action researchers look for ways to share what they've learned with colleagues, their principal, or with special interest groups. This step is not the end but the beginning of a new cycle (see Online Resource 2.5: *Analysis leading to action*).

Variations

School districts and teacher education programs throughout the country have embraced action research and chosen from a variety of structural approaches to customize the process to their own contexts.

Schoolwide research. Some districts implement schoolwide action research where the entire staff studies a school issue or problem of interest to everyone. Action research has great potential to affect a school's practices when administrators (at building and district levels) and teachers themselves support a schoolwide initiative. When developing this kind of program, it is essential that teachers own what they will study, how they will study it, how they will share findings, and what will happen as a result of what they've learned.

Individual research. Other districts and teacher education programs support individual action research. Individual teachers work on a topic of interest to them in their own classrooms. While this may be a powerful experience for the teacher, the teacher may not have the support, vision, or know-how to extend the effects of the work beyond his or her own classroom.

Collaborative research. Some districts implement collaborative action research, where groups of teachers, principals, and/or support staff come together around topics that are priorities for the school or district. Group members may be from the same school or they may represent schools from around the district. The results of collaborative research are likely to be applicable in a variety of settings.

Challenges and how to address them

Some of the challenges action researchers may encounter are common to many professional learning designs: the need for facilitation, the scarcity of time, and the importance of sustaining important work. However, action research is also challenging because core principles that govern it might be sabotaged by actions that contradict them. Also, action research that is shared — as it should be — requires that peers respect the individual during the group process.

Core principles. Action research can be defined very differently in different contexts — and that is part of the effectiveness of this model of learning. The developers of action research in a district must define principles that will maintain the nature and integrity of this powerful strategy and drive the work forward. Research, articles, and experiences from other districts will help educators identify these principles. If, for instance, it is a core principle that the process is learner-focused and teachers will be able to determine their action research questions and data methods, then district leaders cannot tell teachers exactly what they should be studying or exactly what data they need to collect. While district administrators might have good intentions to support the professional learning of staff, they can unintentionally sabotage these efforts if their core principles are not aligned to their actions.

Facilitation. The success of any action research program is inextricably linked to the quality of the facilitators of the groups. The best action research group facilitators are skilled facilitators who know how to create a safe and open learning environment, who are organized and skilled at planning, who know how to bring all the voices into the conversations, who allow the learners to struggle and come up with their own actions, and who are learners themselves. Any district program should build in a support structure for its facilitators through regular meetings where challenges are discussed, resources are shared, and facilitators have the opportunity to build their skills.

Group process. When action researchers share their work with the group at regular meetings, one of the biggest challenges is dealing with how other group members respond. Often, there are group members who have a hard time letting the researcher struggle with his or her question. They want to offer ideas and strategies that they have used to solve a similar challenge. One of the strongest core principles — and one that facilitators need to constantly reinforce — is that each researcher needs to be doing the inquiry work. The role of other group members is not to tell them what to do nor do the work for them, but to ask reflective questions that assist their colleagues in going deeper into their own research puzzles.

Time. There are lots of challenges related to time and doing action research, but the two biggest areas are finding time for research groups to meet and finding time for teachers to collect data, synthesize findings, and write about or otherwise share their work. District administrators have creatively designed strategies to help action researchers meet, including afterschool meetings, during the school day meetings with substitutes, Saturday meetings, professional learning community (PLC) time, and weekly breakfast meetings. While acknowledging that this is extra time for staff, participants talk about the importance and value of this time for them professionally.

Finding time to do the research is also a challenge for teachers. While some district leaders have been able to provide some released time in addition to the meetings, participants typically will do this work on their own time. Collecting data, including observations of students or interviewing staff, can often fit into the school day. District administrators might try to create incentives, including earning credit and providing opportunities to share the work more publicly, to recognize the work that teachers are doing.

Sustainability. How can action research become part of the culture of the district? How can it move from being an isolated activity to being an integral part of the professional learning of a district? These are the questions that face district educators once action research moves beyond the pilot stage. One of the most powerful strategies is to look for places in the organization where partnerships and collaborations can be built. How can action research help others in the organization accomplish their work? A second strategy is to make sure that the leaders of this work are part of the conversation about future directions for professional learning in the organization so that others understand what action research accomplishes. And a third strategy is to share the work widely and in many different ways. Present at principal meetings, create a website, use the research to inform district directions, share the work on local television, present at statewide meetings, submit articles to journals, and so on. Soon, others will want to be part of this exciting work.

Conclusion

Sarah knew she had questions about the rewards system at her school. She had some beginning ideas that jump-started her initial data collection. Her question wasn't well formed, but experiences and observations of students led her to generate some ideas that moved her along to do some initial data collection. Sarah's revised question, *"How can I challenge a rewards system that is perceived by staff as positive by addressing the inequities and lack of access to opportunities for some students?"* met the criteria for a good action research question. Collecting data helped her continue to refine her thinking, define more clearly what she was learning, and determine what actions to take.

By the end of the school year, Sarah's journey had just begun. After interviewing six staff members who represented different established teams in the school, she learned that most of them were supportive of the system and weren't aware of student groupings at each level of privilege. She designed a survey for all staff and facilitated two student focus groups. Among the many issues both staff and students surfaced, the most critical was institutionalized racism throughout the school. In late spring, Sarah shared her findings with staff, and the school's newly formed Equity Team began to plan for the next school year. The Equity Team's goal was to involve the entire school in thoughtfully discussing practices that kept some students from having equal access to a comprehensive learning and educational experience. While Sarah's question began as a personal need to understand the implications of a school practice, her action research led her to examine a system that needed to be challenged.

One voice, one study, one persistent teacher — one journey can make a tremendous difference in the lives of children.

References

St. Louis Action Research Evaluation Committee. **(1998).** *Classroom action research: Five phases of action research.* Madison, WI: Madison Metropolitan School District. Available at www.madison.k12.wi.us/sod/car/carphases.html.

Watts, H. (1985, Spring). When teachers are researchers, teaching improves. *Journal of Staff Development, 6*(2), 118–127.

Zeichner, K., Marion, R., & Caro-Bruce, C. (1998). *The nature and impact of action research in one urban school district: Final report.* Chicago, IL: Spencer.

ADDITIONAL RESOURCES

Articles

"Advancing professional inquiry for educational improvement through action research," by Donald M. Miller and Gerald J. Pine. (1990, Summer). *Journal of Staff Development, 11*(3), 56–61.

"At last: Practitioner inquiry and the practice of teaching: Some thoughts on better," by Susan L. Lytle. (2008). *Journal for Research in the Teaching of English, 42*(3), 373–379.

"Collaborative action research and school improvement. We can't have one without the other," by Richard Sagor. (2009). *Journal of Curriculum and Instruction (JoCI)*, 3(1), 7–14.

"Holding up a mirror: Teacher-researchers use their own classrooms to investigate questions," by Debra Viadero. (2002). *Education Week, 21*(40), 32–35.

"In defense of action research," by Violet Hughes. (1992, Fall). *Research Forum*, pp. 6–11.

"Professional development through action research," by Jack A. McKay. (1992, Winter). *Journal of Staff Development, 13*(1), 18–21.

"Pulling their own levers," by Kenneth Zeichner, Mary Klehr, and Cathy Caro-Bruce. (2000, Fall). *Journal of Staff Development, 21*(4), 36–39.

"The teacher research movement: A decade later," by Marilyn Cochran-Smith and Susan L. Lytle. (1999, October). *Educational Researcher, 28*(7) 15–25.

"Teacher research leads to learning, action," by Joan Richardson. (2000). *Tools for Schools, 3*(4), 1–6.

Books

Action research facilitators handbook, by Cathy Caro-Bruce. Oxford, OH: National Staff Development Council, 2000. Also available at http://files.eric.ed.gov/fulltext/ED472452.pdf.

The Action Research Guidebook: A Four-Step Process for Educators and School Teams, 2nd ed., by Richard Sagor. Thousand Oaks, CA: Corwin Press, 2011.

The art of classroom inquiry: A handbook for teacher researchers, rev. ed., by Ruth Shagoury Hubbard and Brenda Miller Power. Portsmouth, NH: Heinemann, 2003.

Creating equitable classrooms through action research, by Cathy Caro-Bruce, Ryan Flessner, Mary Klehr, and Ken Zeichner. Thousand Oaks, CA: Corwin Press, 2007.

Digging deeper into action research: A teacher inquirer's field guide, by Nancy Fichtman Dana. Thousand Oaks, CA: Corwin Press, 2013.

Ethical issues in practitioner research, by Jane Zeni. New York, NY: Teachers College Press, 2001.

Inquiry as stance: Practitioner research in the next generation, by Marilyn Cochran-Smith and Susan L. Lytle. New York, NY: Teachers College Press, 2009.

Living the questions: A guide for teacher-researchers, 2nd ed., by Ruth Shagoury Hubbard and Brenda Miller Power. York, ME: Stenhouse Publishers, 2011.

The power of questions: A guide to teacher and student research, by Beverly Falk and Megan Blumenreich. Portsmouth, NH: Heinemann, 2005.

"Practitioner research," by Kenneth M. Zeichner and Susan E. Noffke. In Virginia Richardson (Ed.), *Handbook on Research on Teaching,* 4th ed., pp. 298-332. Washington, DC: American Educational Research Association.

Studying your own school: An educator's guide to practitioner action research, 2nd ed., by Gary Anderson, Katheryn Herr, and Ann Sigrid Nihlen. Thousand Oaks, CA: Corwin Press, 2007.

ADDITIONAL RESOURCES

Websites

http://gse.gmu.edu/research/tr/tr-action. Teacher Research web page of the College of Education and Human Development, George Mason University, defines action research, describes the history of action research and links to related literature and action research websites.

http://teachersnetwork.org/tnli/research/. Teachers Network Leadership Institute: Action Research: Teacher Research provides reports about action research conducted by TNLI MetLife Fellows in the following areas: professional development, curriculum implementation, classroom management and school cultures, assessment and preparation for assessment, parental involvement and immigrant engagement, policy and practice teacher leadership in school change, teacher networks, and teacher preparation and new teacher induction.

https://staffdevweb.madison.k12.wi.us/ node/326. The Classroom Action Research web page of Madison Metropolitan School District (MMSD) offers several resources about action research including guidelines, abstracts and past studies, and info flyer/applications for the 2014 classroom action research groups.

http://blogs.edweek.org/teachers/living- in-dialogue/2012/05/teacher_research_transforms_ a_.html. "Teacher research transforms a school in Oakland," is a blog post by Anthony Cody (2012, May 1), *Education Week.*

http://journals.library.wisc.edu/index.php/ networks. Networks: An Online Journal for Teacher Research includes teacher research reports and accounts detailing the impact of this professional activity on student and teacher learning.

www.naeyc.org/publications/vop/resources. The Teacher Research Resources, web page of the National Association for the Education of Young Children (NAEYC), offers print and online resources about the teacher research process, accounts of teachers conducting research in their own classrooms, and connections with others in the field interested in teacher research.

CHAPTER 3

Assessment as Professional Learning

Collaborative designs and peer reviews honor and enhance
teachers' professionalism, expertise, and collegial learning.

By Jay McTighe and Marcella Emberger

For five days one summer, small groups of teachers worked together to design "authentic"
performance tasks and associated rubrics to allow
students to demonstrate that they could
apply their learning in meaningful ways. The teachers were
introduced to a design process and then spent each morning
working collaboratively on task and rubric development. Each afternoon, the teams shared their drafts with
other teams, listened to feedback, and made suggested
revisions. By the end of the week, all teachers had a
collection of rich performance tasks and appropriate rubrics
to use in their classrooms.

The process provided teachers with more than usable
products. Participants also learned about collaboration, peer
review, using feedback to refine work, reviewing student
work, consistency, and calibration. Here are a few of the
teachers' reflections on what they learned:

I was assigned to this team of teachers I had
never met before. They were from other schools.
Anxious does not quite describe my feeling. I had
never written anything with a team. In fact, I
really didn't believe it was a very efficient use of my
time. I wondered why we couldn't all write separate
tasks — then we would have multiple products.
By the end, I realized I was wrong about a couple
of things. First, I learned more from my colleagues
than I ever imagined I could as a 20-year veteran.
Second, I have this collection of good assessment
tasks and rubrics to take back to school.
— *Sandy, a 3rd-grade teacher*

I was somewhat anxious about meeting as a group
for a peer review of our work. We had a set of
criteria that the facilitator had given us, but I wasn't

really sure what was going to happen. The facilitator reviewed the criteria with us. Then she and several teachers modeled a peer review. The most helpful part of all this is the concept of descriptive feedback — the most helpful, but also the most difficult. Most of us are used to giving our opinions but not really identifying what's behind that opinion. We learned quickly that opinions can interfere with our looking at work objectively. Others saw things in my assessment design that I had not seen. Similarly, I gained many ideas from reviewing other tasks.

— *Khalid, a high school history teacher*

The design teams reconvened for two days during the school year after they had used the tasks with their students. They carefully reviewed student work from the tasks, discussed needed refinements and shared instructional strategies and resources for improving student performance. Here are some of their reflections:

I brought several student papers with me to share with my department design team. I must admit I struggled with the temptation to bring only work from my best kids, but finally selected samples from various quality levels as we were asked to do. After all, we had decided we would try to figure out the range in our grade level, but I hadn't thought about how difficult it would be to share work from my students who are not successful. This whole process forced me to look at those kids who may be slipping through the cracks in my classroom.

— *Carolina, a middle school English teacher*

I really didn't think a veteran like me had so much left to learn. I was wrong. I learned every time my team and I shared. Funny thing was, our students could tell we were working as a team. We spoke to them in one voice. One of our students came up to me after class one day and said, 'I think this is a conspiracy. Like this rubric — it's almost exactly like the one Mrs. R. gave us!' I told him he was right. 'We are conspiring to make sure you learn.' I expect that to happen again this year."

— *Lenny, a 5th-grade teacher*

There's a whole lot of talk about developing professional learning communities, but this is the real thing. I am so impressed with how this process changes attitudes and practices — I now feel we are developing a strong collaborative community here at our school — all based on understanding our students' learning.

— *Mike, a high school assistant principal*

Overview

Typically, professional learning has focused on instructional practices, not assessment methodology. While expanding teaching repertoire and refining pedagogical techniques is unquestionably important, professional learning centered on assessment can be equally rich and impactful. When educators work on the collaborative design and review of performance assessment tasks linked to Common Core State Standards and other standards, and in the evaluation and anchoring of the resulting student work, they also engage in their own professional and personal growth.

The process of collaboratively designing assessments typically begins in the summer when groups of teachers gather with colleagues to design performance tasks that embody the standards. Teachers are introduced to a task design process, then spend each morning working collaboratively to develop performance tasks and rubrics they can use in their own classrooms. Each afternoon, they share their plans with other teams, listen to feedback, and revise the tasks. By the end of the week, each teacher has a collection of rich tasks to use to engage learners and assess their performance.

The process provides teachers with more than usable products. Participants also learn about professional collaboration, peer review, using feedback to refine their designs, reviewing student work, and calibration for consistency in evaluation. Moreover, they leave with a much deeper understanding of new standards along with the type of instruction needed to help learners achieve them.

Rationale

Collaborative design and review of performance assessment tasks help educators take action on the Common Core and the Next Generation Science Standards

(Next Generation). This professional learning design helps educators to shift not only district- and school-level assessments, but also their own classroom assessments to performance tasks. The design also helps educators to realize the following benefits: (1) clarify what is meant by standards, (2) identify appropriate sources of evidence, (3) engage students more fully in their learning, and (4) gain insights they would not otherwise have by looking directly at student work.

A focus on performance assessment

The shift to a standards-based approach in education places a greater emphasis on results. Claiming to be standards-based by agreeing on content standards is not enough. Educators must also agree on what evidence will show that students have learned the knowledge and skills outlined by the standards. The Common Core in English/Language Arts and Mathematics (National Governors Association Center for Best Practices, Council of Chief State School Officers, 2010a), along with the newly released science standards reflect the "next generation" of educational standards. Rather than simply specifying a "scope and sequence" of knowledge and skills, these new standards focus on the *performances* expected of students who are college and career ready. More specifically, the Common Core in English Language Arts (ELA) have been framed around a set of anchor standards that define the long-term proficiencies that students need to be considered "college and career ready." The ELA Standards are unequivocal about the need for literate individuals, who

... demonstrate independence. Students can, without significant scaffolding, comprehend and evaluate complex texts across a range of types and disciplines, and they can construct effective arguments and convey intricate or multifaceted information.... Students adapt their communication in relation to audience, task, purpose, and discipline. Likewise, students are able independently to discern a speaker's key points, request clarification, and ask relevant questions. ... Without prompting, they demonstrate command of standard English and acquire and use a wide-ranging vocabulary. More broadly, they become self-directed learners, effectively seeking out and using resources to assist them, including teachers, peers, and print and digital reference materials. (p. 7)

The Common Core in mathematics declare a similar shift away from a "mile wide, inch deep" (National Governors Association Center for Best Practices, Council of Chief State School Officers, 2010b, p. 3) listing of concepts and skills to a focus on developing the mathematical practices of problem solving, reasoning, and modeling. Likewise, the Next Generation highlights eight practices (processes) that are intended to actively engage learners in "doing" science:

As in all inquiry-based approaches to science teaching, our expectation is that students will themselves engage in the practices and not merely learn about them secondhand. Students cannot comprehend scientific practices, nor fully appreciate the nature of scientific knowledge itself, without directly experiencing those practices for themselves. (National Research Council, 2012, p. 30)

The pattern is clear: Standards are focused on developing learners who can perform with knowledge, not simply remember a body of knowledge. McTighe and Wiggins (2013) echo this point:

This performance-based conception of standards lies at the heart of what is needed to translate the Common Core into a robust curriculum and assessment system. The curriculum and related instruction must be *designed backward* from an analysis of standards-based assessments; i.e. worthy performance tasks anchored by rigorous rubrics and annotated work samples. We predict that the alternative — a curriculum mapped in a typical scope and sequence based on grade-level content specifications — will encourage a curriculum of disconnected "coverage" and make it more likely that people will simply retrofit the new language to the old way of doing business.

Thus, our proposal reflects the essence of backward design: Conceptualize and construct the curriculum back from sophisticated tasks, reflecting the performances that the Common Core Standards demand of graduates. Indeed, the whole point of anchor standards in ELA and the practices in mathematics is to establish the genres of performance (e.g. argumentation in writing and speaking, and solving problems set in real-world contexts) that must recur across the grades in order to develop the capacities needed for success in higher education and the workplace. (pp. 14–15)

Needed shifts in assessment

The new emphases of the Common Core and Next Generation Standards call for a concomitant shift in assessments — both in large-scale and classroom levels. The widespread use of multiple-choice tests as predominant measures of learning in many subject areas must give way to an expanded use of performance assessments tasks that engage students in applying their learning in genuine contexts. Indeed, the national assessment consortia, Smarter Balanced Assessment Consortium and Partnership for Assessment and Readiness for College and Careers (PARCC), promise to expand their repertoire to include performance tasks on the next generation of standardized tests.

While it is encouraging to see changes in external testing, the most natural home for the increased use of performance assessments is in the classroom. Since teachers do not face the same constraints as large-scale testing groups (e.g. standardized implementation, limited time, and scoring costs), they can more readily employ performance tasks along with traditional assessment formats. Performance assessments such as writing an essay, solving a multi-step problem, debating an issue, and creating an informative website ask students to demonstrate their learning through actual performance, not by simply selecting an answer from given alternatives. Performance tasks are typically open-ended to allow students more choices in how they respond. Educators need to set classroom tasks in realistic ("authentic") contexts as much as possible so that learners see the relevance in what they are asked to learn. Of course, teachers can and should also use traditional assessments such as selected-response quizzes and tests, observations, and portfolios of student work to provide a complete picture of a student's learning.

Once teachers have recognized the value of performance assessments, they are faced with the challenge of finding or creating tasks and accompanying scoring rubrics because few textbooks provide examples of performance assessments that match the new standards. However, when teachers work together to design performance tasks, they experience significant professional growth. When teachers design assessments together, give each other feedback through peer reviews,

evaluate student work, and plan together for improvement, they are engaged in deep and rich professional learning.

Other benefits of collaborative assessment design

The work of the Maryland Assessment Consortium, as well as similar projects at district, regional, state, and provincial levels, demonstrates four primary benefits of teachers working together to create authentic performance assessments:

1. Assessment opens the door to fundamental questions such as "What do these content and practices standards really mean?" "What must students do to show that they have learned the content and met the standards?" "How will we know that students really understand the important ideas and processes contained in the standards?" "By what criteria will we judge student performance?" "How do we ensure that our judgments are reliable?" "How good is good enough?" "How should we teach so we improve student achievement?" As teachers explore these questions, their content knowledge, assessment skills, and instructional methods improve.

2. Thinking about what evidence will show that students have met standards helps clarify learning goals. When teachers have clear performance goals, they can teach in a more focused and purposeful way. When students have clear performance targets (tasks and rubrics) in advance, they know what is expected and can focus their efforts.

3. Students are more engaged when they see a genuine purpose for their learning and are more likely to try harder on authentic tasks. This effort differs notably from the "minimum compliance" attitude of learners forced into a steady diet of decontextualized practice tests. Students see the performance tasks as worthwhile because the tasks reflect ways that people use knowledge and skills in the world beyond the classroom. And teachers comment that these tasks are "tests worth teaching to" because they call for a rigorous, genuine application of worthwhile knowledge and skill.

4. When teachers regularly use performance assessment tasks in the classroom, they get the most authentic achievement data available — student work. By regularly examining the strengths and weaknesses in student work, teachers do not have to wait for the annual test

score report to know how well they're teaching. The results of regular classroom assessments provide ongoing data to help them plan for continuous improvement (McTighe, 1994).

Stages & steps

Broadly speaking, there are three key stages involved in the collaborative design and use of performance tasks:
1. Collaboratively design performance task and associated rubrics.
2. Conduct peer reviews of the tasks and rubrics.
3. Meet for a group evaluation of student work elicited by the tasks.

STAGE 1: Collaboratively design tasks and rubrics
Stage 1 has four steps.

Step 1: Form and meet in groups
Form collaborative teams to design performance tasks and rubrics, give feedback, and review student work. Typically, teachers meet in grade-level or subject area teams. However, teams that cross subject areas may collaborate to develop multidisciplinary tasks. Small design teams of 2–4 people are better for collaboration and efficiency than larger groups. A facilitator helps teachers form teams and establish norms, and guides the design and review sessions.

Teachers do **not** need to be from the same school or even the same district to collaboratively design performance tasks. This collaborative task design process has been implemented at the state (Maryland) and provincial (Alberta) levels, in large (Boulder Valley, CO) and small (Monomoy, MA) districts, and in regional consortia (six districts in suburban Pittsburgh, PA). Indeed, there is value in such "cross-fertilization" (see Online Resource 3.1: *A process for designing performance tasks*).

Step 2: Decide which standards to assess
Each team, guided by the facilitator, decides which goals or standards to assess. Not every goal requires a performance assessment. For example, if the standard expects students to be able to identify state capitals or to know chemical symbols, multiple-choice or fill-in-the-blank formats provide appropriate evidence of learning. Performance assessments

---

Facilitating assessment teams

To help ensure the design process is successful, the facilitator should:

1. **Use computers when designing tasks and rubrics to make editing and distribution of final drafts easier.** Meet in or near a media center or computer lab with Internet access.

2. **Provide teachers with relevant resources to support their design work.** For example, have content standards documents and curriculum frameworks on hand and provide sample tasks and rubrics to serve as models.

3. **Help teachers use Internet resources related to assessment.** Teachers are masters at adapting ideas and can build on others' ideas rather than starting with a blank slate (see Additional Resources on pp. 76–77).

4. **Schedule multiple opportunities for the group to meet for informal sharing and feedback sessions throughout the design process.** A formal peer review session toward the end of a design workshop should not be the only opportunity for feedback. A gallery walk offers a practical and energizing way to share and get feedback during any part of the process. For a gallery walk, design teams post their draft performance tasks and rubrics on a wall and participants view the works in progress, offering feedback and suggestions anonymously with sticky notes posted to the charts.

---

are needed when the goals are procedural (involve skills or processes such as problem solving) or call for students to understand concepts and principles.

Since they are generally multifaceted, performance tasks can often be used to assess several standards. For example, students might survey people regarding their positions on an issue, tally the survey responses, create a chart or graph to display the results and prepare a persuasive report to communicate to a designated audience (e.g. school board). Such a task reveals students' levels of understanding in organizing, displaying and interpreting data, and communicating the results.

Step 3: Create a task

Teachers consider the kinds of performances needed to provide evidence of learning a given standard or set of standards and develop an authentic situation through which students will demonstrate their knowledge and skills (see Figure 1). The team can brainstorm tasks using the G.R.A.S.P.S. framework (Wiggins & McTighe, 1998) as follows:

Goal: What is the purpose, challenge, or problem (to persuade, to inform, to entertain, to sell)?

Role: What real-world role will the student assume (editorial writer, museum director, artist, business owner)?

Audience: For whom is the student working (newspaper reader, museum visitor, viewer, client/customer)?

Situation: What is the situation or context (a controversial community issue that must be resolved)?

Product/Performance: What will students make or do to accomplish the goal (a letter to the editor, display, mural, business proposal)?

Standards: By what criteria will the product or performance be judged as successful?

Step 4: Develop evaluation criteria

The team develops criteria that teachers and students will use to appraise students' work on the performance tasks. For most complex performance tasks, designers should consider three types of criteria:

1. Criteria to assess the degree of understanding or proficiency (Does the work demonstrate accuracy, thoroughness, thoughtfulness, or efficiency?).

2. Criteria to assess work quality (Is the work well-crafted, mechanically correct, skilled, neat, or creative?).

3. Criteria related to impact or result (Was the letter to the editor persuasive? Was the museum display informative? Did the scientific investigation actually test the hypothesis? Was the role-play convincing?).

These criteria form the basis of one or more scoring rubrics for the evaluation of student products and performances. Rubrics include a performance scale (e.g. 1–4) containing descriptions of the differing levels of understanding, proficiency, work quality, and impact.

Designing performance assessment tasks is not a linear process — teachers typically move back and forth among three components: the learning goals being assessed, the products or performances that provide evidence of

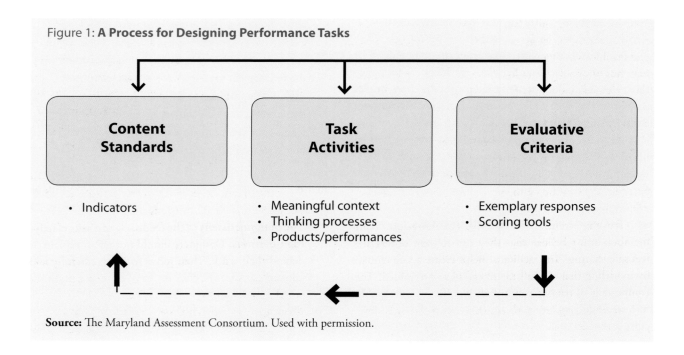

Figure 1: **A Process for Designing Performance Tasks**

Content Standards

Task Activities

Evaluative Criteria

- Indicators

- Meaningful context
- Thinking processes
- Products/performances

- Exemplary responses
- Scoring tools

Source: The Maryland Assessment Consortium. Used with permission.

learning, and the criteria and rubrics by which student work is evaluated, based on the goals.

STAGE 2: Peer reviews of the tasks and rubrics

Educators do not commonly (or critically) review teacher-developed units and assessments. However, structured reviews help teachers improve their designs when peer feedback is descriptive, specific, and criterion-referenced. In addition to the feedback they receive on their assessments, participants in peer review sessions also value the opportunity to share and discuss curriculum and teaching methodology. Indeed, peer review sessions focus attention on the heart of teaching and learning — what it means to learn content; what counts as evidence that students really understand and can use their knowledge and skills; and what and how teachers must teach to enable students to achieve the expected results.

Step 1: Assemble a review team

Peer review teams can be homogeneous — based on content areas or grade levels — or heterogeneous. Both have advantages. In general, homogeneous groups provide more specific feedback about content-oriented criteria, such as whether a task matches content requirements (task validity) and is authentic (related to life outside the classroom). Heterogeneous groups can provide information about whether the task is clear, potentially engaging to students, and feasible to implement. Administrators and teachers who have not helped design tasks can be included as members of the review team. Groups of three to five members work well.

Step 2: Build trust

For peer review to be successful, team members must have a high level of trust so they feel safe when giving and receiving feedback. Creating trust takes time and is built, in part, through practicing the skills of providing descriptive, non-evaluative feedback.

Trust is essential for effective collaboration. Team members must believe that they can rely on others and feel safe sharing. The facilitator helps create a safe climate by modeling that all staff members' ideas are valued. This component of trust is particularly significant since public reviews of colleagues' work are counter to the isolationist culture of teaching.

One method for building trust is practicing peer review sessions using sample assessment tasks and rubrics (see Additional Resources on pp. 76–77, especially websites offering sample tasks, rubrics, and student work with which to practice). Group members need to see others modeling the skills of giving and receiving feedback and practice these skills themselves before they engage in the process with their own designs.

Teams can use the "fishbowl" process to practice. In the fishbowl, participants sit either in an inside or outside circle. The inside circle gives feedback about a performance assessment to the person(s) who created it. The outside circle listens and takes notes about the feedback, including times it is effective and times it is not (such as when the feedback is addressed toward the person who created the assessment, not the assessment itself). One or two vacant chairs in the inside circle permit those in the outside circle to momentarily (enough to make a single comment) join the conversation. At the end of the fishbowl practice session, those in the outside circle provide information about how the review went.

Another approach to trust building is to begin peer review sessions by inviting volunteers to contribute their designs, rather than requiring everyone to participate. Once teachers have observed the process and seen the benefits, they are more likely to want to have their tasks reviewed.

Step 3: Establish ground rules

The group must set ground rules, such as the following, and review them at the beginning of each session.

- **Feedback is specific, descriptive, and guided by the criteria in design standards.** For example, instead of saying, "We liked your performance task," a group member might say, "The task is authentic because it asks students to apply their knowledge in a real-world way."

- **Feedback is de-personalized.** The reviewers provide feedback to help improve the task and rubric and do not praise or criticize the designers.

- **The designer listens to the feedback and asks clarifying questions.** Designers should not try to explain or defend their work. Their job is to listen carefully and take notes. After the peer review, designers can decide whether to incorporate the feedback.

- **Meetings stay on schedule.** Participants must guard against tangential discussions or sidebar conversations.

ADDITIONAL RESOURCES

Article

"Assessment crisis: The absence of assessment for learning," by Richard Stiggins. (2002, June). *Phi Delta Kappan, 83*(10), 758–765.

Books

Core Learning: Assessing What Matters Most, by Jay McTighe. Salt Lake City, UT: School Improvement Network, 2013.

How to create and use rubrics for formative assessments and grading, by Susan M. Brookhart. Alexandria, VA: ASCD, 2013.

How to give effective feedback to your students, by Susan M. Brookhart. Alexandria, VA: ASCD, 2008.

Looking together at student work, by Tina Blythe, David Allen, and Barbara Schieffelin Powell. New York, NY: Teachers College Press, 1999.

Protocols for professional learning, by Lois Brown Easton. Alexandria, VA: ASCD, 2009.

Reflective analysis of student work, by Norene J. Bella. Thousand Oaks, CA: Corwin Press, 2004.

Scoring rubrics in the classroom: Using performance criteria for assessing and improving student performance, by Judith A. Arter and Jay McTighe. Thousand Oaks, CA: Corwin Press, 2001.

The understanding by design professional development workbook, by Jay McTighe and Grant Wiggins. Alexandria, VA: ASCD, 2004.

Websites

www.jaymctighe.com. Jay McTighe offers a comprehensive list of resources for performance assessment and rubrics.

www.literacydesigncollaborative.org. Literacy by Design Collaborative (LDC) is a framework for developing reading, writing, and thinking tasks within various academic disciplines, linked to the Common Core in English/language arts. Tools include practical templates to use in designing literacy tasks.

www.smarterbalanced.org. Smarter Balanced Assessment Consortium is one of two national consortia developing assessments of the Common Core Standards. The website offers information and resources for educators on the Common Core State Standards, an interactive project timeline that illustrates Smarter Balanced activities by school year, and an e-newsletter with Smarter Balanced activities.

www.smarterbalanced.org/smarter-balanced-assessments/#item. The consortium is developing assessment items and performance task specifications to help translate the Common Core State Standards into assessment items.

http://parcconline.org. The Partnership for Assessment of Readiness for College and Careers (PARCC) is a group of states working together to develop a set of assessments that measure whether students are on track to be successful in college and their careers. The PARCC assessments will be ready for states to administer during the 2014–15 school year.

Ultimately, the success of a peer review is determined by the extent to which the designer receives helpful feedback to validate or improve the work.

Step 4: Review assessment tasks

- Select a facilitator or timekeeper to keep the group on task.

- Task designers distribute copies of their tasks and scoring rubrics to review team members. If possible, provide the copies in advance. If the group hasn't seen the copies ahead of time, give the team a few minutes to review the materials.

- The designers provide a brief, two-minute overview of the task, make any specific requests ("I'm not sure if the

ADDITIONAL RESOURCES

Websites, continued

www.p12.nysed.gov/ciai/ls.html. The curriculum, assessment and instruction page of the New York State Department of Education, with standards, performance indicators, and student work samples.

www.ctcurriculum.org. The Connecticut Department of Education website connects readers to state standards and related performance assessment tasks, with examples of student work based on the standards. Teachers also share curriculum ideas.

http://pals.sri.com/. Performance Assessment Links in Science is an online, standards-based, continually updated resource bank of science performance assessment tasks indexed by the national science education standards and other standards frameworks.

www.uwstout.edu/soe/profdev/rubrics.shtml. The University of Wisconsin-Stout School of Education offers links to additional reading about authentic assessments, information about creating rubrics, and examples of rubrics created by classroom teachers for cooperative learning, writing research reports, PowerPoint/oral presentations, multimedia, video, and web projects.

http://rubistar.4teachers.org/index.php. A free tool to help teachers create quality rubrics for project-based learning activities.

www.nwrel.org/assessment/scoring.asp?odelay= 3&d=2. Scoring guides for reading developed by the Northwest Regional Educational Laboratory.

www.escweb.net/tx_bm/science/srubric.htm. A sample rubric for science benchmarks from the Region IV Education Service Center in Houston, Texas.

www.01.sil.org/lingualinks/languagelearning/ otherresources/ACTFLProficiencyGuidelines/ contents.htm. The American Council for the Teaching of Foreign Languages provides a detailed description of the kinds of communication functions, range of vocabulary, degree of accuracy, and flexibility that learners of a language are able to control at different levels in each of the four major language skills (listening, speaking, reading, and writing).

www.fcps.edu/is/worldlanguages/pals/index. shtml#rubric. Fairfax County (Va.) Public Schools performance assessments for language students, including speaking and writing rubrics.

http://learningforward.org/. The Learning Forward website offers a free collection of articles describing ways schools and districts have made time for professional learning.

www.lasw.org/welcome.html. An informative site providing protocols for looking at student work from an association of individuals and educational organizations.

www.wida.us. World-class Instructional Design and Assessment provides can-do descriptors of performance levels for English language learners. The descriptors are free. The assessments and scoring tools may be purchased.

---

second rubric really addresses the identified benchmark. What do you think?"), and leave the room.

- Reviewers spend about 10 minutes *individually* (and silently) reviewing the task, referring to the design standards to evaluate its strengths and weaknesses. Each reviewer makes notes about the task's strengths and weaknesses.

- Review team members spend about 10 minutes discussing their reactions as a group, then summarize in writing the group's feedback and suggestions for the task designers.

Step 5: Offer feedback and suggestions

- The task designers return and the review team gives

Design standards

Design standards define the qualities of effective curriculum and assessment. Design standards are a reference point during design to ensure that the assessment meets the standards, help teachers review and refine drafts, and assist independent reviewers (such as a curriculum committee) before assessments are distributed to other teachers. The Maryland Assessment Consortium developed the following design standards:

To what extent does the performance assessment task:

- Assess student performance on the identified content standard(s) and benchmarks?
- Establish a meaningful context based on issues, problems, themes, or student interests?
- Require the student to apply thinking skills or processes rather than merely recall factual information?
- Establish criteria linked to the standards/bench marks for evaluating student products and performances?
- Contain activities likely to engage students?
- Provide clear, unambiguous directions to students?
- Contain accurate and credible information?
- Use interrelated activities to achieve its purpose?
- Allow for easy use in the classroom?
- Provide feedback to teachers and students about identified goals or content standards?

Optional:

- Integrate subject areas?
- Provide opportunities for students to reflect on and self-evaluate their performance?
- Allow students to revise?
- Allow for a choice of products or performances?
- Use technology appropriately?

From *Developing Performance Assessment Tasks: A Resource Guide* by J. McTighe. Copyright 1994 Maryland Assessment Consortium.

feedback and suggestions for improving the task based on the design standards (see sidebar Design standards).

- The designers listen, ask clarifying questions, and take notes. This step takes about 10 minutes.

STAGE 3: Anchoring student work

When teachers use common performance assessment tasks and rubrics, they review the resulting products and performances to determine how well students understand what they are learning. Focusing on student work increases teachers' ownership of student achievement since the work is a result of their own curriculum, assessment, and teaching. Looking at student work helps teachers focus on the broader goals of student learning and avoid fixating too narrowly on standardized test scores. Structured protocols can help groups examine student work (Arter & McTighe, 2000; Blythe, Allen, & Powell, 1999; McTighe & Thomas, 2003).

Step 1: Use the assessments and collect student work

Teachers use the assessments in their classrooms and collect student work. Teachers should use the performance assessments and rubrics in their own classrooms. They may want students to use numbers instead of names to keep the process in the next step anonymous. They should not put scores on the student work itself; instead, they should keep a separate record of scores.

Step 2: Reconvene the teams

Reconvene the teams that designed the performance assessments and rubrics. Each teacher should bring five to eight samples of student work resulting from the assessments in the previous step, with enough copies of each sample for every team member. These samples should reflect a range of quality, as assessed by teachers using the rubrics in the previous step.

If the assessment required a performance, it should be accessible for viewing (e.g. video) or listening (e.g. recording, podcast). The student work samples should not have a visible score, and students' names should be removed from the work so as to avoid any bias that may occur when names are recognized.

The teams examine the student work to describe, rather than score or grade it, so that those who created the performance assessments and rubrics can make adjustments that are likely to improve the results.

Step 3: Describe the student work on the performance task

Working with one performance assessment and resulting student work — one sample at a time — each team describes what is evident in student work. A recorder makes notes on chart paper so the group can use comments later. Here are prompting questions to use:

- What knowledge and skills are assessed?
- What kinds of thinking are required (recall, interpretation, evaluation)?
- Are these the results I (we) expected? Why or why not?
- In what areas did the student(s) perform best?
- What weaknesses are evident?
- What misconceptions are revealed?
- Are there any surprises?
- What anomalies exist?
- Is there evidence of improvement or decline? If so, what caused the changes?

After finishing one example of student work according to this process, team members repeat the process with the next piece of student work until all samples for a performance task have been described.

Step 4: Evaluate the student work on the performance task

Group members then individually score each piece of student work using the established rubrics. Members of the group compare their individual scores for each sample and discuss the reasons for their scores. This process helps teachers become more consistent in applying the identified criteria and performance levels of the rubric. In some cases, there will be differences among team members. In these instances, the professional development that helped participants build trust comes into play, especially the ability to provide non-evaluative comments.

Step 5: Interpret the results

Use the following questions to further analyze and interpret the results:

- What does this work reveal about student learning and performance?
- What patterns are evident?
- What questions does this work raise?
- Is this work consistent with other achievement data?
- Are there different explanations for these results?

Step 6: Review student tasks

In conjunction with reviewing student work, teams should also examine the performance assessment task itself, particularly the directions given to students, to see if the directions lead students to produce the desired outcome. Task directions that are vague or misleading may cause students to produce a product or performance that fits neither the intention of the task nor the criteria on the rubric.

Step 7: Select anchors

The next step for the reconvened teams is anchoring. Anchoring refers to the process of selecting examples of student work to represent each of the score points on an evaluation scale. In other words, these samples "anchor" the scoring system by providing concrete examples to illustrate the quality or proficiency expected at each level based in the rubric. Anchors help teachers understand and apply the criteria and standards consistently when they evaluate student products or performances. Anchors give teachers and students clear targets that help guide their work and help students understand and apply the criteria when they are evaluating themselves or doing peer evaluations.

There are two models for anchoring the scoring system for performance assessments (see Online Resource 3.2: *Task anchoring process: Two models*).

Model 1 uses established scoring criteria on the rubric, and each team evaluates student responses, products, or performances according to the preset criteria. Next, the group sorts student work by score. The group then selects responses, products, or performances for each score point that illustrates the criteria for that score. Use Model 1 when a performance task and the scoring rubric(s) have been validated through field-testing, reviews, and revision.

Model 2 uses student responses, products, or performances to identify or refine the scoring criteria. The group sorts student responses into three *(high, medium, low)* or four *(excellent, good, fair, poor)* levels based on general quality. The

Tips for successful anchoring

1. Use anchoring to refine performance standards or create them if a rubric has not been designed. When educators choose examples of student work that illustrate the various levels in a rubric, they can easily answer the question, "How good is good enough?" Anchors also help scorers judge work more consistently and help students assess their own work more accurately. With tangible illustrations of what quality work looks like, teachers and students can understand the specific qualities of effective work and get beyond general statements, such as "well organized" or "persuasive."

2. Select several examples for each level. A single example suggests that there is just one best answer or pathway rather than several approaches to an authentic task (diverse excellence). Using several anchors provides a richer set of examples to guide teachers and students.

3. Collect and publish the anchor examples at the grade, school, or district level to promote more consistent evaluations and to help teachers explain scores and grades to parents and students. Many teachers report that grading quibbles virtually disappear when clear rubrics and anchors are available.

group reviews each set and determines the distinguishing characteristics of the responses. They then develop criteria for each level and select several responses to illustrate those criteria. Use Model 2 when a task has been used for the first time and no rubric exists or the rubric is a draft.

Step 8: Identify improvement actions

Ultimately, the goal of assessment is to improve learning, not just measure it. Accordingly, teams should discuss those areas that need improvement and share ideas for addressing these. Here are questions to use:

- What teacher action(s) are needed to improve learning and performance?
- What curriculum adjustments might be required?
- What student action(s) are needed to improve learning and performance?
- What parent action(s) will support improved learning and performance?

Variations

Groups designing and trying performance assessments can vary the process in several ways.

Designing assessments. Teachers from more than one district or school can form a design team and share ideas and resources. A common focus on state standards supports cross-district and cross-school collaborations. When teachers move beyond the comfort zone of the familiar to meet and design assessments with teachers they may not know, they attain a new level of professionalism.

Peer review. The process can be used to review curriculum units teachers have developed, as well as assessments or a district's curriculum. Review teams can adapt the process for lesson study (see "Chapter 14: Lesson Study" in this book) or extend the work into an action research project (see "Chapter 2: Action Research" in this book).

Anchoring. Using the process is valuable professional learning. Although teachers involved in group scoring do not need to anchor their performance assessments to real student work, the process of anchoring increases consistency of teachers' ratings, provides tangible examples for the various scoring levels, and leads to fruitful discussion about the instruction needed to prepare students for the tasks.

Challenges and how to address them

This professional learning design is not for the faint of heart. It asks a lot of educators, but it also delivers a lot in terms of learning for both teachers and students. These are common challenges, which you can anticipate and plan to address in advance.

Sustained effort. When teachers consider these collaborative activities, they wonder, "When are we going to be able to find time for all this?" Yet the question really is, "How do we choose to use the time we have?" Designing performance assessment tasks and scoring rubrics and developing curriculum units require sustained effort, clarity of thought, and time for reflection. These demands are difficult to meet after a full day of teaching when staff members' energy and mental acuity are less than optimal. Using the occasional professional learning day generally does not help produce high-quality products.

Designing and reviewing performance tasks requires two to five consecutive days. The work is best done during the summer when teachers can focus their energy and thoughts, access resources, and reflect without the day-to-day strains of teaching. Some districts have set aside days just before or after student attendance days, in the three days before Thanksgiving, or several days in early January.

While the design work requires uninterrupted time, evaluating and anchoring student work and planning improvements can be done during regularly scheduled professional days (full or half) and at grade-level or department meetings.

Trust. Peer feedback is an essential element to help educators refine their designs. To present work publicly requires a high level of trust that must be created among colleagues who understand the process and can maintain a level of professionalism that focuses on the work rather than the individual.

Understanding. Teachers must understand the need for not only evaluative assessment, but also for ongoing assessments that provide them with feedback to adjust their instruction. Authentic assessments allow teachers to engage students more meaningfully in their learning and get direct, immediate data on the effect of their teaching in time to make changes. They must be willing to gather and use data in their practice.

Additional resources. Administrative support is needed to adjust teachers' schedules and allow for professional learning time. Teams also may need access to the computer lab for meetings to find examples of performance assessments online.

Integration into the school improvement process. The teams participating in designing performance assessments and rubrics, anchoring them, and improving them within individual schools can extend their professional learning by making it part of a continuous process for school improvement. The teams examine multiple sources of data — external test results, student work from assessments and assignments, and information such as student and

ONLINE RESOURCES

3.1 A process for designing performance tasks
3.2 Task anchoring process: Two models

parent surveys — for a more complete picture of student performance. Teams can share what they have learned about student achievement with school and district improvement task forces to look at overall data patterns.

Conclusion

Collaborative designs and peer reviews honor and enhance teachers' professionalism, expertise, and collegial learning. Working in teams to evaluate student work against established criteria, identify models of excellence (anchoring), and plan needed improvements promotes a results-oriented culture of quality. Participating in collaborative processes strengthens teachers' content knowledge, assessment skills, and pedagogical effectiveness. In addition, even the most capable teacher working alone is unlikely to generate the amount and quality of work produced by an effective, competent team.

By designing performance assessments, educators enhance their understanding of content standards and of the evidence needed to show that students really understand the important ideas and processes contained in those standards. Teachers discover that the connection between curriculum and assessment becomes clearer, teaching is more sharply focused, and evaluation is more consistent.

While the focus initially is on assessment, teachers' conversations often quickly expand to include matters of instruction and curriculum — *what* and *how* we should teach to help students perform well on the performance tasks we have created.

By "walking the talk" of standards-based education and reviewing their work against design standards, teachers see the quality of their curriculum and assessments improve. By working together to examine student work and select anchor examples, teachers put performance standards into practice and assume greater ownership for results.

Ultimately, students benefit by having defined learning goals, opportunities to demonstrate their understanding in more authentic ways, and advance knowledge of the evaluation criteria so they have greater purpose in their learning.

References

Arter, J. & McTighe, J. (2000). *Scoring rubrics in the classroom: Using performance criteria for assessing and improving student performance.* Thousand Oaks, CA: Corwin Press.

Blythe, T., Allen, D., & Powell, B. (1999). *Looking together at student work: A companion guide to assessing student learning.* New York, NY: Teachers College Press.

McTighe, J. (1994). *Developing performance assessment tasks: A resource guide.* Frederick, MD: Maryland Assessment Consortium.

McTighe, J. & Thomas, R. (2003). Backward design for forward action. *Educational Leadership, 60*(5), 52–55.

McTighe, J. & Wiggins, G. (2013, February). *From Common Core Standards to curriculum: Five big ideas.* Available at http://grantwiggins.files.wordpress.com/2012/09/mctighe_wiggins_final_common_core_standards.pdf.

National Governors Association Center for Best Practices, Council of Chief State School Officers (2010a). *Common Core State Standards for English language arts and literacy in history/social studies, science, and technical subjects.* Washington DC: Authors.

National Governors Association Center for Best Practices, Council of Chief State School Officers (2010b). *Common Core State Standards for mathematics.* Washington DC: Authors.

National Research Council. (2012). *A framework for K–12 science education: Practices, crosscutting concepts, and core ideas.* Washington, DC: The National Academies Press.

Wiggins, G. & McTighe, J. (1998). *The understanding by design handbook.* Alexandria, VA: ASCD.

CHAPTER 4

Classroom Walk-Throughs for Peers

When peers observe each other in their classrooms and engage in reflective dialogue afterwards, they deepen their learning and commitment to substantive change.

By Carolyn J. Downey

Sam Oden put his coffee cup on the table in the break room at Jackson Middle School and said to his colleague Anita Farley, "I am so excited about this approach to learning! I'm glad we've had the opportunity to visit each other's classrooms. I like being able to stop by for just a few minutes. I would never have guessed how much I learn in that time."

Oden and Farley were discussing classroom walk-throughs with reflective inquiry. They had each visited one another's classrooms at least four times over the last few weeks using an informal walk-through process that allows teachers to learn a lot in a short observation. They used a nonjudgmental approach as they observed each other's practices. Afterwards, they had a follow-up conversation using a reflective dialogue approach.

Oden sipped his coffee and continued, "I remember when we went into each other's classrooms looking for specific instructional practices. I like this better. We get to focus on the decisions and actions we're making in our classrooms."

Farley nodded. "Ditto. We're not doing a 'gotcha,' going in to find the presence or absence of a particular practice," she said. "This is nonjudgmental. I especially like the idea of looking at our curricular decisions, like the objectives we teach and where they occur in the curriculum. I know these walk-throughs have made me think more about the curriculum and especially about where students are in their learning, compared to the district's curricular expectations."

"Me too," Oden said, "I was thinking that one area we might reflect on would be the strategies we use to differentiate the curriculum, as well as what criteria we might use to help us know which strategies fit different circumstances."

Farley and Oden continued to talk, discovering that

they had questions about differentiation of curriculum that were similar, generally, but dissimilar in their particulars. They tried to state their questions as reflective questions. Oden's question was, "When I am planning my lessons and thinking about my curriculum objectives in order to differentiate students' learning and to ensure that the lesson is at the right level of difficulty, what criteria do I use to decide which objective is appropriate for each student?"

Farley said, "That was a focus on curriculum differentiation. I like it, but I'm thinking I might expand it a little for myself: 'When I am planning my lessons and thinking about which strategies to use to differentiate both the curriculum and instructional practices, what criteria do I use to decide on those strategies so each student is accelerating his or her own learning?'"

Oden replied, "Let's go with that one. I want to think about both curricular decisions and instructional differentiation, and the criteria we use to decide on the various strategies to accomplish differentiation. What a great area for reflection! I can see us spending a few months thinking about and discussing this." The bell signaling the change of classes interrupted them, and they left with a vow to get together: "Same time, same place, next week. Right?"

Overview

Walk-throughs are informal, nonevaluative peer observations. They enhance professional learning when followed by a carefully constructed question that leads to reflective, self-directed, and self-analytical dialogue. The term *informal* means that there is no detailed and structured process of data collection during the observation. Instead, there is a five-step observation process that results in data that can be examined through a nonevaluative lens. Only observational data are collected: what students are doing, what the teacher is doing, what's happening in the classroom. The objective of the observation, which lasts for only a short time, is for fellow teachers to get to know the teacher being observed and the types of curricular and instructional decisions that teacher is making. The observation part of the peer informal walk-through is usually unannounced so that peers can observe typical daily routines.

Some history and perspective

The original classroom walk-through model described in *The Three-Minute Classroom Walkthrough: Changing School Supervisory Practice One Teacher at A Time* (Downey, Steffy, English, Frase, & Poston, 2004) was an approach was an approach to supervision wherein principals observed teachers and then engaged them in a reflective question.

The model in this book is similar to the original classroom walk-through model, but it has changed in two significant ways. The first change relates to the model's use for supervision. Unfortunately, supervisors used the walk-through process to see whether teachers were doing what they were supposed to be doing; rather, teacher supervisors should have been using walk-throughs as observations to encourage teachers to reflect. Supervisors cannot — and should not — base judgments about teachers on such a short period of time without knowing what happened before the observation or understanding the larger context of the lesson. Such observers cannot surmise why a teacher has selected one Strategy or practice over another.

Use of walk-throughs for supervision led many teacher unions to become disenchanted with the term. Used for inspection rather than reflection, supervisory walk-throughs eroded teachers' professional positions and prevented them from making meaningful and carefully considered decisions regarding the complex actions of teaching and learning. Teachers became suspicious of this supervisory process and did not see that, if used properly, the walk-through could help them improve as teachers.

Gradually, the walkthrough model has shifted from its supervisory purpose to a mutual learning purpose for peers. This shift led to peer observations that truly helped teachers and those who work with them. After observing one another, teachers discussed their observations. Initially, their follow-up conversations were likely to contain feedback and be judgmental, rather than self-reflective, in nature.

A second change was needed: emphasis on the use of reflective questions rather than feedback. Feedback is not particularly helpful for teacher learning and growth. According to Jill Cosh (1999), supervisory models

> have many weaknesses, and have been widely criticized, notably for their judgmental and threatening nature (Rawnsley, 1993; Richards & Nunan, 1990; Wajnryb, 1992). Unless the staff accepts

Figure 1: **Motivational Paradigm**	
Traditional (Theory X)	**Transformational (Theory Y)**
Feedback	Reflection
Controlling environment	Growth environment
Hierarchical structure	Community of learners (Senge, 1990)
Rewards, bribes, and punishments	Recognition of growth
Extrinsic motivation	Intrinsic motivation
Supervisor control	Inner locus of control
Origin of behaviors — Others	Origin of behavior — Self
Boss-manager (Glasser, 1998)	Lead manager (Glasser, 1998)
Work as task (Deming, 1986)	Work as joy (Deming, 1986)
Approval	Increase capacity
Others validate efficacy	Self-efficacy

them, the only relevance of these schemes is likely to be to accountability, rather than to genuine teacher development. There are, furthermore, many strong educational arguments against these models, and the role of the observer.

Joyce and Showers (1996, pp. 12–16) began their peer coaching models including verbal feedback. After many years of studying their model they did away with any feedback. When teachers try to give one another feedback, collaborative activity tends to disintegrate. Peer coaches told us they found themselves slipping into "supervisory, evaluative comments" despite their intentions to avoid them. Teachers shared with us that they expect "first the good news, then the bad" because of their past experiences with clinical supervision, and admitted they often pressured their coaches to go beyond technical feedback and give them "the real scoop." To the extent that feedback was evaluative or was perceived as evaluative, it was not meeting our original intention. (p. 23)

The model in this chapter builds on the model that was revised by Joyce and Showers (1996) so that it does not include feedback. Rather than provide feedback, principals and peer teachers engage teachers in reflective conversations.

Thus, the peer walk-throughs in this chapter are not about inspection. Instead, the walk-through and resulting conversations are focused on creating a culture of reflection and providing environments that influence a community of learners (DuFour & Eaker, 1998; Senge, 1990). Having peers take the time to be in classrooms can be extremely valuable if the teachers involved see the experience as personally relevant to their practice (Downey, Frase, & Peters, 1994).

Beliefs about motivation

Underlying any approach to peer observation and follow-up conversations is a set of beliefs about the nature of people and what motivates them. Theory X and Theory Y, two alternative theories of motivation proposed by Douglas McGregor (1960), offer a simple way to examine such beliefs (see Figure 1).

A Theory X approach is based on the belief that people have to be coerced to do their work, to do good work, or to grow (Drucker, 1974). Central to Theory X is the belief that people are not intrinsically motivated to grow and change. Theory X requires that people be motivated to change through extrinsic means such as praise, bribes, consequences, etc. The result requires superiors to inspect inferiors' work, to correct workers, and to tell them what to do differently.

The extrinsic approach to motivation and its reliance on inspection is unproductive in bringing about long-lasting change in teacher behavior (Frase, 2005; Peterson, 2000), yet some administrators continue to use such processes with single-minded intensity. They develop and use checklists with ratings, rankings, and built-in degrees of proficiency.

Conversely, a Theory Y approach ascribes to a belief that people put effort into work as naturally as they play. Tenets of Theory Y is that people will apply self-control and self-direction in the pursuit of organizational objectives, without external control. Theory Y recognizes that worker commitment to objectives is a function of reward associated with their achievement; consequently, people usually accept and often seek responsibility. Theory Y recognizes that people generate their own motivation to work, and they widely exert a high degree of imagination, ingenuity, and creativity in solving organizational problems. The result is a participative management style that expects people to reflect with managers and peers to accomplish organizational goals. In practice, the Theory X-based extrinsic approach has migrated into peer observations followed by feedback.

Theory Y (see Figure 1 on p. 85) is about an individually centered, intrinsically motivational approach. Theory Y helps people reflect on their practice, make independent decisions based on that reflection, and grow professionally (Downey, 2007). The value of Theory Y for teacher professionals is that it encourages professional to adjust their practices based on individually gathered input and reflection. Changes then are personally relevant and, therefore, long lasting.

The observation and reflective dialogue process that is most effective in improving teaching and learning reflects a purpose congruent with a Theory Y approach. The approach discussed in this chapter is a Theory Y approach.

The goal of walk-throughs and reflective dialogue

The ultimate goal of short, informal walk-throughs with reflective dialogue is the creation of a culture of reflective practice among colleagues. The goal is adult-to-adult interaction in an interdependent manner. The classroom walk-through is an informal, nonevaluative means to observe teaching; it is meant to encourage reflective dialogue among teachers, mentors, coaches, administrators and other key staff and to encourage educators to learn collaboratively.

Rationale

People have many reasons for visiting classrooms. Short informal walk-throughs allow educators to collect valuable and pertinent information not readily evident from formalized observation structures or processes. For example, peer teachers, coaches, and mentors might use this approach to:

- Observe effective practices that validate teachers' practices;
- Note additional or new practices they might want to use;
- Gain ideas on how to carry out a new practice through one of the powerful ways to learn — see it being done;
- Feel motivated to continually improve teachers' practices;
- Types of curricular decisions being made by individual teachers;
- Note types of instructional decisions being made by individual teachers;
- Compare their own practices with other approaches;
- Note groupings of students and differentiation of learning;
- Ease teachers' apprehension of trying something new;
- Consider possible areas for reflective discussions with colleagues;
- Identify possible areas for individual professional growth; and
- Ascertain the progress one is making in implementing new practices after participating in professional learning (Downey, Steffy, Poston, & English, 2010, p. 140).

As Michelle Israel (n. d.) stated,

Being observed in the classroom can rattle any teacher's nerves. But, teacher observations that serve as vehicles for professional growth rather than performance evaluations have multiple benefits — for teachers, administrators, and the school. More and more, administrators and teachers are viewing peer observation as a form of collaborative professional development. This kind of observation can yield its greatest benefits when used as a means of sharing instructional techniques and ideologies between and among teachers. (paras. 2–3)

As one user of teacher-to-teacher observations stated, they need to "be a tool for professional development and, in turn for student learning" (Israel, para. 4).

Walk-throughs as part of the peer coaching process

The reflective inquiry, which is part of the informal walk-through process, is similar to what educators need to do when they are involved in peer coaching. Peer coaching can be derailed if peer coaches give feedback rather than motivate each other through inquiry. As Teresa Belisle (1999) states:

Peer coaching has come to the forefront in many educational institutions as one key approach to effective professional development. It incorporates three components: self-directed learning, sustained development of expertise, and collaborative professionalism. (p. 1)

Both peer coaching and walk-throughs with reflective questions result in the following:

- Better understanding of teaching and improved teaching performance;
- Improved self-analysis and sense of efficacy;
- Improved sense of professional skills and desire for self-improvement; and
- Increased sense of efficacy, collaboration, and mutual respect (Rattray, n.d.).

Metacognitive thinking

Finally, the model in this chapter focuses on the metacognitive thinking of the peers when using reflective dialogue. According to Australian business school professors Richard Ladyshewsky and John Ryan (2006) writing about peer coaching in the business world,

Metacognition is defined as the self-communication a person engages in while thinking about something. It is knowing what you know, how you came to know what you know, and the ability to retrieve and use what you know to think and plan strategically (Pesut & Herman, 1992). Knowledge is developed using cognitive strategies, which are described as follows (Boud & Walker, 1988):

- Association: connecting ideas and feeling that are part of an experience and tying it to existing knowledge.
- Integration: processing associations to see if there are patterns or linkages to other ideas.
- Validation and validity testing: testing the internal consistency of emerging concepts and tying these to existing beliefs and knowledge.
- Appropriation: making new knowledge an integral part of how one acts or feels. (p. 2)

What these researchers write about in the business world applies to metacognition among educators engaged in classroom walk-throughs with reflective dialogue.

Stages and steps

Before considering the stages and steps involved in the classroom walk-through with reflective inquiry approach (Downey & Frase, 2003; Downey et al., 2004), consider the following assumptions that make walk-throughs with reflective inquiry most effective:

- **Teacher as decision maker:** The teacher is the decision maker in teaching, one with an inner locus of control. The observer — peer teacher, coach, or administrator — does not tell the teacher what to do expecting that he or she will follow that advice.
- **Respect for being involved in process:** The teacher has the choice to be involved in such a process.
- **Professional learning about how to do walk-throughs and reflective inquiry:** Learning and practice must occur in terms of both the observation structure to be used and the reflective conversation, with ongoing debriefing of the process.
- **Informal approach:** It is important that the entire process be informal. Participants don't collect or keep data. Certainly, observers might take notes to help their memory, but never make a checklist or written report of what has taken place.
- **Nonevaluative model:** In both aspects of the model — the observation and follow-up conversation — no judgment is acceptable. The observer identifies teaching actions and decisions without judging their quality. The reflection question is designed with nonjudgmental words and framed into a larger reflective conversation. Focusing on reflection is critical and very difficult to do if teachers have a mindset that is oriented toward giving and getting feedback.
- **Respect for choice:** It is important to recognize that a teacher almost always has numerous choices of teaching actions to make — such as focusing on one objective

rather than another, one strategy instead of the other — and therefore needs to be conscious of these choices as well as personally accountable for those choices.

- **Customized reflection:** Walkthroughs put the observed teacher in control of the reflective dialogue because the teacher formulates — with the help of peers — his or her own reflective question. Teachers who are able to the reflective dialogue around their own needs ensure that their professional learning will be especially applicable to practice.

- **Belief that the teacher uses criteria:** For rational decision making, the teacher uses criteria to select one practice over another and, in any given situation, the teacher's priority for these criteria. Sometimes a teacher is not even aware of the criteria used. Bringing these criteria into the open means teachers can begin to evaluate what they are doing in light of the criteria and determine if they are getting the desired results.

- **Time for reflection-for-action:** The reflective question and dialogue are not about a teacher's decision about a particular lesson or lessons taught in the past, but they are reflections about general practice and the decisions a teacher makes for future actions. Time for reflection is essential.

- **Understanding of context:** The teaching and learning act is complex, as complex as each individual student and teacher. Situations vary within lessons, which, in turn, influence each teacher's choices.

- **Analysis, synthesis, or evaluation of cognitive types:** Teachers are asked to reflect on the criteria they use, whether there is fidelity in using the criteria, whether the criteria are yielding the desired results, etc. The content of the dialogue is to be at the higher levels of thinking.

- **Positive presuppositions:** The observer peer assumes the teacher is thinking about and doing what is presented in the reflective question.

- **Honor what was observed:** The reflective question often poses examples of a selected teaching practice, and often includes the teacher's frequently observed habits.

- **Desire to affect student learning:** The reflective question is often stated with the presupposition that the teacher's decision and actions about both curricular and instructional practices are based upon his or her desire to impact student achievement (cause and effect).

- **Personal relevance in the question:** Each peer teacher selects a teaching practice around which to form a reflective question. The number-one priority is that teachers view the area for reflection as highly meaningful and beneficial to them, one that is personally and professionally relevant.

- **Intrinsic motivation:** The dialogue and interactions are designed to promote intrinsic rather than extrinsic motivation. Proactive dialogue and reflection promote a sense of efficacy.

- **Lead to self-direction, self-analysis, and reflective behavior:** Ultimately, the goal of the walk-through is to enhance a person's conscious reflection leading to self-direction and self-analysis for growth.

The steps that follow are divided into two stages:
Stage 1: Conducting walk-throughs with nonjudgmental observations.
Stage 2: Engaging in dialogue based on a reflective question.

STAGE 1: Conducting walk-throughs with nonjudgmental observations

Walk-throughs are very informal and short, lasting one to five minutes in each classroom. Stage 1 consists of preliminary decisions that ensure that participants understand the conditions of the walk-through and how to conduct a walk-through with reflective inquiry.

Determine the conditions of the walk-through. Participants need to make several decisions before starting walk-throughs with nonjudgmental observations. For example, school educators need to determine the conditions of the walk-throughs; more specifically, principals, coaches, mentors and teachers need to determine who will be involved in walk-throughs followed by reflective inquiry. If possible, participants need to volunteer, and they should form teams of 3 to 4 people. Walk-through teams may be subgroups of larger groups, such as grade-level or subject-area professional learning communities. They can also be small vertical teams (grades 2, 3, and 4, for example) or interdisciplinary teams (English, social studies, science, for example). Don't forget to include library media specialists, special education teachers, and special area teachers (i.e. art, music, and physical education). Administrators can be on teams, as equal members in terms of status, as can classroom aides. These teams should meet regularly for at least a year, doing walk-throughs together, or individually within their groups, and meeting as soon as possible afterwards. Team members may visit classrooms within their team individually or in small groups.

They also need to decide how often to observe. Teams must determine how frequently the peer team members will visit each other's classroom and how many short visits will typically take place before the team gets together to reflect. Together, the teachers need to set a time frame for three or four short visits to each team member's classroom — not actual dates or times but a time span, such as "within the next month." Visits are usually unannounced, but all members of a group know the time frame for them.

Another important preliminary action is to build an understanding of walk-throughs with reflective inquiry. Participants need to cultivate a nonjudgmental mindset. It is important they learn and practice the walk-through with reflective dialogue in a safe setting. Participants need to know how to conduct the observation and then how to form a reflective question and conduct a dialogue based on reflective questions. They need to honor a mindset that assumes teachers always are doing their best and are using the practices that make the most sense to them at any given time.

The facilitator of participants' learning processes needs to model nonjudgmental statements and identify when he or she makes one. The ability to be nonjudgmental when observing in classrooms is a significant paradigm shift for many educators. Moving away from that traditional paradigm may be difficult, but remember: Judging precludes a teacher's need to think about his or her own actions.

Everyone needs to practice and adjust the walk-through process. If possible, the facilitator should model the walk-through process with participants in their own classrooms and then debrief it with them. The same should occur in terms of forming reflective questions and engaging in reflective dialogue. Then, participants should practice the walk-through process, including forming the reflective question and engaging in reflective dialogue. Then, they should debrief the experience and modify as needed.

The walk-through process itself consists of the following five steps:

Step 1: Observe students' orientations to work

When walking into classrooms, observers should be as unobtrusive as possible. Teachers report that they like educators in their classrooms, but not if they are disruptive (Blase & Blase, 1998). Visitors must not distract from the work at hand, even if students attempt to engage them. Although there may be times when engaging with a student is acceptable, those times need to be for a specific purpose.

As the peer observers move into the classroom, they quickly note in one or two seconds, and to the best of their ability, what students are doing and whether or not this is what the teacher has asked for them to do. They are looking at student attending behavior. Are they sitting quietly, writing, reading, doing exercises, talking with other students? This is not a time-on-task count, which would require repeat visits since the classroom visit itself might be a distraction to students.

Step 2: Observe curricular decisions

Observers look for **curricular objectives**, in terms of these three dimensions:
1. what is actually taught;
2. what is intended; and
3. alignment with the objectives to district expectations.

Very little needs to be written down. Observers may refer to their notes to find a few key words to remind them of the objective or a note on the calibration. Observers look for "taught" and "intended" objectives and, later, with the observed teacher, they consider the fit with district curriculum.

Taught objectives become apparent when observers notice, as specifically as possible, what students are doing. For example, rather than thinking, "Students are learning about patterns," an observer might think, "The student is identifying the next number in a repeated addition pattern by writing it down."

Intended objectives might be written on the board or in the teacher's plan book or stated by the teacher for the students. The taught objective might be different from the intended objective.

Curriculum alignment happens later during the reflective dialogue. If observers can be specific about the taught objective (and, if observable, the intended objective), the peer group can help the observed teacher decide whether the taught objective was aligned with the system's curriculum standards or expectations.

The observer next discerns the **context** of the curriculum objective — the situation under which the student will demonstrate the learning (e.g. given a pattern of 2, 4, 6, 8, and a blank, the student is to write the next number or is to fill in the circle next to the correct response). One thing that could be discussed later is that the more context levels in which students demonstrate or practice their learning, the more likely they are to be able to transfer that learning to new situations or contexts (Thorndike, 1932). This is critical for teaching Common Core State Standards.

Next, the observer notes the **cognitive type** (often known as levels of thinking, such as *application*) of students' learning (Anderson & Krathwohl, 2001; Bloom, 1956; Erickson, 2007). District leaders need to choose among several similar taxonomies of cognition and their various interpretations in order to standardize a district-wide approach to cognitive levels."

Step 3: Observe instructional decisions

A peer observer will note the teacher's instructional strategies, such as the use of nonlinguistic representations, grouping strategies, differentiated instruction techniques, or practice activities. Again, the observer may use this information to inform the reflective dialogue following a few walk-through observations. One of the goals of reflective peer dialogue is to help teachers become familiar with their teaching style and their use of powerful instructional practices (Downey, 2004; Evertson, Emmer, & Worsham, 2003; Good & Brophy, 2000; Marzano, Pickering, & Pollock, 2001; Resnick, Hall, & Fellows of the Institute for Learning, 2001; Walberg & Waxman, 1983).

Step 4: Walk the walls

Peer observers should pay attention to what appears on the walls, bulletin boards, easel pads, or electronic devices, etc. The walls can provide data from which observers can derive information about curricular objectives, and how a teacher uses students' work in instruction (e.g. for models, recognition, or cueing). The commercial material teachers put up also reveals their instructional decisions. Observers also might see student portfolios that could be examined, a quiz the teacher is going to administer after the observer

leaves, student work in a box in the room, or artifacts on the walls. Observers should not judge the quality of student products or determine whether the teacher is using the walls and the room to the greatest advantage.

Step 5: Observe safety and health

Peer observers should note the general health and safety conditions of the classroom. This step occurs naturally. For instance, they may notice extreme room temperatures, poor lighting, a torn carpet, or power cords that represent a hazard. Observers may bring these concerns to the attention of the appropriate person.

Besides following Walk-through Steps 1–5, team members who are being observed can identify other things about which they want information. The peer-group members will want to learn more about one another's interests (such as how to make sure students understand) so that conversations about decisions may focus on encouraging reflective thought. This helps avoid any "gotcha" feelings and gives the observed teacher the opportunity to identify an area of focus that interests him or her (see Online Resource 4.1: *Five-step observation structure of the Downey Walk-Through in question form,* and Online Resource 4.2: *Five-step observation lens of the Downey Walk-Through in direction form*).

STAGE 2: Engaging in dialogue based on a reflective question

Professional learning really occurs during reflective dialogue among peers. A classroom walk-through without reflective conversation does not necessarily lead to learning for anyone on the team. Dialogue among team members is crucial to the process.

At first, peer teams may find such reflective conversations mechanical and uncomfortable, but eventually the conversation will become more natural. The reflective question's positive presuppositions will probably be the most awkward, since they call for unusual language and sentence structure (see Online Resource 4.3: *Suggested collaborative-interdependent reflective conversation structure and sample peer conversation*). There's a good reason for the structure of the reflective questions, however, and participants need to be aware of this reason. The structure moves educators to think analytically about aspects of teaching and learning that they might otherwise not consider. Working with peers on creating the reflective question and then having a dialogue about it are critical for professional learning.

Step 1: Schedule a reflective dialogue

After three or four unannounced observations have taken place in a teacher's classroom over a two- or three-week time frame, the team of peer observers is ready for a reflective conversation with that teacher. The team may schedule reflective conversations with more than one team member if these team members have all had the requisite three or four unannounced observations during the time frame.

Thirty minutes per person is usually sufficient for each teacher who is ready to engage in the reflective dialogue. If more than one member is ready, the group schedules an additional half-hour for each person who is ready. A half hour may sound too short for substantive work, but — especially if people are ready (see Step 2) — this time is ideal for sharing reflections and engaging in dialogue to formulate and refine a reflective question. The reflective dialogue is not about answering the reflective question; however, through the dialogue process everyone — including the observed teacher — will come to understand the question deeply and have direction for answering it. If a reflective question can be answered on the spot, then it is not difficult enough. Reflection means taking time to ponder the question.

Step 2: Prepare for the reflective dialogue

Before the reflective dialogue, each observed peer needs to think about his or her teaching generally (not limited to the observed lesson) and come up with one or two areas to discuss with peers. For example, a teacher might be thinking about how to tell if students have understood a concept. In the reflective dialogue, with the help of the peer group, the teacher may refine this consideration into a fully formed reflective question about formative assessment.

At the same time, observing peers who are not ready for the reflective dialogue might think about areas of discussion that were triggered by their observations of the other peers. The purpose of this is to get everyone thinking reflectively.

Step 3: Begin the dialogue with a psychological frame

Once team members have gathered and checked in with one another, they talk briefly about the psychological frame for reflective dialogue. This is equivalent in other designs to talking about norms.

First, they should recollect that the team of observers provides for a positive recognition — not about teacher performance, but about everyone's desire to reflect and improve, so that all students learn.

Second, they are all both observers and observed teachers. All team members are to come to all dialogues (see Step 2) — not just the one focused on them after several observations — having thought of their own possible areas for reflection.

Third, team members need to remind themselves they will be taking a nonjudgmental approach. Many teachers are used to "feedback" of some kind after every observation. They often expect to hear a judgment of their performance; they may even be eager to hear what observers think about their actions. However, the peer team must set aside this perspective if the dialogue is going to work. They need to see this process as one of self-analysis and metacognitive thinking.

Fourth, team members may offer observations from classroom walk-throughs only if these observations validate the thinking of the observed peer or help to clarify statements with examples of criteria or strategies. They should not be offered or construed as feedback; they should be as nonjudgmental as possible. They should be seen as information.

This point cannot be emphasized enough. As Robert Garmston (2000) said, "When mentors, coaches, and supervisors report their observations [as feedback] to teachers, they build the teacher's dependence on that input, and that actually robs the teacher of working the internal muscles necessary to improve their ability to self-reflect" (pp. 63–64). Introducing feedback from one peer to another interferes with teachers' learning to manage their own deliberations and decision making.

Examples of nonjudgmental statements are as follows:
- All the students at the science learning station were engaged in taking apart the model.
- The north wall of the classroom is filled with student writing.
- Three students asked for a repeat of the instructions.

- The group of students at the back of the room asked for help.
- Students copied the worksheets that their teammates were completing.
- No one talked while the teacher demonstrated the note-taking strategy.

Step 4: Explore possible areas for reflection

Once the group has focused on the psychological frame, team members can begin the reflective dialogue itself. Teachers who are ready for reflective dialogue take turns sharing the areas they would like to explore. Teachers describe what caused them to identify this teaching practice as one of interest. Other team members can validate the teacher's ideas by providing two or three specific examples from visits or comments made by the teacher; their job is to bring precision to the question.

An example of a teaching practice that a teacher might choose is "How I scaffold learning for students." Another example is "How I group students." A third example is "What I do when students don't understand" (see Online Resource 4.4: *Examples of teaching practices for the 2nd presuppositional phrase of the Downey Reflective Question*).

Do not overdo this segment, as reflective dialogue is geared toward the present and future, not the past. If teachers are critical of what they did in observed lessons from the past, their teammates need to help them recognize that reflective dialogue is not a critique of past performance, and it is not judgmental from anyone's point of view.

However, a peer might say: "You have picked transfer strategies as your area of reflection. When thinking about my observations in your classroom and the issue of transfer, I noticed that you used approaches to activate prior knowledge and learning relevant to the new learning, such as [name specific example]. Another time, you were giving examples to students about how they might use their prior knowledge."

Clarify the teaching practice with an example ("such as") to be more specific. Help the teacher develop a reflective question by asking for more examples.

Step 5: Set up the idea that the reflection is about the criteria used for a specific teaching practice

Before setting up a reflective question in Step 6, the group should discuss the importance of criteria, a part of

reflection that may baffle even experienced teachers. Members of the group should discuss the importance of surfacing criteria for decision making because criteria affect all teaching decisions — past, present, and future. They can be changed with learning — which is what happens in a reflective dialogue.

Criteria determine how teachers select one strategy over another. A team member might lead this discussion by building on the area of dialogue explored in Step 4. For example, a team member might say, "Let's reflect about the criteria we consider in deciding how to set up our lessons for multiple transfer effects."

Step 6: Form reflective questions

The reflective dialogue then continues with development and refinement of one teacher's reflective question, repeating this process for other teachers if they are ready. Team members choose to consider a question that stretches their thinking and takes them out of their comfort zones (Downey et al., 2004). The best questions create some cognitive dissonance in order to provide teachers with an opportunity to change how they think and to grow in their practices. Here is a process that will help form the question:

a. **Focus on the teacher's selected area of reflection.** Working with one teacher at a time, peer observers help one another deepen their thinking about each chosen area of reflection.

b. **Outline a reflective question based on the selected teachings practice.** When outlining a reflective question, peers help plant a seed in team members' thoughts or raise awareness that each one is making important decisions about teaching practices. The reflective question should have five components:

- *Situation/condition.* Identify when and where the teacher makes the decisions and any contextual conditions that might influence the decision related to practice (e.g. types of students, content of the objective).
- *Teaching practice.* Identify a clear and precise teaching practice, with examples.
- *Criteria.* Identify the criteria that the teacher(s) uses in selecting one strategy over another. Please remember that the focus is not on strategies used, but why one strategy is used over another in any given situation.

Table 1: **Five Components of the Reflective Question**	
Phrase	**Sample language**
Phrase 1: Situation (S) Describes the issue to be examined and reflected upon, and, if desired, the **condition or context (C)** of the situation	Start the phrase with the word *"When...".* For example: (S) *"When* planning my lessons,..."; (S) *"When* teaching my lessons,..."; (C) *"...*aligned with the district curriculum standards..."; or (C) *"...*recognizing that I have a diverse set of learners in my classes...".*
Phrase 2: Teaching practice Includes the idea of thinking about the practice, choice of approaches, the teaching practice itself, and examples of the approaches	Start the phrase with the words *"And thinking about...".* For example: *"... And thinking about* the many ways I could [insert teaching practice here] such as plan for differences or assess readiness, or measure understanding.
Phrase 3: Criteria Focuses on the multiple criteria one can use when planning lessons. It is this phrase that moves the question to one of analysis	Start the phrase with *"What,"* but do not begin the reflective question with this phrase; combine it with Phrase 2. For example: "And thinking about the many strategies I could choose to ..., *what criteria do I use ...?"*
Phrase 4: Decision Recognizes that criteria are used for the purpose of making a decision	Connect this phrase with Phrase 3. For example: "...What criteria do I use to *decide on the strategies* I might use...?"
Phrase 5: Student impact Emphasizes that we make all these decisions to make a difference in student learning	Usually start this phrase with *"in order to"* or *"to. "* For example: "... what criteria do I use to decide on the strategies I might use in order to *influence the student learning* of the objective?"

- *Decision.* Acknowledge the peer teacher's opportunities to make a choice and one's responsibility regarding teaching actions.
- *Student impact.* Connect the teacher's decisions and actions with one's intention to impact student learning (Downey, et al., 2004).

The first four components are about teacher thoughts and actions (cause), while the last one is about the impact of those actions (effect). The reflective question is always stated in the present tense. The reflective question is not centered on a teacher's decision about a lesson or lessons taught in the past, but is a reflection about the teacher's practice in general and decisions for *future* actions.

c. **Form a draft reflective question.** The question includes a series of five phrases, all of which are positive presuppositions. This means that the peer teachers' positive presuppositions assume that a teacher is thinking about and doing what is presented in the question. To form the question, peers include a phrase representing each of the five components (see Table 1: Five Components of the Reflective Question). When working on a question in a reflective conversation, they begin with naming the specific teaching practice. As peers refine the final version of the question, they acknowledge that all components may not all be used at the same time, but interspersed throughout the dialogue. However, at some point in the conversation, peer teams should use

Table 2: **Sample Reflective Questions**	
Question elements	**Instructional example**
1. Situation and context of the situation	When I am delivering my lessons based on the district curriculum and related to the critical attributes of the objectives....
2. Teacher reflection on instructional teaching practice	...AND thinking about the variety of ways I could have students respond,
3. Criteria	...what criteria do I use
4. Decision (refer again to the teaching practice in a general way)	...to decide which type of student response approaches I will use
5. Student impact	...to help each student learn the attributes of the objectives?
Question elements	**Curricular example**
1. Situation and possible condition	When planning my units around the district curriculum...
2. Teacher reflection on curricular teaching practice	...AND thinking about the learning objectives I might select to teach in the unit,
3. Criteria	...what thoughts go on in my mind
4. Decision (refer again to the teaching practice in a general way)	...about which objectives to select from all the possible objectives which could be taught in the unit?
5. Student impact	...to have a high likelihood that each student learns the objectives?

all five components so the observed peers do not think that the question focuses on past actions or that there is a correct answer (see Online Resource 4.5: *Hints on forming reflective questions*).

Table 2: Sample Reflective Questions gives two examples of fully formed reflective questions that a team might help a teacher develop. The first focuses on instruction. The second focuses on curriculum (see also Online Resource 4.6: *Additional examples of curricular and instructional reflective questions* and Online Resource 4.7: *Preparing the Downey Reflective Question*).

At first, peer teams may find that using these phrases is awkward, but they need to remember they are using this set of phrases orally in a conversation, not writing them. (For an example of how a real conversation might go, see Online Resource 4.3 *Suggested collaborative-interdependent reflective conversation structure and sample peer conversation*). While it may be tempting to shorten the question to make it easier to say, all components are needed, and generally in the order

they are presented. Changing the order of the components will change the question. For example, beginning a question with the criteria component creates a direct question, not a reflective one. Thus, if you start with "What criteria do you use...?" you'll get an answer based on fact, rather than one derived from reflection (see Online Resource 4.8: *Examples of five elements in sequence*).

Many educators have found that the dialogue arising from a single reflective question might continue to provoke thinking and discussion over a long time period. That's why peers' reflective questions need to be robust enough to stimulate thinking over time. In fact, if teachers can answer the reflective question immediately, there is no opportunity for deep reflective thought; this immediate response suggests a failure in selecting a meaningful area for reflection. The reflective question needs to be at the right level of difficulty for the teacher, thus requiring time to ponder (see Online Resource 4.9: *Criteria for reflective questions*).

Step 7: Test the reflective question using all five of the positive presuppositions

Peer group members begin to pull the conversation together around the reflective question. Sometimes, when people are first learning to use a reflective question, they simply state the five phrases, and there is no real conversation. Team members should work to embed the components of the question in the reflective conversation as a whole. Near the end of the conversation, teachers might want to put all the phrases together.

After working singly and with colleagues through the iterations of the process, ultimately, each teacher will be able to make the following statement about his or her area for reflection:

> So, here is the reflective question: When I am planning my lessons aligned with district standards, and thinking about the many ways I could use the varied contexts of my practice activities to impact multiple transfer scenarios, such as transfer to high stakes tests or transfer to the real world, what criteria do I use to decide on the type of practice contexts I will use to assist students in their transfer of learning to various settings? (see Online Resource 4.10: *Brief examples of peer teachers in a follow-up reflective conversation*)

Repeat Steps 3–7 in Stage Two with each teacher who has had sufficient observations to engage in reflection with the help of peers.

Step 8: Use the draft reflective question to deepen dialogue

Members of the peer group continue working on the reflective question with one observed teacher at a time. The bulk of the dialogue will be on clarifying the teaching practice on which the teacher reflects. Each group member should provide several examples based on observations (not feedback) during walk-throughs in the observed teacher's classroom and helping that teacher reflect.

Then based on their own experiences, they begin to examine criteria they apply in deciding to use the selected teaching practice. One teacher might say: "Share with me some of the criteria you might apply to decide on using this teaching practice. For instance, when you have the students do a warm-up activity in a test-like format, what thoughts

go through your mind?" The observed teacher responds, and the dialogue continues.

Variations

The classroom walk-through with reflective inquiry approach is adaptable to multiple situations and contexts. For example, teams can be made up of a variety of observers. Observations can be conducted by individuals or by small groups, as long as the observed teacher is prepared for a group.

In addition, the observational data from walk-throughs can be supplemented by other types of data — attendance records, grade reports, dropout rates, turnover rates, parent participation records, student work, exhibitions, and even tests — as long as these create conditions for reflection.

Challenges and how to address them

All of the assumptions in this chapter (pp. 87–88) bring with them challenges, and these challenges cannot be ignored if educators are to succeed in implementing walk-through practice with reflective inquiry. However, within those assumptions are the seeds of solutions to the challenges teachers and teacher leaders, study groups, etc. will face as they implement a reflective inquiry approach. Here are a few of the most important assumptions and suggestions about addressing them.

Teacher as decision maker. The teacher is the decision maker in teaching, one with an inner locus of control. The principal or coach does not tell the teacher what to do, expecting that he or she will follow that advice. This is a paradigm shift that educators may find uncomfortable at first. Culture change happens one interaction at a time until what is unusual becomes commonplace. Educators committed to peer walk-throughs can recognize the teacher as decision maker in their peer groups first and then see the notion begin to spread throughout the school.

Respect for choice. This, too, can be problematic until the culture shifts. The teacher almost always has numerous choices of teaching actions — such as focusing on one objective rather than another or one strategy instead of another — and therefore needs to be conscious of and personally accountable for these choices. The peer groups, again, can serve as the impetus for culture change, respecting choice through the framework of the reflective question and the dialogue process and, gradually, making choice part of the vocabulary of all teachers.

Belief that the teacher uses criteria. Here is where the teaching as art or craft comes into play. The belief that teachers use criteria for decisions needs to be honored. Helping educators surface the criteria they use will change the culture. Also, educators must believe that priorities and circumstances change, and a good teacher will adapt to those with a bevy of appropriate criteria.

Time for reflection-for-action. Like most powerful professional learning designs, this is not a one-off situation. Classroom walk-throughs followed by reflective dialogue takes time throughout a year. More schools each year are instituting Professional Learning Communities (PLCs; see "Chapter 18: Professional Learning Communities"). The work PLC members do in their groups can focus on or include classroom walk-throughs followed by reflective dialogue.

Two additional challenges warrant discussion: justification versus understanding and neutrality.

Justification versus understanding. Educators are used to feedback, which often drives them into a defensive position. They may try to justify an action, for example, when all they need to do is to understand it. Again, the culture changes gradually — peer group by peer group — so that reflective questions and dialogue are not about a teacher's decision about a particular lesson or lessons taught in the past but are reflection about general practice and the decisions a teacher makes for future action.

Neutrality. This challenge is related to the problem of feedback. Observers need to identify teaching actions and decisions without judging their quality. Recipients of observations only — not judgments — may at first be put off by the process. "Just tell me whether the lesson was good or not," is a common complaint as educators get used to observer neutrality. The process in this chapter helps peer groups establish and achieve the norm of neutrality. And, as walk-throughs with reflective dialogue become the norm, educators will be more interested in the details of what happened during a lesson than any single person's evaluation of it.

Conclusion

Educator reflection on practice, based on data, needs to become a norm in schools. Classroom walk-throughs with reflective dialogue is one way to enable that norm. When educators are able to say, "Of course, we observe one another and reflect on what we saw," the culture of learning in a school will change. Learning — for educators and their students — will be exponential.

References

Anderson, L. W. & Krathwohl, D.R. (Eds.). (2001). *A taxonomy for learning, teaching and assessing: A revision of Bloom's Taxonomy of educational objectives.* White Plains, NY: Longman.

Belisle, T. (1999). *Peer coaching: Partnership for professional practitioners.* Available at www.carla.umn.edu/immersion/acie/vol2/May1999_PeerCoaching.html.

Blase, J. & Blase, J. (1998). *Handbook of instructional leadership.* Thousand Oaks, CA: Corwin Press.

Bloom, B. (Ed.). (1956). *Taxonomy of educational objectives: The classification of educational objectives. Handbook I cognitive domain.* White Plains, NY: Longman.

Cosh, J. (1999). Peer observation: A reflective model. *ELT Journal, 59*(10), 23.

Del Prete, T.A. (2013). *Teacher rounds: A guide to collaborative learning in and from practice.* Thousand Oaks, CA: Corwin Press.

Deming, W.E. (1986). *Out of the crisis.* Cambridge, MA: MIT Press.

Downey, C.J. (2004). *SchoolView: Gathering trend data on curricular and instructional practices.* Johnston, IA: Curriculum Management Services.

Downey, C.J. (2006). *The three-minute classroom walk-through: A multimedia kit for professional development.* Thousand Oaks, CA: Corwin Press.

Downey, C.J. (2007). *Mentoring the reflective principal: Participant's manual.* October 2006 Walk-Through Colloquium, Johnston, IA: Curriculum Management Systems.

Downey, C.J. & Frase, L.E. (2003). *Participant's manual for conducting walk-throughs with reflective feedback to maximize student achievement: Basic seminar* (3rd ed.). Johnston, IA: Curriculum Management Systems.

Downey, C.J., Frase, L.E., & Peters, J. (1994). *The quality education challenge.* Thousand Oaks, CA: Corwin Press.

Downey, C.J., Frase, L., Poston, W.K., Jr., Steffy, B., English, F., & Melton, R. (2002). *Leaving no child behind: 50 ways to close the achievement gap.* Johnston, IA: Curriculum Management Systems.

Downey, C.J., Steffy, B., & English, F. (2003). *Participant's manual for conducting walk-throughs with reflective feedback to maximize student achievement: Advanced Seminar.* Johnston, IA: Curriculum Management Systems, Inc.

Downey, C.J., Steffy, B., English, F., Frase, L. & Poston, W.K., Jr., (2004). *The three-minute classroom walk-through: Changing school supervisory practice one teacher at a time.* Thousand Oaks, CA: Corwin Press.

Downey, C.J., Steffy, B., Poston, W. K., Jr., & English, F. (2010). *Advancing the three-minute walk-through: Mastering reflective practice.* Thousand Oaks, CA: Corwin Press.

Drucker, P. (1974). *Management: Tasks, responsibilities, practices.* New York, NY: Harper & Row.

DuFour, R. & Eaker, R. (1998). *Professional learning communities at work: Best practices for enhancing student achievement.* Bloomington, IN: Solution Tree.

Erickson, H.L. (2007). *Concept-based curriculum and instruction for the thinking classroom.* Thousand Oaks, CA: Corwin Press.

Evertson, C.M., Emmer, E.T., & Worsham, M.E. (2003). *Classroom management for elementary teachers* (6th ed.). Boston, MA: Allyn & Bacon.

Frase, L.E. (2005). Refocusing the purposes of teacher supervision. In F. English (Ed.). *The Sage handbook of educational leadership.* Los Angeles, CA: Sage. DOI: http://dx.doi.org/10.4135/9781412976091.

Garmston, R.J. (2000). Why cats have clean paws. *Journal of Staff Development, 21*(3), 63–64.

Glasser, W. (1998). *The quality school: Managing students without coercion.* New York, NY: Harper & Row.

Good, T.L. & Brophy, J.E. (1978). *Looking in classrooms* (2nd ed.). New York, NY: Harper & Row.

Israel, M. (n.d.). Teachers observing teachers: A professional development tool for every school. *Education World.* Available at www.educationworld.com/a_admin/admin/admin297.shtml.

ONLINE RESOURCES

4.1   Five-step observation structure of the Downey Walk-Through in question form

4.2   Five-step observation lens of the Downey Walk-Through in direction form

4.3   Suggested collaborative-interdependent reflective conversation structure and sample peer conversation

4.4   Examples of teaching practices for the 2nd presuppositional phrase of the Downey Reflective Question

4.5   Hints on forming reflective questions

4.6   Additional examples of curricular and instructional reflective questions

4.7   Preparing the Downey Reflective Question

4.8   Examples of five elements in sequence

4.9   Criteria for reflective questions

4.10 Brief examples of peer teachers in a follow-up reflective conversation

Joyce, B. & Showers, B. (1996). The evolution of peer coaching. *Educational Leadership, 53*(6), 12–16.

Ladyshewsky, R.K. & Ryan, J. (2006). Peer coaching and reflective practice in authentic business contexts: A strategy to enhance competency in post-graduate business students. In A. Herrington & J. Herrington (Eds.), *Authentic Learning Environments in Higher Education* (pp. 61–75). Hershey, PA: Information Science Publishing.

Marzano, R.J., Pickering, D., & Pollock, J. (2001). *Classroom instruction that works: Research-based strategies for increasing student achievement.* Alexandria, VA: ASCD.

McGregor, D. (1960). *The human side of enterprise.* New York, NY: McGraw-Hill.

Peterson, K.D. (2000). *Teacher evaluation: A comprehensive guide to new directions and practices.* Thousand Oaks, CA: Corwin Press.

Rattray, D. (n.d.). Peer coaching [Web page]. Available at www.canteach.ca/elementary/fnations17.html.

Resnick, L., Hall, M.W., & Fellows of the Institute for Learning. (2001). *The principles of learning: Study tools for educators.* [CD-ROM]. Pittsburgh, PA: Institute for Learning, Learning Research and Development Center, University of Pittsburgh.

Senge, P. (1990). *The fifth discipline: The art and practice of the learning organization.* New York, NY: Doubleday Currency.

Thorndike, E. (1932). *The fundamentals of learning.* New York, NY: Teachers College Press.

Walberg, H.J. & Waxman, H.C. (1983). Teaching, learning, and the management of instruction. (ERIC Document Reproduction Service No. ED237458). In D.C. Smith (Ed.). *Essential Knowledge for Beginning Educators* (pp. 38–54). Washington, DC: AACTE.

CHAPTER 5

Coaching Principals

The result of high-quality coaching for principals is
high performance by staff and high student achievement.

By Kay Psencik

Pam Jones was an experienced principal and a highly
successful one. All central office staff knew it.
Every time there was a seriously troubled elementary school in the district, they would move Pam
to that school so that she could "turn it around." Though she
stayed several years in one building, she felt as though she
was being moved constantly. Just when student achievement
began to increase and the learning community was working
well, she would be asked to move to another school. Her
other frustration was that principals placed in the schools
she had turned around often dismissed the work that she had
done and initiated their own direction; as a result, student
achievement had fallen.

She loved her district and was passionate about student
learning, but, again, this year, she was faced with another
move. When her superintendent talked to her about the
move, she pleaded with him many times to allow her to stay

and sustain the outcomes of her work. He praised her for all
she had done for the district and how much he admired her
leadership, but he said she was needed in a new school. She
felt trapped and helpless. Furthermore, she was emotionally
and physically exhausted.

Luckily for Pam, she had a professional coach. Let's
listen in to their conversations:

"Pam, it's so good to see you. It's been a while."

"Cody, it *has* been a long time. I'm so glad you could
see me again. I'm struggling with another shift in job assignments. I have been moved again to another really challenging
school, and I have no energy for it."

"Well, let's talk. You remember the ground rules.
Everything we discuss is between the two of us and no one
else unless you wish to share it. Right? My coaching you
is best when you make a commitment to make changes in
your life that best match your values and your dreams and

aspirations. My job is to ask good questions. Still OK with these two rules?"

"Yes."

"You know I'll be taking notes. We will end each session with a plan of action that includes steps you will take before you see me again. You also know that if I think you need help other than what I can provide you, I either must seek it for you or recommend someone to you. Still OK with these rules?"

"Yes."

"Let's get started. Tell me what you're experiencing."

"Cody, you know that I have been sent to two turn-around elementary schools to raise performance of staff and students over the last 10 years. I have really worked hard and long hours. It's a good thing my husband is so supportive of me, and we have no children, because I don't go home at night until really late. The work is fierce. I've had to hire many new staff members, including my assistant. A lot of staff left. I was sad that they didn't stay and become a strong team, but many folks just don't want to work as hard as I expect them to work. Raising achievement of children who are tremendously behind is challenging, to say the least. There were kids in my current school who were never in class; they just walked the halls. They were rude to adults and bullies to each other. They had no commitment to their own learning.

"I've had to build discipline policies, re-educate parents while building trust with them, instill in the students a desire and commitment to learning, and, most important, I've had to build a learning community where none existed. I am proud to say we are well on our way. Staff are collaborative, student focused, data driven, and learning from each other. Student achievement isn't where we want it yet, but it is close. We are becoming a model for the district.

"In the last visit from my superintendent, he said he needed to talk to me. He shared how proud he was of me and that he had announced to the district board of trustees that he would be moving me to another school next year. My heart sank. I could not hear another word he said. I've talked to him many times about wanting to stay where I am to enjoy the benefits of my hard work and to see it through. He assured me I would have that opportunity. Now he has violated my trust in him and I am seething inside. I don't know what he said after that. I need coaching!"

"What have you done since the conversation?"

"I have gone home early several afternoons, sick. I can't eat. I can't face the staff. I am ill with the news. I feel helpless."

"What do you do when you are home?"

"I am reliving that conversation with my superintendent over and over and over again, like playing a tape over and over, trying to figure out what I could have done differently and dreading the future. I am telling myself every day that I cannot do this new job, but I don't have the energy or passion for starting over again. I can't even imagine it!"

"Is this a healthy decision you are making? Is it helping you in any way?"

"No."

"So before we start work on your future, do you want to start thinking about your present condition and your health?"

"No, I have to get past this depression."

"How do you want to do that?"

"Well, maybe it is a mental and physical health issue. I quit going to the gym and have been eating junk food. Let me come back to have this session next week. You're right about my body not being able to show up and think of new actions today. See you next week!"

The following week

"Hey, Pam, welcome back! How was the week?"

"Great! I exercised every morning and am back on healthy eating patterns. I also made a point to visit with all staff members this week to tell them how proud I am of them. I hosted a celebration of successes at the staff meeting. Everyone came with their favorite story of success from their classrooms and their teams and shared. It was such a treat. I visited classes and talked to students. I even substituted one day. The children renew me."

"OK. Sounds like you have already made some good decisions for yourself. Now let's talk about this move. First, do you think you have really explored with your superintendent your wish to stay, at least enough that he will allow you to do so?"

"Yes, I do think that he has his mind made up and will not change it. I have seen that look before."

"You see him closing the door on another conversation, right? Are you sure he would do that? Could things turn out differently? How else might you think about this?

What options do you have?"

"Well I could go talk to him when I'm not so hurt and angry. And the more he talked the angrier I got! I am sure he knew it."

"Well what would you want to talk about? What would you say? How would you approach him?"

"I would want to remind him about his promise to me and my passion for the work I'm doing right now. I would want to tell him I'm not finished!"

"What if he says, 'No, the decision is already made'? How will you react this time? What will you do to keep from allowing your emotions to hijack you so that you cannot think? If he chooses to let you stay, what responses do you want to make to him?"

Pam was silent. Cody waited a minute and then said, "Want to practice? Let's videotape your practice and you can observe yourself. OK?"

"Sure."

"Now, do you want to call his office and get an appointment right now or do you want to do it later this afternoon?"

"I think I want to do it now so that I don't get cold feet and put it off."

"OK. I will step out while you make the call."

A few minutes later, Cody returned and said, "Now let's do the videotape. You can try out what you are going to say a variety of times, and we can review the tape and choose the best response."

Before seeing her coach, Pam did not see a positive outcome for herself. She felt powerless in the situation, and she developed a sense of distrust of her superintendent.

After making the appointment and the videotape, Pam and Cody explored all of her options, including leaving the district. At each session, Pam clarified her feelings, attitudes, and aspirations; she determined small steps and actions she could take to prepare for the choices she made. Coaching Pam to see options, move from her initial attitudes and feelings, and to think clearly about her future was not a short-term event. It took many sessions of structured conversations in which she and Cody uncovered issues and gaps in her thinking, considered options, and selected value-driven, powerful goals for herself.

Effective coaches expect those they coach ("coachees") to establish long- and short-term goals, develop clear plans of action that can be evaluated as to their effectiveness, and

practice new skills so that they are successful. Eventually, Pam realized she was choosing the new school instead of quitting; she saw a change in her attitude and regained energy.

Through several months of coaching, Pam began to imagine herself in the new school, and she began to get excited about the opportunity. Even though she knew she should be moving boxes and files and getting to know staff, she and her husband decided to take a cruise — the dream of a lifetime — before starting the new year.

Coaching made a significant difference for Pam. She was once again energized; she became excited to start a new school year and eager to face the challenges of a new school.

Overview

Coaching is a professional learning design that facilitates coachees' seeing in new ways, thinking differently, and opening up to and trying on new possible actions. Coaching is a personal and precise practice that inspires coachees to take courageous actions and to transform their leadership through learning.

Effective districts ensure a successful program of support for principals. For example, they provide in-depth learning experiences for all principals around the skills of effective leadership. They engage them systematically in study teams and action research with their peers. Most importantly, they ensure that principals have the opportunity for professional coaching.

In order to provide professional coaching for their principals, district leaders need a clear definition of coaching and parameters or norms for the use of coaching in the district. Think about how Pam was coached: The coach assisted her with matters that were totally private — working with her superintendent — and absolutely personal — her attitude toward changing schools. No study team or focus group could have done what Pam and her coach were able to do. Her peers might have talked negatively about their superintendent or fallen into commiserating with her, but those conversations may have just led to Pam being even more distrustful and dissatisfied than she was. It was the coach who helped Pam to make different observations of the world and to look forward to her new experience.

Definition and description

Coaching is a unique skill because it helps others to find themselves, to discover their dreams and aspirations, and to generate the courage to achieve them. Here is a summary of what effective coaches do:

- Help principals use constructivist strategies, namely those that guide principals to create their own solutions and to design their own plans of action.

- Generate powerful, strategic, and focused learning for the coachee.

- Assist principals with personal as well as professional issues.

- Challenge the assumptions that keep a person "stuck." They ask thought-provoking questions. They facilitate people in owning their own problems, learning their own way, practicing for mastery; they also assist coachees in being accountable for the decisions they make and the actions they wish to take (Hargrove, 1995; Psencik, 2011; Rock, 2006).

As with many teaching relationships, coaching is more art than skill. There are distinct skills of coaches: listening from another's point of view, asking the right questions that spur the coachee to think differently, and facilitating goals setting and effective planning so that learning occurs. However, these skills may not be the most important aspects of an effective coach. Effective coaches do not impose their experiences or their assumptions and ideas on their coachees; the coach is other-centered. The coach is fully present with the coachee — there is no multitasking. Coaches take notes, listen between the words, and work hard to understand what is causing the breakdowns in thinking for their coachees. Though effective coaches empathize, they are not drawn into the "story," and they do not lose their objectivity. They expect the best from their coachees and have faith in them that they will achieve whatever goals they set, even if the coachees themselves sometimes lose their courage.

A participant in a training session for coaches said, "But what if I, as a coach, have had this experience myself and I do have an idea for a solution? Why shouldn't I tell my coachee my solution?" The facilitator said most candidly, "You have never had the exact experience; you are making connections to your own life. These teachers are not **your** teachers; these students are not your students. These are your coachee's experiences. Listen to her. You have absolutely no

solution that will be of value; help the coachee find her own way. She will not only own the problem; she will own the solution. She will grow in confidence that she can solve her own problems. Don't rob her of that by telling her what to do."

Two online tools for this chapter can help district leaders and principals define administrative coaching for their own environments. Figure 1 (see p. 103), which is also Online Resource 5.1: *Definition and critical attributes of effective principal coaching*) is a template that helps district leaders clarify their definition of coaching. It is based on Joellen Killion's KASAB formula for outcomes (Killion, 2008) in which the *K* is *Knowledge, A* is *Attitude, S* is *Skills, A* is *Aspirations, and B* is *Behavior.* This template is best used after the district team has engaged in some research and study about effective executive coaching.

Online Resource 5.2: *Innovation Configurations (IC) map for coaches,* provides a description of coaching skills at different levels. This tool is valuable as a self-assessment for those who want to coach principals, and it is also helpful to district leaders in understanding coaching. An Innovation Configuration is an established and well-researched rubric that was developed by experts in a national research center studying educational change (Hall & Hord, 2010; Hord, Rutherford, Huling-Austin, & Hall, 1987). An IC Map identifies and describes the major components of a new practice and describes various uses along a continuum, ranging from ideal implementation to nonuse.

Desired outcomes

The IC maps identify three desired outcomes for coaching:

- The coach builds a safe and nurturing environment in which those being coached are comfortable sharing work challenges, establishing strategies for building shared vision in their schools, and implementing purposeful innovations;

- The coach structures the learning to ensure that leaders develop knowledge and the skills to create and lead learning communities in which all students and staff are learning; and

- The coach continuously learns in order to improve.

Rationale

Today's principals are challenged to achieve complex goals in tremendously short timelines. Principals deal with literally hundreds of brief tasks each day, sometimes 50 to 60 separate interactions in an hour (Peterson, 1982, 1988). Their greatest challenge is, of course, to make a positive impact on student learning, for which they are ultimately accountable.

In order to be accountable for student learning, school principals are challenged to find solutions to 21st-century issues. Not only must they meet the expectations of their communities, districts, and states, but they must also build meaningful relationships with their students and staff members so that everyone owns the challenges and engages in strategies for success. They must build a shared vision with staff members around compelling, complex goals that may require dramatic changes in all or many practices; establish aggressive, passionate communities of learners; and build collective responsibility for the success of all students. They must meet the needs of an increasingly diverse student population, keep students motivated, engage them in a global curriculum designed to meet the demands of a complex world, and ensure a safe school environment in a world that is increasingly apathetic and violent. Anyone who accepts a principalship faces challenges to meet the demands of the job (Marzano, Waters, & McNulty, 2005; Psencik, 2011).

According to a report by the National Association of Elementary School Principals (Protheroe, 2008), "Principals must have time and resources to develop the knowledge and skills they need to lead high-performance schools, as well as the resources to function effectively as instructional leaders in their buildings" (p. 19). Though school leaders are trained and certified, they rarely have sufficient support once they accept a principalship. If there is support, it is often a short-term mentorship to acclimate the new leader to the district. Yet, such short-term support does not close the leadership knowing-doing gap. It is one thing to know about leadership; it is another to lead a school to high levels of performance. Effective principals, like all professionals, are engaged in long-term, purposeful professional learning throughout their career. District leaders ensure principals have access to long-term

Figure 1: Definition and Critical Attributes of Effective Principal Coaching

Effective coaches are characterized by the following (with blanks in each category for the district to complete):

Knowledge: They deeply understand that
- Coaching is other centered;
- Adults have learning preferences;
- _____

Another example: Coaches avoid offering advice or engaging the coachees in their own stories.

Attitudes: Their disposition is characterized by
- A sense of optimism and hope;
- A sense of positive intent in their coachee;
- _____

Another example: Living in joy and accepting every setback as temporary.

Skills: They have high levels of proficiency in
- Listening fully;
- Being fully present;
- Questioning with focus and precision;
- Paraphrasing and reflecting with coachees;
- _____

Another example: Using a coaching cycle that leads the coachee to commit to new practices or attitudes.

Aspirations: They have great hope for their coachee and hold expectations high for them by
- Not letting them "off the hook!";
- Watching for assessments that keep them "stuck";
- _____

Another example: Being hopeful that the coachee will learn, change his/her practices, and see new possibilities and choices.

Behaviors: Actions that lead to coachees' achieving their goals through
- Walking coachees through an effective process of declaring breakdowns through taking new actions;
- Generating powerful actions and focused learning for the coachee;
- _____

Another example: Staying focused on the goal of the coachee until he/she achieves it.

professional learning, including communities of other principals and coaching.

Coaching as a strategy for support

Coaching may be a district's most effective strategy for supporting principals over time. Through coaching, principals have the personal and precise conversations they need and the space to learn.

So what is the added value of coaching? Consider the following:

Outdated leadership modes. Effective coaching helps coachees break the barriers of outdated modes of leadership. Coaching fits precisely to the needs of the learners and the goals they have set. Coaching is just-in-time and personalized. Effective coaching brings depth and focus to particular challenges precisely when principals need such focus. The effective coach becomes a confidante, a thinking partner for support and guidance when coachees are dealing with complex people issues, and a questioner who helps the principal see new options and think in new ways.

The isolation of school leadership. Though principals may attend meetings with peers, few districts have structures or systems in place to build a principal professional learning community. If they exist at all, such communities of principals can effectively work through many complex issues. Communities can also help address the needs, concerns and aspirations of the many people who work in the school and who have diverse opinions, skills, attitudes, and hope and visions for their schools. Most principals' work, however, is lonely work. There is little, if any, support for them throughout their career. An effective coach inspires principals to learn new skills, and like any coach, asks strategic questions and gives precise feedback when requested. Coaches develop in their coachees the capacity to build win-win opportunities, to lead and facilitate effective learning communities, to help staff develop a collective responsibility for student learning and use a cycle of continuous improvement, to challenge their own assumptions that may be holding them back, and to inspire them to face challenges.

Learning and proficiency. In any field, mastery is a satisfaction that evolves through precise practice and commitment. Training alone is insufficient to develop mastery in anything. So often, a seasoned coach is able to add insights, precise feedback, wisdom, technique, encouragement, experience,

and the observer's eye and listener's ear. Often, when individuals significantly improve their performance, they trace that mastery to close relationships with their coaches. Top executives choose their coaches carefully because much depends on the synergy between the two of them. When a brilliant coach and a brilliant leader become partners, extraordinary outcomes and unparalleled achievements result.

In summary, principals need visionary central support. In an interview with former executive director of NSDC Dennis Sparks (2003), Michael Fullan noted, "Investment in leadership development is important. Getting beyond resignation and the passive dependency that has been created by the prescriptions of the past 10 years requires a different kind of socialization for principals" (p. 56). Those in school districts responsible for principals must value principals' work — and value their learning. School leaders need in-depth, structured learning experiences, collaboration, and just-in-time professional learning. When district leaders focus on intense leadership development, they help school leaders develop a shared vision around the district's mission and vision, as well as an understanding of how various innovations are designed to achieve those goals (Marzano & Waters, 2009). When districts have an intense focus on leadership learning, they ensure that each principal has a powerful coach who can mentor, model, question, encourage, and inspire — a coach who works side-by-side with the leader, inspiring the principal to focus on strengthening individual skills, deepen his or her understanding of professional learning communities, and to develop the attitudes and aspirations needed for leading and learning.

Steps

The following process steps will help a district establish a coaching program for principals.

Step 1: Develop a deep understanding of the Learning Forward Standards for Professional Learning

Districts have a moral obligation to focus on the learning of principals. Districts spend considerable energy on teacher learning and professional learning communities. However, little will change in schools unless principals can lead and facilitate teacher learning. Without central office

ADDITIONAL RESOURCES

Articles

"Executive coaching enhances goal attainment, resilience and workplace well-being: A randomised controlled study," by Anthony M. Grant, Linley Curtayne, & Geraldine (2009, September). *The Journal of Positive Psychology. 4*(5), 396–407.

"Making sense of principals' work," by Kent D. Peterson. (1982). *The Australian Administrator, 3*(3), 1–4.

"Realities and reform: Living with the daily realities of principals' work," by K. D. Peterson. (1998, May). *Instructional Leader, 11*(3).

Books

Assessing impact: Evaluating staff development (2nd ed.), by Joellen Killion. Thousand Oaks, CA: Corwin Press, 2008.

Blended coaching: Skills and strategies to support principal development, by Gary S. Bloom, Claire L. Castagna, Ellen R. Moir, & Betsy Warren. Thousand Oaks, CA: Corwin Press, 2005.

Coaching matters, by Joellen Killion, Cindy Harrison, Chris Bryan, & Heather Clifton. Oxford OH: Learning Forward, 2012.

The Coach's Craft: Powerful Practices to Support School Leaders, by Kay Psencik. Oxford, OH: Learning Forward, 2011.

Cognitive coaching: A foundation for renaissance schools, by Art Costa and Robert J. Garmston. Norwood, MA: Christopher-Gordon, 2002.

Leadership coaching for educators: Bringing out the best in school administration by Carla Reiss. Thousand Oaks, CA: Corwin Press, 2007.

Leading for results (2nd ed.), by Dennis Sparks. Thousand Oaks, CA: Corwin Press, 2007.

Results coaching, the new essential for school leaders, by Kathryn M. Key, Karen A. Anderson, Vicky S. Dearing, Edna Harris, & Frances Schuster. Thousand Oaks, CA: Corwin Press, 2010.

Shaping school culture: The heart of leadership, Terence E. Deal, & Kent D. Peterson. San Francisco: Jossey-Bass, 1998.

Trust matters: Leadership for successful schools, by Megan Tschannen-Moran. San Francisco, CA: Jossey-Bass, 2004.

Training institutes for coaches

The following organizations offer institutes for coaches. A district can also hire coaches from these organizations. Learning Forward and Coaching for Results, Global, for example, have certified coaches who also have been school administrators.

http://coachingforresultsglobal.com/
Coaching for Results, Global

www.learningforward.org
Learning Forward

www.newfieldinstitute.com.au/
Newfield Institute

---

support and an intense focus on the learning of school leaders, a district will fail to achieve its moral purpose, dreams, and aspirations. When district leaders understand how adults learn and what professional learning really is, they begin to align the systems of support for principals with the Standards for Professional Learning.

The Standards for Professional Learning, which are included in Part I, "Design: Form and Structure for Learning," are guideposts for district leaders. They assist district leaders in making thoughtful decisions about professional learning for principals. The standards paint a vision

of effective professional learning and help leaders achieve complex, challenging goals. District leaders (including principals) can use Online Resource 5.3: *Understanding the Standards for Professional Learning* to develop deep understanding of the standards and make connections to actions for achieving high levels of student and staff learning.

District leaders should study the standards carefully in order to understand results-oriented, purposeful professional learning and to think about how they can apply these ideas in their work.

Step 2: Develop a deep understanding of coaching

Before initiating coaching for principals, district leaders need a deep understanding of what executive coaching really is. Reading books about coaching helps. There are several valuable resources on the market now (see Additional Resources on p. 105 for some examples related to effective coaching). *The Coach's Craft* (Psencik, 2011), for example, describes a system for developing coaches that also assists district leaders in understanding coaching and its structure. When district leaders use this book in a book-study process, they deepen their understanding.

Please note that coaching a principal or CEO is not the same system as coaching for instruction. Though there are similarities in all coaching, instructional coaching tends to be used to ensure instructional frameworks are followed or certain instructional strategies are used with fidelity. Principals and CEOs shape their own goals and directions and design their own processes and protocols.

Observing coaches at work can be helpful. When district leaders have the opportunity to observe coaching of CEOs, talk to other leaders who use coaches to facilitate the principal learning, and observe videos of coaching sessions, they begin to realize the structure and power of coaching. Given the personal nature of coaching, such observations are sometimes difficult to access. At least, coachees need to grant permission for observation; nevertheless, district leaders need to know how coaching is structured, when it is most effective, and what the attributes are of a highly effective coach. Because they will have developed a deep understanding of professional learning in Step 1, they begin to see how coaching adds precision and personalization to their professional learning program for principals.

District leaders may want to hire coaches for themselves, so they have the experience of being coached. They may read and study the attributes of executive coaches, but there is nothing more valuable than personal experience. Organizations that offer training and certification of coaches (see Additional Resources on p. 105) may be a great asset to district leaders as they work toward understanding coaching.

What district leaders need to understand is that coaching is a personal experience built through developing trusting relationships between the coach and coachee.

Coaches of principals are not information sources for the coachee's supervisor. For example, recall Pam's coaching experience. Although the district fully supported and financed Pam's coach, it would have been inappropriate for the superintendent to say to her coach, "Cody, I know you are coaching Pam. How is she doing with the move to her new school?" If he had, Cody might have said, appropriately, to the superintendent: "You know I am her coach; I really can't respond to your question. You'll need to talk with her."

Coaches may be expected to report the hours of coaching per coachee to ensure follow-through, and they may be evaluated through a coachee's reflections on the coaching experience. But, it is unethical for a supervisor to request regular reports from coaches on what is happening during coaching sessions.

Step 3: Establish a learning program for principal professional learning

School district leaders want to be very thoughtful about how they establish a learning program for principal professional learning. They want to be sure they are grounding their work in the principles of adult learners; aligning the design with the Standards for Professional Learning (see Step 1) and with the leadership expectations in the district; and being intentional about developing systems that lead learners to change behaviors, skills, and dispositions. The program ensures that principals work with one other in a community of learners around common goals and systems of change and have an opportunity for coaching. Online Resource 5.4: *Template for establishing a principal professional learning program,* is a "thinking" template that district leaders can use to ensure they have thought about all the issues.

Figure 2 (see p. 107) is an example of a learning program for principal professional learning. District leaders can modify it according to their own beliefs about principal professional learning, but they should be careful to consider each element of this program as they work on their own. Each component has a purpose in the program. Being specific about the leadership expectations of principals makes it clear to everyone what principals are to do and do well. Self-reflection and authentic goal-setting lead principals to shape their own learning and own it. Though districts

Figure 2: **Essential Components of a Professional Learning Program for Principals**

often have principals engage in intensive summer institutes, leaders may not think about the follow-through essential for principals to implement what they have learned. Follow-through comes through when a principal continues to focus on what was learned with peers in study teams and when they are coached. The entire program is designed to develop new skills, attitudes, and behaviors of all to high levels of mastery.

Step 4: Test the learning design with a theory of change and a logic model

Once the district leadership team has established the essential elements of the district's professional learning program for principals, the team will want to work through a theory of change and logic model to ensure each element is implemented authentically (Killion, 2009). A theory of change *defines all building blocks required to bring about a given long-term goal.* It answers the question, "What will it take to get us from where we are to where we want to be?" Online Resource 5.5: *Example of a completed theory of change*

template, provides a sample theory of change for implementing an effective coaching process. District leaders may wish to use the model to begin their conversations about their own theory of change.

A logic model *is a graphic depiction of the logical relationships between the resources, activities, outputs and outcomes of a program.* While there are many ways logic models can be developed, the underlying purpose of constructing a logic model is to assess the "if-then" (causal) relationships between the elements of a program. For example, a logic model would posit that, if the resources are available for a program, then the activities can be implemented. If the activities are implemented successfully, then certain outcomes are achieved. If those short-term and long-term outcomes are achieved, then the organization accomplishes its goal.

Developing a theory of change and a logic model to initiate an innovation helps district leaders be thoughtful about their approaches and uncover possible breakdowns before they begin implementation. Online Resource 5.6:

A logic model worksheet, gives an example of a logic model for initiating coaching and Online Resource 5.7: *Theory of change template* provides a blank template district leaders can use to create their own logic model.

The template and example logic model both use a backwards mapping design strategy to ensure district leaders begin with the results in mind. Through the development of their theory of change and logic model, district leaders will address such issues as how long coaches serve, how they will be evaluated, how they will be paid, what types of ongoing training and support will occur, who will train them, what competencies they must demonstrate before beginning their service as a coach.

Use these models and examples to stimulate thinking. Every leadership team needs to develop its own logic model based on the unique characteristics of the district. There is no one way to do a logic model; it's the thinking that is significant.

Step 5: Develop a strong cadre of coaches for principals

One of the biggest challenges facing district leaders is to ensure that those who coach have the skills to do so in today's world. Districts may want to hire retired principals to serve as coaches; however, retirees who achieved remarkable success in the past, may find the world in which principals operate today significantly different from the world they experienced. Retirees can be most effective if they receive extensive support. In fact, they may be the perfect choice when they have the wisdom to allow their coachees to grow.

Another source for principal coaches may come from among principals themselves. High-achieving principals in the district may not want to advance their careers by moving to district-level positions but be willing to serve as coaches for other principals. Again, districts must be careful to support the coaching skills development of these individuals so they become proficient coaches.

Another option is to hire outside coaches. This strategy may be the best process for starting coaching in any district. Districts may also choose to use a combination of strategies. They might hire outside coaches for some of the most challenged school leaders and use in-district coaches for others.

Step 6: Establish a system to match coaches with coachees

District leaders need to give careful thought about how they match coachees and coaches. They can examine rich, available data sources to determine a principal's need for coaching and how to address that need. For example, they may have staff surveys or walk-through data, reflections related to principal evaluation systems, and goal-setting systems and portfolios. Of course, principals can be invited to consider these data sources and identify a need for coaching themselves.

In effective systems, coachees learn best when they have control over who coaches them. Districts may want to allow all coachees to select their coaches. Some districts may want to assign certain coaches to certain school leaders. Even under the best of circumstances, however, this situation may be difficult for the coach and the coachee. When district supervisors assign coaches, the principles and practices, confidentiality, and commitments of ethical coaching cover interactions and are understood at the district level. Here is an example of an interaction that a coach and coachee might experience when the coach is assigned to a principal.

Tomicka is a skilled coach; she has just been assigned five coachees by her district. Her first thought is that developing these new relationships will be very difficult. Then she realizes that she is limiting her own thinking. She attends each session prepared to work through the trust issues, very hopeful and optimistic, and with the positive intention to build relationships that lead each principal to success. With four of the principals, the first sessions are positive. With the fifth principal, however, the initial session does not go well. After a few words, the coachee begins to cry.

Tomicka asks gently, "Is there something we need to discuss before we really begin this relationship?"

"I cannot believe I have been assigned a coach! I always thought I would be doing your work — coaching other principals. I am totally embarrassed about this. I cannot go to staff meetings without being ashamed. I really don't know why you're here."

Tomicka lets herself think a bit before responding to this anguish. "First, I am here because those who supervise you asked me to be here. They are concerned that, in the last two years, your students' test scores have continued to slide. Do you think there is something we can learn together that would change that trend? Is there anything in which a thought partner might be helpful to you? I am not here to tell you what to do or to report what we do to anyone, but to listen and ask questions that might open up other ways of thinking or other opportunities for you. We are working together on this. And, what we do and discuss are confidential, not to be shared with anyone else. I can't help you though unless you want me here. It's about you getting everything you want from me."

The principal is quiet for a while. "You know, I would like a thought partner. I've been all wrapped up in myself, and this is not helping at all! I haven't been focused on student and staff needs. I have been focused on myself and all of my strange feelings. I do want you to know I am most upset about the scores as well. Let me show you what I am doing and what I am thinking. I would like to talk it through with you. Maybe together we can think of other ideas. . . ."

Coaching is not part of a system for removal of ineffective principals. Coaching relationships are built on trust, and all sessions are confidential. Consequently, district leaders cannot use coaching sessions to generate evidence that can be used for nonrenewal of a contract. Evaluation systems are in place to serve that purpose. Coaching is an investment for effectively accelerating the learning of principals.

Step 7: Assess impact

Assessing impact does not betray the trust coaches and coachees develop because coaches do not report to district supervisors what is happening within the coaching relationship — neither what is discussed nor what is done. However, the impact of coaching must be assessed because coaching represents a substantial investment of human and fiscal resources. Continued investment of these resources, therefore, needs to be based on the effects of coaching.

District leaders need to determine what they want to know about the impact of coaching. They probably initiated coaching on the basis of data, so they need to collect new data to help them understand whether or not coaching has been successful. To do so, they may use the same data collection tools or new ones.

They will probably want to survey the principals themselves to ascertain whether they perceive any changes in their own knowledge, attitudes, skills, aspirations, and behaviors. They may also use an instrument such as the Standards

Assessment Inventory 2 (SAI2, available at http://learning forward.org/standards/standards-assessment-inventory-sai#) to survey staff in schools. The SAI will help them know whether and how well coaching is building a high-performing learning community at their schools. Another resource is *Assessing Impact* (Killion, 2008), a valuable tool to guide district leaders in establishing a thoughtful, manageable evaluation system.

If district leaders have conscientiously developed a learning program based on goals and outcomes, a thoughtful change theory, and a logic model to achieve their goals, they have many places to begin a conversation around assessing the impact of coaching on student and staff learning.

Variations

One variation on this design is to hire coaches from certified organizations. The organizations mentioned in Additional Resources: Training institutes for coaches on page 105 give district leaders a place to start looking for skilled coaches.

In another variation, district leaders may want to ask one of these organizations to help them identify and contact a district that has a strong system of support for principals, including coaching, to understand how they developed their system, what barriers they overcame, how the system is working now, what they are learning, and what measures they are using to evaluate effectiveness.

Challenges and how to address them

Hiring the right people to coach. One of the greatest challenges is to hire and develop skilled, proficient coaches. The quality of the outcomes from coaching will be dependent on this critical element. Making a poor personnel decision about who coaches principals can have devastating outcomes. District leaders who take their time, are thoughtful, understand coaching, and study carefully those who aspire to coach will have the greatest opportunity for success.

Training, practice, and support. All coaches, as do all administrators, need ongoing training and support to ensure they continue to develop their skills and proficiencies. An essential key to a coach's success is being able to work with others who coach. A cadre of principal coaches can observe one another coaching, with permission from coachees, and give each other feedback. In this way, coaches develop their skills throughout their coaching experiences. With permission from the principals they are coaching, they can even videotape sessions and then work with their colleagues to evaluate effectiveness.

Coaches who want to be successful learn continuously and they practice, practice, practice. District leaders may choose to send two or three future principal coaches through training for certification by the International Coaching Federation. Although these trainings are expensive, they may be a powerful investment in the long run.

Coaching as a component of a coherent program of support. Coaching alone will dramatically increase the success of a school principal. However, when districts value principal learning, coaching is only one strategy in a well thought-out program of support and professional learning. As teams of principals work together to achieve aggressive goals for themselves and learn new strategies, they learn together. Accordingly, in addition to receiving coaching principals can participate in study groups and principal professional learning communities (PLCs) or critical friends groups (CFGs). They can also participate in action research, online networking, online protocols, etc. (See other chapters in this book for more ideas.) Ultimately, principals need a coherent program of support that includes coaching.

Clearly articulated norms and roles. As district leaders develop coaching as a support system, they quickly realize that coaching only works if the coachee has great respect for and trust in the coach. If coachees are uncomfortable or feel their coaches are reporting to their supervisors, coaching will be of no value. If everyone in the organization understands this essential component, the support system will be of great value to the school leaders in the district. Thus, it is important for coaches and coachees to develop norms and clarify their roles with each, other from the beginning.

Assessment of impact. A district will always want to know if coaching matters. After investing in establishing a learning design and developing highly skilled and proficient coaches, they will want to answer the question, "Does coaching really make a difference?" Using data from multiple resources about shifts in principal practice is a key element: Are staff using new strategies? Has the leadership

ONLINE RESOURCES

5.1   Definition and critical attributes of effective principal coaching

5.2   Innovative Configurations (IC) map for coaches

5.3   Understanding the Standards for Professional Learning

5.4   Template for establishing a principal professional learning program

5.5   Example of a completed theory of change template

5.6   A logic model worksheet

5.7   Theory of change template

team taken on new responsibilities? Are students achieving more? These may be the driving questions. Like all assessments, evaluation systems need careful design.

Conclusion

Masters in every field have coaches — in sports, acting, singing, art, music, speech, politics, religion, medicine, and leadership. In fact, a very few experts achieve greatness on their own; successful people usually have a formal or informal coach, mentor, or many such people in their lives. If districts are honestly concerned about student and adult learning, they will ensure principals likewise have highly skilled, wise coaches.

References

Hall, G. & Hord, S. (2010). *Implementing change: Patterns, principles, and potholes* (3rd ed.). Upper Saddle River, NJ: Pearson.

Hargrove, R. (2012). *Masterful coaching* (3rd ed.) New York, NY: John Wiley & Sons.

Hirsh, S. & Hord, S. (2012). *A playbook for professional learning: Putting the standards into action.* Oxford, OH: Learning Forward.

Hord, S.M., Rutherford, W.L., Huling-Austin, L., & Hall, G. E. (1987). *Taking charge of change.* Alexandria, VA: ASCD.

Killion, J. (2008). *Assessing impact: Evaluating staff development* (2nd ed.). Thousand Oaks, CA: Corwin Press.

Learning Forward. (2013, Spring). Understanding the Learning Communities standard. *The Learning Principal,* *6–7.* Available at http://learningforward.org/docs/default-source/learning-principal/principal-spring-2013-low-res.pdf/.

Marzano, R.J., Waters, T., & McNulty, B.A. (2005). *School leadership that works.* Alexandria, VA: ASCD.

Marzano, R.J. & Waters, T. (2009). *District leadership that works: Striking the right balance.* Bloomington, IN: Solution Tree.

National Association of Elementary School Principals. (2008). *Leading learning communities: Standards for what principals should know and be able to do* (2nd ed.). Alexandria, VA: Author.

Peterson, K.D. (1982). Making sense of principals' work. *The Australian Administrator, 3*(3),1–4.

Peterson, K.D. (1998, May). Realities and reform: Living with the daily realities of principals' work. *Instructional Leader, 11*(3).

Protheroe, N. (2008, March–April). *NAESP's 10-year study of the K–8 principal: A historical perspective.* Alexandria, VA: National Association of Elementary School Principals.

Psencik, K. (2011). *The coach's craft: Powerful practices to support school leaders.* Oxford, OH: Learning Forward.

Rock, D. (2006). *Quiet leadership: Six steps to transforming performance at work.* New York, NY: HarperCollins.

Sparks, D. (2003, Winter). Change agent (Interview with Michael Fullan). *JSD, 24*(1), 55–58.

CHAPTER 6

Collaborative Analysis of Student Learning

Through the Collaborative Analysis of Student Learning, teachers move away from using uniform best practices and toward tailoring culturally and linguistically responsive approaches to meet the learning needs of students as they master complex academic standards.

By Amy B. Colton and Georgea M. Langer

Imagine a middle-school student, Nika, who is struggling to engage in class discussions and writing assignments during a unit on westward expansion. Sue, his teacher, has been taking his work to her Collaborative Analysis of Student Learning (CASL) study group for the last few months to inquire into how she might more effectively help him succeed. Even after her experiments with several strategies, his writing is still disappointing.

Sue, who is generally successful with her students, is baffled and frustrated. Many students in her class are engaged and working hard to meet her high expectations She used to feel she could reach all students, but now she is not so sure. In fact, she finds herself wanting to blame Nika for his lack of engagement and sloppy, incomplete work. Many teachers might have given up at this point and let Nika find his own way.

Fortunately, Sue is a teacher committed to the success of every student and refuses to let Nika fail. Acknowledging she can't meet this challenge on her own, she decides to share Nika's most recent written assignment with her study group.

As Sue and her colleagues analyze Nika's work sample, they talk about his most recent classroom behavior, his heritage, and his prior life experiences. As they consider several explanations for his performance and sources of data available, one idea in particular catches Sue's attention.

Perhaps Nika, who is Native American, is aware of how disruptive and painful the westward expansion was to the lives of his people. Since the Native American elders often share their oral histories, he has probably heard such stories from his grandparents. Nika may be expressing anger and frustration that the textbook ignores the sacrifices of his people. In fact, it focuses only on the economic benefits of the westward expansion, and how the American Indians actually helped the pioneers navigate across the country.

Through the conversation, Sue and her colleagues come to understand Nika's point of view. They talk about how Nika's reactions might be influencing his classroom behavior and the quality of his work. They use these insights to consider how Sue might be more responsive to his learning needs and draw on his prior experiences, as well as those of other students with diverse backgrounds.

Based on recommendations of a few colleagues, Sue decides to have her students read and discuss several primary sources depicting the experiences of the American Indians and slaves during the westward expansion. She also invites Nika's father to share some of his people's oral history from this time. Finally, she revises the expository writing assignment to include both the positive impact on the country and the negative consequences to Native Americans and African-American slaves.

In the absence of collaborative inquiry, Sue may have chosen either to lower her expectations for Nika or give up

on him. Instead, she fulfilled the two central purposes of CASL: Excellence with equity. She maintained the same high standard for all her students and designed new paths to learning that were responsive to Nika's background and needs.

The story of Sue and Nika illustrates how the collaborative analysis of student learning not only improves teachers' effectiveness, but also alters teachers' beliefs about their students and their practice. Such *transformative learning* is particularly critical in contexts in which students' linguistic, cultural, and socio-economic values are different than those of those of their teachers.

Overview

The CASL professional learning design provides the necessary social context for *transformative* teacher learning to occur. In small study groups, teachers analyze student work samples that "provide windows into students' understanding

ADDITIONAL RESOURCES

Books

The adaptive school: A sourcebook for developing collaborative groups (2nd ed.), by Robert J. Garmston and Bruce M. Wellman. Lanham, MD: Rowman and Littlefield, Publishers, 2013.

Assessment-centered teaching: A reflective practice, by Kathryn DiRanna, Ellen Osmundson, Jo Topps, Lynn Barakos, Maryl Gearhart, Karen Cerwin, Diane Carnahan, Craig Strang. Thousand Oaks, CA: Corwin Press, 2008.

Biography-driven culturally responsive teaching, by Socorro Herrera. New York: Teachers College Press, Columbia University.

Classroom assessment for student learning: Doing it right - Using it well (2nd ed.), by Jan Chappuis, Rick J. Stiggins, Steve Chappuis, and Judith A. Arter. New York: Pearson, 2011.

Collaborative analysis of student work: Improving teaching and learning (2nd ed.), by Amy B. Colton, Georgea M. Langer, and Loretta S. Goff. Thousand Oaks, CA: Corwin Press, in press.

Culturally proficient instruction: A guide for people who teach, by Kikanza J. Nuri Robins, Delores B. Lindsey, Randall B. Lindsey, and Raymond D. (Dewey) Terrell. Thousand Oaks, CA: Corwin Press, 2012.

How to create and use rubrics for formative assessment and grading, by Susan M. Brookhart. Alexandria, VA: Association of Supervision and Curriculum Development, 2013.

Professional learning communities by design: Putting the learning back into PLCs, by Lois Brown Easton. Thousand Oaks, CA: Corwin Press and Oxford, OH: Learning Forward.

of key ideas and skills" (Langer & Colton, 2005, p. 22). In the process of the inquiry, teachers surface assumptions that may be limiting their capacity to give full attention to the needs of the student. They identify potential solutions and test, analyze and refine them through a systematic inquiry process.

Pursued within a structured learning community, CASL tasks (a) build teachers' capacities to make effective instructional judgments based on thoughtful analysis, problem solving, reflection, experimentation, and assessment (Colton & Sparks-Langer, 1992; Langer, Colton, & Goff, 2003); and (b) transform teachers' practices and beliefs so they persist in addressing inequities within the school context. Consequently, the collaborative analysis of student work allows teachers to find equitable ways for all students in the present and future to reach standards of excellence.

The CASL system has six distinct and essential features. Together these facilitate transformative learning that leads to increased teaching effectiveness and results for all students. The features are:

1. A focus on standards of excellence;
2. Inquiry over time;
3. Case study for equity;
4. Structured inquiry;
5. Collaboration; and
6. Facilitation and support.

A focus on standards of excellence

The primary CASL inquiry is "How do specific students' understandings of complex academic standards evolve over time, and how can teachers use that knowledge to personalize instruction and resources to facilitate learning?" Teachers begin the inquiry by clearly defining the standard of excellence that they plan to achieve. The more specific teachers are about the learning outcomes they wish to promote, the more effective and targeted their instruction and assessments will be.

Inquiry over time

Collaborative inquiry is most powerful when teachers look at individual students' work over time because deep learning of complex outcomes rarely results from a single learning experience. Educators usually agree that it is much easier — and faster — to teach a fact in history,

for example, than a concept such as racism. Single learning experiences may be sufficient for facts but they are insufficient for concepts.

Through longitudinal studies of students' evolving understandings, teachers test various strategies and scaffolded learning experiences. Based on the results, they reconstruct their theories of how best to help *individual* students reach the learning targets (Putnam & Borko, 2000). An additional benefit of this long-term experimentation and reflection is that teachers discover gaps in their own knowledge and skills, which leads them to identify their own professional learning needs.

Case study for equity

Learning to teach is not easy, partly because no one approach works for every student or for all outcomes. The challenge then is to figure out which strategies work for whom, and in what combination and sequence. Such expertise is called "case knowledge" (Shulman 1987). Teachers usually connect their instructional insights to *specific cases* of student learning rather than to uniform best practices.

For this reason, teachers in a CASL study group select a focus student from their class who represents a cluster of students who exhibit similar learning challenges in the Target Learning Area (TLA). What teachers discover about facilitating the learning of the focus student will help them personalize instruction for others in the cluster. Furthermore, each teacher in a study group selects a student with different learning challenges so that everyone in the group learns how to address multiple learning needs.

Structured inquiry

The CASL study groups follow five structured Inquiry Phases (see Figure 1 on p. 116, The Five CASL Inquiry Phases; also see Online Resource 6.1: *The five CASL inquiry phases*). Each Inquiry Phase has a specific purpose, a focus of inquiry, and a protocol that provides task directions and the responsibilities of the study group members.

The design of each Inquiry Phase is guided by the "Framework for Teachers' Reflective Inquiry" (Colton & Sparks-Langer, 1993), which describes the theoretical underpinnings for the CASL system. The Framework portrays the skills and knowledge necessary for responsible and effective teaching (Langer et al., 2003).

Figure 1: **The Five CASL Inquiry Phases**		
Phase 1	**Establishing a focus for CASL Inquiry** • Define the Target Learning Area (TLA). • Assess the TLA. • Reflect on learning and collaboration.	• What might be the most important Target Learning Area (TLA) for our inquiry? • What are the essential concepts, questions and processes to develop in our students so they reach excellence in the TLA? • How might we assess our students' current level of performance in the TLA?
Phase 2	**Refining teachers' inquiry focus and professional learning needs** • Analyze whole-class performance in TLA. • Select focus students. • Reflect on learning and collaboration.	• What are my students' strengths and areas for growth in the TLA? • What are the common characteristics of my struggling students? • Which focus students will yield the most valuable learning for equity and excellence for me and for my study group?
Phase 3	**Inquiring into teaching for learning** • Analyze focus student work samples. • Experiment with responsive approaches and resources. • Continue the Inquiry Cycle Protocol (Observe, Analyze, Plan, Act). • Reflect on learning and collaboration.	• How do specific students construct understanding of complex academic content? • What teaching approaches/resources are most responsive to the strengths and needs of our focus students and others? • Which teaching approaches/resources contribute to every student reaching proficiency in the TLA? • What values and beliefs about my students and myself influence my practice?
Phase 4	**Assessing progress** • Analyze whole-class performance on TLA. • Reflect on learning and collaboration.	• What progress have our students made toward the TLA? • What areas of learning have improved, and for which students? • What areas of learning still need improvement, and for which students?
Phase 5	**Reflection and celebration**	• What have we learned about student learning and our own strengths and needs?

Source: *Collaborative Analysis of Student Learning* by A.B. Colton, G.M. Langer, & L.S. Goff (in press), Corwin Press.

Teachers engage in each Inquiry Phase through the Inquiry Cycle Protocol, adapted from Kolb's (1984) experiential learning theory, which describes how teachers build much of their professional knowledge. The Inquiry Cycle Protocol has four steps: Observing, analyzing, planning, and acting.

Observing. Teachers observe and gather information and typically make split-second decisions to respond to what they see. In this step of the Inquiry Cycle Protocol, teachers learn to refrain from jumping to conclusions by collectively describing, without judgment or interpretation, what they see in student work. As they share different perspectives, teachers begin to broaden their lenses for observing the work, resulting in increased layers of meaning (Carini, 1979).

Sue's colleagues helped her see how Nika used negative adjectives when describing the "white men" and positive adjectives when referring to the Native Americans. These observations proved to be just the clues Sue and her colleagues needed to crack the case about Nika's learning needs.

Analyzing. In the next step of the Inquiry Cycle Protocol, teachers entertain several possible explanations for the most significant observations. Examining multiple interpretations before deciding what to do about a learning challenge is a central feature of CASL's inquiry process. This analysis allows teachers to adequately frame the problem they are facing before setting a course of action.

While Sue thought the adjectives in Nika's writing were based on class discussions or the textbook, her colleagues suggested they could represent Nika's strong alliance with his people and his feelings about what the pioneers did to the Natives. As the group checked out this hunch by examining the book and resources, Sue acknowledged that the heavy bias toward the settlers in them could have angered Nika. This insight shifted Sue's assumptions about Nika as a learner, and caused her to change her course of instruction.

Planning. After choosing the interpretation that seems to make the most sense, the study group devises a plan of action. As the scenario suggests, Sue worked with her colleagues to select some primary sources and revise her final assignment. She also talked through what she was going to ask of Nika's father.

Acting. Finally, the teacher puts the plans into action and collects results from the next work sample to share with the study group so that everyone can learn from the experience. Sue brought to her study group the final essays of **all** of her students because she was so proud of what they, including Nika, had written. In addition to the improved quality of the writing, each paper showed great empathy for the struggles of the minorities. The other minority students, who had struggled in a similar fashion to Nika, also benefited from her new approach to the unit as evidenced from their papers. The other teachers asked whether Nika's dad might also come to their classes. Sue left the study group committed to using more primary sources to personalize her instruction in the future.

Collaboration

The way teachers interact when they are not in the classroom influences the success of CASL (Darling-Hammond, 1998; Sparks, 2002). The most productive environments are those in which teachers regularly engage in collaborative conversations around meaningful and relevant issues. "During such times, assumptions are revealed and examined, and teachers allow their thinking to be open to the influence of others" (Langer et al., 2003, p. 44).

Collaborative dialogue is a central process of the CASL system because it invites multiple interpretations, helps teachers examine limiting assumptions, and unleashes teachers' "expertise and creativity" (Love et al., 2008, p. xi). A major consequence of collaborative inquiry is *collective efficacy* — a sense that teachers can overcome learning challenges when they rely on one another's expertise (Goddard, How, & Hoy, 2000).

Collaboration, however, does not happen automatically. For teachers to move beyond a "culture of polite conversation" toward deep analysis of teaching and learning, groups need to develop, practice, and reinforce norms and skills of collaboration intentionally. This evolution toward collaboration is possible through facilitation and other organizational resources.

Facilitation and support

Few innovations are sustained without organizational support. The CASL facilitator guides teachers to the kinds of thinking, problem posing, and analysis necessary for transformative learning (Langer et al., 2003). A skilled facilitator can ensure that group norms are developed and followed, that everyone develops the necessary communication and analytical skills, and that teachers keep their focus on student learning. The facilitator also helps teachers reflect on their assumptions, identify their own learning needs, and seek additional support when necessary.

Support from school administrators is also critical to the success of the system. Leaders should continuously assess the school culture. In doing so, they can determine how to support teachers in the improvement of their practice through analysis of student learning. They can render such support by providing readiness activities, meeting space, and regular times to meet; engaging teachers in the analysis of assessment data; setting high expectations and holding teachers accountable to them; and providing incentives and effective feedback.

Rationale

Researchers (Croft et al., 2010; Darling-Hammond, 2009; Hawley & Valli, 1999; Hord, 2009) have found higher levels of teacher expertise and student achievement in schools where professional learning:

- Focuses on learning of important content;
- Is sustained over time;
- Facilitates a cycle of continuous improvement where teachers assess students, share expertise, and find solutions for authentic problems of practice;
- Is school- or classroom-based, and integrated into the workday; and
- Develops collaborative teams with collective responsibility for student learning.

Such professional learning moves teachers away from working in isolation and toward implementing sustained powerful learning teams (Blank & de Alas, 2009; Darling-Hammond, Wei, Andree, Richardson, & Orphanos, 2009; Desimone, Porter, Garet, Yoon, & Birman, 2002; Garet, Porter, Desimone, Birman, & Yoon, 2001). For this kind of professional culture to take root in a school, however, leaders have to build capacity in individuals, teams, and the organization to be both learners and leaders (Learning Forward, 2011).

Since the CASL system aligns closely with the research on effective professional learning, it is not surprising that research on CASL has yielded impressive outcomes. Since 1999, nine studies of 272 elementary and secondary teachers in CASL study groups (Goff, 1999; Gray, 2009; Langer & Colton, 2001, 2006, 2007, 2008, 2011; Loyd, 2006) show the following benefits:

Benefits to students
- Improved student learning in writing, reading, and content areas; and
- Increased student clarity about intended learning.

Benefits to teachers
- Commitment and confidence in ability to promote student learning;
- Analytical and reflective inquiry skills;
- Growth in professional knowledge: content; student development and learning; personalized instruction (pedagogy); assessment design and interpretation; and contextual factors;
- Alignment among classroom standards, assessments, and instruction;
- Collaborative and group facilitation expertise;
- Awareness and self-assessment of professional practice and needs; and
- National Board for Professional Teaching Standards certification.

Benefits to parents and organizations
- Parent clarity about learning targets and student progress;
- Curriculum alignment within and across grade levels;
- Professional learning targeted to teachers' needs; and
- Ongoing, institutionalized collaborative inquiry into student success.

Phases and steps

A CASL process occurs in five phases, usually over a year (see Figure 1: The Five CASL Inquiry Phases on p. 116; also see Online Resource 6.1: *The five CASL inquiry phases*).

PHASE 1: Establishing a focus for CASL inquiry

The purpose of Phase 1 is for teachers to identify the area of the curriculum that has been consistently challenging for them to teach as evidenced in their school and classroom performance data. In Phase 1, teachers address the following questions:

- What might be the most important Target Learning Area (TLA) for our inquiry?
- What are the essential concepts, questions and processes to develop in our students so they reach excellence in the TLA?
- How might we assess our students' current level of performance in the TLA?

The most powerful Target Learning Areas (a) integrate concepts and skills found in complex content-area standards; (b) are developed over time and applied in a variety of situations; and (c) have posed instructional challenges for teachers.

To initiate this phase, teachers need disaggregated and organized test data, curriculum materials, and local grade-level formative and summative assessments and scoring rubrics with work samples, if possible.

Step 1: Define the Target Learning Area

After selecting the area for inquiry, teachers define the Target Learning Area (TLA) by describing how students will ultimately demonstrate their proficiency in the specific learning outcomes. Next, teachers deconstruct the broad outcomes into enabling objectives, including prerequisite skills.

Step 2: Administer initial assessments

Next, teachers design and administer an initial assessment with prompts, student directions, teacher procedures, and scoring rubrics to determine (a) the current status of their classes' learning in the Target Learning Area (TLA), and (b) where student learning should begin.

Step 3: Reflect on learning

At the conclusion of this phase, teachers reflect on their insights about the learning required to reach proficiency in the TLA, the design of assessments for complex processes, and their adherence to group norms and use of collaborative skills.

PHASE 2: Refining teachers' inquiry focus and professional learning needs

In Phase 2, teachers narrow their inquiry by examining their own students' performance in the TLA, and selecting students who will be fruitful to study for maximum teacher growth. (See Online Resource 6.2: *Phase 2 protocol questions*.) They consider the following inquiry questions:
- What are my students' strengths and areas for growth within the TLA?
- What are the common characteristics of my struggling students?

- Which focus student(s) will yield the most valuable learning for equity and excellence for me and for my study group?

Step 1: Complete student performance grid

To begin Phase 2, teachers bring their initial assessment prompts, directions, procedures, scoring rubrics and a class set of scored student responses to the prompt. But the scoring of the performances is just the beginning of this phase.

The developers of the CASL system believe that a numeric score from a rubric reflects only a small part of what the teacher needs to know to address a struggling student's needs. Teachers, therefore, use the Student Performance Grid (see Online Resource 6.3: *Student Performance Grid*) to "look within the score" for both specific strengths and misunderstandings. For each piece of work showing low or uneven proficiency, teachers record on the grid the name, the student characteristics, the strengths in the work, and the student's specific struggles.

Step 2: Analyze the grid for patterns

Initially, teachers use color-coding to highlight common student struggles with the understandings and skills assessed. They share their findings and discuss why these patterns might exist.

Because each teacher will study a different focus student, it is important that the selected students pique the teachers' curiosity about both common content difficulties and teaching for equity.

Sue's study group's Phase 1	Sue's study group's Phase 2
Sue's group engaged in this Phase by using grade-level expectations, resources, and assessments to define, in detail, the enabling objectives within expository writing. They designed and administered the initial assessment to determine each student's specific struggles with this Target Learning Area. As a result of their final reflections, they fine-tuned their rubric to further delineate the critical attributes of various levels of performance.	When Sue analyzed her grid, she found that many students were struggling with organizing their thinking in writing. She also discovered a group of students who were very quiet and rarely participated in class discussions or small group activities. Most of these students were also African- or Native Americans. Sue's inquiry question became: "How do students like Nika, who are extremely quiet, and who don't seem actively engaged in most lessons, learn to organize their thinking in writing when composing an expository essay?" The patterns found in other teachers' classroom assessments led them to frame questions around their own content challenges and student characteristics.

Step 3: Select focus student and identify inquiry question

Next, teachers look for common characteristics among the students of concern, for example, their prior experience, ethnicity, cultural background, language proficiency, neighborhood, interests, academic proficiencies, and home values. Finally, they ask, "How are these students' cultural backgrounds or experiences the same as or different from my own experience?" and "Which student might yield the most learning for me and the group?"

Teachers craft an inquiry question that frames their professional learning goal: "How do students like ___ (focus student's name), who are (characteristics as a person and learner), learn how to (enabling objective) in order to successfully achieve (Target Learning Area)?"

Step 4: Begin student biography

After selecting a focus student, the teacher begins a student biography through observation, engagement with the student, family interviews, and talking to the student's other teachers who know the student well. The biography includes information such as the student's cultural background, prior experiences, passions, learning style, current level of performance (including academic strengths), language proficiency, and friends.

Teachers who are committed to being culturally and linguistically responsive place their students' biographies at the center of their practice so they can "personalize their instruction" in an equitable manner (Herrera, 2010).

Step 5: Reflect on learning

At the conclusion of Phase 2, teachers share the characteristics of the struggling students within their own classrooms and across the classrooms studied. They reflect upon the patterns of student proficiency, and ways to fill in the gaps for those lacking prerequisite skills, knowledge, and dispositions. Finally, the group assesses how consistently they followed the norms and used the collaborative skills.

PHASE 3: Inquiring into teaching for learning

The purposes for Phase 3 are to (a) discover what each student needs to succeed, (b) decide what strategies are most responsive to those needs, and (c) examine and transform any assumptions or beliefs that may be hindering progress with students. Teachers fulfill these purposes by addressing these inquiry questions:

- How do specific students construct understanding of complex academic content?
- What teaching approaches are most responsive to the strengths and needs of focus students and others?

Sue's study group's Phase 3	Sue's study group's Phase 4
The Overview described how Sue's group engaged in *observing* and *analyzing* Nika's work sample and *planning* Sue's next steps with Nika. At the end of that session, teachers reviewed their use of the collaborative norms, and decided to be more deliberate about taking time to examine each interpretation of the work before adding a new idea to be considered.	When Sue's group analyzed their students' responses to the final assessment, they found that students' abilities to write expository essays had advanced in specific ways. Sue's class, in particular, showed vivid use and organization of ideas related to the advantages and disadvantages of westward expansion.

- Which teaching approaches contribute to every student reaching proficiency in the Target Learning Area (TLA)?
- What values and beliefs about my students and myself influence my practice?

Step 1: Analysis of student work samples

This phase extends over a few months as teachers meet regularly to analyze each focus student's most recent work. The presenting teacher begins by sharing the student biography and giving each member a copy of the work sample. As the facilitator leads the group through each step of the Inquiry Cycle Protocol, the recorder writes the group's observations, analyses, plans, and emerging questions on a study group record. They share a copy of this information with the building administrator to communicate their progress and needs. When teachers go back to the classroom, they act on the plans made. After using the new approaches and resources with the focus student, they return to the group with a work sample that shows progress.

Step 2: Reflect on learning

At the conclusion of each study group session, group members discuss what they have learned that might help other students learn, and how the use of the Work Analysis Protocol and collaborative skills influenced the group's professional learning.

PHASE 4: Assessing progress

Although the group members have been focusing on the learning of their selected focus students during the months of inquiry, they've also been using their insights to personalize their instruction for their other students. In Phase 4, group members step back and look at the progress made by the entire class in the TLA.

Phase 4 leads teachers to address the following questions:
- What progress have our students made toward the TLA?
- What areas of learning have improved, and for which students?
- What areas of learning still need improvement, and for which students?

Step 1: Analyze student performances

First, teachers design their final assessment, administer it to their classes, score it, and complete a final Student Performance Grid. Then, they use color-coding to identify patterns of content understandings — both strengths and areas needing growth. They also compare the students' final performances against their initial assessment to see how much progress has been made. For those students not reaching the target, teachers reflect on why those patterns exist and how they can be more responsive.

Sue's study group's Phase 5	Reflection on Sue's experience
The energy level in the room as Sue and the other teachers shared their success stories was noteworthy. Every teacher saw impressive gains in their student's expository essays. Sue shared what she learned about using primary sources as a way to present multiple perspectives in history. She also pointed out how she was able to actively engage more students when she took the time to get to know them as people so she could connect their backgrounds to the content being taught.	Sue's level of efficacy had soared as a result of her CASL inquiry. She ended the year believing that, with the help of her colleagues, she can tackle any future challenge that comes her way. Her group's inquiry not only enriched her professional knowledge about how to teach history and writing, her study of Native American students revealed how limiting one's own cultural lenses can be when setting student expectations and designing lessons. As a result, Sue left the school year with a long summer reading list around issues of culturally proficient instruction. Sue's study group also grew in collective efficacy as they now are more effective in addressing instructional challenges and providing equitable, culturally sensitive teaching-learning approaches for their students.

Step 2: Reflect on learning

As teachers share their findings, they note changes to make next time in the instructional path toward the Target Learning Area (TLA) and in the assessments and scoring guides. Finally, they consider their use of the norms and collaborative skills.

PHASE 5: Reflection and celebration

In Phase 5, the group members ask: "What have we learned about student learning and our own strengths and needs?"

As they look back at their CASL inquiry, teachers identify their own growth and their future professional learning needs with an eye toward greater success with students who struggle in the TLA.

Many schools have a "CASL Teacher Roundtable Exhibit" during which teachers share with others not in their study group the initial and final performance grids, focus student work samples, and their insights about teaching students like the focus students in the TLA.

Variations

Two important variations have to do with teachers' needs, and the use of student work samples in teacher evaluation.

Tailoring CASL for teacher needs

Phases 1 and 2 (defining and assessing a TLA, and selecting focus students) are best completed during the beginning of the year or semester. Phase 3 (analyzing focus student work samples and experimenting with strategies) extends over a period of months. Most groups analyze each focus student's most recent work three to five times. Phases 4 and 5 (final whole-class assessment and reflection) are usually conducted toward the end of the semester or year.

Just as CASL leads teachers to personalize their instruction for specific students, so must the system be tailored to teachers' learning needs. Although the greatest benefits come from studying teachers' influence on focus students' learning over time (Phase 3), Phases 1 and 2 can be extended as necessary to respond to the following teacher needs.

Lack of knowledge of content and standards. Teachers who lack deep understanding of the standards for their grade level will need more time in Phase 1 to define their TLAs. In this case, examining work samples showing various levels of proficiency can be quite helpful.

Need for assessment design expertise. Many teachers need a review of the essentials of assessment before they can assess their students' initial learning in the TLA. Teachers who are designing and revising their assessment prompts, procedures, directions, and scoring rubrics will find the use of actual student work helpful in this process.

Reliance on commercial classroom assessments. Student learning may suffer when teachers use an assessment with blind faith that it matches (a) their teaching materials and methods, (b) their students, and (c) their own definition of the standard. In this case, close examination of the assessment prompt, student directions, procedures, and scoring is necessary, preferably alongside student work taken from the teacher's own classroom.

Lack of collaboration or trust. In school cultures where transparency about individual classroom learning has been lacking, teachers might begin by analyzing a work sample from an anonymous student. This activity allows teachers to experience the excitement of inquiry with no worry over their own status among the others. Gradually, as teachers move into Phase 2, they will want to select and study their own focus students.

Teacher evaluation

CASL is a valuable part of teacher supervision, as one can best assess teachers' reflective thinking and commitment to excellence with equity by hearing them analyze a work sample from a struggling student. Protocols for this process are available from the authors.

Challenges and how to address them

Several issues challenge staff members who engage in collaborative analysis of student learning. Educators and school leaders who are committed to supporting CASL groups have found ways to overcome these challenges.

Finding time. The number one challenge is finding time for CASL groups to meet. Many principals have dedicated staff meeting time to CASL inquiry. They put announcements and other procedural information in bulletins and emails. They also allocate

ONLINE RESOURCES

6.1 The five CASL inquiry phases
6.2 Phase 2 protocol questions
6.3 Student performance grid

all or part of their professional learning days for study group meetings.

Finding facilitators. Facilitation is another challenge due to the need for expertise in promoting collaboration within the study group. It is best to have a specially trained facilitator. Many groups appoint a person who has the necessary skills; others rotate the facilitator role. Rarely is the principal the best facilitator for a group.

Finding ways to include teaching specialists. Although the ideal is to include special education and specialist teachers in the study groups, the mechanics of scheduling them often make this impossible. One solution is to provide substitute teachers so that special education and specialist teachers can participate in the CASL inquiry.

Conclusion

Excellence with equity. Teachers' engagement in CASL's long-term, structured analysis of students learning leads to achievement of these two purposes. As small groups of teachers analyze student work and engage in other inquiry related to content, instruction, and assessment, they discover how students' learning evolves and how they, as teachers, can most effectively promote this learning.

In the process of the inquiry, teachers discover assumptions that may be limiting their capacity to give full attention to the needs of each of their students. They identify, test, analyze, and refine potential solutions through a systematic and structured inquiry process. Consequently, the collaborative analysis of student work allows teachers to find equitable ways to ensure that all students will continue to reach standards of excellence.

References

Blank, R.K. & de la Alas, N. (2009). *Effects of teacher professional development on gains in student achievement: How meta-analysis provides scientific evidence useful to education leaders.* Washington, DC: Council of Chief State School Officers.

Carini, P.F. (1979). *The art of seeing and the visibility of the person.* Grand Forks, ND: University of North Dakota Press.

Colton, A.B., Langer, G.M., & Goff, L.S. (in press). *Collaborative analysis of student learning.* Thousand Oaks, CA: Corwin Press.

Colton, A. & Sparks-Langer, G.M. (1992). Restructuring student teaching experiences. In C. Glickman (Ed.), *Supervision in transition* (pp. 155–168). Alexandria, VA: ASCD.

Colton, A. & Sparks-Langer, G.M. (1993). A conceptual framework to guide the development of teacher reflection and decision making. *Journal of Teacher Education, 44*(1), 45–54.

Croft, A., Coggshall, J.G., Dolan, M., & Powers, E. (2010). *Job-embedded professional development: What it is, who's responsible, and how to get it done well.* Washington, DC: National Comprehensive Center for Teacher Quality.

Darling-Hammond, L. (1998, February). Teacher learning that supports student learning. *Educational Leadership, 55*(5), 6–11.

Darling-Hammond, L., Wei, R.C., Andree, A., Richardson, N., & Orphanos, S. (2009). *Professional learning in the learning profession: A status report on teacher development in the United States and abroad.* Oxford, OH: NSDC.

Desimone, L., Porter, A., Garet, M., Yoon, K., & Birman, B. (2002). Effects of professional development on teachers' instruction: Results from a three-year longitudinal study. *Educational Evaluation and Policy Analysis, 24*(2), 81–112.

Garet, M., Porter, A., Desimone, L., Birman, B., & Yoon, K.S. (2001). What makes professional development effective? Results from a national sample of teachers. *American Educational Research Journal, 38*(4), 915–945.

Goddard, R.D., Hoy, W.K., & Hoy, A.W. (2000). Collective teacher efficacy: Its meaning, measure, and impact on student achievement. *American Educational Journal, 37*(2), 479–507.

Goff, L. (1999). *Teacher and administrator perceptions concerning the use of teacher portfolios for professional development and evaluation.* (Unpublished doctoral dissertation). The University of Southern Mississippi, Hattiesburg.

Gray, S. (2009). *A study of teachers' professional learning and student outcomes.* (Unpublished master's thesis). Grand Valley State University, Allendale, Michigan.

Guerra, P.L. & Nelson, S.W. (2009). Changing professional practice requires changing beliefs. *Phi Delta Kappan, 90*(5), 354–359.

Hawley, W.D. & Valli, L. (1999). The essentials of effective professional development: A new consensus. In L. Darling-Hammond & G. Sykes (Eds.), *Teaching as the learning profession: Handbook of policy and practice* (pp. 127–150). San Francisco: Jossey-Bass.

Herrera, S. (2010). *Biography-driven culturally responsive teaching.* New York, NY: Teachers College Press.

Hord, S., Roussin, J.L., & Sommers, W.A. (2009). *Guiding professional learning communities: Inspiration, challenge, surprise, and meaning.* Thousand Oaks, CA: Corwin Press.

Kolb, D.A. (1984). *Experiential learning: Experience as the source of learning and development.* Englewood Cliffs, NJ: Prentice-Hall.

Langer, G. (2001). *Portfolio analysis of 40 Michigan teachers' collaborative Analyses of student learning.* (Unpublished evaluation study).

Langer, G.M. & Colton, A.B. (2005). Looking at student work: Growing schools' capacity for learning. *Educational Leadership, 62*(5), 22–27.

Langer, G. & Colton, A. (2006). *Collaborative analysis of student learning in Paddock Elementary School, Milan, Michigan.*(Unpublished evaluation study).

Langer, G. & Colton, A. (2007). *Evaluation of collaborative analysis of student learning professional development system in Adrian, Michigan middle schools.* (Unpublished evaluation study).

Langer, G. & Colton, A. (2008). *Study of collaborative analysis of student learning in four Ann Arbor, Michigan elementary schools.* (Unpublished evaluation study).

Langer, G. & Colton, A. (2011). *Evaluation study of collaborative analysis of student learning professional development system in Forest Hills School District, Michigan.* (Unpublished evaluation study).

Langer, G.M., Colton, A.B., & Goff, L.S. (2003). *The collaborative analysis of student work: Improving teaching and learning.* Alexandria, VA: ASCD.

Learning Forward. (2011). *Standards for Professional Learning.* Oxford, OH: Author.

Love, N.B., Stiles, K.E., Mundry, S.E. & DiRanna, K. (2008). *The data coach's guide to improving learning for all students: Unleashing the power of collaborative inquiry.* Thousand Oaks, CA: Corwin Press.

Loyd, J.W. (2006). *Collaborative learning communities: Influences on teacher and student learning.* (Unpublished doctoral dissertation). Wayne State University, Detroit, Michigan.

Putnam, R.T. & Borko, H. (2000, January/February). What do new views of knowledge and thinking have to say about research on teacher learning? *Educational Researcher, 29*(1), 4–15.

Shulman, L.S. (1987). Knowledge and teaching: Foundations of the new reform. *Harvard Educational Review, 57*(1), 1–22.

Sparks, D. (2002). *Designing powerful professional development for teachers and principals.* Oxford, OH: NSDC.

Yero, J.L. (2002). *Teaching in mind: How teacher thinking shapes education.* Hamilton, MT: MindFlight Publishing.

CHAPTER 7

Critical Friends Groups

In Critical Friends Groups, teachers learn together, pool knowledge, and expand their abilities to reach all students.

By Stevi Quate

It has been a long day, but Louie wants to be on time to his Critical Friends Group (CFG). For several years, he has met monthly with seven high school colleagues, four of whom were there from the start of their collaboration. Because of retirement and a maternity leave, two teachers left, and Maggie, a new teacher at the school, joined the group at the start of the school year.

When first approached about joining the CFG, Louie hadn't been sure that it would be worth his time. Part of his initial resistance was that the group of teachers represented a variety of disciplines: three taught English, one taught science, one taught math, another taught social studies like Louie, and one was the school's media specialist. Even though Louie enjoyed the company of each person, he hadn't been convinced that he would grow professionally by looking at English or science assignments. Always game to improve his teaching, however, he hesitatingly agreed. Now after four

years of collaborating, he recognizes how narrow his initial perspective had been. Each time he studies an assignment or student work from a different subject than his, he learns something new.

Reflecting on their time together, he thinks about how each member of his CFG has grown professionally. In particular, when the group decided to focus on issues of equity, teaching practices gradually changed as they figured out what culturally responsive teaching and differentiation looked like with their students. As a result, they saw that in their classes the achievement gap between Latino and Anglo students was narrowing and that their students seemed more engaged than they had in the past.

Today is Louie's turn to bring work to the group. The day before he had met with Jeannie, the CFG coach, to refine his inquiry question and select a protocol to guide the conversation. Even though she is the coach, Jeannie doesn't always facilitate the CFG, but this afternoon she will. When Louie walks into the meeting room, he recognizes Jeannie's efforts. The well-worn chart paper with the group's norms is posted on the wall, refreshments are sitting on a table, and the chairs are arranged in a circle.

Promptly at the designated time, Jeannie welcomes everyone and quickly reviews the agenda. "We'll start with Connections and then hear an update from Juan. After that we'll jump right into thinking with Louie. Tim has agreed to be our process observer today to help us think about how we're doing as a group. All set?"

Each CFG begins with about 10 minutes of Connections, a routine that gives the group a means to settle back into work together and to create a chance for each person to share what is foremost on his or her mind (see Online Resource 7.1: *Ideas for connections*).

After closing Connections, Jeannie turns to Juan. "Juan, why don't you update us about what's happened since last month. At that time we talked about students needing models of good work. How did that make a difference?" A couple of years ago several members of the group talked about how they were curious about what difference their feedback had made, so they agreed that each meeting would include checking in with the former presenter. With a slight grin, Juan explains how using models had boosted the quality of work his science students are doing, especially the boys.

Jeannie directs the group's attention to Louie. "Louie, you wanted to try a protocol for tuning a plan to discuss an upcoming assignment. So let's look over this protocol and begin." Even though they had used variations of this protocol before, Jeannie reviews the steps and then invites Louie to explain his dilemma.

"In my American history class, I'm working hard at inquiry, but I'm not happy about what I'm seeing students do. Often their questions are superficial and disappointing. I want to think about what I can do to get a better inquiry question out of all of them. Look at this opening activity for our upcoming Vietnam War unit. I'd like you to check this assignment to see if I'm clear and if it makes them dig deep."

With that background, the group dives into the rest of the protocol. Jeannie guides the group into asking clarifying questions to make sure everyone understands Louie's dilemma. "Remember that clarifying questions are questions that will help you understand what Louie is wrestling with. These

are questions that Louie should be able to answer easily and are frequently questions about facts. Make sure you're not asking leading questions since we'll have time to explore our thoughts about his dilemma later in the protocol." Quickly members of the group pose questions:

"How many students are in this class?"

"How many times have they done something similar in your class?"

After a few minutes of asking clarifying questions, Jeannie urges the group to take the next five minutes to study the assignment while keeping Louie's goals in mind. When the five minutes are up, she invites them to discuss what they noticed. "Now that you've had a chance to think about it, let's talk about Louie's assignment. Louie, you get a chance to listen for the next few minutes." She turns to the group while Louie scoots back and opens up his computer to take notes on the conversation. "Remember that we want to look at what worked, as well as what he should work on. Let's begin with the strengths of the assignment."

"I appreciate the choice he offers students," Sami begins. "Remember that article we read a few months ago about student engagement and how choice seems to be an important variable? This task brings to life what we read about."

The group looks carefully at the assignment over the next few minutes, pointing out its strengths. At times one or another comments, "Oh, I hadn't noticed that" or "That's a great idea. I hadn't thought about it that way before."

Jeannie moves the group forward: "Let's look at concerns that we have or gaps that we've noticed. This is the time for us to offer cool but not cruel comments. Keep in mind Louie's hopes: When students are through with this assignment, he wants them to have a meaningful inquiry question. What do you think? Will that happen? What gaps do you see? What's missing?"

Juan, who has been quiet for some time, says, "I wonder how much background knowledge Louie's kids have about the Vietnam War. I'm curious whether they know enough about the war to pose an inquiry question at this point."

"When we were thinking about student engagement last month," says Lisa, "we talked about how background knowledge fuels curiosity. This could be one of the problems Louie is facing."

After a few minutes, Jeannie prompts them to think about ways to strengthen Louie's assignment.

Jo begins, "Louie wants to make sure his students are thinking at a high level. Do you think the verbs in the directions get them into the kind of thinking or the level of inquiry that he wants?" The group looks closely at the verbs Louie had used in his instructions to students. Louie continues taking notes as the discussion moves to an end.

After glancing at the clock on the wall and hearing a lull in the conversation, Jeannie says, "Our 15 minutes for feedback are up. Let's invite Louie back in and hear his comments."

Louie thanks the group for the comments and refers to his notes. "I hadn't thought about the verbs," he says. "I knew what I wanted from the students, but I'm asking them to do one kind of thinking while I really want another kind." He continues, generally agreeing with the group's responses.

After Louie's feedback, Tim, their process observer, gives the group feedback about its work. "Well, we're getting better at clarifying questions. Listen to these questions that we asked." Reading from his notes, Tim lists a series of questions the group had asked early in the protocol. Then he adds, "There was one point, though, when we seemed to move beyond clarification. When we raised questions about his grading system, I think we were hinting that the rubric was missing. What do you all think? Were we probing or clarifying?"

After the group explored the nature of their questions, Tim continues with his observations. As he finishes, Jeannie asks the group, "Based on this discussion, what should we work on next month?"

The group decides they were cutting one other off. They review the norms posted on the wall and decide to focus on letting each speaker finish his or her own sentence. They select the facilitator, presenter, and process observer for the following month.

It is almost 5:30 p.m. "I can't believe we've been at this for two hours," Juan says. "I'm exhausted and energized. Here's to another good month!"

Overview

When educators first hear the term *critical friends,* they frequently snicker, "Who needs another critical friend? I have enough of those." After they've experienced a CFG, most shift away from the negative connotation of the word *critical*

and recognize how *critical* means "vital" or "necessary" for their professional growth.

Reflecting Learning Forward's Standards for Professional Learning (see Part I, "Design: Form and Structure for Learning"), a CFG is a unique form of professional learning community that focuses on problems of practice and leads to robust student learning. An effective CFG supports the capacity of its members to engage in significant work that matters for all students. Grounded in a commitment to equity, CFGs address the challenging issues confronting educators as they build schools that work for all students. As explained on the website of the School Reform Initiative (SRI), CFGs are guided by a set of principles. Members should:
- Be accountable to their colleagues to continually improve their practice for the benefit of their students and share their actions with their colleagues;
- Engage in public, collaborative assessment of student and adult work;
- Work in ways that challenge each other's assumptions about educational excellence and equity; and
- Examine their beliefs and question how these beliefs are enacted in their practice (School Reform Initiative, n.d.).

These principles result in a collective commitment to children by making teacher and student work public, committing unwaveringly to all students, and believing that educators learn best in community. Because of the safety that they have built within their CFGs, educators can bring their most daunting challenges to trusted colleagues for candid feedback. As Gene Thompson-Grove, one of the original co-directors of the School Reform Initiative, reminded participants at the 2005 annual winter meeting of the National School Reform Faculty, CFGs are "relatively simple structures, within which complex ideas can take hold" (see Online Resource 7.2: *SRI keynote speech*).

Within this safe community, 8 to 12 teachers meet regularly to examine student work, reflect on teacher practice, and collaborate on professional dilemmas. Using s, or structured ways of examining and reflecting on problems of practice, CFG members think deeply about student work and examine assumptions about teaching and learning. Protocols are the tools that keep the group on track and deepen the conversation while at the same time build the group's collective knowledge and skills. Some educators

What are the purposes of a Critical Friends Group?

Critical Friends Groups are designed to:

- Create a professional learning community;

- Make teaching practice explicit and public through conversation about teaching;

- Help people involved in schools to work collaboratively in democratic, reflective communities;

- Establish a foundation for sustained professional development based on a spirit of inquiry;

- Provide a context to understand our work with students, our relationships with peers, and our thoughts, assumptions, and beliefs about teaching and learning;

- Help educators help each other turn theories into practice and standards into actual student learning;

- Improve teaching and learning.

Source: From "Critical Friends Groups," para. 3, Voices for Education [Website]. Available at www.voicesforeducation.org/index.php?option=com_content&task=view&id=105&Itemid=86. Used with permission.

new to CFGs resist protocols until they discover their purpose: to develop a culture that allows educators to do serious, meaningful work. As Thompson-Grove has written,

> [protocols] permit a certain kind of conversation to occur — often a kind of conversation which people are not in the habit of having. Protocols are vehicles for building the skills — and culture — necessary for collaborative work. Thus, using protocols often allows groups to build trust by actually doing substantive work together. (Southern Maine Partnership, n.d, para 1, ll. 4–7)

Protocols provide a safe way for colleagues to discuss what matters most to them: student learning and their own teaching.

A CFG is much more than a protocol, however. For it to be a CFG and not just a group that uses protocols, the same group of people must meet regularly with the goal of strengthening their practice for the sake of the students. A CFG is not a drop-in event with shifting membership, nor is

it an occasional gathering of educators. Instead, membership must be consistent, just as meeting times must be regular and predictable. In her keynote address at the 2005 winter meeting of the National School Reform Faculty, Gene Thompson-Grove noted the difference between CFGs and other professional learning communities:

> So, a group of people reading together can be useful work, but that's a book group, not a CFG. People coming together to research best literacy practices is important work, but that's a study group, not a CFG. People learning to look at student work on a professional development day can produce new insights and new learning, but that's a workshop, not a CFG. Faculty participating in teambuilding and conflict resolution activities might be vital to the health of a school, but that's not a CFG. People being told by the district to bring curriculum units to a district wide meeting to be tuned might produce better alignment of the curriculum to the standards, but it is not a CFG (see Online Resource 7.2: *SRI keynote speech*).

The book club, the study group, the faculty meeting may all be using protocols, but they are not CFGs. Thompson-Grove reminded the group that CFGs "use the protocols to create and sustain professional learning communities" (see Online Resource 7.2: *SRI keynote speech*). Rotating membership and irregular meetings do not create the robust kind of professional learning community that a CFG does.

Members of CFGs play different roles that help the learning community grow: coach, facilitator, presenter, responders, and sometimes process observer (see Online Resource 7.3: *Roles in a Critical Friends Group*). Frequently, the coach, who has been trained in facilitation skills and CFG processes, supports the group. The coach attends to the group's logistics by making sure reminders of meetings are sent out on a timely basis and checking in with the presenter before the meeting. Sometimes the coach facilitates the meeting, moving participants through each part of the agenda and ensuring that norms are followed; however, it's not uncommon for CFGs to rotate the role of facilitator. Even though the roles of coach and facilitator can be interchanged, it's vital that one person has been trained in coaching CFGs.

At each meeting one member of the group is the presenter who brings work for the group to reflect on and poses an inquiry question to guide the discussion. Often, but not always, another member acts as a process observer in order to track the group dynamics. The process observer pays attention to aspects of group work such as focus, interruptions, domination, and depth of discussion and reports his or her observations at the end of the meeting. Other members act as responders, discussing the work the presenter has brought.

Faculty members in elementary and secondary schools conduct CFGs, as do those in higher education settings. In elementary schools, group members may teach the same or different grades, while CFG members from secondary schools often teach different subjects and work in various roles. In some schools, principals and other administrators are active members of CFGs, while in other schools or districts administrators participate in their own CFGs.

Rationale

Anthony Alvarado, the former superintendent of District 2 in Manhattan, frequently remarked, "isolation is the enemy of improvement" (Wagner, 2013). This is particularly true for educators. Teachers historically have worked alone. However, research on schools that beat the odds reveals that collaboration improves school climate (Little, Gearhart, Curry, & Kafta, 2003), student achievement (DuFour & Eaker, 1998; Fullan & Hargreaves, 1991) and teachers' energy to teach (Graves, 2001). Collaboration broadens teachers' perspectives, increases their repertoire of teaching strategies, and nourishes reflective practice. Participating in a CFG helps educators improve their teaching by studying together and giving and receiving feedback on day-to-day practices. When teachers wrestle with sensitive issues such as equity, they can find support in a collaborative team for examining unspoken assumptions and unintended — or even intended — consequences of their decisions.

In addition to what happens within the CFG itself, the culture of the school is nurtured by staff collaboration. Trust grows leading to teacher investment in school policies and an increase in innovative practices (Little, Gearhart, Curry,

& Kafta, 2003). As a bonus, teachers who work in learning teams, such as CFGs, report that this effort feels less like work. Collaborating seems to restore teachers, nurturing the energy to teach (Graves, 2001).

Furthermore, unlike professional development days scattered throughout a school year, CFGs give teachers a means to continue to grow their practice. Dennis Sparks has joked about inservices, by citing this comment from a cynical teacher: "I hope I die during an inservice because the transition between life and death would be so subtle" (Sparks, 2007). Perhaps it's the delivery of the content that leads to such cynicism. Perhaps it's the lack of relevance of the content. Perhaps the timing is simply off. Whatever the reason, too many inservices miss the target of increasing professional knowledge. And even when they hit the target, typical inservice sessions don't often change teaching practice. Despite their best intentions, many teachers drift back to familiar and comfortable ways of teaching. However, because of the support offered within a CFG, new practices are more likely to take hold and become part of a teacher's repertoire. The CFGs provide opportunities for teachers to learn new teaching practices and to get support needed to implement those practices in a way that makes a difference for students.

Stages and steps

Although any individual or small group of staff members can start a CFG, at least one member needs to be trained as a coach. Go to the website for the School Reform Initiative (SRI) to find out more about training to coach and facilitate CFGs.

Once a coach has been trained, this person invites others to an introductory meeting to explain CFGs and shares the rationale and the process of a meeting. Later, the coach establishes meeting times and places (about two hours for each meeting, in school or a participant's home) and facilitates the conversations.

The coach and the facilitator may be the same person or different people, depending on the wishes of the CFG. Coaches may or may not participate in CFG meetings; if they do not participate, they frequently serve as process observers. Facilitators do not generally participate in CFG meetings, except to facilitate them.

STAGE 1: Preparation

The most successful CFG meetings are those in which everyone is well prepared.

Step 1: Arrange the meeting

The coach arranges the meeting, including securing a location and disseminating the agenda, articles for discussion, reflection sheets, and other materials. If a member of the group other than the coach is the upcoming facilitator, the coach checks in with the facilitator.

Step 2: Meet with the presenter

The facilitator, who may be the coach, and presenter meet in advance to discuss the work to be presented.

Select the work to present. Together the coach and presenter reflect on the work that the presenter wants to bring to the group. When possible, the work should include samples of student work with student names removed. The work might be a collection of work from one class, with the assignment sheet and standards, or a single assignment from one student.

Determine reasons for sharing the work. The facilitator and presenter explore the reason for bringing this work to the group: What is troubling about the work? What is there about this work that keeps the presenter awake at night? Based on this conversation, they frame an inquiry question that will guide the discussion.

Select the protocol. The two then select the protocol that holds the best promise to produce the results the presenter seeks. Each of the many protocols meets a specific need. Some work best to probe the depth of student thinking, for instance, while others work well to define an imprecise problem. Some protocols yield advice, while others are intended to probe the presenter's thinking so the presenter can find his or her own solution (see Online Resource 7.4: *Matching the work to the protocol*, as well as Online Resource 7.5: *Five protocols for CFGs to use*).

Assign the reading. Before the CFG meeting, everyone closely reads the assigned texts.

STAGE 2: The CFG meeting

Although the model has many variations, a CFG meeting often includes four steps.

Step 1: Begin with an opening activity

Typically CFG meetings begin with some kind of an activity that provides a chance to get everyone's voice in the room. Often this activity creates a transition between the hectic pace of a teaching day and the reflective time that is an essential element of a CFG. A common activity is Connections, which takes about 10 minutes (see Online Resource 7.1: *Ideas for connections*).

It is important that this activity not bog down the group. The facilitator of a new CFG may be tempted to spend time on team-building activities to develop the group's sense of community. Experienced CFG members recognize how structured conversations around matters important to the group *are* the team builders. They argue that the joint work, not the activity, builds community.

Step 2: Set norms

During the first meeting of the year, the CFG sets norms (see Online Resource 7.6: *Microlab for setting norms*). At the start of subsequent meetings, the group would be wise to review the norms. The facilitator or coach should always check in with the group about whether or not the norms provide the framework needed for the group to do the work that they want to do. If not, the group should revise or amend the norms.

Step 3: Use a protocol with a text

For about half an hour, the group uses a protocol to discuss an agreed-upon text to build the group's common understanding (see Online Resource 7.5: *Five protocols for CFGs to use*). The text can be an article, a book, video, or even school data. The important aspect of the selection is that it addresses an issue important to the group. For example, a CFG at one high school decided to focus on high-yield instructional strategies, so members read *Visible Learning* by John Hattie (2008). Then, at one meeting, they watched a video of a teacher conferring with students and listened carefully for the quality of the feedback she offered students. They used the video for their text-based discussion and explored how students responded to her feedback. At another school, the CFG spent one meeting looking carefully at data from state assessments. Studying these data led group members to note serious gender gaps in literacy, so they set goals to address this gap throughout the year.

Step 4: Use a protocol to discuss the presenter's work

The group moves on to about an hour of structured conversation, again using a protocol, about the presenter's work (see Online Resources 7.4 and 7.5).

Open the discussion. The facilitator opens this discussion with an overview of the steps of the protocol and a brief introduction to the presenter's work. In most protocols, the next step is for the presenter to provide the context for the group and to pose the inquiry question.

Ask clarifying questions. In most protocols, the following step is for group members to ask clarifying questions that help them understand the dilemma. The facilitator's job here is to make sure that participants ask only clarifying questions and that the rest of the group avoids asking probing questions or making suggestions disguised as questions (see Online Resource 7.7: *Types of questions*).

Use probing questions. In some protocols, probing questions follow the clarifying questions. Probing questions are intended to challenge the presenter's thinking and to encourage her to think about the dilemma in a new way. The presenter may answer the probing questions or save them to think about later.

Discuss the work. The participants discuss what the presenter has brought to them. At this point, the presenter retreats from the group to listen to the group discussion and may not respond to the comments. The group is discouraged from talking directly to the presenter.

The facilitator's role is to ensure the group follows the steps of the selected protocol and to remain vigilant about the direction the discussion takes so that the presenter's needs are met and so that everyone is learning and growing. If members speak directly to the presenter, the facilitator nudges them to talk to the group only. If the group veers away from the presenter's concern, the facilitator redirects the group.

Step 5: Debrief the group's work

The group debriefs its own work for about 10 minutes. This step is one that many groups are tempted to overlook. It is important, though, that the group reflects on its work together. If the group has a process observer, this is the time for the process observer to share observations about how the group worked together. In debriefing, group members explore process issues such as whether everyone's comments were valued and what the "take-aways" were for each participant. This is the time participants identify growth they've made over time and develop goals for their continuing evolution as an effective learning community (see Online Resource 7.8: *Tips for debriefing*).

Step 6: Plan the next meeting

Finally, group members spend about five minutes planning for the next meeting. They focus on when and where they will meet, what article they might want to study, and who will present student work or teacher practice. The facilitator or coach notes these plans.

Variations

Two variations affect the conditions under which a CFG may convene, but they do not change the basic principles governing how a CFG operates.

CFGs beyond the school context. Even though many CFGs are housed in schools, CFGs exist in other contexts also. What matters is not that the CFG members are from the same setting, but that they commit to working together over time in order to grow their practice. For example in Denver, Colorado, a group of university professors from three different universities met for about five years. Each participant was involved in a teacher preparation program, but the programs differed greatly. Despite the differences — or because of those differences — the group was able to provide feedback that would not have been possible within their institutions.

Because of changes in jobs, this CFG disbanded, but a new CFG emerged and still exists. Six educators with very different professional roles meet at a coffee house for two hours a month in order to learn and grow together. One person coaches in a public school of choice while others work with private schools as staff developers and curriculum directors. A few are independent coaches and work with schools across the nation while another person writes curriculum for a national organization. United by a commitment to urban education and students traditionally underserved, the group has found that their varied backgrounds add richness to the conversation. In their time together, they have provided

ADDITIONAL RESOURCES

Articles

"How are professional learning communities created? History has a few messages," by Bruce Joyce. (2004, September). *Phi Delta Kappan, 86*(1), 76–83.

"The 'things' children make in school: Disposable or indispensable?" by Steve Seidel and Joseph Walters. (1994). *Harvard Graduate School of Education Alumni Bulletin, 39*(1), 18–20.

Books

At the Heart of Teaching: A Guide to Reflective Practice, by Grace McEntee, John Appleby, JoAnne Dowd, Jan Grant, Simon Hole, Peggy Silva, and Joseph Check. New York, NY: Teachers College Press, 2003.

Clock Watchers: Six Steps to Motivating and Engaging Disengaged Students Across Content Areas, by Stevi Quate and John McDermott. Portsmouth, NH: Heinemann, 2009.

The Facilitator's Book of Questions: Tools for Looking Together at Student and Teacher Work, by David Allen and Tina Blythe. New York, NY: Teachers College Press, 2004.

Going Online With Protocols: New Tools for Teaching and Learning, by Joseph P. McDonald, Janet P. Zydney, Alan Dichter, and Elizabeth A. McDonald. New York, NY: Teachers College Press, 2010.

The Just-Right Challenge: 9 Strategies to Ensure Adolescents Don't Drop Out of the Game, by Stevi Quate and John McDermott. Portsmouth, NH: Heinemann, 2013.

Leading for Powerful Learning: A Guide for Instructional Leaders, by Angela Breidenstein, Kevin Fahey, Carl Glickman, and Frances Hensley. New York, NY: Teachers College Press, 2012.

"Learning from looking," by Steve Seidel. In Nona Lyons (Ed.), *With Portfolio in Hand: Validating the New Teacher Professionalism* (pp. 69–89). New York, NY: Teachers College Press, 1998.

Looking Together at Student Work: A Companion Guide to Assessing Student Learning, by Tina Blythe, David Allen, and Barbara Schieffelin Powell. New York, NY: Teachers College Press, 1999.

The Power of Protocols: An Educators' Guide to Better Practice, by Joseph P. McDonald, Nancy Mohr, Alan Dichter, and Elizabeth C. McDonald. New York, NY: Teachers College Press, 2003.

"Wondering to be done," by Steve Seidel. In David Allen (Ed.), *Assessing Student Learning: From Grading to Understanding* (pp. 21–39). New York, NY: Teachers College Press, 1998.

Websites

www.lasw.org. Looking at Student Work includes individuals and education organizations collaboratively studying student work.

www.schoolreforminitiative.org. The School Reform Initiative is the national center for Critical Friends Groups and other collaborative work. The website offers valuable information, including protocols, research on learning communities, and seminars about CFGs.

feedback on meeting agendas, reflected on school improvement plans, tuned capstone projects, and examined assumptions about leadership. Because of relationships, forged over time, they can share their vulnerabilities, knowing that they will receive support and will be challenged, and it's the challenge that brings them back month after month.

Online CFGs. Through technology such as Google Hangouts, GoToMeeting, and Skype, CFGs can exist in cyberspace, linking educators from different parts of the country. In an interview with Ruth Whalen Crockett, a coach from Parker Charter School in Massachusetts, she said she found that online CFGs work best if the members have time to meet face to face before meeting online. This is when they build relationships and develop their agreements for how they will collaborate. At the same time echoing the concerns of Thompson-Grove (see Online Resource 7.2: *SRI keynote speech*), Crockett is cautious about some online groups that identify themselves as CFGs. If the groups haven't established norms and aren't focusing on examining assumptions and practices that directly affect student learning, they may be more about learning a program or studying the tenets of a practice than doing the work of a CFG. For example, one group she works with is learning strategies for language acquisition. A teacher at one school hosts weekly online groups; however, the focus is on learning the practices of the organization rather than teachers determining their agendas based on the needs of their students. The work is good and necessary, but it is not a CFG.

Challenges and how to address them

Context determines time to meet. Creating time for a CFG can be challenging and regularly scheduled time is vital to the success of CFGs. Rarely is one hour sufficient for the group to do the thoughtful work that is possible within a CFG. It takes time for people to reflect with depth on student work and on teacher practice. This kind of depth also requires ongoing, regular meetings so that groups can develop the high level of comfort and trust necessary for substantial work and, as Crockett points out, time for members to develop the stamina needed to look with depth at student work.

> ## ONLINE RESOURCES
>
> 7.1 Ideas for connections
> 7.2 SRI keynote speech
> 7.3 Roles in a Critical Friends Group
> 7.4 Matching the work to the protocol
> 7.5 Five protocols for CFGs to use
> 7.6 Microlab for setting norms
> 7.7 Types of questions
> 7.8 Tips for debriefing

Principals across the nation have found creative solutions to find time for teachers to engage in the work of a CFG:

- Three or four times a year one administrator hires substitutes for all teachers to meet simultaneously in their CFGs for the entire day.
- Monthly, another administrator hires substitutes for an entire day. CFGs meet for two hours during the day, and the substitutes rotate from one teacher to another throughout the day. Because the substitutes are regulars, they know the teacher and the students well so there is little disruption of learning.
- At another school, the administrators bundle one-hour meetings into two hours monthly so that CFGs have adequate time to be reflective and not feel rushed.
- In several schools, administrators provide eight half-day early release days for each CFG.

In addition, some administrators encourage teachers to meet before or after school and pay them for this additional work time.

Training. A well-trained coach makes it easier to implement a successful CFG. Although learning the steps of the protocols seems easy, coaching a group of colleagues as they learn to engage in deep conversations about their practice is not. Crockett believes that an important element is careful planning so that over time a critical mass of educators is well-trained and well-skilled. She described how her school accomplished such development through a tiered system. The first tier of coaches trained one summer. The second tier joined the CFGs started by the coaches, and over time their coaches supported them in understanding strategies, processes, and ways of thinking that would develop them into future coaches. As a result, the second tier, trained and mentored, could themselves start and work with new CFGs. Additionally, teacher leaders throughout the school, including department chairs and team leads, trained during the summer at institutes hosted by a local educational institution.

A collaborative school culture. A CFG works best when it is part of a school culture in which collaboration is the norm. Without such a culture educators may resist working in a CFG or participate superficially. Interestingly, CFGs can shape and build this kind of school culture. Parker Charter School provides just one example. Because of the training, mentoring, and coaching that has resulted from an ongoing commitment to CFGs, the culture of the school is one in which everyone grows — students and staff.

Voluntary attendance. Although administrators may be tempted to mandate CFGs, inviting participants is more effective. Teachers who are required to attend when they don't want to can sabotage the group. In one group, for example, the presenting teacher brought in an assignment that she had found to be successful in the past. Presenting the assignment to her colleagues required no risk on her part because it was a stellar example of an assignment with which no one could argue. Her reason for presenting such safe work became apparent during the discussion. In the feedback part of the protocol, one social studies teacher made his resistance obvious through his body language. Tapping his pencil, watching the clock, and sighing loudly, he deflated the group's energy without saying a word. The group's discussion of the teacher's work was perfunctory and superficial.

In a more successful approach, the principal modeled a CFG meeting by inviting several teachers to join him in a fishbowl discussion (using one of the protocols) about a schoolwide issue. After the staff discussed what they observed, he showed a video that illustrated a CFG at work. Then he invited staff to form a CFG. That year, one group of eight teachers met regularly. Because of their enthusiasm, new CFGs formed each subsequent year.

Norms. At the outset, groups must create agreements or norms for working together. Often groups have implicit norms, but being explicit about how group members agree to act enhances the group's ability to work successfully.

Building and attending to norms is a way to prevent groups from being side-trapped by congeniality. Even though relationships are important in effective CFGs, when a group becomes too congenial, members may resist tackling tough challenges with the mistaken belief that "playing nice" is what they need to do to preserve their friendships (Fullan & Hargreaves 1991).

One process for setting norms is the norm-setting microlab (see Online Resource 7.6: *Microlab for setting norms*). Other CFGs use norms developed by groups such as Adaptive Schools (Garmston & Wellman, 1999) or books such as *Courageous Conversations about Race* (Singleton & Linton, 2006).

Rotating roles. Another successful practice is rotating roles (see Online Resource 7.3: *Roles in a Critical Friends Group*). In new groups, a coach often facilitates the meeting, but this role can be shared so responsibility for the group's success is spread among the members. CFG members can take turns acting as the process observer, the person who helps the group reflect on how members worked together in a particular meeting. The process observer records interactions and shares the observations so the group can reflect on its own work, self-correct as needed, and celebrate successes.

Authentic work product. The work presented at a CFG meeting — often a professional dilemma, an upcoming assignment, or student work — must be authentic for the presenter. When possible, assignments and dilemmas should include samples of student work. For instance, one teacher had been surprised when a typically successful student struggled over what the teacher had thought was an easy task. When her CFG studied the student work with her, she was able to unravel the mystery of the unexpected challenges her student faced. In another CFG, a teacher wanted her students to begin a community service project that would also address the state's new standards. Since this was a new undertaking for her, she needed feedback from more experienced peers. Along with bringing the assignment sheet, she also brought a transcript of the student discussion she had recorded.

Conclusion

When teachers learn together, they pool knowledge and expand their abilities to reach all students. They create a bank of knowledge that deepens their own and the group's understanding and changes practice. Because an important focus within a CFG is on what matters most to teachers — their students' work — they are likely to be invested in exploring new ideas. As Ruth Whalen Crockett noted, when teachers begin their work with CFGs they want answers to questions, but over time they become more curious and recognize big issues that deserve their attention. This curiosity has led many into realizing that through their work in CFGs they must address issues of equity, acknowledging the students who are traditionally underserved, and being thoughtful about what teachers can do that matter for them and for all.

In May, Louie's CFG convened for the last meeting of the year. Toward the end of the meeting, Louie summed up the year's work: "This has been one of the most difficult years that I've had, but our CFG has made all the difference in the world. You made me think harder about the work that I was asking students to do and consider its impact on their learning. I'm a better teacher now. It might take the summer to rest up, but I can hardly wait until we start again next year."

References

DuFour, R. & Eaker, R. (1998). *Professional learning communities at work: Best practices for enhancing student achievement.* Bloomington, IN: Solution Tree.

Fullan, M. & Hargreaves, A. (1991). *What's worth fighting for?* Andover, MA: Regional Laboratory for Educational Improvement of the Northeast and Islands. Available at http://files.eric.ed.gov/fulltext/ED342128.pdf.

Garmston, R.J. & Wellman, B.M. (1999). *The adaptive school: A sourcebook for developing collaborative groups.* Norwood, MA: Christopher-Gordon.

Graves, D. (2001). *The energy to teach.* Portsmouth, NH: Heinemann.

Hattie, J. (2008). *Visible learning.* London, England: Routledge.

Little, J.W., Gearhart, M., Curry, M., & Kafta, J. (2003, November). Looking at student work for teacher learning, teacher community and school reform. *Phi Delta Kappan, 85*(3), 184–192.

Singleton, G. & Linton, C. (2006). *Courageous conversations about race: A field guide for achieving equity in schools.* Thousand Oaks, CA: Corwin Press.

Sparks, D. (2007, November). What it really means to learn. *Leading through learning, 1*(3). Available at www.learningforward.org/docs/pdf/sparks1107_1.pdf?sfvrsn=0.

School Reform Initiative. (n.d.). [Website]. Available at www.schoolreforminitiative.org/.

Southern Maine Partnership. (n.d.). A rationale for protocols. [Website]. School Reform Initiative. Available at www.schoolreforminitiative.org/download/Documents%20to%20Support%20the%20use%20of%20Protocols/rationale_for_protocols.pdf.

Voices for Education. (n.d.). Critical friends groups. [Website]. Available at www.voicesforeducation.org/index.php?option=com_content&task=view&id=105&Itemid=86.

Wagner, T. (2013, January 12). What does it mean to be a "change leader" in education? [Blog post]. Available at www.tonywagner.com/1191.

Curriculum as Professional Learning

Teachers who collaboratively create challenging assignments linked
to the Common Core State Standards engage in professional learning
and see students' skills and engagement rise dramatically.

By Eleanor Dougherty, Stacy Galiatsos, and Anne C. Lewis

Secondary history teacher Sara Ballute wanted to make the 10th-grade curriculum for her Global Studies course more engaging for students — as she called it, "grabbing kids' attention" — while addressing the New York state standards. She wanted to move well beyond the "memorization of facts" too often seen as necessary to pass the State's Global Regents Exam required for graduation. How could she enliven the standard that asked students to "investigate key events and major turning points in world history to identify the factors that brought about change"? Moreover, how could she do this in a way that both challenged and supported her 100 students at Brooklyn's High School for Service Learning, including a large number of ELL and special education students? In a video entitled "Literacy Matters," Ballute relates her experience teaching a Literacy Design Collaborative (LDC) assignment, called a module, and relates her learnings from the experience (www.ldc.org/resources#About-LDC).

Working with fellow teacher Timothy Lent, Ballute decided to teach their students the art of the argumentative essay as a way to engage them in the British Industrial Revolution, a topic that could be potentially dry for 15- and 16-year olds. They chose the academic essay because it offered them opportunities to teach students a variety of literacy and historical thinking skills, all of which are necessary in preparing them for postsecondary opportunities. The results? The teachers saw that their students learned "a lot": how to analyze multiple texts, argue their viewpoints, and write coherent essays. "My own expectations changed," Ballute said. "It is almost as though I saw them transform into more rigorous students." She had gotten her students' attention.

Ballute and Lent started their process by focusing on a state history standard and transforming it into an *engaging assignment*. Their comprehensive three-week approach included a challenging prompt and an instructional plan in which students studied almost two dozen resources to address the question: "Were the achievements and growth of the Industrial Revolution Era worth the cost to society?" The instructional plan consisted of minitasks, or small assignments centered on skills required to complete the product, an essay. To help their students move through the reading and writing processes, Ballute and Lent developed a step-by-step writing packet.

Ballute's students were required to research and synthesize information and to organize that information to address the prompt. Working in pairs or sometimes in larger groups, the students learned to articulate their ideas and listen to different viewpoints. By the time the students drafted their final arguments, they had researched child labor and environmental issues, assessed economic benefits, discussed the impact of technology on society — and practiced the skills of note-taking, synthesis, outlining, and revising of drafts.

Because of the scaffolding of the lessons and student minitasks, the assignment stayed focused, and Ballute and Lent received clues about the skills that needed more attention as they moved through the reading and writing processes. Their students were so caught up in the process of producing a good written product that Ballute reflected, "I saw students teaching the skills to each other when the classes were doing peer editing." At the end, 94 of Ballute's 100 students, many of whom before had shunned any writing assignment, submitted final essays. Not only did Ballute and Lent make the history standard more engaging, they assured their students met the literacy standards in the Common Core State Standards (Common Core).

They may not have labeled it as such, but Ballute and Lent were engaged in powerful professional learning. Their learning was embedded in their practice, beginning with student learning needs and resulting in a successful assignment that affected every aspect of teaching and learning in their classes. Ballute and Lent had deprivatized their classrooms and worked collaboratively. They had transformed their own learning in order to transform students' learning.

Overview

Ballute and Lent achieved this transformation with the use of teacher tools developed by the Literacy Design Collaborative

(LDC). Their school was one of 11 schools in the New Visions for Public Schools network in New York City that participated in LDC, a community of tens of thousands of teachers in 34 states dedicated to implementing literacy instruction in the subject areas. Ballute and Lent used the LDC tools to help them create their assignment and instructional plan so that it was aligned to the Common Core State Standards.

The framework

The LDC framework, launched in 2010 by a small group of practitioners and curriculum developers, is a flexible system in which teachers participate in the crafting of an assignment. It is not a program or script. At its core is a firm belief that the task, specifically an assignment that teachers ask students to complete with a written product, determines what students learn. As one educator has said, "The task predicts performance." All LDC templates involve writing in response to reading, and partners such as the National Paideia Center include speaking and listening standards as part of their LDC modules.

Once they had assessed the student work from their assignment and refined the process, Ballute and Lent worked with other teachers on creating LDC modules. Teacher leadership and collaboration around curriculum characterize the New Visions work related to the LDC modules. "The collaborative nature of these projects has really brought our schools together," according to Lent, "and put some very sharp minds to solving common problems." The LDC modules and system for creating effective assignments involve educators in the heart of professional learning as they are "working on the work," the purposeful effort related to teaching and learning, what Phillip Schlechty called "WOW" (Schlechty, 2002).

The template system

Teacher learning that results in effective assignments is guided by the LDC system that specifically involves students in writing in response to reading. The core of the LDC system is the template task. A template is a fill-in-the-blank prompt into which teachers insert one or more texts and content to create what LDC calls a *teaching task*. The template tasks are aligned with the Common Core and include rubrics for scoring student work.

The second element of the LDC framework is the module, a template that teachers can use to identify the skills students need to complete the task and then design their instructional approach so that the identified skills are taught and students successfully complete the teaching task. The LDC partners provide example modules that teachers can adopt or edit so that they do not have to identify literacy skills or create their instructional plans from scratch.

The third element is "LDC courses or linked modules" in which teachers and LDC partners are able to link modules within a course or across subject areas or grades as a larger instructional approach that ensures literacy-rich learning experiences. Teachers can create modules using Core Tools on the LDC website or find modules to use or adapt created by other teachers (Literacy Design Collaborative, 2014c).

Finally, LDC includes a jurying system in which partners work together to identify and share modules deemed as "good to go" or "exemplar," as well as benchmarked student work samples. For full details on the system, take a look at the *1.0 Guidebook for LDC* (Crawford, Galiastos, & Lewis, 2011) and the LDC website (www.LDC.org); the website includes video observations of Ballute and her students working on the assignment.

Argumentative, informational/explanatory, and narrative templates

There are three categories of template tasks and module templates based on the CCCS for writing: argumentation, informational/explanatory, and narrative. Using these categories, the LDC developers originally prepared 29 template tasks for teachers to use. Based on ongoing feedback from teachers and partners, the original collection has been revised and is called LDC Template Task Collection 2. Within each of the writing categories, there are two types of template tasks: One is designed for a research assignment and the other for a reading task that focuses on developing close reading skills using one or two texts or a small group of short texts (Literacy Design Collaborative, 2014b). The examples in Table 1: LDC Template Tasks from Collection 2 on page 140 provide a glimpse of the types of LDC template tasks found in Collection 2.

It is important to note that this collection is just the beginning. LDC partners are also producing additional template task collections to submit to the collaborative and for others to use. (All collections are available on the LDC website and can be used without requesting permission.)

When teachers select a template, they are selecting a set of literacy standards they want to teach or emphasize based on the College and Career Readiness Anchor Standards. For LDC Template Task Collection 2, these include recursive standards, or ones that are always addressed in reading and writing instruction. The LDC deems these the **"built-in" standards,** for example R1, R2, and R4, W4, W8, L1 and L2. Others are noted as **"when-appropriate" standards** because their alignment to a task varies with the content teachers choose as they complete the template (see Online Resource 8.1: *Built-in standards*). Each of the template task categories also includes a rubric — co-designed with Measured Progress, SCALE at Stanford University, LDC partners and teachers — for assessing and providing feedback on student work. When teachers decide on a module template, they find all the elements of an assignment that document instruction: prompt, skills, standards, rubric, and instructional plan. Once they fill out the blanks and customize the instructional plan to fit their prompt, they have documentation of their assignment for future use or use by other teachers.

LDC supports

Since LDC began its work, it has sought partners to expand and deepen this approach to teaching secondary school literacy. The LDC partners have developed resources and/or worked directly with teachers, districts, and states on adopting the LDC system for student assignments. Aware that professional learning and support for teachers will increasingly be conducted online, the partners and core LDC planners are exploring how best to use technology. The array of partner supports includes:

- Module Creator designed by MetaMetrics, an education research and development corporation. This web-based tool guides teachers in designing their tasks, suggests appropriate texts, and offers a Lexile system that evaluates the readability and complexity of the texts.

- A minitask online bank, developed by University of California, Berkeley researchers and New Visions for Public Schools.

- New template tasks and module templates designed by subject-area organizations. These include:

  > EduCurious at the University of Washington that designs science-specific templates, as well as

Table 1: **LDC Template Tasks from Collection 2**

Argumentation (Literacy Design Collaborative Template Task Collection 2.0, p. 6)
Task 2 Template: [Insert optional question] After reading _____ (literature or informational texts), write a/an _____ (essay or substitute) in which you that addresses the question and argue _____ (content) and support your position with evidence from the text(s). (Argumentation/Analysis)
Task 2 ELA Example: Would you recommend _A Wrinkle in Time_ to a middle school reader? After reading this science fiction novel, write a review that addresses the question and support your position with evidence from the text. (Argumentation/Analysis)
Task 2 Social Studies Example: How did the political views of the signers of the Constitution impact the American political system? After reading _Founding Brothers: The Revolutionary Generation_ write a report that addresses the question and support your position with evidence from the text. (Argumentation/Analysis)
Informational or Explanatory (in LDC Template Task Collection 2.0, p.8)
Task 11 Template: After researching _____ (informational texts) on _____ (content), write a _____ (report or substitute) that defines _____ (term or concept) and explains _____ (content). Support your discussion with evidence from your research. D3 What _____ (conclusions or implications) can you draw? (Informational or Explanatory/Definition)
Task 11 Social Studies Example: After researching articles and political documents on government lobbyists, write a report that defines "lobbying" and explains who and what lobbyists are and the role they play in our political system. Support your discussion with evidence from your research. (Informational or Explanatory/Definition)
Task 11 Science Example: After researching scientific articles on magnetism, write a report that defines "magnetism" and explains its role in the planetary system. Support your discussion with evidence from your research. (Informational or Explanatory/Definition)
Narrative (in LDC Template Task Collection 2.0, p. 11)
Task 27 Template : [Insert optional question] After reading _____ (literature or information texts), write a _____ (narrative or substitute) from the persective of _____ (content). (Narrative/Description)
Task 27 Social Studies Example: What can historical accounts teach us about someone's struggle for dignity? After reading historical documents and accounts about The Trail of Tears, write a narrative article from the perspectives of a Choctaw and George Gains. (Narrative/Description)

Source: All samples of templates and examples can be found in the Literacy Design Collaborative (LDC) Template Task Collection 2.0 Available at www.ldc.org/resources#LDC-Task-Template-Collection-2.

projects incorporating modules that engage students by focusing on student science interests such as their pets' genetics or a biology unit based on plants from their backyards.

> Paideia's LDC modules that hardwire in the Socratic Seminar approach to engage students in the speaking and listening skills described in Common Core.

Their work includes designing a series of modules that build sequential skills across a full school year.

• Scoring protocols and benchmarks for student work designed by Measured Progress, co-designer of the LDC student work rubrics.

• New types of online systems for teachers to share ideas and strategies.

• Virtual professional development led by Lee Kappes and Cathy Feldman, co-founders of REACH Associates (and members of the core LDC team). REACH is exploring the feasibility of taking the attributes of personal coaching to scale using technology. Working with about 500 teachers, coaches and administrators, REACH is offering different levels of support to teachers through facilitated peer collaboration and online coaching that matches experienced LDC coaches to teachers based on their subject areas and needs. Like the LDC philosophy from the very beginning, the REACH Associates leaders and coaches emphasize the importance of collaboration of teachers around student work as the key component of producing high literacy skills among students. Researchers at the University of Pittsburgh are conducting ongoing research on this strategy, which focuses on certain states (Kentucky, Louisiana, and Colorado) and selected school districts including Erie, Pennsylvania; Washington, DC; and Hillsborough, Florida.

Rationale

The reason the LDC came into being as a co-project of the College-Ready initiatives of the Bill & Melinda Gates Foundation (with similar support for math instruction) is that teachers had little to work with as they tried to engage with and implement the Common Core. Moreover, the new literacy standards shifted a focus to teaching the reading of factual texts within subject areas such as science and social studies. The Common Core involve using evidence to support text-based responses in writing or in other venues, as well as student use of more formal language in their responses. To ensure students are taught these skills, LDC is designed to teach fully developed student academic work products, complete with text-based evidence and well-organized prose. For LDC modules, the final proof of student learning is their ability to write well, in response to reading, whether in ELA, science, social studies or other disciplines.

Why LDC?

Traditionally, middle and high school literacy instruction has taken place almost entirely in English and language arts classes. The limitations of this on learning and practice

for students are well known, but the only major effort to distribute responsibility for literacy among teachers has been writing-across-the-curriculum strategies. These were layered upon the curriculum, often sporadically, if at all. Common Core revealed the shortcomings of this practice and the need to reverse it. Because of the strong emphasis in Common Core on using factual texts in different areas of study, it was clear that literacy instruction had to become part of social studies, science, and other disciplines at the secondary level. Literacy needed to be the foundation for subject-area content, not an afterthought placed on top of content. As Vicki Phillips, director of Education, College-Ready, at the Gates Foundation, and Carina Wong, deputy director, wrote in *Phi Delta Kappan*:

> Based on our experiences as classroom teachers and as state and district administrators, we knew we wanted to invest in really well-designed tools and supports that could find the right balance between encouraging teachers' creativity and giving them enough guidance to ensure quality. And we wanted to ground these tools in evidence about what really powerful teaching aligned with the Common Core looks like. (2012, p. 31)

With an eye on the timeline — the adoption of Common Core by most states and the rolling out of Common Core-based assessments — teachers needed a lot more than off-the-shelf advice (even if it were available). The Gates Foundation asked a small group of curriculum and practice experts to begin the design of a new approach, based on their experience with standards-based instruction at district and state levels. Using this "strawman" design, the Foundation brought together more than 200 expert teachers from different districts and partners in 2010 to pressure test the emerging LDC framework and contribute their feedback and thoughts in a co-design effort. They spent three days in discussions and working together in a design process in which the next iteration of the LDC template tasks and module templates emerged for piloting and further testing.

The LDC moved to a pilot phase with five districts and a handful of partners for a year and then to a scale effort involving numerous statewide and districtwide LDC initiatives within three years. The implementation and impact of LDC has been researched and evaluated by Research for Action since the pilot stage. Using survey data, observations, and interviews, Research for Action has documented the progress of LDC in interim reports, annual reports, and case studies, which are available on the Research for Action website (www.researchforaction.org) and the LDC website (www.LDC.org/results).

The latest results (*Scale Up and Sustainability Study of the LDC and MDC Initiatives*, September 2013), based on survey data from more than 1,800 teachers using LDC and more than 500 of their administrators, as well as interviews and focus groups, found high levels of buy-in to LDC initiatives and evidence of positive impact on instruction and student learning. More than 80% of educators surveyed found the LDC tools effective; among teachers, more than 90% endorsed them as effective in teaching literacy skills in secondary classrooms. Endorsement of LDC has increased from one annual research report to the next one. While the full impact of LDC on students' abilities to master the Common Core probably will not be known until the results of state assessments based on the Common Core are available, the continued confidence of teachers and administrators in the LDC initiative indicates it is a sustainable tool for the nation's secondary classrooms. Consistently, LDC teachers have found that the tools resulted in higher quality writing (80%), supported student college readiness (87%) and helped prepare students for current assessments (75%). Teachers, however, want more help on differentiating instruction for varying student skill levels.

Although the research finds that districts are still challenged to provide the time for formal professional learning around the LDC strategy, LDC has resulted in increased opportunities for teachers to participate in small group work with a focus on literacy skills across subject areas and use student work to determine instructional next steps. These groups function much like PLCs with a focus on curriculum development (see "Chapter 18: Professional Learning Communities" in this book). The success of this type of professional learning is "good news," say the researchers, because "high percentages of teachers also rate this form of professional learning opportunity as effective" (p. 65).

Steps

One of the most important features of the LDC design is its flexibility. The sample LDC teaching tasks (see p. 143, Step 2) illustrate the universal aspect of the template task strategy and its links to skills described by Common Core. No matter if the class is ELA, social studies, science or career-technology or grade level, by filling in the blanks of an LDC template task teachers are asking students to:

- Think in ways that prepare students for success in college and the workplace;
- Read, comprehend, and analyze texts as specified by the Common Core;
- Write products as specified by the Common Core; and
- Apply Common Core literacy standards to the content they are studying.

It is also important to note that using the template tasks requires that teachers make deliberate decisions about content and context for teaching and learning. To design a strong assignment, educators must bring to bear a strong knowledge of text and subject area content, along with a solid understanding of the skills needed to produce a discipline-specific product involving reading and writing. Again, LDC is not a script or program, but a system that provides guidance as well as flexibility for teachers in their efforts to deliver high-quality instruction. The system is composed of a process for teachers to follow and a set of templates for them to use as they engage in their own professional learning in order to create assignments that engage students and result in achievement of standards.

As teachers fill in the template task blanks, they are making it clear to students that they must produce a written product to demonstrate evidence of their content understanding and literacy skills. Through the design of their assignment, teachers are also able to control the complexity of a task, challenging students to learn new skills and practice ones teachers already have taught or students have learned in previous modules or coursework. In addition to the Common Core Anchor Standards that are built in, and the ones that teachers can select to address in their task, teachers can also add grade-specific Common Core, speaking and listening Common Core and state content standards if they choose to.

The bottom line is that each blank in the teaching task template calls on teachers to make instructional choices related to skills and content. The discussion in this section is meant to help teachers make choices that justify the time and effort teachers and students will spend in completing an LDC task. The beauty of the LDC process is that it provides ways for teachers engage in professional conversations that help them make choices about teaching and learning so students succeed; they learn from each other about how others make choices about curriculum, instruction, and assessment.

Step 1: Choose a mode: argumentation, informational/explanatory, or narrative writing

The LDC template tasks and module templates are grouped by writing modes. Teachers working in their small groups choose the mode carefully because their choice relates directly to the type of product students will produce and the skills the teacher will teach.

In Template Task Collection 2, the templates begin with asking teachers to fill in a question. While constructing an opening question of the teaching task is optional, it helps to clarify for students the purpose of their response, whether to compose an argumentation, informational/explanatory, or narrative response. For example, an argumentation task question might be "Is fusion or fission a better option for energy?" In contrast for an informational report on the same topic, the question might be "How do fusion and fission compare as forms of energy?" Teachers can also craft a teaching task without a question to signal the mode. For example, "After researching science articles, write a report in which you define 'fusion' and 'fission' and explain their potential and challenges in creating nuclear energy" requires an informative/explanatory response.

Part of what teachers do in this step is share data, if available, or information about skills students need to be introduced to or need to practice. Then they choose the mode based on how that mode lends itself to learning those skillsand what type of product they will produce. Whichever mode teachers choose for their teaching task, they should use the appropriate rubric when scoring.

Step 2: Choose an "after reading" template or an "after researching" template

Within the argumentation, informational/explanatory and narrative categories, LDC Template Task Collection 2 provides two template types: *After reading* templates designed for one text or close reading of a few texts and *after researching* templates designed for research tasks with multiple texts.

Teachers will want to continue their dialogue about student needs and bring into consideration which approach best fits those needs. They'll want to discuss what they want the task to be: based on a text or a theme. For example, a teacher could select a text, such as *The Metamorphosis* by Franz Kafka, and ask students to describe how the author uses the major tenets of existentialism in the text. Or, a teacher focusing on the topic of "isms" in literature could choose a theme, such as asking students to research essays and articles on existentialism, and then write an essay explaining its key themes. The "text or theme" decision helps to drive which template type is selected.

If teachers choose an after reading template task, they need to craft a question that relates specifically to the text(s) and topic. Teachers should save global, essential, or open questions for full units, choosing a narrower question for the assignment they are writing. They should also double-check that the question is clearly in the mode of the template task: argumentation, informational/explanatory or narrative. Finally, they should determine whether or not the question forces a bias or a specific response from students. The best questions in this template type relate directly to a text and include a reference to the author, issue, character, theme, or some other aspect of the texts that students are reading. In other words, questions are constructed from the text, not forced upon it.

The after researching templates were designed for researching multiple texts. Those skills might include selecting texts that are relevant and credible, identifying relevant evidence from a set of texts, and using techniques for embedding evidence and citing in student work products. Teachers need to be careful when using this template task so as to not overload the task with too many texts. If teachers select only a few texts, they can teach research skills such as annotation methods and selection of appropriate evidence more successfully than if students must wade through several texts. Limiting the number of texts also allows teachers to know them well so they can score with knowledge of the text and for traits in the student works. Next teachers discuss whether they want to focus within their chosen mode on reading a single text — or just a few — or researching a concept with several texts." Continue with info about the two types of focus.

Step 3: Choose texts

Continuing their work in small groups, teachers should choose an appropriate text or multiple texts (see Online Resource 8.2: *Possible texts*). Texts are the central focus of the

Common Core Standards; the abilities to understand and analyze a text and cite evidence are the key skills. Teachers should choose texts that allow them to teach a set of skills that challenge students as well as involve them in content. To prepare for their own selection of text(s), the group of teachers might discuss these examples of assignments and texts. Likely, they'll find that the first task does not involve students in reading texts or content that is relevant to the study of literature nor does it ask students to read appropriately complex texts. The second example allows teachers to focus on textual analysis, and the third example is text-based and relevant to a social studies curriculum (Literacy Design Collaborative, 2014a).

Sample 1: Should middle school students be able to use cell phones? After reading editorials on this topic, write your own editorial in which you address the question and support your position with evidence from the texts (Task 2).

Sample 2: Which event most influenced western expansion in the 1800s? After researching primary and secondary texts about this period in American history, write a report in which you address the question and support your position with evidence from the texts (Task 2).

Sample 3: After reading Mark Twain's "On Running for Governor," write an essay in which you explain what stylistic devices he used to create a satire (Task 19).

The emphasis in the Common Core on text complexity means that teachers will need resources to access the texts that allow them to address the skills described in the reading standards. For example, Standard RI8 requires students in 8th grade to "delineate and evaluate the argument and specific claims in a text." In Standard RL7 high school students must have the resources — texts and media — to manage the demands of this standard, which involves comparing a text to its counterpart in a medium. States and education organizations provide a variety of text complexity rubrics, but at the core of this idea of complexity is the stipulation that a text should offer rich ideas, ones that provoke thoughtfulness and skill in extracting meaning.

Step 4: Choose a student product

Next, teachers work together to choose a student product. A product is an important choice because it determines skills sets that must be taught and students must demonstrate in their final submission. (See Online Resource 8.3: *Possible products.*) The unique language and structure of writing require a commitment from the writer that is very different from talking about something, and each product sets the stage for that commitment by requiring specific features. A product, such as essay or memo, contains clues about writing traits, including audience, structure, formality of language, tone, mode, and purpose. Below are descriptions of four common types of student products. Students should understand what each product requires in order to make their own decisions about what and how to address the charge in the task.

- **Essay:** The essayist style tends to explore ideas in an argumentation or explanatory mode to an academic audience, although the essay is also a popular type of text. Other features might include either a deductive or inductive structure with distinct sections, discipline- specific language, and reasoned and logical use of textual evidence to support the controlling idea. The term essay is often used as a catch-all and is often mistaken for the five-paragraph essay. In fact, it can appear in many forms. Professor Barrie Olson's (2014) research on discipline-specific student products at the college level provides important insight into the different types of essays — and their requirements — found in various subject areas.

- **Report:** A report tends to be informative or explanatory, but it can be argumentative as in arguing for a practice or a product. It tends to be the term used in the workplace and in science, social studies, technical, and business fields. Its audience is often peers, and its function is to report on some topic using a deductive structure with distinct sections and discipline specific language. The memo is a business version of this with a distinct protocol. Reports are also expected to be reasoned and logical and use textual evidence and data to support a controlling idea.

- **Feature article:** A feature article is journalistic and can be written in any mode, including narrative. Its audience is general and it uses either a deductive or inductive structure with distinct sections, often delineated by subheadings. It is written in plain English to explain technical topics and is logical. It refers to but doesn't formally cite textual and experiential evidence to support the controlling idea.

- **Editorial:** An editorial is intended to convince the reader, using an emotional appeal as well as a reasoned one. It is also written in a journalistic and personal style and can be argumentative or explanatory. Editorialists often use narrative techniques to engage a general audience. Its structure is more informal and the punch line is often at the end of the editorial. Language is conversational. The editorialist sometimes uses textual and experiential evidence to support a controlling idea but relies more on credible reasoning than on facts.

- **Narrative:** The LDC narrative template tasks are designed for two purposes: (1) to give an account of an event based on historical research or interview, and (2) to write directions or about processes. An LDC narrative's main feature is its chronology or sequencing in either purpose, whether it's an account of a battle or directions for assembling a gadget. The key to writing a narrative is its chronological structure and its use of descriptive language to help the reader imagine an event or follow a series of steps.

Step 5: Choose content

Teachers continue the LDC process by working collaboratively to choose content for their assignment. The LDC template tasks are designed not only to teach literacy skills but also to teach how to think about content, particularly when it is appropriate for students to examine a central theme, concept, event, or issue in the discipline by reading about it and then writing about it. "Clear writing is clear thinking," according to William Zinsser (1998) in his seminal book, *Writing to Learn* (p. 192). Teachers can create opportunities for students to develop clear thinking by focusing on some aspect of the curriculum's content that, in the process, teaches them *how to learn.*

It is important that teachers frame content for its value to the study of the discipline and show its worth for the time and effort teachers and students will engage in while producing the product. The Common Core reading standards can help teachers determine how to frame content. The blanks in the LDC template task allow teachers to extend the LDC verb to include other demands. For example, in the LDC Template Task Collection 2.0, template task 20 reads, "…write a _____that analyzes_____." Teachers can add to the complexity of this template and address demands in the grade-level standards by "complicating" the analysis, focusing on Common Core RIST9.6–8: "…write a _____that analyzes *the article by distinguishing among facts, reasoned judgments, and speculation.*"

> **Exemplary Modules, LDC CoreTools**
>
> In LDC CoreTools, readers can access banks of sample modules by visiting the LDC website (**www.ldc.org/sample-curricula**) and creating a free account. Example modules include the following:
>
> **Existentialism and Kafka** (https://coretools.ldc.org/#/mods/f3ca3046-98ee-4ede-bc78-a6d58432183c)
>
> **Power of Language** (https://coretools.ldc.org/#/mods/cfc856c8-d792-4e43-b492-f754d78acdfe)
>
> **Springfield High School Social Studies — The Treaty of Versailles** (https://coretools.ldc.org/#/mods/3c84f22d-5f2b-4aac-a308-a0f113aa15ff)

Following are examples of how the ELA standards can help teachers choose content topics that work well with LDC modules. (To access sample modules, see sidebar above.)

- **Common Core Standard RL1.6–12:** This is the most important standard for reading because it describes skills that all readers must use to understand a text as the author intended. The best way to address this standard squarely is to assign a text that lends itself clearly to content. In the study of literature, for example, content would include genre studies, and an example is a task that asks students to connect a cultural movement (e.g. existentialism) to an author's theme. The LDC module, "Existentialism and Kafka," does just that.
- **Common Core Standard RL5.8:** This standard calls for students to "compare and contrast the structure of two or more texts and how the structure of each text contributes to its meaning and style." In the LDC module, "Power of Language," students analyze structures (i.e. a poem, a recipe, prose selection) affects meaning about the same topic.
- **Common Core Standard RIHSS9:9–10:** This standard involves a basic historical skill, to "compare and contrast treatments of the same topic in several primary and secondary sources." In the LDC module, "Springfield High School Social Studies — The Treaty of Versailles," students read a selection of articles and passages from the document to write an argumentative essay on the topic. They can use the same set of skills to examine other documents and their historical significance.

CHAPTER 8 ■ CURRICULUM AS PROFESSIONAL LEARNING

Table 2: **The LDC Prototype Minitask**

Skill objective	Minitask product and prompt	Minitask scoring rubric	Instructional strategies
2. Essential vocabulary Ability to identify and master terms essential to understanding a text.	**Vocabulary list** In your notebook, list words and phrases essential to the texts. Add definitions, and (if appropriate) notes on connotation in this context.	• Lists appropriate phrases. • Provides accurate definitions.	• Lists appropriate phrases. • Provides accurate definitions.

This step is critical in that "filling in the blanks" is much more than just filling in the blanks. It is a purposeful approach based on the Common Core or district and state content standards as well as the core concepts of a discipline.

Step 6: Teach the task using an LDC module

Once teachers are satisfied with their teaching task, they have the option of using the LDC module templates. The module is designed to lead instruction through a process of teaching the skills necessary to produce a product in which students must write in response to reading or research. This process takes place in an LDC module using a series of "minitasks," which teachers will recognize as formative assessments. In LDC, the minitasks enable learning by providing teachers and students with feedback as learning proceeds and ensure students stay focused. The minitask system helps teachers decide if something needs to be re-taught or if students are ready to move on or tackle another skill. An example of a minitask for reading is, "List the key points in each paragraph of the article." One for writing is, "Write an outline and develop a structure for your essay." An example of an LDC prototype minitask involves the alignment among four elements: the skill objective, the minitask prompt, a short success rubric, and a few notes on instruction strategies. It will also include estimated pacing time (See Table 2, The LDC Prototype Minitask.)

As mentioned, New Visions is working with researchers at the University of California, Berkeley, to develop criteria for effective and relevant minitasks. Part of their research involved an in-depth case study of the Industrial Revolution module designed by Ballute and Lent. They found that the teachers' successful minitasks:

• Provided scaffolding toward the culminating written product;

• Required students to actively construct knowledge, instead of reciting or regurgitating information;

• Required students to refer back to texts for evidence, whether those texts were written within the reading or writing packets or notes they took themselves; and

• Were structured to provide known content when a new skill was being introduced or emphasized, and known skills when the content was new.

Scoring minitasks should be viewed as feedback to students, rather than a summative score. For that reason, most minitask scoring guides involve only the must-have features of a response for quick scoring. Teachers who have used the module system of minitasks have arrived at ways to keep the scoring manageable, such as sampling student work on minitasks from each class each day, adjusting minitasks to student skills (more capable writers, for example, may skip intermediate minitasks between an outline and a first draft), or coaching students to conduct peer evaluations. Ultimately, a taught module documents thoughtful, quality teaching to include the template task, the teaching task, the standards, a rubric, and an instructional plan with a collection of student work.

Variations

The LDC is by its nature an evolving system because is essentially teacher driven. In this sense it will never be finished. Teachers not only share modules and minitasks but also create them in partnership with other teachers; they also provide feedback and create new templates and other tools for a variety of purposes to ensure their instruction aligns with standards and academic practices. Many teachers are currently active within networks and on web-based resources, communicating so they can support and learn

146 ■ **Powerful Designs for Professional Learning**   **Learning Forward**

from each other. For example, the Teaching Channel, the National Paideia Center, the Southern Regional Education Board (SREB), and the National Writing Project have created web-based resources for teachers to share their work and support each other. In the process of this collaboration, new LDC tools are emerging for a variety of purposes, some by subject and others by grade levels., Teachers are trying out ways to sequence minitasks and modules to create LDC units and courses. Because assignments are the centerpiece of a challenging curriculum, the LDC system can be seated in any curriculum design. Such flexibility offers potential for any number of variations, including project-based learning and STEM.

Challenges and how to address them

Research for Action (2012) has conducted several studies of the implementation of LDC. Findings show that teachers overwhelmingly report that LDC engages students and that student learning of both literacy skills and content knowledge has improved through LDC. The Research for Action studies also outline challenges expressed by some teachers across sites and offer potential solutions suggested by teachers themselves.

Finding time to include literacy. It is important to note that finding time for literacy is a common challenge identified by LDC and non-LDC teachers alike as they are introduced to the Common Core State Standards. The Common Core "set requirements not only for English language arts (ELA) but also for literacy in history/social studies, science, and technical subjects" (p. 3). The Common Core is clear in its demands that literacy is taught within these subject areas. Common Core Standards "are not meant to replace content standards in those areas but rather to supplement them" (p. 3). They require shifts in instruction from ELA and content teachers alike.

At first, these new changes do demand an investment of time — time to learn about the new expectations, to think through what they mean in a subject area, to plan and collaborate, and to test and refine new strategies. For LDC, Research for Action found that "teachers are concerned about science and social studies teachers having the time to teach literacy" (Research for Action, 2012, p. 6). Others believe that LDC modules compete with their curriculum and view them as "add-ons" to their current approach. And, while

ONLINE RESOURCES

8.1 Built-in standards
8.2 Possible texts
8.3 Possible products

"teachers value the module development process . . . they also find it demanding and time-consuming" (Research for Action, 2012, p. 18).

Strategies of professional learning. So, what are a few strategies for finding time and supporting teachers as they learn about LDC and use the LDC tools to implement the Common Core in their classroom?

* First, the *Scale-up and sustainability study* (Levin & Poglinco, 2013) highlights the importance of teacher leaders, administrators, and LDC partners in helping teachers understand how LDC can work within their courses. The study recommends a role for district administrators "in facilitating [LDC] tool use by ensuring that teachers understand: the purposes of the tools; how the tools should work hand-in-hand with the curriculum; and where best to place the tools in the overall pacing of instruction" (p. vii).

* For Research for Action, Levin and Poglinco (2013) also identify ongoing professional learning and teacher collaboration as a means for successfully implementing LDC:

  Our research provides evidence that, while collaboration is an essential component in implementing and scaling the [LDC] tools, many teachers do not have regular time together to discuss tool development and implementation. Principals and district leaders should support teachers in scheduling time to work together as they learn to use the tools and continue to refine their practice. (p. viii)

* Teachers also benefit from professional learning about LDC. LDC teachers report the need and benefits of small group learning or personalized learning for understanding LDC (Levin & Poglinco, viii). In addition to district and state supports, the LDC organization

and LDC partners such as The Teaching Channel are proving to be helpful by offering online learning. They offer videos, tools and a peer community that teachers can access when it is convenient for their schedule and when they need them. LDC also provides exemplar modules and a library of minitasks that save teachers time as they share and borrow proven ideas and strategies from each other, allowing teachers to customize based on their students' needs and interests.

- Finally, the instructional shifts demanded by Common Core lend themselves to thinking differently about time during the school day. It becomes difficult for teachers to engage students in deep reading, research, writing and speaking and listening work during a typical 40–45 minute period. Organizations such as TimeWise Schools are helping schools maximize time within their given budget allocations and district/state policies. Using the TimeWise approach, school leaders and teacher teams can design their own schedules that repurpose time to better support LDC and similar strategies in the classroom.

Like many of the powerful designs in this book, such as lesson study, the LDC process takes time but rewards teachers through greater learning, both for themselves and their students. Between 78% and 86% of teachers engaged in the LDC process believed that their own learning led to an increase in student learning, including improved writing (Research for Action, 2012, p. 27).

The more involvement teachers had in creating LDC modules, the better their implementation. In fact, Research for Action found that teachers who created modules wanted to create more modules, became better at creating them, and implemented them skillfully.

Conclusion

The LDC began four years ago as a small design team and with a few volunteer districts. In 2013 the Collaborative grew to include tens of thousands of teachers in 34 states. In 2014, it became a nonprofit organization led by Chad Vignola, former vice-president of New Visions for Public Schools in New York City. He has set as his priority the refinement of LDC as an effective professional learning resource, primarily through communicating quality standards of practice. Successful LDC teachers, he believes, must be paired with an effective professional learning system to support their growth.

References

Crawford, M., Galiatsos, S., & Lewis, A. (2011). *1.0 guide to the literacy design collaborative framework.* Available at ldc.org/sites/default/files/LDCBook_web.pdf.

Levin, S. & Poglinco, S.M. (2013). *Scale-up and sustainability study for the LDC and MDC.* Available at www.researchforaction.org/projects/?id=89.

Literacy Design Collaborative. (2014a). Grades 6–12 LDC Module Templates 2.0. [Website]. Available at www.ldc.org/resources#Grade-6-12-LDC-Module-Templates-2.0.

Literacy Design Collaborative. (2014b). LDC template task collection 2.0. [Website]. Available at www.ldc.org/resources#TASK-TEMPLATES.

Literacy Design Collaborative. (2014c). Literacy matters. [Videotape]. Available at www.ldc.org/resources#About-LDC.

Olson, B. (2014, November). *Academic writing across the curriculum.* Available at http://ldc.org/resources#LDC-Framework-Guides.

Phillips, V. & Wong, C. (2010, April). Tying together the common core of standards, instruction, and assessments. *Phi Delta Kappan.* Available at http://slcschools.org/departments/curriculum/language-arts/documents/CCSSarticleforWS.pdf.

Research for Action. (2012). *Brief Two — Robust implementation of LDC: Teacher perceptions of tool use and outcomes.* Available at www.researchforaction.org/projects/?id=89.

Schlechty, P. C. (2002). *Working on the work: An action plan for teachers, principals, and superintendents.* San Francisco, CA: Jossey-Bass.

Zinsser, W. (1988). *Writing to learn.* New York, NY: HarperCollins.

CHAPTER 9

Data Analysis

Teachers examine each type of data by itself and then study how the data sets relate to one another to create the whole.[1]

By Victoria L. Bernhardt

Benjamin Franklin Middle School teachers believe they are getting the best results they possibly can from the students they teach every day. Staff members are adamant they cannot work any harder — and they certainly do not have time to add even one more thing to what they are doing. With state and federal accountability, however, even schools with good results must get better results. All schools are expected to improve — not just those classified as underperforming.

The principal and the professional development data team believe staff members have done a good job of looking at student achievement scores for ways to improve but think they may be missing information from other data.

They decide some outside assistance may help. They invite Jane from the Regional Education Service Center to facilitate learning about data that are important for continuous school improvement, why these data are important for school improvement, and how to analyze all the data, independently and together.

When teachers arrive for the professional learning day to look at data other than student achievement results, many are reluctant to spend more time on the matter. They feel they are doing a fine job and there is nothing else that can be done. Jane, however, has decided that — after a quick overview of the different types of data — it would be good to start the data analysis process by looking at another school's data.

Jane begins the session by reviewing **four categories of data** — demographics, perceptions, student learning, and

---

[1] Adapted from *Data Analysis for Continuous School Improvement* (3rd ed.), by Victoria Bernhardt. Larchmont, NY: Eye on Education, 2013. Copyright, Eye on Education. All rights reserved. Used with permission.

school processes — and why each of these types of data is important for continuous school improvement. Of course, some teachers are still thinking, "Test results are what we're accountable for. Why look at anything else?"

Jane then declares, "Let's see what it looks like when a school gathers each of these data types." She introduces them to Magnolia Middle School. The first type of data they consider for Magnolia is demographics. Demographic data tell them not only about students and teachers, but also how Magnolia aligns staff to work with different groups the school is attempting to serve. Demographics set the context for everything educators do. Demographics also give educators a glimpse into their processes, educational philosophy, and system.

Working in teams, the teachers review the demographic profile of Magnolia, a school that had gotten good results over three years but still struggled to improve. Benjamin Franklin Middle School staff members look for strengths and potential challenges and list implications for Magnolia's continuous school improvement plan. They also talk about other demographic data they think Magnolia should consider.

Soon they begin discussing how accessing additional data makes sense. Franklin educators like the idea that additional data can give them some direction in improving student achievement results.

Next, each Franklin team reports what it sees in the Magnolia data, and Jane helps them merge the various ideas. Teachers begin speaking up. "It was frightening to me to know that I did not see *half* of what we saw collectively," one says. "We have to pull our demographic data together so we can see what we look like to others — and to ourselves."

With less reluctance now, a teacher who has been talking with others at her table raises her hand and says, "So tell us what perceptions can do for us." After Jane provides a quick overview of why perceptions are important and how to use questionnaires, the teachers and administrators review Magnolia's student, staff, and parent questionnaire results. The teachers are getting excited about what climate questionnaires can tell them.

The group next considers Magnolia's school process data. School processes include a school's procedures, policies, and programs, namely, how the school does business. Schools have to know the processes the school uses to

understand how educators there get the results they are getting. An examination of processes helps educators know what is working and what is not working.

Jane comments, "If you want different results, you have to change the processes that create the results. That does not mean that, if you do not like the results you are getting in reading right now, you have to drop your current program and buy a different one. It means that you have to understand what and how processes are being implemented. You also need to understand for which student groups they are working and when they are not."

Jane tells the staff that processes to consider include curriculum (what we teach), instruction (how we teach), assessment (how we know students understand what we are trying to teach), environment (how everyone treats everyone else), policies (what rules we follow, requiring parents to call the office to report an absence by 9 a.m.), and procedures (how we conduct school business, such as sending home mid-term report cards).

In small groups, the Benjamin Franklin Middle School staff makes a list of implications for Magnolia's continuous school improvement plan based on what they know about the programs, processes, and procedures operating there. The groups share their findings and their impressions about Magnolia's programs, processes, and procedures that need to be stopped, implemented differently, or evaluated further.

The last of the four categories of data is student learning. Before Franklin educators look at student scores, however, they summarize what they now understand about Magnolia in the other categories. The staff members revisit their earlier conclusions about demographics, perceptions, and processes and surmises how these data might affect the example school's improvement plans. Then they look at Magnolia's graphs of student learning data. The teachers appreciate seeing the disaggregated student achievement data in "picture" form.

Franklin educators see few surprises in the Magnolia student learning results.

One staff member says, "We knew what the student achievement results would be by looking at the school's demographics, perceptions, and school process data. We almost didn't need to review the student learning results." Another says, "We knew what they should do in their continuous school improvement plan . . . even before looking at student scores."

One of them volunteers, "I think school plans look different if staff look only at the student learning results without the other data categories." Someone responds, "Definitely!" Another says, "No wonder Magnolia is getting the same results over time." "They weren't looking at all their data, and it is all there!" says a third. Three people said, nearly in unison, "We need to look at all *our* data."

The teachers begin to see how critical it is to understand where any school is right now and over time within each of the data categories, and how seeing where the categories intersect brings them a deeper understanding of the impact of the teaching and learning processes.

Jane then encourages staff members to look more specifically at the implications for Magnolia's continuous school improvement plan across the four types of data. They see the relationship of decisions made in all the categories to student learning results and recognize that a few big things could make a big difference in the example school's results.

By the end of the day, staff members set deadlines and assign individuals responsibilities to gather a complete set of their own data for the next meeting. As they identify actions the example school could take to improve, the staff grows more excited about gathering and analyzing their own data. Benjamin Franklin Middle School educators are not only ready to examine themselves, they already have begun.

Overview

Data are "facts or information used usually to calculate, analyze, or plan something," according to the Merriam-Webster online dictionary (www.Merriam-Webster.com). That dictionary also defines *analysis* as "a careful study of something to learn about its parts, what they do and how they are related to each other; an explanation of the nature and meaning of something" (www.Merriam-Webster.com).

Putting the definitions together pinpoints exactly the process of data analysis. Educators examine the data, each type by itself — i.e. demographics, perceptions, student learning, and school processes — and then study how the data sets relate to each other to create the whole (see Online Resource 9.1: *Multiple measures of data*). They do this to understand how to improve their work to get better results.

As Benjamin Franklin Middle School educators learned, no one type of data is sufficient for understanding a school's

current state or for seeing changes in that state over time. Four data sources are necessary: demographic, perceptions, processes, and achievement.

Demographic data provide descriptive information about the school. Demographics provide the context for understanding all other data. One cannot understand another piece of data without context. Demographic data also help educators understand the impact the educational system has on all groups of students when the data are disaggregated by gender, ethnicity, or other subgroups.

Perceptions data help educators understand what students, parents, teachers, and the community think about the learning environment. Perceptions can be gathered in various ways, including through questionnaires, interviews, and observations. The perceptions of those associated with a school are important to understand since people's actions follow what they believe, perceive, or think. One way to change actions is to change perceptions. If educators want to change a group's perceptions, they have to know what those perceptions are. Student perceptions can shed some light on what motivates them to learn. Staff perceptions can suggest possibilities within the school with respect to improvement/change.

School processes define what staff members are doing to get the results they are getting. School processes include programs, instructional strategies, assessment strategies, classroom practices, procedures, and how standards are implemented. Routine though they may be, processes both reflect and affect all aspects of a school, and changes in processes can affect perceptions as well as student achievement. For example, instituting a new reading program that supports the identified needs of students confirms a school's dedication to literacy as well as increases students' abilities with text. Documenting processes can help school staff build a continuum of learning that makes sense for all students.

Student learning describes the results of the educational system, including scores on norm-referenced tests, criterion-referenced tests, standards assessments and formative assessments, as well as teacher-given grades, and ratings of student work. Schools use a variety of student learning measurements. The important thing is for schools to use assessments that measure what it is the staff want students to know and be able to do.

Rationale

Data analysis is a powerful form of professional learning. Data are critical for understanding how a learning organization is doing in terms of its processes, procedures, and student learning results. Understanding data leads to knowing what to do to improve those results. To turn data analysis into meaningful action, all staff must understand the data and know what they personally must do for the system to improve. The power of data analysis as a professional learning activity comes from many facets:

- Data are real; therefore, the work is real.
- Most teachers do not typically see their whole school's data, so they might not know the health of the organization and what they and their colleagues can do to improve it.
- The focus is on improving learning for *all* learners.
- The focus is on improving the quality of the work done in the organization at all levels.
- The professional learning is collaborative.
- The work that is done is in the context of a professional learning community.
- Analyzing data honors the staff's expertise, experience, and professional knowledge.
- Data analysis requires reflection and inquiry.
- The work helps uncover findings that lead to change.
- When staff review what the data are telling them to change, they start changing.
- Data analysis conversations can be built into the work week.
- Data analysis includes all staff in the work, and every stakeholder's voice is heard through the data.
- Data analysis leads to improved learning for *all* students.

Steps

Data analysis works best when:

- A teacher, school or district administrator, or member of the community that the school or district serves has identified a *need* for data collection and analysis and makes this need known to others. A need might become evident as a result of an accreditation report or because of an undesirable condition, such as a high drop-out rate or poor performance on a student achievement examination.

- A district or school administrator *commits* to collecting and analyzing data.
- Using this chapter or other resources, a group of people, sometimes called a *data team,* creates a plan for collecting and analyzing data.
- A data team, working on its own or with a facilitator, collects and pre-analyzes the data so members can appropriately facilitate the analysis of data with the staff.
- The data team facilitates the analysis of data with the entire staff.

Preliminary actions

Steps 1–4 usually can be accomplished in one day and should involve the whole group. Steps 5–7 are accomplished by the deadlines set by the whole group and involve individuals or small teams. Steps 8 and 9 involve the whole group again.

Before the first meeting, the data team completes the following actions. Team members work together to do the following:

- **Identify those to be involved.** Early in the data process, the data team should communicate with all those who will be affected so they have a voice in how the strategy is implemented. Involve the whole school, including administrators, special area teachers (such as art), counselors, classroom assistants, support staff (especially if data analysis might lead to changes in their work), and students. Concerned members outside the immediate school staff (such as the superintendent, district director of curriculum, parents, and other community members) also should be involved.

- **Plan to include a large group in the process.** Have everyone involved in Steps 1–4, and 9–11 meet in a room large enough for the entire group. Not everyone needs to be involved in steps 5–8 (gathering or graphing the data, pulling together a report, and planning a meeting). However, everybody should participate in steps 9–11 during which decisions are proposed and made on the basis of data. Step 11 is the action step, which is completed by individuals or small groups (see sidebar Summary of steps).

- **Identify a meeting location.** Use a location with computer access to expedite the group's work.

Summary of steps	
Preliminary Steps (Data team)	
• Identify those to be involved. • Plan to include a large group in the process. • Identify a meeting location. • Outline procedures.	
The First Day (Whole group)	
Step 1	Help all staff understand what data analysis entails, why it is important, and how it can make a difference.
Step 2	Show an example.
Step 3	Make lists of the data to gather for your own school.
Step 4	Set up subcommittees to gather the data.
Subsequent Days (Subcommittees)	
Step 5	Gather the questionnaire data.
Step 6	Graph the data.
Step 7	Compile the results in a report.
Step 8	Plan for the whole staff to get together to analyze the results.
The Analysis Day (Whole group)	
Step 9	Use a half-day for the whole group to review results
Step 10	Determine what absolutely has to be in the continuous school improvement plan.
Step 11	Implement and follow up on ideas.

Having someone in the group who knows computers well also helps.

- **Set a time.** Plan a whole day of work for the first meeting.
- **Outline procedures.** Typical meeting procedures will help data analysis meetings proceed smoothly. Use:
  - Introductory activities;
  - Norm setting;
  - Opening and closing activities;
  - Nametags and name tents; and
  - A written agenda and time to revise the agenda as needed.

By the end of the first day, participants will have:
1. Analyzed demographic data for the example school.
2. Analyzed perceptions in the example school.
3. Analyzed school processes in the example school.
4. Analyzed student learning in the example school.
5. Formed subcommittees, chosen leaders, and planned their own data collection processes for all four data categories.

Step 1: Help all staff understand what data analysis entails, why it is important, and how it can make a difference

This step should be accomplished in a single day. Data collection and analysis do not happen magically by themselves. The strategy requires careful planning and implementation. Staff must understand why data are important and how data analysis can lead to continuous school improvement. All staff members need to get involved in this work and understand how the analysis will affect each aspect of the school from classrooms to school culture.

At the first meeting, the data team presents the need and gets consensus from participants that data collection and analysis will address the need. The facilitator helps the group understand that the process entails looking independently and interdependently at four categories of data: demographics, perceptions, student learning, and school processes (see Online Resource 9.1: *Multiple measures of data*).

Step 2: Show an example

This should also occur on the first day the whole group meets. Since the group has decided to use data analysis, participants must develop an understanding of what is involved.

Teachers sometimes declare that they are not using specific strategies (like cooperative learning) because they do not know what these ideas look like in practice. In the case of data collection and analysis, the solution is to show teachers an example of data gathered in another school and model how to analyze the data in the sample. As your example, you can use data from a school called Magnolia Middle School, which the Benjamin Franklin Middle School educators used in the narrative that began this chapter (see

What subcommittees need to do:

1. Compile the demographic, perceptions, student learning, or school processes data.

2. Design, test, and arrange for any questionnaires to be administered. (e.g. the Questionnaire Subcommittee)

3. Make an inventory of the processes the school is using. (e.g. the School Processes Subcommittee)

4. Graph the data and include clear titles and legends. (each subcommittee)

5. Organize the graphs in a logical sequence, such as most general to most specific data, following the example school (Magnolia) profile. (each subcommittee)

6. Write narratives about the graphs. (each subcommittee)

7. Set up the reports, perhaps online, for all staff to review. (each subcommittee)

Online Resource 9.2: *Magnolia Middle School case study*). The handout includes multiple pages and many charts for the four types of data.

Many teachers and administrators do not think they can analyze data until they actually analyze data. Teachers and administrators have no trouble analyzing another school's data quite comprehensively, and are much better at looking at their own data after analyzing data from another school. Use the study questions (see Online Resource 9.3: *Data analysis study questions*) to help with this analysis.

One good way to accomplish this step is by dividing the group into teams of not more than seven people to allow adequate airtime for each person. The outside facilitator or data team member who is facilitating the process distributes Online Resources 9.2 and 9.3 to each team member. Teams analyze data according to the questions on Online Resource 9.3. Each team can then record its findings on chart paper and merge these with other small-group findings into the whole group findings.

School process data may be hard to analyze by itself, unless the school has created an inventory of school processes. School processes show up in the other categories of data, however, and they need to be considered within the context of the other categories to make the most sense. Looking at data from Magnolia, the Benjamin Franklin teachers saw a lot of process data in the demographic and questionnaire data. For example, the number of students identified as learning disabled or gifted and the number of students getting high school credit for middle school work implied processes. Consequently, the Franklin staff members wanted to know more about how students were identified for these programs. Magnolia Middle School seemed to have a strong academic intervention program. The school had a very strong arts program, but not much was said about math and science.

When you begin data analysis, you will find school processes data by looking through all the Magnolia School data, as well as your own data.

Step 3: Make lists of the data to gather for your own school

This step should also occur on the first day and involve the whole group.

Having looked at data from the example school, have staff members decide about the data they want to gather for their own school. Online Resource 9.4: *Guiding list of demographic data possibilities* provides typical sources of demographic data to gather, including data elements that most schools use in a comprehensive analysis.

Step 4: Set up subcommittees to gather the data

This step should also occur on the first day. Not every participant has to get involved in gathering each element of data. All must understand, however, that the purpose of gathering the data is to use these data to improve learning for all students, not to place blame or to criticize individuals.

For this step, the facilitator or data team member encourages participants to divide the labor and sign up for at least one data gathering subcommittee. One group of staff members can be in charge of pulling together the demographic data. Demographic data such as attendance and discipline are gathered every day in schools, but the information is usually not captured or presented well enough to use as it is. To make demographic data most usable, someone needs to graph it and organize all the demographic graphs from most general information to most specific information. Use the Magnolia case study (see Online Resource 9.2: *Magnolia Middle School case study*) as a guide.

Another group can be in charge of questionnaires — determining which questions to use and when and how the questionnaires will be administered; they should also oversee administering the questionnaire. If the school personnel already administered questionnaires, gather the results for review. Another group can make a list of school processes, and another can gather and graph student achievement results.

After all participants have volunteered for at least one data-gathering subcommittee, the subcommittees meet to plan their work. One of the first questions the subcommittees should address is, "Who should lead us?" Another good question is, "Who should help the leader?" The subcommittee members should make sure that at least two individuals in each subcommittee volunteer to take on leadership roles. Leaders are responsible for:

- Setting meeting times;
- Finding meeting space;
- Setting deadlines;
- Setting specifications for data;
- Reporting on progress to the whole sub-committee; and
- Working with leaders from other subcommittees to pull together a report on all the data.

The whole group should decide and commit to a deadline for the work, perhaps setting benchmark deadlines before then during which subcommittees will report progress.

Step 5: Gather the questionnaire data

A subcommittee will accomplish this step according to the established timeline. The subcommittee might consider administering questionnaires online. Free downloadable questionnaire files and tools to help you set up questionnaires online are available at http://eff.csuchico.edu/html/questionnaire_resources.html. See the resource list on the website for additional resources for questionnaires, graphing templates, and tools for putting the questionnaires online.

Online administration results in quick returns. Staff members get a real boost when they see the data flowing in quickly. Start with the staff questionnaire so staff can know what they need to do to help administer the questionnaires to students and parents. Consider giving the student questionnaire during school, and the parent questionnaire at parent-teacher conferences, or other times when parents are present.

Step 6: Graph the data

Gathering data is important. Graphing the data is equally important. Graphing the data turns the information into a picture that everyone can see at the same time. Graphs are easier than raw data for most people to comprehend.

Demographic, perceptions, and student learning data can be graphed. Process data may be presented in a list or chart. The subcommittees in charge of demographic, perceptions, and student learning data — or a special subcommittee designated to graph all data — take charge of presenting information in picture form, according to deadlines set by the whole group.

Subcommittees can choose how to present pictures for the data they collect using graphing templates that allow committee members to find the appropriate graph, enter the numbers, and watch the graphs build. If they are creating the graphs from scratch, Microsoft Excel is a great, commonly used tool.

Step 7: Pull the results together in a report

Leaders from the subcommittees can pull all the data together into one report that will be easy for staff to read and analyze. The report should have some narrative, and many graphs, but no conclusions yet. It is important for the staff to see the story of the school as told by the data.

Communicating the results in a meaningful way is extremely important to the analysis of the data if staff members are going to use the data to make decisions about continuous school improvement. While staff members are the most important recipients of these results, members of the larger community (district administrators, board members, parents, and community members) also need to understand why the school is collecting and analyzing data, and how they may use the information to develop new strategies to improve student learning.

Step 8: Plan for the whole staff to get together to analyze the results

Plan at least a half-day of professional learning for all of the initial participants (see Step 1) to analyze the results together. Having a facilitator (a data team member or outside facilitator) and a recorder for the whole-group activities can help keep this meeting focused.

ADDITIONAL RESOURCES

Books

Data Analysis for Continuous School Improvement (3rd ed.), by Victoria L. Bernhardt. Larchmont, NY: Eye on Education, 2013.

From Questions to Actions: Using Questionnaire Data for Continuous School Improvement, by Victoria L. Bernhardt and Brad Geise. Larchmont, NY: Eye on Education, 2009.

Using Data, Getting Results: A Practical Guide for School Improvement in Mathematics and Science, by Nancy Love. Norwood, MA: Christopher-Gordon, 2001.

Using Data to Improve Student Learning in Elementary Schools, by Victoria L. Bernhardt. Larchmont, NY: Eye on Education, 2003.

Using Data to Improve Student Learning in High Schools, by Victoria L. Bernhardt. Larchmont, NY: Eye on Education, 2005.

Using Data to Improve Student Learning in Middle Schools, by Victoria L. Bernhardt. Larchmont, NY: Eye on Education, 2004.

Using Data to Improve Student Learning in School Districts, by Victoria L. Bernhardt. Larchmont, NY: Eye on Education, 2006.

Publications

Journal of Staff Development (2000, Winter). The whole issue is devoted to data. Oxford, OH: NSDC.

Websites

http://eff.csuchico.edu. Education for the Future is a nonprofit initiative located on the California State University, Chico campus that builds the capacity of learning organizations to gather, analyze, and use data to continuously improve teaching and learning.

http://learningforward.org. The Learning Forward website includes myriad resources, including articles, links to other sites, and related books.

Step 9: Use a half-day for the whole group to review results

Have the group review the four categories of data one at a time and report its findings. One way to accomplish this step is to have all individuals independently read one section of the data report (perhaps beginning with demographics) and jot down their thoughts about strengths, challenges, implications for the school improvement plan, and suggestions of other data that should be gathered (about 12 minutes). Then in small groups, have individuals share their thoughts about this section. Have a member of each small group serve as recorder/reporter to collect the group's thoughts about the data on that section on chart paper (about 20 minutes).

The facilitator should bring the small groups back into the large group to merge their thinking (about 30 minutes) about a section until the whole group has one complete list of ideas. One way to do this is with a round-robin process during which one small group presents its ideas on strengths, challenges, implications, or other data. Succeeding groups mention ideas that haven't been mentioned. The result is a complete list of ideas about a single section from all groups.

Repeat this process with another data section, perhaps perceptions. By the end of this process, all groups will have presented their analysis of information for all four data categories (see Online Resource 9.5: *Steps in analyzing results*).

Step 10: Determine what absolutely has to be in the continuous school improvement plan

After the whole group has analyzed all sections of the report, the group should reflect on the relationship of the results of the different data categories to each other. Participants need to see the big picture of data relationships across the four categories to make informed plans that will help the school get different results.

Participants may be excited that different types of data say the same, or similar, things. To begin, the facilitator asks participants to look across the different categories for *commonalities* in the implications for the continuous school improvement plan. For example, the group may notice that demographic data showing a high attrition rate for 6th graders is matched by data showing student decreases in achievement in that grade level. Have staff examine apparent *contradictions,* which may require additional data collection and analysis to resolve. For example, the group may notice that attitudes about bullying in 4th grade are not matched by similar attitudes in 3rd and 5th grades and may want additional information.

The process for Step 9, from individual writing to small-group sharing, ending with a round-robin process, works for this step, too.

As a result of this step, participants need to fit what they have learned into their current school improvement plan or one that they will create from their data analysis. By creating or revising a plan from information obtained from all categories of data, participants in this process will avoid focusing on one narrow aspect of data, such as the lowest scoring subtest on the state test. A better school improvement plan will result because the school focused on analysis of data across a wide spectrum.

Step 11: Implement and follow up on ideas

Data analysis is just the beginning. Complete the cycle by actually implementing and monitoring changes, according to a continuous school improvement plan, then collecting and analyzing new data. The goal of data analysis is be able to understand how working differently will achieve different results. If members of a school's community don't change their actions, their results will be the same, year after year, no matter how much data are gathered.

Variations

Variations depend on the type of data support the school is given.

Creating data sets. If a school district has someone whose job is to graph data, and who can give staff members all the data they want in the format they want it, professional learning could focus entirely on Steps 7–11. Staff members need to analyze the results, however, to ensure they understand each piece and how the pieces work together to tell the whole story of the school.

Level of analysis. The type of data analysis discussed here is a whole-school analysis. However, this design can be used by those involved in a whole district, a grade level, a subject area, or an individual class. If data analysis involves multiple schools, individual schools could

ONLINE RESOURCES

9.1 Multiple measures of data
9.2 Magnolia Middle School case study
9.3 Data analysis study questions
9.4 Guiding list of demographic data possibilities
9.5 Steps in analyzing results

analyze each other's data before looking at their own results. The important element is getting everyone involved in the analysis.

Questionnaires. While everyone is in the room on the data analysis day, staff could take the online staff questionnaire. In 15 minutes, it's possible to get a 100% response rate.

Challenges and how to address them

Managing for successful and productive data analysis and usage requires that schools and districts address several challenges.

Data availability and organization. The most challenging element in this approach is to have all the data available at one time. To look only at demographic data or questionnaire results is meaningful, but looking at demographic, questionnaire, school process, and student learning results together is powerful and satisfying. By looking at all four categories of data together, staff can discover trends, patterns, and anomalies and can leverage strengths to create continuous school improvement plans that improve their schools. Analyzing information in isolation results in school improvement plans that miss the boat.

Pulling the data together into a data profile for the first time can be pretty labor intensive depending on the data tools and support available to the organization (school, district, etc.). However, the benefits of having all staff review the data together is worth the effort. Updating the data profile over time will be much easier once there is a comprehensive start. By parsing the work to the subcommittees, analysis becomes a doable job. In addition, all staff members have a stake in looking at the data because they took part in pulling it together.

Whole staff involvement. Another challenging but critical element to the success of this process is having the whole staff review the data and perform the analyses. Allowing a district-level staff person to analyze and summarize the data and then tell staff what has to change will not result in a powerful professional learning experience for staff. Nor will it gain the improvements that can come when everyone realizes what must change to get different results. A district person can organize and graph the data, but the staff must review the data and come up with meaningful implications. When staff members review the data, they see different things in the data; that diversity of viewpoint is why they all need to be a part of the review. The process leads all staff members to see, at the same time, the things that have to change. Staff involvement is much more likely to lead to implementation and real improvement.

Focus on continuous improvement. With high-stakes accountability, it is easy to fall prey to the practice of locating gaps and focusing all planning efforts on closing those gaps. With this comprehensive approach of looking at all the data, staff will see the system and be able to consider how to move all students forward at the same time. Addressing all of the gaps in a system is only possible with a comprehensive approach. Additionally, the comprehensive data analysis sets schools up for needs assessments, monitoring processes, and evaluation. Do the hard work once, but use it for everything.

Conclusion

Data analysis is a powerful professional learning tool that can lead to continuous school improvement. Professional learning that focuses on data analysis lets staff members assume leadership roles in gathering and analyzing data and gets them to look collaboratively at critical information about the whole school. The more often all staff members are involved in analyzing data, the more likely they are to get involved in implementing changes demanded by the results.

The beauty of data analysis is that it tells the story of a school. If you do not like the story, especially the ending, you can change it; but you have to know the details of the story first.

CHAPTER 10

Dialogue

Genuine dialogue strategies such as Socratic seminar help build trust, community, and shared understanding and can be used to foster professional learning related to the Common Core State Standards.

By Oscar Graybill

Rudy Garcia, principal of Horizons Elementary School, knows that the conversations in his building are not effective. He has been Horizons' principal for many years, knows his teachers well, and knows that they care about kids. He likes his teachers, and they like him. They truly are wonderful people who are friendly and hardworking. Yet, when conversations turn to fundamental beliefs about teaching and learning, teachers' resistance emerges, communication falters, and walls go up. For example, when Rudy wants them to talk about how they might embrace the six shifts of literacy in the Common Core State Standards (Common Core), no one really engages in the conversation.

Horizons has impressive mission and vision statements that Rudy and the staff created when he first arrived, but he realizes that these are just statements. He understands that the demands of the Common Core require immediate and significant changes in the beliefs of his staff. He is especially interested in having teachers talk about their beliefs so they can begin to understand the impact the Common Core will have on their instruction. He suspects that, once teachers talk about their beliefs, they'll discover that they view literacy in much the same way as the writers of the Common Core. Thus, they'll be more invested in the instructional changes that they'll need to make to implement the new standards.

Rudy has little to complain about with his staff. When push comes to shove, they do what he asks them to do. In a word, they are compliant. He, however, realizes that excellence does not happen in a culture of compliance. He wishes he could create a culture of commitment.

Rudy wants to do so much in his school. He fully embraces the new standards. He believes that all students can achieve at high levels. He believes that there is much to learn from recent brain research about how to improve instruction and student learning. He believes that instructional improvements are at the heart of the changes needed at Horizons Elementary School. He knows, however, that it is not enough for him to believe; his entire staff has to believe.

An experienced principal, Rudy knows and understands that changing beliefs about teaching and learning does not happen overnight. His district has created online learning communities, but he's not sure that they have created the conversations and community building that he knows his school needs. Frankly, he feels that too much time has been spent sitting in front of computers, and not enough time has been spent in deep, meaningful face-to-face conversations with each other. He is determined to change the culture in his building and he believes that face-to-face learning will make the difference.

Since reading *Leading for Results* by Dennis Sparks (2007), especially Chapter 10, "Genuine Dialogue," Rudy discovers a way to improve the face-to-face conversations in his building: dialogue. He decides to bring genuine dialogue into his school so that people will talk with each other, face to face, and build the relationships that determine the culture of the school. He reflects, "It is how educators talk to each other in and out of meetings that make the difference." Rudy wants his staff to share in his *aha* moment, so he decides to engage them in dialogue, reading Sparks' book together. He begins by helping his staff understand the clear differences between dialogue and debate; he also reviews some norms of collaboration, and establishes ground rules for dialogue at Horizons. Then teachers participate in two structured dialogue protocols related to Sparks' chapter on dialogue. After this session, in which they practice the norms of collaboration, his teachers are ready for the more advanced experience of a Socratic seminar.

The day before the Socratic seminar, a long-time teacher at Horizons sees Rudy and tells him, "The article you gave us to read on authentic pedagogy raises a lot of questions for me."

"I'm glad it does," Rudy responded. "I look forward to hearing your questions at tomorrow's Socratic seminar!"

"I really appreciate what you're doing to try to get us talking better with each other," the teacher said. "This staff has a lot of different personalities. It's always been so hard to get a word in edgewise. What you presented to us about getting away from debate hit home for me."

The teacher continued, "Using discussion protocols to get us to share our ideas and questions about the Sparks article on genuine dialogue felt comfortable, and I learned a lot about the ideas in the reading, about my colleagues, and what we have in common."

Rudy is eager to engage his teachers in an open dialogue using Socratic seminar, but he keeps in mind what his own trainer and coach emphasized — to trust the process and to be sure to have the group reflect on the experience. He knows conversation at Horizons already is beginning to change as a result of the dialogue on the Sparks' chapter; he knows it will continue to change with their first Socratic seminar.

Since Rudy's goal is to engage in dialogue to create shared knowledge and understanding, he chooses an educational journal article that presents the philosophy behind the Common Core. The group reviews the purpose and guidelines for Socratic seminars, and then Garcia poses this opening question: "How does the article add both clarity and uncertainty about how Common Core State Standards can increase student achievement at Horizons Elementary School?"

Rudy is pleased with how quickly engaged his teachers are as they share their thoughts about statements in the article. His staff has a history of getting into debates, but the Socratic seminar process with its emphasis on dialogue seems to defuse the tendency to debate. Teachers state ideas, ask each other questions, consider their own assumptions, and generally are open to considering others' viewpoints.

Then the physical education and art teachers speak up. They say engaging students in higher order thinking skills, as suggested by Common Core, should be part of *academic* classes, but they're not sure that asking kids to synthesize and evaluate is feasible in a *skills* class, such as art or physical education.

After a long moment of silence, another teacher poses a question of pure inquiry. "What should be the role of higher order thinking skills in our skills classes? How much do athletes and artists need to analyze, synthesize, or evaluate?" This question launches the group into a deep conversation about higher order thinking skills in both academic and skill-based classes. Around the room, people are engaged, thinking, changing their minds, and contributing new ideas.

As the Socratic seminar comes to a close and the group reflects on the experience, teachers express how comfortable they felt to disagree civilly, and that their closer listening to others' views enlarged their understanding of the ideas in the article.

Rudy Garcia realizes that the teachers had worked together to achieve the purpose of the Socratic seminar — shared knowledge and new understanding. Although they hadn't reached any conclusions or made any decisions about the role of Common Core across the curriculum, their conversation had changed. Future conversations would result in decisions and action.

Overview

Genuine dialogue is a reflective learning process in which group members seek to understand one another's viewpoints and deeply held assumptions. Genuine dialogue affects the way people think and act. With consistent practice, dialogue leads to collective meaning and shared understanding (Garmston & Wellman, 1999). While the end goal of discussion and debate is a decision, the end goal of genuine dialogue is shared understanding and team learning.

Dialogue and debate

Dialogue is significantly different from debate and

Dialogue	Discussion/Debate
See the **whole** among the parts	Break issues/problems into **parts**
See the **connections** among the parts	See **distinctions** among the parts
Inquire into assumptions	**Justify/defend** assumptions
Learn through inquiry and disclosure	**Persuade, sell, tell**
Create **shared** meaning among many	Gain agreement on **one** meaning

Source: *Dialogue: Rediscover the Transforming Power of Conversation* by Linda Ellinor and Glenna Gerard. New York: John Wiley & Sons, 1998. Used with permission.

discussion. Dialogue is collaborative, with participants who hold multiple points of view working toward shared understanding. Debate is oppositional, with participants from opposing sides trying to prove each other wrong. In dialogue, participants listen to understand, make meaning, and find common ground. In debate, participants listen to find flaws, spot differences, and counter arguments (see sidebars Dialogue and Discussion/Debate and Ways of Talking).

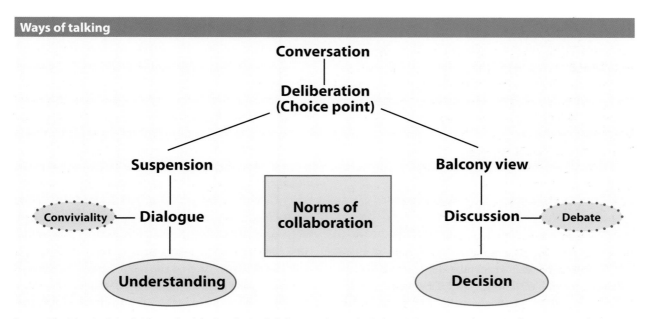

Ways of talking

Source: *The Adaptive School: A Sourcebook for Developing Collaborative Groups,* by Robert J. Garmston and Bruce Wellman. Norwood, MA: Christopher-Gordon, 1999. Used with permission.

In dialogue, participants submit their best thinking, expecting that other people's reflections will help improve rather than threaten that thinking; in debate, participants submit their best thinking and defend it against challenges to show that their thinking is right. Many people have pieces of answers in a dialogue, and cooperation can lead to a greater understanding. In debate, one person has the right answer. Dialogues respect all participants, and participants try not to alienate or offend. Debate participants rebut contrary positions and may belittle or deprecate others.

In dialogue, participants open up problems, issues, or topics, getting as many new and different perspectives and viewpoints as possible. Discussion or debate narrows the conversation to one idea, perspective, or viewpoint.

Purpose and qualities of dialogue

Dialogue serves the dual purpose of developing shared understanding and helping individuals to clarify personal thinking to ground their actions. Effectively facilitated dialogue leads to shared understanding that is the foundation for conflict resolution, consensus, and community. When group members feel left out or have their ideas discounted by the group, decisions often don't stay made. Dialogue gives voice to all parties and all viewpoints (Garmston & Wellman, 1999).

General qualities of dialogue are:
1. Suspension of judgment;
2. Release of the need for specific outcomes;
3. An inquiry into and examination of underlying assumptions;
4. Authenticity;
5. A slower pace with silence between speakers;
6. Listening deeply to oneself, others, and for collective meaning (Ellinor & Gerard, 1998).

The heart of dialogue is a simple but profound capacity to listen. Stephen R. Covey (1989) reminded readers of the importance of listening in his national bestseller *The Seven Habits of Highly Effective People*. Habit 5, "Seek first to understand, then to be understood," suggests that listening first is the key to improving communication. The practice of dialogue encourages participants to learn to listen to each other. Listening to each other is important, yet difficult. William Isaacs (1999) aptly describes this challenge:

"Listening requires we not only hear the words, but also embrace, accept, and gradually let go of our own inner clamoring" (p. 83). Regular practice of dialogue requires intentional and repeated work in becoming a better listener to each other — and to oneself.

Forms of dialogue

There are two main forms of dialogue: planned (includes structured and open) and spontaneous.

Planned dialogue. Planned dialogue simply means that people know in advance that the intended type of conversation is dialogue rather than discussion or debate. Planned dialogue is distinguished by its use of specific ground rules, guidelines, or protocols that all participants are expected to adhere to. Because its communication and expectations are clear, school leaders who announce in advance that a meeting will be a dialogue — and carry through on that promise — earn the respect and trust of their staffs. Planned dialogue may be either structured or open.

Structured dialogue. Structured dialogue is a type of planned dialogue that uses protocols (see "Chapter 17: Online Protocols" in this book). The value of protocols is that they direct who talks and for how long. Protocols often determine the type of questions and comments to be made when it is a person's time to speak. A protocol creates a structure that makes it safe for people to ask challenging questions of each other; it also ensures some equity and parity in terms of how each person's issues are attended to.

Using protocols helps people with little experience in dialogue achieve many of the benefits of dialogue without formal training. For example, one quality of dialogue is to slow the pace of conversation with periods of silence between speakers. Many people find this difficult to do when first attempting dialogue. Strictly adhering to the guidelines of a protocol requires that participants listen deeply to others, practice pausing and silence, and slow down the pace of the conversation. Paradoxically, with structure, participants experience the freedom to honestly express themselves.

Open dialogue. Open dialogue, the second form of planned dialogue, has benefits and challenges not present in structured dialogue. While there are clear expectations and ground rules for an open dialogue, there are no strict guidelines that determine how much or when a person talks. The intent of open dialogue is for participants to experience all the qualities of dialogue but through a free flow of conversation with questions and comments from everyone. One of the most powerful open dialogue formats is the Socratic seminar (see sidebar Socratic seminar).

Some of the major benefits of open dialogue are the diversity of comments and questions that surface from a large group, the new understandings and connections that emerge, and the sense of community and shared understanding that grow. While everyone is made aware of the goal and guidelines of the dialogue, people new to dialogue find it challenging to follow the guidelines.

Spontaneous dialogue. Spontaneous dialogue comes to those who regularly practice structured and open dialogue. In one sense, spontaneous dialogue is the ultimate goal and benefit of regularly practicing dialogue. Many of the most important conversations in schools are unplanned. In schools, as in life, people cannot always anticipate when an important conversation will take place. Students, parents, staff, or community members often just "show up at the door." In such spontaneous moments, genuine dialogue can be the most important skill to practice. Practicing dialogue allows people to look for common ground, to listen closely to others, to suspend judgments, to surface assumptions for examination, and to step back and consider the whole picture.

Rationale

Human beings want to be heard, understood, and valued. Schools where administrators, teachers, students, parents, and community members are heard, understood, and valued are places where trust grows. As trust grows, so does shared understanding and professional community.

Faculty members must trust each other before they can agree on shared mission, vision, values, and goals — all characteristics of professional learning communities (DuFour & Eaker, 1998). Effectively developing shared mission, vision, values, and goals starts with establishing shared understanding. Dialogue is the foundation for this work. Dialogue creates shared understanding by honoring, respecting, and supporting people as they reexamine long-held beliefs and assumptions. Dialogue requires that people think together

Socratic seminar

The Socratic seminar is a highly motivating form of intellectual and scholarly discourse facilitated with students or adults. Socratic seminars usually last from 30 to 90 minutes. Socratic seminars grew out of the early work of Mortimer Adler and the Paideia program (Roberts, 1998). The goals of a Socratic seminar are collective inquiry and shared understanding through dialogue.

Participants in Socratic seminar create dialogue and, therefore, engage in fostering active learning, critical thinking, and shared understanding; they explore and evaluate the ideas, issues, and values in a particular article, chapter, or book. A Socratic seminar is always text-based, which distinguishes it from discussion protocols.

An effective seminar consists of four interdependent elements: the text being considered; the questions raised; the seminar leader; and the participants.

The text. A seminar text can be drawn from a story, article, chapter, or book in literature, history, science, math, health, philosophy, education, or from works of art or music. Socratic seminar is perfect for dialogue.

The question. An opening question has no right answer; instead it reflects the leader's genuine curiosity. A good opening question has no single or "right" answer, but is framed to generate discussion. An effective opening question leads participants back to the text as they speculate, evaluate, define, and clarify the concepts and ideas present. Responses to the opening question generate new questions from the leader and participants, leading to new responses. In this way, the line of inquiry evolves on the spot rather than being predetermined by the leader.

The leader. In a Socratic seminar, the leader plays a dual role as leader and participant. The seminar leader consciously demonstrates habits of mind that lead to thoughtful exploration of the ideas in the text (see Online Resource 10.10). As a seminar participant, the leader actively engages in the group's exploration of the text.

The participants. In a Socratic seminar, participants and the leader share responsibility for the seminar's quality. Effective seminars occur when participants closely study the text in advance, listen actively, share their ideas and questions in response to the ideas and questions of others, and search for evidence in the text to support their ideas.

in relationship as they listen to one another. People learn to no longer take their own position as final. They relax their grip on certainty and listen closely and deeply to the possibilities that come from simply being in relationship with others, possibilities that might not otherwise have occurred (Isaacs, 1999).

Linda Ellinor and Glenna Gerard (1998) point out that,

As dialogue is practiced over time, we discover (1) greater levels of authenticity showing up; (2) better decisions being made; and (3) improved morale and alignment forming around shared work. More personal initiative and leadership are exercised outside of the formal hierarchy. As people begin to see more of the whole of what is being accomplished together, they each see where he/she can add more value. People stop waiting for someone else to tell them what to do. (p. 18)

Peter Senge and colleagues (2002) emphasize that dialogue is the most important element in creating a professional culture that truly learns and improves. Dialogue encourages deeper learning, shared knowledge, and shared understanding. The more dialogue is practiced, the stronger the sense of community by those involved. In short, genuine dialogue is what makes a professional learning community.

Stages and steps

Genuine dialogue is best achieved by having participants engage in a series of planned conversations, starting with structured dialogue protocols and culminating with open dialogue, the Socratic seminar. A facilitator — the principal, another staff member, a consultant, or a trusted central office person — carefully plans this series of converstions so that participants have the opportunity to learn the fundamental skills of dialogue as they progress.

The series of planned conversations can be thought of as stages of development. Within each stage, the facilitator helps participants go through a series of steps to learn and practice dialogue skills and then participate in a dialogue itself. As much as possible, the facilitator should adhere to the given time limits for each step.

STAGE 1: Learning and practicing dialogue skills

Step 1: Prepare the room and divide the group
(5–10 minutes)

Arrange for a room that is large enough to hold the number of participants expected in groups of four.

Divide staff members into groups of four so that both paired conversations and small group conversations can be quickly and easily assigned. If groups of four are not easily divisible, several groups larger or smaller also can work well.

Step 2: Provide an introduction to and rationale for dialogue (10–20 minutes)

Use the overview and rationale in this chapter to help participants recognize that genuine dialogue can make conversations more productive.

Step 3: Present ways of talking (10 minutes)

Give each participant a copy of Online Resource 10.1: *Ways of talking*. Have participants talk in pairs or trios for five minutes, paraphrasing for each other what they read.

Step 4: Guide group members' understanding of dialogue and debate (15–20 minutes)

Give each participant a copy of Online Resource 10.2: *Dialogue and debate*. Emphasize that, according to the *Ways of talking* in Step 3, debate is an extreme form of discussion. The differences between dialogue and *discussion* may be less obvious, but this activity will help participants detect even fine differences between the two types of conversation.

Ask the same pairs (or trios) as in Step 3 to take a minute to scan the two columns. One member of each pair or trio should choose a sentence from either column to begin the paraphrasing process. After that member has paraphrased one of the sentences, the other member should paraphrase the paired sentence from the other column. Continue with one member of a pair or trio paraphrasing either a dialogue or a debate sentence and the other(s) paraphrasing the paired sentence. The facilitator keeps time and moves the pairs from sentence to sentence.

At the end of this process, group members might decide on the most personally meaningful pair of sentences, the pair that might be most helpful in remembering how dialogue and debate are different.

Step 5: Review the seven norms of collaborative work (10–15 minutes)

Provide each participant with a list of the seven norms of collaborative work (see Online Resource 10.3: *The seven norms of collaborative work*). Have the pairs and trios from the previous two steps paraphrase to each other their understanding of these norms. Remind the group members that these norms help foster both dialogue and discussion.

Step 6: Establish a sample set of agreements for dialogue (10–15 minutes)

In the initial stages of learning about and starting to practice dialogue skills, it may be helpful to provide a sample set of agreements and ask that participants follow them (see Online Resource 10.4: *A sample set of agreements for dialogue*). Review each point and clarify any misunderstandings or questions.

As a group grows in its understanding and use of dialogue, the group can create its own unique set of ground rules. To develop ground rules with a more experienced group, use a process (see Online Resource 10.5: *Forming ground rules*).

Step 7: Practice easier forms of structured dialogue (75–95 minutes; varies)

Use the following two protocols sequentially to practice structured dialogue.

The Final Word Protocol (10 minutes to read; 30 minutes for the protocol): Give each member of the group a copy of Chapter 10 of Dennis Sparks' book, *Leading for Results* (2007) about genuine dialogue (see Online Resource 10.6: *Use genuine dialogue* for an excerpt). Have each member silently read this chapter and highlight key passages.

Use the Final Word Protocol (see Online Resource 10.7: *The Final Word Protocol*) to engage staff members in their first structured dialogue. It is best to introduce this process by having one timekeeper/facilitator for the entire group so that all groups start and finish at the same time.

Three Levels of Text (35–45 minutes, depending on the number of participants): This is the next protocol to try with an article, chapter, or book before engaging in open dialogue (see Online Resource 10.8:

The Three Levels of Text Protocol). Select an article or chapter about the Common Core State Standards that does not encourage participants to take sides on an issue. Text selection is important. When groups are first learning the qualities of dialogue and are practicing dialogue skills — especially suspending one's beliefs and surfacing assumptions for examination and evaluation — dialogue is more difficult if participants have a history with or are passionate about the text.

This protocol gives participants experience in aspects of open dialogue while still providing structure so that all voices are heard.

STAGE 2: Participating in dialogue

Step 8: Host an open dialogue using the Socratic seminar process (30–90 minutes)

A well-facilitated Socratic seminar is genuine dialogue at its best. The most effective leaders of Socratic seminars have been formally trained and have experience leading Socratic seminars with a variety of people. In the absence of training in Socratic seminar leadership skills, following the guidelines for leaders of Socratic seminars (see sidebar on p. 166, Guidelines for leaders of Socratic seminars) helps a new leader facilitate a seminar that creates shared understanding. (See Online Resource 10.9: *Socratic seminar*.)

Step 9: Reflect (10–15 minutes for group and whole staff reflection)

After each dialogue session (Step 7 — both protocols — and Step 8), whether structured or open, have participants reflect on the experience. If people are too busy to reflect, they are too busy to improve. Be sure that each group reflects on such questions as:

- *What did you find to be the best part of this protocol?*
- *What did you find to be your least favorite part of this protocol?*
- *What would you consider changing about this protocol that would better encourage dialogue?*

Variations

Dialogue protocols can be applied to the examination of issues and group learning in various formats.

Guidelines for leaders of Socratic seminars

Before the Socratic seminar:

1. Announce in advance to participants that they will engage in a Socratic seminar. Remind them that a Socratic seminar is an open dialogue conversation aimed at shared understanding and professional learning and not a format for making decisions.
2. Select an appropriate and engaging text and provide it in advance for participants to read.
3. Develop an opening question. (See Online Resource 10.11: *Forming good opening questions.*)
4. If the group is larger than 35 participants, decide whether to include everyone in the work of the seminar. With groups as large as 100, consider having an inner circle of participants and outer circle of observers for the first half of the time, then switch.
5. Arrange for space and furniture. Ideally, everyone is seated in a circle at tables and chairs. Groups of 35 or more may not need tables and chairs if participants can be in a circle facing one another.
6. Provide name tents or tags for all participants.

Starting the Socratic seminar:

1. Welcome everyone.
2. Distribute and review Socratic seminar ground rules before opening the seminar. (See Online Resource 10.9: *Socratic seminar.*) Remind participants that the goal is shared understanding, not a decision or agreement.
3. Allow participants a brief time to review or reread the text.
4. Present the opening question on a projection screen or on large chart paper for all to see during the seminar.
5. Ask participants to spend five minutes talking with a partner next to them in the circle (or an outer circle participant) about the opening question.
6. After five minutes, invite everyone in the Socratic seminar to share thoughts, ideas, and questions around the opening question.

During the Socratic seminar:

1. Model qualities of dialogue.
2. Model habits of mind (see Online Resource 10.10: *Habits of mind*).
3. While participants should not look to the leader to decide who speaks, be prepared to offer time to quiet participants and to ask the dominant participants to allow others to speak.
4. Stay with the text.
5. If needed, follow answers with another question, building on the answer just given.
6. Rephrase questions, if necessary, until they are understood.
7. Wait three to five seconds, or even longer, for participants to reply to questions; thinking is OK.
8. Draw out from participants the reasons for and the implications of their answers.
9. Insist that answers be clear and adequately explained.
10. Do not insist on agreement in matters of opinion; encourage participants to discuss differences.
11. Take a stand to provoke genuine disagreement, but not to start an argument. Stay open. Remember what was said of Sen. Robert Taft: "He had the best mind in the Senate, until he made it up."
12. Remember that there is no need to reach resolution, compromise, synthesis, or closure.
13. Recognize listening as a form of participation.

After the Socratic seminar:

Provide a personal and collective reflection on the process. Possible questions to address:
   a. How well did we, as a group, follow the guidelines or agreements?
   b. Which quality of dialogue did we best achieve, and which did we have the most trouble achieving?
   c. How could we have improved the Socratic seminar?

Book study. The dialogue process may be centered around reading an entire book. Book study is more than reading and discussing material in a group. To deeply study a selection means to examine closely, carefully analyze, deliberate, and question. Book study occurs over a period of time (as much as a year), sometimes a chapter at a time. A book study is, in fact, a series of genuine dialogues.

Dialogue without texts. Another variation is to hold structured dialogue protocols without any written texts. Powerful and rich dialogue can result from interactions without texts. Check the website of the National School Reform Faculty, www.harmonyschool.org, for hundreds of protocols. Also see the website of the School Reform Initiative (www.schoolreforminitiative.org).

Examining student work. Another variation is to use dialogue protocols to examine student work. The use of the Tuning Protocol, described in the second edition of this book, is one such method. Also see "Chapter 17: Online Protocols" in this book. The interaction that participants have during the participant discussion in the Tuning Protocol usually takes the form of a dialogue.

Challenges and how to address them

Facilitators of Socratic seminars may encounter certain challenges, which they can address with training, practice, and resources such as committed leaders and sufficient time.

Training and practice. Leading planned dialogue — either structured or open — is a skill best learned through training and practice. The leadership skills necessary for powerful Socratic seminars, particularly, come from training, practice, and experience.

An appropriate text or topic. Engaging people in structured or open dialogue depends on providing readings on topics that elicit deep thought and meaningful conversations. Yet, for people to openly share their beliefs and assumptions, they must feel safe. Starting with topics and readings that are interesting and provocative without being threatening provides needed comfort and safety for group members to start learning the skills of dialogue.

Willing leaders. Genuine dialogue affects a school's culture. The resulting power shift breaks down traditional, hierarchical leadership. Leaders who value having the last say will discover dialogue does not support this stance. Leaders also must consider that topics and ideas presented in dialogues could be viewed as criticisms of the leader's previous behaviors. Leaders must let go of their defensiveness as dialogue takes hold in the school. Additionally, an announced dialogue sometimes turns into an emotional debate with little collective inquiry and shared understanding, even if participants have experienced many successful dialogues. Leaders must remain committed to staying on the path of dialogue. Tremendous growth occurs after unplanned debate when leaders take the group through an honest reflection on the debate to explore how the next dialogue can be improved. Dialogue is about the leadership of ideas.

Time. Learning and practicing dialogue takes time. Schools that understand and value the benefits of a culture of shared understanding do not find the time; they make the time for teachers to practice structured and open dialogue. Schools must place a high value on creating and maintaining shared understanding; otherwise, investing the time in dialogue yields no benefits.

Conclusion

The practice of genuine dialogue transforms the way people talk, relate to, and understand each other. The promise of powerful professional learning is realized in schools where educators engage in genuine dialogue as they study books, share ideas, and examine issues important to all. While the qualities of dialogue can be applied to online conversations like blogs and forums, using dialogue regularly in the face-to-face professional learning conversations in a school yields shared understanding that can lead to common vision, mission, and goals. Genuine dialogue focuses participants on meaningful conversation and is a practice that can be learned, rehearsed, and improved upon in all schools.

Today's educators face important decisions. The Common Core State Standards require changes to teaching and learning that not all staff members fully understand and realize. The practice of genuine dialogue can be instrumental in increasing understanding of content standards as individuals work together to create a shared vision of powerful learning for all kids. The trust and shared understandings of genuine dialogue transform teaching and

ADDITIONAL RESOURCES

Articles

"Socratic Seminars: Engaging students in intellectual discourse," by Linda Tredway. *Educational Leadership, 53*(1), 26–29.

Books

The Constructivist Leader (2nd ed.), by Linda Lambert, Deborah Walker, Diane P. Zimmerman, and Joanne E. Cooper. Foreword by Maxine Greene. New York, NY: Teachers College Press, 2002.

Crucial Conversations: Tools for Talking When Stakes are High, by Kerry Patterson, Joseph Grenny, Ron McMillan, and Al Switzler. New York, NY: McGraw-Hill, 2002.

Dialogue: The Art of Thinking Together, by William Isaacs. New York, NY: Doubleday, 1999.

The Dialogue Game, by Peter Gryffon Winchell. San Rafael, CA: The Invisible Press, 2006.

The Different Drum: Community Making and Peace, by M. Scott Peck. New York, NY: Touchstone, 1987.

The Habit of Thought: From Socratic seminars to Socratic Practice, by Michael Strong. Chapel Hill, NC: New View Publications, 1996.

Leadership and the New Science: Discovering Order in a Chaotic World, by Margaret J. Wheatley. San Francisco, CA: Berrett-Koehler, 1999.

On Dialogue, by David Bohm. New York, NY: Routledge, 1990.

The Performance Assessment Handbook, Portfolios and Socratic Seminars: Designs from the Field and Guidelines for the Territory Ahead, by Bil Johnson. Larchmont, NY: Eye on Education, 1996.

Socrates Café: A Fresh Taste of Philosophy, by Christopher Phillips. New York, NY: W. W. Norton, 2002.

Socratic Seminars in the Block, by Wanda H. Ball and Pam Larchmont Brewer. Larchmont, NY: Eye on Education, 2000.

Turning to One Another: Simple Conversations to Restore Hope to the Future, by Margaret J. Wheatley. San Francisco: Berrett-Koehler, 2002.

Websites

www.nsrfharmony.org. The National School Reform Faculty offers a variety of protocols under its quick links to practice facilitation skills.

www.schoolreforminitiative.org. School Reform Initiative provides information about Critical Friends Groups, protocols, and other reform issues.

http://socraticseminars.com. Socratic Seminars International provides additional information about Socratic seminars, dialogue leadership, and best practices.

http://ncdd.org. National Coalition for Dialogue and Deliberation provides information, news, blogs, and perspectives to foster higher-level conversations.

learning in ways that result in higher achievement for all students.

References

Covey, S.R. (1989). *The seven habits of highly effective people.* New York, NY: Simon & Schuster.

DuFour, R. & Eaker, R. (1998). *Professional learning communities at work: Best practices for enhancing student achievement.* Bloomington, IN: Solution Tree.

Ellinor, L. & Gerard, G. (1998). *Dialogue: Rediscover the transforming power of conversation.* New York, NY: John Wiley & Sons.

Garmston, R.J. & Wellman, B. (1999). *The adaptive school: A sourcebook for developing collaborative groups.* Norwood, MA: Christopher-Gordon.

Isaacs, W. (1999). *Dialogue: The art of thinking together.* New York, NY: Doubleday.

Roberts, T. (1998). *The power of Paideia schools: Defining lives through learning.* Alexandria, VA: ASCD.

Senge, P.M., Cambron-McCabe, N., Lucas, T., Smith, B., Dutton, J., & Kleiner, A. (2000). *Schools that learn: A fifth discipline fieldbook for educators, parents, and everyone who cares about education.* New York, NY: Crown Business.

Sparks, D. (2007). *Leading for results: Transforming teaching, learning, and relationships in schools* (2nd ed.). Thousand Oaks, CA: Corwin Press.

ONLINE RESOURCES

10.1 Ways of talking
10.2 Dialogue and debate
10.3 The seven norms of collaborative work
10.4 A sample set of agreements for dialogue
10.5 Forming ground rules
10.6 Use genuine dialogue
10.7 The Final Word Protocol
10.8 The Three Levels of Text Protocol
10.9 Socratic seminar
10.10 Habits of mind
10.11 Forming good opening questions

CHAPTER 11

Digital Teacher Portfolios

Collect, select, and reflect: Using portfolios to demonstrate
your vision of an effective educator.

By David Niguidula

There are moments when you just know that what you're doing is working. At Sousa Elementary School in Port Washington, New York, two third graders were looking at the work they had done as part of a science unit. In front of a video camera, one student was interviewing the other, and asked, "Brad, can you describe your illustration to me?" Brad motioned to his drawing of a rainforest scene, and pointed out trees and flowers in the picture. Then, the moment hit: Brad said, "My favorite part is this. It was very hard to observe and I never knew I would do something this good."

The moment takes less than 10 seconds of online video. But the moment represents the culmination of a years-long process involving interdisciplinary curriculum, principal leadership, teacher professional development, community partnerships, grant proposal writing and logistics. Getting

Brad to that moment of insight — about something that he had learned AND about his own abilities — is what all of us who work in schools are trying to achieve. This video is a terrific example of the kind of work that should go into a student portfolio; the work that led to this moment is what belongs in a professional portfolio.

Consider Dave Meoli, the principal of Sousa Elementary School. Like many educators, he recently found himself trying to figure out how to comply with his state's new educator evaluation system. In this case, it is New York State's Annual Professional Performance Review (APPR). New York's system has multiple components, many of which are determined locally. The administration within Dave's small district convened many meetings to figure out how to comply with the regulations in a way that wouldn't drive them crazy. It was clear that the new process was going to be demanding, so the administrators (including the seven principals) decided to go first. They would create their own portfolios — evidence of their work as "effective" educators (to use the state's language). This year, the administrators would experience the evaluation process before asking teachers to go through the same process next year. Dave took it one step further, volunteering to create his portfolio digitally.

Dave thought about the work he had been doing as a principal and an educator. He considered what was going to demonstrate the standards — in his particular case, standards set by the state, expectations set by the district — and professional goals that he set himself. He also considered the audience; in this case, the evaluator (his boss, the superintendent), but also his colleagues who might provide some peer guidance.

One compelling piece of evidence that demonstrated many of these standards was a project called "Drawn to Science." Dave had written the grant proposal for this project. In essence, it brought artists-in-residence to his school's classrooms, where they would develop — and co-teach — a set of units with elementary classroom teachers. The units addressed different topics, from the change of the seasons to the skeletal system of the human body, all of which came from the district's curriculum maps. What the units would have in common is a unifying essential question: "How do we observe?" The notion of observation is critical to both scientific and artistic endeavors; by addressing these topics at the same time, students would be able to combine multiple intelligences and improve their skills as both artists and scientists. Thus, the "Drawn to Science" project became a candidate piece of evidence for Dave's portfolio.

Dave gathered the artifacts related to "Drawn to Science." This included the original grant proposal; documents from the professional development activities he led with the teachers; correspondence with the artists; the original curriculum maps from the district; and the actual student work. In this last case, it helped that the school was already engaged in creating digital *student* portfolios. Some of the teachers had scanned student artwork or taken video of students discussing what they did in class. The pieces Dave gathered included some terrific "before" and "after" examples, such as a first grader's illustration of a leaf prior to the unit (which essentially looked like an oval with a single,

straight line representing the stem) and the same student's detailed composition of a leaf after the unit (where the leaf now had contours, symmetry, and there was purpose behind each line and curve).

Dave uploaded these pieces to his online portfolio. He then needed to reflect on this work. First, Dave decided which standards this unit demonstrated. He linked the work to state Domain #2: School Culture and Instructional Program (Strategic Planning) and to several District Goals for Teaching and Learning ("Implement effective teaching strategies to engage and challenge all students," "Enhance instruction through the integration of technology," and "Support ongoing professional development to strengthen teaching and maximize student learning"). Then, Dave wrote a short narrative including captions for the specific pieces of work and a general reflection about what this unit meant to him, visiting artists, teachers, and students.

Dave continued this process of collecting, selecting, and reflecting on his work throughout the year. The standards provided a framework for the data he collected; he knew he would have to find demonstrations of each of the state and district expectations. Dave gathered different pieces, including work from faculty meetings, strategies for introducing new policies to the school, and communication with parents. The portfolio process makes educators more conscious of documenting activities. All three parts of the portfolio process, but especially the reflection part, helped Dave learn through examination of his own practice as a principal.

In all, Dave added 20 entries to his portfolio, linking to all six of the state's Domains and all seven of the district's Goals for Teaching and Learning. Since the portfolio was digital, entries could be linked to multiple goals and domains; the page for State Domain #3 could list some of the same entries as the page for District Goal #4. The reflections showed how the entries demonstrated each domain or goal.

During the spring, Dave presented his portfolio to the superintendent. Some of the evidence in the portfolio was already familiar to the superintendent; other entries were new. By displaying artifacts, such as animations, scanned student work, and video (including Brad's insight), Dave was able to paint a richer picture of his overall work, and thus provide the superintendent a more rational basis for assessing his skills and providing feedback. He also had created a sample that both the teachers in his building and the other principals in his district could use as a model for their own digital portfolios.

After Dave completed his portfolio, he shared it with his staff members so they could begin preparing their own portfolios. They discussed their visions of what makes an effective teacher, and Dave shared his process of collecting, selecting, and reflecting on their best work — ideas that you can read about later in this chapter. As the teachers began to document their work, Dave was able to guide them thoughtfully, since he had done it himself.

Overview

A digital teacher portfolio is a *purposeful* collection of a teacher's (or principal's) professional work. It's tempting to think of a digital portfolio as simply an online folder of work, and certainly there are organizations that define portfolios that way. The word "purposeful" is the key; the entries in the portfolio are there to achieve some purpose or to tell a specific story. The purpose needs to focus on teachers' improvement; as educators engage in the portfolio process, they enhance their own professional learning. Otherwise, it isn't a portfolio; it's a scrapbook.

Figure 1: **Cover Page for Digital Teacher Portfolio**

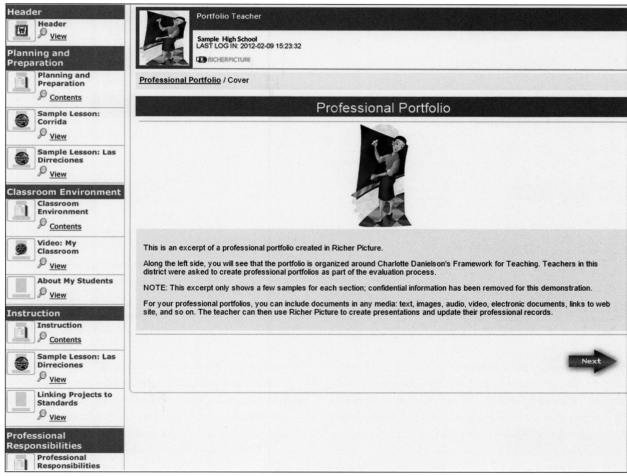

Source: Created with Richer Picture software, copyright 2013 Ideas Consulting, Inc. Used with permission.

Organization of contents

Typically, a portfolio is organized around a set of standards or expectations. One common set of expectations comes from Charlotte Danielson's *Framework for Teaching* (Danielson, 2007), which lists four broad categories:

1. Planning and Preparation;
2. Classroom Environment;
3. Instruction; and
4. Professional Responsibilities.

These four categories can apply to administrative portfolios, too, but administrators in a district may want to work together to devise their own categories. The four items in this list suggest that the portfolio has four sections in which educators can demonstrate their abilities. Of course, these categories break down into parts, but it helps to have a list of categories that an educator can keep in short-term memory. Figure 1: Cover Page for Digital Teacher Portfolio on page 173 shows the cover page from a sample digital teacher portfolio. Note that the contents of the portfolio are listed on the left side with each section corresponding to the four categories from the framework.

Figure 2: **Contents Page for One Section of Digital Teacher Portfolio**

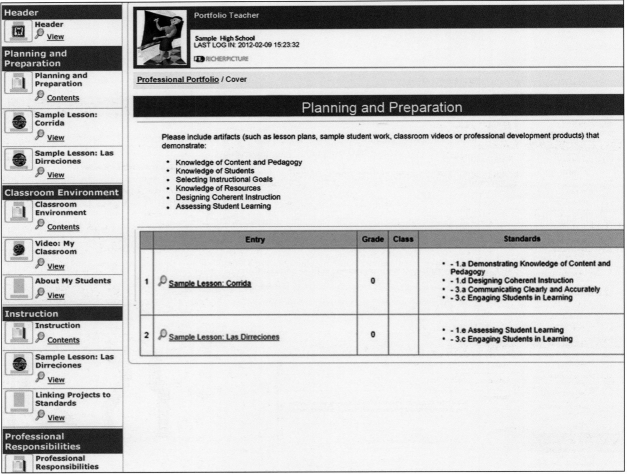

Source: Created with Richer Picture software, copyright 2013 Ideas Consulting, Inc. Used with permission.

Contents

Within each section, educators add entries to demonstrate their skills. Thus, each section typically has a contents page, listing the entries within it (see Figure 2 on p. 174).

In teachers' portfolios, the entries include any documents that help illustrate their work. In a digital form, of course, these documents can be in any medium that makes sense: video, audio, links to websites or blogs, scanned images, or even word processed documents. For example, to demonstrate an effective classroom environment teachers have used simple video technology, such as a camera phone, to show how they have decorated their classroom walls. One teacher stood in the middle of the room, and while taking a 360-degree video, simply talked about the significance of each wall's displays. Figure 3 shows a different sample entry; in this case, the entry includes both teacher slides and sample student work.

The left side of this teacher portfolio page contains an overview, including the summary and goals met by the entry; the right side shows screen shots from a teacher's slide presentation and sample student work.

Entries can be linked to multiple standards. A description of an effective classroom unit could easily demonstrate specific goals within both "Planning and Preparation" and "Instruction." In the digital teacher portfolio, that entry should appear in the contents page for both sections, but it can link to the same entry, so the entry only needs to be added once.

Each entry can have several components:

- A **summary** is a brief description of the entry. This is just a factual description of what the entry contains, such as, "This entry describes my English 11 unit on Greek mythology. Students read several myths, submitted an

Figure 3: **Sample Entry from Digital Teacher Portfolio**

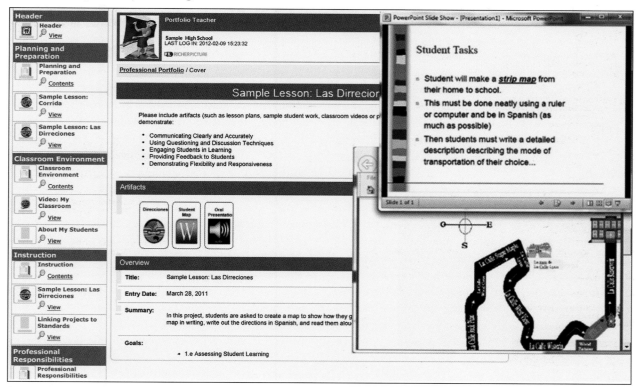

Source: Created with Richer Picture software, copyright 2013 Ideas Consulting, Inc. Used with permission.

in-class paper about what they read, engaged in class discussions, and worked in groups to create a video about a myth of their own creation."

- The **artifacts** are the actual documents. In the case of the Greek mythology entry, the artifacts could include the assignment issued by the teacher, a link to the actual myths, and sample work done by the students (see Steps later in this chapter for more information about artifacts).

- Entries should contain the list of **standards** that are demonstrated by the artifacts. Most states have student and teacher standards and, if the entry in a teacher portfolio is a lesson or teaching unit, most teachers will identify both the student standards (such as the Common Core) and the teacher standards that the lesson or unit addresses. Many states now have administrator standards, which administrators would reference in their portfolio entries. As noted above, the list can come from multiple standard categories; that is, any one entry can be used to demonstrate many standards.

- All portfolios need to contain **reflections** from their creators: teachers or administrators. There are two typical ways to set up the reflections: one is to include a brief reflection for each entry, through which the educator describes how the artifacts demonstrate the selected standards. Another is to have a reflection for each *category of standards,* through which the educator describes how the body of evidence in this section of the portfolio shows the overall level of skill in this area.

Review

An effective portfolio system isn't just about the educator assembling work into an online form. The early research on digital portfolios in K–12 schools (Niguidula, 1998) indicated that the most critical component of a portfolio system isn't the specific technology or portfolio structure; it's the feedback. In a school setting where time is at a premium, educators need a compelling reason to take on any additional tasks. If they take the time to assemble thoughtful, reflective portfolios, educators are going to want more than a perfunctory check mark on some form. The value of the portfolio as a strategy for improving education depends on the value of the feedback educators receive for their efforts.

Many lists of professional standards, such as the Danielson framework or those issued by state departments of education, include rubrics. As educators assemble the work for the portfolio, they can use a rubric to help decide what entries will be most relevant, and which components of the artifacts they should highlight. The rubric can also guide the reviewer (principals, supervisors, or peers) through the portfolio, providing a structure for what to look for, and to determine whether the entries are meeting the expectations.

Marks on a rubric, however, are not enough to constitute a review. Since portfolios are often reviewed once a year (and sometimes, even less frequently), the review should provide an opportunity for discussion between the educator and the reviewer. This discussion can focus on the educator's growth, how the evidence in the portfolio demonstrates educator's strengths, and the areas where the educator could use more effort.

It's worth noting that this process is called a "review" rather than an "evaluation." There is no doubt that digital portfolios can be useful in the teacher or administrator evaluation process, and indeed, there are schools that are using them very effectively. At the same time, recent developments have made the evaluation process, at least in certain states and districts in the U.S., cumbersome and politically fraught. In terms of teacher evaluation, even some of the administrators most admired for improving teacher skills are finding themselves overwhelmed with the demands of these new evaluation systems.

All of these trends suggest that the supervisor need not be the only person conducting the review. Peers can be involved in reviews of digital teacher portfolios within a professional learning community (PLC) setting, using any of a number of protocols, some of which can be found elsewhere in this volume, or in selected resources (McDonald, Mohr, Dichter, & McDonald, 2007 or Easton, 2009). Whether to include peer review in the formal evaluation is an issue for each school and district to address; in some situations de-coupling the review from the evaluation can lower the stakes associated with the portfolio. Still, no matter who reviews the portfolio, the process should be a time for reflective, thoughtful conversations. The structure of a digital portfolio can help push the process in that direction.

Rationale

At the fall meeting to launch teacher portfolios, Dave shared with his staff some good reasons for instituting teacher portfolios. Teachers are expected to assume many roles: professionals who have a passion for their craft, coaches who can extract performances (in any subject) from their students, effective communicators with parents, enforcers of policies...and the list goes on. Helping students understand and learn requires teachers to understand their subjects as well as have a talent for working with children and adolescents. Teaching requires a complex set of skills, and inevitably each teacher is stronger in some skills than others.

Digital portfolios offer a way for teachers to reflect on where they are effective, and where they can improve. They are tools for self-reflection, so that teachers can tell their own stories; they are also tools for provoking professional conversations, so that educators can get feedback. The portfolio process exemplifies the best type of professional learning because it is personally relevant, embedded in practice, action-oriented, and engages educators in the collection and use of data.

Earlier research on digital portfolios (Niguidula, 1997; Niguidula, 2010), establishes a set of essential questions that schools can address to make portfolio development more worthwhile for teachers and administrators. Dave used these questions related to vision, evidence, and review to help Sousa teachers understand more about the powerful reasons for engaging in portfolio development and feedback processes.

Vision: What makes an effective educator?

The portfolio system needs to be guided by a vision of an "effective" teacher — but what does that term mean? Glib answers such as "one who gets kids to learn" are not helpful to teachers who want to improve. A different question can guide the definition of effectiveness: How do teachers get students to learn in this specific situation? Context matters; the environment of the school (and, indeed, the environment and individuals within any given classroom) determines the priorities of teachers and students. Thus, the whole faculty should begin the process of defining effectiveness by considering the critical skills, knowledge and attitudes that are most important to create and promote a schoolwide vision of *effective*. Then, individual educators, in their specific roles, may need to establish personal goals for the coming term,

year or decade. Addressing the essential question of "What makes an effective teacher/principal?" provides clarity to the entire portfolio endeavor — and in turn, focuses the portfolio process on the most important aspects of educator work.

Evidence: How do teachers and principals show that they are fulfilling that vision?

For too long, the education community has relied on essentially two pieces of evidence for evaluating teachers: officially sanctioned classroom observations, and the (informally documented) number of complaints received. These criteria are a variation of what the *Shopping Mall High School* (Powell, Farrar, and Cohen, 1985) called "classroom treaties" where "little is usually expected" (p. 184); "the only common understanding is that passing...is contingent on orderly attendance rather than on mastery of anything" (p. 4). The inadequacy of these pieces of evidence has led many states in recent years to generate new teacher evaluation structures. Many states allow some form of portfolio to be a component of this evaluation.

An effective portfolio allows educators to collect, select, and reflect upon their work. The evidence of an educator's effectiveness comes from documenting the daily work in the classroom and school; this creates a more compelling view of a teacher's work than relying solely on external measures (such as test scores). In the case of teacher portfolios, teachers can collect samples from a broad set of activities, simply storing them digitally as they occur. Essentially, the portfolio stores the handouts or deliverables that the teacher already is generating or recording and allows the teacher to organize them online in one place. In addition, the teacher can describe one teaching unit in detail, showing the process of teaching from initial planning to reviewing student work.

From this collection, teachers can select a subset of these documents and reflect (in writing or on video) about how the artifacts connect to the goals. In this way, teachers are able to provide their own evidence of how they fulfill the vision.

Review: How do educators get feedback on their work?

A portfolio system isn't just about the assembling of the documents in order to "write" the portfolio; there must be an audience that is able to "read" the portfolio. The engagement between educator and reviewer provides the motivation for doing the portfolio in the first place. In order for the portfolio to be more than just "one more thing to do," reviewers need to provide feedback; and just as teachers provide feedback to students, reviewers need to think about the process of review. If the portfolios will be reviewed using rubrics, do the rubrics emphasize the right areas? Do educators receive feedback on their specific areas or interests?

In the end, the portfolio process is about providing a feedback loop for continuous improvement. Collecting, selecting, and reflecting on work — and the critical component of someone providing feedback — is worth the time if educators see it as a way to grow professionally.

Steps

Step 1: Clarify your vision

In the months following their launch of digital teacher portfolios, Dave guided Sousa teachers through the steps he had taken to develop his administrative portfolio. At the end of the year, he learned that principals of other schools in the district had used these steps to develop their own portfolios, with only the particulars changed. Here are the steps, directed toward teachers. Before educators begin creating digital teacher portfolios to demonstrate effectiveness, they need to ask, "What is our vision of an effective teacher (or administrator)?" The word "our" is important here; both the creators and the readers of the portfolio need to share this vision. It needs to be clear to both writers and readers what the portfolio will illustrate (see Online Resource 11.1: *Digital teacher portfolio samples*).

The starting point for the vision can be the state's or district's list of standards; after all, these lists are intended to describe what makes an effective teacher. However, many such lists are simply too long; with explanations and rubrics, printouts of state guiding documents can require dozens of pages. Of course, one can make an argument that every item on the state's list represents a reasonable sign of effective practice (and in fact, someone on the state's committee probably made such an argument). Practically, however, asking teachers to demonstrate every aspect of effective teaching in one short time period is like asking chefs to show their skills by preparing breakfast, lunch, dinner, and desserts simultaneously.

Thus, to clarify the vision for the portfolio, teachers and reviewers might agree to focus on a few key areas. A beginning teacher may want to focus on classroom management and creating compelling lessons; a more experienced teacher may want to focus on experimenting with new strategies, or working with different student populations. The school or district may have its priorities; for example, if improving discipline or literacy issues is a collective goal, teachers' portfolios could contain evidence of how they are contributing to achieving that goal. In any case, teachers should go into the development of the portfolio saying, "My portfolio will demonstrate what I know and am able to do in the areas of x, y, and z."

Step 2: Collect and select

The bulk of the time required for the portfolio is spent gathering evidence. Here is where the digital aspect is particularly useful. Current technologies make it easy to capture events in classrooms, and much of teachers' and students' work may already be in a digital form.

The most common entry in a digital teacher portfolio is a teaching unit. Consider which of your units is going to be a good demonstration of the teacher effectiveness standards you selected in Step 1. You probably don't want to select a unit that is simply a student review of older material; this should be an opportunity to see how teaching and learning unfolds in your classroom. Consider choosing a unit that caused you to learn as a professional and will continue to prompt your learning.

Each entry should include these components:

- **A description of the unit.** What is the topic? Where does it fit in the context of the class? How many class days are spent on this? What student standards (such as Common Core) does this unit address?

  The actual artifacts for this description might include whatever documents you share with your students (such as assignments, readings, or PowerPoint overviews), or your lesson plans (whether done as formal plans, curriculum maps, or narrative descriptions).

  The point of this artifact is to give the reader an overview of the unit, and some sense of what skills and knowledge you want the students to gain.

- **Assignments.** What will students actually produce in this unit? The assignment may be something simple (an in-class response to a reading); it may have complex parts (a complete research paper or lab report; or it may be a combination of formative assessments and group projects). Your reviewer should be able to tell what you've asked the students to do.

This section might also include some less formal assignments but still provide a sense of student activities. For example, you may have structured time at "stations" within your classroom or organized discussions in the classroom or online. Don't overlook these "casual" assignments; they can show a reviewer how you have created an environment for students to learn in multiple ways.

- **Assessment.** How do you give feedback to the students? For each assignment, you should include rubrics, scoring guides, or whatever process you use to assess the student work. How much weight you give to each item will demonstrate the priorities of the specific assignment.
- **Student work samples.** It's very useful for a reviewer to see what the students actually produce. You don't need many samples; one or two can suffice. However, if you are showing your skill as a teacher, it may not be to your advantage to show only the most brilliant example of student work. It may be more useful to the reviewer to see the work of a student who struggled a bit, or had something that needed revision.

You will want to include your assessment of this particular student's work — the completed rubric or score sheet, along with any comments that you've made. (As you are collecting the work, you can collect a range of samples; then, later, when you are selecting the specific artifacts to display to a reviewer, you can select the one or two that will lead to the best demonstration of *your* skill as a teacher.)

- **Classroom video.** Depending on the unit, it may be useful to capture some video of your classroom activities. You can show how you interact with students or use video to illustrate the process you've set up. These videos do not have to be very long; you may need only a minute or two to get the point across. Because of the logistics of the classroom, many teachers will simply set up a camera and record a whole class period. Consider, however, that a reviewer may not have time to watch

the entire video. A more effective method is to point to a particular clip (such as telling the reviewer to start at the 5 minute mark) or better yet, use a video editor to put the clips together. You don't have to be an Oscar-caliber director with your video; simple cutting and pasting with your computer's free video editing software will usually be good enough to highlight the key elements of your classroom activity.

- **A note about student work.** You may want to be cautious about how you handle the student artifacts, including any video or audio. If possible, you should see if you can remove or black out student names from any scanned documents. When dealing with students on video, you can minimize any identifying information. Much depends on how you're storing the video and audio; you don't want to simply post student video on an unprotected YouTube account. There are secure ways of using video in digital teacher portfolios, and it's a common feature of most commercial portfolio systems. Still, it helps to be aware of your school's policy (which may be as simple as getting permission from the students and their parents), and to keep those policies in mind as you collect the work.

Classroom units aren't the only types of entries you can have in your portfolio. You may also consider:

- **Pre- and post-test results.** Standardized tests have, unfortunately, become the primary indicator of student progress and of teacher effectiveness. Digital teacher portfolios can put the test scores in context, especially if you are able to indicate what the test results mean to you, and what insights, if any, you gather from these data points. Quantitative data can have its place in a portfolio, but as with all other entries, you need to make the link between the data to the goals that you are trying to demonstrate.
- **Work with individual students.** Often, the professional problem that keeps teachers up at night is how to reach a particular individual student. You can use one entry in your portfolio to tell the story of a specific issue faced by a student — how you and the student identified the issue, and how the two of you worked toward a resolution. Your ability to be a student's coach can provide powerful evidence of your effectiveness as a teacher. (Even if you don't have a specific story, you may

consider including ways you reach students individually, such as student-led conferences.)

- **Professional learning activities.** The portfolio can contain examples of your own learning. Think about the professional learning activities you participated in — whether these were part of your district's normal schedule, a formal graduate course or your work in a professional learning community. How did these activities relate to your practice? Were you able to apply your learning in your classroom or with your students? What happened? These entries do not have to be elaborate; simple descriptions of the activities, and reflections of what you learned can be enough.

- **Work you have done with other adults.** Hours that you spend in support of your school, district or department should also count as part of your professional activities. How did your contributions help your organization, as a whole? You may also be participating in communities of educators, either online or face to face. What ideas were generated from those interactions? Were you able to get feedback from your colleagues?

Clearly, just about anything you do professionally could become a useful entry. This is why you'll want to be selective about what you decide to put into your portfolio. The vision you are attempting to demonstrate (from Step 1) should help guide your selections. You may put together some entries as you go through your school year and decide later which ones will be most relevant for this year's review.

As you go through the year, make it a habit to capture at least some of your work electronically; use your camera phone to take pictures of student events or maintain a folder on your computer for the lessons and other documents you generate. Bookmark ideas you get from an Internet resource or take a screenshot of an interesting project. By documenting as you go, you will make it that much simpler to select the entries most relevant for displaying your growth.

Step 3: Reflect

Reflection is your opportunity to tie the entries you selected in Step 2 with the vision you established in Step 1 and reflect on your learning. Essentially, you can structure this section as follows. For each goal you selected in Step 1:

- What entries demonstrate your progress toward this goal?
- How do these entries, collectively, demonstrate this progress?
- What did you learn during the process of connecting what you did as an educator to goals?

For some teachers, reflection comes very easily; for others, reflection can be a chore. Teachers in the latter category might find it helpful to break down the reflection question into component pieces:

- What activity was most effective in your classroom?
- What would you do differently (or not at all) next time?
- Which students got the most (and least) out of this lesson/activity?
- What did you learn that will help you improve professionally?

Questions such as these can help some teachers articulate what worked well and what needs improvement.

The reflection is typically written, although it could also appear as a video blog or in a podcast format. The format is less important than the content. While brief, the **Reflect** step is just as important as the **Collect and select** step. The ability to use the evidence in the portfolio to demonstrate growth is a critical skill. Peer critiques and principal comments can help teachers identify what is "good" about a particular entry, and how it ties into school or district goals.

Step 4: Review

The review is critical (see pp. 176–177). In fact, the review process may determine whether educators perceive the digital portfolio as a useful professional learning design or just another thing that has to be done.

Just as any assignment for students needs to include information about how student work will be evaluated, the review process should be established before the work begins. Portfolios are built for audiences, and it's only fair that teachers and reviewers agree on what they will look for within the portfolio and agree on the rubric (or other assessment instrument) that will be used.

Even though the digital portfolio is online, most schools prefer to have their reviews take place face to face. Typically, the teacher will begin by going over the teaching effectiveness standards being addressed. For each standard, the teacher may find it useful to go over the reflection first and then go into the details of the entries. This way, the presentation stays focused on the "big picture" — how the teacher is meeting the expectations — while the actual entries are used as supporting evidence. In the other order, the conversation may get hung up on a detail of an entry that isn't the most critical indicator of the standard being addressed.

The amount of time for the presentation can vary, but in a half hour, the teacher should be able to discuss five or six entries in some detail. The presentation might be limited to 15–20 minutes, allowing the rest of the time for the reviewer to provide feedback and steps for improvement. If the review is attached to a formal evaluation, then the reviewer may need more time to look over all the required entries for the portfolio.

Ideally, the reviewer should be able to look at the portfolio ahead of time, before the reviewer and the teacher meet. The teacher may still want to do a brief presentation, highlighting certain elements of the portfolio, but given the paucity of time teachers get for actual feedback, as much time as possible should be devoted to conversation. Both the teacher and reviewer should focus on the effect of the portfolio process on the teacher's professional learning

In a peer group setting, the teachers are usually also the reviewers; that is, every member of the group will present to the others. There are a couple of ways to organize the sessions. One way is to have a session devoted to one teacher, presenting his or her portfolio to the group, and getting responses. Another strategy is to devote each session to one section of standards; for example, using the Danielson framework, one meeting will focus on "Planning and Preparation" and another on "Professional Responsibilities." In this version, each teacher in the group might have 5 minutes to present entries from this section, and then the group has 5 minutes to collectively respond. After everyone has presented, the group can discuss the qualities of entries that define a "good" demonstration of the standards. (Even better, principals or supervisors can join the peer group — and act as both presenters and reviewers.) The presenter of the portfolio will not be the only one who learns from a peer group review; participants come away from such sessions feeling as if they benefitted from the process, too.

ONLINE RESOURCE

11.1 Digital teacher portfolio samples from www.richerpicture.com

---

Variations

Some teachers are able to create portfolios for themselves, and provide their own self-reflection on their work. Self-evaluation and reflection is a terrific process for thinking about how to improve one's own practice. It may also be particularly useful to review a past portfolio to see if goals for improvement were actually accomplished. Still, the review from a colleague or a supervisor provides a different perspective.

Portfolios are by no means limited to teachers; principals and other administrators are engaging in this process as well. The overall strategy — clarifying a vision, collecting and selecting, reflecting and reviewing — remains the same; what varies are the specific goals and entries that are used to demonstrate them. Often, professionals within the same building only have a vague notion of what other people's jobs involve. Having administrators present some of their work to colleagues, or other staff members, can help illuminate the work that goes into the daily running of a school or district.

Challenges and how to address them

Time. With the increasing demands on teachers and administrators, time for anything new is hard to find. There's no denying it; assembling and reviewing portfolios takes time.

However, it's worth noting that you can minimize that time commitment by focusing the conversation. One way is by limiting what teachers need to demonstrate: if teachers are gathering information for a couple of domains of teacher effectiveness, rather than all of them, then that will require less time.

Similarly, another option is to ask teachers to begin their portfolio work by selecting one unit of study and one additional activity (such as a parent conference or faculty committee) to document. Those two entries may not cover all of the standards, but they will provide a starting point for the review conversation.

Technology. Even today, technology may scare away some educators. For one thing, technology changes rapidly. However, each iteration of smartphone, laptop and software tools makes it that much simpler to document everything. Capturing student work (from paper) doesn't mean having to find a high-end scanner; a picture taken with a smartphone can be sent directly to a portfolio tool on the web. Tablets, laptops, and digital cameras make it possible to assemble documents quickly. The conversation should focus on *how* teachers can use the technology. What are the most important things to capture? How can you present those artifacts in the best way?

One strategy for dealing with both the time and technology issues is to have a "portfolio assembly" session for the teachers. Reserve a computer lab specifically for the faculty piloting this process and ask them to bring the pieces that they want to include in their portfolios. You can have your resident technology experts wander through the lab, providing guidance on assembling the portfolio — and help with more advanced skills (such as video editing) as necessary.

Culture. Do teachers trust that they are going to get valuable feedback? Do reviewers believe that they will get an honest picture of a teacher's abilities? Digital portfolios can lead to an interesting conversation about how "good" is "good enough." Sometimes, a culture of mistrust has kept teachers and administrators from having straightforward conversations with each other, and the portfolio process has been blamed. Difficulty in implementing a portfolio process may signal a deeper malaise in the culture.

One way to move toward a more trusting culture is to have a "showcase" review of a portfolio. One volunteer teacher might work with an administrator to demonstrate a review publicly, live or on video. Most reviews, of course, are expected to be private but producing a model, demonstrating how the teacher and the reviewer will interact, can help to ease anxieties about what the portfolio process will actually mean.

Conclusion

There's a story, perhaps apocryphal, about Pablo Picasso. In his later years, he was at an event and a matron of the arts asked him to do a sketch. Picasso obliged, and while she watched, he created an illustration. He handed over the sketch, and said, "That will be $10,000." The woman was taken aback. "But that sketch only took you five minutes," she objected. Picasso replied, "No, that sketch took me a lifetime."

The entries teachers and administrators create for their portfolios are sketches; moments of time that represent a component of teaching and learning. Collectively, the sketches come together, and the portfolio, as a whole, begins to capture the lifetime of skills and knowledge that make those moments possible.

References

Danielson, C. (2007). *Enhancing professional practice: A framework for teaching.* Alexandria, VA: ASCD.

Easton, L.B. (2009). *Protocols for professional learning.* Alexandria, VA: ASCD.

McDonald, J.P., Mohr, N., Dichter, A., & McDonald, E.C. (2007). *The power of protocols.* New York, NY: Teachers College Press.

Niguidula, D. (1997, November). Picturing performance with digital portfolios. *Educational Leadership, 55*(3), 26–29.

Niguidula, D. (1998). A richer picture of student work. In D. Allen (Ed.), *Assessing student learning: From grading to understanding* (pp. 183–198). New York, NY: Teachers College Press.

Niguidula, D. (2010). Digital portfolios and curriculum maps: Linking student and teacher work. In H. H. Jacobs (Ed.), *Curriculum 21: Essential education for a changing world* (pp. 153–167). Alexandria, VA: ASCD.

Powell, A.G., Farrar, E., & Cohen, D.K. (1986). *The shopping mall high school: Winners and losers in the educational marketplace.* Boston, MA: Houghton Mifflin.

CHAPTER 12

Instructional Coaching

Deliberate, intentional processes and procedures ensure effective
coach-teacher and coach-principal relationships.

By Chris Bryan, Heather Clifton, and Cindy Harrison

Silver Mountain Elementary has begun to implement new curriculum standards based on the Common Core State Standards, and the instructional coach and the principal know that teachers need support to make the shifts in instruction called for in these standards. Since teachers have not experienced planning for or implementing new curriculum, they are nervous about how successful they will be with this initiative.

Roshanda and Clara

Roshanda, an instructional coach at Silver Mountain Elementary, is about to start a coaching session with Clara, a 24-year veteran teacher at the school. Clara was reluctant to be coached last year, and Roshanda is a bit nervous about this interaction. This year, Clara did, in fact, request Roshanda's help, but only after the principal set clear expectations that all teachers engage in continuous instructional

improvement. The principal required each teacher to develop an improvement plan, which included working with a coach.

For more than five years at Silver Mountain Elementary, Roshanda has assumed teacher leadership roles working with grade-level teams, facilitating grade-level data teams, and helping grade-level chairpersons develop leadership skills. This is only her second year working with individuals as an instructional coach.

She feels that she is well prepared for the instructional coach role, based on professional learning she experienced through Learning Forward's summer coaching academy and the ongoing professional learning sessions in her district every Friday afternoon for the last two years. Roshanda has continued to improve the craft of coaching through onsite practice and learning from her peers. Every Friday she has time to share ideas with other instructional coaches, as well as to expand her knowledge and skills in a variety of areas.

She participates in coaching labs where she gets to practice coaching with a peer and receive feedback.

Silver Mountain has a diverse population. Each year the school has improved its student learning results as measured by various teacher-made common assessments, as well as district and state assessments. Students in most classrooms have demonstrated growth in reading and math. Clara's students, however, have shown little growth; a large academic achievement gap exists between the Hispanic and Caucasian boys in her class. She has resisted jumping on what she sees as bandwagons of innovations introduced to the staff; indeed, she included coaching in her improvement plan only because she was required to do so. Yet, realizing there are some problems in her classroom, Clara finally has acknowledged that she needs to improve her skills.

Roshanda established a goal last year to learn more about motivating and teaching males at the elementary level. Her coaching champion, the person who gives **her** coaching and support, was able to refer her to various resources, including people with expertise in this area and articles from educational journals, to help her in her quest for knowledge.

Roshanda and Clara, therefore, have a common interest: They are both concerned about the boys in the school whose achievement gap is larger than that of girls. At their first coaching meeting, they decide they will begin dealing with the issue by working on a science and writing lesson about life cycles. This will be the first time Clara has attempted to integrate two content areas into the same lesson.

As Roshanda and Clara plan the lesson, they pay special attention to student engagement; they want to ensure that students do the thinking. When Roshanda asks Clara about aspects of the lesson about which she would like to have feedback, Clara lists the following:

- General student engagement;
- Levels of thinking, especially for the boys; and
- Success of the curriculum integration.

Roshanda agrees to take notes on student engagement related to specific parts of the lesson. In terms of the second and third areas for feedback, Roshanda talks about the importance of looking at student work to see whether students have learned. Together, they design a prompt that calls on students to apply what they have learned by writing about a hypothetical life cycle.

Clara teaches the lesson as Roshanda watches and takes notes on engagement, correlated to what Clara was doing at the time. They make a videotape of the lesson to serve as backup in case they want to dig deeper into some data. Clara collects the writing. They determine the time for a follow-up conversation.

During the follow-up conversation, Roshanda and Clara go over the data: Roshanda's notes about engagement during various parts of the lesson and the student writing. Roshanda does not evaluate the lesson; instead, through her questions, she encourages Clara to think about the data. Together, they determine the following:

- Students were intensely engaged during small group work but not as engaged when Clara was talking (no surprise!).
- Two-thirds of the boys had trouble beginning the writing; they were taking up to two minutes longer to get started than the girls.
- Overall, the boy's responses were shorter than the girls' responses, in some cases, less than half the length.
- Two boys drew pictures rather than write responses to the prompt.
- Two boys misunderstood the assignment and replicated the life cycle that was described during the lesson rather than creating a hypothetical life cycle.

Roshanda and Clara use these data to establish some hypotheses. For example, they wondered if students needed to practice orally what they would later write. "Perhaps," said Clara, "students could have described to a partner the hypothetical life cycle they had in mind. Or, partners could have created the hypothetical life cycle together and then written about it individually."

Roshanda and Clara make plans for another lesson. They decide to see if changes related to the life-cycle lesson would make a difference. The coaching cycle (plan, observe, feedback) continues through a few more lessons. After several iterations, Clara has a chance to end the relationship with Roshanda, but she doesn't. Instead, Clara requests that Roshanda work with her for the rest of the year. This request indicates that coaching has been successful for Clara. Roshanda also feels very successful. She has been rewarded by seeing the various teachers she has coached use student data, plan lessons effectively and teach them well, respond to feedback, and then plan next steps accordingly.

Overview

Instructional coaching is a design for professional-learning that, when implemented well, promises the useful application of new learning in actual practice (Joyce & Showers, 1995, p. 112).

As schools and districts face more complex and demanding changes, coaching becomes increasingly important as a design for supporting individual and organizational change so that students learn at higher levels. For example, as states adopt the new standards, teachers are required to make instructional shifts that necessitate significant changes in content knowledge, instructional practice, and pedagogical content knowledge. Coaching can provide needed support to individual teachers, teams of teachers, and the whole school.

Other important changes in the classroom relate to the shifting roles of the teacher and the students in engaging in the learning. Table 1 illustrates these changes.

Table 1: **Shift in Roles**

Shifting from	Shifting to
Teacher owns the learning	Student owns the learning
Teacher does the thinking	Student does the thinking
Teacher-directed learning	Student-generated problem solving

Other areas in which coaches are needed to support teachers include the following:
- Co-planning instructional units and lessons;
- Selecting instructional methodologies to teach the knowledge and skills embedded in the standards;
- Adapting instruction to meet the needs of English language learners, students with special needs, and learners at advanced performance levels;
- Designing rigorous assignments and learning tasks that provide opportunities to differentiate learning in real-life situations;
- Working collaboratively to increase the efficiency and effectiveness of team instructional planning;
- Using data regarding student performance to reflect on and refine practice;
- Reducing variance across classrooms so that all students have equitable opportunities to learn and succeed;

- Supporting learning teams in the use of the collaborative inquiry model to affect teacher practice and student learning;
- Modeling, implementing, and fostering reflective practice; and
- Aligning teachers' instructional decisions with evidence-based practices.

The impact of coaching is not solely dependent upon hiring effective, dynamic individuals for coaching positions. Coaching programs are successful because leaders thoughtfully hire and place coaches, clarify their roles and responsibilities, support their ongoing professional growth, and ensure effective relationships between the coach and teachers and principals. Coaching makes an impact when leaders give thoughtful consideration to aligning the coaching program with the school's or district's goals and take steps to define an evaluation process for both the program and the individual coaches before the implementation begins.

The focus of the work of the instructional coach is on strengthening the quality of teaching in all classrooms, including those of the learning specialists and electives teachers. Coaches focus on management issues only as they relate to establishing the environment in which students can thrive as learners.

Rationale

As educators face increasingly complex challenges and changes such as teaching to the Common Core State Standards and linking teacher evaluation to student achievement measures, education leaders must invest in professional learning practices that have the greatest possibility of bringing about desirable results in student achievement. Education leaders who choose the professional learning practices in which to invest must begin with this theory of change: Teacher use of more effective instructional practices leads to higher levels of student achievement. When educators adopt that straightforward theory, they are likely to realize that coaching programs are an important means for achieving desired results in both adult and student learning. If they believe that the teacher is the single most important factor within educators' locus of control for improving students' learning, leaders must ensure that teachers become reflective about their practices and make the most of their

ADDITIONAL RESOURCES

Articles

"Coaching can benefit children who have a higher hill to climb," by Penny Reddell (2004, Spring). *JSD, 25*(2), 20–26.

"Coaching in the K–12 context," by Joellen Killion. In S. Fletcher & C. McMullen (Eds.). *The Sage handbook of mentoring and coaching in education* (pp. 273–294). London, England: Sage, 2012.

" 'Hope is not a strategy': Coaching is effective at closing the gap in a Georgia school," by Joan Richardson. (2008, September). *The Learning Principal, 4*(1), 1, 6–7.

"Instructional coaching: Eight factors for realizing better classroom teaching through support, feedback, and intensive, individualized professional learning," by Jim Knight. (2006, April). *The School Administrator, 63*(4), 36–40.

"Leadership for literacy coaching: The principal's role in launching a new coaching program," by Lindsay Clare Matsumura, Mary Sartoris, Donna DiPrima Bickel, and Helen E. Garnier. (2009). *Educational Administration Quarterly, 45*(5), 655–693.

"*Principals as partners with literacy coaches: Striking a balance between neglect and interference,*" by Jacy Ippolito. Literacy Coaching Clearinghouse, June 23, 2009. Available at www.literacycoachingonline.org/briefs/Principals_as_Partners.pdf.

"See me, hear me, coach me," by Marcia L. Rock, Madeleine Gregg, Pamela W. Howard, Donna M. Ploessl, Sharron Maughn, Robert A. Gable, and Naomi P. Zigmond. (2009, Summer). *JSD, 30*(3), 24–32.

Books

Cognitive Coaching: A Foundation for Renaissance Schools, by Art Costa and Robert J. Garmston. Norwood, MA: Christopher Gordon, 2002.

Group and Team Coaching: The Essential Guide, by Christine Thornton. London, England: Routledge, 2010.

Instructional Coaching: A Partnership Approach to Improving Instruction, by Jim Knight. Thousand Oaks, CA: Corwin Press, 2007.

Instructional Coaching: Professional Development Strategies that Improve Instruction. Available at http://annenberginstitute.org/pdf/instructionalcoaching.pdf.

Short on Time: How do I make time to lead and learn as a principal?, by William Sterrett. Alexandria, VA: ASCD, 2013.

Reports

Jefferson County Public Schools Instructional Coach Program Review, by Cindy Harrison, Heather Clifton, and Chris Bryan. Golden, CO: Jefferson County Public Schools, 2010.

MetLife Survey of the American teacher: Challenges for school leadership. by Available at https://www.metlife.com/assets/cao/foundation/MetLife-Teacher-Survey-2012.pdf.

MetLife Survey of the American teacher: Teachers, parents and the economy. MetLife Foundation. New York, NY: Author, 2011. Available at http://files.eric.ed.gov/fulltext/ED530021.pdf.

Primary sources: America's Teachers on Teaching in an Era of Change. By Scholastic and the Bill & Melinda Gates Foundation. Available at www.scholastic.com/primarysources/PrimarySources3rdEdition.pdf.

Supporting Literacy Across the Sunshine State: A Study of Florida Middle School Reading Coaches, by Julie A. Marsh, Jennifer Sloan McCombs, J. R. Lockwood, Francisco Martorell, Daniel Gershwin, Scott Naftel, Vi-Nhuan Le, Molly Shea, Heather Barney, and Al Crego. Santa Monica, CA: RAND Corp., 2008.

ADDITIONAL RESOURCES

Websites

www.edutopia.org. The website of the George Lucas Educational Foundation provides resources to help educators implement project-based learning, social and emotional learning, comprehensive assessment, teacher development, integrated studies, and technology integration.

www.facebook.com/instructional.coaching. The Facebook social media presence of The Instructional Coaching Group, (http://instructionalcoaching.com/), is committed to one goal: that every student receives excellent instruction, every day, in every class. They partner with schools, districts, states, and provinces to achieve that goal in three ways: (a) sharing high-impact teaching strategies, (b) proven instructional coaching practices to support implementation of those practices, and (c) system change strategies.

www.instructionalcoach.org. The purpose of the Kansas Coaching Project is to study factors related to professional learning and how to improve academic outcomes for students through supports provided by instructional coaches.

www.literacycoachingonline.org/tools.html. This website provides tools that help literacy coaches, reading coaches or instructional coaches reflect more deeply on their work and come to new insights that enhance the quality of their efforts.

www.instituteforinstructionalcoaching.org. The Pennsylvania Institute for Instructional Coaching is a statewide model designed to provide the uniform and consistent delivery of sustainable professional development around instructional coaching and mentoring.

own learning as they do for the learning of their students. Instructional coaching programs, when well designed and well executed, create opportunities for high achievement for all children.

The research of Bruce Joyce and Beverly Showers indicates that, when compared to the learning designs of presentation, modeling and practice with feedback, coaching is five to eight times more likely to influence teachers' ability to change their practices and engage in productive problem solving (2002, p. 78). The authors' personal experiences working with educators across the United States and Canada substantiate Joyce's and Shower's claim. Coaching makes significant differences in changing and improving teachers' instructional practices and ensuring full implementation of new initiatives.

Based on extensive experience in working with school and district coaching programs, the authors have ascertained that instructional coaching programs characterized by specific qualities and conditions have the most positive impact on student performance. At this stage of the research, findings suggest that whether coaching works, or not, depends on how it is implemented, the longevity of coaching practices, the support provided by principals, the culture of the school, and the preparation of coaches (Borman, Feger, & Kawakami, 2006).

Steps for creating a coaching program

The planning process for creating an effective instructional coaching model may last from six months to a year, depending on the current culture and practices of the district. Typically, the process for creating a coaching program begins with a person or a small group of people who believe that instructional coaching is a strategy for moving teachers' practices to higher levels of effectiveness.

Step 1: Explore the possibilities

Often an individual or team of people conducts some preliminary work to become familiar with effective coaching models. They may actually observe coaching models in action and follow up by talking with teachers, principals, and the teacher's association in the district they visited about implementing an instructional coaching model. Then, of course, they talk with each other and teachers, principals, and the teacher's association in their own district about what they learned. Involving representatives from the teachers union/association generally garners greater support for the program if it is done before or at the start of the program. Another appropriate starting place might be to study the book *Coaching Matters* (Killion, Harrison, Bryan & Clifton, 2012) or other resources listed in this chapter (see Additional Resources on pp. 186–187).

Creating an effective coaching program requires that decision makers examine the research on coaching, various coaching models, and components of effective coaching programs. Building foundational knowledge is essential to making effective decisions regarding the direction and structure for the coaching program.

Consider student needs. As educators begin this process it is important that they consider student achievement needs within the district, along with instructional implementation gaps that might have contributed to the achievement issues. The decision to implement an instructional coaching program (as with any other new initiative) usually results from analyzing these gaps, researching a variety of approaches to closing the gaps, and determining what form of professional learning is most likely to address the gaps in a significant way. Learning Forward put it this way in its Implementation Standard: "Professional learning that increases educator effectiveness and results for all students integrates theories, research, and models of human learning to achieve its intended outcomes" (see a summary of the Learning Forward Standards in Part I, "Design: Form and Structure for Learning"). Indeed, instructional coaching is a model of professional learning that addresses all of these aspects.

Identify some desired outcomes. Before actually beginning the design of a coaching program, leaders need to identify the desired outcomes for the program. What do they want the program to accomplish? What are the measurable goals? An overall goal might be to positively impact the learning of all students. A more specific goal might be to close the achievement gap between English language learners and the rest of the student population in writing. Another might be to support teachers as they fully implement new standards or differentiate instruction for all learners in their classrooms.

Consider a theory of change. A theory of change embedded in the decision to implement a coaching program very likely reflects the following thinking:

- Student learning is directly impacted by teacher effectiveness;
- Positively impacting classroom instruction will positively impact student learning; and
- Instructional coaching is the professional learning strategy that can best impact teacher practices in the classroom.

Leaders who adopt this theory of change will likely see the rationale for implementing a coaching program.

Step 2: Establish a steering committee

One result of initial work done by interested individuals can be that district leaders become interested in establishing a coaching program. They then begin the formal process by setting up a steering committee, which might include members of the initial interest group. One reason for forming a steering committee to design the instructional coaching program is to ensure that a variety of perspectives is considered in the design. An effective steering committee consists of representatives of all stakeholder groups, including teachers, principals, and central office personnel. Often the team also includes resource teachers whose current jobs incorporate some sort of coaching. It is important to pay attention to diversity among team members regarding length of time in the district, types of schools the teachers and administrators represent, content areas and grade levels represented, and any special interests that hold influence in the district. If the position of coach is to replace another current position in the district, then representation from that position on the team is also important.

Including representatives of the teachers union/ association on the steering committee contributes to the program's success. Providing opportunities for these representatives to ask questions, offer input, and engage in the design leads to smooth implementation of the program. The steering committee might very well comprise 15–20 people, along with a skilled facilitator who designs and facilitates the process for all meetings. The facilitator can be a person from within the district or someone external to the organization. Enlisting an internal facilitator offers the following advantages: incurs less expense, offers easier access, and brings knowledge of district culture. On the other hand, an external facilitator who does not engage in the politics of the district may provide a fresh perspective.

Step 3: Write a charge statement

Writing a clear charge statement is one of the keys to creating an effective program. A team convened to create a program needs a clearly defined charge so that the process and outcomes of the program are aligned with the intended purpose of the program. A charge statement includes the roles and responsibilities of team members, the products expected, the desired outcomes, parameters for the project, and the level of decision making that the team will use.

A suggested format for the charge statement includes the following:

- Overall purpose of the steering committee;
- Questions to answer in the process;
- Membership;
- Parameters; and
- Timeline.

The charge statement can serve as a method for leaders to later determine the extent to which the steering committee's work is aligned with its intended purpose.

State purpose of the steering committee. The first element of the charge statement answers the question, "What is the fundamental reason for pulling the team together?" What is the intended function and purpose of the team? An example might be:

To provide a structure to support high levels of teacher success with current and prospective changes and expectations (e.g. Common Core State Standards, teacher evaluation) by designing a powerful instructional coaching model that makes a positive impact on student achievement (see Online Resource 12.1: *Sample charge statement*).

Draft questions to address. The charge statement includes questions for the group to research, discuss, and answer; thus, it is an effective way to focus the work of the team. These questions provide structure for the agendas and conversations that need to take place during the committee meetings. Table 2 includes examples of possible questions.

Determine parameters. Recording parameters as part of the charge statement serves as the frame around the entire

Table 2: Example Questions to Guide Steering Committee

1. What do we want to be the desired outcomes for instructional coaching? Year 1? Year 3?
2. What main roles will instructional coaches assume? Should these roles change over time? If so, how?
3. What is the job description for instructional coaches?
4. What are the characteristics of instructional coaches that are likely to make a difference in student achievement?
5. How is coaching defined? What coaching practices are expected or appropriate?
6. How will coaches stay current with effective classroom practices?
7. What will be the process for hiring instructional coaches?
8. How will the instructional coaching program be evaluated?
9. How will confidentiality be defined as it pertains to coaches' work?
10. How will instructional coaches communicate with others about their work?
11. Who will supervise and evaluate the work of instructional coaches?
12. Who will provide training for instructional coaches? How often?
13. Who will receive coaching services?
14. What is the process for addressing conflicts between instructional coaches and teachers or administrators?
15. How will coaches receive feedback from others on the impact of their work?
16. What is the relationship of the instructional coach, new teacher mentors, instructional coordinators, reading specialists, etc.?
17. What will be the same about the model for all levels? What will be different for the elementary level? Middle school level? High school level?

"picture" of the design of the coaching program. Parameters define the limitations for the work of the group; they are the givens within which decisions need to be made. No matter how well the charge is stated, specifically defined parameters ensure greater clarity about the scope of the work of the committee and assist committee members avoiding pitfalls. Following are examples of parameters:

- The proposed model must be able to operate within existing funds/FTE allocations. No additional positions may be requested.
- The instructional coaching positions must be fully open positions available to all staff by application. No person will be grandfathered into the position without meeting all of the qualifications described in the job description.
- The steering committee will make a recommendation to the superintendent who will make the final recommendation to the school board.

The steering committee can avoid unnecessary complications by establishing and conveying these parameters at the start of the process.

Devise a timeline. The steering committee will improve its efficiency by including a timeline in the charge statement. Often the timeline includes a year for designing the program, followed by a year of monitoring the program after implementation commences. It is useful to have the committee stay together through at least one year of implementation to assist in solving problems that might arise (see Online Resource 12.2: *Sample timeline*).

Step 4: Define the roles and responsibilities of the coaches

One of the most important factors that drives the entire coaching program is a clear delineation of the roles and responsibilities of coaches. When the role is poorly defined and lacks specificity, coaches spend much of their time attempting to determine what work will be "most impactful" or simply engaging in any tasks that are requested of them. Implementing the 10 roles defined by Killion and Harrison (2006) is one way to approach the task of clearly defining the work of coaches. Coaches cannot effectively implement all roles simultaneously. The steering committee can identify three or four roles that are aligned with the school goals so coaches can focus on them, especially in the first year, to increase the likelihood that their work has the

greatest promise of positively affecting classroom practice and student learning (see Online Resource 12.3: *The roles of the learning support coach*).

Step 5: Select and place coaches

A clear job description, along with a system that allows provision of evidence about candidates' knowledge, skills, and other qualifications and a rigorous selection process, will ensure the best-qualified candidates are placed in the coaching positions. Including multiple people in the interviewing and selection process will generate high levels of commitment. The district-level administrator who has ultimate oversight responsibility for the coaching program must take an active monitoring role in this process.

One way to structure this is to create a central pool of best applicants and then engage building-level principals and teachers in the selection of the best applicant(s) for their respective buildings. Having principals and teachers define school needs that a coach might address ensures a better match. Likewise, it would be ideal for potential coaches to describe the kind of school that might best match their skill sets because matching a candidate with building culture is an important consideration in the placement of coaches.

Designating each coach for one specific building is generally a more effective model than employing district-level coaches to work at two or more buildings. One coach who works with several teachers in a single school, rather than with the same number of teachers in different schools, can establish a presence in that school. The coach in a single school is more likely to have frequent points of contact with staff and students and deeply understand the culture of the school. School-based coaches who spend time in one school, engaging with its teachers and students, can build trust quickly and observe their impact on teacher and student learning. District-level coaches who visit several schools sometimes find it challenging to build relationships in each school. Since the goal of the coaching program is to make a positive impact on classroom instruction and student learning, then coaches — either single-school or district-level — must be accessible enough to the teachers to build a high level of trust. Having multiple opportunities to interact with individuals and teams of teachers is essential to making an impact.

Step 6: Develop partnership agreements

Effective coaching programs begin with ensuring that time is allocated for the coach, the principal, and teachers to develop partnership agreements. A partnership agreement involves a conversation that results in a mutual agreement between coaches and those with whom they work. The purpose of the partnership conversation is to provide clarity and build trust between coaches and their clients. These agreements, especially those between the coach and the principal can be formalized, written, and signed (see Online Resource 12.4: *Coach and principal agreement sample;* also see Online Resource 12.5: *Partnership agreement between principal and instructional coach*).

It is important for the coach to be clear about the principal's expectations, the coach's own needs, commitments each makes to the other, and clarification about what the coach will and will not do. It is important to include expectations about confidentiality in this conversation. Coaches can talk about the work they are doing, who they are working with, and how much time they spend with teachers; however, if they stray into conversations that include comments or data that could be considered evaluative, they risk breaking the trust they have worked so hard to build with teachers. The challenge for coaches is to schedule time to have this conversation, which requires honesty and transparency from both the coach and the principal. It is also sometimes a challenge to convince the principal of the importance of this conversation. Sometimes the principal lacks full understanding of how necessary nonevaluative support is for the coaching program. Without an opportunity to align coaching with the vision of the principal, coaches' work is disconnected from school goals.

As a result, teachers often interpret coaching as a professional learning opportunity in which they may or may not choose to engage. Astute coaches and principals are also aware that, when the principal asks the coach to work only with teachers who need to improve their practice, the danger is that teachers view coaching through a deficit lens. Faculty may believe that, if the coach is working with a teacher, there must be something wrong or something the teacher needs to fix. The expectation should be that every teacher works with the coach (see Online Resource 12.6: *The teacher's roles in coaching as a reflective practitioner;* also see Online Resource 12.7: *Sample teacher/coach partnership agreement*).

With teachers, the agreements are often more informal and can be renegotiated each time they work together. When creating a partnership agreement with teachers, coaches need to be sure that they and teachers clarify expectations of each other, support and resources needed, identification of roles, where and when the coaching will take place and for how long, and a focus for the coaching. Engaging teachers in a partnership agreement conversation affords the coach an opportunity to ensure the teacher that they are entering into the partnership as equals, not as the teacher and the expert. Coaches who believe they need to have all the answers may find that they are not as likely to be invited into teachers' classrooms. When teachers have an opportunity to share where, when, how, and about what topics they want coaching services, they are more likely to form a productive partnership with their coaches.

Step 7: Provide initial training for coaches

Training in necessary knowledge and skills provided for coaches before they actually begin to implement the program ensures that they get off to a good start. Coaches benefit from developing or enhancing a good skill set before they begin their work. A few days of well-designed training in the summer before the start of the program is useful and includes such basic topics as partnership agreements, the change process, roles and responsibilities of coaches, and effective communication skills. Joint participation of the principal and the coach in this training ensures that appropriate decisions are made about implementation at the school level. The schedule of the six-day training of Learning Forward's Coaches' Academy is included as Online Resource 12.8: *Coaches' Academy agenda overview.*

Step 8: Roll out the program

School leaders who successfully implement a coaching program begin with thoughtful consideration about how they introduce the program at the building level. From the start they communicate about the desired outcomes for the program, the structures that will be used at each site, and the expectations for how teachers and coaches will work together.

Connecting the coaching program to professional learning, one principal introduced the coaching program by stating that all teachers are expected to be learners and to be growing continually. This principal stated that one of the best methods for continuous learning is work with a coach. If the principal does not convey strong expectations that teachers work with the coach — that is, if coaching is framed as a voluntary option — teachers will not access this resource. School leaders or steering committees should describe clearly the coach's roles and responsibilities; to help target the work of the coach, principals may even provide a list of what the coach does and does not do. Principals can introduce the coaching program to staff members by inviting them to offer ideas about ways for the coach and individual teachers or teams of teachers to work together. Principals and coaches who operate according to a 30/60/90-day plan can make sure that their actions to institute the plan are deliberate and effective (see Online Resource 12.9: *30-60-90-day action plan*).

By giving staff members opportunities throughout the year to request services from the coach, as well as give feedback on services received, principals increase staff investment in the program. Implementing a coaching program that responds to staff and building needs increases the likelihood that staff members will use the coaching services.

Step 9: Identify support systems for the instructional coach

The coach's own professional learning is as important as that of teachers. As lead learners, coaches model effective practices by continually striving to increase their knowledge and improve their skills. Optimally, an extensive network of support for the coach is in place. The entire program is more effective when a variety of professional learning opportunities, ranging from training sessions to virtual professional learning networks, are available to coaches. The steering committee should designate mentors for new coaches and provide ongoing personal coaching so that coaches can improve their skills (e.g. classroom coaching or working with teams of teachers on data-informed classroom decision making), which leads to greater success for coaches.

Ongoing training is essential to the continuous learning of coaches. Many districts plan training for a half-day each week. Many district leaders choose Fridays because sometimes there seems to be a lower level of use of coaching services at the end of the week. To support the coaching work, district leaders need to be sure that time is set aside for coaches to share practices with one another, as well as time for coaches to practice skills with feedback. Scheduling opportunities for coaches and principals to learn together is also effective, especially for the implementation of large district initiatives. In many instances, coaches are perceived as the building-level arm of district professional learning; therefore, they are an integral part of introducing new initiatives at the building level. Finally, it is essential that leaders think about the number of areas on which coaches are asked to focus if they are to prevent coaches from being overwhelmed by too many district initiatives.

Step 10: Create an evaluation system to assess the coaching program and individual coaches

Another essential step is designing an evaluation plan for the coaching program before beginning implementation. Part of the steering committee's work is to create an outline of a plan that identifies the desired outcomes, as well as periodic benchmarks that indicate whether the program is focused on the right work and having the desired impact. Coaches need to maintain logs that delineate the types of work in which they engage with various clients and the impact of that work so that program evaluators (perhaps the steering committee) can incorporate data about time allocations and usage of coaching services.

Program evaluators can gather perception data from users through surveys and focus groups in order to understand how clients perceive the services and to identify ways to improve the coaching, and increase the levels of use for coaching services. Evaluators examining the impact of coaching can include observing teaching practices, talking with students about their learning, and listening to the conversations of teachers in team meetings to assess the level of collaboration. With an active plan for collecting continuous feedback from principals and teachers, coaches can revise program services on a regular basis (see Online Resource 12.10: *Mid-year coaching reflection*).

Likewise, a system for formal evaluation of individual coach performance is necessary. Ideally the evaluation is aligned with the expectations described in the job description. Often coaching champions and principals collaboratively evaluate the coach's performance (see Online Resource 12.11: *Post-coaching surveys*).

Step 11: Implement, monitor, and revise the program

The coaching program achieves greater success when the program design includes a plan and a timeline for program rollout and regular, periodic benchmarks for assessing the program's effectiveness. When the original steering committee members remain in place for the first year of the program, they can serve as additional sets of eyes and ears for determining the effectiveness of the program, as well as providing assistance in solving problems that surface (see Online Resource 12.12: *Program evaluation benchmarks*).

A log is an effective tool for measuring the impact of the coach's work on the outcomes of the program. Coaches' logs assist educational leaders in the monitoring and revision of the coaching program. Logs enable program managers to assess how time is spent and assess the impacts of actual time spent. They also enable coaches and the program managers to identify the level of fidelity to the defined roles and responsibilities of coaches (see Online Resource 12.13: *Example coach's log*).

Variations

Coaching is a supple form of professional learning, adaptable to a variety of school needs.

School-based or district-based. There is no uniform agreement about which are more effective, school-based or district-based coaches. Districts usually make decisions based on the goal for the coaching program, available staff, and budget. Generally, school-based coaches are more readily available to work with teachers consistently over time. When they are considered part of the teaching staff, coaches find it easier to develop trusting relationships with those they coach. A variation for this model is designating a single coach to be responsible for more than one school. Another variation is to house coaches at the district or a regional support center.

Content-specific or generic. One factor that influences the success of the coach is a definition of parameters for their work. When beginning a coaching program, districts should be sure that the parameters are clearly stated in the charge statement, which defines the expected outcomes for the coaching program. When the outcomes are clear, then districts can make good decisions about how the coach's work should be defined. Content coaches focus their work on content-specific planning, instruction, and assessment. They support teachers in their development of content knowledge and how best to teach their content to all students (pedagogical content knowledge).

Generic instructional coaches interact with teachers about all aspects of general instruction, including planning, differentiating instruction, and assessing the learning of students with a focus on meeting the needs of diverse learners.

Challenges and how to address them

Regardless of their preparation and experience, coaches encounter daily challenges. Examples range from understanding how to support educators moving through the change process, implementing a new innovation, and facilitating team-based learning, to providing classroom support through the gradual release model, facilitating data conversations, thinking through how to engage others in critical feedback conversations, partnering more effectively with their principals, or evaluating the effectiveness of their coaching and their coaching programs.

District leaders can address these coaching challenges by providing a system of support and ongoing professional learning, ensuring that coaching is part of the district and school strategic plan with defined criteria and parameters, and allocating resources including time that helps create conditions in which coaches are able to build safe, trustworthy relationships with teachers.

Support for the coach. Coaches need access to support for problem solving and opportunities to obtain tools for addressing a range of challenges. Coaches benefit from coaching services themselves. Ideally, a *coach champion* — a person who understands the goals of the coaching program and supports the coach — provides this kind of support. Coach champions are usually district-level people who understand and support the coaches and the coaching program. They typically take a lead role in providing professional learning for coaches. They will often be the people to mediate challenges coaches might face with teachers or the principals with whom they work. Although coach champions might also evaluate coaches, ideally they do not, since the perception of the evaluation process sometimes mitigates the level of trust needed to engage in frank problem solving and other areas of support.

In rural school districts a coach champion may not be available. In situations where this face-to-face support is absent, coaches can benefit from a master coach by participating in an online coaching program designed to help coaches tackle challenges they face (see "Chapter 15: Online Coaching" in this book). Ideally, the support coaches receive online is from someone with whom they form a relationship over time.

Ongoing professional learning. In addition to support, instructional coaches need professional learning if they are to enhance the quality of their clients' instruction. The coaching program is only as effective as the individual coaches within the system. Too often, coaches receive little or no professional learning to develop their knowledge and skills about coaching or opportunities to reflect on their own beliefs about teaching, learning, and collaboration.

Effective coaches receive ongoing opportunities to develop and strengthen their coaching skills, including strong interpersonal skills, well-developed listening and communication skills, the ability to build and maintain relationships, and the ability to build and maintain trust with their clients. If their role is content specific, they need professional learning geared toward developing their content knowledge. If their role is to provide generic instructional coaching, they need to develop knowledge and skills about effective instruction for all students.

Vision and goals. Another challenge for instructional coaches is defining and focusing their work around the roles that align with the vision and goals of the coaching program, which should align with the vision and goals of schools and the district. The vision and goals of the coaching program should be based on what educators in the system need to learn to better meet the learning needs of students. If the work of coaches is not focused on improving instruction to meet student needs, the impact of coaching will be disappointing.

Coaching, therefore, needs to be one part of a district's strategic plan. The coaching program should fit with other efforts to help educators in the system learn what they need in order to help all students learn (see Online Resource 12.14: *A sample district strategic plan,* which includes the role of coaches).

Coaches often assist teachers with implementing vision-related innovations, which they may understand at a cognitive level but cannot translate into classroom practice. In order for coaches to engage teachers and promote change aligned with district, school, and coaching goals, coaches must develop expert listening skills. They also need the ability to collaborate with their clients, a deep understanding of the change process, and strategies for responding to those with whom they work based on where those teachers are in the change process.

One of the most influential ways coaches can affect teachers' learning is working directly with them in the classroom. In the classroom-supporter role they engage in work that involves co-planning, co-teaching, providing demonstration teaching followed by a debriefing session, and engaging teachers in the coaching cycle (plan, observe, feedback). By providing job-embedded professional learning, coaches can bridge the knowing-doing gap for teachers.

Criteria for coaching. Vision and goals translate into criteria for effective coaching. Effective coaching programs have a clearly defined focus for coaches' work based on data used to inform leaders about areas for improvement and initiatives. It is important, therefore, for district leaders to identify the knowledge, skills, and belief sets coaches need to be successful.

It is important, therefore, for district leaders to identify the knowledge, skills, and belief sets coaches need to be successful. Although Joellen Killion and Cindy Harrison (2006) have identified 10 roles for instructional coaches (see Online Resource 12.15: *Roles of coaches*), good coaching programs narrow the possibilities to two or three roles that best align with district or school goals, at least at first. These roles shift over time as the work of the coach makes an impact on teachers' practices.

Relationships and trust. Effective coaches need to build strong relationships with their clients. Teachers don't want to be "fixed"; rather, they want to be understood and supported. One mistake coaches sometimes make is presenting themselves as the experts and responding to clients from that perspective. Teachers are not usually impressed by a coach's level of content expertise or the extent of knowledge about effective pedagogy.

Instead of presenting themselves as experts, coaches must develop the ability to support clients in the process of reflection on their practice. The ultimate goal of coaching is to build the capacity of the teacher to improve his or her own teaching practice. What engages teachers in coaching is a relationship in which they are equally partnered with a coach in a learning process.

Confidentiality. If coaches are to be effective in their work, it is essential for them to build trust with their clients. One important way they accomplish this is by maintaining confidentiality with their clients. This can be a challenge if the principal expects the coach to share information about teachers with whom they work. A remedy for this challenge is to engage the principal in a partnership conversation that clarifies roles, responsibilities, and expectations of each other, including their agreements about confidentiality.

Joellen Killion and Cindy Harrison (2006) have identified four "T's" that can be shared in coach-principal conversations. These are the *time* the coach spends working with a teacher or a team of teachers, the *tasks* they work on, the *topics* they discuss, and the *teachers* they work with. If the coach and principal honor the four T's, the coach will be able to maintain the kind of confidentiality needed to establish and preserve trust with clients. When more than one coach works with a staff, the challenge is to make sure each coach is adhering to the same agreement about confidentiality.

Time to coach. Still another challenge that requires creative thinking by coaches is how to solve the dilemma of finding sufficient time to coach. As Tom Many (2009) says,

> There is no closet in which schools store extra time or secret drawer holding a stash of reflective moments. Simply put, because we are never going to find more time, if we want to ensure that teachers work in teams we have to make time for collaboration. (p. 9)

Making time for job-embedded professional learning is one of the most frequently cited challenges with implementing change in education (Killion, 2013, p. 7).

Learning Forward's (2011) Standards for Professional Learning include the Resources standard. This standard states:

> Professional learning that increases educator effectiveness and results for all students requires prioritizing, monitoring, and coordinating resources for educator learning. (p. 32)

ONLINE RESOURCES

Coaches can make the most of allocated school time by working side-by-side with teachers in their classrooms or in their team meetings. Coaches and teachers need to engage in creative thinking about how to re-allocate existing time so that they can have a pre-conference, debrief after an observation, co-plan, or solve problems.

In her article, *4 Places to Dig Deep to Find More Time for Teacher Collaboration,* Kristi Khorsheed (2007, Spring), suggests educators reconsider funding, time, staff, and student grouping to prioritize and coordinate the resource of time (see Online Resource 12.16: *4 places to dig deep to find more time for teacher collaboration*). Another valuable resource is the recent Learning Forward publication, *Establishing Time For Professional Learning* (Killion, 2013), which describes a seven-step process for establishing time within the school day.

Coaches' documentation of their work, including how the time is spent, and identification of the outcomes of the work help district leaders monitor the use of time to collaborate. Making time for job-embedded professional learning is one of the most frequently cited challenges with implementing change in education.

Conclusion

School- or district-based coaching programs result in greater success when they are designed with an intentional focus on ensuring the conditions described in this chapter. No doubt, designating highly skilled teachers to be coaches is of critical importance to the success of any coaching program. However, even the most sophisticated, highly qualified coach is likely to be less effective when there are no deliberate, intentional processes and procedures in place that ensure effective coach-teacher and coach-principal relationships. Thoughtful attention to hiring and placing coaches, clearly defining their roles and responsibilities, and establishing structures for their ongoing support is critical for the success of the program. Ultimately, the students served by these programs bear the consequences. Paying attention to what matters most can make a lasting difference in how much impact a coaching program will make.

References

Borman, J., Feger, S., & Kawakami, N. (2006, Winter). Instructional coaching: Key themes from the literature (white paper). Available at www.brown.edu/academics/education-alliance/sites/brown.edu.academics.educationalliance/files/publications/TL_Coaching_Lit_Review.pdf.

Killion, J. (2013). *Establishing time for professional learning.* Oxford, OH: Learning Forward. Available at http://learningforward.org/docs/default-source/commoncore/establishing-time-for-professional-learning.pdf.

Killion, J. & Harrison, C. (2006). *Taking the lead: New roles for teachers and school-based coaches.* Oxford, OH: NSDC.

Killion, J., Harrison, C., Bryan, C., & Clifton, H. (2012). *Coaching matters.* Oxford, OH: Learning Forward.

Joyce, B. & Showers, B. (1995). *Student achievement through staff development: Fundamentals of school renewal.* White Plains, NY: Longman.

Joyce, B. & Showers, B. (2002). *Student achievement through staff development* (3rd ed.). Alexandria, VA: ASCD.

Khorsheed, K. (2007, Spring). 4 places to dig deep to find more time for teacher collaboration. *JSD, 28*(2), 43–45; 64–65.

Learning Forward. (2011). *Standards for Professional Learning.* Oxford, OH: Author.

Many, T. (2009, May/June). Make time for collaboration. *TEPSA News, 66*(3). Available at www.allthingsplc.info/files/uploads/make_time_for_collaboration.pdf.

CHAPTER 13

Instructional Rounds

An instructional rounds practice focuses on classroom learning and teaching as part of a purposeful, systematic, and collective improvement process.[1]

By Lee Teitel

Principal Randall Lewis stood at the front of the school library, where members of his district's instructional rounds network had gathered for coffee, muffins, and conversation before the official start of the day's visit. "Welcome to Jefferson Middle School. We're excited to have you here today to help us with our problem of practice. We're also a little nervous, but that's okay. I've told the teachers that this is about my learning and the network's learning, and that we're going to get lots of good information from having so many eyes and ears in our classrooms."

Randall described the "problem of practice" on which he and the teachers had asked the visitors to focus. "We noticed that, when our students were faced with reading something unfamiliar on our state exam or in other places, they froze up. They didn't have the literacy attack skills they need to understand what they were reading. Last spring, we rolled out a new literacy initiative that required a radical shift in teaching strategies for many of our teachers. It was across the board — not just in English/language arts classes. We used big chunks of our professional development time so that all teachers could learn how to teach these skills to our students. A year later, we're trying to understand what we've learned and what we haven't, and whether it's translating into different kinds of learning for students."

---

[1] Portions of this chapter are adapted from Chapter 1 "Overview of the Instructional Rounds Practice, its Impacts and Philosophy" in *School-Based Instructional Rounds,* by Lee Teitel (Harvard Education Press, 2013). Some draw on *Instructional Rounds in Education: A Network Approach to Improving Teaching and Learning.* By Elizabeth City, Richard Elmore, Sarah Fiarman, and Lee Teitel (Harvard Education Press, 2009). Copyright © 2013 and 2009, respectively, President and Fellows of Harvard College. All rights reserved. Used with permission.

The visitors listened carefully as Randall and several of the teachers on the instructional leadership team shared the detail of the instructional strategies with which they had been working. Visitors had lots of questions. "Should we expect to see these in all classes?" asked a principal from a neighboring school. "What exactly should we be taking notes on during our observations?" asked a visiting teacher. The host team answered each question: "Yes you should be able to see it in all classes. Please take notes on how you see the students using the attack skills, as well as how you see that teachers are weaving them into their lessons."

Satisfied that they understood what the host school was asking them to look at — and as the time to go into classrooms was fast approaching — the participants broke into prearranged observation teams of four or five. As they greeted the other members of their observation teams and gathered maps and papers for notes, there was a buzz of anticipation — much like a group of scientists about to embark on field work for data collection.

At 9:00 a.m., the observation groups fanned out through the school to begin conducting observations. They spent 20 minutes in each of four classrooms, filing as unobtrusively as possible into the back of each one. They observed whole group lessons, small group discussions, and independent work by students. During the small group and independent work, the observers watched what students did and to what materials they referred when they got stuck reading something. Occasionally the observers asked students questions like: "What are you doing? What happens to your work after you finish it? What do you do when you need help?" Scribbling furiously, the observers tried to capture direct quotes and detailed observation notes on all they saw and heard that was relevant to the problem of practice.

By 10:30 a.m., the observing groups reassembled in the library, helping themselves to some more coffee and getting ready for the next step, which was to debrief their observations.

Overview

Randall Lewis and his colleagues were spending the day doing something that an increasing number of educators are starting to do: going on an instructional rounds visit. That

is, they were looking at classroom instruction in a focused, systematic, purposeful, and collective way. The goals of these observations are not to provide supervision or evaluation for specific teachers, but to look closely at what is happening in classrooms and to work together systematically to try to provide high-quality teaching and learning for all children. Along with other principals, teachers, union leaders, and central office personnel, Randall was learning about improving instructional practice by participating in instructional rounds, an idea adapted from the medical rounds model used by doctors.

The instructional rounds improvement cycle starts well before the actual visit described at the beginning of this chapter.

Before the visit

Several important things had happened weeks and even months before the visitors started drinking coffee in the school library at Jefferson, the pseudonym for one of the schools in the Ohio Leadership Collaborative.

The network. In a sense, this visit had started months before when the district formed a network that brought together principals and teachers from seven schools, along with central office and union leadership to develop a rounds practice to support improvement in the district. The roots go back even further, since educators from the district had participated in an exploratory cross-district network the previous year before deciding to launch the in-district networks, including the one that Jefferson is in.

Since this was the third visit for the network, a certain amount of norming and calibration had already been done; the visiting teams were familiar with the idea of a problem of practice that would focus their observations. They had practiced taking detailed, nonjudgmental observational notes by watching videos of classrooms, and they had done some reading and discussion of the importance of centering this work in the instructional core — the connection among students and teachers in the presence of content. They came to Jefferson eager to learn, eager to help, knowing that their own schools would be visited later in the year.

Prior to a visit, a network may explore common challenges among its members and agree on a common focus for the year. For example, in its first pilot year the Ohio Leadership Collaborative composed of mixed teacher and leadership teams from five districts, decided to focus on a broad common issue: the teaching and learning that was going on in each of the districts to support higher-order thinking skills. This focus not only shaped the visits that took place over the year, but it also became the topical aim for reading, discussion, and other professional experiences that the network members undertook to support their learning. Also, this focus required educators from all the districts to calibrate — to agree on a very descriptive level — what students and teachers would be doing in classrooms that exhibited different levels of higher-order thinking. Not all networks choose to have a common focus for their visits, but success in rounds requires keeping a focus on both the learning of the network and of the schools that are hosting the visits.

Networks also typically work both before and after visits to hone and improve the rounds and improvement practices that they use, to maximize their learning as a network, and to maximize the impact of each visit on their member schools and districts.

The host school. The work at Jefferson — at the school itself — had started about four weeks before the visit. Randall and the four teachers on the rounds team had done their best to prepare their colleagues for the visit by explaining its nonjudgmental nature and involving many of the other faculty members at Jefferson in the identification of the problem of practice that would be used to guide the visit. Knowing how important it was for this not to be a performance or a dog-and-pony show, Randall and the other teachers held a voluntary after-school briefing session on rounds and distributed a few short articles that highlighted rounds as a learning activity rather than an evaluative one.

The more engaged the staff is in the development of the problem of practice, the greater the likelihood is that the rounds visit will contribute to school improvement. Consequently, many schools use faculty meetings, instructional leadership teams, and other ongoing school structures to help identify an issue that the staff truly owns and cares about. If there are already strong school improvement processes in place, the problem of practice for a visit might draw from and connect with them. In addition, before the visit many schools will provide some sort of exposure and optional training in the process for school staff.

Since making rounds takes a very different approach from traditional top-down administrative walk-throughs, it is very helpful if teachers understand the nonjudgmental, collegial nature of the visit before it occurs. Teachers who are involved in identifying and who care about the problem of practice, and who understand the purpose and the processes of the rounds visit, are much more likely to learn from the results, as opposed to feeling judged by them (see Online Resource 13.1: *Additional examples of problems of practice.*).

Once the problem of practice had been identified, Randall and his team worked together on the logistics of the schedule, identifying teachers to be observed, preparing maps, ordering food. In addition, Randall and the staff identified three teachers to "visit" their own school as full participants in the visiting team (see Online Resource 13.2: *How to schedule a rounds visit: Notes for the host school*).

During the visit

Several events occur during visits: sharing the problem of practice, observation of practice, the observation debrief, analysis, prediction, and the next-level-of-work.

Sharing the problem of practice. On the visit day, someone (the principal or a teacher leader) shares the problem of practice with the visitors at the start of the day, along with background information and context about the school that will help the visitors to make sense of their observational data and more specific and targeted suggestions at the end of the day. As the opening vignette illustrates, typically the principal and a team of teachers from the school take 30 to 45 minutes at the beginning of the day to explain the problem of practice, where it came from, what data led to it, what the school has already done to address it, and where the school feels stuck.

If time permits, they will also give some background information about the school's improvement processes — its teaming structures, how it uses data, and when and how professional learning takes place. Visitors have time for clarifying questions and making sure they are calibrated on the kind of data to collect during their observations.

Observation of practice. A central part of any visit is the observation of practice. Typically groups of four or five visitors observe in three or four classrooms for about 20 minutes each. The classrooms are selected by the host site to reflect the problem of practice. Since Jefferson's literacy strategies were supposed to be embedded in all classes, the visits covered a wide range of classrooms and grades. In another setting, a focus on mathematics might bring visitors to a narrower swath of classes. Observers learn to take specific and nonjudgmental descriptive notes and to pay special attention to students and the tasks they are doing — not just what students are being *asked* to do, but what they are *actually* doing. Because visitors in their networks will already be familiar with the instructional core presence of content, they will not just be looking at what teachers do, but observing and talking to students and looking at the work they are doing.

The visitors are guided by the host school's problem of practice. At Jefferson, they were given a one-page summary of 14 literacy strategies that teachers had been trained to use and asked to look for evidence and patterns of student use of these strategies.

The observation debrief. The next step of the rounds process is the observation debrief, in which participants sift through the evidence they collected together. There are three stages in the debrief process: description, analysis, and prediction.

Description. The *description* stage keeps the focus on a factual description of what visitors actually saw — not their reactions, judgments, or inferences. In the debrief, observers, who have taken copious and specific notes during their observations, typically sit quietly for 10 to 15 minutes to select data from their notes that they think would be particularly useful in focusing on the problem that the school has identified. They transfer the selected, focused data to sticky notes, which they share with their fellow observers. Colleagues give feedback on these notes to ensure that they are specific and nonjudgmental before moving forward to the next step.

Analysis. In the *analysis* stage of the debrief, the team looks for patterns within and across the classrooms they saw. In this step, and throughout the process, the visitors are aggregating up — not focusing as much on the practices they saw in any one class, but looking across classes to see what they notice about, for instance, the use of literary strategies at Jefferson.

Prediction. Groups then build on these patterns to move to the *predictive* stage of the debrief, where the goal is to connect teaching and learning. Participants ask themselves, "Based on the patterns that we have just seen, if you were a student at this school and you did everything you were expected to do, what would you know and be able to

do?" By linking the task and teacher's instruction directly to student learning, network members tackle the central question, "What causes the learning we want to see? What specific teaching moves, what kinds of tasks, what forms of student engagement lead to powerful learning for students?"

This process ultimately helps host schools identify potential areas for improvement and offers clues about *how* these areas could be improved, including the specific strategies and techniques that teachers could use and what the school or district could do to support them. Taken cumulatively, these debrief practices allow participants to describe the specific behaviors and structures they see that cause, enable, or at times constrain learning.

At Jefferson, the patterns that emerged in the *analysis* section of the debrief were clear and quite consistent across the dozens of classrooms visited. Visitors saw teacher use of one or more of the literacy strategies, but they saw almost no independent student use of the strategies. This led to the *prediction* that students in these classes will be able to follow directions in using specific literacy strategies *when asked to do so by their teacher.*

The next-level-of-work. The final step of the rounds process on the day of the visit is identifying the next-level-of-work when network members think together about what kinds of resources and supports teachers and administrators would need in order to move instruction to the next level. That particular phrase — *next-level-of-work* — is a reminder that school improvement is not a linear process. There are often flat points, plateaus, or even dips, along with rises on the journey to improvement. The phrase acknowledges that the work that school staff members have already done to get to their current position may need to change in order to get it to reach the next level.

Here again, the more specific and precise the suggestions, the more helpful they are. At Jefferson, the visitors suggested that the school be more explicit with students about the goal of having them using these strategies in their own reading, writing, and thinking. Concrete suggestions included giving students a version of the one-page summary of 14 literacy strategies and having them track their own use of the strategies, combining this with teaching students about metacognition, and making explicit to students and teachers alike that the goal is to have students use the strategies, not just teachers. In this particular example, most of the suggestions were based at the school level because they involve improvements and interventions that were doable with the current resources at the school. In other cases, visitors on rounds may make specific suggestions that can be addressed at the district level as well.

After the visit

Arguably, the most important part of the improvement cycle takes place after the visit.

Work at the host school. Teachers and administrators at the host school and district need to make sense of the observations, patterns, predictions, and advice that the visitors have left them. They need to make plans to translate the learning that they have engaged in that day into action in ways that connect with and support the ongoing improvement efforts at the school and in the district. They also need to figure out how to engage all members of the faculty in these improvement efforts — not just the handful of members who were on the visit.

Work the network does. At the same time, the network needs to consolidate and incorporate its learning from the visit into its ongoing improvement work. After the visit at Jefferson, not only were members of the Jefferson staff making plans to implement the suggestions from the visit, but teachers and administrators from other schools and districts in the network were also discussing how they could improve the specificity of their guidance to and support of students in learning in other content areas. Administrators from Jefferson's district discussed what they had learned about how they can better support literacy work in all their schools.

Randall Lewis knew that, at the next network meeting, he and the teachers from the school would be expected to describe briefly how the findings from the visit had been shared with the faculty, and what specific follow-up steps were being taken. In addition, because every visit contributes to the learning of the network as well as at the host site, Randall knew that the visit at Jefferson, along with the other two visits made by the network that year, would be discussed at the next network meeting. Network members would look for common themes that emerged across the three visits, check for calibration of norms and instructional rounds practices, and see what improvements needed to be put into place before the next three visits.

Recognizing the importance of follow-up and the

ways hosts and visitors continue to learn from the leadership moves that occur after a visit, some networks set up mini-revisits by a subset of the network. For example, in the Connecticut Superintendent Network within three months of the network visit, two peer superintendents come back to the school and the district for half a day to discuss the follow-up.

In instructional rounds work, the school visit always gets the most attention. Rounds is a high-energy event that brings insiders and outsiders to the school together to do some observations, patternmaking, and deep collegial problem solving. But the visit can never stand alone. It should be understood as a key and highly visible part of the improvement process for the host school and for the network (see Online Resource 13.3: *The rounds visit supports the learning cycle of the network and the host*).

Rationale

The goal in doing instructional rounds work is to help schools and districts develop effective and powerful teaching and learning at scale — not just isolated pockets of good teaching in the midst of mediocrity. Accordingly, at a rounds visit, the network's suggestions for the next-level-of-work are never about "fixing" any one teacher or group of teachers. They are about developing clarity about good instructional practice and about the leadership and organizational practices needed to support this kind of instruction at scale. Suggestions in typical cross-site network rounds for the next-level-of-work are, if anything, intended more for administrators and other leaders than for individual teachers.

How does this bring about improvement? People often ask, "Will doing rounds lead to an increase in student learning? Will it raise test scores?" The short answer is: "By itself, no." Although the rounds process is not a silver bullet that will single-handedly lead to better test scores or increased learning for students, it is a powerful accelerant of school and district improvement efforts.

Districts and schools that are improving teaching and learning at scale have developed in three important areas. They have:

- A clear idea about what high-quality teaching and learning should look like.

- A coherent and strategic approach to systemic improvement.
- A collaborative approach to adult learning that is embedded in practice and relies on engagement and inquiry rather than compliance.

Although these sound relatively simple, each actually requires deep cultural change as educators need to learn new ways of working with one another.

Agreeing what high-quality teaching and learning look like

This is a complex, value-laden task that moves educators away from the atomized individual practice that, for many, is the cherished norm. The fact that rounds focus on what goes on in classrooms anchors improvement efforts to the instructional core. The calibration that takes place in visits forces educators to define more clearly what they mean. Unlike many educators who call for "increased rigor" or "critical-thinking skills" with only a vague idea of what these terms mean, rounds network members work together to develop detailed lists of what those abstract ideas look like in real classrooms. They develop agreements on what teachers and students would be saying and doing if critical thinking skills were being demonstrated, or what students would be working on if their tasks were really rigorous. And when they don't see these signs of critical thinking or rigor, they don't blame teachers, students, parents, or other external factors. Instead they look within the school and district to suggest new and powerful ways educators can work together to achieve the high student learning outcomes they desire. Of course instructional rounds aren't the only approach that is pushing for this level of clarity. Often districts and schools integrate rounds with other efforts connecting to instructional frameworks like those of Charlotte Danielson (1996), or taxonomies for higher-order thinking like those of Benjamin Bloom (1956) or Robert Marzano (2000).

Getting strategic and coherent

Being strategic and coherent is a major departure for many systems. It is, sadly, not uncommon for a school district (and even a school) to have a variety of loosely connected initiatives in place that are poorly coordinated with one another and that lack clear feedback loops on their efficacy in making an impact on what happens in the classroom.

The rounds process encourages educators to use theories of action to articulate and test causal connections between a given improvement initiative and the impact that it has on learning and teaching in classrooms. Rounds participants state their theories of action as "If…, then …"propositions, in part to stress the causal nature of the statements, and in part to reinforce the idea that these are testable propositions that should be subject to revision if educators are working hard at learning their practice.

For example, under the overall goal of increasing literacy in Jefferson Middle School's district, school staff members developed a theory that might be articulated as, "If teachers learn literacy strategies to teach their students, then student reading skills in all their classes across the curriculum will improve, thus contributing to their overall improved learning."

This is a school theory of action; for other examples, see Online Resource 13.4: *Two theories of action — One from a district and one from a school within it.* Educators who look closely at classrooms through rounds get access to a key source of data and a powerful feedback loop to inform them whether their improvement efforts are actually reaching students, and if not, how to modify them to achieve better effects.

In the Jefferson example, the school learned that parts of its theory of action were working — teachers had learned the literacy strategies and were teaching them to their students. There was, however, a break in the chain, since the students only seemed to be using them when directed by a teacher. By making this theory explicit and visible to the observers, the rounds visit helped the school identify next steps in addressing the weak links of the causal chain.

A collaborative approach to adult and organizational learning

This approach embeds adult learning into practice and relies on engagement and inquiry rather than compliance. For many schools and school systems this is an enormous shift in culture. It requires moving from a top-down hierarchical system where administrators and other outside "experts" make the important instructional decisions and then check to ensure that teachers are implementing them. A collaborative approach suggests new roles for administrators in relationship to teachers, and to teachers in relationship to each other and to new systems of vertical and lateral accountability. It requires changes in deep-seated norms of practice by moving learning in schools and school systems from a primarily individual, isolated activity to a collective activity that can be examined, discussed, and improved.

With a nonjudgmental, descriptive approach, the rounds process makes it easier for professional learning to occur because it separates the person from the practice. Trust and a sense of collective efficacy are key elements for organizational and instructional improvement. The shared experience of developing a common language for describing and analyzing instructional practice and articulating common norms for collective learning creates opportunities for the development of trust. Repeated practice of instructional rounds creates collective efficacy among teachers and administrators around student learning. The collaborative learning approach used in rounds networks creates norms that support adult learning and make organizational learning possible. These efforts are similar to, and reinforce, the cultural changes called for in establishing and sustaining professional learning communities; however a great deal of change in the default culture has to take place for these efforts to work.

The rounds approach is countercultural to most educational improvement efforts. Making rounds is really about professionalization of education and educators. Educators engaged in rounds move from a default culture where teachers and administrators mostly operate in a bureaucratic and compliance-oriented culture to that of a "profession, with a shared set of practices, a body of collective knowledge, and a set of mutual commitments that define professional accountability" (City, Elmore, Fiarman, & Teitel, p. 185).

Steps

If an instructional rounds practice is implemented as a series of protocols or separate processes that are not integrated into a purposeful whole, educators can get good at "doing rounds" but will realize only limited gains and impacts on teaching and learning. For that reason, any set of implementation steps has to begin with larger questions connected to common definitions of high-quality teaching and learning, strategic purpose, desired impacts, and theories of action, as well as theories of adult learning, for achieving improvement goals. These big-picture underpinnings for the rounds practice also shape choices a school or district will make about implementation, since the rounds process is more of a practice than a fixed program.

Step 1: Clarify why you wish to engage in the instructional rounds process and how, specifically, it will intersect with and support your improvement strategy

An instructional rounds process needs to be a carefully designed complement to other strategic approaches to improvement. If the rounds process stands alone or the school or district does not have a strategic approach to improvement, the investment in the rounds practice will not have a sufficient payoff to be worth the trouble. To engage in this step properly, you need to articulate the improvement initiatives in place in your district (and your school), explain how they are strategically connected to one another, and then explain how the rounds practice will be integrated with those efforts and will support them.

To get traction on this important first step in schools and school districts where this language is unfamiliar, some educators use a protocol for extrapolating their strategy from an inventory of their initiatives. One way of doing this is through the process described in Chapter 1 of *Strategy in Action* (Curtis & City, 2009).

Another approach is to have a facilitator put the phrases "improvement strategy" and "instructional rounds" near each other on a large piece of butcher block paper and have educators from the district or the school conduct a "Chalk Talk" so they can graphically and literally make the connections. See the websites of the National School Reform Network (http://www.nsrfharmony.org/system/files/protocols/chalk_talk_0.pdf; www.nsrfharmony.org/sites/default/files/2008.SpringConnections.ProtocolsInPracticeTripleChalkTalk.pdf) and the School Reform Initiative (www.school reforminitiative.org/download/Protocols/Extending%20Practice/chalk_talk.pdf).for information on doing a "Chalk Talk." Those who are unfamiliar with drafting and then improving a theory of action can use Chapter 2 of *Instructional Rounds in Education* to practice developing an articulate and clear connection that links the rounds process with system strategy and shows how rounds will enhance the desired outcomes.

Step 2: The rounds practice helps improve teaching and learning at scale; make sure you clarify how the rounds practice will connect with any existing system frameworks that define high-quality teaching and learning

If you already have a clearly established instructional framework, you need to be clear about how it will be used to guide rounds and create a common focus on problems of instructional improvement. It is important to make sure that the rounds process keeps the focus on continuous inquiry and improvement of instruction and does not just help teachers share practice — a good thing, but one that could be achieved with a much less time-consuming peer observation approach. A rounds practice should be designed to deepen and improve learning and teaching. You need to think through how a rounds process will retain a focus on all aspects of the instructional core — teachers, students, content — and not just focus on teacher behavior (a drawback of some instructional frameworks). You must consider how you will ensure that the practice of rounds does not become so specific about classroom practices that rounds visits become implementation checks rather than continued inquiry. If a clearly established instructional framework is not in use in your district or school, you need to think through how rounds can calibrate the learning of educators to help them develop common understandings of what good teaching and learning should look like in their setting.

Step 3: Develop a customized design for rounds implementation that meets the challenges and opportunities of your setting; make sure it is consistent with your theories of action and theories about how adults, teams, and organizations learn best

Instructional rounds practice takes place in various formats that can be customized to meet the specific needs and improvement theories of action in your setting. Rounds can be conducted in networks that include only school-based administrators, only central office personnel, or only classroom teachers. Other networks deliberately mix teachers, administrators at all levels, and union personnel. Some educators conduct rounds across schools within a district (and some across districts); others conduct them within schools by teachers, administrators, and sometimes students.

Different approaches to the organization of rounds practice are discussed in more detail in the Variations section. The combinations and permutations that undergird the structures you put into place for your instructional rounds practice are not random or introduuced by happenstance; they need to be thoughtful and deliberate. At this stage, there are three items, in addition to your improvement strategy, to consider: development of organizational and improvement capacities; a culture of learning and improvement; and a theory of individual, team, and organizational learning.

Developing organizational and improvement capacities. How do you approach development of organizational and improvement capacity in your school(s)? Specifically, how will the rounds practice go beyond the focus on the visit day to really connect with a school's continuous improvement cycle? In addition, since an improvement strategy doesn't mean much unless there is the organizational capacity to enact it, anticipate how the organizational improvement capacity of the school (e.g. its use of teams, data, instructional leadership) will interact with the instructional rounds process. Otherwise, as some districts have discovered, instructional rounds visits can highlight next steps for improvement in schools, but the improvement capacity is so weak that nothing constructive comes from the process.

Developing a culture of learning and tangible improvement. How do you develop a culture of learning that is reinforced by improvement cycles that lead to a powerful sense of collective efficacy among educators? One of the most important aspects of improvement in any organization is the engagement of the individuals within the setting in identifying problems or "stuck points" in their work, figuring out improvements, trying them out, and then reflecting on the outcomes and starting the whole process again. This process, which shows up in management literature as the plan-do-study-act or the Toyota lean approach, is a fundamental underpinning of the rounds improvement cycle.

Follow-up and frequency are key. If teachers and administrators see that the next-level-of-work suggestions are implemented and lead to improvement, their engagement in this positive feedback loop is reinforced. On the other hand, if no clear and consistent steps are put into place for following up or checking back to look for impacts and outcomes, people are likely to disinvest, a result that underscores the importance of the next process.

Theory of adult, team, and organizational learning. What is your theory for how adults, teams, and organizations learn? It is useful to keep in mind that teachers who are observed in the rounds visit do not learn something from being observed. Rounds practices — whether they are network or school-based — need to develop clear structures and processes for learning from a visit that lead to changes in teaching and learning in classrooms.

Step 4: Make the long-term implementation commitments necessary to start and sustain the work

The learning processes taking place at Jefferson Middle School described at the beginning of this chapter do not just happen. The rounds process is facilitated, not just on the day of the visit, but before and after it. Facilitators need to be trained, supported, and paid or released from some of their other activities. An instructional rounds process requires a commitment of time, one of the scarcest of resources in schools. If teachers are involved, they need substitute coverage, except in some models of school-based rounds, where creative scheduling can obviate the need. Organizational support, logistics, food, and other supplies are needed. These are not short-term, temporary startup costs; they are ongoing and need to be sustained for the long haul.

Just as important as the resources outlined above are the commitment and connection of the rounds processes to the improvement work of the school or district. The rounds process cannot stand alone as a separate improvement approach and have any significant impacts on improvement. Rather, you must think about how all the items mentioned in the previous steps can be — and need to be — integrated into the other improvement processes of your district or school.

For example, large districts that have implemented instructional rounds have taken the core idea of a problem of practice and included it as a clear expectation for all the schools — not just those that might be visited that year. Districts have embraced the ideas about developing inquiry into the instructional core and have connected rounds to other ideas discussed in this book: professional learning communities, data teams, action research, and coaching approaches. They build in the expectation of and committment to supporting the school-level improvement capacity. They realize that while the rounds process can shed light

on the gaps in the local school's improvement processes, it alone cannot fill those gaps.

Step 5: Continue to learn about rounds and improvement

The rounds process is an evolving practice: "You learn the work by doing the work." Any steps taken toward implementation of rounds must build in reflective cycles. Usually these are done at network levels, where participants examine, for example, the process and the content of the last four rounds visits. They pay attention to patterns that might have emerged across several of the different schools visited, and what the implications might be for systemwide improvement as a result of the patterns. At the same time, they reflect on their processes: Have they gotten better as a network in developing powerful problems of practice or deep, reflective, and actionable next level-of-work suggestions? The notion of continuous learning is a key element for instructional rounds practice and needs to be designed in from the outset.

Variations

Conducting instructional rounds is not a program with a rigid set of protocols, but a practice with core guiding principles and key processes that are connected to organizational strategy and theories of learning for individuals, teams and organizations. In most settings, the network uses rounds practice to bring together educators from across schools within a district, or across districts to work together on instructional improvement. Rounds participants represent all types of educators.

Most of the models described in *Instructional Rounds in Education* (City, Elmore, Fiarman, & Teitel, 2009) are role-alike superintendent and principal networks, or mixed-role networks where teachers, union leaders and administrators visit a series of schools together. A typical school in one of these networks might get visited once a year; the improvement focus for many of these networks is as much on the district, system, or the broader network as it is on any individual school.

For a significant number of schools (as well as some districts) the models for cross-school networks articulated in the 2009 book did not provide a sufficiently close and continuing focus on schools and classrooms. Educators began to experiment with and adapt the principles and practices of instructional rounds to conduct rounds repeatedly in a single school context.

An unexpected outcome of the success of the 2009 book has been the widespread interest in and use of **school-based** instructional rounds (SBIR) — a structure and approach that is barely mentioned in it. Some saw developing an SBIR as a natural progression from having a rounds practice that engaged those who were relatively far from classrooms (as in a superintendent network) to involving those closest to them (like teachers). Working on their own and mostly in isolation, those engaged in SBIR have been developing significant variations on the rounds practice. Some have set up structures that dramatically increase the frequency of rounds visits; others have replaced the portions of the next-level-of-work process (where visiting teams make suggestions for systemic improvement) with an internal commitment process (where school-based teacher teams decide how they want to modify their work to help address their problem of practice). Some districts have aligned or "nested" school-based rounds with their district-wide or cross-school rounds practices to try to get the benefits of both practices (see Online Resource 13.5: *School-based instructional rounds* for more information on models and benefits of SBIRs).

Challenges and how to address them

When integrating rounds into their improvement processes, districts will face challenges. Some challenges are connected to the extent to which districts have been able to make changes in the three qualities of high-performing school districts mentioned previously: (a) agreement on what high-quality teaching and learning should look like, (b) a strategic and coherent approach to improvement, (c) and a collaborative approach to adult and organizational learning. Others have more to do with the instructional rounds practice itself and how it has been implemented in these settings.

Qualities of high-performing school districts. Of the three qualities of high-performing school districts, probably the most progress is being made on developing and articulating clear ideas about what high-quality teaching and learning should look like. Many districts have addressed this challenge by adapting or adopting existing frameworks like those of Charlotte Danielson or by developing their own and starting to use them.

Another challenge exists in terms of district development of a coherent and strategic approach to systemic improvement. Some district leaders have used the theory of action idea to good effect. Some have used it side-by-side with *Strategy in Action* (Curtis & City, 2009), or with other coherence-making approaches like that of *DataWise* (http://datawise.org/). But what many district leaders have found is that an improvement strategy is more than a blueprint or set of ideas that live in the heads of system and school leaders. It must include development of the organizational capacity to deliver on the promise of improvement. In the last few years leaders have developed clearer notions about what that improvement capacity needs to look like at the school level.

Factors like instructional leadership, teaming structures, availability and use of data, collaborative engagement of teachers and administrators in the work of improvement and a concomitant sense of efficacy and accountability are critical. When schools have well-developed capacity in these areas and a clear understanding of what good teaching and learning looks like, they are much more likely to enact a strategy developed in the system at the school and classroom level.

The norms about adult and organizational learning have proven very difficult to change. The culture of schools is very strongly oriented around a *status* mindset that can best be summarized by the belief that, when it comes to a knowledge, skill, or individual or organizational attribute, "you either have it or you don't." This stands in sharp contrast to a more *developmental* approach, which acknowledges the gradual and sometimes incremental learning used in other settings that characterizes individual and organizational growth. Philosophically, the developmental approach draws on the work of Carol Dweck (2006). Victoria, Australia, uses a developmental approach for student and teacher learning, as well as for organizational development (www.eduweb.vic.gov.au/edulibrary/public/staffdev/bastowinstitute/DLFposter.pccation).

And, although schools and districts report some progress in "separating the person from the practice" and getting educators to move out of the "land of nice" to actually name and address the real challenges and "stuck points" that they face, the analyses often don't go below the surface. Furthermore, the norms for follow-up still need to be strengthened. Rather, educators seem pleased to be able to see and learn from each other's practice (and consequently enjoy and are enthusiastic about participating in rounds), but in many settings, the next-level-of-work suggestions are not as deep and context specific as they could be.

The rounds practice itself. This challenge is related to an overly developed focus on the visit, with not enough attention to the overall improvement cycle that the visit represents, including the importance of what happens before and after.

Also, educators participating in rounds may lack clarity about exactly who should be learning from the rounds process and how they should be learning. Are rounds visits primarily for the benefit of the network visitors or for the host school? What, when, and how do the observed teachers learn? Since most of those who get to participate on the visit team describe it as a powerful learning opportunity, how can rounds be scaled up to provide the experience for more teachers?

There may be tensions, especially in medium and large districts, between how localized and how centralized aspects of the process should be. For example, a district can see the advantages of coherence and districtwide learning if all of its schools focus on the same problem of practice. On the other hand, schools that have not engaged in and have ownership of their problem of practice may end up viewing the whole process as a perfunctory compliance activity.

The rounds practice, which cannot replace an improvement strategy and the capacity to implement it, does have a strong symbiotic relationship with it. When schools and districts have more developed improvement practices, rounds can more easily take root and accelerate them. In districts with less developed improvement practices, the rounds process can highlight the gaps.

Incorporating instructional rounds as a practice that may change deep-seated culture in service of organizational and instructional improvement is slow, evolutionary work. Those involved in rounds need to take more of a developmental mindset about improvement; it is not "all or nothing." Schools and districts are not in either the default top-down compliance culture or the engaged organizational learning culture; rather, they move along a continuum.

ONLINE RESOURCES

13.1 Additional examples of problems of practice
13.2 How to schedule a rounds visit: Notes for the host school
13.3 The rounds visit supports the learning cycle of the network and the host
13.4 Two theories of action — One from a district and one from a school within it
13.5 School-based instructional rounds
13.6 Author's note on the evolution of the work
13.7 The Five Whys Protocol

A developmental approach means that problems of practice should not be framed with questions such as "Are teachers asking higher-order thinking questions?" Instead, the question should be "In what ways are teachers asking higher-order thinking questions?" as a way to move from a yes/no question, to focus on the actual practice, and to recognize the developmental nature of the continuum. It's important to see pockets of improvement, to learn from them and to use ideas from them to move the practice of others along the continuum. Organizational capacity for improvement (e.g. the use of teaming, data, instructional leadership) is developmental, and developmental rubrics can help educators name where they are in developing the capacity.

For an example of how Akron (OH) Public Schools integrates these ideas into a developmental rubric, see pages 84–88 in Teitel (2013), *School-Based Instructional Rounds*. A root-cause analysis like the Five Whys Protocol (see Online Resource 13.7: *The Five Whys Protocol*) can help participants go below the surface in addressing the challenges that are identified during the rounds process.

It's critical to weave the school's assessment of its improvement capacity into the next-level-of-work discussions so the suggestions made by the visiting team can be realistic and tied to local capacity. It's also imperative for educators to be explicit in teaching about and modeling adult learning. Every next-level-of-work suggestion requires some form of adult learning, since improvement can only take place with adult learning. Consequently, participants need to have clear ideas for how adults learn, which can be woven into their follow-up suggestions.

The practice of rounds can succeed when participants are clear about the importance of the work before and after a visit. Based on the root-cause analyses, the next-level-of-work suggestions can go deeper, and link contextually to the school culture and improvement structures. They can also be more specific about the kind of adult learning that will be necessary to help the school move to that next-level-of-work. This is work on making deep cultural change; it requires teachers and administrators to think differently about learning, mindsets, accountability and how they work in very different ways with each for improvement.

The author continues to learn about challenges related to using rounds to support instructional improvement. See Online Resource 13.6: *Author's note on the evolution of the work* for the story of what he and his colleagues are learning about challenges of and strategies for using rounds to support instructional improvement.

Conclusion

Educators participating in rounds need to realize how important it is to go through the "big picture" steps before and during the implementation and development of any rounds practice. If schools and districts are not clear about why and how instructional rounds will support their improvement efforts, their investments in the practice may not pay off. Since all improvement in the educational setting is contingent upon increased learning — by individuals, teams, organizations — it's important to emphasize theories of learning and how they connect with theories of action.

The emergence of variations on the structures of the practice, like school-based instructional rounds, leads to new emphasis on the design considerations. One size does not fit all. Variations such as "nested" rounds can be used to incorporate the outside perspectives and other system benefits of cross-school networks with the frequency and ability to increase and deepen the engagement of teachers that comes from school-based rounds. The big takeaway here is the importance of this understanding: The goal is not to "do rounds," but to support organizational and instructional improvement. Educators need to be intentional about

using instructional rounds as a part of their overall strategy for improvement. As the various forms of the instructional rounds practice continue to evolve, rounds can be used as one of many approaches to use to improve schools and districts, professionalize education, and offer all students the high-quality teaching and learning experiences they deserve.

References

Bloom, B. (1956). *Taxonomy of educational objectives.* Boston, MA: Allyn & Bacon.

City, E.A., Elmore, R.F., Fiarman, S.E., & Teitel, L. (2009). *Instructional rounds in education: A network approach to improving teaching and learning.* Cambridge, MA: Harvard Education Press.

Curtis, R. & City, E. (2009). *Strategy in action.* Cambridge, MA: Harvard Education Press.

Danielson, C. (1996). *Enhancing professional practice: A framework for teaching.* Alexandria, VA: ASCD.

Dweck, C. (2006). *Mindset: The new psychology of success. How we can learn to fulfill our potential.* New York, NY: Ballantine Books.

Marzano, R.J. (2000). *Designing a new taxonomy of educational objectives.* Thousand Oaks, CA: Corwin Press.

Teitel, L. (2013). *School-based instructional rounds: Improving teaching and learning across classrooms.* Cambridge, MA: Harvard Education Press.

Tyack, D. & Cuban, L. (1995). *Tinkering toward utopia: A century of public school reform.* Cambridge, MA: Harvard University Press.

CHAPTER 14

Lesson Study

Lesson study focuses on the heart of the educational process:
what actually happens between teacher and students in the classroom.

By Catherine C. Lewis

Six teachers are gathered around a table at a northern California elementary school. They have spent the past week at a summer workshop on mathematics and lesson study. They have solved algebra problems, analyzed state math standards, and identified the components of elementary mathematics that lead to success in algebra.

Today the group begins talking about a lesson study focus that will help students identify patterns and represent them mathematically.

"I think students are pretty strong in seeing patterns," says one teacher, "but not necessarily in going to the next step of establishing a rule and writing an equation, at least at the beginning of 4th grade. We don't always take them on to 'How would we represent this with numbers?'"

Over the next 10 days, the lesson study team works through two lesson study cycles of planning, teaching, observing, and reflecting on a research lesson (see Online Resource 14.1: *Lesson study cycle*).

Although lesson study is sometimes portrayed as a way to polish lessons, it actually provides a way groups can work not just on improving the lesson but on deepening their own understanding of content, in this case, mathematics; their understanding of students; and their understanding of teaching.

They begin to plan the research lesson by comparing textbooks and analyzing lessons designed to build students' mathematical representation of patterns. They choose one lesson and modify it to provide a real-world context (see Figure 1 on p. 211). They focus their instructional planning on an immediate goal — to help students recognize and mathematically represent patterns — and a long-term goal — to help students become curious, eager learners.

Several days later, one team member teaches the

research lesson to a class of 4th graders while the other team members and about a dozen invited outsiders (including several mathematics specialists) observe. Each team member takes detailed notes on the learning and behavior of one selected student, recording how that student's learning progressed (or failed to) over the course of the lesson, and what helped or hindered the learning. While the team members often lean in close to capture student work and conversations, they are careful not to disrupt student work or sight lines to the teacher.

Following the "Triangle Tables" research lesson, the team members take a brief break to organize their notes, and then have a colloquium in which they follow a structured discussion protocol (see Online Resource 14.2: *A protocol for observing and discussing a research lesson*) to present their observational data to teammates and the invited outsiders. The discussion dwells on an interesting contradiction in the data: Most students filled out the worksheet (see Figure 1: Triangle Tables Lesson on p. 211) correctly, suggesting that they grasped the mathematical rule that was the teacher's objective. In addition, when talking with tablemates, some students discussed the mathematical rule. But few students could articulate the meaning of the pattern in the worksheet with respect to the original problem, as the following excerpt from the end of the class reveals:

Teacher (asking class to guide her in writing the equation on the board): *The number of tables plus two equals what?*

The teacher pauses, seeing only a few hands raised.

Teacher: *The number of tables plus two got us what?*

The teacher pauses again, still sees few hands raised.

Teacher: *What are we trying to figure out?* [Pause]
What are we trying to figure out here? [Pause]
We already know the number of tables. Jamie tells us we have to add two. What's that going to get us?

As the instructing teacher comments during the colloquium, "At the very end, when I was trying to get them to say the number of tables plus two equals the number of seats, there was a lot of confusion. It's easy for them to just go 'plus two,' 'plus two,' 'plus two,' and they sort of lose the whole picture of what the plus two is representing." She notes that the worksheet may have spoon-fed the pattern to the students. Another team member explains how her observation of students changed her own thinking about the problem by revealing the geometric reason for the plus-two pattern:

"I noticed kids counting the seats different ways, and this was a kind of a big 'aha' for me. . . . When I've done the problem myself, I've always counted [she shows how she counted around the edge] and it didn't occur to me there was another way of counting it. . . . But [student name] had laid out 20 triangles. . .and she was counting [demonstrates counting top and bottom alternately, followed by ends] and then it looked totally different to me. I could see there are 10 triangles on top, 10 on bottom, and a seat on either end. Now I was seeing the pattern a different way. . . . That's why I thought it might be helpful to have kids talking about how they're counting it."

In meetings that day and the next, the team decides to modify the lesson in several ways. The teachers eliminate the worksheet and give students strips of paper with the number of tables filled in and the number of seats left blank.

Students each receive a unique number of tables, for which they are asked to figure out the number of seats, share data with tablemates, and find and write about a pattern that will help them solve the problem. The team also builds into the lesson an opportunity for students to show publicly how they counted, because counting may reveal geometric reasons for the plus-two pattern that other students have not noticed.

Two days later, another lesson study team member teaches the revised research lesson to a different 4th-grade class. Once again the remaining team members observe, record student work and behavior, and report their observations during the colloquium following the research lesson. Their reports suggest that the redesigned lesson, in which students were forced to organize the data without the worksheet, better promoted student understanding of the meaning of the plus-two pattern. As students worked in their table groups, they made comments like, "There's one seat for each triangle and one extra for each end."

The teacher who taught the first lesson sums up the difference: "Having taught the first lesson, I would much rather have taught this lesson. . . . The student-driven activities are so much more powerful. They discovered it. I wasn't pouring it into their ears. . . . It's their own personal information."

Another teacher adds: "The learning was so much more effective this time. It wasn't about teaching; it was about learning. To me, as a teacher, going back and looking at lessons and lesson plans, that idea can be used anywhere — to make sure that students are always the learners in the classroom.

Figure 1: **Triangle Tables Lesson**

We have a long, skinny room and triangle tables that we need to arrange in a row with their edges touching, as shown. Assuming each side can hold one seat, how many seats will 1 table, 2 tables, 3 tables hold? Is there a pattern that helps you figure out how many seats 10 tables will hold?

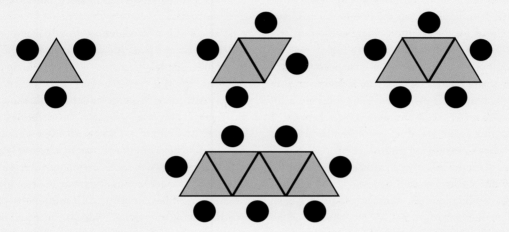

STUDENT WORKSHEET

Triangle Rule Macine   Name_____

INPUT
Number of triangle tables   ☐

RULE
☐

OUTPUT
Number of seats   ☐

INPUT *Number of triangle tables*	OUTPUT *Number of seats*
1	3
2	4
3	
4	
5	
6	

Source: *Lesson Study: A Handbook of Teacher-Led Instructional Change,* by Catherine C. Lewis, Philadelphia: Research for Better Schools, 2002. Used with permission.

We're not necessarily the teachers."

The next day, the lesson study team members consolidate their learning by looking back at the two research lessons, recording the changes they made, and reflecting on what they learned from revising the research lesson and teaching it a second time. They concur that the second lesson gave them a better understanding of student thinking.

The instructing teacher from the first lesson suddenly recalls: "The focus on the counting. Having the kids talk about their counting. That was a big improvement. Because we started to talk about the process of what's happening here."

Another teacher adds, "Having the students have to describe their counting really got at their thinking a lot more, and it also made the lesson more accessible to other kids. It gave other kids a lot of opportunities to hear and think about what was going on in the lesson."

The instructor of the first lesson said: "And just a personal 'aha' for me. When you had said . . . in the first debriefing, that we should really spend some time on having the students' share [their counting], at first I thought 'Who cares about that?' I did not see that as important because I personally did not see the pattern, that the ends are the plus-two. So it just shows that in everything we teach, we're only as effective as our level of understanding. So we have to keep pushing ourselves to delve into . . . the why, the how come. That's the challenge. . . . Especially in the elementary grades, the stuff is relatively simple."

Overview

Originating in Japan, lesson study is a cycle of instructional improvement focused on planning, observing, and discussing research lessons and drawing out their implications for teaching and learning more broadly. Research lessons are classroom lessons that provide an opportunity for teachers to (1) bring to life their ideas about effective teaching and (2) carefully record student learning and behavior and give each other feedback on the research lesson, the students, and on teaching and learning. In lesson study, teachers work together to:

- Form goals for student learning and long-term development. Teachers study existing curricula and standards and discuss the qualities they would like students to have five to 10 years later.

- Collaboratively plan a lesson designed to bring to life both immediate and long-term goals.

- Teach the lesson, with one team member teaching and others gathering evidence on student learning and development.

- Discuss the evidence they gather during the lesson, using it to improve the lesson, the unit, and overall instruction.

- Teach the revised lesson in another classroom, if they desire, and study and improve it again (Lewis & Hurd, 2011).

Through this cycle, teachers deepen their knowledge of content, pedagogy, and student thinking, and increase their access to knowledgeable colleagues. As illustrated in the story of the California teachers, closely examining student learning and behavior during research lessons helps teachers find effective ways to teach particular subject matter, and also yields broader lessons about teaching and learning. As one team member commented, "I learned that a worksheet can be a dangerous thing." Another noted, "I learned that students need to do the work, not the teacher."

Observations during the research lesson also reveal the student qualities and habits of mind that support or undermine student learning in one's own setting. For example, teachers may discover that students who focus on filling out the worksheet may not be attending to the mathematical content. This discovery may deepen their lesson study work, as teachers seek to design research lessons, and then their own lessons, in ways that promote students' curiosity and eagerness to learn.

Throughout the process of lesson study, teachers have opportunities to deepen their own content knowledge as they compare various curricula and standards, select and modify a lesson, try the problem themselves, anticipate student thinking, and analyze student responses to the lesson.

Rationale

Lesson study focuses on the heart of the educational process: what actually happens between teacher and students in the classroom. Although it makes sense that observation and improvement of actual classroom instruction should be the foundation for instructional improvement, U.S. teachers actually have few opportunities to observe classroom lessons or to be observed by others, resulting in an unstable basis for instructional improvement.

During lesson study, teachers collect data on the supports and barriers to students' learning during actual classroom lessons, share these data so they form a picture of the whole class's learning, and use the resulting information to improve their instruction — not just the single lesson under study, but instruction more broadly. Lesson study is a teacher-led process. Ideally, teachers actively draw on the best available expertise from outside as well as within the school.

Many promising educational reforms fail when educators implement superficial features of the reform without clearly understanding the reform's essential elements. The activities outlined in this chapter — setting goals, reviewing existing curricula, and developing, observing, discussing and revising a research lesson — are useful only when they create opportunities for teachers to learn about subject matter, teaching, and students. When asked how lesson study benefits their practice, experienced Japanese and U.S. teachers say lesson study has provided opportunities to:

1. Think carefully about the goals of a particular lesson, unit, and discipline.
2. Study the best available curriculum materials.
3. Deepen knowledge of subject matter and of instruction.
4. Think carefully about long-term goals for students and connect those with daily practice.
5. Strengthen collaboration with colleagues.
6. Develop the eyes to see students.

The point of lesson study is to create continuous learning along each of these pathways.

Research about lesson study has focused on single or multiple case studies. Case studies have looked at the effects of lesson study within a particular school context. They have provided "local proof" of effectiveness (Lewis, Perry & Murata 2006). Only recently, large-scale studies have also been conducted to test the impact of lesson study. A recent experimental study (Lewis & Perry, 2014) focused on three groups of teachers, randomly assigned to treatments. Results demonstrated that the group assigned to conduct lesson study supported by mathematical resources significantly improved students' learning of fractions (Gersten et al., 2014; Lewis & Perry, 2014, March). Lesson study supported by mathematical resources also significantly increased teachers' mathematical knowledge, teachers' perception of the usefulness of collegial work, and their expectations for student achievement (Lewis & Perry, 2014, March; Lewis & Perry, in press).

Steps

Lesson study is a simple idea. If you want to improve instruction, what could be more obvious than collaborating with fellow teachers to plan, observe, and reflect on lessons? While it may be a simple idea, however, lesson study is a complex process, supported by collaborative goal-setting, careful data collection on student learning, and protocols that enable productive discussion of sensitive issues. The first step is to form a group.

Step 1: Form a lesson study group

Recruit group members (four to six is optimal), make a time commitment, and agree on a schedule and ground rules for working together (Lewis & Hurd, 2011). There are no hard and fast rules about membership. Depending on your goals and situation, it may make sense to work with teachers from the same or adjoining grade levels, or with teachers who share a content area focus. Teachers may come from the same or different schools.

Some lesson study groups find it useful to work with an outside content coach, facilitator, or university-based researcher. *Lesson Study Step by Step* (Lewis & Hurd, 2011) provides a more detailed discussion of group formation strategies. Lesson study, because it requires trust and commitment on the part of teachers, is most likely to succeed if teachers participate willingly. Beginning with a small group of trusted colleagues and allowing the concept to spread over time is likely to be more effective than a top-down mandate. That said, schoolwide lesson study is extraordinarily powerful, and it makes sense even when beginning with a small group of volunteers to lay out the welcome mat for the whole school — for example, to plan a research lesson open to the school, or to invite the whole school to share in developing the long-term research theme. A whole-school lesson study case is provided in Lewis & Hurd (2011).

Step 2: Focus the lesson study

Lesson study focuses on specific content goals and also broad, long-term goals for student development. For example, the California teachers introduced at the beginning of this chapter focused on helping students learn to represent patterns mathematically, and also on helping them become eager, curious learners. Team members need to consider both types of goals as they shape their lesson study work.

Consider long-term goals for student development. What qualities would you like your present students to have five or 10 years down the road? What is the gap between these qualities and who they are now? These are the classic questions that begin lesson study. You can focus your lesson study work using Online Resource 14.3: *Choosing a lesson study theme.*

For example, the Japanese elementary school teachers featured in the videotape *Can You Lift 100 Kilograms?* (www.lessonresearch.net) wanted their students to be active learners who developed their own perspectives and ideas. But the teachers felt their students were often passive learners, perhaps as a result of the time spent watching TV and playing video games. As one teacher commented, "When they hear another student's answer, particularly if it's a smart student, they just figure 'That's good enough; I'll go along with that,' rather than thinking deeply for themselves." The teachers also noticed that some students preferred solitary computer play to interacting with classmates. The teachers chose as their long-term goal: "For students to value friendship, develop their own perspectives and ways of thinking, and enjoy science."

Choose a content area and topic. Your group may form with the intent of working in a particular content area (language arts, mathematics, science, social studies, etc.) or, especially in elementary schools in which one teacher usually teaches all subjects, you may make this decision after you form the group. Lesson study can be practiced with any content area or aspect of school life. In fact, lesson study practice in Japan often focuses on areas we find surprising (music, art, physical education, moral development, class meetings, schoolwide events, and so forth). What content area does your group wish to target?

Within a particular content area (such as mathematics or language arts), you will need to home in on a particular topic for your research lesson. For example, the California teachers focused on students' mathematical representation of patterns. When choosing the focus of your lesson study, you may wish to concentrate on areas that are:

- Fundamental to subsequent learning;
- Persistently difficult for students (or disliked by them);
- Difficult to teach; and
- New to the curriculum.

Student work, test data, and standards may be important resources in helping you select the focus for your lesson study work.

Step 3: Plan the research lesson

The planning that leads up to a research lesson differs from the lesson planning familiar to U.S. teachers. Online Resource 14.4: *Template: Plan to guide learning* guides research lesson planning. As teachers work through this resource, they will want to create a plan to guide learning, a document that serves three purposes: to guide teaching the research lesson; to guide collecting data and informing outside observers; and to document the research lesson to be used in later reflection by the lesson study team. Some unfamiliar features of the research lesson planning process are highlighted in this section.

Study existing curriculum materials and build on them where possible. The California teachers began by studying mathematics standards, comparing how different textbooks teach the topic of mathematical patterns, and selecting an existing lesson to use as a starting point for the research lesson. Whenever possible, teachers should build on the best available lessons, rather than writing a lesson from scratch. In this way, the curriculum can steadily improve as teachers "stand on the shoulders of giants."

Consider the whole unit plan. Lesson study is not about a single lesson in isolation. The plan to guide learning (see Online Resource 14.4: *Template: Plan to guide learning*) includes a space for teachers to describe the unit of study in which the research lesson falls. Even though teachers may observe and collect detailed data on just a single research lesson, they consider the larger unit context of the lesson, creating a brief outline of the number of lessons in the unit, the major learning within each lesson, and where the research lesson falls within the unit.

Try the task and anticipate student thinking. When teachers themselves try the task or problem they plan to give to students, they can explore the academic content in ideas students may bring to the task. For example, when the California teachers took out triangles and tried the task themselves, several teachers struggled to make sense of the plus-two pattern in the table. Their confusion led to a discussion in which they collectively made sense of both the horizontal pattern in the table (two more seats than tables) and the vertical pattern (one seat is added each time a table is added). Anticipating that some students might not arrange the triangles in a straight line, the teachers explored the problem to see what would happen and found that different arrangements of a given number of triangles could lead to different numbers of seats.

A New Jersey teacher involved in lesson study describes research lesson planning: "It is challenging to try and think about the students' solutions to the problem before they do it and to try and get all of the answers they might come up with. You have to think about things from the student's point of view, and that is a big change." She goes on to contrast research lesson planning with the planning that previously went on at her school:

> . . .[now] we think a lot more about the motivation for the lesson and making sure that the kids have the prior knowledge that they need before we teach each lesson.…Before we did lesson study, we really didn't think about what the student responses would be to the questions. When we posed a problem we never really thought about what the kids would come up with. It was . . . "Well, we hope they get the right answer, and if they don't, then we will deal with it." Now we are really thinking about, "Well, what if this answer were to come up? How would we deal with it?"

If your effort to anticipate student thinking doesn't provoke a rich discussion, two lines of action may be productive.

- *Examine your student task.* Do you have a task that reveals student thinking? If not, can you revise it so that it is more of a thought-revealing task (Lesh, et al., 2000)? In the work of the California teachers, students revealed much less about their thinking when they filled out the table than when they discussed and wrote about the pattern.
- *Investigate several students' current thinking by using an open-ended problem or interview.* Knowledge of student thinking may help you design a better task.

Eventually, your plan to guide learning should include goals at four levels:

1. Goals specific to the lesson.
2. Goals specific to the unit.
3. Broad goals for the subject area.
4. Long-term goals for student development.

The simultaneous focus on specific and broad goals makes lesson study confusing to newcomers. People sometimes ask in exasperation, "Which is the real focus of lesson study? Teaching specific topics like fractions or long-term goals like love of learning?" The answer is both. This makes sense if you consider that long-term goals like scientific habits of mind and love of learning are built up through daily lessons. Students who fill out worksheets in science class day after day are likely to have a very different attitude toward science than students who are challenged to move a 100-kilogram sack that has suddenly appeared in the middle of their gym (Lewis, 2000). And, in turn, student qualities and basic disciplinary habits of mind strongly constrain what teachers are able to teach. If you have any doubt about this, think about what you were able to teach to the most and least motivated classes you have ever taught.

The levers lesson, "Can You Lift 100 Kilograms?" (Lewis, 2000), for example, was designed to build the students' motivation to learn more about levers (a lesson goal); their understanding of the factors that affect the lever's functioning (unit goal); students' willingness to develop their own scientific ideas (broad subject area goal); and their enjoyment of learning and friendship (long-term goals for student development).

You need not worry that these goals are set in stone. Over the course of their lesson study cycles, the California teachers who refined the "Triangle Tables" lesson also refined their thinking about what it meant for students to understand mathematical patterns.

Make a data collection plan. Data collected during the research lesson enable team members to see how selected students' learning progressed — or failed to — over the course of the entire lesson, and how each element of the experience (lesson design and materials, prior knowledge, personal qualities, fellow students, etc.) supported or interfered with their learning. The students observed should represent a range of achievement levels and backgrounds so as to reveal diverse points of view on the lesson. A complete narrative record of everything the selected students said, did, heard, and saw is helpful. For example, if students made calculations or notes that they then erased, a record of the writing and erasure should be made. Students' nonverbal behavior and activities should also be described or sketched, and student work collected or copied. Many teachers also like to videotape or audiotape selected students or groups to facilitate later study of the research lesson; however, these records are not a substitute for the careful written observations and artifacts that can form the basis for the post-lesson colloquium.

The specific data collected will depend on the study team's goals. For example, the team that planned "Can You Lift 100 Kilograms?" was interested in helping students value friendship, so they collected data on how frequently the quietist students spoke up and when this occurred (i.e. whether it happened in response to particular design features of the lesson).

Consider inviting outsiders to the research lesson and colloquium. If you wish to invite outsiders to your research lesson and colloquium, there are several groups you might want to consider (see Online Resource 14.5: *Outsiders to invite to lesson study*).

Arrange logistics. The class to which the research lesson will be taught needs to be arranged for in advance. Most often it is the instructing team member's class, but it is also possible to borrow a class, as the California teachers did, taking advantage of a year-round school that was in session during their summer workshop. Substitutes may need to be arranged for the period during the research lesson (and the colloquium following, unless it is held after school).

Students need to understand the basic facts of the research lesson: that teachers are studying the lesson to improve the lesson and their own teaching, not to judge students. Students should also be told in advance that the observers are there to gather data, not to help or teach them. (Otherwise students may think they have encountered an exceptionally unhelpful group of teachers.) If the lesson will be videotaped or audiotaped, teachers should check on any district requirements for parental consent or notification.

Step 4: Conduct the research lesson and colloquium

When the lesson study team has finished writing the plan to guide instruction (see Online Resource 14.4: *Template: Plan to guide learning*), members will have prepared

carefully for the research lesson by studying existing curricula and standards, trying the student task themselves, anticipating student thinking, refining the lesson design, and planning the data collection that will reveal student thinking. Yet, as one Japanese lesson study group has noted, teaching is like polar exploration: You never know exactly what you will encounter once in the field. Like a polar explorer, the instructor of the research lesson has studied the terrain carefully through collaborative work on the instructional plan but still may encounter unexpected situations. In these situations, the team member teaching the lesson should exercise his or her own professional judgment, just as in daily teaching.

One lesson study team member teaches the research lesson while the rest of the team members closely observe student learning and behavior to gather the agreed-upon data. In addition to the lesson study team members, others may observe the lesson. The team gives all observers the plan to guide instruction ahead of time, and observers carry it into the research lesson on a clipboard along with any special data collection forms (such as a seating chart).

While the teacher is teaching the research lesson, the observing teachers should not help or teach students, or interfere with their learning (for example, by blocking the child's view of the teacher). Observers also should respect the classroom atmosphere by arriving and leaving on time, refraining from side conversations, and paying attention to the lesson's "points to notice" (see Online Resource 14.4: *Template: Plan to guide learning*) for later discussion.

The post-lesson colloquium can occur after a brief break of 20 minutes or so, or after school on the day of the research lesson. Any lesson artifacts (such as the problem posed to students, visual aids, and student work) should be posted for the team and observers to see during the colloquium. The colloquium follows a structured agenda that typically starts with comments from the instructing teacher (see Online Resource 14.2: *A protocol for observing and discussing a research lesson*).

Data presentation is a key part of the colloquium. One member of the team should serve as facilitator, to keep time and move the discussion along. Often team members or a facilitator will formulate several questions to guide the discussion. For example, in the case of the California teachers, one team member asked, "What is the evidence that students understood the plus-two pattern?"

If outside observers have been invited, the team must provide a brief overview of why the lesson was designed as it was and orient them to a process for the colloquium and how it differs from more familiar discussions.

The purpose of the research lesson colloquium is not to evaluate the teacher but to share data on students' responses to the lesson. U.S. teachers will need to create this shared understanding by developing group norms and protocols, such as:

- Post and review the agenda and ground rules for the discussion so all attendees understand the research.

- Have a discussion chair who keeps time and facilitates, and agree in advance on how the facilitator will handle lengthy or inappropriate comments.

- Have a well-conceived plan for collecting and presenting data to support a rich discussion.

- Have one group member take notes, which the lesson study group will use later to think about where to go next. "We've got that in our notes" can be a great way to move the discussion on.

- Reflect in speech that the research lesson belongs to the group, not just the teacher who taught it. The instructing teacher needs to feel supported. It is our lesson, not my lesson.

- The teacher who actually taught the research lesson speaks first and has the first chance to point out any difficulties in the lesson. (And there seems to be an unwritten rule that teachers don't further criticize something that's already been identified as a problem.) Next, if outsiders are attending, one member of the lesson study team explains to everyone the thinking and planning behind the lesson.

The heart of the colloquium is discussion of the data collected during the research lesson. The data collection focus is decided in advance (and noted in the instructional plan, under "points to notice," Online Resource 14.4: *Template: Plan to guide learning*). It almost always includes a detailed narrative record of the learning of selected students in order to document how their thinking changed over the course of the lesson and what supported or impeded change. Observers talk specifically about the data that were collected, not impressionistically about the quality of the lesson. So, for example, they might say, "Forty-seven percent of the students raised their hands at some time during today's lesson" rather

than, "Few (or many) students raised their hands."

After each team member has had a turn to present data, the colloquium may move into a discussion format. Often, the discussion focuses on questions developed in advance by the team or facilitator. The point of these questions is generally to encourage further thinking about the research lesson, the data collected, possible directions for lesson revision, or the broader implications for instruction.

The California teachers asked what students' manipulative use revealed about their thinking, and what evidence was available that students understood the plus-two pattern. Other examples of organizing questions include: What motivated students' learning today? How did blackboard use (or journal use, student presentation of ideas, etc.) contribute to student learning? What did the lesson suggest are the strengths and challenges of our students as scientific (or historical) thinkers? What does the lesson tell us about our reciprocal reading program? The questions will vary greatly depending on the goals of the lesson, the goals for student development, and the teachers' interests.

If outside observers are present, the team may want to allot time for them to ask questions and make comments. A protocol common in Japan may be useful in the United States: speakers there begin their comments by thanking the instructor and team members and noting something they learned from the lesson. The facilitator can list and, perhaps, organize observers' comments so that the lesson study team can consider the major themes that arise, rather than responding to each comment individually.

An hour or so is generally sufficient for a colloquium, and free discussion is best kept to a small portion of that time. Although this may seem brief, the end of the formal colloquium is not the end of the learning from the research lesson. As one teacher said at the end of the colloquium following a research lesson: "The research lesson is not over yet. It's not a one-time lesson. Rather, it gives me a chance to continue consulting with other teachers."

Step 5: Consolidate learning. Plan next steps

You've now completed one cycle of lesson study, from thinking about goals to bringing them to life in an actual lesson and seeing how students responded. Now consider what you have learned about subject matter, students, and instruction (see Online Resource 14.6: *Reflection on the lesson study cycle*). Team members should write a brief afterword to the instructional plan that summarizes what they learned from planning, teaching, observing, and discussing the research lesson. Remember that the California teachers, reflecting on what they gained from their lesson study cycle, learned not only about representing mathematical patterns, but about the ways that firsthand messy work with data builds students' understanding.

What would your group like to do next? Would you like to modify this lesson and teach it again, trying out some of the suggestions made at the colloquium?

Often, the data gathered during the first time the research lesson is taught suggest important design changes, and team members derive great satisfaction from seeing the re-designed lesson's impact on students (Fernandez & Yoshida, 2004). Another option is to move on to another topic. In any case, just after the first research lesson is an excellent time for the team to reflect on the goals of the lesson study effort and on the successes and rough spots of the work. Several questions may help team members reflect on the lesson study cycle and think about next steps:

1. What aspects of our lesson study work are valuable? What aspects are challenging?
2. Is lesson study helping us develop our knowledge of subject matter and of student learning and development?
3. Is lesson study leading us to think in new ways about our everyday practice?
4. Are we working together in a productive and supportive way? Do all members of our group feel included and valued?

Finally, don't forget to celebrate. You are pioneering a new form of professional learning in the U.S. Embrace this Japanese tradition that has become a favorite with many lesson study groups in the U.S. Have a party or dinner out following the research lesson, with team members treating the lesson instructor.

Variations

There is no single right way to do lesson study. Lesson study is a flexible approach that Japanese teachers adapt to their own needs and circumstances. The remarkably diverse contexts for lesson study in Japan include the following:

- Teachers create private, voluntary circles to pursue an issue of interest (e.g. integrating human rights education into the elementary curriculum). They collaboratively study existing resources, plan how to bring the new form of instruction to life, visit each other's classrooms for research lessons when feasible, and share videotapes, student work, and other data about their instruction.
- National teachers' groups (such as the science teachers' or history teachers' associations) center their annual conferences on lesson study rather than meeting in a hotel. Attendees fan out to cooperating local schools to observe and discuss research lessons.
- Instead of writing a final report to a funding agency, teachers conduct "open-house research lessons" to show what they have learned, for example, integrating technology into the social studies curriculum. Hundreds of teachers visit to see the lessons and hear the teachers talk about what they learned over the course of their funded work.
- Twice a month, students go home an hour early and all teachers in a district engage in district-sponsored, cross-school lesson study groups focused on various content areas (e.g. math, language arts, science, art, music, etc.). Teachers choose the content of most interest to them. Twice a year, these groups conduct research lessons open to all educators in the district.
- A whole-school lesson study effort focus has as its goal building students' experience of the school as a community. Teachers conduct and study cross-age buddies activities, schoolwide festivals, and class meetings in much the way that they study research lessons in academic disciplines.
- A junior high with a high truancy rate adopts a lesson study theme of "instruction that connects students to school." All teachers agree to conduct a research lesson at least once a year, and teachers agree on a set of instructional principles to enact across all subject areas (such as opportunities for students to discuss ideas with classmates and to see how their learning is related to life outside school).
- Nationally active teachers in mathematics education submit instructional plans on a specific topic (area of parallelograms, for example) to their national association. Five selected teachers explain the rationale for their instructional plans during a panel discussion

at the association's national meeting; the 1,000 audience members choose the approach they want to see implemented with the waiting class of 5th graders. They watch the lesson, taught on stage, by video projection.

The heart of lesson study is careful study of actual instruction in order to improve it in the future. Teachers who have developed successful lesson study efforts have not viewed lesson study as a blueprint to be implemented, but as a set of practices to be studied and refined continuously to promote learning along all the pathways mentioned at the outset of this chapter. The California teachers took a research stance, not just toward their teaching but toward the process of lesson study itself by frequently reflecting on what worked well and what needed to be refined in their lesson study work. Some of their modifications include the following:

- Inviting math content specialists to join their work;
- Shortening the planning period before the first teaching of the research lesson because the data gathered during that lesson enabled much more thoughtful planning;
- Introducing the norm-setting so that groups would think early on about the norms that would guide their work;
- Studying existing curricula and standards to begin the lesson study process; and
- Actively collaborating with Japanese practitioners and others knowledgeable about lesson study.

Challenges and how to address them

Educators who are beginning to use this learning design may find themselves confronted by challenges of social capital and tangible resources, both of which may be addressed by development that comes from commitment to the process.

Teacher interest. Lesson study is driven by teachers' interest. Participating teachers must be willing to invest time and energy in the hard work of lesson study. Small, committed efforts that spread through teachers' enthusiasm may ultimately prove more able to "go to scale" than efforts mandated from the top down. In a well-designed effort, teacher commitment to the process grows steadily over time.

A learning stance. Precisely because there is no blueprint for lesson study, teachers and administrators who would make it succeed must take a learning stance.

For example, they would be wise to:

- Use and build on existing protocols and curricula rather than reinventing the wheel;
- Learn from others, including Japanese colleagues, content specialists, and experienced lesson study practitioners;
- Regard instruction as work in progress that can always be improved; and
- Continuously reflect on their work to see what can be improved.

Willingness to collaborate. A fundamental benefit of lesson study comes from seeing instruction through others' eyes and from developing strong collegial networks that can be drawn on in daily instruction. The Japanese have a saying that "when you gather three people, you have a genius." When asked what attitudes were essential to the success of lesson study, teacher Jackie Hurd answered: "That you can always get better at teaching. That you're never at the end of the road. . . . If you came into [lesson study] and you were [acting] like 'I'm the hottest thing out there and I've got all these great ideas and I'll share them with you guys'. . . you're not going to get anything out of it."

High-quality content resources. In lesson study, teachers collaboratively study the curriculum and how to teach it. Their study will be useful to the extent that high-quality resources are accessed — for example, well-designed curricula, relevant research, and expertise within the group or from the outside (for example, a district-based or university-based "knowledgeable other"). Recent research documents, for example, how Japanese curriculum materials include information about the development of student thinking and the rationale for instructional tasks that is often lacking from U.S. curriculum materials (Lewis, Perry & Friedkin, 2012) and that can provide a crucial catalyst for teachers' learning during lesson study (Lewis, Perry, Friedkin & Roth, 2013). Likewise, a recent randomized trial of lesson study with high-quality mathematics resources on fractions (drawn from Japanese curriculum materials and U.S. research), demonstrates a significant impact of lesson study supported by mathematical resources on both teachers' and students' learning of fractions (Gersten et al., 2014; Lewis & Perry, 2014, March).

Administrative support. Administrative support and resources (such as substitute time, meeting time, and/or stipends) are needed for many lesson study efforts. While the critical elements are foundations for lesson study, they should also be built up through lesson study. Teacher interest, learning stance, and willingness to collaborate should all increase over time in successful lesson study, and indeed there is some evidence this is the case (Lewis & Perry, 2014; Lewis, Perry & Hurd, 2009). In Japan, lesson study allows teachers to have a central role in policy implementation and to rapidly build and spread knowledge about a new curriculum or approach to education (Lewis, 2010), an application of great potential usefulness outside of Japan as well.

Lesson study impact. A growing body of research suggests that lesson study can make an impact on teachers' knowledge, professional community, teaching practice, and student learning (Hart, Alston, & Murata, 2011; Lewis, Perry, & Hurd, 2009; Lewis, Perry, Hurd, & O'Connell, 2006; Lo, Chik, & Pong, 2005). Much of this research is what might be called "local proof" (Lewis, Perry & Murata, 2006); that is, lesson study is shown to be effective in a particular setting, as demonstrated by beneficial effects on teachers' knowledge, teachers' beliefs (such as the belief that students can learn), teaching practice, and/or student learning. Recently, some general proof of the effectiveness of lesson study has also emerged, such as a randomized controlled trial in which lesson study, supported by a mathematical resource kit on fractions, was shown to have a significant impact on teachers' and students' knowledge of fractions, as well as to increase teachers' belief that students can learn, teachers' belief in the usefulness of collegial collaboration, and so forth.

Conclusion

It is surprising to hear that many people think that they know everything they need to know about lesson study because they have watched a video, read a book, or attended a workshop. This is like assuming one can learn everything one needs to learn about teaching from a book, video, or workshop. Resources are a great way to start learning about lesson study (see Online Resource 14.7: *Additional resources*).

Like teaching, one learns to do lesson study skillfully by working at it over time. Lesson study is a much richer and more varied practice than most educators outside Japan realize. So it behooves educators to keep studying Japanese

lesson study models as well as models emerging around the world (e.g. WALS, 2012).

It is natural for newcomers to lesson study to think of it in terms of its surface features: planning, conducting, observing, and revising research lessons. This is a starting point for thinking about lesson study, but it is a bit like thinking about teaching as a set of activities (passing out materials, posing a problem, writing on the blackboard, asking questions, and so forth). The crux of successful lesson study is to plan, observe, and discuss the research lesson in ways that strengthen the pathways of learning for teachers:

- Teachers increase content knowledge and pedagogical knowledge as they study the best available curricula and standards, solve and discuss the problems that will be given to students, and analyze student thinking.
- Teachers improve their "eyes to see students" by anticipating student thinking, carefully observing students during lessons, and hearing other teachers' observations;
- Teachers develop stronger networks with each other so they can better use each other's knowledge and resources;
- Teachers make stronger connections between their daily practice and their long-term goals for students;
- Teachers increase in motivation to improve instruction and their sense of efficacy as they have opportunities to look closely at student learning and redesign instruction in more effective ways.

Lesson study is a way for teachers to help one another slow down the act of teaching in order to learn more about students, subject matter, and their own teaching. As Kazuyoshi Morita, a Japanese teacher at Tsukuba Attached Elementary School, said:

> A lesson is like a swiftly flowing river. When you're teaching, you must make judgments instantly. When you do a research lesson, your colleagues write down your words and the students' words. Your real profile as a teacher is revealed to you for the first time.

And as Jackie Hurd, a U.S. teacher, said of lesson study:

> One of the things that I really love about it is that it puts a professional part back in teaching that we have to battle for all the time. ... Being able to say, "This is like a science, and we can figure these things out and get better at them."

References

Fernandez, C. & Yoshida, M. (2004). *Lesson study: A case of a Japanese approach to improving instruction through school-based teacher development.* Mahwah, NJ: Lawrence Erlbaum Associates.

Gersten, R., Taylor, M. J., Keys, T. D., Rolfhus, E., & Newman-Gonchar, R. (2014). *Summary of research on the effectiveness of math professional development approaches.* Washington, DC: US Department of Education, Institute of Education Sciences, National Center for Educational Evaluation and Regional Assistance, Regional Educatioal Laboratory Southeast. Available at http://ies.ed.gov/ncee/edlabs/projects/project.asp?projectID=391.

Hart, L., Alston, A., & Murata, A. (Eds.). (2011). *Lesson-study research and practice in mathematics education: Learning together.* New York, NY: Springer.

Lesh, R., Hoover, M., Hole, B., Kelly, A., & Post, T. (2000). Principles for developing thought-revealing activities for students and teachers. In A. Kelly & R. Lesh (Eds.). *Handbook of research design in mathematics and science education* (pp. 591–646). Mahwah, NJ: Lawrence Erlbaum Associates.

Lewis, C. (2000, April). *Lesson study: The core of Japanese professional development.* Paper presented at the meeting of the American Educational Research Association, New Orleans, LA. Available at www.lessonresearch.net/aera2000.pdf.

Lewis, C. (2010, September 15). A public proving ground for standards-based practice. *Education Week,* pp. 28–30.

Lewis, C. & Hurd, J. (2011). *Lesson study step by step: How teacher learning communities improve instruction.* Portsmouth, NH: Heinemann.

Lewis, C. & Perry, R. (2014). Lesson study with mathematical resources: A sustainable model for locally-led teacher professional learning. *Mathematics Teacher Education and Development, 16*(1), 22–42.

Lewis, C. & Perry, R. (in press). A randomized trial of lesson study with mathematical resource kits: Analysis of impact on teachers' beliefs and learning community. In E.J. Cai & J.A. Middleton (Eds.), *Design, results, and implications of large-scale studies in mathematics education.* New York, NY: Springer.

Lewis, C. & Perry, R. (2014, March). Lesson study to improve fractions instruction: A randomized, controlled trial. Manuscript submitted for publication. Abstract can be downloaded from www.lessonresearch.net/ies_study/11IESAbstract.pdf.

Lewis, C., Perry, R., & Friedkin, S. (2012). Using Japanese curriculum materials to support lesson study outside Japan: Toward coherent curriculum. *Japanese Journal of Educational Research, 79.*

Lewis, C., Perry, R., Friedkin, S., & Roth, J. (2012). Improving teaching does improve teachers: Evidence from lesson study. *Journal of Teacher Education, 63*(5), 368–375.

Lewis, C., Perry, R., & Hurd, J. (2009). Improving mathematics instruction through lesson study: A theoretical model and North American case. *Journal of Mathematics Teacher Education, 12*(4), 285–304.

Lewis, C., Perry, R., & Murata, A. (2006, April). How should research contribute to instructional improvement? The case of lesson study. *Educational Researcher, 35*(3), 3–14.

Lewis, C., Perry, R., Hurd, J., & O'Connell, M.P. (2006, December). Lesson study comes of age in North America. *Phi Delta Kappan, 88*(4), 273–281.

Lo, M., Chik, P., & Pong, W. (2005). *For each and everyone: Catering for individual differences through learning studies.* Hong Kong: Hong Kong University Press.

Mills College Lesson Study Group (Producer). (2000). *Can you lift 100 kilograms?* [Video]. Order at www.lessonresearch.net/canyoulift1.html.

ONLINE RESOURCES

14.1 Lesson study cycle
14.2 A protocol for observing and discussing a research lesson
14.3 Choosing a lesson study theme
14.4 Template: Plan to guide learning
14.5 Outsiders to invite to lesson study
14.6 Reflection on the lesson study cycle
14.7 Additional resources

Perry, R. & Lewis, C. (2011). Improving the mathematical content base of lesson study: Summary of results. Available at www.lessonresearch.net/IESAbstract10.pdf.

World Association of Lesson Studies (WALS) (2012). *World Association of Lesson Studies International Conference 2012: Programme and Abstracts.* Singapore: Author.

Online Coaching

Online coaching offers anytime, anywhere support.

By Joellen Killion

Richard is a risk taker. Throughout his nearly 15-year career as a middle school math educator, he has actively pursued opportunities that challenged him professionally. After three years of teaching, he transferred to a different school to work with underperforming students. He then took a position in a rural school when his family decided to purchase a small farm so they could raise their own food. Richard loved his new life in the country yet felt isolated as the only middle school math educator. The two math educators in the high school also coached different sports, so they had little time for collaboration.

The year after Richard moved to his new home, the state implemented new math standards. The standards and the resulting curricular changes meant that Richard was teaching content he had never taught before and using instructional practices that were unfamiliar to him. Even the new

assessments required students to demonstrate their learning in ways that were unfamiliar to Richard. He always had felt confident as an educator, yet these changes were daunting. With little or no support and only the elementary educators available as content collaborators, Richard began to doubt his efficacy.

Fortunately, the regional center that provided professional learning to school districts in his geographical area was piloting an online coaching service for educators in ELA and math. The service was voluntary and available between noon and 8:00 p.m. via a web link. The regional center coordinator asked only that educators try the service a minimum of three times in the first three months of school so they could provide input about the effectiveness of the service and help determine if it should be continued.

Richard wasn't certain online coaching was the right thing for him. He wanted a workshop on the new standards and some strategies to teach them. Unfortunately, he was unable to participate in the summer session and another would not be offered until after the winter break.

When he encountered the geometry portion of his curriculum, Richard knew he wanted help. He felt fairly comfortable with the content, yet he was uncertain about how to weave together the various content areas and to design classroom tasks that engaged students in constructing understanding and explaining their thinking in writing. He decided to try the coaching service.

After the last period of the day, he logged in using his assigned log-in, not certain what to expect. On the screen, up popped a picture of Mike, his session coach, and a greeting. After getting some basic information from Richard, Mike asked him about the focus of their coaching session. Richard shared the situation; Mike asked clarifying questions; together they formulated a goal statement for the session.

Soon, Mike was asking Richard questions that challenged him in an intellectually stimulating way. Richard found that he was explaining his understanding of the mathematical concepts he was teaching, the theoretical framework of the new state standards, and his own beliefs about his role as a math educator.

About 15 minutes into the conversation, Mike asked Richard if the conversation was helping him think about goals and whether they needed to change directions or continue. Richard asked for assistance in mapping out a lesson. Together Mike and Richard worked on the whiteboard writing essential questions and designing a series of learning tasks. Mike listened carefully to how Richard was making decisions, and he periodically suggested other considerations. They then worked through the tasks together. As Mike listened to Richard think out loud about the math, he again suggested some quick ideas to help Richard get clearer on the math. At the end of the 45-minute session, Richard had planned a lesson, chosen two new strategies for engaging students, and demonstrated a clearer understanding of two key concepts embedded in the lesson.

Richard connected with the online coaching service about once a week. He enjoyed being able to reflect on his teaching with someone who was a skillful coach. He grew more confident in his own understanding of the content and the pedagogy required. He became more willing to identify

challenges in his classroom that he might not have articulated previously. Most importantly, he grew more efficacious and he knew his students were getting his best teaching every day.

Overview

Coaching is based on a simple principle. Practice and feedback improve performance. People seek help from peers, experts, and the Internet when they want to learn or improve. YouTube has become a quasi-coaching resource for those who want to know how to texture drywall, pack dishes for moving, or restring a favorite necklace. Online coaching is increasingly more common in education.

The value of online coaching rests within the value of coaching. Others have written about that in this book. When most people hear the term *coach,* they immediately think of athletics. Dancers, educators, speakers, executives, musicians, and people with health issues have coaches who guide them in improving their performance. Coaching provides the feedback and guidance for achieving excellence.

Definition and description

Defining online coaching requires exploring its two parts — online and coaching — and putting them together for meaning.

Coaching. In education, coaching is a form of professional learning in which one person guides and supports an educator or a team of educators to achieve goals. Essential in this definition is the phrase *to achieve goals.* The guide or coach is someone with expertise in the processes associated with coaching, such as providing constructive feedback, gathering and analyzing data, listening to understand needs and concerns, questioning and probing to elicit thinking (Killion & Harrison 2006; Killion, Harrison, Bryan, & Clifton, 2012).

Coaching is a process in which clients initiate the learning process by identifying a desire for professional growth. In most coaching situations, coaches — often people with expertise in coaching — interact with *clients,* people who request support to extend their practice and impact. In education, clients can be any member of the education workforce, including superintendents, who often receive executive or leadership coaching; educators who receive content or instructional coaching; administrators who receive coaching to develop leadership skills; or others who receive role-specific coaching.

Coaches and clients may develop a trusting relationship over time when they have regularly scheduled interactions. One image of a coach that resonates with many is Lionel Logue, King George VI's voice coach. In the movie *The King's Speech,* Geoffrey Rush portrays Logue, a coach who blended an authentic, nonhierarchical, and honest relationship, clear and focused communication, persistent emphasis on practice and reflection to change habits, and intense belief in the potential of his client. Coaching, whether in person or mediated by technology, unleashes potential.

Online. The *online* aspect of online coaching is more complex. Online coaching has evolved from other forms of online professional learning that supports individual and team learning: structured courses, massive open online courses (MOOCs), brief webinars, and TED talks. Online coaching, like other online learning designs, represents migration from a traditional face-to-face learning design to the web or another technology to accomplish the same results.

Like other learning designs that are now mediated by technology, there are several features common to online coaching. One is physical space. The term *online* conveys that the coach and client are not physically in the same place; they are connecting from a distance. The brief scenarios below demonstrate the range of how technology is used to seek and receive support.

- A principal writes a letter to a parent about an unfortunate situation that occurred in the school and emails the draft letter to several colleagues for feedback before she sends it out. She also sends it to the district's communications officer for his review and recommendations. Very quickly the principal receives expert and peer feedback using the simple medium of email. While this example points to occasional interactions for support and feedback, the principals discover that giving feedback helped them all learn and ask if they can use one another for other communications support such as their monthly parent newsletters and weekly staff letters.
- A district math coach just finishes facilitating a team coaching session with a group of high school educators. She is uncomfortable about an exchange that occurred among several educators in the meeting and is eager

to process her facilitation skills with a neutral party. She makes a note to dial into Coaches' Connect, a district-provided service that offers coaching for coaches. She logs on when she gets back to her office at 4:30 p.m. A coach greets her and then listens thoughtfully to her description of the situation. The coach prompts her to consider her own role and influence, engages her in exploring potential alternative interpretations, and asks her to consider multiple other strategies to use in similar situations to expand her repertoire.

- It is 5:00 p.m. and time for Martin's weekly call with his executive coach. For the past several weeks they have been working on how Martin is conducting personnel performance reviews. Martin plans to share his successes and get some assistance with a particularly challenging staff member. He celebrates with his coach and explains his perspective of the situation with the staff member. His coach uses a strategy that helps Martin see the situation from the perspective of the staff member. Through the experience Martin discovers how he might alter his approach to align it more with the staff member's communication and learning style.
- A school secretary is grappling with the district's new data system. She calls the data office for the client-support specialist who provides real-time support to users. The specialist asks to share screens with the secretary and soon they are walking through the process together with the specialist modeling the process on the secretary's computer.
- The primary education specialist who coaches teams of K–3 educators across three elementary schools meets with her team of eight kindergarten educators in Google Hangout at 11:30 a.m. on two Thursdays a month. They convene during the regularly scheduled collaborative planning time for kindergarten educators. During the 40-minute meeting, the educators focus on writing essential questions for their lessons. They review the characteristics of good essential questions, look at several they have written, comment on them, and develop new essential questions for the next two weeks' math lessons.
- The head custodian receives a shipment of the new floor product and can't remember how to store it. He recalls special instructions all custodians received in last week's

meeting about this floor product. He reads the label carefully and doesn't see any information. He logs onto the product website for the online advisor, writes a question in the chat box, and gets a visual image of a smiling person dressed in a Dickies uniform with the company logo, wearing a tool belt, and holding a clipboard. This avatar greets the custodian by name and says he is glad to be asked about the special storage requirements. He then explains why is it best to store the product in a cool place without much sun and shows several pictures of appropriate places. He also asks whether the custodian needs to know anything else about the product, and signs off with a cheery wave when the response is no.

As technology advances, the opportunities for connectivity increase. Coaches and clients may continue to meet face to face, and now have the opportunity to meet in real time across great distances. Technology makes it possible for a coach in California to meet face to face with a client in New York and share resources just as if the coach were reaching into her bookshelf or file cabinet to grab a resource to share with the client who is sitting next to her. She and her client can also create text, diagrams, doodles, or notes together in real time across distances.

Another aspect of the *online* portion of online coaching is the determination of who serves as the coach. Online coaching makes it possible for the coach to be an avatar or electronic coach rather than a human. Businesses have been using electronic coaches to provide coaching for many years and are creating more intelligent avatars to respond to requests for assistance, guidance, resources, and information. The avatars are often named and have physical features, voice qualities, and *intelligence* to emulate a trustworthy, knowledgeable person. The custodian in one of the scenarios was working with an avatar coach.

According to Grace Ahrend, Fred Diamond, and Pat Gill Webber (2010),

> having an online coach ready 24/7 — including when work is actually being performed — with rich content, suggestions, practice ideas, tips, techniques and other direct coaching advice is ideal. An electronic coach can serve as a lower-cost tool that replicates the benefits of a live session while allowing the content to be accessed privately and conveniently — at any time. (p. 44)

Avatar coaching is relatively new to education yet not new in other fields. An IT staff member who needs to know how to address a particular problem can immediately query the online coach who has answers, suggestions, or advice related to the specific situation with which the staff member wanted assistance. Companies have created repositories of brief videos that provide encouragement, support, specific guidance, and important information that are accessed through a query-based system. For example, a young employee, feeling threatened by a superior, turned to the online resources to ask for suggestions and met "Sally," an avatar, who offered information about employee rights, several strategies to use if she were in similar situations, and details about the company's policies and procedures for addressing the situation. At the end of the *coaching* session with "Sally," the young employee had the confidence to take appropriate action.

Bringing the two parts together: Coaching + online. Online coaching, then, is a form of professional learning in which a human or avatar coach provides personalized support to a client who is physically removed from the coach and who seeks to strengthen his or her practice and increase its impact.

While this chapter is about online coaching, the nomenclature for this form of professional learning includes other terms that are often used to describe the same or similar processes. *E-mentoring* refers to a coach or mentor working with a novice in a school or school system. *Web-enabled coaching, e-coaching, telecoaching,* and *telementoring* are other terms that appear in the literature.

Background

Neither coaching nor technology is new, yet the intersection of the two is relatively new to education. It is not surprising that online coaching is growing rapidly in all arenas as a means of supporting one or more people who want to adopt new behaviors. Health professions, corporate leadership, skilled technical fields, and education are tapping into online coaching to support employee development and bottom-line performance.

Companies such as IBM have used online coaching routinely for nearly two decades as part of their employee development programs, particularly for leadership development, and especially in soft skill areas such as communications and building relationships. In its four-tier e-learning model for management development, IBM uses online simulations and the IBM Coaching Simulator to develop capacity. Brandon Hall and Jacques LeCavalier (2000) explain that the coaching simulator "alone presents 8 different real-life situations; with nearly 100 decision points and over 5000 screens of actions. The design is sophisticated — based on the Institute for Learning Sciences' Goal-Based Scenario model — but the implementation is simple . . ." (p. 58). According to Hall and LeCavalier (2000), "new managers are supported not only by extensive material contained online, but also by coaching from the 2nd-line manager, who learns the IBM Coaching Model via a simulator and online coaching materials" (p. 59).

As learners engage in the scenarios and make decisions, the software coaches them, records their responses for deeper analysis, and uses their decisions as a teaching tool. With their human coach, they reflect on their decisions and gain a deeper understanding of how their decisions influence results. A study of the IBM management development program reported positive results including enthusiasm for learning, five times more material learned compared to more traditional learning models, and demand for continued access to the material and networks of colleagues developed through the four-tiered learning process.

Technology now allows clients to access coaching when and where they want, thereby expanding access to coaching and to continuous improvement. Advances in technology make it a dynamic rather than static medium for communication. With these advances, those seeking support can turn to human or electronic coaches when and where they want. Simple technologies such as a telephone or more advanced technologies such as specially designed coaching platforms create opportunities for clients to reach coaches. When clients have access to on-demand coaching, they may be more likely to access a coach since they are able to reach out when they want rather than at a pre-arranged time.

Rationale

Student success depends on educator effectiveness. Developing expertise requires not only completion of preparation programs, traditional or alternative, it also requires years of practice, reflection, and continuous improvement.

Coaching helps educators develop expertise, and online coaching increases access to coaching. When it is designed to align with both educator performance standards and expected student outcomes, as the Learning Forward Outcomes standard emphasizes (see Part I, "Design: Form and Structure for Learning," for a list and description of the standards) this design for professional learning accelerates implementation of professional learning and results. Online coaching is an appropriate learning design for educators who seek to improve student results, refine professional practice, and address issues emerging within their school systems, schools, or classrooms, and meet individual professional learning goals (Killion, 2000). Online coaching offers personalized, just-in-time support for educators on the issues they want to address when they want to address them.

Foundational principles

Assumptions driving online coaching are grounded in the research on gaining expertise, professional learning, and learning.

Gaining expertise requires practice and feedback. Traditional designs of professional learning frequently fail to incorporate processes to implement learning into practice. K. Anders Ericsson, Michael J. Prietula, and Edward T. Cokely (2007) note, "New research shows that outstanding performance is the product of years of deliberate practice and coaching, not of any innate talent or skill" (p. 114). Researchers and practitioners report that it takes approximately 10 years or 10,000 hours to attain the level of expertise that allows an individual to compete in national or international competition and that coaching from someone who will provide constructive feedback is essential to the process of developing expertise (Ericsson, Prietula, & Cokely, 2007; Gawande, 2011).

"Real experts are extremely motivated students who seek out such feedback," Ericsson, Prietula, and Cokely (2007) report. They go on to describe the learning traits of "real experts":

> They're also skilled at understanding when and if a coach's advice doesn't work for them. . . . The best coaches also identify aspects of your performance that will need to be improved at your next level of skill. If a coach pushes you too fast,

too hard, you will only be frustrated and may even be tempted to give up trying to improve at all. (p. 119)

Benjamin Bloom (1985) intensively researched factors that contributed to the development of high levels of talent in students. This research led to further research that began to debunk long-standing theories. After rigorous scientific study, Bloom's conclusion was that three factors contributed to talent. All the superb performers he investigated had practiced intensively, had studied with devoted educators, and had been supported enthusiastically by their families throughout their developing years. Later research building on Bloom's pioneering study revealed that the amount and quality of practice were key factors in the level of expertise people achieved. Consistently and overwhelmingly, the evidence showed that *"experts are always made, not born"* [emphasis added] (Ericsson, Prietula, & Cokely, 2007, p. 115).

Personalization increases relevance and results. Aligning learning to the unique needs of learners increases the meaningfulness and relevance of the learning situation. Too much professional learning is designed as one-size-fits-all and assumes that all learners need the same content and learning processes. In Part I, the essay "Design: Form and Structure for Learning" discusses Learning Forward's Standards for Professional Learning (p. 15). The Data standard stresses that using educator, student, and system data to design the learning experience is essential in selecting appropriate learning designs. For example, the Learning Designs standard stresses that leaders of learning address characteristics of the learner, such as years of teaching experience, current level of understanding, past learning experiences, prior and current student achievement, school and community contexts, performance expectations, and degree of confidence and efficacy to select appropriate learning designs. According to the Outcomes standard, leaders of learning need to align the content of professional learning to course or grade level taught, curriculum, standards, and/or performance expectations.

Learning is a social process. Great learning theorists concur that learning and thinking are social processes. Lev Vygotsky (1978), Paulo Freire (1998) and John Dewey (1916) emphasize that learning is a process of constructing knowledge; constructing knowledge requires language

for thinking and interacting about the knowledge being constructed. As educators construct knowledge and implement new instructional, leadership, or other role-specific practice; reflect independently and with colleagues about the effects of their practice; and examine results related to their effectiveness from a variety of assessment tools, they identify areas for refinement and improvement in the knowledge, skills, practices, and dispositions appropriate to their role. Learning, according to many cognitive psychologists, is a process of making meaning that is enriched by working with others.

Coaches are more knowledgeable others. Vygotsky (1978) emphasized the importance of a *more knowledgeable other* as a partner in the learning process. While Vygotsky's work focused primarily on young children, many of his theories apply to adult learners as well. In conceptualizing the zone of proximal development, Vygotsky discovered that the most sensitive point for instruction or guidance to accelerate or enhance learning occurs within a zone determined by need to know, desire to know, and commitment to know. Learning is enhanced during that span of time when a skillful tutor, mentor, or coach provides guidance in the form of social interaction that is cooperative and collaborative. Supporters provide scaffolds that they withdraw (gradual release of responsibility) as the learner becomes more proficient. More knowledgeable others have knowledge that the learner does not and some experience in applying the learning.

Through technology, more knowledgeable others now may even be avatars who hold information or can provide guidance to learners. Educators want support from peers and more knowledgeable others whom they perceive to have extensive experience and who can both appreciate and understand the complexities of teaching and student learning. Online coaches are skillful and, most often, well-prepared experienced educators who connect their coaching services directly to their client's context, curriculum, and school environment.

Learning requires construction. Countering the transmission model of education that assumes learners are simply receptors of information, coaching uses a constructive or critical pedagogy theory of knowing. Paulo Freire's work (1998) laid the foundation for critical pedagogy. Freire pairs praxis and dialogue. Praxis refers to a cycle of theory, application, evaluation, reflection, and new or adjusted theory. Dialogue (see "Chapter 10: Dialogue" in this book) is the process of working collaboratively and respectfully with one another to listen, question, and construct understanding. Freire emphasized that learning cannot be separated from its cultural and political environment, that it requires reciprocity between the roles of educator and learner, and continually involves evaluation, relearning, reflection, and application.

Learners share ownership for their learning. Through a dynamic interactive process that occurs in coaching, all parties — the client, coach, and the client's clients, students — share responsibility for increased educator effectiveness and student success. The ever-changing interactions, for example, between educators and students, influence student success. The support principals give educators influences educator and student success. Systems of support available from central office staff simultaneously influence principal, educator, and student success. The relationships are dynamic, interconnected, and unique to the school, district, and community setting, and the political and social environment within which they are positioned. Another equally important influence on these relationships is the culture within the work environment — as defined by shared vision and beliefs, peer relationships, individual beliefs and goals, sense of trust and appreciation, levels of satisfaction and commitment, and available support for continuous improvement.

In seminal studies of the impact of learning on educator practice, Beverly Showers (1984) and Bruce Joyce and Beverly Showers (1988) report that learners are significantly more likely to use new learning to address challenges in their work if they receive coaching or peer support or participate in a study group. Newer studies by Bruce Joyce and Emily Calhoun (2010) confirm similar findings.

Coaching followed by application of the practice and ongoing reflection builds educators' efficacy to succeed in their roles, and increased efficacy influences student success. When educators seek support to be more efficacious in their roles and apply new practices to increase efficacy, students benefit.

Cognitive psychologist David Kolb (1984) stated that experience is the source of learning and development. His experiential learning theory stressed that learning is a process in which knowledge is constructed through experiences and that abstract concepts are applied in context. Kolb described a four-stage learning process:

- The first is *concrete experience* in which learners experience a new situation.
- The second is *reflective observation* in which learners observe and reflect on the experience and note any discrepancies or inconsistencies between what they experienced and what they understand.
- The third is *abstract conceptualization* in which learners refine or modify their understanding of the abstract concepts they hold.
- The last stage is *active experimentation* in which the learner applies the newly refined or modified concepts to real-world situations and observes the responses.

Practical realities

Online coaching makes sense for multiple practical reasons. Online learning in general offers several benefits, including expanded access, flexibility in learning content and design, cost, and ability to collaborate with fellow learners across distances and at different times (Killion, 2000). When educators have limited time for their own learning, their daily schedules provide only small time periods for learning. Accessing place-based learning means traveling great distances or through congested metropolitan areas. For these reasons, online learning makes sense because, with the exclusion of connectivity limitation, most online learning is available anywhere, 24/7.

Online coaching done in real time (synchronously) depends on the availability of both the coach and client. A client who can connect with a coach only at 9:00 p.m. on the East Coast may find it easier to connect with a coach who is available in the early evening on the West Coast. Or, through uploaded materials (including artifacts, such as classroom videos) clients can connect with their coaches asynchronously. The coach who is available at 9:00 p.m. may review these materials then and provide support for the client who awakens to them on another continent.

Online learning allows learners to design their own learning, including selecting the most relevant content, the sequence of the learning, the pace of the learning, the design of the learning, and the time and place for learning.

Online learning, particularly with the use of online coaching, may have a fiscal advantage over face-to-face coaching because there is no travel or travel time involved. Certainly, electronic coaches will be less expensive than human coaches; however, the initial investment in programing and the requisite ongoing revision and helpdesk support may equal or exceed the cost of human coaching.

Online coaching, like online learning, permits interaction with coaches who are remote from the client, increasing opportunities to interact with coaching in different locations and with different areas of expertise. Learners are able to interact with peers through networks and collaborative groups who work in widely diverse settings and benefit from different perspectives. Those who wish to engage in peer or expert coaching have more opportunity through technology to connect with coaches or peers worldwide.

Allison Rossett and Gerald Marino (2005) cite several reasons for e-coaching, the term they use for online coaching.
- Coaching online lingers.
- Coaching matches needs and resources.
- Coaching expands the role of the manager and supervisor.
- Coaching goes where the action is.
- Technology makes coaching affordable (pp. 47–48).

The empirical research on the effects of online coaching and mentoring is limited, yet some researchers report "positive benefits including acquisition of new skills, abilities, and perspectives; improved performance; better goal-setting-setting; and adaptability" (Ensher, Heun, & Blanchard, 2003, p. 268). Others report that online business coaches "enable clients to set and achieve business goals and reach a balance between work and family priorities" (p. 268).

Coaching, if done well, aligns with Jane Vella's principles of adult learning (1994). As a learning design, coaching aligns with the following principles:
- Begins with understanding what the learner's needs are;
- Provides a safe, confidential place for learners to learn;
- Is grounded on the educator's belief that the coach is an advocate for the learner;
- Is practical, focusing on what the learner needs at this moment;
- Promotes reflection and self-analysis;
- Engages the learner in the coaching process by stressing the learner's responsibilities; and
- Places accountability for learning on the learner.

Steps

Expanded from the theory of change developed by Tutor.com for its MyLivePD program (Killion, 2012), an on-demand coaching program piloted for educators of algebra, the theory of change depicted below demonstrates how online coaching works and how it produces results for educators and students. The theory of change maps the process between an educator's desire for support to change practice through to results for students.

Terms such as *educator, principal, coach, educator leader, district curriculum coordinator, superintendent,* or any other role title can be substituted for *educator* throughout this theory of change.

The following steps describe the process of coaching. While there are minor variations between face-to-face and online coaching, the process applies in both situations. In online coaching, for example, the relationship building is likely to be less authentic than in face-to-face coaching. The type of technology also may influence the process. For example, if the coaching is done via email with an exchange of documents, the coaching interaction may occur over a period of several days or more, rather than in a compact time period. An example of the latter is when the coaching occurs via a web-enabled coaching platform using audio, video, or a combination of both.

Step 1: Identify the situation

The educator identifies a student learning, instruction, curriculum, assessment, human relations, community, or family issue to address; when appropriate or available, he or she uses evidence from student data, educator practice, or other system data to define the issue. Recognition and acknowledgement of an issue to address begins the process of reflection, analysis, learning, and action.

This step of the process aligns with both the Learning Forward Learning Communities and Data standards. Identifying a situation demonstrates a commitment to continuous improvement and sharing in collective responsibility for student success. Using student, educator, and system data as the basis for identification of the situation creates a data-based situation rather than one based on opinion.

Figure 1: **The Theory of Change that Links an Educator's Desire for Support to Change in Practice and Results for Students.**

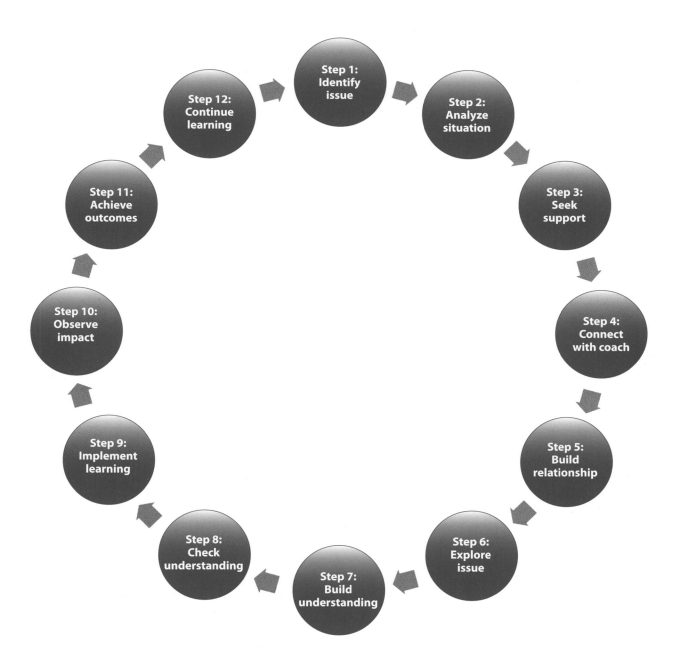

Step 2: Analyze the situation

In this step, educators consider if they have strategies to address the issue. If they want to broaden their existing repertoire of practice, confirm their approach, or check perspective with a more knowledgeable other, they may opt to seek support from a peer or a coach. Through this process, educators apply self-analysis skills to reflect on and assess their own abilities.

This step aligns with both the Learning Forward Data standard and the Outcomes standard. It uses data as the basis for examination of the situation and benchmarks improvement to student outcomes and educator outcomes to specify the learning focus.

Step 3: Seek support

Educators who are seeking coaching support as a routine part of their practice or to address a unique issue become coaching clients. The need or desire for support not only motivates a coaching client to seek support, it also shapes the purpose or focus of the coach-client interaction (see Online Resource 15.1: *Initiating a coaching session*).

This step aligns with the Learning Designs standard because it places the learner in control of the type of learning design chosen to address the learning need. It also aligns with the Learning Communities standard because it acknowledges the importance of collaboration. Availability of coaching services to a client meets the Resources standard because it prioritizes, monitors, and coordinates resources to support educator learning. This step also demonstrates the Leadership standard because the availability of coaching support is evidence that leaders have created the supporting systems and structures for educator learning.

Step 4: Connect with a coach

The educator and coach connect using the available or appropriate technology. The coach may be a peer, an electronic coach, or a real-life coach. Coaching may be regularly scheduled or may be on an as-needed basis.

In this step, the support of a coach who facilitates learning meets both the Leadership and Learning Designs standards. The coach applies learning theories, research and strategies; engages the learner; and personalizes support tailored to the client's learning preferences and outcomes.

Step 5: Build a relationship

The coach uses a set of strategies to build a relationship with the educator to establish a climate of safety and productivity. Some communication strategies such as listening carefully, paraphrasing, and questioning may contribute to more open communication and trust between the coach and client, thereby creating a safe and risk-free environment in which clients can disclose information and feelings, examine their values and beliefs, and generate new ideas.

Step 5 demonstrates attention to the Learning Designs Standard. Coaches use technology to personalize, differentiate, and deepen learning.

Step 6: Explore the issue

The educator provides information to the coach about the issue to help the coach understand the specific situation, the educator's learning need, and the specific support the educator is seeking. The coach asks probing questions to elicit more information and to clarify the situation or the client's feelings and response to the situation. The coach may use observations or questions to elicit and understand the client's perspectives, understanding, or beliefs related to the situation.

Depending on available technology, the client may stream video, share student work, or use a whiteboard to help the coach understand the specific situation. Protocols for opening the session, identifying the type of support desired, and for closing a session are offered in Online Resource 15.2: *Identifying the situation.*

Step 6 addresses the Learning Designs standard by promoting active engagement, with the coach and the client interacting to make meaning. In Step 6, the coach encourages the client to have an active role in the professional learning process, shaping the learning to fit the need.

Step 7: Build understanding

The coach applies a broad repertoire of communication, assessment, and relationship skills; job-specific and content knowledge; an extensive, immediately accessible resource bank available through the technology; and disposition to develop an educator's expertise to address the identified issue. The coach may find opportunities to integrate additional support to address related issues if given permission to do so. The coach focuses on the areas specific to the educator-identified issue. For example, if the client is a teacher, the coach focuses on the teacher's content knowledge, pedagogy, and pedagogical content knowledge to provide requested or appropriate additional support.

Step 7 also integrates the Learning Designs standard by promoting "deep understanding of new learning" and increasing "motivation to implement it." This step helps the coach and client explore "individualized and collective experiences" so they can "actively construct, analyze, evaluate, and synthesize knowledge and practices" (p. 42).

Step 8: Check understanding

The coach checks that the educator has defined appropriate next steps and understands the rationale for them before ending the coaching session. The coach's goal is to develop the client's independence and capacity to self-coach by making the coaching process transparent to the client and even coaching the client in self-coaching (see Online Resource 15.3: *Checking for understanding*).

Step 8 integrates the Learning Designs standard and prepares the client for applying his or her learning, thus demonstrating attention to the Implementation standard.

Step 9: Implement learning

The educator reviews and applies what he or she learned during coaching. Application of learning promotes contextual understanding and allows the client to make appropriate adaptations to fit his or her unique circumstances.

In this step, such adaptation is a core component of Kolb's (1984) experiential learning theory and aligns with the Implementation standard.

Step 10: Observe impact

Coaches support educators as they reflect on the results of their practice using appropriate, available data as evidence. Because educators' clients (students, teachers, peers, etc.) respond differently in different situations, studying the effects of educators' practice on their clients is a part of the coaching process (see Online Resource 15.4: *Closing coaching session*).

Step 10 aligns with the Implementation, Outcomes, and Data standards. By implementing new learning and observing for impact, the educator is more likely to gather relevant

information to adjust and refine practice, to extend and sustain learning, to achieve desired outcomes, and to measure the effectiveness of his or her own learning using appropriate data.

Step 11: Achieve outcomes

Clients of the coaching client, including leaders, teachers, and students, increase their effectiveness as demonstrated by a variety of observational and other data related to performance indicators and assessments.

Step 11 demonstrates that effective coaching establishes measurable outcomes, thus connecting to both the Outcomes and Data standards.

Step 12: Continue learning

Educators engage in continuous reflection on their practice and its results, independently and in collaboration with peers and supervisors, to identify the next area of focus for their continued development. An educator may seek additional coaching to refine the practice or to expand his or her expertise by identifying a new area of focus. Through the process of reflecting, receiving coaching and feedback, and analyzing practice, educators deepen their understanding, refine their practice, and expand their capacity to achieve high levels of performance and make an impact on student success (see Online Resource 15.5: *Following up*).

The process of continuing to learn builds on all seven standards, and specifically the Learning Communities standard, which supports the disposition of continuous learning for all educators as a means of improving student learning.

Variations

Coaching can vary considerably in terms of who, what, when, where, why, and how.

Who is involved? As client, any educator who wants to engage in continuous growth; as coach, a nearby or faraway person or even an avatar. Coaches also coach coaches.

What do coaches and clients do? They explore learning that leads to improvement and results, for both the client and the client's clients, for example, students.

When and where? Online coaching permits coaches and their clients to be next door or on the other side of the world. When they engage in coaching depends, of course, on what the coach and client decide. They can engage synchronously or asynchronously. "Anytime and anywhere" is what makes online coaching supple.

Why? The purpose is to achieve outcomes related to improved learning for both adults and young people, leading to positive results.

How? Coaching uses any means needed, from dialogue to decision making, from cameras in the classroom to ear-buds, from reviews of educator and student work to problem-solving, and from links to online resources to scanned materials.

Challenges and how to address them

With the advantages of technology-facilitated coaching come challenges, however. Communications between a coach and client require more explicit listening, clarity of speaking, and probing for clarity. In a study of communication in e-relationships, Elaine Cox and Patricia Dannahy (2005) explore how communication is changing in the virtual world. They suggest that the purpose of e-mentoring, for example, may stay the same as traditional mentoring, yet the "way in which the relationship is conducted is quite different and requires adjustments to be made to communication styles" (p. 39).

Some authors suggest that the anonymity of e-relationships may impede the development of openness and trust (Anthony, 2000; Clutterbuck, 2004; Sztompka, 1991) particularly if the relationship is conducted via chat or email as was the focus of the Cox and Dannahy case studies. Their study focused on the use of nonviolent communication (NVC), a framework for communicating affective information, particularly that which might be expressed most often nonverbally in face-to-face communication. The NVC framework follows four steps, including observation without judgment or evaluation; feeling related to what is observed; needs related to the feelings; and requests related to the feelings or observation. The researchers conclude, "The most noteworthy indication of NVC's ability to facilitate electronic dialogue is illustrated through the speed at which in-depth relationships were forged with students, thus allowing them to address significant mentoring issues in the online relationship" (p. 49). NVC has potential to encourage trusting personal relationships characterized by openness in e-relationships, but further research is needed on many aspects of electronic communication.

ONLINE RESOURCES

15.1   Initiating a coaching session
15.2   Identifying the situation
15.3   Checking for understanding
15.4   Closing coaching session
15.5   Following up

Conclusion

The world of education is changing rapidly. Educators face significant changes in nearly every aspect of their work. Continuous growth designed to expand and refine their professional expertise and to sustain efficacy is essential. Coaching, especially online, provides the ongoing support that allows educators to engage in a highly effective learning design that provides personalized, just-in-time, and cost-efficient support as educators implement new practices.

References

Ahrend, G., Diamond, F., & Webber, P.Q. (2010). Virtual coaching: Using technology to boost performance. *Chief Learning Officer, 9*(7), 44–47.

Anthony, K. (2000). *The nature of the therapeutic relationship within online counselling.* Available at www.onlinetherapyinstitute.com/wpcontent/uploads/2011/02/thesis2000Anthony.pdf.

Bloom, B. (1985). *Developing talent in young people.* New York: Ballantine.

Clutterbuck, D. (2004). *Everyone needs a mentor.* London: Chartered Institute of Personnel and Development.

Cox, E. & Dannahy, P. (2005). The value of openness in e-relationships: Using Nonviolent Communication to guide online coaching and mentoring. *International Journal of Evidence Based Coaching and Mentoring 3*(1), 30–51. Available at http://ijebcm.brookes.ac.uk/documents/vol03issue1-paper-04.pdf.

Dewey, J. (1916). *Democracy and education: An introduction to the philosophy of education.* New York: The MacMillan Company.

Ensher, E., Heun, C., & Blanchard, A. (2003). Online mentoring and computer-mediated communication: New directions in research. *Journal of Vocational Behavior, 63*(2), 264–288.

Ericsson, K., Prietula, M., & Cokely, E.T. (2007). The making of an expert. *Harvard Business Review, 85*(7/8), 114–121.

Freire, Paulo. (1998). *Educators as cultural workers: Letters to those who dare teach.* Translated by D. Macedo, D. Koike, & A. Oliveira. Boulder, CO: Westview Press.

Gawande, A. (2011, October 3). Personal best: Top athletes and singers have coaches. Should you? *The New Yorker.* Available at www.newyorker.com/reporting/2011/10/03/111003fa_fact_gawande?printable=true&currentPage=all.

Hall, B. & LeCavalier, J. (2000). *E-learning across the enterprise: The benchmarking study of best practices.* Sunnyvale, CA: Brandon Hall Group.

Joyce, B. & Calhoun, E. (2010). *Models of professional development: A celebration of educators.* Thousand Oaks, CA: Corwin Press.

Joyce, B. & Showers, B. (1988). *Student achievement through staff development* (Rev. ed.). White Plains, NY: Longman, Inc.

Killion, J. (2000). Online staff development: Promise or peril? *NASSP Bulletin, 84*(618), 38–46.

Killion, J. (2012). *Live online coaching theory of change.* Available at www.tutor.com.

Killion, J. & Harrison, C. (2006). *Taking the lead: New roles for teachers and school-based coaches.* Oxford, OH: NSDC.

Killion, J., Harrison, C., Bryan, & Clifton, H. (2012). *Coaching matters.* Oxford, OH: Learning Forward.

Kolb D. (1984). *Experiential learning experience as a source of learning and development.* Upper Saddle River, NJ: Prentice Hall.

Learning Forward. (2011). *Standards for Professional Learning.* Oxford, OH: Author.

Rossett, A. & Marino, G. (2005, November). If coaching is good, then e-coaching is . . . *T&D, 59*(11), 46-48.

Showers, B. (1984). *Peer coaching and its effects on transfer of training.* Eugene, OR: Center for Educational Policy and Management.

Showers, B. (1984b). *Transfer of training: The contribution of coaching.* Eugene, OR: Center for Educational Policy and Management.

Sztompka, P. (1991). *Society in action: The theory of social becoming.* Chicago: University of Chicago Press.

Vella, J. (1994). *Learning to listen, learning to teach: The power of dialogue in educating adults.* San Francisco: Jossey-Bass.

Vygotsky, L.S. (1978). *Mind in society: The development of higher psychological processes* (14th ed.) Cambridge, MA: Harvard University Press.

CHAPTER 16

Online Courses

Start with sound design principles to get the most out of your instruction.

By John D. Ross

R ichard was pleased to see Toni and her new colleague, Abby. Richard worked in educational technology but had a background in instructional design, and he and Toni worked on projects together before she came to the state department of education. He enjoyed chatting with her, and she always had good stories or jokes to share. Whether working through the details of a project or sharing stories, Toni always proved to be fun.

This time should be easier, Richard thought, contemplating the new design project. The first time that Toni and Richard had worked together was with a Department team developing an online course about assessment strategies. That team, nicknamed the ASC team for Assessment Strategies Course (pronounced *ask*), had been an interesting first experience. The project manager for ASC had charged right into wanting to make videos — in which she starred — employing a video crew even though there had been no conversation about why video was right for that project.

At the first ASC meeting to which Richard was invited, the group was "ooh-ing" and "ah-ing" over what Richard thought was a lackluster performance of the project manager starring in the first video. She had been meticulously (and obviously) reading from a teleprompter and preaching about the importance of the assessment strategies. The video was no more than the project manager as "talking head," filmed in front of a blank white wall. Richard couldn't imagine anyone intentionally sitting through that video.

"It's great to be able to work together again, Toni," Richard said, pulling himself back from his recollections. "Maybe we can find some time to hit that Korean barbecue place for lunch. I haven't been in a while."

"It's closed," she sighed. "You gotta move fast around here, right Abby?"

As the new kid on the block, Abby smiled knowingly. Richard understood that smile.

Again, he thought back to ASC: *That's true in a number of ways.* He remembered that first team and the rush to produce video without even knowing how the course would be delivered. Like many other projects around the Department, ASC had moved at a rapid pace. At the time, Richard thought that the problem was there didn't seem to be any consensus on where the project was going, or even what the project was going to look like when it was done. There was no clear framework and people weren't working toward a clear goal. It was hard to see how all the parts fit together.

That was why his supervisor had asked Richard to join the ASC team mid-project. She had noticed that, while the team members worked well together, they didn't really have a clear vision of what the online courses would be. She had wanted him to provide instructional design support.

That meeting of the ASC team had appeared to be ending when Richard had spoken up, "Excuse me, I hate to interrupt, but since I'm new to this group I'm hoping I might get a little background information." Willing to ask lots of naïve questions, he had continued. "I've been listening to your conversations, but I'm not really sure what this course is all about. Or whom it's for. Or how they're going to get to it. And, while it's nice you have this video, I'm not really clear on how it fits with other content that's being developed. Or if other content *is* being developed? Isn't this course supposed to launch in just a couple of months? Could you fill me in on just the general background?" Richard remembered just barely being able to see Toni lower her eyes from across the table.

"Well," the project manager had said, "it's obvious this is a course on assessment strategies. The audience is classroom teachers — *all* classroom teachers across the state, and beyond the state for that matter. If you'll note the meeting agenda, ..."

"Yes, I get that," Richard said, interrupting her, "but that's a pretty big topic, and an even larger audience. When I work with elementary teachers I go about it differently from when I'm working with middle school teachers, or high school for that matter. I use different examples and maybe even different language for some things. I try to be specific, and relevant, for each group. I wouldn't use a generic math example for all grades, just like I wouldn't expect a language

arts teacher to be interested in my science example."

"Of course we know that," the ASC project manager had replied, perhaps not too sympathetically. "That'll all come out in the details."

"But what details?" Richard had even more questions. "How do you know who your audience really is? Who wants this course? Why would they take it? What might one group want that's different from others? Not to mention how you'll get the course content to them?" He had paused just enough to take a breath. "How *will* you get the course to them?"

"Well, online, of course. Isn't that what you're here for? You're the technology guy."

Zing! There it was. It was all too familiar. It was just a different room with a different group of people, but the plot usually ran about the same. A well-meaning group — and, yes, this group meant well — sought to disseminate information they felt was important. Most groups he had worked with felt their information was important. But, instead of relying on what the education community generally understands is good instruction, somehow putting things online was supposed to be different. *"We come up with the content,"* was what they seemed to be saying to Richard, and *"you put it online."* Somehow.

"It's not just about putting things online," he stated. "That's the easy part. First we have to design good instruction, and there are several things we need to consider before even thinking about whether we're going to use video, or a blog, an online journal, or whatever. Maybe you can tell me a little bit about what you expect this course to look like. Have any of you taken online courses before?"

While all had a background in education, few had ever taken an online course, and so all had different ideas of what they thought the course could be. They knew they wanted to get some information out there. And they were experts in their content areas; the conversations had focused more on the importance of the content. Online courses were mysterious things to them, so they chose the content and a medium with which they were somewhat familiar (video) rather than first determining what their audience wanted or how best to get it to them.

"Maybe we can have a discussion board," one staff member had said. "We used those in my graduate classes."

"I like our video. Maybe we can videotape some classrooms?" another had offered.

"It has to be rigorous," said one. "Teachers really need to understand the research behind it and work through the steps in order."

"Well, whatever it is," the project manager had said, "it has to be engaging and interactive."

There they are, thought Richard, *"engaging"* and *"interactive."* He could have provided that part of the script himself. In every online course project he had worked on, someone always said that, whatever they did, it had to be engaging and interactive. Of course, he had agreed silently, *but what does that mean in this case?*

"That's good," he'd said. "We can start with that. How about over the week we all determine what we think would be engaging and interactive for our audience? Let's also think about what's engaging and interactive about our content, too. We know it's important, but before we decide what technologies we'll use to deliver the course, let's work from the position of making our content engaging and interactive to those who are going to experience it. If it's okay, I have some ideas about how we can do that, and I'll share those ideas via email so we can dig deeper next week. Let's begin with what our audience wants and then we can go from there."

"What are you thinking about?" Toni asked, bringing Richard back to the present.

"Oh nothing," said Richard. "Just remembering. Hey, why don't we get started? Tell me some more about this new project."

"Well," said Toni, "we're not sure how we're going to do this yet, but because of your help with the last online course, we're hoping you can help develop an online course for our literacy coaches. Abby's an excellent literacy coach and has lots of good ideas. We just need your help to get them online."

"Yeah," Abby chimed in, enthusiastically. "We want it to be really engaging and interactive!"

Overview

What is an online course?

This obvious and seemingly simple question doesn't have one clear answer. An online course can be many things. One online course can look and feel very different from another, but both can be effective. That's the best part. It doesn't matter which technologies create that look and feel

and are used to support online learning, because it's not the technologies themselves that make a course successful. It's how they're used that's important. And many different technologies can be used to support effective online learning.

The general perception of an online course is likely one that grew out of the use of early learning management systems (LMSs) that proliferated in education, first in higher education. These software applications allowed student users to log in to their courses and view course content, such as lecture materials created in presentation or word-processing software and supporting documents and textbook readings; they could interact with the course facilitator and other students through a discussion board and a messaging system. Some LMSs had a quizzing tool and a place for students to submit their work. Some also bundled management features such as registration/enrollment, course scheduling, grade reports, and course completion. LMSs proved to be a handy tool for presenting and organizing content; LMSs also organized the people who used them (see Online Resource 16.1: *Evaluating a management system*).

As the Internet became more user-friendly through the introduction of Web 2.0 tools and a wide range of media, including access through mobile phones and other devices, the functionality of LMSs grew too. The modern LMS can support:

- audio and video, whether previously recorded or streamed live;
- collaborative spaces and student and teacher tools that go beyond text-based discussions and can include videoconferencing and shared documents; and
- connection through mobile devices.

Is online learning effective?

Research on online learning has grown over the past few decades, and a shift is now apparent (Abrami, Bernard, Bures, Borokhovski & Tamim, 2011). Early studies focused on comparing face-to-face and online delivery and, despite the variation in the design and efficacy of those studies, the general consensus was that online learning can be effective. The shift in research about online learning is on *how* online learning can be effective and in what settings.

Types of learning. Basically, professional learning can occur online, face to face, or in a blended format with some online and some face-to-face settings.

In a comprehensive meta-analysis of online and blended learning using only experimental or quasi-experimental studies with statistically controlled participant groups, Means, Toyama, Murphy and Baki (2013) confirmed that, on average, students perform modestly better in online rather than face-to-face settings. The impact was greatest for students in blended learning settings, in which at least 20% or more of the learning occurred online. Part of the reason blended learning settings may have had the most impact on learning was that these settings tended to include opportunities for additional time spent on learning activities, varied instructional resources, and interactions among learners (student-to-student).

Wholly online settings offer a benefit that is relevant to many decision makers and funders; they can cost less than face-to-face or blended learning formats. Cost savings can occur through reduced staff and facility requirements — if a course has enough paying participants. Costs for developing a course can be similar whether presented online or face to face, but a higher return on investment can be seen online when more people enroll in an online course over time (Cavalluzzo, Lopez, Ross, & Larson, 2005). It's often less expensive to deliver an additional section of an online course than to add another in-person session. Also, unlike face-to-face settings, having more participants may lead to less cost per person.

Blended learning, on the other hand, does not usually result in the same level of cost savings because a face-to-face component, even limited, is required and must meet the same strictures as face-to-face instruction regarding staffing, facility, and some resource requirements.

Effectiveness criteria. Mashaw (2012) proposed a model of interrelated components that educators can use to determine whether an online course will be effective. Students in an online course can be motivated to succeed through factors related to design and delivery:

- Clear objectives;
- The modular presentation of content with clear connections among modules; and
- Encouragement of exploration and discovery.

The author also found that the course and its content can actually inspire students to continue or persevere.

However, students can suffer from demotivational factors. While the correlation for the motivational factors were all strong, demotivational factors were less so, perhaps because students often volunteer to take a course online and may expect some problems simply due to the setting and use of technology. The most important factor that discourages learning, however, is boring content or activities.

Mashaw (2012) and others have found that the effectiveness of a course is less dependent on the technology used and more dependent on the design of the course and the quality of the learning experience. It's how the selected technologies are used to deliver well-designed content to inspire learning that will impact the effectiveness of an online course.

Why instructional design?

Instructional designers are advocates for the most important constituent in learning — the learner (Cennamo & Kalk, 2005). Instruction is designed to help the learner acquire new knowledge or skills, and an instructional designer draws upon different strategies to find the best fit between the content and the needs of the learner to help the learner succeed.

Models of instructional design. Instructional design practices truly embody the intent of the Learning Designs standard (in the Standards for Progessional Learning) as they integrate theories, research, and models of human learning to achieve intended outcomes. Regardless of the medium or setting, design depends on three factors: (1) who the audience is, (2) what the content is, and (3) the media available to deliver it (Ross, 2011).

Educators can consider several popular instructional design models, including the early ADDIE (analysis, design, development, implementation, evaluation) model developed for military use; models that view learning as a complex interrelated system, like the *Systematic Design of Instruction* (Dick, Carey, & Carey, 2008); and models that incorporate rapid prototyping that leverages new technologies to improve the development process (Cennamo & Kalk, 2005). Another model that educators can apply to online settings is the popular *Understanding by Design* (Wiggins & McTighe, 2005). And while not all designers adhere completely to every step described in a model every time they design instruction, experienced instructional designers report that they do rely on knowledge of a model as a heuristic or general guideline for course development (Ertmer, York, & Gedik, 2009). Once familiar with instructional design models, educators use the models' guidelines or suggestions to organize instruction, suggest learning activities, and solve issues or problems that arise during the development phase. Models are resources designers use to make decisions about instruction.

Gibson and Dunning (2012) from Troy University noted that a peer-reviewed assessment process helped their university improve the design of online courses by:

- emphasizing the establishment of standards that align learning outcomes and the method and types of instruction and assessments used to achieve them;
- encouraging the development of community; and
- providing multiple opportunities for student feedback from each other and the instructor.

One strategy for supporting these instructional design components is making assessment criteria explicit during the design process in order to create opportunities for students to demonstrate their learning.

Putting engagement and interaction into perspective. *Engagement* and *interaction* are two often-stated goals for online instruction, but these goals may be directed toward aspects of technology rather than design. Well-designed instruction is engaging and interactive regardless of the setting or medium.

Engagement. Engagement is the focus of Schlechty's (2002) popular *Working on the Work (WOW)* series. Independent of setting — online, face to face, or in some combination — two key assumptions undergird the WOW framework for increasing student engagement. One assumption is that the level and type of engagement is dependent upon the qualities built into coursework; the other is that teachers can directly affect student learning by creating instruction that is highly engaging to students.

These same principles apply in online courses. It is not the medium that is engaging; the work that learners do online and how that is structured impacts engagement. Incorporating pretty pictures, different colors, various fonts, or even video in lackluster instruction will do little to promote deeper engagement.

Robinson and Hullinger (2008) identified several elements in online courses that may link directly to student engagement. The researchers noted that students in online courses from three universities reported working harder than expected, a statement commonly made about many online courses. The participants — at least in these courses — engaged in a variety of activities that encouraged critical and analytical thinking, activities commonly associated with engagement. In addition, the researchers noted that the use of asynchronous communications, which are common to many online courses, can impact student engagement through increased opportunities for higher order levels of thinking in three ways:

1. Asynchronous communications provide learners more time to think critically, reflect, and craft responses that use higher levels of cognition, such as analysis, synthesis, and supporting their positions.
2. Multichannel communications, or the use of a variety of media to present and communicate about information, promote thinking.
3. Participants in an online course often generate some form of community which the researchers suggest are really communities of inquiry that support thinking.

Interaction. The second half of the "holy grail" of online learning is interaction. Interaction in online courses has changed from the days when the image of online learning was of an isolated individual sitting in front of a computer screen for hours at a time reading and clicking buttons. Just as the ways people can interact with each other have blossomed through the use of technology (e.g. mobile phones for voice, text, and data; video- and web-conferencing; blogging and micro-blogging) so too have the types of interaction in online courses.

Interaction is generally framed around three components: the instructor/facilitator, the learner, and the content. Moore's (1989) often-cited paradigm of interaction described these three types: (1) interaction between the learner and content, (2) interaction between the learner and the instructor, and (3) interaction among learners.

Kanuka (2011) noted that the design and development of online learning are key factors for promoting all three types of interaction and that specific kinds of online instructional strategies (especially debates and WebQuests, but also other strategies) can promote more effective interaction.

Rationale

Even though online learning is not new to education and is indeed growing in popularity in education and training, many organizations are still new to the process of designing and delivering online learning that is engaging and effective. For some reason, when it comes to moving instruction online, many people struggle with making appropriate decisions about professional learning that meets the needs of the educators with whom they work. They often focus on the technology and lose sight of what makes good learning. However, educators know many things about how people learn. They know how to provide instruction that addresses different learning needs. They know what they want their learners to know and be able to do and can identify activities and resources that not only help promote but demonstrate mastery of that learning. Unfortunately, much of that knowledge seems to be forgotten when technology comes into the picture. For some, technology has a blinding effect (Ross, 2011). One purpose of this chapter is to help developers focus, first, on designing good instruction and, then, on making sound decisions about which technologies to use and how — in essence, overcoming the blinding effect of technology.

The technologies used to deliver professional learning have changed rapidly and will likely continue to do so. However, sound instructional design that meets the needs of adults and motivates them to be successful learners will never become outdated, no matter what technologies are used. Using effective design principles can help educators get the most out of available technologies (see Online Resource 16.2: *Online PD module template* for a PowerPoint related to course development).

One of the main reasons many organizations turn to the online delivery of professional development is the hope that it will save money. This can happen, of course, and is certainly a reasonable goal. But simple cost estimates are not the whole story. It's not just the inputs that must be considered. To truly be cost-effective, an online course must yield a return on investment. Such a return should consider measures of how many participants actually gain the knowledge and use the skills presented in the course. How does the course impact practice? And how do those practices yield return in terms of student learning?

If a course is going to truly be cost-effective, it must first be an effective learning vehicle. It may seem cheaper to have all the teachers in a district take an online course rather than having a consultant or trainer physically visit every school and offer multiple face-to-face workshops, but if the online course is designed poorly and the course isn't relevant to what teachers need for their daily practice, they won't use it. In that case, there's no return on that investment. Good design can improve return.

Steps

Step 1: Determine the need

This may be one of the most overlooked steps in developing online courses. Is there really a need or is it just someone's opinion that the online course is necessary? Or that going online is the right strategy? An online course may be someone's pet project, but without a real need, the course can result in frustration and wasted time and money. Usually, some trigger suggests that an online course is necessary, but developers should still evaluate true need. With the growth of online learning and the evolution of technology that supports it, online learning can often be justified.

A common method for determining need is through a needs assessment, using any of a variety of strategies from the fields of organizational development, the military, and instructional design. Needs assessments can be intense and involved or quick and easy to conduct if there is extant data to suggest need. A needs assessment can be conducted by internal staff or contracted out to others that specialize in this process.

Triggers such as new policies, addition of new staff, adoption of new instructional resources or methods, changes in standards, or inadequate student performance may signal need. A trigger should lead to data collection and analysis to determine if there really is a need for professional learning (that may or may not be an online course); data analysis may even point to how the professional learning should be shaped and provided. Data can be collected through surveys, interviews, or focus groups, offering an opportunity for decision-makers to connect with the primary audience — the learners. A needs assessment can be an early public relations step to promote the project. There may be several rounds of data collection as information is understood and new questions are posed.

Ross (2011) suggested that a needs assessment for online professional learning should be informed by four questions:

1. *What's the trigger?* What action, change, or performance suggests a need for online courses?

2. *Who should be at the table?* Include representatives or information from key stakeholders, especially the learners.

3. *How will online professional learning align with existing initiatives?* Consider existing offering professional learning offerings and whether an online course will supplement or supplant other professional learning.

4. *Are you ready for online professional learning?* Consider whether members of the system for whom the course is intended are ready for online learning and have the desired technology access and skills.

Step 2: Know your audience

Because instructional designers are advocates for learners, they must try to learn as much as possible about them. One process for doing this is called an *audience analysis.* Whenever possible, instructional designers visit, interview, observe, or otherwise learn as much as they can about the audience. They need to learn how a course might meet their needs. When actual audience members cannot be interviewed, an instructional designer may create an audience profile. This can be a narrative about the audience, describing potential motivational factors as well as reasons for nonparticipation. A profile may also involve images or video. No matter how the information is compiled, the intent is to understand the needs of the audience (see Online Resource 16.3: *Audience analysis for the West Virginia Department of Education*).

Sometimes, designers will involve actual audience members in the design process. Called *participant-based design* or simply *participant design,* this strategy requires designers to collect input from audience members during interviews or focus groups as well as later during the actual design process when designers test prototypes or otherwise evaluate components of the course.

Another approach, which comes from software development and the field of human-computer interaction, is *scenario-based design* (Rosson & Carroll, 2002). Designers develop stories or scenarios that describe how users — audience members — will ultimately interact with the product — the online course. Scenarios go beyond simply describing functionality of the course; they describe how one or more audience members might actually use the course, addressing motivational as well as demotivational factors. People and the interactions they have with a product such as an online course are complex, and scenarios help designers better understand that complexity and consider alternate solutions (see Online Resource 16.4: *Bill Squandered storyboard* for an example of a scenario based design).

Designers should also consider *why* the audience will participate. What will they get out of it? What will motivate them? Responses to this question can help decision-makers determine what kinds of incentives might be necessary to encourage enrollment (see Online Resource 16.5: *Motivation and design.*)

Regardless of the methods used, designers should determine the audience's current level of knowledge about the content so that the online course is matched to their level of need. The content shouldn't be too easy nor too far beyond their current level of understanding. The audience analysis should also determine the audience's access to technology and proficiency with those technologies. Courses that rely on video can fail if the audience is in a district that blocks streaming media.

Step 3: Determine what the audience will know and be able to do

Every day, teachers determine learning outcomes for their students — what students should know and be able to do. Classroom teachers use standards, curriculum frameworks, and pacing guides to help determine what it is their students should learn. One process an instructional designer can use is an *instructional analysis* (Dick, Carey, & Carey, 2008).

An instructional analysis lays out the desired learning outcomes in a hierarchy, generally starting from the ultimate goal of the course, so the connections between all the learning outcomes can be clearly seen. This process helps the designer determine scope and sequence of the content, usually working backwards from the ultimate goal by repeatedly considering what the learner needs to know or be able to do to achieve that goal. The designer breaks down component skills and knowledge until identifying skills and knowledge that learners should already possess. These are prerequisite or entry-level skills and knowledge.

Subject-matter experts (SMEs) are critical in this process so that appropriate skills and knowledge are identified. Sometimes, however, an instructional designer may have to streamline or organize subject matter based on the needs of the learner. SMEs are usually passionate about their content and often want to include as much as possible. The instructional designer, as the advocate for the learner, may have to diplomatically determine how much of the content the learner will actually need, or want. For example, an SME may want to bring in extensive citations of research or theory to emphasize the importance of particular content when the learners already accept the fact that the new skills or knowledge are important and just want to learn how to use new materials.

An instructional analysis is a good strategy for developing content (based on subject matter or other outcomes) from scratch, but that may not always be necessary. Sometimes, online courses can be purchased or material from existing courses in another setting can be repurposed for online delivery. In a popular article early in the current generation of thinking about online learning, Klemm (2001) suggested that converting an existing course might be a good first step for those interested in creating online learning. Conversion can allow the developer to become better acquainted with the tools and processes associated with creating an online course without also having to tackle new content. The content and activities may need to be modified, of course, but at least the developer is working with familiar content.

Klemm also supports the notion that content should be the focus of the course, not the technology, but that developers should take advantage of the networked state of information online and shouldn't be afraid to connect with other resources of note. The content developer or instructor does not have to be the sole font of information, for high-quality information is now readily available from numerous reliable sources on the Web. Regardless of where the content comes from, early on the designer must still determine what the learners will need to know and be able to do. Converting or linking to outside content has to directly support the learning outcomes.

Step 4: Determine how learners will demonstrate their new knowledge and skills

Several instructional design models encourage the development of assessments prior to designing instructional activities. Many educators are familiar with *Understanding by Design* (Wiggins & McTighe, 2008) that advocates "backwards design." The benefit of designing assessments first is

that the assessment dictates which and how much content must be provided within the course. According to the logic of this model, the learner should be able to complete the assessment successfully with the content and activities provided, and developing the assessments first gives the designer targets for determining how much content is necessary and which activities will prepare the learner for the assessments. Assessments, in this case, do not have to be formal assessments but can include instructional or reflective activities that allow learners to monitor their own growth (see "Chapter 3: Assessment as Professional Learning" in this book).

Assessment should be dictated by the learning outcomes, not by available technology. While online quizzes graded by the computer are convenient, they may not be appropriate for all types of learning outcomes. If an online course is designed to help teachers incorporate a new lesson plan process or a pedagogical technique, the assessment should require development of a lesson plan or demonstration of that technique. If it's designed to help administrators conduct classroom walkthroughs, then administrators should do the walkthroughs and report results. With the many digital technologies available today, designers can likely find a technology for appropriately assessing outcomes.

Step 5: Consider the visual design

Online courses are a visual medium. Whether it is primarily text-based or includes graphics or video, every course will have a visual design, intended or not. Fonts used and their colors, sizes, headings, and other treatments influence the visual design. The types of images selected, whether photos or graphics, including the quality of the imagery and the subjects in them, also impact the visual design. The course interface (what the user sees and interacts with onscreen) — the basic colors, layouts, buttons, and other features — affects visual design, and visual design affects learning. A poor or distracting visual design can have a negative impact on learning (see Online Resource 16.6 *Visual elements* for a PowerPoint on visual considerations).

Not all project budgets can afford a graphic designer, but there are some things anyone can consider in terms of designing a more successful visual design. The first is to look elsewhere for designs. Popular presentation software, such as PowerPoint and Keynote, are actually collections of different design samples that coordinate background images, fonts, and colors. Other websites, whether online course websites or not, are also sources for potential designs. Also review relevant print and digital publications, such as trade magazines that are popular with the target audience. What design elements best represent the target audience? Several different organizations give out awards for web and graphic design and post links to the winners. There are also templates available for use with different applications, such as blogs, LMS, and even videos; template sites exist online with free and low-cost designs (see Online Resource 16.7: *Additional resources*).

Gather input from project team members about their preferences for the visual design. Have each collect examples of the design elements that they feel best represent the course. These elements may include colors, fonts, buttons, and types of images. Team members should consider how each relates to the target audience. If the audience is teachers, what kind of images might they like best? Should the visual design be thematic, based on a little red schoolhouse? Or maybe a modern computer lab? From a review of the different examples, the team may be able to come to consensus on design elements.

When in doubt, less is more. Generally avoid using too many fonts, perhaps sticking with two or three different treatments within the same font family for the main text, headings, and accent fonts. Black or dark text on a white or very light background often works best for readability. Two complementary and one accent color can result in a very effective design palette.

Step 6: Match media to learning outcomes

Learning outcomes — and what they look like when operational — should guide designers in terms of selecting technology. Of course, available technology may limit what can be used. For example, a district may have invested in an LMS that supports text-based discussions but not real-time collaborative spaces; another district may prohibit the use of social media sites or streaming video on the district network. Designers should identify technology limitations during the audience analysis process and keep the focus on giving learners an appropriate method to access the content and demonstrate learning.

Media used in an online course is dependent on the types of learning desired, and some media are better suited to some outcomes rather than others. Mayer (2001) has identified general principles of media design shown to support or hinder learning:
- Principles for reducing extraneous processing;
- Principles for managing processing; and
- Principles for fostering generative processing (for details, see Online Resource 16.8: *General principles of media design for learning*).

Many online courses are text heavy. The amount of text that is necessary should influence its formatting. Shorter passages are best for reading online. Longer passages can be made downloadable. Images should support text and appear with or near relevant supporting text. Video, if incorporated, should be used to demonstrate processes or give the learner an idea of how something works. Video is for showing, not talking. Other options, such as animations or narrated presentations, may be a cheaper and easier alternative to develop for a course than a video — and have just as much impact. (For ideas on matching outcomes to media, see Online Resource 16.9: *Matching outcomes to technology*, as well as "Chapter 11: Digital Teacher Portfolios," "Chapter 22: Videos," and "Chapter 24: Webinars" in this book.)

Designers can think beyond traditional forms of media used in online courses and investigate the potential of new and emerging technologies to support learning. In proposing alternate approaches to the use of discussion boards — ubiquitous to many online courses — van Aalst (2006) noted that student posts in an online class are often minimal, and few students return to a threaded discussion after making their initial post and meeting their participatory obligation. The author suggested rethinking the way discussion lists and collaborative work are used.

While most online courses encourage the use of discourse for academic purposes, van Aalst suggests that nongraded social discourse can be important in terms of establishing trust and a sense of community among participants. In fact, social discourse may be needed *before* course participants can get to the point where they can successfully collaborate with and learn from each other under the pressure of obtaining a grade. Both social and academic discourse are necessary in an online course. Social discourse helps students build a sense of community and may not always be supported by an activity-based discussion that is graded. Both can strengthen a course experience.

Step 7: Motivate the learners

Successful courses motivate learners by design. Since learners come to an online course motivated by different factors, instructional designers leverage these factors to motivate learners to be *successful* in the course. The instructional design should contain elements that increase student engagement and encourage participants to persevere and succeed. Part of the equation with adult learners is understanding a few key aspects of *andragogy* (Knowles, 1990), which relates to designing relevant instruction for adults.

The audience analysis should provide some background on the proficiency and skill level of the target audience — for both the content and the technologies used. These can be fairly sophisticated for educators. Adults generally enjoy some autonomy in their learning and need to know why an online course is relevant. Adults, especially busy practitioners, want solutions to their problems and are more likely to appreciate developing skills or learning how to use resources they can apply immediately in their practice, rather than watching presentations of research and theory.

Design elements, too, can be leveraged to motivate learners. Using a simple framework, the ARCS Model, Keller (1987) suggested that designers consider the four key motivational principles of *attention, relevance, confidence, and success* (see Online Resource 16.10: *ARCS motivational design module;* also see Online Resource 16.11: *Supporting the ARCS model*). Designers must engage the learners by gaining and keeping their attention as they progress through the course. They must make relevance apparent and emphasize it throughout the instruction. Designers can build confidence with the language and examples they use, trying to relate the content to the target audience as much as possible. They can also design activities so that all learners experience success early on; then designers can incorporate incremental challenges over time. Pintrich (2003) provided implications for the design of instruction that are consistently found in the literature related to motivational science (review Online Resource 16.5: *Motivation and design*).

Step 8: Monitor

Even though this is listed as the eighth step, ongoing evaluation of the online course needs to be considered early. Whenever possible, members of the target audience should preview sections of the online course to provide feedback before the course is given. SMEs might also be consulted about whether content and activities are relevant. This formative assessment approach can help strengthen the product, providing information so that designers can hone major structural components; it can ensure that the product is relevant and appropriate.

Formative assessment may be affected by the restrictions of time and money. Ideally, course designers would preview all of the content and media at least once, but the reality is that, because of schedules and budgets, they may be able to preview only excerpts from the content or prototypes of media elements.

Because the course is online, course reviewers can provide feedback from anywhere with an Internet connection, but course developers can get additional insights by observing users in person. Reviewers can find it overwhelming to review an entire course before it goes live; however, they can provide reviews of specific tasks or sections, and they can also provide focused feedback through a user scenario.

Evaluators and course developers can easily update most content online; therefore, they can think of all evaluations as formative to some degree. Responding to a few survey questions at the end of a course or module, course participants can give feedback to course developers. Course developers also can provide a direct link for comments, the optimum way of obtaining this feedback.

Course developers should include evaluation in the budget from the beginning. Previewers usually receive some form of compensation, which can include access to materials, copies of curriculum materials, or a fee. Once the product launches, evaluation occurs on a relevant relevant schedule, such as annual reviews of evaluation data, and developers should update or revise content accordingly. Very little content remains relevant year after year, and ongoing review and revision can keep content fresh and incorporate new information, as needed.

Step 9: Promote your project

Another step that is not so much a final one as an ongoing step is getting the word out while courses are being developed. Multiple forms of communication will probably be necessary, perhaps included in a professional learning catalog or announced by relevant organizations. Consider both print and online marketing and making presentations at meetings or conferences. Simply posting an announcement online, even on a company, school, or department website, might not reach potential participants.

Marketing material should answer all key questions the audience might have, such as why the course is important and how participants can use the information immediately in their positions. Don't forget to include cost information, technology requirements, and incentives that might attract participants to the course. It may be possible to post a sample of the course, or an agenda or syllabus. People respected by members of the target audience can also serve as champions to promote the effort.

Variations

The only "absolute" in this chapter is that course designers attend to the principles and practices of effective instructional design. Otherwise, almost everything else about an online course can be varied to suit the audience and the purpose of the course — including the technology through which the course will be delivered.

Challenges and how to address them

Using an instructional design model and incorporating the steps described in this chapter are strategies for overcoming many of the pitfalls that are commonly associated with developing and delivering online courses.

Inadequate resources. Two pitfalls that commonly plague the development of online courses are inadequate time and money budgeted for the project. These challenges occur when decision makers do not understand how much time must be spent on developing high-quality content or how long development takes. Designers themselves, especially when new to the process, do not always understand the time and money challenges. Over time, as design teams become familiar with both instructional design principles and available technology, development timelines can be shorter and costs diminished. Time truly is money, in that the time people spend working on developing online courses has to be charged somewhere. Repurposing media or using templates or processes developed from earlier courses can help the design team be more effective and reduce costs. Limited timelines, however, can result in boring content that is developed more to meet deadlines than to meet the needs of the learners.

ONLINE RESOURCES

16.1 Evaluating a management system
16.2 Online PD module template
16.3 Audience analysis for the West Virginia Department of Education
16.4 Bill Squandered storyboard
16.5 Motivation and design
16.6 Visual elements
16.7 Additional resources
16.8 General principles of media design for learning
16.9 Matching outcomes to technology
16.10 ARCS motivational design module
16.11 Supporting the ARCS model

Lack of formative assessment. Another challenge occurs when online courses are developed without any formative assessment. Designers who rush projects to the finish line and don't take the time to have the course previewed throughout the development process can find more than errors in content and programming. Gaining user feedback may seem time consuming, but feedback can actually improve the product and the process. After the course has launched, it's too late to find out that audience members can't access course videos or that the LMS interface is difficult to use. Despite the best intentions of content experts and project managers, lackluster content that doesn't engage the learner or that has no relevance to their practice won't be used.

One basic suggestion for developers of online courses is to enroll in one. Learning through experience can help design teams better understand what to do and what not to do in terms of designing their own courses. There are many opportunities for participating in an online course, many for free. There are several state and national organizations that offer online courses for educators on a variety of topics — including online courses about designing online courses. And massive open online courses, or MOOCs for short, which show growing enrollments among universities, are becoming another way to experience an online course.

Conclusion

Online courses are proliferating in many settings, including professional learning for educators. The increasing availability of digital technologies, their decreasing cost, and expanding power and functionality make it a greater possibility that most teachers may, one day, turn to online courses for part of their professional learning experiences. This chapter focused on the incorporation of sound instructional design practices intended to improve the quality of online courses. The use of instructional design models not only supports the Learning Forward Standards for Professional Learning but can actually result in online courses that bring them to life.

References

Abrami, P.C., Bernard, R. M., Bures, E. M., Borokhovski, E., & Tamim, R. M. (2011, December). Interaction in distance education and online learning: Using evidence and theory to improve practice. *Journal of Computing in Higher Education, 23*(2–3), 82–103.

Cavalluzzo, L., Lopez, D., Ross, J., & Larson, M. (2005). *A study of the effectiveness and cost of AEL's online professional development program in reading in Tennessee.* Charleston, WV: Edvantia.

Cennamo, K. & Kalk, D. (2005). *Real world instructional design.* Belmont, CA: Wadsworth Publishing.

Dick, W., Carey, L., & Carey, J. O. (2008). *The systematic design of instruction* (7th ed.). Upper Saddle River, NJ: Pearson.

Ertmer, P., York, C.S., & Gedik, N. (2009). Learning from the pros: How experience designers translate instructional design models into practice. *Educational Technology, 49*(1), 19–27.

Gibson, P.A. & Dunning, P.T. (2012). Creating quality online course design through a peer-reviewed assessment. *Journal of Public Affairs Education, 18*(1), 209–228.

Kanuka, H. (2011, December). Interaction and the online distance classroom: Do instructional methods affect the quality of interaction? *Journal of Computing in Higher Education, 23*(2–3), 143–156.

Keller, J.M. (1987). The systematic process of motivational design. *Performance & Instruction, 26*(9), 1–8.

Klemm, W.R. (2001). Creating online courses: A step-by-step guide. *The Technology Source.* Available at www.technologysource.org/article/creating_online_courses/.

Knowles, M. (1990). *The adult learner: A neglected species* (4th ed.). Houston, TX: Gulf Publishing.

Mashaw, B. (2012). A model for measuring effectiveness of an online course. *Decision Sciences Journal of Innovative Education, 10*(2), 189–221.

Mayer, R.E. (2001). *Multimedia learning.* New York, NY: Cambridge University Press.

Means, B., Toyama, Y., Murphy, R., & Baki, M. (2013). The effectiveness of online and blended learning: A meta-analysis of the empirical literature. *Teachers College Record, 115*(3), 1–47.

Moore, M.G. (1989). Three types of interaction. *The American Journal of Distance Education, 3*(2), 1–6.

Pintrich, P.R. (2003). A motivational science perspective on the role of student motivation in learning and teaching contexts. *Journal of Educational Psychology, 95*(4), 667–686.

Robinson, C.C. & Hullinger, H. (2008). New benchmarks in higher education: Student engagement in online learning. *Journal of Education for Business, 84*(2), 101–109.

Ross, J.D. (2011). *Online professional development: Design, deliver, succeed!* Thousand Oaks, CA: Corwin Press.

Rosson, M.B. & Carroll, J. M. (2002). Scenario-based design. In J. Jacko & A. Sears (Eds.), *The human-computer interaction handbook: Fundamentals, evolving technologies and emerging applications* (pp. 1032–1050). Hillsdale, NJ: Lawrence Erlbaum Associates.

Schlechty, P.C. (2002). *Working on the work: An action plan for teachers, principals, and superintendents.* San Francisco, CA: Jossey-Bass.

van Aalst, J. (2006). Rethinking the nature of online work in asynchronous learning networks. *British Journal of Educational Technology, 37*(2), 279–288.

Wiggins, G. & McTighe, J. (2005). *Understanding by design* (2nd ed.). Alexandria, VA: ASCD.

Wiggins, G. & McTighe, J. (2008, May). Put understanding first. *Educational Leadership, 65*(8), 36–41.

CHAPTER 17

Online Protocols

Protocols help us develop the habits we wish we had.[1]

By Alan Dichter and Janet Mannheimer Zydney

Marty, an experienced principal, kept talking about how nervous he was and how he felt like a new teacher as he led professional learning sessions at his school. The thought of starting a staff meeting with a warm-up or launching into a text-based protocol made him physically ill.

Then, when working with some colleagues on his own development as a leader, he announced he had had a break-through. He realized what was haunting him — at times, paralyzing him — and he had to face and overcome his fear. He said, "I needed to overcome my fear of eye-rolling!" Everyone instantly knew what he meant: The silent groan from the teacher who is never pleased. The mumbling "What are they doing to us now?" In fact, he realized, as most teachers do, it was as much about his confidence in

the soundness of what he was doing as about his technical skills at facilitating.

Anyone facing a school faculty who has not engaged in truly sustained successful professional learning knows Marty's fear of eye-rolling. What Marty needed was to take some risks and not worry about the eye-rollers in his crowd.

Marty learned some worthy lessons along the way. What Marty learned was that using protocols didn't just allow all voices to be heard but provided structures that actually helped more people to participate. He learned that multiple perspectives shared in a respectful way inspire participation. The eye-rollers were the minority who managed to silence and dishearten the vast majority of staff who actually wanted to engage with colleagues. Marty found that taking the risk to introduce and use structured protocols may not have stopped

---

[1] McDonald, Mohr, Dichter, McDonald, 2013, p. 23.

the eye-rolling, but it meant that eye-rolling didn't stop the rest of the people from happily participating. Other important habits Marty came to develop and appreciate were getting feedback regularly and being transparent about how he modified what he did based on that feedback. He also needed to remember, and remind people, that whining is not feedback.

Marty and his team learned, for example, that the Tuning Protocol helps everyone develop the habit of giving balanced feedback and helps people move beyond their fear that all they will get is criticism. They learned from various openers and protocols that, when individuals have strict time limits, participants relax because they know that one or two people won't dominate the discussion and that people won't talk over one another.

In the world of **online** professional learning, the equivalent fear is the moment of dead silence. Anyone who has facilitated online knows this feeling too. Are the participants taking notes, pausing for a moment of reflection, or have they left the room to go to the bathroom? Or are they perhaps multitasking — checking email, for example — and no longer paying attention? In some cases, facilitators might even prefer the live eye roll. At least, it provides some feedback as opposed to the empty space of the online world.

When they learned how to engage in the online Tuning Protocol, Marty and his team established an order and made sure to be explicit about things like no multitasking. Because of their preparation, online participants came to believe that conversation would be productive and they would have a chance to contribute when it was their turn. By setting up norms, Marty and his team learned that participants would stay focused and learn, through the various listening segments, that their colleagues actually had some interesting things to say. Participants would also come to understand that they would be listened to more closely themselves.

Marty and his team grew to appreciate how protocols are structured so that sufficient time is given to participants to understand the nature of a dilemma. Also, through the structure of live and online protocols, participants could trust that they wouldn't be quickly (and mistakenly) judged.

Although seemingly different types of fears manifest themselves in online and face-to-face professional learning, both these and similar challenges can be addressed through the use of protocols combined with good leadership and effective facilitation moves.

Overview

Protocols, as the term is used here, are strategies for having structured communication to enhance problem solving, encourage different perspectives, and build shared knowledge. The protocol process helps leaders and staff developers empower and build community. The use of the term *protocols* by educators became popular in the 1990s. Reformers, needing tools to help them engage in the difficult work of strengthening practice and forming vibrant professional learning communities, began to construct ways of looking together at student and educator work, learning from text, and collaboratively solving problems.

More recently, educators have begun to use protocols to facilitate professional learning in online spaces — partly because people need to connect from different places but also to take advantage of new environments for learning. For example, asynchronous tools, such as discussion forums, blogs, Google+, etc., where participants post messages to one another at different times, can extend a conversation over a week or two. Participants can take advantage of the additional time to reflect and give more thoughtful feedback to one another.

Synchronous tools, such as WebEx, Skype, or Google Hangouts, allow participants to talk or text at the same time from places all over the world. They can immediately share their own practices as educators through real-time video, for example, showing a classroom in action on Skype. They can also share student work, current teaching dilemmas and educational issues and, through a protocol, gain insight and become more thoughtful about what they are doing.

Blended environments, which use a combination of online (both asynchronous and synchronous) and face-to-face time, allow participants to take advantage of different spaces for different purposes. Thus, professional learning leaders can strategize how to maximize the time the group has together physically when a richer and more constructive discussion is needed and use the online spaces when participants cannot get together physically or when they need more time to reflect and process experiences and information.

Whether the protocol is face to face in real time, online (either synchronously or asynchronously), or a combination of these formats, professional learning leaders need to consider three important factors that lead to success: facilitation, trust, and equity.

The work of the facilitator

Facilitation is an important part of any protocol. While protocols are designed for collaborative work and promote shared responsibility, facilitators, who may also participate, must always keep part of their focus on the process and goal. Joe McDonald, Nancy Mohr, Alan Dichter, and Elizabeth McDonald (2007) note:

> At its heart, facilitating is about promoting participation, ensuring equity, and building trust. This is true whether the facilitating involves a protocol or another kind of meeting format. The difference is that protocols are deliberately designed with these tasks in mind, while most other meeting formats are rife with opportunities for ignoring them. We all know the result: the faculty "meeting" that turns into a monologue by the principal or the chairperson, the "whole group discussion" that two or three people dominate, or the task force that manages to suppress divergent thinking. (p. 15)

Successful facilitators realize that it would be difficult to facilitate professional learning and *not* pay attention to promoting participation, ensuring equity, and building trust. For example, it's difficult to imagine ensuring equity without having trust. For that matter, it's difficult to imagine building trust without ensuring equity. Some people might think of them as sequential (i.e. first trust and then equity), but when they examine the ideas closely and reflect on them, they are likely to see that trust and equity are all part of a web of conditions that allows for and promotes professional interaction and meaningful participation.

Facilitators can sense when these conditions are present and, then, it all seems so easy. Veteran facilitators have probably also experienced the terror when, suddenly, trust and equity seem to evaporate. Good facilitators must be vigilant and establish rituals and routines that promote these conditions and have safeguards and strategies built in for when the conditions appear to erode or the group needs some direct attention.

While protocols themselves help prevent things from going wrong by providing an overarching structure that participants can trust, things still happen that require intervention. Facilitators using protocols early in a group's development might hear, "Why don't we just talk?" Facilitators find it helps to ask participants to go with the process and remind them that they can share their feedback at the end. It is also about this time when the facilitator who spent a few minutes on norms can gratefully reference them, and the facilitator who skipped doing norms remembers why that was a mistake.

Many participants are eager to make sure that a group hears all voices. The skilled facilitator knows that the hearing of all voices is more than just being equitable with time and making sure as many points of view as exist are heard — and structures conversations accordingly. Facilitators also want to make sure that the group can come to know more than any one individual in the group can possibly know. Protocols explicitly value the collective — not over the individual, but because of the presence of the individuals. McDonald and colleagues (2007) explain:

> When a facilitator promotes a group's trust, it is not to help everyone trust every other individual member *as an individual,* but rather to help each trust the situation that has been collectively created. The purpose is not trust in general, but trust sufficient to do the work at hand. Nor is the goal to make everyone feel comfortable. Given trust, a group of individuals can learn from one another and their work together even when the work creates *dis*comfort — as work involving worthwhile learning often does. (p 17)

Much has been written about the role of the facilitator (see *The Power of Protocols* by McDonald et al., 2013, and *The Facilitator's Book of Questions* by Allen and Blythe, 2004), but it is critical for anyone seeking to lead professional learning or build professional community to remember to pay attention to these three interdependent aspects of work of the facilitative leader: equity, trust, and participation.

The importance of being explicit about equity

In addition to valuing differing viewpoints, groups engaging in protocols must explicitly recognize and value different life experiences based on race, sexual orientation, ethnicity, class background, nationality, ability/disability, geographical locale, etc. Surfacing these differences and addressing their impact can often create volatile situations.

Protocols were designed with just this need in mind, however, allowing groups to engage with equity concerns in relatively safe and productive ways.

Most protocols have built-in reflection steps at the end. This is one of those times that doing things online has its advantages because working asynchronously can allow participants greater time to pause and reflect on what's happened. Groups that take the time to pause and reflect at the end of a protocol — regardless of whether the closing is online or in person — are developing an excellent habit. Even if they're in a business meeting, they can make sure that at the end of the meeting there will be a round of feedback. The facilitator who makes sure that all voices are heard will almost always broaden everyone's perspective on what just happened. And then the leader can transparently apply that feedback to strengthen things at the next meeting or to take action between meetings. Closure with reflection is empowering for the group and promotes a virtuous cycle.

Rationale

Marty was working with some colleague principals on developing their own facilitative leadership capacity. Based on his research and experience, Marty had come to believe that, in order to lead a collaborative organization, these leaders needed a different set of leadership skills and dispositions. Those who seek to lead collaborative organizations know that the notion of a strong collaborative leader is not an oxymoron. In fact, it takes great strength and some very specific skills to successfully lead such a group. What is often referred to as "facilitative leadership" (Hord, 1991) is an approach that many successful collaborative leaders adopt — sometimes without even being able to name it.

Protocols are extremely valuable tools for those seeking to develop facilitative leadership skills themselves and to embed facilitative leadership within an organization. What becomes clear though, to workshop leaders and to principals and teachers seeking to lead professional learning in their own communities, is that overcoming some initial resistance on the part of some to working with protocols is going to take work and persistence. The structure of the protocols creates a safe and equitable environment, helping leaders take these steps.

What educators have learned is that the ability to apply the principles behind good protocols is critical not only for protocols but for successful professional learning. The very habits that protocols help develop are those that assure that time when professionals gather is maximally productive. This is the case for weekly staff meetings, teacher team meetings, retreats, and seminars, regardless of whether they are in-person, online, synchronous or asynchronous.

It might be useful to consider that protocols "help us develop the habits we wish we had" (McDonald et al., 2013, p. 23) and, by using protocols, leaders and participants are supported in developing the habits needed for strong successful professional community. While most who have engaged in good professional learning have no doubt experienced some excellent activities or ways to interact and process information, unpacking those strategies and understanding the principles behind them allow educational leaders to select, create, or customize structures/protocols to best meet their needs.

Steps for a variety of effective protocols

Many protocols have been found to be very effective tools to support professional learning. This section describes four of them, providing purposes, guidelines, steps, facilitation tips, variations, and online versions of the protocols, as appropriate.

PROTOCOL 1: A protocol for getting started — the Clearing Protocol or Connections Protocol

Sometimes facilitators can be tempted to skip the warm-up, or opener, especially when working in a school where time is always limited. Participants might say, "Let's just get to work. Anyway, warm-ups are silly and a waste of time, even if we sometimes have fun." Don't underestimate the importance of a few minutes at the beginning to reconnect: "Time is always an issue in the facilitation of groups. In our experience, however, a little investment of time up front saves a lot of time later" (McDonald et al., 2007, p. 18). The opening is even more critical, and for some reason not done very often, in online environments where people are more likely to feel disconnected and isolated from one another. Having fun together builds rapport, and rapport turns out to be a critical asset when things get a little sticky. Giving and getting feedback will be more honest and effective the better participants know each other.

Good openers are connected to the work and task at hand — even if that task, early on, is getting to know more about the richness each participant brings to the learning. But, that doesn't mean that there aren't some warm-ups that are silly and may be better off being skipped:

> Disconnected openers provoke the "touchy-feely" accusation, and seem as incongruous as an off-color joke at the start of a serious speech. It matters, too, that the scale of the opening move fit the scale of the meeting: short moves for short time frames; longer ones for half-day sessions or day-long retreats. (McDonald et al., 2007, p. 18)

Using a food metaphor, warm-ups are appetizers and are best tasty and minimal and should complement the rest of the meal.

It is also important to remember to set norms. How you approach this depends on the purpose, length of time, and how well members of the group know each other. There are many examples of approaches to set norms. Most important is to make sure at least some attention is given to setting norms.

Purpose of the Clearing or Connections Protocol. People come to meetings or leave them with things on their minds, and they need time to transition from there to here. This protocol, used by many facilitators of on-going groups at the beginning of every meeting, has two names. Some call it *Clearing* and others call it *Connections*. When it is used as a Clearing, it is intended to clear your mind of things that might distract you. These are things that can be unrelated to the work at hand. Maybe you were in a fender bender this morning and have been getting annoying calls or dread going home to tell your son that the car he thought he was using tonight is in the shop. Maybe you just made reservations for a great vacation. Whatever it is, it's on your mind and the idea is that if you share it or clear it you will be freer to attend to the work of the group.

Those who call this protocol Connections rather than Clearing may think of it as a way to connect more fully with members of the group and all they bring to the table. Some facilitators actually think of it as reconnecting, and group members may voice lingering thoughts from prior discussions. In fact, "This is an especially good opener for an

Network for educators interested in protocols

To join other educators interested in using protocols visit the School Reform Initiative (SRI) website at : www.schoolreforminitiative.org

after-school workshop when people come in still connected to some earlier events or for groups that meet periodically. People get better over time and find this routine way of starting to be very centering" (McDonald, 2003, p. 23).

Details and guidelines for the Clearing or Connections Protocol. Review these guidelines and the following steps with participants before beginning. Also, see Online Resource 17.1: *Summary of steps for the Clearing Protocol or Connections Protocol.*

- Set a time frame. Depending on the size of the group, between 5–10 minutes is usually best.
- DO NOT try to connect to what someone else has said, despite the fact that some people call this Connections,.
- There is absolutely no dialogue or conversation.
- Nothing is too irrelevant to share.
- Each person talks only once unless everyone else has spoken.
- No hand-raising.
- No going in order.
- It's perfectly fine not to say something.
- Silence is to be expected.

Steps for the Clearing or Connections Protocol

1. The protocol begins when the facilitator says, "We will take five minutes. Clearing (or Connections) is now open."
2. Participants speak following the guidelines above.
3. When there is a minute left, facilitators may tell the group that time is almost up and invite people who haven't spoken, and may want to, to use the time now.
4. When time is up, the facilitator announces "Clearing (or Connections) is now closed," and the group moves on with no debrief or discussion.

Online version of the Clearing or Connections Protocol. Here's an example of how a skilled facilitator, working online, was able to use this protocol. Donna Isaacs was facilitating a virtual Critical Friends Group (CFG) with classroom teachers (see "Chapter 7: Critical Friends Groups" in this book). Teachers were linked via video conferencing and sitting in their own classrooms. Donna wanted to use Connections and realized she had a unique opportunity. She asked members to take a few minutes to find something in their space that had meaning and bring it back to the group. Each member then got to speak for one minute and in a specific order. Note that in an online world there are no nonverbal signals to indicate whose turn it is to talk. People may try to talk at the same time, or each waits for the other to start talking again, leaving long, awkward silences. The facilitator needs to let participants know who will start and how others will be invited to speak, perhaps named by the current speaker.

While the possible confusion of who speaks is a constraint of the online world, there are also some advantages. The facilitator of a face-to-face CFG can ask people to bring artifacts, but there is certainly something about the ability to be spontaneous and in the moment in an online CFG that is desirable. Donna Isaacs' CFG is an example of an online CFG that wasn't just compensating for not being in the same room, but taking advantage of being in different spaces.

See *The Power of Protocols* (McDonald et al., 2013) and *Going Online with Protocols* (McDonald, Zydney, Dichter, & McDonald, 2012) for more openers.

PROTOCOL 2: A protocol for working on problems of practice — the Descriptive Consultancy

Most protocols are flexible, and can be used or adapted for multiple purposes. The original Descriptive Consultancy[2] developed by Gene Thompson-Grove, Paula Evans, and Faith Dunne in their work at the Coalition of Essential Schools and the Annenberg Institute for School Reform, is a protocol designed to support collaborative problem solving. One of the key aspects of this protocol, and all its variations, is that advice, if given at all, is withheld until a thorough examination of the challenge takes place. All variations of the original Consultancy have very specific times for particular sorts of questions, reflection on what people have

---

Probing questions

For more information about probing questions, see http://schoolreforminitiative.org/doc/probing_questions_guide.pdf

---

heard and, perhaps, but not always, recommendations. As a professional learning tool, it is one of the best for helping people develop the habit and skill of asking good questions.

The use of probing questions, considered by many to be the most powerful dimension of this protocol, is a skill that practitioners find they readily apply in all sorts of professional (and personal) interactions. The key behind a good probing question is that it is asked to help the person answering the question to think more deeply and expansively about the issue; it is not about questioners imposing their own interpretations or solutions. Probing questions often help people gain insight into a problem that is far more helpful than suggestions. It is also true that, once the presenter shares those additional insights, whatever suggestions are made are far more likely to be on target. Following is one variation of the original Consultancy.

Purpose of the Descriptive Consultancy. In this variation, presenters gain the opportunity to learn how others frame their dilemmas. Nancy Mohr, who designed the protocol, used it especially to help groups of educators become facilitative leaders. Over a series of meetings, these educators presented a number of dilemmas to each other for descriptive consultation. In the process, they not only obtained better perspectives on their own problems, but also became better consultants to each other.

As with the original Consultancy, the Descriptive Consultancy has two purposes — helping practitioners think through a dilemma that they present, and expanding their power to address it. Both involve learning how to engage in what many scholars in the social sciences call re-framing or frame reflection.

Details and guidelines for the Descriptive Consultancy. The protocol requires approximately one hour for

---

[2] From *The Power of Protocols: An Educators' Guide to Better Practice* (2nd ed.), by Joseph P. McDonald, Nancy Mohr, Alan Dichter, and Elizabeth C. McDonald. Copyright 2007 Teachers College, Columbia University. All rights reserved. Adapted by permission of the publisher.

the exploration of each dilemma, though overall times vary depending on the number of participants. The setting typically involves either one group of 10 to 12 or smaller groups of three to five participants each, meeting in a space where multiple conversations can be carried on simultaneously. Smaller groups — using a more constrained time frame — might consult on all its members' dilemmas in turn.

Steps for the Descriptive Consultancy

1. *Presentation.* The presenting member of the group describes the dilemma, laying out its different dimensions as he or she sees them, including previous attempts to address it if relevant. (10 minutes)

2. *Clarifying questions.* Other members of the group (acting in the role of consultants) ask questions designed to elicit information the "consultants" think they need in order to consult more effectively. (5 minutes)

3. *Reflecting back descriptively.* The presenter is silent while each of the consultants describes the content of the presentation beginning with the facilitator's prompt, "What did you hear in this presentation?" The facilitator then adds prompts to spur additional go-rounds in order to ensure the fullest possible description of the problem and its complexities. Such prompts might include, "What seems important to the presenter?" "What if anything surprised you?" and "What does this problem seem to be about?" Participants in the go-rounds are asked to pass if someone else has already offered their reflection. (10–15 minutes total)

4. *Response.* The presenter briefly responds to the consultants' expressed understandings of the problem and provides further clarification of the problem as needed. (5 minutes)

5. *Brainstorming.* The presenter is again silent while the consultants brainstorm possible solutions or next steps, saying things like this: "What if. . . ?" "Have you thought about. . . ?" This step often takes the form of open conversation among the consultants, and sometimes in the third person (as if the presenter were not in the same room), a strategy that often helps the presenter to listen more fully and the consultants to speak more freely. (10–15 minutes).

6. *Response.* The presenter responds again, this time to answer any questions that might have arisen in the brainstorming and to acknowledge any shifts in how he or she now views the problem. Here the presenter does not so much answer the group's questions as present his or her new insights gained during listening. (5 minutes)

7. *Debriefing.* The facilitator asks the presenter and participants about their roles: "How did it feel to be the presenter?" "How did it feel to be the consultant?" The facilitator ends with, "Sometimes people other than the presenter learn something important from the Descriptive Consultancy — something useful in their own context. Does anyone have something to share along those lines?" (5 minutes)

Facilitation tips for the Descriptive Consultancy. When the Descriptive Consultancy is conducted in multiple small groups, the facilitator oversees the process as a whole, having first modeled the process by allowing participants to observe an abbreviated or full version. During the process, the facilitator should monitor the groups' use of the steps, not hesitating to intervene if they are not being followed. In explaining and monitoring, the facilitator should especially emphasize the importance of Step 3 — reflecting back a description, rather than making a judgment or proposing a solution. The watch phrase should be, "No rush to advice before it's time." This is a delicate step for the facilitator, who must gently nudge the group to remain descriptive.

The facilitator should also emphasize Step 4, which involves the presenter's listening to the way the consultants frame the problem. "The reason we reflect back," the facilitator might tell the group, "and listen carefully to the reflections is to acknowledge that people inevitably have different takes on a complex problem. The power of the Descriptive Consultancy is in learning from these different takes." The facilitator may ask the presenter at the end of Step 4 if he or she wants to reframe or restate the problem at this time.

Sometimes it is useful for a team to present a problem for consultation. This helps team members — say, a leadership group at a college — to become clearer about the problem as they think through how to present it.

Online version of the Descriptive Consultancy. This online version is for use in a blended environment with the first part happening asynchronously using a discussion forum and the last part taking place face to face, although the protocol can be done completely online, if necessary. The protocol requires two online weeks and finishes with a face-to-face meeting at the end of the second week.

The purpose of the online protocol is the same as the face-to-face consultancy but allows participants more time to reflect on reframing of the problem. This version is for groups of up to about 10 participants. In the online directions, the facilitator must allow enough time for participants to ponder the dilemma the presenter describes prior to posting responses in the discussion forum. This protocol tends to run smoothly with few interventions, though monitoring for timeliness and attention to directions is always important. It might be helpful to do the face-to-face version before trying this online version.

The steps for the online version differ from those for the face-to-face version:

1. *Organization.* Before the first of the two online weeks, the facilitator recruits or invites a member of the group engaged in the Descriptive Consultancy to present a dilemma. With information from the presenter, about a week before the beginning of the two week-long Consultancy, the facilitator creates a new discussion forum with the title of the presenter's dilemma (such as "Writer's Block in Adolescent Boys"), a few words to describe it, and directions for the protocol.

2. *Problem presentation.* In the meantime, the presenter has pondered the issue and prepared a presentation of the dilemma. Within two days of the facilitator's creation of the discussion forum, the presenter posts the presentation of the dilemma as a new thread.

3. *Clarifying questions.* Consultants read through the problem presented and post a response with any clarifying questions they want to address to the presenter. Answers to clarifying questions address gaps in understanding and fill in missing details. Consultants title these "Clarifying Questions." These clarifying questions are due two days after the initial posting, and the presenter should answer them by the end of the first week.

4. *Brainstorming.* All consultants post a response to the presenter's dilemma. In their responses, they write suggestions for possible solutions or next steps. They title these "Suggestions." This posting is due in the middle of the second week.

5. *Reactions.* If done in a blended setting, where participants can come back together at the end of the second week, the presenter reads the replies to his or her dilemma before the meeting and prepares a reaction to share with everyone. The presenter is encouraged to share any new insights that he or she has gained as a result of reading the brainstorming suggestions. Alternatively, if participants cannot come back together for a face-to-face meeting, the presenter writes a reply to his or her original thread with his or her reaction to the suggestions. This post should be titled "Reaction." The posting is due at the end of the second online week.

6. *Debrief.* Finally, if participants are able to come together to debrief the process, then this step is done at that time. Otherwise, if the group cannot come together face to face, the facilitator creates a new thread called "Insights," and all participants post a reflection on the problem-solving process. They respond to the questions: "How did it feel to do the consultancy online?" "Would you use this type of protocol in the future for your own work?" This posting is due at the same time as the "Reaction" posting.

See Online Resource 17.2: *Summary of steps for the Descriptive Consultancy.*

PROTOCOL 3: A protocol for learning from experts — the Panel Protocol

Facilitators often find themselves in retreats for which a panel has been scheduled. The usual "everybody talks for 10 minutes (which typically becomes 20), then we'll have each panel member discuss the topic, and finally open the floor to questions (when there's little time left for any)" is often a horrible way to spend precious professional learning time.

Here is a protocol that requires some advanced planning but actually energizes participants and leads to far greater involvement and learning. In addition, the presenters generally love it too.

Purpose of the Panel Protocol. The main use of the Panel Protocol[3] is to make sure that a group of educators gets

---

[3] From *The Power of Protocols: An Educators' Guide to Better Practice* (2nd ed.), by Joseph P. McDonald, Nancy Mohr, Alan Dichter, and Elizabeth C. McDonald. Copyright 2007 Teachers College, Columbia University. All rights reserved. Adapted by permission of the publisher.

to interact meaningfully with some outsiders whose expertise it needs, instead of being bored by talking heads. The protocol's additional purpose is to help the experts think about and frame their expertise so that they best meet the needs of the people they are trying to help. All too often, experts are hastily briefed and arrive with too limited a perspective on how they might best contribute.

Details and guidelines for the Panel Protocol. The protocol generally takes about two hours. The size of the overall group can vary substantially, as can the size of the small work groups. The panel can similarly come in many sizes, although three to four panelists seems ideal. If the room is very large, a wireless microphone is helpful.

Preparation of the experts is essential. They need to know that this panel will be quite different from the usual, and they need to prepare for the panel by developing a written case study focused on a problem of professional practice. Panel members may use a case study written by someone else, as long as the cases are more or less complex depending on the time that will be available for wrestling with them. A one-page case for a two-hour protocol is appropriate. The cases should be written in a way that highlights the ambiguities and uncertainties of professional practice and should end with questions to prompt readers to identify next steps.

The following, for example, are good closing questions:
- "In light of the information you have, what action would you take?
- "Was there any action that should have been taken earlier but was not?
- "What additional information do you need to act?
- "How would you proceed to get that information?"

The facilitator also explains the steps in the Panel Protocol, especially in light of expectations for panel members. For example, during the expert consultation part of the protocol, panel members will respond to questions from the groups but should avoid giving elaborate responses to these questions and avoid providing overall solutions to the case problems. During the panel reactions part of the protocol, panel members will have 10-15 minutes each to focus on the strengths and weaknesses of the various action steps proposed for the case they wrote and point out what they think the groups may have overlooked. They can reinforce principles they think should guide decision making in practice.

Steps for the Panel Protocol

1. *Introduction.* The facilitator explains the steps to follow and asks the experts to introduce themselves and give a brief description of their area(s) of expertise.
2. *Case reading.* Small groups each receive a prewritten case, with each case going to at least two groups. The facilitator allows ample reading time and encourages note-taking.
3. *Case interpretation.* For a two- to three-hour protocol, group members get 20–30 minutes to work collaboratively on interpreting the case and trying to solve the problem it highlights. During this time, they also prepare a two- or three-minute presentation. This presentation should include an answer to the question, "What is this a case of?" The answer will help participants in other groups who did not read the case to understand the rest of the presentation. The presentation should also include a short list of action steps and an acknowledgement of either the group's consensus or not regarding them.
4. *Expert consultation.* During work time, groups may call over the experts to answer specific questions. When they are not engaged in answering call-overs, the experts wander the room and listen in. They do not provide solutions, nor do they make elaborate presentations.
5. *Presentations.* Following the small group work time, the facilitator announces the first case, calling on all the groups who worked on it to make their presentations in turn. Following all the presentations on the case, the facilitator invites all participants to react or ask questions. Presentations continue in this fashion until all the cases have been presented and discussed (5–15 minutes *per case*).
6. *Expert panel reactions.* After a break, the experts assemble into a panel to react to what they have heard. Each expert, in turn, gets a maximum of 10–15 minutes of reaction time. The facilitator suggests that they focus especially on the strengths and weaknesses of the various action steps proposed for the case they wrote, and that they take the opportunity as well to point out what they think the groups may have overlooked. The facilitator has privately suggested to them that this format offers them an opportunity to reinforce principles they think should guide decision making in practice. Each

expert, in turn, gets a maximum of 10–15 minutes of reaction time.

7. *Questions and comments.* Participants react to the experts' perspectives.

Facilitation tips for the Panel Protocol. The facilitator must meet with the experts beforehand. It is crucial that they understand their role and how it departs from the ordinary. They may need assurance that they will have plenty of time in Step 6 to share their expertise, and that the participants, having wrestled with the cases they wrote, will be far more receptive to learning from this expertise than they would be if they had walked cold into a conventional panel-of-experts presentation. The experts should be encouraged to use Step 4 as an opportunity to discern what the participants already seem to know, and also what they still need to know.

If the group is very large, it may not be possible for all the teams to report out. Instead, the facilitator may ask one team to report and give a few minutes at the end for other teams working on the same case to offer another viewpoint or crucial action step if one comes to mind

In handling the final questions and comments, Step 7, the facilitator may encourage the experts to take 5–10 questions before answering any of them. Not only does this allow the experts a chance to synthesize their responses, often focusing on themes and reinforcing broader issues, but it decreases the likelihood that the panel as a whole will get stuck on one point (see Online Resource 17.3: *Summary of steps for the Panel Protocol*).

PROTOCOL 4: A protocol for learning from text — the Final Word Protocol

Daniel Baron and Patricia Averette developed this versatile protocol for the National School Reform Faculty. It is useful for exploring any kind of text, including controversial ones.

Purpose of the Final Word Protocol. The purpose of the Final Word Protocol[4] is to expand the interpretation of one or more texts by encouraging the emergence of a variety of interests, viewpoints, and voices. By forcing everyone to offer an interpretation and to listen closely to and reflect back others' interpretations, Final Word ensures the emergence of diverse perspectives on texts. It also helps participants feel safer in proposing what may be offbeat or dissident interpretations because the protocol implicitly avoids consensus building. It is okay in this protocol to end a session with as much difference of interpretation in the air as there was at the start. The point is to get different interpretations into the air.

Details and guidelines for the Final Word Protocol. Final Word generally takes from 30–60 minutes (depending on group size) and is best done in groups of three to six. It works especially well when the facilitator wants a large group to engage with the same text and breaks the whole group into smaller groups. Participants must have copies of the text(s). Texts may have been read in advance, or they may be read on the spot (although then they must be short, and the facilitator must allow for varied reading times and for a bit of mulling over). A watch or phone with a countdown timer can be a very helpful tool for this and other protocols with tight time lines.

Steps for the Final Word Protocol

1. *Introduction and selection.* The facilitator introduces the whole protocol, providing copies of a short list of the steps involved. Then he or she asks all participants to select from one of the texts a short passage that has particular meaning for them, a meaning they would like to call attention to.

2. *Arrangement.* The whole group breaks into tight circles of three to six participants each. The facilitator assigns an order of presentation for participants in each circle — for example, "The person in your group whose back is most turned to the door is number one, and the person to his or her right is number two, etc. One member of each circle needs to be a strict timekeeper." Alternatively, the facilitator can serve as timekeeper for the entire room, calling out the time switches.

3. *Presentation.* Presenter number one presents the passage he or she has identified, reading aloud and

---

[4] From *The Power of Protocols: An Educators' Guide to Better Practice* (2nd ed.), by Joseph P. McDonald, Nancy Mohr, Alan Dichter, and Elizabeth C. McDonald. Copyright 2007 Teachers College, Columbia University. All rights reserved. Adapted by permission of the publisher.

having people follow along on their copies. The presenter speaks for two or three uninterrupted minutes about it (with the timing clear in advance).

4. *Reflecting back.* Each listener in turn has one uninterrupted minute to reflect back on what the presenter has said. Reflecting back means exploring the presenter's interpretation of the passage, not adding one's own interpretation. A listener might begin, "From what you said, I can see that you are concerned about . . ."

5. *Final word.* The round ends with a one-minute uninterrupted time for the presenter to react to what has just been said.

6. *Round repeats.* Rounds two, three, etc. follow until all members of each group have presented and had their final word.

7. *Written reflection.* Following the rounds, the facilitator asks everyone to write for five minutes about what they have learned from the rounds about the text(s) as a whole. This might be followed by a go-round asking each member to share one observation or insight. In a group with some history and trust, the facilitator might ask volunteers to share something they heard from someone else that they found surprising, moving, or provocative.

Facilitation tips for the Final Word Protocol. When the facilitator keeps the time, he or she risks feeling like an intrusive announcer ("May I have your attention, please. Time to switch presenters!") or the caller in a square dance ("Readyyy? SWITCH presenters!"). However, when the groups do their own timing, there is the probability that they will finish at different times. There is also the risk that they will succumb to the temptation to dispense with artificiality. But without the contrived times, Final Word becomes a small-group discussion, which is a different learning vehicle.

Groups may be bigger than three, and bigger groups raise more viewpoints and more possibility of hearing diverse interpretations. But, of course, the process takes longer, with more rounds as well as more time per round.

Facilitators should take particular care with Step 4. This is where presenters can experience really being heard — a crucial (and often unusual) experience for many. It helps in describing Step 4 to say, "It's not what *you* think about *the presenter's* passage. It's what you think you heard the presenter

say (and think and feel) about the passage."

Some facilitators find it disconcerting that they cannot hear what all the conversations touch upon. They need to get over that and recognize the beauty of the conversation they are having.

Online version of the Final Word protocol. Just as with the face-to-face version, the online version of this protocol encourages different perspectives on and interpretations of a complex text. The ability to connect with colleagues on a text asynchronously over a period of time encourages deep reflection on the part of the participants. It offers the advantage that everyone in the group can read through all the threads, enabling a full understanding of the text. Another benefit to the online version that takes advantage of this medium is that the texts don't have to be written ones — for example, participants can interpret a podcast or YouTube video.

The Final Word takes two online weeks to facilitate and is best done with group sizes between 10 and 20 participants. Participants must have online access to the texts that will be discussed in the forum and have enough time to review the text prior to making their first post. Facilitators need to monitor the forum to make sure that everyone posts on time and follows the directions. The facilitator can email or instant message participants with friendly reminders as needed.

Online steps are somewhat different from the face-to-face version of this protocol:

1. *Organization.* Prior to the first online week, the facilitator should create a new forum on the discussion board with a title related to the assigned text(s).

2. *Introduction and selection.* The facilitator posts the directions for the protocol. In these directions, the facilitator assigns half the participants to complete the first postings, explaining that the other half will contribute the first postings in the second week of the protocol.

3. *Presentation.* The posting participants select brief quotes from the text (or transcribed excerpts from the audio or video) that they think are meaningful. Participants are encouraged to post excerpts that are a maximum of three sentences, provide the page number (or number of seconds in) to give context, and explain their reasoning for selecting the particular excerpt. The forum is monitored carefully to make sure that no one posts the same excerpt. If this happens, participants are asked to

delete the excerpt and repost something else. Posting participants include the excerpt and their explanation as a new thread within the forum and title it with the first few words of the excerpt, so that other participants can quickly scan the forum and see what excerpts have already been chosen. This initial posting is due three days into the start of the online week to give everyone a chance to review the text.

4. *Reactions.* All participants (including the ones who contributed the passages) reply to at least one other participant's excerpt. The participants provide an interpretation of the excerpt and how it relates to the larger topic. The facilitator encourages participants to pick excerpts to react to that have fewer than two responses already, so that everyone who posted receives at least two reactions. The reaction posting is due two days after the initial posting.

5. *Final Word.* The participants who originally posted the quotes provide their reaction to others' interpretations and how they might apply this to their future work. The Final Word posting is due at the end of the online week.

6. *Round repeats.* The entire protocol is repeated the following week with the other half of the participants posting the selected excerpts from a related text (see Online Resource 17.4: *Summary of steps for the Final Word Protocol*).

Variations

Every protocol has its variations, and online use of protocols only adds more variations. One caution in terms of varying protocols is that the person who modifies them needs to know the protocol very well in its original form before varying it. Each of the seemingly simple protocol steps serves a purpose, and changing them may very well change the culture of the protocol and render it useless in terms of learning.

That said; here's an example of how a protocol may be changed. These notes from McDonald et al. (2007) suggest: sometimes Final Word facilitators ask speakers in Step 4 to provide their *own* reactions to the text passage, rather than reflect on the presenter's. This has the advantage of getting more interpretations into

the open, but the disadvantage of not attending fully to any one interpretation. However, there may be times when this makes sense. A protocol called Save the Last Word for Me takes this variation further and offers still other benefits. In Save the Last Word, each presenter merely reads the passage or passages selected, withholding any comment until the listeners have first had their turns to comment. Then the presenter's "last word" incorporates not only his or her original interest in the passage but also what he or she has learned about it from the other members of the circle. This variation is useful in encouraging presenters to pick particularly complex or ambiguous passages — perhaps ones that they think are important, but do not feel they fully understand. It has the added advantage of increasing the likelihood that the conversation will remain more "text-based" with no initial interpretation to respond to. (pp. 37–38)

Challenges and how to address them

Sometimes getting started is the most difficult step. Here are a few suggestions summarized from McDonald et al., 2007; 2012:

*   Try these protocols in both face to face and online environments. Offer to facilitate and make sure to get feedback. Committee meetings, virtual team meetings, and classrooms (with students) are all good places.
*   While co-facilitating can bring special challenges, having a partner can be extremely useful, especially in online environments, where one person can focus on the technology support and troubleshooting.
*   Form a CFG group to support one another. Meet regularly and make agreements, which you can stick to, about what you will do between meetings to try to use protocols online.
*   Find someone to act as your coach who will observe you in a face-to-face setting or lurk in an online environment and give you feedback.
*   Observe other facilitators, especially when they are facilitating a new protocol or with technologies that you haven't used.

ONLINE RESOURCES

17.1 Summary of steps for the Clearing Protocol or Connections Protocol

17.2 Summary of Steps for the Descriptive Consultancy

17.3 Summary of steps for the Panel Protocol

17.4 Summary of steps for the Final Word Protocol

- Take workshops to learn how to use the new technologies and to gain exposure to the relative advantages of one technology over another. Use that knowledge to make informed decisions of which one to use.
- Set expectations with the group so they realize that they may have problems at first when trying a new technology. Set a norm to keep a sense of humor about technology glitches.

Conclusion

Marty isn't afraid of eye-rolling anymore. That doesn't mean he never sees it, but he knows not to be afraid. It's information. He now believes "that most of the wisdom to be gained will come from the participants" (McDonald, et al., 2003, p. 102). He understands that maximizing participation and gaining new perspectives are crucial to everybody's learning. Marty has developed good habits and some routines that have served him well. He also has processes to use to reduce uncomfortable silences online and has learned to laugh a little when they do happen. For example, he has learned that it is critical never to skip the norms. Establishing norms is particularly important for online groups, where miscommunications can happen much more easily due to the lack of nonverbal cues. Online groups need to establish norms for simple logistics, such as when, where, and how frequently to check in with one another (McDonald et al., 2012). One of the most important norms is to promote risk-taking. As part of risk-taking, he has learned to jump in and get started and others will follow this lead. He "remembers that there are very few mistakes you can make that would be (as our computers sometimes warn) 'fatal errors.' Maybe mild embarrassment" (McDonald, et al., 2003, p. 102).

While facilitating, he has learned to listen, take notes, and summarize what he has heard so that participants know he is listening. This is especially useful in online environments where participants can feel isolated and disconnected from one another (van Tryon & Bishop, 2009). To wrap things up, he remembers to include time for reflecting/debriefing afterwards. This helps participants be aware of what they have learned and helps Marty learn more about facilitating (McDonald et al., 2003). Most importantly, he has learned to have "the courage, above all, to do business differently, to be a learner, to be a leader, to educate yourself" (McDonald et al., 2003, p. 102).

References

Allen, D. & Blythe, T. (2004). *The facilitator's book of questions: Tools for looking together at student and teacher work.* New York, NY: Teachers College Press.

Hord, S. (1992). *Facilitative leadership: The imperative for change.* Austin, TX: SEDL.

McDonald, J.P., Mohr, N., Dichter, A., & McDonald, E.C. (2003). *The power of protocols: An educator's guide to better practice.* New York, NY: Teachers College Press.

McDonald, J.P., Mohr, N., Dichter, A., & McDonald, E.C. (2007). *The power of protocols: An educator's guide to better practice* (2nd ed.). New York, NY: Teachers College Press.

McDonald, J.P., Mohr, N., Dichter, A., & McDonald, E.C. (2013). *The power of protocols: An educator's guide to better practice* (3rd ed.). New York, NY: Teachers College Press.

McDonald, J.P., Zydney, J.M., Dichter, A., & McDonald, E.C. (2012). *Going online with protocols: New tools for teaching and learning.* New York, NY: Teachers College Press.

School Reform Initiative. (2013). SRI school reform initiative: A community of learners. Available at www.schoolreforminitiative.org.

van Tryon, P.J. & Bishop, M.J. (2009, November). Theoretical foundations for enhancing social connectedness in online learning environments. *Distance Education, 30*(3), 291–315.

CHAPTER 18

Professional Learning Communities

PLCs are not just about learning; they are about doing.

By Lois Brown Easton

ookies, again! Nothing like chocolate chip cookies to help an afternoon pass swiftly. Delia was the second person to enter the small meeting space outside the English Department offices. Tomás was arranging cookies on a plate; Delia sent him a "hey" and put on the table the water pitchers she had carried from the kitchen. Soon, six other teachers arrived, greeted each other, and settled into places around the table, helping themselves to the cookies with "thank-yous" to Tomás.

Fed and watered, the group looked ready to begin this session of the Clemons High School Engagement Professional Learning Community (PLC). Karen, serving as this session's facilitator, welcomed everyone and asked people to check in with a story of student engagement that they had seen since the group had last met. The stories were mostly "laser," but Delia had a longer story to tell of a student who had nearly dropped out of 9th grade between first and second semester. "I don't know whether we have him forever," she said, "but he has decided to pursue our civil rights unit from the point of view of his culture, and he is really jazzed. He keeps bringing me stories from his extended family, and he's doing research on the Internet. He comes before class and stays after because he wants to share what he's learning." Smiles and a little applause from her colleagues.

Karen then asked them to use a quick protocol to discuss one of the chapters in the book they had been reading, *Engaging Youth in Schools: Evidence-Based Models to Guide Future Innovations* (Shernoff & Bempechat, 2014). She asked them to call out a letter from the alphabet; Carla Rae called out the letter *p*. Opening a dictionary to a page with words beginning with *p*, Karen called out the first word she saw: *profile*. Then, another page and another word: *perceive*. And, a third word: *plough*. Others chose one or more of the words and framed what they said about the chapter around their choice(s). The most interesting was Cameron's description of engaging students' imaginations by thinking of imagination as fertile ground, needing only a bit of ploughing (stirring up) and seeds of "what if" questions. Several minutes of discussion ensued, with some debate about teachers' roles as conservators versus transformers.

Then, the PLC launched into its business. The group had decided it needed more data about student engagement, this time from the students themselves. Each group member had written or researched possible survey questions. Delia talked about the *2009 High School Survey of Student Engagement (HSSSE)* (Yazzie-Mintz, 2010) which described engagement as actions students take to learn: Time devoted to a task and the importance of the task to the student, which represent student effort; rigor and relevance, which relate to the challenge of classes, the focus of the work, and how it contributes to growth; and relationships, support, and connection, which are affected by the beliefs of teachers, support from adults and peers, safety and fairness, and connection to school community (p. 11). She wondered if these might be the basis of the questions. Delia, Tomás, and Rondi agreed to take everyone's questions and put them into the HSSSE framework for everyone to examine at the next meeting.

Karen ended the PLC meeting, 90 minutes after its start, by asking each member of the group to state a research question to be explored before the next meeting. She offered her own question as an example: "I want to know if beginning each class with a provocative or outrageous question on the board and an invitation to students to write about it will engage them. The question has to be about the subject area we're going to delve into, and I think I'll count how many people are writing two minutes and five minutes into the period."

The Engagement PLC was not the only one meeting during this half-day early-release time every other week. In fact, all faculty and administrators at Clemons were meeting in some kind of a PLC. That's the way the mandate had come down from the district office: "Thou shalt belong to a PLC." According to Rondi, the good part was that everyone was given a choice. Some people linked around topics, such as engagement, and some connected around a grade level or a subject, but everyone participated. Once formed, the PLCs themselves decided everything except when to meet, which was established by the whole faculty when they proposed next year's schedule the previous spring. PLCs met for 90 minutes on the early-release days every other week.

Most importantly, PLCs decided precisely what they would study, often finding a need to dig deeper into data they had or get information they didn't have. Once they knew enough, they decided what to do to address issues revealed in the data. And then they collected more data, which launched them into the next cycle of study and action.

All PLCs were accountable twice a year to the whole faculty and staff, making presentations of learning and sharing portfolios of work. Individual PLC members also made shorter announcements at faculty meetings, blogged, set up a Wiki, or contributed to a graffiti board outside the teachers' lounge.

A schoolwide design team with a representative from each PLC kept things coordinated, meeting once a month to report what PLC members were learning and doing and to address conflicts such as when the Parent Relations PLC wanted to schedule a Data Dessert on the night of a board meeting. The most important thing the design team did was to connect each PLC's work to the work of other PLCs and to connect all the PLC work to school and district goals. Thus, the PLC structure at Clemons was both tight and loose. The tight part was that everyone participated and focused on universal goals. However, within that mandate, everyone could choose what to do as well as how and with whom.

Delia, for one, liked this structure — and the chocolate chip cookies.

Overview

Definition and description

The definition of professional learning community can be pared down to three parts. A PLC is

- A group of educators who meet regularly to engage in professional learning . . .
- For the purpose of enhancing their own practice as educators . . .
- In order to help all students succeed as learners.

In terms of absolutes, educators in PLCs need to:

- Focus on professional learning activities;
- Focus on what educators can do, what's happening in classrooms and schools and how educators can get better in terms of what they do; and
- Focus on helping all students succeed.

Other than these absolutes, PLCs can differ considerably, for example in terms of:

- Group size;
- Members of the group;
- How often they meet and for how long; and
- What they call themselves.

In terms of the last of these variables, what groups call themselves, WestEd lists some 30 names for PLCs (see Online Resource 18.1: *Names for PLCs*). Other names include simply *professional community* or *learning community;* also, *school-based learning community, school learning community, site-based learning community,* even *school accountability community.* One school insisted on calling its PLC *Eaglewise* after the school mascot. It doesn't matter what a group calls itself as long it is focused on the learning of all of its members and on applying that learning to improved student learning.

Another way to understand PLCs is to see them as a *structure* or *format* for professional learning. As such, PLCs can house a variety of professional learning designs, such as those in this book. Educators in PLCs can engage in everything from action research to watching webinars together. PLCs are internal networks for learning.

Some history

PLCs are not new to education, although the term is relatively new. They are similar to quality circles developed in the 1970s on the basis of the work of W. Edwards Deming in both the United States and Japan. Quality circles were mixed job-role teams focused on improving the quality of the workplace — the environment and the system — in order to achieve quality outcomes. One of the theories behind quality circles is known as Theory Z, based on Deming's 14 Points, a set of ideas about management and motivation (Deming, 1986, 2000).

A structure invented by the Coalition of Essential Schools in the 1980s, Critical Friends Groups (CFGs) are still popular in some schools today. As described by the Coalition, CFGs (see "Chapter 7: Critical Friends Groups" in this book) are peer groups that engage in text-based discussions, look at student work together, and lead school reform according to the Ten Common Principles (originally nine) from the Coalition under the leadership of Theodore (Ted) Sizer.

A decade later, Peter Senge's *Fifth Discipline: The Art and Practice of the Learning Organization* (1990) introduced the world to the concept that a business or nonprofit could be a learning organization if it used systems thinking along with four other strategies for learning: personal mastery, mental models, team learning, and shared vision. Senge's ideas were applied to the contexts of educational organizations in *Schools That Learn (Updated and Revised): A Fifth Discipline Fieldbook for Educators, Parents, and Everyone Who Cares About Education* (2012). The discipline of team learning pointed the way to PLCs.

Jean Lave and Etienne Wenger (1991) described communities of practice that naturally united people around common interests and a need to know.

In the mid-nineties, professional learning communities gained that name and a set of characteristics. For example, Sharon Kruse, Karen Seashore Louis, and Anthony Bryk (1994) described PLCs that engaged educators in reflective practices, deprivatization of practice, a collective focus on student learning, collaboration, and shared norms. Shirley Hord (1997) described similar communities of learners that featured supportive and shared leadership, shared values, collective learning and application, shared personal practice, and supportive conditions. Richard DuFour and Robert Eaker (1998) described PLCs that had a common mission, vision, values and goals; worked to ensure achievement for all students, including systems for prevention and intervention; focused collaborative teaming on teaching and learning; used data to guide decision making and continuous improvement; and built sustainable leadership capacity.

Theories behind PLCs

Organizational and management theories from business plus a socio-constructivist theory provide the construct for PLCs. Margaret Wheatley addresses the organization of PLCs: "We see a need. We join with others. We find the necessary information or resources. We respond creatively, quickly. We create a solution that works" (Wheatley & Kellner-Rogers, 1996, p. 37). The most effective PLCs are self-organizing and energized by management theories related to Peter Senge's seminal work on learning organizations, especially his ideas about mental models, building a shared vision, and team learning.

PLCs are more about learning than teaching, the learning of both the adults within the PLCs and the young people with whom they work. As such, PLCs operate according to the theory of social constructivism, which maintains that people "make meaning" or learn with others; learning is contextual and situational. PLCs are sensitive to adult learning needs, as summarized in Part I, "Design: Form and Structure for Learning."

Seeing an organization as a *learning* organization is key to understanding PLCs. In fact, as Linda Darling-Hammond and colleagues from the School Redesign Network at Stanford asserted in the title of a report written in 2009 for the National Staff Development Council (now Learning Forward), *Professional Learning in the Learning Profession,* it seems absurd to think of schools as nonlearning organizations.

Research

Early research, such as studies reported by Shirley Hord (1997); Sharon Kruse, Karen Seashore Louis, and Anthony Bryk (1994); and Fred Newmann and Gary Wehlage (1995) showed positive effects for both teachers and students. Since then, both experimental and qualitative research have shown effects on student learning, achievement, and behavior; also on teachers, generally, and on teacher beliefs, behavior, content-related knowledge, otherwise known as pedagogical content knowledge, and general pedagogy. PLCs have also helped to change classroom and school climates and cultures as well as management, including conversations, processes, reform orientation and decision making. PLCs have helped ideas spread within and beyond districts. See Online Resource 18.2: *Summary of research on professional learning communities* for specific details related to research.

Rationale

Side-by-side caves. That's one description of schools that privilege autonomy. Teachers paper windows and keep doors closed. Yet, some of the best-performing countries on international assessments, such as Japan and Finland, and cities such as Shanghai, make collaboration a natural part of the school day.

Tony Wagner, co-director of the Harvard Change Leadership Group, proposed seven survival skills, including collaboration, that all students need to be prepared for the 21st century. These are:

- critical thinking and problem solving;
- collaboration and leadership;
- agility and adaptability;
- initiative and entrepreneurialism;
- effective oral and written communication;
- accessing and analyzing information; and
- curiosity and imagination (Wagner, 2008).

Their teachers need these skills, too, and PLCs help them gain and use them.

Another argument for PLCs can be found in the literature about self-efficacy. Simply understood, self-efficacy is closely linked to job satisfaction. In 2012, the MetLife Foundation discovered that, at a time when more than ever the need for an effective teacher in every classroom is critical, "teacher job satisfaction [in the United States] has dropped 15 points since 2009, from 59% who were very satisfied to 44% who are very satisfied, the lowest level in over 20 years" (MetLife, 2012, p. 7).

In a deeper sense, self-efficacy is about professionalism. Teachers who are treated professionally — who have high self-efficacy — are likely to succeed in teaching and work well with students. They respond creatively and effectively to problems and persist despite them. They are less likely to "burn out" than teachers without feelings of efficacy.

Professionalism is also important for attracting people into teaching. In some countries, including the United States, teaching is not highly respected as a career; not enough people are attracted into teaching at precisely the time that teacher shortages are occurring, which may mean lower standards for who is accepted into teacher preparation programs. Elevating the professionalism of teaching through structures such as professional learning communities helps to attract young people into teaching and, eventually, raises the bar for who enters the field.

Innovation is another reason PLCs are important. Reference 21st century skills and you'll likely see innovation, or a synonym, as one of the necessary skills for this century. It is challenging for teachers who are not encouraged to be innovative themselves to prize innovation in the classroom. PLCs help teachers innovate; they also help teachers value innovation from outside the school. PLCs themselves can be seen as an innovative structure that encourages innovative practices.

Steps

Step 1: Start a PLC

This step may seem obvious: Just start! But, consider both the many ways to start a PLC and the various configurations PLCs can take.

Ways to start a PLC. Some ways to start a PLC are especially effective; some are less so. Probably the most effective way is "bottom-up" when teachers become aware of a need or an issue and decide to address it. They may meet informally and take steps within their own contexts to improve the situation. Of course, they'll want to keep the appropriate administrators notified of their work. If members of the PLC want to enlarge the domain of their work — from their classrooms to the whole school, for example — they will need to secure administrative support.

Another effective way to start a PLC is both "bottom-up" and "top-down." Here are its steps:

- The principal hears about PLCs from faculty or from outside school.
- The school's faculty has also heard about PLCs.
- The principal and interested faculty meet to discuss PLCs.
- They form a design team to study PLCs.
- The design team presents a report to the entire faculty.
- The design team has the faculty complete a "Why" survey and shares results with them. See Online Resource 18.3: *Survey: Why educators might want to engage in PLCs.*
- Faculty who are interested join a PLC; other faculty do not (that's OK).
- The principal is part of one or more school PLCs; the principal may belong to a PLC of principals, as well.
- PLCs begin to meet and spread the word about what they're doing.
- Other faculty members hear about the work being done in PLCs and join (not all may join, however).

At Clemons High School, PLCs began through this process:

- The principal had a district mandate to form PLCs with some options in terms of how to do so.

- The principal presented the concept to faculty, and faculty members studied it and visited and talked with people from schools with PLCs.
- The faculty identified issues or topics they wished to address — such as eighth-grade mathematics, engagement, and reading circles — and faculty members chose according to topic which PLC which to join.
- Everyone was part of at least one PLC.
- The PLCs established their own ways of working together and were accountable to each other within and outside the PLCs.

In contrast, here is one less-than-effective way to start PLCs:

- The principal is mandated by the superintendent/other district staff to form PLCs.
- The principal mandates that all teachers will be in a PLC and determines how PLCs will be organized and who will be in them.
- The principal mandates what the PLCs will learn and do (e.g. differentiated instruction).
- Faculty and staff members participate in PLCs as a "duty."

Possible configurations of a PLC. It is possible to have everyone in the whole school be in a single PLC, especially if the school has 10 to 15 faculty members. Otherwise, whole-school PLCs usually break into special action teams or interest groups in order to work on parts of a process such as how to involve students in formative assessment. Another popular configuration involves the whole school in PLCs organized according to grade level or subject.

Members of whole faculty, department, or grade-level PLCs should take care not to mix business with professional learning. One way to do this is to have separate meeting times (and places, if possible) for the two purposes of meeting.

The ideal PLC (or working group formed from a whole school PLC) is between 3 and 12 people. Having two people in a PLC will work, but having at least three allows for a bit more diversity; having more than 12 makes it hard for everyone to have sufficient air time and may make it harder to organize logistically. Department or grade-level PLCs are effective, and vertical vertical learning teams in the same subject area or interdisciplinary teams in middle and high schools also work. Also, faculty can form a PLC based on common interests, such as using formative assessments. Principals can be active members of PLCs, as long as they do not "pull rank" during PLC time and concentrate on learning along with others.

You can find information about possible PLC configurations in Online Resource 18.4: *Possible configurations of PLCs.* Online Resource 18.5: *A Planning menu* might be helpful in terms of considering the logistics (Who, What, Where, Why, and How) of PLCs.

Step 2: Attend to relationships

This is not a one-time-only step. PLC members need to attend to relationships early in the formation of PLCs and continue to do so throughout the work of the PLC. Relationships can make or break a PLC. Not everyone will like everyone else — the goal is not conviviality — but everyone needs to be able to respect, trust, and work with each other toward common purposes. Attention to relationships is not especially effective if it is separate from work related to the purposes of the PLC. In other words, conducting a trust walk (where pairs, with one of the pair blindfolded, take turns leading each other) or similar team-building activities is not enough and, in fact, may be seen as superficial or silly.

Use real work as a way to get something meaningful done and simultaneously focus on relationships. For example, early in the life of a PLC, engage people in a discussion of their preferences for learning and doing. Then, have them apply what they have learned about themselves and others to a real agenda item. One good way to accomplish this task is Four Corners (also known as Four Compass Points). See Online Resource 18.6: *Directions for Four Corners.*

Continue to focus on relationships by ensuring that everyone has a voice in every PLC gathering, at a minimum, through check-in at the beginning and closure at the end. Use the skills of dialogue (see "Chapter 10: Dialogue" in this book) to engage everyone in dialogue before discussion. Use protocols (see "Chapter 17: Online Protocols" in this book; also Easton, 2009) to guide the course of dialogue and discussion so that everyone has a time to talk and a time to listen.

Make sure the working agreements honor participants; one way to do this is by incorporating into these agreements the seven norms devised by Robert Garmston and Bruce Wellman (1999). You will find these on Online Resource 18.7: *Seven norms for collaboration.* Discuss what these norms really mean: What would you see and hear if they were honored? What would you not see and hear? Be sure that you have a mechanism for talking about norms that need attention; one of the best ways is to allow for anyone to call "norm check" when people do not seem to be following the norms. Reference the norms at the beginning of a PLC meeting, evaluate members' adherence to the norms at the end, and prepare to revise norms when they do not appear to be working

Step 3: Determine purpose and passion

One of the first actions PLCs need to engage in is finding purpose and passion. The survey (Online Resource 18.3) is a good way to find purpose and passion. A PLC is only as strong as its purpose and passion. A weak purpose or one ordained by outsiders can erode a PLC.

Although many school reformers advocate for the careful construction of a mission or vision statement, PLC members benefit more from identifying PLC purposes and articulating beliefs. Purposes and beliefs tend to be more to-the-point, descriptive, and detailed. "We can't let our students drop out of school" is a robust and passionate purpose, but hardly the stuff of a mission or vision statement. Purpose answers a series of important questions:

1. "Are we doing the best we can in terms of educating young people?"
2. If not, "What do we need to change or improve?"
3. Next, "Why do we believe these changes will result in an affirmative answer to the question, 'Are we doing the best we can in terms of educating young people?'"
4. Ultimately, "How can we make needed changes or improvements?" (Easton, 2011, p. 34).

Passion comes from "pain in the system." Use the chart on page 269 to focus on what gives your PLC passion and purpose.

Finding purpose and passion may require deep probing into data that have been collected. PLC members may also need to collect additional data and similarly engage with these data in thoughtful analysis (see "Chapter 9: Data Analysis" in this book). Be sure to look for demographic changes and consider alternative ways of looking at achievement, such as examining

Focus on passion and purpose		
What's not working as well as it could?	**Evidence**	**Purposes**
Example: Students aren't engaged.	They don't pay attention in class. They don't do classwork. They don't do homework. They don't appear to like what they are doing.	Discover how to help students become engaged in their own learning.

actual student work or student portfolios. Consider surveys of students, faculty and staff, faculty and staff from other schools, parents, community members, etc. Consider focus groups and interviews and, above all, examine the processes — what the school is currently doing — to understand what might have led to current data.

Purpose and passion will be specific to each PLC, but both should align to school and district goals. For example, a PLC's passion about vocational education may not work in an elementary school district that does not fund vocational programs. That passion may, however, be reconsidered as hands-on, service learning and, understood this way, may align with school and district goals.

The best way to center on purpose and passion is through dialogue (see "Chapter 10: Dialogue" in this book). Adhere to the customs of dialogue to find agreement about purpose and passion; then go on to discussion about how to address both.

Step 4: Formulate a plan of action based on purpose and passion

Again, engage in dialogue to discover all possible actions before discussing them and deciding what to do. Do not devise a five-year or even a two-year strategic plan. Keeping in mind purpose and passion, devise a First Steps Plan (see Online Resource 18.8: *First-steps plan*). Be ready to change the plan as one task is accomplished and new data are collected and analyzed.

Step 5: Engage in effective learning during PLC sessions

Although your PLC should focus on your plan of action and the purpose and passion that are driving it, your meetings should be productive in many ways. Here are some agendas that help PLCs accomplish important tasks and thrive as learning organizations:

A first meeting agenda
- Establish *norms* or rules of engagement (including a norm about what to do when norms are broken). See Online Resource 18.9: *Some starter norms or working agreements,* including norms for collaboration from Garmston and Wellman (1999).
- Determine *purpose* and *passion* — what matters and why — of the PLC .
- Relate these to school and district goals.
- Set *dates, times,* and *places* for meetings well in advance (at least a semester).
- Establish *procedures* (facilitator rotations, for example).
- Determine ways to be *accountable* (e.g. sharing results of learning with the entire faculty; keeping a PLC journal or portfolio; publishing what happens).

A basic agenda for all meetings
- Provide a way to check in (ranging from a simple "How are you today?" to having individuals select objects on a table and check in by comparing themselves to that object).
- Remind each other of norms and agree to follow them at the beginning of the meeting.
- Learn.
- Do (Task Focus).
- Remind participants of the date, time, and place of the next meeting.
- Decide on who will facilitate the next meeting.
- Determine specifics related to the learning activities for the next meeting.
- Check on how well the group met the norms during the current meeting.

Sample agenda #1

- Check-in/Opening activity

- Review of norms

- **Learning Focus: Socratic seminar (dialogue) related to an article**

- **Task focus**

- Details about next meeting (when and where)

- Decision about activity for next meeting

- Decision about who will facilitate next meeting

- Decision about sharing what was learned at this PLC meeting with others

- Group evaluation of how norms were kept

- Closure activity

Sample agenda #2

- Check-in/Opening activity

- Review of norms

- **Learning activity: The Tuning Protocol on student work sample**

- **Learning activity: Dialogue on a relevant article**

- **Task focus**

- Details about next meeting (when and where)

- Decision about activity for next meeting

- Decision about who will facilitate next meeting

- Decision about sharing what was learned at this PLC meeting with others

- Group evaluation of how norms were kept

- Closure

A developmental approach to agendas

- The first few PLC meetings might focus on more objective activities, such as book or article study.

- More subjective activities, such as looking at student work can be woven into PLCs as the group matures.

The Check-in/Opening Activity is important to bring everyone's voice into the room, get the group focused on the work, and uncover any problems that may be occurring within the group. Other ideas for check-in include "1–10" ("What number are you right now in terms of learning? And why?") or responding to selected postcards or items on the table in terms of what they mean for the individual and the work being done.

Reviewing the working agreements or norms at the beginning and end of the meeting is important, with minds open to changing them. The end of the meeting is a good time for personal review of norms ("How did I do?") and group review ("How did we do?"). These can be done aloud or on paper. In a mature group, individuals will be able to say, "I don't think we did very well in terms of paying attention to our needs and others' needs. For example, I was distracted by the ringing of cellphones even though we have agreed to turn off our cellphones, but I didn't say anything about it." Permission needs to be given within the norms for anyone to say what needs to be said about how the group functioned; this permission should, in fact, be a norm.

Doing some *learning work* as part of a PLC session is essential. If possible, it needs to be related to the passion, purpose, and tasks deemed important by the PLC. For example, PLC participants engaging in the Tuning Protocol on a sample of student work might want to examine it for their passion — higher-order thinking — and purpose — having students think deeper about subjects through writing — and one of their tasks — a poster in each room that addresses how to engage in higher-order thinking through writing. Another activity, such as dialogue about an article, might be based on an article related to higher-order thinking.

A list and description of a variety of PLC learning activities, many of which are described in this book, can be found as Online Resource 18.10: *PLC learning activities.*

Doing some *task work* is also necessary. PLCs are not just about learning; they are about doing. As a result of identifying passion, purpose, and tasks, PLC members have an improvement focus as well as a learning focus. During one part of each PLC meeting they also need to examine a "doing" focus: "What have we done so far? What results have we had? What do we need to do next? How will we know we're making a difference? How will we know we're making progress?" In addition, members need to spend time at each PLC meeting to plan the next step with enough detail to make it happen. Or a subgroup needs to plan the next step separately, get feedback about the plan from the entire group, execute it, and bring back information to the whole group.

The next meeting needs to be discussed, at least briefly. Who will facilitate? Some PLCs have rotating facilitators or paired facilitators, one who takes the lead one meeting and then passes along the lead to the other at a subsequent meeting. Other roles may need to be determined; see Douglas Reeves' list of leadership assets and a list of leadership roles on Online Resource 18.11: *Leadership assets and roles.*

An effective PLC also needs to provide a chance for members to focus on their own learning: "What was your most important learning, your 'ah-ha' today?" This might be done as a closure activity. And, an effective PLC needs to think about accountability to others. Thus, the question, "How can we share what we have learned?" is important, and it can be answered in a variety of ways. One good way of being accountable on an ongoing basis can be accomplished through technology. One member of the PLC can blog about what happened, what was learned, and progress being made by the PLC, perhaps on an all-school PLC blog. Establishing a Wiki is another way a school can collect the learning and activities of multiple PLCs as they work. For a low-tech solution, consider a graffiti wall near the teacher workrooms.

Step 6: Understand the change and school improvement processes

At some point early in the process (within six months of start-up), PLCs need to examine the change process (see Part I, "Design: Form and Structure for Learning") from a number of different points of view. They need to make this a big part of a regular meeting and then refer later to what they learned during this meeting as they engage in change themselves and ask their colleagues to make change.

They also need to understand the school improvement process as it applies to PLCs. Basically, the logic model for change embraced by PLCs looks like Figure 1: The Logic Model on page 272.

The vertical center of the model is what concerns PLCs: What educators learn, what they do with their learning, how they change their own behaviors, and as a result, how their students' behaviors change to lead to improved student achievement (and well-being). PLC members need to be aware of the multiple contexts, such as state and regional organizations, that surround this process, however. They can influence these contexts by what they do, but PLCs are also going to be influenced by these contexts, no matter what they do.

It's important for members of PLCs to have a dialogue about this model (or other models of the school improvement cycle) and to refer to it as members work on both learning and doing. It's also important for PLC members to dig deeply into other models summarized in Part I, "Design: Form and Structure for Learning."

Step 7: Be accountable

The best way of looking at accountability is through the concept of mutual accountability and commitment. PLC members commit to each other to learn and to do something to make a difference in their environments; they are accountable to each other in this way. PLCs also need to be accountable to individuals in other PLCs and to the PLCs as change groups. They need to be accountable to the school and district (which may have supported PLCs by providing time and resources) and ultimately to students and their families and the community.

Accountability is much more than simply posting the minutes of a PLC meeting. It goes way beyond saying, "We met."

One key to accountability is relationships. People who have connections with each other are more likely to feel accountable to them. Also, when adults have a voice in what they are doing — such as working in a PLC — and a choice about what to do, they are more likely to feel accountable. Being treated as professionals is also important in terms of accountability. Judy Wurtzel (2007), a senior fellow at the Aspen Institute working with its Education and Society Program in Washington, D.C., describes the "old" professionalism as *autonomy*: "freedom to make decisions about what, how, and sometimes even whom to teach," which, unfortunately, does not lead to instructional improvement (pp. 30–31).

Figure 1: **The Logic Model: School Improvement Cycle**

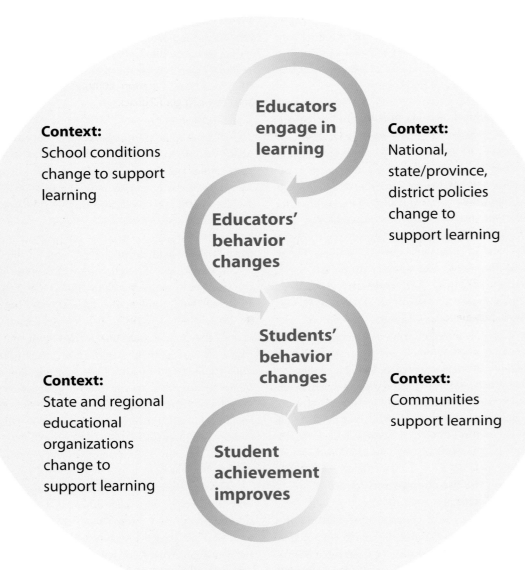

From *Professional learning communities by design: Putting the learning back into PLCs* by L.B. Easton, p. 161. Copyright 2011 Corwin Press, and Oxford, OH: Learning Forward. Used with permission.

Some who entered the profession "back in the old days," did so because they expected to shut the door and teach what and how they wanted. However, according to Wurtzel, what's needed in today's schools is "robust teacher professionalism [that] . . . places accountability for results and the use and refinement of effective practices at the core of teaching" (p. 31).

Here are Wurtzel's (2007) six tenets of the new professionalism:

1. A professional owes her primary duty to her clients — in the case of educators, to students.
2. Professionals are accountable to the profession for results.
3. A professional has a duty to improve her own practice.
4. A professional has a duty to improve common or collective practice in the profession.
5. Professionals adhere to a body of specialized knowledge, agreed-upon standards of practice, and specific protocols for performance
6. Professionals are expected to exercise professional judgment. (pp.32–33)

PLCs can choose how they want to be accountable — in the spirit of voice and choice — but there should be no doubt in anyone's mind that each PLC will be accountable. Some PLCs may choose to keep portfolios related to what members learn and do. They may have someone in the group serve as the archivist for the portfolio. The most important aspect of a portfolio is not really the artifacts of the work; it's the reflections on learning regarding those artifacts. This means that the archivist should command 5–10 minutes every few meetings so that PLC members can reflect on the artifacts being collected into the portfolio.

Presentations — or exhibitions — of learning are important for students . . . and adults. At least twice a year, as part of the portfolio process or not, PLCs should make presentations to each other about what they have learned and what they are doing as a result of the learning. PLCs that have portfolios can spread their contents out and do a "poster session" including reflections on the contents for other PLCs. Or, they can summarize and reflect on their learning in short PowerPoint presentations.

These summative forms of accountability need to be bolstered by formative types, as well. When several PLCs operate within a school, PLCs should serve as "critical friends" to other PLCs. Especially when they get to the point of planning an action, PLCs need feedback from others. Using some kind of protocol, perhaps the Triad Protocol (Easton, 2009), PLCs might give and get feedback.

When the whole school is a PLC, members can divide into two groups and use a protocol such as the Inside/Outside Protocol (Easton, 2009) to present planned actions and give and get feedback.

An ongoing blog and threaded conversations can help PLC members keep others current with what they are doing and what they are learning — and provide a regular means of feedback.

Use of simple online surveys can keep PLCs from becoming too insular. For example, a PLC that is working on a schedule change to allow more time for students to do group work will want to access the ideas of others on a regular basis. A simple item could ask teachers to rate the ideal time period for group work: 30 minutes, 45 minutes, 60 minutes, 90 minutes, etc. An open-ended question that would help a PLC considering this type of work might be "What are the downsides to a class period that goes longer than 60 minutes? What are the upsides?" A PLC that does not engage the whole faculty and staff in terms of important changes, such as schedules, is foolish.

Of course, no PLC will have the power to implement anything that affects more than its members without going through an already established decision-making process.

Variations

Designers create PLCs so they are variable. PLCs thrive if those within them are given the autonomy to determine, not only the logistics of meetings, but why they are meeting (the passion), what they want to focus on (the purpose), what they'll do (the tasks) and how they will work (the learning and improvement). So, there are infinite variations to the steps described above. What should remain true, however, are the parts of the definition. PLCs should be about adult learning. Groups of adults should meet regularly. They should apply what they are learning to what they do (individually or collectively) as educators. What they do should be focused on helping students learn.

Challenges and how to address them

Buy-in. One of the often-mentioned problems in terms of any kind of change in education is "buy-in" (a five-letter word that may as well be a four-letter expletive). Buy-in is an issue when someone wants someone else to do something and *like* it. In other words, buy-in is an issue when people do not have a voice or choice in terms of what they're doing. If people have voice and choice, buy-in is usually not much of an issue, so it is important in terms of PLCs not to force people to participate or, if they are required to participate in PLCs, give them lots of choices. Participants should have a voice in terms of how PLCs are formed, what they do, and how they work.

Ideally those who do not want to participate will not be forced to do so. It may be that, over time and, as they witness the excitement of learning in PLCs, they'll elect to join a PLC, but they should not be forced.

If forced to be in a PLC, resistors cannot be persuaded to buy in. People who have no choice about something will not be persuaded by attempts to get them to buy in. Resistors might be invited to form their own PLCs and to find a purpose that benefits the school, or they can reside as observers in other PLCs. They might also be involved in other aspects of school improvement, such as doing research for PLCs.

PLCs without the learning. In the United States, PLCs are at risk of becoming another fad. Some PLCs "have proven disappointing, and the concept as a whole is in danger of fading like many initially exciting structures for change, such as small schools and block scheduling" (Easton, 2011, p. 49).

> In some cases, professional learning communities are just a new name for doing the same things as before. As one teacher commented, "Professional learning communities are just meetings dressed up in their Sunday best." "It's business as usual," another teacher reported. "We discuss things, but we do nothing. Nothing changes." "It's a gripe session," a disillusioned principal reported. "All they do is argue and bellyache, moan and groan." (Easton, 2011, p. 50)

As long as the middle word in PLC is the central, main word for this professional learning design, it can be stopped from disintegrating into "business as usual." Learning is powerful enough for educators as well as their students to keep them engaged in worthwhile work, likely to make a substantive difference in the world.

Conclusion

Internationally, educators turn to the United States to learn about PLCs. While many Asian countries have a history of teamwork and collaboration, many European and other countries do not. PLCs are still a viable and exciting structure for adult learning in the United States. They still have great promise in terms of promoting better student and adult learning and well-being.

References

Deming, W.E. (1986). *Out of the crisis.* Cambridge, MA: MIT Press.

Deming, W.E. (2000). *The new economics for industry, government, education* (2nd ed.). Cambridge, MA: MIT Press.

DuFour, R. & Eaker, R. (1998). *Professional learning communities at work: Best practices for enhancing student achievement.* Bloomington, IN: Solution Tree.

Easton, L.B. (2009). *Protocols for professional learning.* Alexandria, VA: ASCD.

Easton, L.B. (2011). *Professional learning communities by design: Putting the learning back into PLCs.* Thousand Oaks, CA: Corwin Press.

Garmston, R.J. & Wellman, B.M. (1999). *The adaptive school: A sourcebook for developing collaborative groups.* Norwood, MA: Christopher-Gordon.

Hord, S. (1997). *Professional learning communities: Communities of continuous inquiry and improvement.* Austin, TX: SEDL. Available at www.sedl.org/pubs/change34/.

Kruse, S., Seashore Louis, K., & Bryk, A. (1994, Spring). Building professional community in schools. Available at www.wcer.wisc.edu/archive/cors/issues%5Fin%5FRestructuring%5FSchools/issues_NO_6_SPRING_1994.pdf.

Lave, J. & Wenger, E. (1991). *Situated learning: Legitimate peripheral participation.* Cambridge, England: Cambridge University Press.

ONLINE RESOURCES

Wagner, T. (2008). *The global achievement gap: Why even our best schools don't teach the new survival skills our children need — and what we can do about it.* New York, NY: Basic Books.

Webster-Wright, A. (2009). Reframing professional development through understanding authentic professional learning. *Review of Educational Research, 79*(2), 702–739.

Wheatley, M. & Kellner-Rogers, M. (1996). *A simpler way.* San Francisco, CA: Berrett-Koehler Publishers.

Wurtzel, J. (2007, Fall). The professional, personified. *JSD, 28*(4), 32–35.

Yazzie-Mintz, E. (2010). *Charting the path from engagement to achievement: A report on the 2009 High School Survey of Student Engagement.* Bloomington, IN: Center for Evaluation & Education Policy.

MetLife Foundation. (2012). *The MetLife survey of the American teacher: Challenges for school leadership.* New York, NY: Author. Available at https://www.metlife.com/assets/cao/foundation/MetLife-Teacher-Survey-2012.pdf.

MetLife Foundation. (2009). *The MetLife survey of the American teacher: Collaborating for student success.* New York, NY: Author. Available at http://files.eric.ed.gov/fulltext/ED509650.pdf.

Newmann, F. & Wehlage, G, (1995). *Successful school restructuring: A report to the public and educators.* Madison, WI: Center on Organization and Restructuring of Schools.

Senge, P.M. (1990). *The fifth discipline: The art and practice of the learning organization.* New York, NY: Doubleday Currency.

Senge, P., Cambron-McCabe, N., Lucas, T., Smith, B., & Dutton, J. (2012). *Schools that learn: A fifth discipline fieldbook for educators, parents, and everyone who cares about education.* New York, NY: Crown Business.

Shernoff, D.J. & Bempechat, J. (2014). *Engaging youth in schools: Empirically-based models to guide future innovations. A National Society for the Study of Education yearbook.* New York, NY: Teachers College Press.

CHAPTER 19

Shadowing

Shadowing is the process of following a student or educator through part of a day, a whole day, or longer, learning how that person experiences school.

By Michael Soguero, Dan Condon, Colin Packard, and Lois Brown Easton

The Urban High School (UHS) group arrived a few minutes before morning gathering at Eagle Rock School. Meeting the group at the door, Rachel, the director of professional development, led them to the hearth area where the whole-school gathering is held and helped them find seats among students on the floor or steps. Although the five teachers, one administrator, and a counselor had arrived the previous night and experienced an orientation, they had not yet met students. Today, they would be with students all day. Rachel was gratified to see students make room for the newcomers, introduce themselves, and welcome them.

When Rachel introduced the group during the announcements portion of gathering, students applauded for them and raised their hands to signal that they wanted to have someone from the UHS staff shadow them. After the gathering, the educators walked away, paired with students,

and conversations were in full swing even before the pairs had gotten outside onto the Esplanade.

After second period and before lunch, students brought their shadows to the Professional Development Center. Rachel listened as the shadowing pairs said farewell (for the moment, at least). The UHS staff members seemed both appreciative and excited.

When visitors come to Eagle Rock, the professional development staff turns them over to students as soon as possible because Eagle Rock's belief is that student voices need to be heard in school restructuring conversations. Student voices are powerful. Staff members have found that they can say exactly what students say, but visitors really hear student voices. An adult talking about the need to personalize schools is just one more voice in the clamor for school reform. But when a teen describes feeling like nobody in a 3,000-student high school ("Nobody would notice if

I didn't show up one day"), adults listen. They listen both cognitively and emotionally; sometimes, they remember how they felt as well — or better, what they learned — when they engage in the hard work of improving their own schools.

Now, the seven educators who just shadowed students were gathered on the couch and in easy chairs in front of the hearth in the Eagle Rock Professional Development Center. "Would you like some time to write and reflect on your shadowing experience?" Rachel asked. They nodded and began to write. After a few minutes, she asked if they wanted to share their experiences: "You've each gotten a couple of snapshots of what we do here. It's nothing like the full-length feature film, but through sharing you might be able to create an album of your morning." They began talking — about the Holocaust class during which students profiled each other, about the hydroponics class during which students assessed the health of their tomato plants and researched how to help them grow, about the memoirs class during which students read aloud selections from their writing and received feedback, about the mathematics class in which students made plans to build an accessible fishing pier at Lake Estes.

To broaden their examination of the morning, Rachel asked, "So, what were you struck by? What caught your attention? What did you notice?" The UHS staff members volunteered these reactions:

"I was struck by how independent the students were."

"They were fully engaged. Nobody had to discipline them or try to get them working."

"They were so polite and courteous. And they wanted to know about me and my school."

"They love Eagle Rock and they love talking about it."

"They really support each other's learning; they're not competitive at all."

"They seemed to want to learn. Learning was cool to them."

One of the most telling comments was this one: "These students are like our very best students." Rachel had to remind them that Eagle Rock students are the students in the proverbial "back of the classroom," who dropped out or were expelled, and got into trouble.

That comment broadened the inquiry: "I wonder why they do so well at Eagle Rock?" They suggested a number

of reasons, including an engaging curriculum, and Rachel suggested a few others, and then it was time for lunch.

The UHS staff would shadow different students in the afternoon and reconvene for another debrief in the Professional Development Center. At the afternoon debriefing, Rachel hoped to take them to another level of processing their shadowing experience. She wanted them to look at what they *were already doing* at Urban High School to keep students in school, engage them in learning, and graduate them to purposeful lives afterwards. Then she wanted them to probe what they *could do*, based on their Eagle Rock experiences. Before they left the following the day, Rachel hoped they would agree to some first steps as a result of shadowing, even if those first steps merely involved having more UHS educators (and perhaps, students and their parents, and district staff members) shadow at Eagle Rock. Or perhaps they could shadow in their own school to see what their own students experienced each day.

Overview

Shadowing is the process of following a student or educator through one day, part of a day, or longer, experiencing what that person experiences for the purpose of professional learning. Shadowing is neither new nor limited to the field of education. Historically, shadowing is the first step in an apprenticeship; today, people interested in a particular career often shadow someone accomplished in that field. Pre-med students shadow doctors to understand what it takes to be a doctor, and interns shadow medical specialists when they are considering narrowing their focus from general medicine. The purpose of shadowing in a school is similar; teachers shadow students or other teachers to discover what their school lives are like.

Educators, including building and district administrators, can shadow in their own or other schools, individually or in a group. Non-educators also can benefit from shadowing. Parents, community members, business leaders, and policy makers can learn through shadowing how school works from a student or educator perspective (see Online Resource 19.1:*Options for shadowing*).

Those being shadowed benefit, too. School staff members have said one advantage to having a shadow is that they have to be prepared. They have said they learn a lot through

About Eagle Rock School and Professional Development Center

Eagle Rock School and Professional Development Center is an initiative of the American Honda Education Corporation, a nonprofit subsidiary of the American Honda Motor Company. It is a full-scholarship (free tuition, room and board) school for high-school age students from around the country and a low-cost professional development center for adults. Eagle Rock is located in the mountain resort community of Estes Park, Colorado, gateway to Rocky Mountain National Park.

Eagle Rock opened in the fall of 1993 and, since then, has admitted and graduated students three times per year. A year-round residential school, Eagle Rock is purposefully small with a capacity of 84 students.

Its students are admitted between the ages of 15 and 17 and can stay until they graduate; the oldest graduating student was 21. About half are of color and half are male. Typically, they have not experienced success in "regular" (mostly public) schools, and most have dropped out with no expectation of graduating from high school.

The school year is comprised of three 13-week trimesters and 3–5 week breaks in between each trimester). Most students take between 8 and 14 trimesters to graduate (2 and 2/3 to 4 and 1/3 years).

Many, but not all, students stay to graduate from Eagle Rock. Some leave on their own volition or leave after breaking a restorative practices contract they've entered into after breaking a non-negotiable (no violence, sex, tobacco, drugs, or alcohol). Some of those who leave recommit to their education at Eagle Rock, apply to return through a process called Second Chance, and graduate. Most who leave but do not come back are able to graduate from their home or other schools, or get their General Equivalency Diplomas (GEDs). Approximately 90% of all students who entered Eagle Rock not expecting to graduate from high school are able to obtain diplomas.

In a culture that does not prize testing, especially large-scale testing using standardized, multiple-choice formats, Eagle Rock students do well, with the differences between pre- and post-test scores at a *significant, highly significant,* or *very highly significant* level (Easton, 2008, p. 2). Their performance on SATs and ACTs matches the profile of high school students anywhere.

Many graduates go on to college or university, but not all. A few have gone on to obtain graduate degrees. As in pubic high school populations, not all ERS students stay in college; some leave and some return at some later date. In addition, some serve in the military, get jobs, and/or start families.

Eagle Rock is also a professional development center (PDC) that works with interested educators on issues of school reform, renewal and reinvention. One way the Eagle Rock PDC does this is through hosting educators on the campus and providing shadowing experiences. The PDC staff also share successes at Eagle Rock with others through conference presentations, but this is not the heart of the work, which is to assist organizations and public high schools across the country in their own settings. For example, PDC staff have been working with the Leadership High School Network through the New Mexico Center for School Leadership in Albuquerque, New Mexico.

PDC staff members optimize their reach by working primarily through organizations that convene large numbers of schools and touch the lives of hundreds, sometimes thousands, of students. The PDC approach is to discover clients' aspirations, surface assets that already exist in their settings and, through facilitation, engage local expertise in a process of continuous improvement toward vision. This contextual, strengths-based and facilitative approach constitutes what Jim Collins (2011) would call a "hedgehog strategy" (p. 9).

visitors' questions and comments. "It's almost like having a mirror held up to what I'm doing," said one staff member. Staff members in a host school appreciate visitors who are purposeful and really want to learn as opposed to those who are merely curious or forced to visit.

Staff members of Eagle Rock have also said that having shadows provides a strong stimulus to get better. One staff member commented, "Having visitors in my classroom all the time makes me want to figure out how to teach better." Another: "I make an effort to live up to the standards of the school as an innovative school." They see benefits in their classrooms, as well. "Students usually perk up; they become real learners, even show-offs, when visitors are present." Finally, they have said that they really appreciate it when visitors work with students, participating in the activities of the classroom, helping students learn.

Students, too, benefit from having shadows. They practice presenting themselves, polish listening skills, and learn others' viewpoints. They learn how to relate to different kinds of people. Students also say they understand better what they are sharing with adults as they try to explain it. The murky becomes meaningful. They get to show off the school and relate their pride in it. In fact, their pride grows as they see their school through another's eyes. "It's not such a bad place," one student said about his Eagle Rock experience after having a teacher from another school shadow him.

Older students at Eagle Rock have even networked through their shadows, making contacts with visitors that have led to information sharing, jobs, and college possibilities.

Rationale

Shadowing is a type of job-embedded professional learning (Croft, Coggshall, Dolan, & Powers, April 2010) in the sense that it "takes place in the classroom, in real time, with current students, and is centered on issues of actual practice" (p. 3). Like all forms of embedded professional learning, shadowing begins with a real-life experience in a school or district and ends in another school or district when participants take what they learned and implement it as a way to help students succeed.

Shadowing is an effective form of professional learning because it provides an authentic, not just a theoretical or hypothetical, experience of school. Ann Webster-Wright (June 2009) compares professional learning for educators to professional learning in other professions, calling for "authentic professional learning" (p. 702). She argues for "the experience of learning" and cautions that the "lived experience" must be holistic rather than atomistic (p. 704). Shadowing provides a holistic, authentic professional learning experience for educators. Being in a school for a substantive length of time — and learning from that experience — can help educators become more authentic when they talk about what needs to be improved in education.

Shadowing is experiential and, according to early work by David A. Kolb (1984), results in knowledge, understanding, and the ability to change things because of both the concrete experience and reflection on it (p. 41). That's why shadowing by itself is not enough; those who shadow need to engage in reflection and, eventually, concept formation and a plan to take action. According to Kolb, shadowing can, thus, be transformative.

As in the best of experiential learning, shadowing is both cognitive and emotional. Daniel Goleman's (1995) research on emotional intelligence emphasizes that the emotional impact of an experience can strengthen learning by making it more memorable. Educators who face challenges while trying to implement a strategy learned through shadowing may recall the emotional impact of the shadowing experience. When they recall how something felt, they are likely to be able to recall the specifics of the experience, become encouraged and sustain the change effort. As visitors who have shadowed at Eagle Rock or in other schools implement changes in their own curriculum, for example, they remember the impact those innovations had on students at their host schools, and they persevere.

Many shadowing experiences are eye-openers. Often, those who shadow — educators and others — comment that they did not realize what it is like to be a student today. Because the experience injects reality into the proceedings of a committee or task force, shadowing can result in changed plans, sometimes in rethinking reform initiatives.

Steps

This section is divided into two parts, one for schools hosting shadows and the other for educators who are shadowing. The first part focuses on what **schools** can do before, during, and after hosting shadows. The second focuses on what **visiting educators** can do before, during, and after shadowing in their own or another school.

PART 1: Steps for schools hosting shadows

Step 1: Prepare to host

Before hosting visitors, a school community should discuss its reasons for doing so to be sure that shadowing will provide real benefit.

Role of the visitors. School staff need to determine in advance the role they want visitors to play while shadowing:

- Will they simply observe?
- Will they sit in the back of the room and take notes?
- Will they participate in classroom activities?
- May visitors question students or teachers? During class? Between classes?
- Will the shadows join the students in their courses only?
- Will they go to lunch with the students they shadow? After-school activities?

How shadows capture their experiences. Host staff decide acceptable ways for visitors to record what they see and do:

- May they videotape or audiotape the class?
- Are there questions they may not ask students? Teachers?
- May students ask visitors questions or for help with their work?
- Should visitors use a pre-designed form to record their observations?
- Would the host school staff provide these forms?
- Does the school community (students and staff) desire feedback in another form?
- Does the school community want to meet to debrief the shadowing experience from their point of view?

How hosts expand the shadowing experience. In addition to hosting visitors the staff may invite them to join students in dialogue and discussion:

- What about a panel discussion featuring students or teachers or both from the host school?
- What other events might be appropriate and helpful to visiting educators?
- Schools may need to consider the possibility that visitors may want to shadow teachers or administrators. Is that permissible? How would this form of shadowing work?

At some point — sooner rather than later — the school staff needs to involve students in the decision to have shadows. Students will want to know why adults are shadowing them. They will want some say in the logistics of the shadowing to keep their classrooms and lunch lines from becoming congested. Ultimately, they will want to know, "What's in this for us (individually and as a school)?"

The next step for the school is deciding which students the shadows will accompany. A sound practice to begin with is to ask for student volunteers to be shadowed. Depending on the particular interests and goals of the visitors, certain students may be more ideal candidates than others for shadowing. Should students be required to have shadows? The answer for most schools is probably no; students should be allowed to volunteer to host a visitor. However, what if visiting schools want to shadow particular types of students — for example, male students? How does the host school want to handle creating intentional matches between visitors and students to provide a richer experience for both groups?

Schools also will need to decide if the students who might have shadows need an orientation to shadowing. At some schools, students are accustomed to having visiting educators on campus and to having shadows. They know what to do because, as is the culture at Eagle Rock and schools with similar professional learning programs, they pass along to each other a protocol for shadowing: to introduce themselves fully (name, age, where they're from if it is a residential school, and how long they've been at the school). They shake hands and ask the shadow to identify himself or herself. This initial introduction can be a moment of wonder for visitors being hosted at schools like Eagle Rock and ones serving similar populations — some of the students are former gang members coming from all over the country. The polished and polite demeanor of students who are practiced in professional interactions often dispels any assumptions visitors may be carrying and opens their minds for the remainder of their shadowing experience.

A host school needs a contact person to facilitate productive visits. This person schedules the visit and is the school intermediary for the visit. The contact person needs to know enough about the school and education in general to assist during the visit. At first, the contact may be someone in the principal's office or even the principal, but as visitors become more frequent, a full-time contact may be needed.

Schools sometimes have a parent, group of parents, or retired staff members serve this function. When visits are daily, the school may want to charge enough for a part-time salary.

Step 2: Prepare for the visit

After an initial contact from an individual or a group that wants to shadow, the host school's contact person sets up the shadowing experience by:

1. Talking with educators at the visiting school to discern the purpose of the visit and visitors' expectations.
2. Sending materials about the school — fact sheets, copies of newsletters or articles, and other background information.
3. Linking visitors to the school's website.
4. Customizing the visit, if necessary. For example, a group that wants to learn more about service learning might be scheduled for a service-learning project and be seated at lunch with students and staff involved in that project. An individual who wants to research portfolio assessment might spend some time watching videos of students presenting their portfolios.
5. Alerting staff and students about how many people will visit, for what purposes, when, and for how long. Kitchen staff may need to be notified that they will need to prepare for lunch guests.
6. Arranging for students or staff to be shadowed and for special interviews, discussions (such as pairings or groupings over lunch), or focus groups.

Step 3: Prepare for the shadowing experience

If possible, the host school contact person gives visitors an orientation at the beginning of their shadowing experience. The distance that visitors are traveling may dictate the timing of their orientation. An orientation on the evening prior to the start of their visit can allow for a more detailed exploration of the host school's demographic, environment, culture, program, and mission. However, that is not always possible and a brief introduction on the day of the visit can be enough to provide essential knowledge before shadowing begins.

The host school contact might spend 90 minutes discussing the school, its culture, and mission with the visitors. The contact can offer useful questions for the visitors to ask students they shadow at the beginning of their experience to ease both into the shadowing process:

- How long have you been a student at this school? What school did you go to before this school?
- What is the best thing about this school? What is the worst?
- What did you really like about your school experience before you came here? What did you dislike?
- What do you want to accomplish this year as a student? In the next few years?

Students want to know similar things about their shadows:

- Where are you from?
- Why are you visiting our school?
- What do you do professionally? Where did you go to school?
- What do you like to do on your own time?

At the start of the school day, introduce visitors to a group of students (in the case of Eagle Rock this group consisted of the whole school), ask students to volunteer to have a shadow, and link visitors with students. Students who volunteer can choose a visitor or be assigned for intentional matches. Often pairing happens in the rather opportunistic way that adults in professional learning sessions match themselves for learning — proximity or making eye contact and then moving together.

Step 4: Debrief

As in any experiential learning, the experience is only one part of gaining new knowledge; reflecting on the experience is at least as important. The debriefing is best while the shadowing experience is fresh, both cognitively and emotionally.

When individuals or groups visit for an entire day, the host school contact person asks the students to bring visitors to a central place before lunch for a debriefing. Also, the host school contact person can ask the visitors to gather for another, longer debriefing at the end of their day. If the visit is more than one day, do the two debriefings on the first day and just one on the following days. Debriefings usually proceed like this:

1. **Write.** Ask visitors to write about their shadowing experience. Since many were active during classes, they may not have captured their thoughts on paper. Writing also prepares them to have something to say as the debriefing proceeds.

2. **Share observations.** In a brief shadowing experience, shadows have seen only isolated episodes of learning in their host school so the contact person needs to invite them to share those episodes. Visitors begin with a simple description of what they experienced. They may talk about the person they shadowed, what happened in the classes they attended, what students were doing, what teachers were doing, what they did. They may comment on the culture or atmosphere of the class, anything descriptive.

3. **Consider the "what."** The contact person then asks shadows to think about what they were struck by, moving beyond description to themes, trends, patterns, and generalizations. At this point, the host school contact person can begin to assess the cognitive and emotional value of the experience.

4. **Consider the "so what."** At this stage, the host school contact person asks visitors to ask themselves, "So what does this mean to me?" After inviting them to do so, the host school contact can somewhat withdraw from the dialogue that ensues. Visitors may talk among themselves, with only occasional prompts from the host school contact person, such as "So, what would this look like in your school?"

5. **Consider the "now what."** It's important for the host school contact person to help visitors think about what they will do first when they get back to their own environment. When visitors exclaim something like, "Hey, we could do this at our school!" it is a good sign that they are ready to think about "Now, what we need to do at our school. . . ." From there, the contact person can ask a few implementation questions to capitalize on that energy (see Online Resource 19.2: *Steps in shadowing*).

The debriefing is somewhat different when an individual is shadowing. The school contact person partners with the individual, helping this person engage in the same steps. The individual can present the descriptive and "struck by" parts of the debriefing, but probably will need collaboration to move to the "so what" and "now what" stages. The contact person can ask questions such as: "What connections are there between what we do at our school and what you want to do in your school? What differences would there be? How would you adapt what we do? What are some of the barriers? What are some of the challenges? Who might support your

ideas?" It helps to encourage the individual to make the next step a matter of asking, "Who else needs to be here?" so the individual is not alone in contemplating change.

At the end of the debriefing — with groups as well as individuals — when the shadows' first steps are relatively clear, sometimes the host school contact person will add another step: How can we help? Often the best help the school can provide is welcoming another group to shadow on the campus. The current group may say, "The rest of our staff needs to experience this." Sometimes the initial group decides that people in other roles need to shadow students: district staff, students, parents, policymakers, for example. Sometimes the initial group wants students and staff from the host school to come to the visiting school to make a presentation. Both are positive steps toward the growth of active learning communities.

The best-laid plans, of course, are hard to implement when the realities of any school environment roll over and flatten them. The host school contact person can call or email people who have shadowed at a school to see what they've been able to do as a result of their learning experiences. Through the call or email, the contact person can encourage visitors to recall their experience at the host school, remember their insights, and refocus on their implementation plans. Here is another good time for the contact person to ask, "How can we help?"

Debriefing is not all about the visitors. After visitors leave the host school with new insights and energy with which to return to their own schools, educators at the host school need to consolidate their own learning. The contact person can capture visitors' reflections, ideas, and comments during the visitors' debriefing sessions and then share them via email or voicemail. Better than that, the contact person can share them face to face, as part of a regularly scheduled meeting, such as a staff, grade-level, or subject-area meetings, inviting the host school's staff to engage in their own reflection on the feedback.

Staff and students are interested in what visitors have to say. With their comments, visitors hold up a mirror to a school's culture and practices. The mirror may show a school that is doing what it hopes to be accomplishing; or, it may *not* reflect what the school believes should be clearly visible, difficult as that might be to accept. Both are powerful stimuli for continuous improvement.

PART 2: Steps for educators who are shadowing

Step 1: Prepare

Educators preparing to shadow need to:

1. Know why they are visiting another school or shadowing in their own school. The Urban High School visitors had done some data analysis and were distressed about the progress of their male students who they thought could be classified as "at risk." Their purpose in visiting was to see how male students at Eagle Rock functioned in their classrooms and the school as a whole. Also they wanted to discern what engaged them in terms of program (curriculum, instruction, and assessment).

2. Review the host school's demographics, environment, culture, program, mission/vision, curriculum, and key elements. Those shadowing within their own school should prepare by studying the context of the environment as if they were outsiders.

3. Establish critical questions to ask.

4. Decide who will make the visit. Having the appropriate administrator in the visiting group is extremely beneficial. The group needs a sponsor or champion for what may happen as a result of shadowing. The UHS principal knew Eagle Rock well and already had indicated his sponsorship by arranging the visit. He decided to visit with the team, and his decision was especially helpful when the team debriefed and began planning. Having a counselor as part of the team also was very helpful because counselors see the student's perspective in a different way than administrators and teachers do.

5. Be clear about what they can and cannot do as shadows at the school they are visiting. Inquire in advance whether videotaping or audiotaping classes or taking pictures of students is permissible, for example. Understand the role of the shadow and rules for a shadowing (see Step 1 for Schools Hosting Shadows for some questions to consider). The contact person from the school probably can help with understanding the nuances of a visit (see Online Resource 19.3: *Preparing to shadow*).

Step 2: Shadow

Throughout the shadowing experience in another school, educators need to keep in mind the following:

1. The school we are visiting is not our school. We can't replicate the entire school. We can't do exactly what they are doing. We probably wouldn't want to.

2. At the same time, we also need to avoid thinking that the school we visit is not like our school and, therefore, nothing is applicable.

3. What's happening in this school might be helpful as applied to our own needs. Educators can ask themselves: What are the differences and similarities between our schools? How would something from the school we are visiting translate to our own school? What would change? What would remain the same? Why would we want to make the change? Who would support the change? Who might block it? What would be the system repercussions of that change?

Those shadowing in their own school need to take the same approach, acknowledging that they are visiting their own school but looking at it objectively, as if it were a different site. Use Online Resource 19.4: *Observation form* for visitors to record their observations.

Step 3: Debrief

The school contact probably will have a formal debriefing session with the visiting group. However, visiting group members will want to check with each other to determine:

1. The different experiences members had and the impact of these experiences;

2. New thoughts or ideas those experiences have inspired;

3. New questions that have arisen from those experiences;

4. Applications that will improve their own school.

At some point, the visitors will need to determine how to roll out their shadowing experience with colleagues who were not able to participate. Their colleagues will be curious and may feel left out of an important process, especially if participants in the shadowing experience make plans for implementing significant change. Nothing sabotages school improvement more than the feeling that some are privileged in the process, and some are not (see Online Resource 19.5: *Prompts for debriefing and implementation*).

Step 4: Implement

At the very least, those who shadow should describe their experience to others, perhaps in staff, department, or grade-level meetings. If they are serious about change based on a shadowing experience, they need to involve others.

Implementation may start with the simple step of communicating with others and making sure they have experiences that get them "on board" with change.

The shadowing group should also seek sponsors or advocates for the change, perhaps the administrator who was part of the shadowing team, perhaps another person in power. The next step for shadows is actually implementing a change, a process that can be planned in a linear fashion but usually occurs in a very iterative way. This sets a foundation for a cycle of critical analysis and action for school improvement.

Finally, the shadowing group should keep in mind that school improvement is contextual. The process involves adaptation not adoption. Few approaches to teaching and learning translate wholesale from one context to another.

Variations

Several variations have already been mentioned: individuals or groups; teams of teachers or mixed role teams; individuals or groups of non-educators. Any of these groups or individuals can shadow someone other than a student. Shadowing a teacher can be an eye-opener for administrators, for example. Shadowing a principal or another building administrator can awaken teachers, district-level administrators or others (such as board members) to the work at a building level.

One variation that is particularly effective when visitors can stay longer than one day is a research activity (see Online Resource 19.6: *Become an action researcher while shadowing*). Visitors become researchers in teams or as individuals, identifying on the first day an essential question, one that intrigues them and one for which there is no simple or right answer. They develop a hypothesis and collect data during the day to answer their questions. They get their data through interviews with individuals or groups, focus groups, panel presentations, observations of classes, or artifacts they request (such as a student handbook, portfolios, etc.).

At the end of the visit, the host school contact person sets aside time (perhaps five minutes per group or individual) for visitors to share the results of their research with the rest of their group and with students and staff from the host school. Visitors' presentations are often eye-openers for the host school and give visitors a greater purpose for shadowing.

In another variation, students can shadow adults to see what their lives are like as well. In addition to typical job

shadowing, students can travel to conferences or participate and assist in staff-led workshops and presentations. They get an idea of what it is like to interact with adults, especially adults who are engaged in their own learning. Students who shadow teachers and principals usually begin their debriefing with, "I had no idea it was so hard!" and then share their newfound respect for the educators in their own lives.

Challenges and how to address them

Purpose. Visiting educators must be serious about shadowing. Visitors must want to make changes in their own schools in order to benefit from shadowing in another school. The school's contact person can ascertain visitors' seriousness of purpose through an interview with the person arranging a visit; if educators from the visiting school or district are really serious, they may agree to form a design team and to do some pre-visit work, such as reading materials about the school they want to visit. With clear and serious purposes in mind, both the host school and the visitors benefit from the experience.

When there is little or no evidence of seriousness of purpose, both students and staff at a host school may feel abused, especially when visits are frequent. One student's description of his shadow epitomizes how it feels to have visitors who are not serious about their visit: "She just sat there in my class, the whole time, reading her magazine." He never again volunteered to have a shadow.

Attention to all steps. Simply shadowing is not enough. All the steps are critical for a powerful result. Shadowing, like any other experience, loses its power over time despite the emotional impact. Those who shadow must be helped to make meaning and take steps forward in their own environments as a result of the experience.

A coordinator. Someone in the school who has other, full-time responsibilities will not be able to handle the shadowing process if visitors become more than occasional. At some point, someone who can devote the requisite time to handling visits needs to respond to requests to shadow, set up visits, and help visitors debrief and plan next steps. The role is not clerical. It requires someone knowledgeable about the school and its innovations (the reasons other educators might want to visit) as well as some expertise in education and education reform.

A learning community. The school that creates a shadowing program must be a true learning community.

The most important benefit of shadowing to the school that hosts visitors is the opportunity for its staff and students to learn from visitors. Staff and students must be willing to become learners — and also to become teachers. Staff members expand their work to include teaching visitors; students become teachers when they have shadows.

Affective challenges. Students and staff involved in hosting visitors describe several challenges of having shadows. Students dislike feeling like they're in a fishbowl when there are many visitors, one group after another. They need breaks between the visits. They resent their more crowded classes. They wonder whether they are getting special instruction because visitors are present. (Since Eagle Rock has visitors nearly every day, they are always getting special instruction!) They resent nosy questions and rude people. They find it tough to deal with people with opposite viewpoints. They chafe at having an overcrowded lunchroom and fewer spaces for them to relax and not be "on" all the time. An Eagle Rock student claimed, "We are always on the spot. We have to learn and be smart."

Staff members declare it both an advantage and disadvantage that they always have to be prepared. They can't have a bad day; they feel the pressure to be "on" every day. They can be embarrassed by students. When they have teaching fellows or student teachers, they worry about having visitors when the teachers-in-training are leading the classroom.

Conclusion

Despite these challenges, the consensus among students and staff at Eagle Rock is that a shadowing program improves the school and creates a true learning community. A school that hosts shadows experiences a change in culture. It is hard to remain static when visitors hold up a mirror to what is actually happening in a school, good and bad. Staff members learn from the questions and comments of shadows. Staff become learners. Students become teachers to their shadows.

The UHS team experienced its own cultural shift. Several other small UHS groups visited Eagle Rock to shadow both students and staff. The debriefings were the most important part of their visits as they began to plan changes within their building. An assistant superintendent visited and liked what she saw. She supported summer planning, including another trip to Eagle Rock. The UHS principal

ONLINE RESOURCES

19.1   Options for shadowing
19.2   Steps in shadowing
19.3   Preparing to shadow
19.4   Observation form
19.5   Prompts for debriefing and implementation
19.6   Become an action researcher while shadowing

retired before the team could implement its plans, but the assistant superintendent's support and the faculty's strength helped the school make a significant change in curriculum. This change affected the whole system and led to changes in assessment and the district's use of time and resources. Now UHS welcomes shadows to its building and shares both what has worked and what the school community still is working on.

References

Collins, J. (2011). *Good to great: Why some companies make the leap...And others don't.* New York, NY: Harper Business.

Croft, A., Coggshall, J.G., Dolan, M., & Powers, E. (2010, April). *Job-embedded professional development: What it is, who is responsible, and how to get it done well.* Issue Brief. Washington, DC: National Comprehensive Center for Teacher Quality.

Easton, L.B. (2008). *Engaging the disengaged: How schools can help struggling students succeed.* Thousand Oaks, CA: Corwin Press.

Goleman, D. (1996). *Emotional intelligence: Why it can matter more than IQ.* New York, NY: Bantam Books.

Kolb, D.A. (1984). *Experiential learning: Experience as the source of learning and development.* Upper Saddle River, NJ: Prentice Hall.

Webster-Wright, A. (2009, June). Reframing professional development through understanding authentic professional learning. *Review of Educational Research, 79*(2), 702–739.

CHAPTER 20

Social Media

Teachers engage with digital technologies to build professional learning networks, forge relationships with other educators, access and share resources, and collaborate to learn.

By Lynmarie Hilt

When Jay Cole began his career as an elementary principal in northwest Pennsylvania, he quickly realized that the role of educational administrator was a lonely one. "As the school leader, I longed to establish connections with others who were 'living' the role of principal on a daily basis. As the principal, you're expected to be everything to everyone, and it's overwhelming at times. I sought a support group of other educational administrators to help me grow in my profession. I knew there was a lot to learn, and not a lot of time to learn it," Jay said.

Jay turned to social media, specifically the use of Twitter, to connect with other educational leaders. He noticed that teachers and principals across the country and beyond were communicating online via the social network to ask questions, share ideas and resources, and offer support to one another. Jay first heard of Twitter in 2007 at an educational technology conference, but at the time, he considered the tool to be a frivolous one, void of any educational value.

"I really didn't think Twitter could help me perform my job better in any way," Jay recalls. "I opened the account but didn't use it. After all, did I really have a need to see what people were eating for breakfast? It seemed to me the things being shared on Twitter were trivial at best."

However, after investing a few hours establishing connections and developing relationships with a handful of key contributors, Jay suddenly saw his role in terms of this medium in a new light. "My isolation quickly waned," he said. "I was suddenly part of a larger community of educators who embraced and supported me and the work I was doing in my school. Through this network I was able to reflect on my role as principal, improve my practice, gain resources for myself and my teachers and students, and help serve as a model for my school community as I interacted digitally with the global educational community."

*　*　*

Lindsay Edwards, a second-year middle school science teacher in Louisiana, knew that reflective practice was an important component of professional growth. She occasionally used sticky notes, riddled with jottings she made between class periods, and stuck them to the pages of her teachers' manuals to help her reflect on her performance and guide future instruction. She realized, however, that this system didn't necessarily translate into improved teaching practice. Also, when asked to share her reflections with colleagues and administrators, she found the sticky notes didn't provide the coherent or concrete evidence of reflection that she desired.

Through simple Internet searches, Lindsay located a number of blogs teachers had written to reflect on their experiences teaching and learning in the classroom. They described and reflected on their practice in detail and shared with the global community through various blogging platforms such as WordPress, Blogger, and Edublogs. Lindsay found other middle school science teachers who shared unit and lesson plans, class resources and materials, and processes for helping students learn. Teachers openly and honestly reflected on their experiences, and through the comment threads on the blogs, other educators provided feedback and additional resources and support.

Lindsay said, "It was evident that these teachers were invested in helping one another learn more about best practices in science instruction, and through the work they shared, other teachers benefited. I was so impressed about how easy it was to share and reflect using a simple platform such as a blog."

Lindsay decided that the use of a blog to post her reflections was a far superior method than using the sticky notes. She was able not only to organize and articulate her reflections but also to share her learning with an authentic audience who would provide her with feedback, additional resources, and support.

"I can't describe just how meaningful blogging has been as part of my professional learning plan. I've learned more through my reflective writing and interactions with other educators in the blogging community than I have in many of the graduate courses I've taken," Lindsay shared. Lindsay

is now taking steps to incorporate student blogging into her classroom activities. While she is not a language arts teacher, Lindsay knows, through her personal experiences with blogging, that writing as a reflective practice can help her science students demonstrate understandings of science content explored in class.

Overview

Social media use is pervasive in daily work and play of adults and children alike. About 72% of adults are now active on at least one social network. Compare that to 67% in 2012 and just 8% in 2005 (Pick, 2013, para. 4). News anchors scroll their Twitter handles onscreen while reporting. Television shows share hashtags so the public can tweet about televised events in shared streams. Children, teens, and adults use Facebook to connect, share, and converse. There are estimated to be 31 million bloggers in the United States (Bullas, 2012). There are 60 million Instagram photos posted daily on average (Smith, 2014, p. 3). And YouTube reaches more adults than cable television (Scott 2013, para. 3).

Just ten years ago, the world was a very different place in terms of connecting, collaborating, and learning. The explosion of digital devices — suddenly available and affordable — combined with the ever-increasing use of social media tools to connect users and ideas around the world has the potential to revolutionize the way people communicate, which in turn can transform the way teachers and other educators engage in professional learning.

At first, educators battled social media, perhaps intimidated by digital advances or seeing them as short-term distractions from learning. Citing the difficulty of keeping students on task educationally, educational administrators and teachers prevented student use of personal cell phones and other devices when first introduced. Educators believed they needed to regulate students' visiting sites such as MySpace, online chat rooms, and instant messaging during school hours. Instances of cyberbullying also convinced school personnel that these tools might do more harm than good.

As social media became more accessible and as teachers became more familiar with the platforms, educators around the world discovered the value of using social media for professional learning endeavors, both for their own personal learning and for engaging students. These educators who have come to be known as "connected educators," began to share with school leaders the importance of allowing students access to a number of open networks and social media platforms. These educators also willingly and openly shared their own learning via social media platforms such as Nings, blogs, Facebook, and Twitter. Connected educators made it their mission to collaborate with other passionate educators to learn, create, read, write, and share in the name of professional learning. Many also used established connections to bring global learning opportunities to their students and schools.

Learning Forward (2011) acknowledges the integral role of technology to support professional learning in the Standards for Professional Learning (Learning Designs):

> Technology is rapidly enhancing and extending opportunities for professional learning. It particularly facilitates access to, sharing, construction, and analysis of information to enhance practice. Technology exponentially increases possibilities for personalizing, differentiating, and deepening learning, especially for educators who have limited access to on-site professional learning or who are eager to reach beyond the boundaries of their own work setting to join local or global networks to enrich their learning. (para. 5)

Anthony Armstrong (2013) of Learning Forward wrote that social media and other digital technologies can help districts provide meaningful professional learning opportunities for teachers by maximizing available funds and time.

Recent attempts to organize professional learning for educators via social media have been quite successful. For example, the Reform Symposium (RSCON) is a worldwide e-conference that has helped engage thousands of professionals in anytime/anywhere professional learning. The RSCON's free, online conference has linked educators annually since 2010 using the Blackboard Collaborate webinar platform. Similar e-conferences, held yearly, such as the School Leadership Summit and the Global Education Conference, help provide professional learning for educators through the use of social networking platforms.

In 2012 the first-ever Connected Educator Month (CEM) organized by the United States Department of Education, linked thousands of teachers. CEM delivered "at least 90,000 hours of professional development to teachers and other educators." The event was even more successful the following year (Connected Educators, February, 2013).

The online learning opportunities facilitated by Connected Educator Month demonstrate that "online social learning and collaboration can complement individual, school, district, and state efforts to improve professional excellence and, ultimately, student learning" (Connected Educators, 2013, p. 1).

The options for connecting, collaborating, and learning via social media are limited only by the imagination.

Theories of social media learning

Several learning theories help shape and explain the power of connected learning.

Connectivism as a learning theory. How do we learn? How do we interact with content, ideas, other people, resources, and networks to learn? How do we shape the creation of knowledge? What is more important, knowledge itself or the process the learner uses to engage in learning? These are the questions educator and researcher George Siemens (2012) addressed in his work on a connectivist learning theory. "Connectivism," Siemens (2012) claimed, "is a learning theory for the digital age" (para. 1).

Siemens and Stephen Downes have researched and shared the ideas that comprise connective knowledge and connectivism as a learning theory. Both Siemens (2003) and Downes (2005) provide the background and rationale for the use of networked learning.

The foundations of connectivism are as follows: Learners have a need to externalize to make sense of what has been learned. They use structures and frameworks for doing so. Powerful learning occurs when learners socialize around knowledge. Learners' minds use patterns to organize and assimilate new information. Finally, people have a desire to extend humanity through technology (Siemens, 2008).

Siemens (2008) identifies these key principles of connectivism:

1. "Knowledge is networked and distributed.
2. "The experience of learning is one of forming new neural, conceptual, and external networks.
3. "Learning occurs in complex, chaotic, shifting spaces.
4. "Our networked experiences are increasingly aided by technology" (p. 8).

Neural/biological, conceptual, and social/external networks all play a role in connected learning. Learning is a process of connecting nodes of information sources. According to connectivism, in order to continue to learn, people must nurture and maintain connections. Understanding these connections will allow educators to improve how they design classrooms, create curriculum, teach, and learn (Siemens, 2008).

Stephen Downes (2012) defined principles of effective e-learning experiences so that others could learn how to make the most of their informal learning experiences. While he is clear that the process varies for individual learners, he suggests that these three components help create a successful online learning experience:

> *Interaction* — the capacity to communicate with other people interested in the same topic or using the same online resource; this encourages human connection, collaboration, and shared creation.
> *Usability* — the tools should be simple in design (easy to access, understand, employ) and offer consistency in their approach to use.
> *Relevance* — the principle that "learners should get what they want, when they want it, and where they want it." (Downes, 2012, p. 50)

Rhizomatic learning and learning communities. Dave Cormier, a Canadian educator with a wealth of experience supporting professional learning through communities, provides another theory related to professional learning via social media. In 2008 he developed the concept of *rhizomatic learning* that explores learning as a chaotic experience that can't be controlled or even defined. A "rhizome responds to changing environmental conditions" (Cormier, 2008, para. 12). So, "in the rhizomatic model of learning, curriculum is not driven by predefined inputs from experts; it is constructed and negotiated in real time by the contributions of those engaged in the learning process" (Cormier, 2008, para. 12). This means that the "community acts as the curriculum, spontaneously shaping, constructing, and reconstructing itself and the subject of its learning in the same way that the rhizome responds to changing environmental conditions (Cormier, 2008, para. 12).

In an audio interview with connected educator Bud Hunt, Cormier elaborates: "Rhizomatic knowledge … is about that connection and the fact that when we connect, we create context with the people we're connecting with, the knowledge we create there is contextual, and it matters that there are real people there" (Hunt, 2008, para. 1).

When educators make the decision to become part of a connected learning community, they are taking the initiative to make their own learning a priority. They do this to grow as professionals for the benefit of their students and school community. Sheryl Nussbaum-Beach and Lani Ritter Hall (2012) explore the methods by which one can become a connected educator. They provide an in-depth look at what connected learning communities do:

> Connected learning communities are designed to support the professional development goals their members have chosen to improve instruction and subsequently bring about increased growth and achievement for the 21st century learner. Members of connected learning communities collaborate and work interdependently to achieve high levels of student achievement, while also focusing on their own professional and personal learning goals. (p. 38)

So how can a method of professional learning be so very individualized, yet rely so heavily on the connections made with others? Enter personal learning networks.

What is a personal learning network?

In 1998, Daniel Tobin published *Building Your Personal Learning Network* on his Corporate Learning Strategies website. It is one of the earliest known mentions of personal learning networks (PLN). Tobin emphasizes the importance of ongoing, job-embedded development and the need for a network of people to support continuous learning. Tobin defines the personal learning network as "a group of people who can guide your learning, point you to learning opportunities, answer your questions, and give you the benefit of their own knowledge and experience" (Tobin, 1998, para. 1).

Personal learning networks not only provide the learner with sources of information, but also help the learner make sense of and apply the information in practice through dialogue and collaboration. David Warlick (2007) has shared some of the earliest work on PLNs as applied to the field of education. He provides this working definition:

A *personal* or *professional* [emphasis added] learning network (PLN) involves an individual's topic-oriented goal, a set of practices and techniques aimed at attracting and organizing a variety of relevant content sources, selected for their value, to help the owner accomplish a professional goal or personal interest. (p. 4)

Educators tend to use the italicized terms interchangeably. The concept of personal learning environment has also been explored in depth; a personal learning environment (PLE) relates to a PLN in that the environment encompasses the interactive tools that individuals use to support learning as well as the personal learning networks they establish.

Steve Wheeler from Plymouth University in the United Kingdom created Figure 1 showing the relationships among personal learning environments and networks, as well as personal web tools individuals use to support learning. Also see Online Resource 20.1: *Anatomy of a personal learning environment (PLE)*.

Alec Couros is another educator who has significantly impacted the open education and connected educator movement. Couros's work was influenced by social learning theory, social constructivism, adult learning theory, and connectivism. Couros developed two images contrasting the "typical teacher network" with that of the "networked teacher," demonstrating the improved connections the networked teacher establishes, connections that are not only more numerous but also reciprocal (see Figure 2 on p. 292 and Online Resource 20.2: *Typical teacher networks and the networked teacher.*)

Figure 1: **Relationships Among Personal Learning Environments, Networks, and Web Tools**

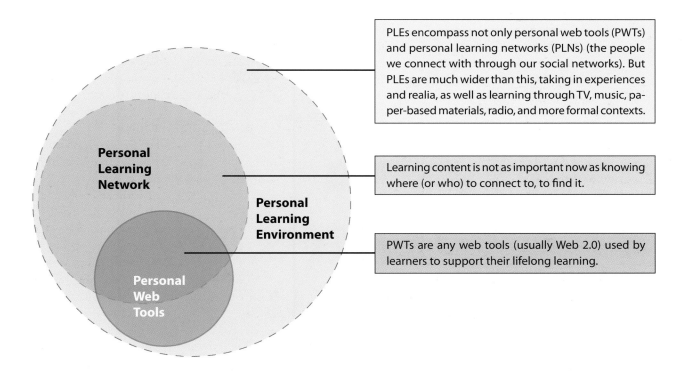

PLEs encompass not only personal web tools (PWTs) and personal learning networks (PLNs) (the people we connect with through our social networks). But PLEs are much wider than this, taking in experiences and realia, as well as learning through TV, music, paper-based materials, radio, and more formal contexts.

Learning content is not as important now as knowing where (or who) to connect to, to find it.

PWTs are any web tools (usually Web 2.0) used by learners to support their lifelong learning.

From *Anatomy of a PLE* by Steve Wheeler, Copyright 2010 by Steve Wheeler. Reproduced with permission.

Figure 2: **Typical Teacher Networks and the Networked Teacher**

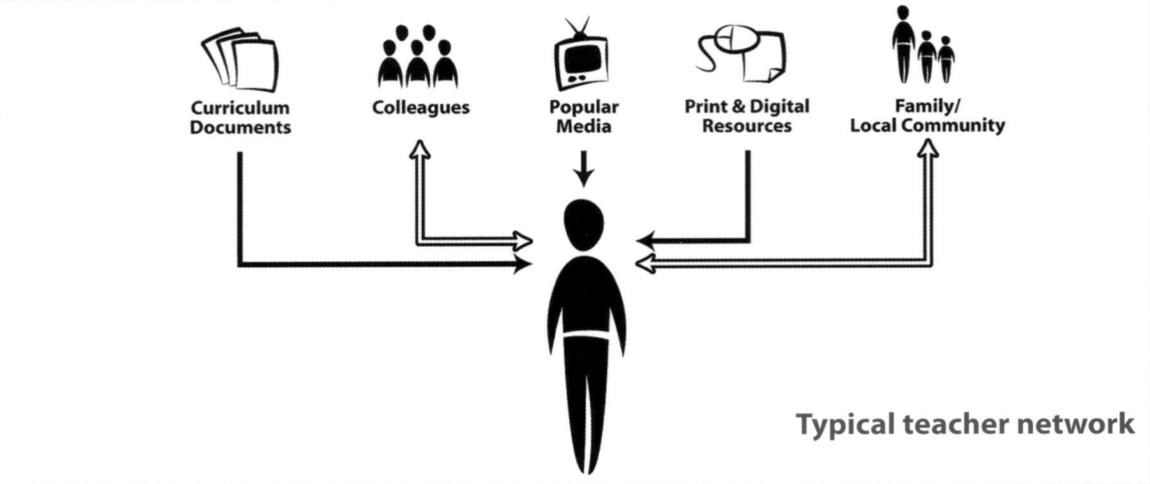

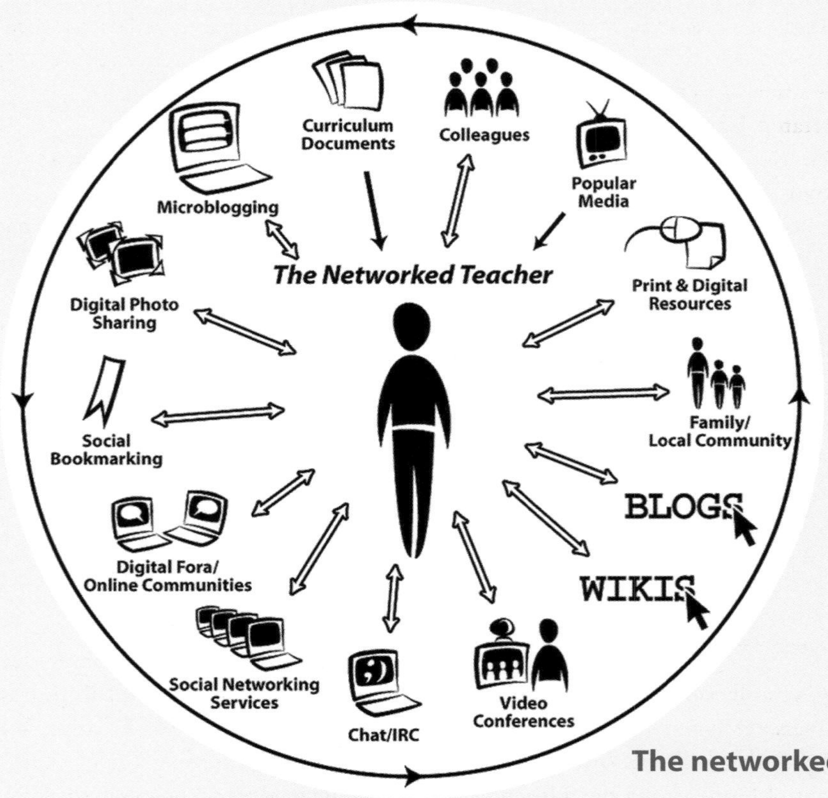

Developing personal learning networks for open and social learning by Alec Couros in *Emerging technologies in distance education.*
Copyright 2010 AU Press. Reproduced with permission.

No longer are teachers influenced by antiquated forms of media, curriculum guides, and those in their local school settings. The networked teacher has access and the ability to contribute back to numerous learning communities and services via social networking. These connections, once forged, offer continuous sources of information, support, feedback, and ideas to the educator.

Researcher and author Kristen Swanson (2013) explored the concepts of the personal learning network and the use of social media for professional learning. She defines "user-generated learning" as:

> learning acquired through active curation, reflection, and contribution to a self-selected collaborative space. This basically means that user-generated learning is something you do, not something you get. You have to actively participate in the process through searching, evaluating, and sharing. In user-generated learning, everyone has something to contribute. We are all experts in our own ways. This doesn't negate the importance of educational research or vetted practices. Instead, user-generated learning reflects that all adults recognize their personal applications of ideas and strategies, and this synthesis and community are a valuable part of the learning process. (p. 5)

Swanson (2013) details the processes by which educators can embrace digital tools and social media networks to establish connections with other educators for professional learning. Through *curation,* educators collect relevant resources. Next, with *reflection,* educators assimilate new information with existing background knowledge. The last step in Swanson's user-generated learning process is *contribution* during which educators share what they have learned with their learning communities.

Rationale

Educators have several incentives to use social media: the needs of adult learners, the variety of ways a user of social media can interact with others, the transparency the process engenders in terms of learning, and the differentiation that is possible. These benefits accrue for educators as well as students.

What do adult learners need?

How can social media best support adult learning? Andragogy, the art and science of adult learning, provides an answer. Andragogy operates under the assumptions that adults are self-directed and display an increasing readiness to learn. As adults mature, they become their own increasing resource for learning due to their accumulated experiences. Adults seek to apply knowledge practically, in a timely manner, and as part of the problem-solving process. An adult learner displays increased intrinsic motivation to learn (Queensland Occupational Therapy Fieldwork Collaborative, 2007, paras. 3–5).

Adult learning designs allow the learner to be actively involved in the planning and implementation of the learning. Learner autonomy is key. Adult learners should be encouraged to make mistakes and apply their own knowledge to new experiences and information learned. Learning opportunities for adults should be relevant, timely, problem-based, practical, and tied to actionable goals (Queensland Occupational Therapy Fieldwork Collaborative, 2007, paras. 6–9).

How can social media address adult learners' needs?

The use of social media can support adult professional learning in the following ways:

- *It puts the learner first.* It is a highly individualized process; therefore educators can choose the best tools to support their unique learning goals. Educators have full control over the networks they establish and the communities in which they choose to engage.

- *It promotes collaboration and builds relationships through the establishment of connections and networks.* Through advances in digital technologies, educators can connect and communicate easily with other educators from around the world. Collaborative platforms such as Skype, Google Hangouts, and webinar software allow for synchronous collaborative learning.

- *It is reflective.* Social media platforms support reflective writing, reading, and sharing. Whether the user shares information using a microblogging platform in small increments or chooses to compose blog posts with more significant content, social networks support opportunities to reflect and receive feedback.

- *It is timely, relevant, and practical.* Social media interactions exist in real time. When educators submit a query via a social network, they are likely to receive feedback immediately and from users with practical experience. Because of the wide range of educators using social networks for learning, teachers can connect with those that specifically address their needs in particular content areas, developmental levels, and geographic areas around the world, making it a highly relevant learning experience for the user.

A variety of participation possibilities

Social media are important for professional learning because they provide a variety of ways users can interact. Every online community and network has its own norms of behavior established by users. For example, on Twitter it is appropriate to include the username of a tweeter when you re-share or "retweet" his or her content. It would be a faux pas to share the exact tweet of another user without giving credit for the original tweet. It is important to get to know how a social network works. This getting-to-know-you phase of social media use is an integral part of the PLN development process. For many users, the first step in participation in social networks is *lurking.*

Lurking, considered by some educators to be a form of "legitimate peripheral participation," (Lave & Wenger, 1991) is often the first step in engagement with an online community or network. Legitimate peripheral participation refers to the process by which new members of a community of practice acclimate themselves to the community, and in doing so, eventually become established members of the group. As newcomers observe the practices of the established members, they learn about the functions of the community, how members interact with one another, and how ideas are shared. As new members begin contributing, they start fulfilling important functions that help the community flourish (Lave & Wenger, 1991).

Steve Wheeler (May, 2013) explores lurking as a valuable exercise in his blog post, Just How Far Can They Go? He created the graphic featured in Figure 3 to display the levels of engagement within a classroom, applicable also to adult learners' engagement in their networks.

While Wheeler considers the ultimate form of engagement to be "the ability to generate one's own

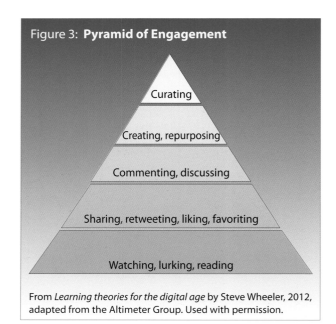

Figure 3: **Pyramid of Engagement**

Curating

Creating, repurposing

Commenting, discussing

Sharing, retweeting, liking, favoriting

Watching, lurking, reading

From *Learning theories for the digital age* by Steve Wheeler, 2012, adapted from the Altimeter Group. Used with permission.

content and then add value to it for others," he believes that lurking is an important precursor to the complex interactions that a more active contributor would demonstrate (Wheeler, 2013, para. 4). See Online Resource 20.3: *Pyramid of engagement.*

So, while many consider lurking to be an essential first step in the process of interacting with social networks, *the eventual goal should always be to contribute and give back to the community as soon and as often as possible.* The acts of sharing and contributing are essential to helping the community thrive.

As Kristen Swanson (2013) shares in her book's chapter on contribution as part of the user-generated learning process,

There is a pronounced need for you to contribute to the learning spaces and people from which you learn. And while you might be asking, "What do I have of value?" the answer is simple: You have your experiences, your classroom, and your teaching to share. In essence, your voice is unique and it offers the network a different perspective. Regardless of your level of expertise, the simple act of contribution builds reciprocal learning relationships that prove very powerful. (p. 64)

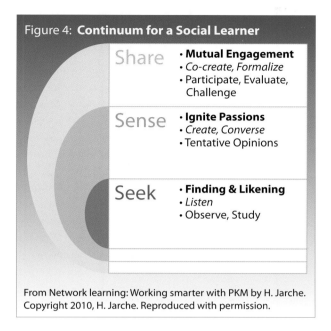

Figure 4: **Continuum for a Social Learner**

Share
- **Mutual Engagement**
- *Co-create, Formalize*
- Participate, Evaluate, Challenge

Sense
- **Ignite Passions**
- *Create, Converse*
- Tentative Opinions

Seek
- **Finding & Likening**
- *Listen*
- Observe, Study

From Network learning: Working smarter with PKM by H. Jarche. Copyright 2010, H. Jarche. Reproduced with permission.

In all of its variations, social media is an informal learning process. According to Jarche (2010), when people engage in informal learning, they are engaged in a continuous process of "seeking, sensing and sharing" (para. 12). Consider Figure 4. It illustrates how a social learner moves along the continuum of acquiring new information, making sense of that information, and sharing with a learning network. Thus the learner grows as a professional while also contributing to the greater good of the learning network.

What is involved in each step of this model?

- *Seeking* – Finding out new information and staying up to date through the connections made in personal learning networks. Information is not only "pulled" by the learner but also "pushed" out by trusted sources.

- *Sensing* – How the learner personalizes and uses the information. Reflecting and applying to practice what has been learned. Requires learning by doing for the greatest impact.

- *Sharing* – The exchange of resources, ideas, and experiences with networks and through collaboration. (Jarche, 2010, para. 12). See Online Resource 20.4: *Continuum for a social learner.*

Benefits of participation possibilities

The variety of participation possibilities results in several kinds of benefits to educator learners.

The benefits of transparency. When educators make the choice to use social media for professional learning, they become *transparent learners.* What does that mean? Educators who tweet, post links, share ideas, write, comment, and publish in open online spaces allow others to see and attempt to understand their perspectives. They assume a level of vulnerability that is not present when sharing privately or personally. They open themselves up to criticism and critique.

Constructive feedback is, of course, an essential element of the learning process. Transparent learners establish trust among colleagues and stakeholders by sharing their learning so openly and readily.

Benefit of differentiation: Anytime, anywhere. Another benefit of the use of technology and social media for professional learning endeavors is that they allow for an incredibly diversified and differentiated learning experience for all teachers and administrators. Social media technologies also embrace the notion of anytime, anywhere learning. Educators understand that teaching and the administrative life are not 9 to 5 professions. Despite their best efforts, educators still have work to do when they depart school for the day. Every educator has responsibilities outside of the school day, including commitments to families, friends, and other extracurricular endeavors.

The beauty of using social media to support professional learning is that the tools are generally accessible from any Internet-capable device. Mobile apps have made it exceedingly easy to access, reflect upon, and share information anytime, anywhere. Are you an early bird, awake in the early hours before the rest of the family? Check your Twitter streams and compose your blog drafts. Are you a night owl, preferring to read and work through the late evening hours? Perfect! Your personal learning network never sleeps. You may even find that new connections from other areas of the world can be established easily as you connect during the work hours of other time zones. You may even find that you can establish new connections in other areas of the world as you connect during the work hours of other time zones.

Benefits of becoming a connected educator. So just what are the benefits of connected learning?

Can't an individual receive equal benefits from participation in a local learning community, or through the stand-alone professional development sessions offered by a school district?

When teachers engage in professional learning, and model that process continuously to their students, they become *lead learners* in classrooms. It is powerful for adults to model and share how they themselves are engaging in professional growth as part of their commitment to life-long learning. The quality of the teacher and that teacher's commitment to professional growth has a profound impact on student achievement. See Online Resource 20.5: *Examples of researchers who have addressed the relationship between professional learning and student achievement.*

Using social media for learning can help educators address system-level goals and also support work in classrooms, on school teams, and within schools and districts.

> Technology-enhanced learning designs can improve engagement with research-based models that improve learning results. On a macro level, incorporating technology into a system of professional learning requires alignment of goals on the individual, team, and system levels, helping ensure coherence in the learning. (Armstrong, 2013, para. 6)

The International Society for Technology in Education (ISTE) has identified a number of skills and competencies that today's teachers should acquire in order to best meet the needs of modern learners. The ISTE standards "are the standards for evaluating the skills and knowledge educators need to teach, work and learn in an increasingly connected global and digital society" (ISTE, 2013, para. 1). ISTE believes "As technology integration continues to increase in our society, it is paramount that teachers possess the skills and behaviors of digital age professionals. Moving forward, teachers must become comfortable being co-learners with their students and colleagues around the world" (ISTE, 2013, para. 2).

Two of the ISTE standards, "Promote and model digital citizenship and responsibility" and "Engage in professional growth and leadership," are especially applicable to achieving system-level goals. These include performance indicators such as:

- Promote and model digital etiquette and responsible social interactions related to the use of technology and information;
- Develop and model cultural understanding and global awareness by engaging with colleagues and students of other cultures using digital age communication and collaboration tools; and
- Participate in local and global learning communities to explore creative applications of technology to improve student learning (ISTE, 2008, paras. 4–5).

Educators must consider their current level of comfort and proficiencies with digital technologies and the impact these have on their students. Are there excellent teachers out there who do not use technology in the classroom? Sure. But could those teachers be better? Could they use technology to delve deeper into learning with communities about certain content areas and pedagogies? Could the *skillful* use of technology enhance and transform classroom practices, assessments, and student learning experiences?

As Swanson (2013) states:

> If you are going to adequately prepare students for modern, technology-rich workplaces, you must be comfortable learning in online spaces yourself. Learning, making mistakes, and experimenting in the online space not only provides meaningful professional content, but also gives you the opportunity to experience successfully, technology-rich educational environments. (p. 13)

Finally, connected educators around the world have turned to their blogs and used Twitter to share how connected learning via social networks has positively affected their practice. Joan Young (2013), an elementary educator from California, recently shared a post titled *7 Ways My Classroom Is Better Because I Connect.* Because she is a connected educator, Young and her students have developed new ways of solving problems. She's learned from the collective wisdom of the members of her PLN, and she has developed a growth mindset as a result of her network interactions. Her students are able to participate in global collaborative projects such as The Global Read Aloud, and they benefit from the shared wisdom of experts from around the world. Because Young is connected, her students receive feedback on their work from an authentic audience. Lastly, Young is constantly energized by her network, and those important interactions and inspiration help her avoid teacher burnout (Young, 2013, paras. 1–10).

Connected learners not only support their own learning, but through connections they also open up a world of collaborative experiences for their students. Teachers may connect with colleagues in another country and establish a collaborative project for their student groups. Global learning initiatives such as The Global Read Aloud, Quadblogging, and Mystery Skype have been created specifically for such powerful student learning endeavors.

Steps

So, you're ready to become a connected educator? Fantastic! These steps will guide you through the process of using social media to enhance your professional learning. Remember that each educator's experience is a personal one. Do not feel pressured to follow these steps exactly — what may work well for one educator may not for another.

Step 1: Set your learning goals and develop a plan to assess the outcomes

What do you hope to accomplish through your engagement in social media? What short-term results do you hope to see? What are your long-term goals? How will you collect evidence of your learning and assess the effectiveness of your efforts?

You can use Learning Forward's *Professional learning plans: A workbook for states, districts, and schools* (Killion, 2013) to find tools and examples to use in developing professional learning plans. Consider adapting example designs to meet your exact specifications and needs or use the frameworks that your district or state provides. Be sure to plan specifically for how the use of social media tools will support your learning endeavors.

Step 2: Explore the available digital tools that will support your learning goals, choosing tools that are the best fit for you

This step can be quite an adventure as you look for digital tools that fit.

Link your plan and goals to possibilities. Educators' personal learning networks are different. That's what makes them personal! The nodes and communities that come together to build a PLN vary from individual to individual. What one person finds to be a valuable resource or community may be a waste of time for another educator.

Determine what you are looking for, in general, before examining possible social network tools. For example, are you looking to find short tidbits of information and links to resources? Delve deeply into blog readings and write reflectively? Connect with like-minded educators, or branch out to a diverse population to expand your horizons? Read and learn from the experiences of other educators? Be a member of a cohesive team of educators who regularly interact online via video conferencing and chat? Participate in a full-fledged course like a Massive Open Online Course (MOOC)?

Then, as you examine various tools, use the following criteria to determine if the tool is right for you:
1. Do I understand how this tool allows me to be part of a learning community or network?
2. Do I have time to commit to using this tool?
3. Do I have the technology necessary to access the community's resources?
4. Will the use of this tool help me achieve my learning goals?

Explore tools and their communities. Twitter, Google+, blogging communities, and Facebook are examples of social media tools for developing a personal learning network. A number of social networks with descriptions and opportunities for use for professional learning are found in Online Resource 20.6: *Social media tools commonly used to support professional learning.*

Step 3: Make an engagement plan, forge connections, build relationships, and contribute

After you have identified the social networks you will use to build your personal learning networks, personalize the experience.

Establish an educational digital presence. If you will use social media primarily to support professional learning, carefully craft your online presence so others know you are an educator interested in connected learning. Your Twitter profile description and photo, the "About Me" page on your blog, and Google+ profile should clearly identify you as an educator.

This is not to say you can't maintain your own personal Facebook profile for connecting with family and friends. Make decisions about how you will use each social media tool. For example, will you share educational resources via your personal Facebook page? Will you follow your favorite celebrities on Twitter in addition to educators who inspire you?

Some educators marry personal and professional social media accounts. Others elect to create separate Facebook profiles for personal and educational use. Others have two Google+ profiles or use Twitter for educational purposes only and save personal posts for a private Facebook page. Keep in mind that the more accounts you create, the more time you will need to invest in updating and maintaining those digital spaces. Consider also that, private accounts or not, educators should *always* be cognizant about the appropriateness and quality of the content they post via social media. Educators wish to instill in their students respect for the public medium and respect for selves. It is up to them, as adults in students' lives and digital role models, to promote respectful creation and sharing practices.

Make connections. Establishing connections within the community is a vital step in the learning process. Even in educational networks, users will want to reveal some personal as well as professional characteristics; doing so helps them form the deep, lasting connections that build trust among colleagues and deepen learning. Educators using social networks will find that over time they become familiar with the names, faces, vocations, areas of expertise, and passions of the members of these networks. Begin reaching out to others in the network to build connections. The process to do so varies slightly for each social network.

During the lurking phase, an educator wishing to become a member of a social community should examine the following:

- How do people share information? What types of information do they share?
- What can I learn by reading the tweets/posts of some key contributors?
- Do I understand how this community functions? Do I feel as though I could be comfortable contributing to, and learning in, this community?

Contribute to the online community. It is important to be a contributing member of the communities in which you engage. Sharing and replying to tweets, retweeting

tweets, posting helpful ideas and links to resources, asking questions, commenting on others' blog posts, and sharing your experiences as an educator are ways you can help your personal learning network flourish. After you have created your accounts and become a connected educator, you must continue to converse with other users, respond frequently to queries, comment on others' blog posts, and actively participate in the learning that emerges within the network. Failure to do so will certainly result in a less-than-ideal professional development experience. Remember, this is not professional learning that happens *to you.* It is professional learning *for you, by you.*

Because each platform varies slightly in its composition and the ways in which users interact with content and with one another, it's useful to share some step-by-step instructions for starting to build your personal learning network. See Online Resource 20.7: *Quick-start guides for Twitter, Google+, and Blogs.* See also Online Resource 20.8: *Additional resources to help you get started.*

Step 4: Get organized and manage your information flow

Upon embarking on the connected learning journey, educators will quickly experience what some deem information overload. Through the connections made via social media, users become inundated with resources, links to articles and blog posts, commentary, images and graphics, and other forms of media at an almost overwhelming pace. Educators who use social media for learning must develop strategies for navigating and making sense of this rapid influx of information.

Determine time commitments. Educators who are introduced to professional learning through social networks are often reticent to engage because of perceived time commitments. It's true: You need to be committed and devote time to build and maintain a social network (PLN). However, once your network has blossomed, it may actually end up saving you time. Through the connections established in your trusted network, resources and information will come to you, thus saving you time in finding them for yourself. The more effort you put into developing your PLN and making logical connections that will add to your learning, the more reward you will see in the long run.

Committing yourself to connect for learning may

mean you make some sacrifices, such as not watching as much TV or playing computer games. Simply substituting 30 minutes of blog reading or tweeting for one 30-minute sitcom viewing could have a profound impact on your professional growth!

Get organized: Tools streamline information flows. Many services help streamline and organize digital learning networks. These tools will help you engage in a *seek-sense-share* process. Educator Bryan Alexander describes this as his "daily info wrangling routine." Alexander's process includes the following steps:

Seeking. Alexander's information input comes from email, his RSS feeds, social networks such as Twitter, and print materials.

Sense-making. Alexander looks for patterns and repetitions among stories and posts he reads. Drawing upon his own experiences and contexts, he reflects both while immersed in the digital world and during offline hours.

Sharing. Alexander shares questions, comments, and reflections via comments on others' blog posts, Facebook and Google+ posts and tweets and by using social bookmarks and writing his own blog posts.

As Alexander (2013) indicates, this is a living process, and it is constantly evolving as new apps and technologies appear and disappear:

> Final thoughts: seeking, sensing, sharing, I developed this routine over nearly a decade, trying out many strategies and often discarding them. It requires some time to monitor and tweak: adding and subtracting Twitter followees, checking time spent on a resource versus rewards gained. (Alexander, para. 19)

The seek-sense-share process of managing information and using it for learning will vary by individual. It can be an overwhelming process for a newly connected educator to read, organize, synthesize, and attempt to share the steady stream of information flowing through social networks.

Consider the use of time-saving tools that help automate and synchronize information intake and output. See Online Resource 20.9: *Tools for managing social media* for social media tools designed to help the busy connected educator connect, curate, and comprehend efficiently.

Step 5: Apply learning to practice

As you spend more and more time engaged in learning within your social network, you will find countless examples of ideas and resources to use in your teaching or administrative role. It is important that you not only locate, evaluate, and curate information and resources, but also that you apply the ideas to classroom and school practice.

For example, Jane, a teacher in California, learned via her Twitter stream that other teachers have begun experimenting with a "Genius Hour" model in which they set aside an hour per week for their students to engage in passion-based project work. After reading the initial tweets and following the links shared within, she connected with Nick, a teacher in Indiana, who had successfully incorporated Genius Hour in his classroom for the past several months. He freely shared his organizational methods and resources so that Jane could apply similar strategies in her classroom. Nick also informed her that a weekly #geniushour Twitter chat was held for educators to converse about Genius Hour practices and related topics.

After gathering resources and making her plan, Jane implemented Genius Hour into her classroom for the first time. While not without its hiccups, the strategy worked in the classroom, and Jane credited her PLN for sharing the information with her. Jane took time to reflect upon the experience and posted her reflections on her blog. She tweeted the link to her blog post and asked other educators who use Genius Hour to read her thoughts and provide feedback so she might improve her implementation of the strategy. Within a few days she received constructive feedback that helped her improve the experience for all involved. She even was able to video chat with another educator via Google+ Hangouts, and they scheduled a time in the future when their classes could present the results of their Genius Hour project work with one another.

Step 6: Assess the effectiveness of the learning experience

Learning via social networks should be as results-oriented as any other professional learning experience. By collecting evidence of change and growth as a result of interactions with their personal learning networks, educators can begin to assess the effectiveness of their engagement plans and interactions with their networks. Are they receiving adequate resources, support, and feedback through their networking efforts? Are they making strides toward achieving their personal learning goals? Is there a noticeable, positive impact on educators' collegial relationships, both online and offline? Has learning through social networks helped educators make constructive changes to their classroom practice, thus resulting in enhanced learning experiences for students?

If the answers are "yes," educators should continue along the designed course, paying careful attention to the quality and breadth of the network interactions. If the answers are "no," educators should re-examine how they are engaging with their social learning networks, and what change(s) they can make to ensure the experience is more beneficial. This may mean ceasing to use a certain platform and trying an alternate service. It may mean devoting more time to establishing connections or pursuing different avenues through which to do so.

Variations

Development of a PLN and engagement in online communities is a personal journey; therefore, the tools and techniques, level of transparency, and action steps taken toward achieving learning goals will vary tremendously among individuals.

Regardless of their personal choices, connected educators will find that any one tool may cease to serve its purpose as the journey continues. Learners should constantly assess the effectiveness of their engagement plans to ensure time is spent toward achieving learning goals and that the tools help serve the tasks at hand. They may need to pursue different networks and communities to achieve desired outcomes. When learning with social media, educators must be flexible and willing to adapt often because technology changes rapidly, and tools come and go.

Challenges and how to address them

Educators who wish to include the use of social media to support professional learning may face a variety of challenges, none of which is impossible to overcome.

In some school districts, school leaders and administrators do not acknowledge the value of using social media or truly understand its transformative properties. For that reason, they may be unwilling to acknowledge teachers' efforts to learn via social media. Teachers may find that their administrators fail to provide continuing education credits, professional learning hours, etc. to help fulfill their contractual requirements.

The Connected Educator Month team makes the following recommendations for school administrators and district leaders wishing to validate online professional learning:

1. Make participation count by developing ways to assess how participation fulfills local, state, and national standards for professional learning and teacher quality; convene state, district, and school leaders, experts in job-embedded professional learning, and online social learning practitioners to discuss and further develop tools, templates, and examples, as well as to examine alignment with professional standards; develop and encourage the adoption of digital badging systems that guide and document development of professional knowledge, skills, and dispositions through online social learning and collaboration.

2. Make participation easier by creating maps and tools that organize online offerings in ways that enable educators to navigate the landscape and make learning plans appropriate to individual needs; build in time for connecting.

3. Broaden and deepen efforts by engaging a diverse group of organizations in planning and collaborating to provide connected online learning opportunities and pushing the boundaries for participation.

4. Strengthen research on the impact of online social learning and collaboration with systematic studies of the impact of online social learning and collaboration on educators' professional practices, attitudes, and effectiveness (Connected Educators, 2013).

Many schools across the country and beyond use their Internet filtering systems to block social media services and do not allow teachers or students to access these sites from school. Blocking these sites sends a message that social media are not valued in supporting the learning process. The message creates a negative impact on teachers and students who could find meaningful connections and collaborative learning opportunities online. District leaders need to familiarize themselves with the benefits of social media use while continuously working to make certain that school policies and infrastructures are in place to ensure the safety of students and teachers who use technology for learning.

Educators who use social media for professional learning may also be challenged by a fear of transparency. Educators are held to a high moral standard because of the work that they do. For that reason, many choose to maintain high levels of privacy in their personal lives. They are uncomfortable with the thought of publicly sharing information via Twitter, Facebook, or other social media networks because they fear sharing will reveal too much about their lives to the public. Educators need to use common sense about what they share, with the expectations that what they post publicly will be read by people who know them personally and professionally.

Others are fearful about contributing because they feel what they have to share won't be useful to anyone else. New Twitter users often think, "Who would want to read what I have to share?" The answer is, *everyone*. Dean Shareski, a Canadian educator and Discovery Education consultant, stresses the importance of sharing in his work, *Sharing: The Moral Imperative*. He quotes Ewan McIntosh, founder and CEO of NoTosh, an innovative educational consulting organization: "Sharing, and sharing online specifically, is not in addition to the work of being an educator. It is the work" (Shareski, 2009, 2:53–3:00). He goes on to cite the work of researcher David Wiley who asks educators to consider the fact that, if teaching is sharing, and there is no sharing, then there is no education (Shareski, 2009, 3:36–3:42)!

As with any professional learning endeavor, teachers may find it difficult to sustain focus and commitment over time. It is natural for someone who engages in social networking for learning to experience an initial thrill upon successfully connecting and collaborating for the first time. This rush will energize educators to the point where they feel almost addicted to the tools and the constant information flow. After several months of these interactions, they may find that initial excitement has waned, so it's important for educators to stay grounded and focused on their learning goals. It's natural to want to take a break from social media now and again, to focus on face-to-face interactions, book reading and reflecting, and other offline commitments. The key to making social

ONLINE RESOURCES

20.1 Anatomy of a personal learning environment (PLE)
20.2 Typical teacher networks and the networked teacher
20.3 Pyramid of engagement
20.4 Continuum for a social learner
20.5 Examples of researchers who have addressed the relationship between professional learning and student achievement
20.6 Social media tools commonly used to support professional learning
20.7 Quick-start guides for Twitter, Google+, and blogs
20.8 Additional resources to help you get started
20.9 Tools for managing social media

networking a substantial contributor to a professional growth plan is to find a healthy balance between online and offline time.

Conclusion

Educators today are asked to do more, be more, and achieve more, often with constraints on budgets and time. Educators are asked to grow professionally and continuously, all the while attempting to meet federal, state, and district mandates and support the academic, emotional and social well-being of the children in their care. The use of social media to support professional learning is a practical, time- and cost-effective practice that supports collaboration and respects the autonomy of the adult learner.

References

Alexander, B. (2013). My daily info wrangling routine [Web log post]. Available at http://bryanalexander.org/2013/12/26/my-daily-info-wrangling-routine/.

Armstrong, A. (2013, November). Leveraging technology in professional learning. *Transform Professional Learning.* Available at http://learningforward.org/publications/transform/2013/11/technology-in-professional-learning.

Bullas, J. (2012, August 2). Blogging statistics, Facts and Figures in 2012 – Infographic [Web log post]. Available at /www.jeffbullas.com/2012/08/02/blogging-statistics-facts-and-figures-in-2012-infographic/.

Connected Educators. (2013, February). *Connected Educator month report: Learning with connected and inspired educators.* Washington, DC: U.S. Department of Education. Available at http://connectededucators.org/wp-content/uploads/2013/02/Connected-Educator-Month-2012-Report.pdf.

Connected Educators. (2013). Connected educators month by the numbers. Available at http://connectededucators.org/cem-2013-by-the-numbers/.

Cormier, D. (2008, June 3). Rhizomatic education: Community as curriculum [Web log post]. Available at http://davecormier.com/edblog/2008/06/03/rhizomatic-education-community-as-curriculum/.

Couros, A. (2010). Developing personal learning networks for open and social learning. *Emerging technologies in distance education.* Edmonton, AB: AU Press.

Downes, S. (2012). *Connectivism and connective knowledge.* Available at www.downes.ca/files/Connective_Knowledge-19May2012.pdf.

Hart, J. (2010). 100 examples of use of social media for learning [Web log post]. Available at http://c4lpt.co.uk/social-learning-handbook/100-examples-of-use-of-social-media-for-learning/.

Hart, J. (2013). The workplace learning revolution. Centre for Learning & Performance Technologies [Web log post]. Available at www.c4lpt.co.uk/blog/2013/05/07/the-workplace-learning-revolution-free-mini-e-book/.

Hunt, B. (2008, November 3). Episode 5: Bonus Conversation 1: Dave Cormier. (B. Hunt, Interviewer/Producer) [Audio file]. Available at http://budtheteacher.com/lieofcommunity/?p=20.

ISTE. (2008). *ISTE Standards Teachers.* Available at www.iste.org/docs/pdfs/20-14_ISTE_Standards-T_PDF.pdf.

ISTE. (2013). Digital age teaching. Available at www.iste.org/standards/standards-for-teachers.

Jarche, H. (2010, October 22). Network learning: Working smarter with PKM [Web log post]. Available at www.jarche.com/2010/10/network-learning-working-smarter/.

Killion, J. (2013). Professional learning plans: *A workbook for states, districts, and schools.* Oxford, OH: Learning Forward. Available at http://learningforward.org/docs/default-source/commoncore/professional-learning-plans.pdf.

Lave, J. & Wenger, E. (1991). *Situated learning: Legitimate peripheral participation.* Cambridge, England: Cambridge University Press.

Learning Forward. (2011). Standards for Professional Learning: Learning Designs. Available at http://learningforward.org/standards/learning-designs.

Nussbaum-Beach, S. & Ritter Hall, L. (2012). *The connected educator: Learning and leading in a digital age.* Bloomington, IN: Solution Tree Press.

Pick, T. (2013, November 12). 103 compelling social media and marketing statistics for 2013 (and 2014). Available at www.business2community.com/social-media/103-compelling-social-media-marketing-statistics-2013-2014-0679246#!qXKoA.

Queensland Occupational Therapy Fieldwork Collaborative. (2007). The clinical educator's resource kit: Adult learning theory and principles. Available at www.qotfc.edu.au/resource/?page=65375.

Scott, M. (2013, October 12). Five surprising social media statistics for 2013. Available at http://socialmediatoday.com/docmarkting/1818611/five-surprising-social-media-statistics-2013.

Shareski, D. (2009). Sharing, a moral imperative [transcript of video]. Available at http://dotsub.com/view/027a4da1-8be2-4ea7-85e9-2e3be140db1a/viewTranscript/eng.

Siemens, G. (2003). Learning communities and learning networks [Web log post]. Available at www.elearnspace.org/blog/2003/09/30/learning-communities-and-learning-networks/.

Siemens, G. (2008). What is connectivism? Available at http://elearnspace.org/media/WhatIsConnectivism/player.html.

Siemens, G. (2012). Connectivism: A learning theory for today's learner [Web log post]. Available at www.connectivism.ca/about.html.

Smith, C. (2014, August 28). By the numbers: 85 interesting Instagram statistics. Available at http://expandedramblings.com/index.php/important-instagram-stats/#.UvO20nlf9G5.

Swanson, K. (2013). *Professional learning in the digital age: The educator's guide to user-generated learning.* Larchmont, NY: Eye on Education.

Tobin, D.R. (1998). Building your own personal learning network. Port Chester, NY: Corporate Learning Strategies. Available at www.tobincls.com/learningnetwork.htm.

Vygotsky, L. (1978). *Mind in society: The development of higher psychological processes* (14th ed.). Cambridge, MA: Harvard University Press.

Warlick, D. (2007). Personal learning networks. Available at www.slideshare.net/dwarlick/personal-learning-networks.

Wheeler, S. (2010). Anatomy of a PLE [Web log post]. Available at http://steve-wheeler.blogspot.com/2010/07/anatomy-of-ple.html.

Wheeler, S. (2013). Learning theories for the digital age. Available at www.slideshare.net/timbuckteeth/learning-theories-for-the-digital-age.

Wheeler, S. (2013, May 10). Just how far can they go? [Web log post]. Available at http://steve-wheeler.blogspot.com/2013/05/just-how-far-can-they-go.html.

Young, J. (2013). 7 ways my classroom is better because I connect [Web log post]. Available at www.edsurge.com/n/2013-09-23-7-ways-my-classroom-is-better-because-i-connect.

CHAPTER 21

Teacher-Led Conferences

TeachMeet Sydney cultivates organic professional learning in Australia.

By Matthew Esterman and Cameron Paterson

We had gathered just before the end of the Australian school year in a library on Sydney's north shore. The people in the room were all volunteering their time to come together and share ideas on what they do, or would like to do, in their classrooms to make learning as relevant, engaging, and valuable as possible for their students. We had called it *TeachMeet Xmas,* and — after a few presentations on technologies, networks, resources, connections, and possibilities, just before the first networking break — a teacher moved to the presentation space.

He stood there, delivering his presentation: Young, keen, constantly moving around the space with an energy that wafted over the crowd in the form of a stream of excited words and phrases. He was talking about things like "collaboration" and "creativity," buzzwords that seem to lose their meaning when spouted by the ubiquitous keynoters

who pervade education conferences. With him, from him, these words had real meaning, tethered to real examples and sketches of how he had tried to fuse them to his students' learning experiences. He flashed images of extended metaphors and clever visual puns, using jokes to draw his audience closer to his argument.

Then, a moment we will never forget: His movement stopped, save for the shakiness that no one had noticed during his vibrant exposition. He looked at us, a group of fellow teachers — some old, some young. Some with great levels of experience and qualifications beyond much of the global population. Some taught students who were just beginning their journey through the schooling system; others taught students nearing the end of their exhausting final year. He looked at us, with all our myriad motivations for being part of the profession. He looked at us, with our different approaches to and philosophies about education. He looked at us, and he began to cry.

This young teacher shed tears of pure appreciation for those in the room, and beyond, who had helped him through his first tumultuous year in what is often a highly demanding role. He thanked those — specifically and more generally — for their offers of advice, resources, strategies, and coping mechanisms that had carried him through and brought him successfully to the close of an academic year that he truly did not think he would survive.

That, in all its raw, affective power, is TeachMeet's real impact on the people who are involved in this thing we call "teaching," and it is the true purpose of organic professional learning communities.

Overview

Richard Elmore stated in a personal communication "Schools are hard-wired, culturally and structurally, to resist systemic practices of adult learning." Much of the dysfunction in schools is a result of the historical isolation of classrooms and schools as compartmentalized hierarchies, which establishes teaching as an individualistic rather than a collegial enterprise. Schools have been bureaucratized and organized around teacher separation rather than teacher interdependence. Many problems identified specifically with ineffective teaching practices are attributed to teacher isolation, and the isolation of cellular classrooms discourages professional interdependence. This professional isolation operates as a bulwark against school improvement.

Unfortunately, professional development — as it has been delivered — has not offered much remedy to the situation. Indeed, Patricia Graham, former dean of the Harvard Graduate School of Education (in Troen & Boles, 2003) quipped, "Professional development for teachers, as we currently define it, is foolishness" (p. 54).

The growth of unconferences, like Edcamps and TeachMeets — agile grassroots professional learning for teachers by teachers — is a direct response to teacher isolation, an over-centralized school system, and unsatisfactory professional development.

The term *unconference* has been applied to a wide range of gatherings that avoid high registration fees, vendors, and top-down organization. An unconference is a democratically organized, user-generated, participant-driven professional learning gathering. Unconferences often use variations of the Open Space Technology format developed by Harrison Owen in the 1980s (see Online Resource 21.1: *What is open space technology?*).

There are multiple models of unconferences, both for educators and for other professions. And although there is no one right way to run an unconference, the Edcamp model is proving particularly powerful and far-reaching in North America and internationally, and the TeachMeet style of unconferencing, which began in the UK and is popular in Australia, is experiencing similar success (see Online Resource 21.2: *Edcamps*). The difference between Teach-Meets and Edcamps is simply in the planning and execution. Both are usually free of charge and both commence with the premise that all teachers have something worth sharing. With TeachMeets there is more work done beforehand to establish a schedule, and the presentations tend to be shorter. However, the purpose of both approaches is to provide a breadth of ideas and the connections to continue learning after the unconference.

It is important to note that in all unconference formats much of the learning takes place informally. The real learning often occurs in the unpredictable conversations and connections formed in breaktimes and at the conclusion of formal presentations. As Professor Daniel Wilson at Harvard noted in a personal communication, "80% of professional learning is informal and incidental." The unconference approach appears to magnify the learning in the informal and incidental connections. A term that applies to all of these types of conferences is *teacher-led conferences*.

Education in Australia

Before learning more about TeachMeets in Australia, you might want to know more about education in Australia. Three sectors govern and manage education in Australia: government or "public" schools, Catholic systemic schools, and independent schools. Students do not pay fees at public schools. Government schools receive funding predominantly from the state governments, with some additional funding from the federal (or "Commonwealth") government. The department of education for the relevant state is in charge of all aspects of employment, finance, operations, and management. Catholic systemic schools are financed and run by the relevant Catholic diocese through a diocesan office. Catholic systemic schools are usually low-fee, funded partially by a mix of state and federal funding. Independent schools, which may be Catholic, owned not by the diocese but by a religious order (e.g. Jesuits, Brigidine sisters, etc.), often charge fees and receive some funding from the federal government.

Australian schools are diverse in terms of governance; however, all Australian schools are required to go through a process of inspection and registration (to varying degrees) and required to teach to the same academic syllabus documents provided by the State Board of Studies or equivalent. For example, every student in New South Wales, where both authors teach, is required to sit the same exam at the end of their schooling for each course that they complete, regardless of what type of school they attend.

Despite the differences that exist between schools in Australia, therefore, the onset of the Australian Curriculum (which requires all schools in Australia to follow a single set of syllabus documents K–12) provides teachers a chance to join in a truly open and vibrant teaching community.

A short history of TeachMeets

TeachMeets began in a small Scottish pub in Edinburgh in 2005. Educators who were also technology enthusiasts came together to share ideas and resources over a beer and a meal. The premise was simple: TeachMeets should be free and organized by teachers and no one person should hog the limelight. Those who attended the first TeachMeet chose when the next one would be. Soon! And, over the course of a few years, TeachMeets became a fixture at the British Educational Training and Technology (BETT) Show, and word began spreading about these teacher-driven events.

Though originally focused on "techie" ideas regarding best practice and innovative pedagogical approaches to learning with technology, the TeachMeet-style event began to spread around the United Kingdom and is now a regular fixture for many teachers, especially in densely populated areas like London. Teachers in the UK now use the TeachMeet wiki site (www.teachmeet.org.uk) to organize and promote their events. Scrolling through the upcoming events will give viewers a clear indication of just how wide-ranging and popular these events can be.

The idea of teachers meeting informally to share support, ideas, and issues is not new in Australia. However, it wasn't until 2010 that Australian teachers began

TeachMeet innovators

Several teachers from all three sectors (see Education in Australia) came together to make TeachMeet Sydney happen, in particular:
- Simon Crook (@simoncrook);
- Mick Prest (@mickprest);
- Jeanette James (@7mrsjames);
- Malyn Mawby (@malynmawby);
- Phillippa Cleaves (@pipcleaves);
- Henrietta Miller (@henriettami);
- Rolfe Kolbe (@rolfek);
- Liam Dunphy (@LiamDunphy);
- Summer Howarth (@edusum);
- Cameron Paterson;
- Matt Esterman.

Though it was not a normal TeachMeet (if there is such a thing), it made hundreds of teachers aware of the potential and power of teacher-led professional learning and resulted in the organization of additional TeachMeets in the subsequent months.

The teacher-run website at http://www.teachmeet.net is still capably run by Natasha Bryceson, a primary school teacher from Western Sydney.

TeachMeet Melbourne is led by Celia Coffa (@ccoffa) and TeachMeet Brisbane by Steve Box (@wholeboxndice).

making a concerted effort to make them happen on a regular basis. Completely unaware of each others' efforts, educators started one TeachMeet in Sydney and another in the western suburbs of Sydney. Through social media, the two groups connected and laid the foundation for the community that is now called TeachMeet Sydney. Both original TeachMeets followed the "rules" (a very fluid term) whereby the events were free, were run by teachers and for teachers, and presentations were short and to the point: either seven minutes or two minutes long. The duration of presentations maximized the number of ideas flowing at the event and led to incredibly complex discussions and debates during the breaks. This format continues to be useful as a way to keep the events running in a timely and productive manner.

TeachMeet Sydney then became a movement — not just a group — whose adherents welcomed new hosts and members all the time and sought to provide opportunities for professional learning to all teachers in Sydney. The key focus was on working out a way to cultivate events so that a teacher could attend one or two TeachMeets per school year without having to drive more than 30 minutes from work or home. And so there were events like "TeachMeet North" and "TeachMeet West" and "TeachMeet Hills," each with its own theme or central concept that pulled the presentations into orbit. Most events were held at schools, but some were held in pubs, libraries, or other locations conducive to the purposes of TeachMeet.

From the very beginning the first few organizers (a list that was growing rapidly) sought to make these events more than just isolated experiences. By using a wiki (http://tmsydney.wikispaces.com), a Facebook group (www.facebook.com/groups/tfcsydney), Twitter hashtag **#tmsydney** and whatever other methods of communication were available, teachers from all three sectors (Government, Catholic and Independent; see Education in Australia p. 306) and all levels of education were soon hearing about TeachMeets and keeping in touch without needing to give away personal contact information. TeachMeets in Australia are also supported by a teacher-run website www.teachmeet.net where any host can have an event posted.

"TeachEats" often follow TeachMeets so that those who don't have to rush home are able to share their passion over a meal. For a burgeoning number of teachers, TeachMeet has become exactly what they had been waiting for: an opportunity to share, to network, and to be inspired but without advertising and egos that can dominate other forms of professional learning.

With the help of dozens of teachers, this momentum culminated — but didn't end — with a massive TeachMeet held at the Australian Technology Park in Eveleigh, in the southern part of Sydney. It was a rainy Friday night, with the wind howling outside and participants streaming in soaked and smiling. With over 300 participants, and more tapping into the live stream and/or Twitter conversation, the event surpassed the expectation of the organizers. The outcome was a TeachMeet that had a parallel hybridity: Some participants moved to rooms with typical TeachMeet-style presentations and networking opportunities, and others moved to a bar area for conversations nudged along by a moderator. Still

others escaped to a room with a useful table where they could share iPad apps in a fast and furious "App Swap" session. Attendees voted with their feet; if they didn't like what they were hearing, they moved.

As of the writing of this chapter, it is estimated that over 3000 individual attendees have participated in TeachMeets in and around Sydney. These include preservice teachers, new graduates, experienced teachers, and veterans. Journalists and education officers from institutions around Sydney have attended to share in the experience. TeachMeets seem to fulfill a need that many teachers have to be heard and to develop support mechanisms beyond their own staffrooms.

TeachMeet groups have been cultivated in other cities and in the virtual sphere. TeachMeet Melbourne and TeachMeet Brisbane are just two of the many TeachMeet groups that have established themselves as new players in Australia. Some TeachMeets have even been hosted online and showed the power of inter-sector collaboration

Happily, hosts and participants in TeachMeets are not answerable to anyone but those who actively participate in the process, a group that is constantly evolving and morphing, with porous "membership" and a highly valuable purpose.

Rationale

The most powerful attraction of the unconference model is the fact that attendance is voluntary; teachers choose to attend in their own time. Robert J. Marzano and John Kendall's (2007) work on engaging the self-system demonstrates that the key determinant of whether people attend to a given type of knowledge is whether they consider the knowledge important. Self-system thinking controls whether or not someone engages in a new task and the level of motivation allotted to the task if they do choose to engage. For many teachers, an unconference is their first experience of taking ownership of their own professional learning. This is a radically different proposition from school or system-mandated professional development. An unconference creates space for peer-to peer-learning and collaboration, and it can be a powerful incubator for creative, innovative ideas.

Another advantage of unconferences is their agility. Unconferences are based on network thinking. There is enormous pressure on teachers to figure out how to take advantage of the opportunities and challenges of an increasingly networked world, where information flows faster and many aspects of the world are flatter. Brafman and Beckstrom (2006) contrast traditional "spider" organizations, which have a rigid hierarchy and top-down leadership, and revolutionary "starfish" organizations, which depend on the power of peer-to-peer relationships. Their metaphor is that if you chop off a spider's leg, the spider will be permanently crippled. However, if you chop off a starfish's leg the starfish will grow another one and the old leg can grow into a completely new starfish. The starfish is a powerful metaphor for the leaderless nature of unconferences and the education unconference network makes an interesting comparison to the Napster and Kazaa challenge to the traditional music industry.

Other reasons that can compel educators toward teacher-led conferences include the need for truly conscious professional learning, interest in social media and connectivity, and need for an innovative environment.

Professional learning

Paolo Freire (1993) was critical of the way that education makes people fit in instead of questioning the world. In his writing about the banking notion of consciousness, he described the teacher-student relationship:

> This relationship involves a narrating Subject (the teacher) and patient, listening objects (the students). . . . Education is suffering from narration sickness. The teacher talks about reality as if it were motionless, static, compartmentalized, and predictable. Or else he expounds on a topic completely alien to the existential experience of the students. (p. 52)

This dismal picture of learning describes professional development. If we are honest, most professional development is the same, the carwash model, "spray and pray." Corcoran (1995) presaged Graham's retort when he wrote: "Conventional forms of professional development are virtually a waste of time" (pp. 3–4). Even education conferences, which are supposed to be meetings of people who "confer" about a topic, increasingly center on expensive high-powered keynote presentations with little thought to a two-way conversation. This is why the concept of unconferences appeals to those who want to learn rather than just listen.

For too long, teachers have been categorized as the passive receivers of professional development rather than active members of the professional learning process. This is ironic considering the push for learner-centered teaching in most current educational publications. Even a lecture or workshop led by a fellow teacher may be sponsored by an organization with an agenda. More often than not, these experiences are also commercial in nature — teachers are on the receiving end of advertising, as if they aren't able to do their work without the same level of branding as a Formula One driver.

Although formalized and traditional professional development still has its place, it is clear that in a world where school gates, national borders, and time zones are being bulldozed by asynchronous social media and other technologies, teachers need to be more active in their own professional growth. If individuals aren't in charge of their own learning, who is?

The fear that teachers will just be talking to themselves about trivia or engaging in mindless group think during teacher-led conferences is unfounded. According to Chatfield (2012), ". . . when everyone is able not only to have their opinion, but to broadcast it, merely individual claims of expertise can start looking flimsy to the point of translucency" (pp. 73–74). The opposite is likely to occur because teachers can see through fabrications about life in the classroom.

Forming professional learning networks (PLNs) or professional learning communities (PLCs), communities of practice or communities of learners, are alternative expressions of socio-cultural learning theories or the idea that people learn best when connected and supported by other learners with shared goals. (See "Chapter 20: Social Media" and "Chapter 18: Professional Learning Communities" in this book.) Educators can each grow individually and at different rates, but TeachMeets demonstrate that teachers of all levels of experience and all types of teaching style and personality are able to come together to learn about and reflect on Common Core purposes.

The distributed leadership and shared responsibility of TeachMeets also encourage a heightened sense of ownership and purpose for those involved. Teachers who attend an event for the first time are more likely to present at an event in the future, or even host one themselves. Rather than have a rigid set of rules that all TeachMeets must abide by, the community shares common values about the free, open, and active role that a TeachMeet should play in professional learning. Ideally, each community would feel both connected and supported within itself but also connected to other communities around the world as part of a larger, global community of educators.

Truly social media

The world is changing, and professional learning needs to change accordingly. Whitby (2013) declared, "The lag time between having a thought and sharing it has decreased dramatically" (p. 6). Lag time between thoughts and communication of them has decreased because of social media and informal networks. Designers of professional learning need to pay attention to social media.

Twitter and Facebook have played a crucial role in maintaining the momentum of TeachMeet Sydney. Social media have informed educators about TeachMeet opportunities and allowed the community to not only be more interactive and connected after the TeachMeets but also to explore possibilities beyond the community. Synchronous Twitter feeds, usually unmoderated, and organic and based on how many attendees are willing to tweet their way through a TeachMeet, allow educators and others from around the world to participate in the discussion by offering thoughts, posing questions and sharing resources. Asynchronous discussions inevitably follow, with teachers wanting to remain connected so as to avoid losing motivation to try new ideas in the classroom.

George Seimens, writer and researcher on learning, networks, technology, and communities in digital environments at Athabasca University in Alberta, Canada, who espouses connectivism, recognizes the beautiful chaos that is often part and parcel of TeachMeets. A TeachMeet requires some structure and organization, but there is little control over how people will react, communicate, participate and remain connected after the event. The TeachMeet itself is often just a catalyst that requires participation as fuel. As a result of participation in a TeachMeet, educators are more connected than before: to ideas, to people and to a greater knowledge of themselves as teachers. In fact, some might argue that it is a responsibility of teachers today to establish and maintain meaningful connections with each other in order to bring relevant learning experiences into their classrooms.

Siemens argues that the pipe is more important than the message, and learning is all about the connections. Whatever you think of his radical argument, it does provide a useful means of discussing the networked nature of learning today. For more on connectivism, start with "Chapter 20: Social Media" in this book or go to www.elearnspace.org/Articles/connectivism.htm.

TeachMeets recognize current realities in society and education: That knowledge is both infinite and transitory. That several aspects of being a great teacher need cultivation and support. That systems and institutions that have existed for more than 30 years often aren't structured to handle the challenges of rapid and myriad change. That school gates no longer dictate where your colleagues are located. That sharing, as we are taught in kindergarten, is a central aspect of society and can be done quickly and easily. That organizations that are truly organic, flexible, and based on the needs of the members, will be as or more valuable than traditional top-down organizations. And, perhaps most importantly, teachers themselves can and should lead the conversation around our practice. Social media allow teachers to develop their collective ideas quickly and easily and address the realities of today.

Innovation time

Growing numbers of schools are creating some sort of innovation time for teachers. *Google's 20% Time* is well known. Google allows employees to spend one day a week focusing on projects based on the personal interest of each employee. Interestingly, 50% of Google's products, including Gmail, have originated from the 20% time allocation for employees' personal interest projects. The concept of a *FedEx Day* began at the Australian software company Atlassian. These are one-day bursts of autonomy which allow staff to work on anything they want, provided they show what they create to their colleagues 24 hours later. Individuals choose with whom they want to work, the task, and the final product/idea, all acceptable as long as they deliver a product or idea by the deadline. These days are called FedEx Days because participants have to deliver something overnight, although FedEx is now requesting that their brand no longer be used in association with this type of learning.

Other workplaces have adapted to their own context by introducing the concept of *Genius Hour* — a sliver of 60 minutes of autonomy each week for staff to work on new ideas or master new skills. Many schools have adapted the concept of innovation time to provide passion-based learning opportunities for teachers.

TeachMeets are part of this constellation of practices regarding innovative and effective professional learning.

Steps

The strategy of TeachMeets

Similar to an effective network using instructional rounds, TeachMeet networks can spread good practice beyond the walls and timings of the classroom to promote excellence and innovation in a supportive and sustainable manner. City, Elmore, Fiarman and Teitel (2011) argue in *Instructional Rounds in Education* that, "There are pockets of excellence throughout our schools and school systems. The students lucky enough to be in the pockets are well prepared to make a good life for themselves and for their community. The students left out of the pockets are not so fortunate. . . " (p. 2). (See "Chapter 13: Instructional Rounds" in this book.)

It is difficult to offer a concrete strategy for success when it comes to informal and organic communities like TeachMeets. By their very nature, these types of organizations grow from within. They are organic.

However, some strategy is needed, and those involved in the process of keeping momentum going must take the initiative and make decisions. However, they do not need to establish traditions or norms that restrict creative experimentation with structure, theme, style or approach.

Their strategy should be fairly simple:

- Provide a platform for professional dialogue and reflection that leads to action.
- Provide a virtual space for organization and communication of events.
- Be adamant about the free, open, and noncommercial nature of TeachMeets.
- Manage the event well so that all speakers have their chance to present and so that participants are nourished, connected, and inspired.
- Make sure attendees spend nothing more than their time on the event. No entry fees should be charged.

Consider these ideas if you have the burning desire to establish more than single, isolated events and you wish to

help foster a community of practice:

- Be inclusive of new members to the community and empower them to host an event.
- Establish social media networks that do not require approval from authorities or governing bodies.
- Make sure that all members of the community are advertising events as often as possible.
- If needed, perhaps establish a core group who can be the key support for new hosts and organizers and who is generous with time and ideas so that momentum is sustained. For TeachMeet Sydney, the core group arranged some semi-regular meetings (over coffee, drinks, or meals) to discuss strategy or possibilities.

Teacher-led conferences can be as informal as the host desires, so there is no 'minimum' organization really. In Sydney, a few TeachMeets have been as simple as "Meet at pub X on this day at this time. See you there."

However, teachers often prefer a little information about what they will be doing in their increasingly precious time. That is why teacher-led conferences need some kind of structure (though it can easily be changed as circumstances require).

Step 1: Decide on a location

The location often dictates the nature of the teacher-led conference. The more formal the location, the more structured and restricted the conference might be. For example, there is a massive logistical and philosophical difference between holding a teacher-led conference in a room at a local pub and holding one in a university lecture theatre. TeachMeet Sydney has done both, and its organizers have learned that the location does change the nature of the event. Both formal and informal settings have their uses, but organizers need to be aware of how structure and style may shift according to location.

Schools. Schools are a natural fit for many educators who want to host a teacher-led conference. Schools are likely to have space and facilities for presenting ideas and cultivating discussion. Teacher-led conferences held at schools require collaboration between the host and teachers from other schools in order for the event to be successful. Schools need to reserve facilities and decide how their own staff and students might be involved. Most educators welcome visitors to their schools, but some may feel some trepidation.

Visiting educators usually find it exciting (and perhaps a bit daunting) to be in another school, but they usually relish seeing new ideas — even the architecture of another school.

Universities. Similar to schools, universities have natural meeting spaces for teacher-led conferences. Universities may be eager to host teacher-led conferences, especially if they understand how their own faculty, pre-service, and graduate teachers can be involved (see Variations, p. 314).

Pubs. There is something very appealing about holding professional learning events in a place close to a bar. When the environment is friendly and informal, those who are struggling through traffic don't have to feel awkward walking in late. Those who want a drink or some food can get up during a presentation that they consider less relevant to them. TeachMeets began in a Scottish pub and have continued in the colonies. Most pubs and other establishments with a space or room available to be booked are happy to support (often for free) a teacher-led conference full of thirsty teachers unlikely to start anything more than a verbal conflict.

In 2012, a "TeachMeet Unplugged" event was held with no formal registration process or speaker list, just a group of keen educators who met at a pub on a quiet Saturday afternoon to share ideas and have practice-based conversations.

Libraries. Most school and public libraries, in terms of design and purpose, are conducive to hosting a TeachMeet. The furniture is often less formal than a classroom or at least a change of scenery for teachers. Teacher Librarians are an essential part of a school community. Some of the most active members of the TeachMeet Sydney community are Teacher Librarians and, in fact, one leading innovator held a TeachMeet-style series of quick presentations at the end of a professional development day for the New South Wales (NSW) Teacher Librarian Association.

A particularly spectacular partnership between teachers and a library occurred on May 1, 2013, when the State Library of NSW facilitated a TeachMeet called "Learning Revolution" (a pun on the fact that it was International Labour Day) that had a distinct history flavour. Many teachers who attended were attracted by the location — in terms of its historical and architectural depth — and also its geographical location in the centre of the city of Sydney.

Museums and other institutions. Any institution that courts the public is likely to be happy to support a teacher-led conference. This is especially prominent in places that hope

students will visit regularly. The general public is sometimes unaware of or apathetic about museums, despite concerted efforts at such places as the Australian Museum or the Power-House Museum (both in Sydney) to attract new and renewed visitors with outstanding temporary exhibitions. These places often have an education officer or department who is keen to have passionate teachers present in their buildings

Staff meetings. Some teachers are so enthusiastic about teacher-led conferences (often suggesting that their passion has been "reignited" or that "I never knew there were teachers like this out there") that they want to transplant this concept into staff professional learning at their schools. Teachers can learn much about their on-site colleagues, people whom they have simply been too busy to ask about on a day-to-day basis. Although teacher-led conferences as staff meetings are valuable, the ideas generated there may go no further than the walls of a particular school, unless teachers use Twitter to share them. Staff meeting conferences may foster a sense of excitement about attending a broader teacher-led conference in the future.

A symbiosis. Sometimes teacher-led conferences can be held in conjunction with other events. TeachMeets have a proud tradition of latching on to other events and forming a somewhat subversive element to promote teacher dialogue. This is what occurred at the Australian Technology Park at Eveleigh in March 2012. The event that occurred during the day had the entire complex hired all night but their sessions finished at 3 p.m. Therefore, the TeachMeet crew for the event were able to move in and use the amazing facilities for a professional learning experience like nothing most attendees had seen before.

Similarly, TeachMeets can crop up in unexpected places. While travelling in the United Kingdom on a study tour in June 2012 (investigating how the UK veterans sustained their TeachMeets), one of the authors of this chapter was lucky enough to meet some other TeachMeet participants who attended the Education Festival at Wellington College, just outside London, England. A small band of teachers met in a room not being used by vendors, presenters, or workshops and spent the hour talking about TeachMeets. Though they had only met through Twitter, taught in quite different education systems, had varying levels of expertise and approaches to learning, the group had a shared sense of community and connection. That is one of the key goals of TeachMeets.

Step 2: Decide on a suitable date

You won't please everyone. Don't try to. What you may like to do is think about which day of the week will influence the type of audience you get. Friday nights are great if you intend for people to stay around for a meal and a drink together after the event, but this may not suit people with families. Often a venue will determine the date, but try to find out from potential presenters and attendees what date would suit them best.

Step 3: Decide style, structure, and focus

Teacher-led conferences can vary in style and structure. Depending on anticipated attendance, the organizers may want to be certain that sufficient rooms are available to allow more presenters and more attendees to have parallel sessions. Perhaps there will be more networking time. Perhaps there will be icebreaker activities so that teachers meet someone and begin to build their PLN (Professional Learning Network) immediately. Some TeachMeets begin with a video to set the scene (think a Ken Robinson TED talk or an inspirational video relating to the kids educators teach today). There are really no parameters that make one TeachMeet work better than another, but hosts have found that two of the key factors are: (a) the variety of presentations and (b) the time available for connecting.

Try not to overload your participants with a solid two- or three-hour block of presentations. Break up sessions with interactive time, especially with refreshments. Plan the conference to include as many interesting and engaging aspects as you think appropriate e.g. music, introductory video, icebreaker games, changing furniture arrangement.

There doesn't need to be a focus if you don't want one. However, TeachMeet hosts have found that teachers appreciate knowing generally what kinds of presentations they can attend, and this can be most easily massaged into place with a core focus. Some TeachMeets focus on skills, for example collaboration, and encourage presenters to share ideas for student collaboration within and beyond the classroom. Some TeachMeets are focused on content areas, though it is an aim of TeachMeets to eliminate the silo effect based on subject areas that pervades most schools and systems.

Step 4: Build a Wikispace for organizing the event

A virtual space is useful for advertising and organization. If presenters, attendees and potential attendees have a single site or space they can go to easily, they are more likely to participate, and the host(s) will find life a lot easier. TeachMeet Sydney uses a Wikispaces site, managed by several teachers and open for editing to anyone who wants to host. Key information, including presenter names and titles of their talks, are useful to help potential attendees create their own schedules of participation. For examples of the structure and style of wiki pages used by TeachMeet Sydney, visit the Wikispace site (http://tmsydney.wikispaces.com) or the TeachMeet Australia site (www.teachmeet.net.), which is used to connect people to their local network.

Step 5: Use a simple tool for attendees' registration

A registration function is also useful: Use a Google Form or similar tool for each individual event so that there is a spreadsheet of attendees and presenters available for potential attendees and presenters (as well as the organizers) to view. By having a hyperlink that attendees can follow to register on a simple form, hosts are more likely to get teachers who are not confident with technology as well as the keen ones who are adept.

The link to the spreadsheet of the Google Form allows attendees to connect before, during, and after the TeachMeet.

Step 6: Begin to gather potential presenters and attendees

Tap teachers on the shoulders and suggest that they share ideas. Remind presenters that they have a limited time to present. A host who has never held an event like this might want to start with the 7/2 model: Presenters can nominate themselves to speak for two minutes or seven minutes. If they want to use a PowerPoint or other presentation display, they can do so but must remain within time. One way to ensure this is to require presenters of seven minutes to time their presentation in PechaKucha format — 20 slides, each timed to transition after 20 seconds (total six minutes and 40 seconds).

Many commercial groups will offer to present. Hosts should reject and, in some cases, actively repel these offers as they do not fit the philosophy of a teacher-led conference.

Step 7: Spread the word via social media and traditional media

A growing number of teachers are using social media such as Twitter, Facebook, and LinkedIn to keep connected, but many are not. Therefore, hosts must seek to communicate and advertise using both traditional and social media. Pamphlets, posters, and letters are useful to drop onto the desks of teachers who might be interested, but worth of mouth is golden. Make sure you ask attendees to register a friend too, as friends will value the advice of their colleagues over a generic email drop.

Step 8: Manage presenters

Make sure you estimate the number of presentations that can occur in the time allowed. Do not go over this number as you will reduce the networking/break time, which is essential to a successful teacher-led conference. Also, add at least one minute to each presentation to cater for technical issues and impromptu interruptions.

Have a timer or countdown clock somewhere that both presenters and attendees can see (e.g. a second projector screen) so that all participants know when the next presentation should begin.

Keep in touch with presenters, especially for larger teacher-led conferences. Confirm availability and make sure that they know the rules (if there are any). A quick email sent a few days before the event will be sufficient.

Step 9: Establish a hashtag on Twitter for backchannel conversations

Encourage a few participants who have Twitter accounts to act as live "scribes" for the event using a set hashtag. For example, the TeachMeet Sydney community has adopted #tmsydney as the generic hashtag for all TeachMeet Sydney events, but other Australian cities and regions have their own hashtags such as #tmmelb (TeachMeet Melbourne), #tmbyron (TeachMeet Byron Bay) or even more specific #tmwr2012 (for the record-breaking TeachMeet World Record in March 2012).

By encouraging teachers to use Twitter, you will advertise the event before, during, and after. You will also engage teachers who are not able to attend and be able to share the learning with colleagues around the world.

Step 10: Enjoy your teacher-led conference

The host should usually say something at the beginning to welcome people, thank them for attending, and give them some house rules. After the final presentation, the host should remind participants to connect with each other via social media and whatever virtual space has been created. Encourage those who write blogs or are connected to other networks to spread the word about their experiences and write about them for professional journals. Also, this is a good time to challenge someone in the audience to host the next teacher-led conference!

Variations

One variation in the teacher-led conference extends convening power to several relevant sponsors and participants.

Universities. Starting in 2012, several Sydney universities planned and/or hosted TeachMeets that focused on connecting "preservice" teachers (those yet to graduate from university with teaching degrees) to the ideas and people who currently inhabit schools. The form and structure, as with every TeachMeet, has varied somewhat.

For example, the first university-based TeachMeet that was hosted by the Education Department at the Australian Catholic University, Strathfield Campus, intentionally organized the presentations to be a mixture of current practitioners and pre-service teachers. Leanne Cameron (@leannecameron) and Miriam Tanti (@miriamtanti) led the organization and opened the door for other universities to join the community. An immediate outcome was that teachers were stunned by the talent of those about to join the ranks. An equally important result was that pre-service teachers could see that teaching is not a tired, antiquated, and static profession but rather brimming with creativity, innovation, and deep love of learning.

StudentMeet. A variant that has excited regular TeachMeet participants is the *student*-led TeachMeet. These may feature student feedback sessions, during which students of various ages offer thoughts and ideas on education to a room full of teachers. When students do this in a forum where ideas rule and egos do not, there is a good chance that some of the ideas will stick in the minds of those present.

At a StudentMeet at Shore School in North Sydney in

2012, students as young as 10 were able to articulate the ways they learn best and what makes school exciting for them. These were not artificial speeches about why the world should save an endangered species for science credit; these were real and meaningful pitches to teachers as to why they need to change (though the endangered species analogy may be more relevant than at first glance.)

In a world where content is now available even faster than the touch of a button, students need to be more involved in the process of education rather than just passive recipients of it. StudentMeets will challenge and confuse many practitioners, but they will lead to excellent discussions about the most effective ways to help students learn. (Read about a StudentMeet in Online Resource 21.3: *Come to a StudentMeet.*)

Online TeachMeets. Though not appealing to 'purist' TeachMeet supporters, the idea of an online TeachMeet (hosted like an interactive webinar) certainly appeals to those who wish they could attend and watch the presentations live, but cannot due so because of location or other factors.

Several successful online TeachMeets have been hosted using software such as Adobe Connect, Google Hangout and Skype. These online TeachMeets play an important role for what Australians call "regional" and "remote" teachers: Those who live a certain distance away from metropolitan areas. There are many teachers living in regional or remote towns who rely on events like TeachMeets for regular interaction with their peers. It is important to acknowledge this reality and facilitate, where possible, some kind of online broadcast either through the already mentioned tools or something like www.ustream.com or YouTube. Educators can engage in Online TeachMeets without a budget because all the tools mentioned in this section are free and require only an online subscription or registration to begin using them.

Challenges and how to address them

Advertising. Commercial advertising is not a part of teacher-led conferences such as TeachMeets. From time to time, well-meaning (and sometimes not so well-meaning) education product companies or representatives of companies will offer to speak at a TeachMeet, set up a table of products, or give food and refreshments in exchange for some time on stage. This may sound as if the company is doing you a favor.

It is not. You do not need cash to run a successful TeachMeet. People become uncomfortable at TeachMeets when someone, even a teacher, appears to be advertising a commercial product. Some TeachMeets encourage participants to raise their hands to object or vote with their feet if a presentation sounds like advertising.

Since the core business of TeachMeets is to share good practice, companies have no part to play in them. Since companies can advertise through other types of conferences and workshops, TeachMeet coordinators believe companies have no part to play in TeachMeets.

Having said all that, if a group or institution supports the TeachMeet and the host wishes to recognize that with a quick acknowledgement, no one really minds. It's only when ideas are commercialized by vendors that teachers object; when commercialisms are featured on posters or in brochures at tables that have been bought — or, more insidiously, in ads that masquerade as seven-minute presentations.

Sponsorship. Does sponsorship change the nature of a teacher-led conference? If so, avoid it at all costs. Some TeachMeets in Sydney have gained local sponsorship in the form of refreshments or gifts for presenters. The host will determine the most appropriate level of sponsorship for an event, but the vast majority of TeachMeets functions on a small contribution from the facility where the event is held. Most facilities seem happy enough to offer enough funds for tea, coffee, biscuits, and other snacks.

There is much debate occurring in the United Kingdom as to whether sponsorship has changed the nature of TeachMeets so far that some events should no longer be called TeachMeets. This is a debate that needs to occur within the community as it evolves.

An order to the chaos. As informal as some TeachMeets are, there needs to be some kind of structure and purpose to the event. Teachers need to know that their time is not being wasted and that the event is far more than a social event. Advertising early and often and supporting a clear structure and focus of presentations will ensure that participants know what they are getting and can feel confident that their time is well spent.

Formal recognition. While TeachMeet communities and the events they host are not intended to fit any kind of state-based or national expectations or standards, many hosts have found that many teachers who attend appreciate knowing that the time they spend at a TeachMeet is recognized in some way. Very few teachers have required formal recognition from organizers, but the registration of attendance (and a sign-on sheet at the TeachMeet) can act as evidence or documentation of participation for professional learning portfolios or programs.

Conclusion

The two key premises of teacher-led conferences are that teachers should be trusted to lead their own learning and they should be expected to learn and share their learning in public. Hiebert and Stigler expressed it like this:

> When teachers recognize that knowledge for improvement is something they can generate, rather than something that must be handed to them by so-called experts, they are on a new professional trajectory. They are on the way to building a true profession of teaching, a profession in which members take responsibility for steady and lasting improvement. They are building a new culture of teaching. (2004, p. 15)

Teacher-led conferences are not social get-togethers. They are possibilities for deep learning connections, where teachers are encouraged to exchange ideas and construct knowledge and learn, not from but with each other. Perhaps it is time to stop thinking of unconferences as innovative and to start expecting this approach to professional learning as the norm. Paolo Freire is said to have remarked that if the structure doesn't allow for dialogue, then the structure should be changed. So true.

In Sydney, Australia, it is clear that, while the teacher-led conference is growing in popularity and value to educators there is a need for more than just a series of events relating to professional learning. TeachMeet Sydney has been established and continues to grow because it is a community, not just an event. It is a community that is sustained from within by the educators involved, beyond location, sector, age of students, or level of experience. Participation is voluntary but volunteers must participate in order to gain the most out of the learning experience, contrary to most professional learning that occurs passively, within frameworks and standards dictated by institutions and groups that are by their nature more rigid, formal, and less inclusive of learners.

ONLINE RESOURCES

21.1 What is open space technology?
21.2 Edcamps
21.3 Come to a StudentMeet

Recall the passion and purpose with which the teacher in the opening scenario spoke. His listeners learned from him but, more importantly, they remembered why they were educators. The future of adult and student learning rests on the connections educators make with each other. Teacher-led conferences are one way to help educators make connections of the mind and heart on behalf of students all over the world.

References

Brafman, O. & Beckstrom, R.A. (2006). *The starfish and the spider: The unstoppable power of leaderless organizations.* New York, NY: Penguin Group.

Chatfield, T. (2012). *How to thrive in the Digital Age.* London, England: Pan Macmillan.

City, E.A., Elmore, R.F., Fiarman, S.E. & Teitel, L. (2011). *Instructional rounds in education: A network approach to improving teaching and learning.* Cambridge, MA: Harvard University Press.

Corcoran, T. (1995, June). *Helping teachers teach well: Transforming professional development.* Philadelphia, PA: Consortium for Policy Research in Education.

Hiebert, J. & Stigler, J.W. (2004). A world of difference: Classrooms abroad provide lesson teaching math and science. *JSD, 25*(4), 10–15.

Marzano, R.J. & Kendall, J.S. (2007). *The new taxonomy of educational objectives.* Thousand Oaks, CA: Corwin Press.

Troen, V. & Boles, K.C. (2003). *Who's teaching your children? Why the teacher crisis is worse than you think and what can be done about it.* New Haven, CT: Yale University Press.

Whitby, G. (2013). *Educating Gen Wi-Fi: How we can make schools relevant for 21st-century learners.* Sydney, NSW: HarperCollinsPublishers.

CHAPTER 22

Videos

Advances in technology make video a tool that can bridge gaps in teaching contexts to increase teacher capacity and lift student achievement.

By Pat Wasley

I put real effort into my teaching and believed that I was pretty good, but my analysis was based on my own reflection and the little bit of feedback I got from my principal. Like almost everyone, I had good days and bad days. I talked with colleagues about what I was doing and what they were doing, but I couldn't always tell from their descriptions of their work whether the strategies they were using were effective. As in many schools, kids evaluated their teachers and shared their perceptions with their favorite teachers, but again, I wasn't always sure that kids' perceptions were accurate — whether they were based on quality of teaching skill or on personal relationships.

Because I could not compare my own efforts or even examine a good record of my teaching after having taught a lesson, I found myself *hoping* that I *was* good and, because I wasn't completely sure, reticent to have others come into my classroom. When I talked about my teaching with other teachers, I could control the narrative — ensuring my own sense of efficacy. But by practicing that way, I missed many opportunities to really *learn*. I gradually became afraid that, if others did come in, I might discover that, despite all my effort, I wasn't very effective. This syndrome is not something teachers surface to conscious thinking very often. Rather it is a worry, a fear. Over the years, many teachers have admitted to feeling just this way, too. The worst part about this syndrome is that fear of learning the truth closes classroom doors more tightly, reinforces the conditions of isolation, and further complicates every teacher's efforts to grow.

* * *

A number of years ago, I taught a group of 6th graders who were attending Bank Street's School for Children in New York City. They provided me with the very best example of how children learn in a variety of ways than I have ever encountered. Our class activity makes a very clear case for why teachers need a broad repertoire of approaches to teach important skills and strategies: We decided to do a project that required the students tutor younger students in reading at a neighboring high-needs school. As we were thinking about what we would need to do to prepare, one of the boys said, "We can't teach reading! Our teachers go to college and some of them go to graduate school to learn to teach reading. We don't know enough!" One of the girls, Elissa, said quickly, "Of course we know how to teach reading. We all learned didn't we?" and she moved to the board. "Emily, how did you learn to read?"

"My grandmother read me the same story every day when I came home from preschool. Every day. I'd snuggle up in her lap and then one day, like a miracle, I don't know what happened, but the words began to make sense to me, and all of a sudden I could read!"

Back to Elissa, "Jon, how did you learn to read?"

"My mom and dad made us do flash cards at the dinner table every day. C-A-T. CAT. We had to sound the words out, say the letters, and then read the word. It was sooooo boring — but it worked."

Emily: "LaTasha, how did you learn to read?"

"Me and Michaela learned to read from Carmine. She'd lay on the floor with us and show us the pictures and then show us the words. We'd go back and forth between the pictures and the words and eventually, it made sense."

Around the room of 25 children Emily went, and she wrote the method that worked for each child on the board until there were 14 different strategies.

I suggested that we agree on the three most helpful strategies, learn them well as a group, and then use those strategies to help the younger students. Emily looked at me like I'd lost my mind. "Did you say that we want to make sure that we help all the kids learn to read? If we leave any of these strategies out, someone won't learn!"

Out of the mouths of babes. Emily had identified key criteria in raising the achievement level of all of our students: teachers need a wide range of strategies in their pockets for helping young people develop the skills and abilities they need.

* * *

I watched an experienced teacher who had been trained to use the Socratic method of instruction. (A video example of this method can be seen at www.teachingchannel.org:

Socratic Seminar: Supporting Claims and Counter-claims. (Also see "Chapter 10: Dialogue" in this book.) She was excited about the training she had received; she was eager to try the method of evidence-based, Socratic dialogue in her classroom. She told her students that they would each have different roles in the discussion and that they would need to provide evidence from the text for any point they wished to make. She gave them a brief on the Socratic method: Socrates educated his students by asking provocative questions that didn't have simple answers and then he required his students to assemble the evidence for their answers. She moved the desks into a circle in order to facilitate student-to-student discussion. She reviewed the roles and, after students had a chance to read the text she had assigned previously, they began.

Unbeknownst to herself, the teacher reverted to her most common method of conducting a discussion: Elissa, what does the author say about X? Tom, what did you think when you read Y? Back and forth she went from one student, to teacher, to the next student, back to teacher, while asking questions that were less than robust. At the end of the lesson, she asked her students how they liked the new method and they told her that they liked sitting in a circle. That was, in fact, the only change she actually made. Because she was working alone and had no feedback, she had no idea that she had not demonstrated the full potential of the new method. This happens for many of us; learning new approaches requires practice, feedback and more practice. Had she had a video of herself, she may quickly have seen what the students saw: all she had really changed was the room arrangement. She had lapsed into her own most comfortable teaching method (Wasley, Hampel, & Clark, 1996).

It is also true that she was a novice at this new technique. While she was a very experienced and good teacher, she reverted to novice status when trying the Socratic seminar method. Few of us are generally facile at using new approaches the first time we try them, regardless of our years of general experience. Effectiveness usually comes with practice. So, having a feedback tool can prevent teachers from missing the full benefit of trying something new. This aspect of learning is precisely why focusing on improving teacher education is insufficient to growing teacher accomplishment. Teachers must continue to grow throughout their careers.

And if that is the case, each year they should be focused on learning something new. The act of learning something new throws them back into the role of a novice.

Overview

The three vignettes that introduced this chapter point to the need for video for professional learning. The use of video is important to teacher growth for three important reasons.

Video and teacher growth

Video provides teachers with images of the various ways in which teaching can be approached. This helps teachers to understand that there is more than one way to teach almost everything. This is key to enabling teachers to serve the diverse needs of the students who arrive in their classrooms. Because students' learning needs and preferences differ so significantly, approaching a class with a broad number of approaches for teaching and learning the subject matter makes it more likely that a teacher will be able to support the diverse learning needs of her students.

In recent years, a number of organizations have developed important video libraries, and all are being used around the country:

- **The Annenberg Institute for School Reform** developed an early series on learning math and science that is still widely in use.
- The **School Improvement Network** developed a video library after its founder, a teacher who had previously worked in film, discovered that video taping other teachers really helped him to learn his craft. Other teachers asked to see what he was taping and he discovered that teachers loved seeing how others were approaching various dimensions of subject matter and learning. (Personal Communication with SIN, 2013)
- **Teachscape** has created a video library that enables teachers to see and distinguish the characteristics of high quality teaching.
- **Teach for America** developed a terrific website that provides beginning teachers with images of what a novice, an experienced and a master teacher look like using their teacher quality rubric.
- **Teachers Media** has a wonderful collection of BBC

quality 30-minute films that show what's happening in classrooms all over Britain.
- The **Washington DC Public Schools** has captured an excellent collection of videos of their teachers.
- The **Academy of Urban School Leadership,** Chicago's School Turnaround organization, has 60+ videos of their signature strategies.
- The **University of Michigan's Teaching Works** houses the **Measures of Effective Teaching Extension Library.**
- The **National Board for Professional Teaching Standards** has an extensive library of videos and reflective essays that teachers have submitted as part of their board certification process collected in **Atlas.**
- **Teaching Channel** has a video library of 800+ videos that are designed to enable teachers to see a strategy or a method in action.

Teachers all over the U.S. and in 30 other countries are sending messages every day about how they are using the strategies they have adapted from these videos. It is clear that teachers are searching for great ideas about how to teach in order to learn new approaches.

In the best of these videos, teachers can see what other teachers do, what moves they make, how they explain their approach, and what kids are doing in response. Video can be surrounded by materials like lesson plans, research articles that review the efficacy of the approach, samples of student work, and teacher reflections, so that a teacher viewing the video can get a much more detailed understanding of what was involved for the teacher to engage the way he/she did.

Watching video of other teachers' classrooms is unquestionably helpful, but it is also essential that teachers video themselves in action, upload these videos, and share them with colleagues or a coach for feedback. Being able to analyze their own performance to better understand how they are implementing strategies and approaches and to see how their students are reacting is crucial to implementing a teaching strategy effectively.

It is also true that video provides an evidence base for professional learning. Everything a teacher does on video is captured and can be revisited and looked at through a variety of lenses. Having a visual record allows teachers to learn from an actual record of practice, rather than from their memory or their personal narrative of what happened.

Rationale

For the last 30 years, educators have been trying to find effective ways to lift student achievement in the United States. They have created multiple sets of standards — the latest, the Common Core State Standards (Common Core) and the Next Generation Science Standards (Next Generation) — have real promise. States have invested billions of dollars in new standardized assessments and again, those currently under construction by the two assessment consortia, the Partnership for Assessment of Readiness for College and Careers (PARCC) and the Smarter Balanced Assessment Consortium, are aimed at lifting student achievement to new levels.

The problem is that there has not been an aligned and consequential investment in professional learning to match investments made in standards and assessment. In order to enable *teachers* to learn the skills they need to prepare *students* for more rigorous standards and more complex and demanding assessments, teachers need new forms of professional learning.

Currently, the dialogue in the U.S. about teachers is both too narrow and not thorough enough. Policymakers complain about two major issues: (1) that colleges of education are not adequately preparing teachers and (2) that administrators need to force out bad teachers, which has led to state-by-state activity to build more rigorous teacher evaluation systems. In general it is true that most colleges of education need to re-examine their programs to suit the current context in which teachers are teaching. While administrators do want to make sure that poor teachers move on, and educators do want more effective evaluation systems, these measures alone are not going to ensure that the remaining teacher work force has the skills needed to lift student performance.

What is missing from the national debate is the realization that for over 100 years, the U.S. has persisted in putting teachers into a teaching culture that curbs their growth, which consequently curbs the achievement of students. This problematic working context is not the fault of teachers, of course, but nonetheless has a large influence on their long-term efficacy.

The third and necessary arm to the American strategy to lift student achievement is providing teachers with scalable, online, asynchronous tools to help them meet the challenges required of them. This important third investment, along with the current development of standards and assessments, will provide teachers with the timely and modern tools they need to analyze their own classroom performances using an evidence base.

How the context prevents teacher growth

The conditions within which teachers work, characterized by isolation and limited feedback, have remained constant for teachers for well over 100 years. (Lortie, 1975; Goodlad,1990; Wasley,1994). Since the days of one-room schoolhouses, teachers teach alone in classrooms with little opportunity to watch colleagues in action or get feedback on their own work beyond their annual evaluations. Only recently, with the steady development of new technologies, have teachers had the chance to both watch others teach and to see themselves in action in the classroom. Unfortunately, only a small percentage of the 3 million public school teachers in the U.S. have had access and encouragement to use these new tools.

There are real consequences resulting from these working conditions that influence student achievement. The first consequence is that many teachers teach the way they were taught as children simply because their own schooling is their greatest apprenticeship in learning how teaching is done. Mirroring how one was taught as a child generally means merely *telling* children what they need to know — one of the least effective methods for ensuring that students retain what they've learned or can use that knowledge in new contexts.

The second effect of continuous isolation is that many teachers develop a very narrow repertoire of practices that they use with kids over and over again; as a result, school quickly becomes routinized for youngsters. Most people recognize this phenomenon because the routines used today were present when they went to school. In English: Read a book or poem or essay; have a discussion; write a paper. In math: Review homework from the night before; learn the next steps in the algorithm and start on the homework for the next day; take a test. In science: Do the vocabulary; read the chapter; answer the questions; do a lab that the teacher has demonstrated with a predictable outcome; take a test.

Such routines exist in every discipline. Kids figure out the routines and then they learn how to put forth the minimum amount of effort. Many of today's adults did that too: They divided up the homework or they got one person to summarize the book or they divided up the vocabulary words. Kids today get bored when school is predictably routine — just as today's adults did — and that affects the effort they make to learn (Clark & Wasley, 1999).

The third critical consequence of so little feedback and so little exposure to other ways to teach is that many teachers find themselves living in a variation of the imposter syndrome. The *imposter syndrome* is a psychological condition in which accomplished people cannot recognize their success and, therefore, believe themselves to be frauds. As the opening scenario shows, educators stricken with this syndrome don't know for sure if they are executing as well as they might; as a result, they become more afraid of external feedback and reticent to have outsiders come into their classrooms.

These problematic conditions work against providing teachers with what they need to help students learn. Adults who have their own children know that kids have different passions, strengths, weaknesses, and dispositions. The kids in classrooms are just the same! Some love school; some hate it. Some understand math easily and to others it looks like ancient Egyptian script. If teachers use a narrow band of approaches, they can't possibly unlock the learning of all the kids in their rooms. When they use a narrow band of repetitive strategies, kids figure out the strategies and cut to minimal performance. Most adults did just that when they were kids! If educational leaders don't provide teachers with the tools they need to grow and develop in evidence-based, rigorous ways, they will not be able to fulfill the promise of the new standards.

The third leg needed to lift student achievement

Fortunately, it is true that there are great teachers who use a wide range of approaches with kids. These teachers do understand that learning is related to freshness, to piqued interest — their own and their students' — when they try something new. These teachers develop a more sophisticated repertoire that keeps students awake and present to learning. These teachers exist all across the country in all kinds of schools, but they are the exception, rather than the rule. For example, an English teacher moves from reading a poem,

having a discussion and writing a paper to a Socratic Seminar. After she finishes that unit, she asks students to create an evidence-based essay and uses creative circles to enable them to get feedback on their work before they submit it (Wasley, Hampel & Clark, 1997). (See Sarah Wessling's feedback to students via podcasting at www.teachingchannel.org: *Podcasting to Personalize Feedback*.) When teachers use this kind of pedagogical repertoire, their students learn more approaches for processing and interacting with material. They literally can't cut to minimal performance because the approaches the teachers are presenting are new. These are the teachers whose classrooms are always in demand by parents and students alike. Kids describe classes that look like this as engaging and compelling:

"Like in electronics," said Sean. "First we learned about charges by making a bunch of them. Then we did airwaves. Then we worked on understanding transmitters. It's sort of one step at a time, but everything builds." Students are able to see the connection between techniques, approaches and the curriculum and it makes sense to them. (Wasley, Hampel, & Clark, 1997, p. 46)

And the teachers who do this are some of the most enthusiastic about their craft; they see more to learn and learning new things is engaging for them, interesting and challenging. More teachers would strive to teach like this if they understood its importance in relation to student learning. And, if they had the support to develop in a robust learning context themselves.

So, there is convincing evidence that suggests that teachers are restricted in their capacity to help students succeed by: (1) the isolation in which they work; (2) the limited feedback they receive; and (3) the lack of regular collaboration. These key questions logically follow:

- How do educational leaders change these detrimental conditions that have prevented teachers from growing?
- How do educational leaders provide teachers with the opportunity to grow the approaches and methods they use with students to meet the demands of all of our state standards and to lift student achievement?
- How do educational leaders make a consequential investment in teacher development so that teachers can work with the new standards and the new assessments to grow student success?

Video: A growing solution

The answer to these questions is to create a profession that is continuously growth-oriented and that provides teachers with the resources they need to guide student learning to successful accomplishment of the standards. Video is not a new tool, but it has advanced to a place where it can reliably and affordably provide teachers with an evidence-based resource to foster their own growth.

Over the last 20 years a number of initiatives have engaged teachers in collaborative groups to learn from their own videos and those of others. Various university researchers and practicing teachers have been working together to video teacher performance because videos provide an actual evidence-based record. The first ground-breaking study was done by Magdalene Lampert and Deborah Ball (1998) when they videotaped every minute of a year in their classrooms with multiple cameras. In addition, they scanned every assignment and all student work into a database so that anyone interested could study what was actually happening with the students' learning in relationship to the teacher's actions. That database became an incredible tool for investigating both teaching and student learning and was used with both beginning and experienced teachers, as well as in teacher preparation programs across the country.

A growing set of organizations emphasizes the use of video in teacher development. The National Board for Professional Teaching Standards (NBPTS), founded in 1987, requires that teachers submit a video of their work in order to demonstrate their actual skills and abilities inside the classroom. The board also requires an essay to accompany the video to ensure that teachers are reflecting on what they see. The Education Teacher Professional Assessment (EdTPA), developed by Stanford's Center for the Assessment of Learning and Equity (SCALE), is now required in 24 states as an entry requirement for beginning teachers. EdTPA requires that student teachers videotape themselves in action and reflect on what they see with an eye toward better understanding what kids are doing in reaction to their efforts.

In a study funded by the Bill and Melinda Gates Foundation (2013) entitled *Ensuring Fair and Reliable Measures of Effective Teaching: Culminating Findings from The MET Project's Three-Year Study,* researchers were looking for the most consistent measures of teacher effectiveness and included video as one of those measures. The teachers who participated in the study found that they grew enormously from examining their own teaching by watching video clips of themselves in action (Bill & Melinda Gates Foundation, 2013). This study has influenced new state teacher evaluation systems, and many systems now require video as a data source.

The new technologies embedded in iPads, tablets and smart phones have made the use of video much easier. Teachers no longer need expensive and cumbersome equipment to do a reasonable job filming, and several new tools facilitate the analysis of the captured video. Companies like Torsh, Edthena, and Teaching Channel provide video upload tools that are faster and more easily shareable so that teachers can get feedback from colleagues, principals, and coaches.

Steps: The Learning from Video Process

From Teaching Channel, here is a simple learning cycle for working with video, which greatly enhances a teacher's ability to develop a more sophisticated repertoire. The cycle requires that teachers move through several steps; the order of steps is variable, depending on what the teacher is working on. In this chapter a step is added for reflection. Teachers who experience this cycle note that it is nearly impossible to not learn a great deal about whatever skill they are trying to master if they move through all the steps. If the goal is to have teachers develop a broad repertoire of approaches for working with kids so that more kids succeed, then the design principles for the process suggest that teachers need to:

- **Collaborate** in order to gain a broader perspective:
- **Learn** by trying things in their own classrooms with their own students;
- **Get feedback** on their fledgling efforts;
- **Practice frequently** in order to move from a novice to an expert.

While video provides the content or the focus for working together, videos of great teaching practice and videos of one's self in action using web-based collaboration tools enable teachers to change the stale working conditions that have prevented teacher growth. They can move into a contemporary learning context to learn in Professional Learning Communities (PLCs). See "Chapter 18:

Figure 1: **The Learning from Video Process**

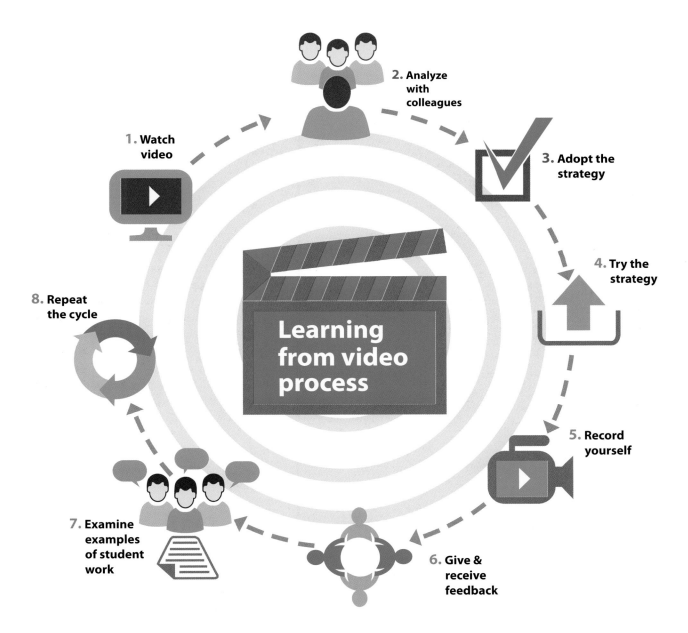

Source: The Teaching Channel. Used with permission.

Professional Learning Communities" in this book.

After identifying a likely strategy for use with students — perhaps through watching several videotapes of promising strategies — teachers follow the basic eight steps of The Learning from Video Process and add a step allowing them to "Reflect" within PLCs. The cycle occurs on an interactive, asynchronous collaboration platform that allows teachers to form study groups across their districts or states and work with colleagues throughout the cycle.

Step 1: Watch videos

Watch, annotate, and analyze one or more videos to understand an instructional strategy or the method, preferably in the company of PLC members. If teachers watch and analyze a video in collaborative groups, discuss the embedded strategies, outline the teacher moves and examine what is happening for kids, they will find that their understanding of what they see expands.

Step 2: Adapt the strategy

Members of the PLC adapt the strategy for their own classrooms, grade levels, and subject areas in order to try it themselves in their own context.

Step 3: Try the strategy

Teachers try the strategy in their classes and videotape their fledgling attempts.

Step 4: Review your videotape

Teachers review their own videos, select an interesting (NOT a perfect) short clip, and send them to members of their PLCs.

Step 5: Watch others' videotapes

PLC members watch the clips from their colleagues.

Step 6: Receive and provide feedback

PLC members receive feedback from their colleagues and provide feedback to them.

Step 7: Upload student work.

Each member of the PLC uploads samples of student work from their classes and the PLC as a whole analyzes the samples collaboratively. This is important because teachers see different things in student work. PLC members help each other link teacher actions to student outcomes and focus on what needs to be tweaked in order to get the kind of performances they want from kids.

Step 8: Reflect

The PLC as a whole reflects on the strategy itself; members address what is required to make sure that this particular approach is effective in helping teachers improve their work with students.

Step 9: Repeat.

Repeat the cycle to build greater expertise.

Teachers are more likely to use new strategies with greater facility and in ways that are more likely to support student learning if they engage in this kind of practical, but evidence-based approach to professional learning. Deep, transformative, thoughtful learning only occurs when teachers have the opportunity to engage with a strategy, figure it out in their own context, and determine how it works with their students (Donovan, Bransford, & Pelligrino, 1999).

Learning Forward has created the Standards for Professional Learning which support this approach: "The professional learning that occurs when these standards are fully implemented enrolls educators as active partners in determining the content of their learning, how their learning occurs, and how they evaluate its effectiveness."

The good news is that this form of learning can be delivered online and asynchronously so that already busy teachers can fit this kind of collaborative work into their day according to their learning preferences and the demands on their time. In addition, they can work in cross-district and even cross-state collaborative groups — something teachers find compelling.

As an example, Sarah Wessling, the 2010 Teacher of the Year from Johnston, Iowa, is using The Video Learning Cycle on Teaching Channel's Teams platform to asynchronously lead a group of teachers from all over the United States. They are in a boot camp to help one other understand the shifts embedded in the Common Core. For the first time, teachers can mobilize one other to continue to grow and learn so that each year of their professional lives they become stronger at supporting student learning — just as a learning profession ought to do.

Variations

Learning from video can take place in a number of ways:

Learning in video groups

Considerable research has been done on video clubs in the last 20 years (Borko et al., 2006; Erickson, 1982; Sherin 2004; 2007; Sherin & Sherin, 2007; Sherin et al., 2010). In video clubs, teachers form collaborative working groups to look at pieces of video they shoot in their own classrooms to help each other interpret, strengthen, and celebrate the work going on inside their classes. The benefits of this work are that teachers begin to actually *see* what they are doing from a variety of perspectives, because no two teachers see exactly the same thing in a video. Further, they develop stronger analytical skills and receive more feedback than they normally would by engaging their colleagues.

Hilda Borko and her colleagues paralleled and incorporated the findings of Miriam Sherin (2004) and others on video clubs in their 2006 study. After two years of working closely with a group of teachers in video clubs, teachers reported they found value in having their classrooms recorded and discussed with teacher colleagues — as a way out of the isolation syndrome many teachers feel and as a way toward a greater understanding of where student and teacher learning coincide:

> When I watched other teachers' videos, it wasn't critiquing. It was seeing what they do in their classroom and realizing that a lot of what's going on in their classroom is what's happening in mine. Or this person really does a great job at opening a lesson. Maybe I could try something they're doing (Linda, final Year 2 interview, June 2005). (Borko, Jacobs, Eiteljorg, & Pittman, 2006, p. 434)

In a recent study conducted by Nicole Kersting, Karen Givvin, Francisco Sotelo, and James Stigler (2010), teachers who analyzed their teaching through video became much more analytical of their work and as a result, have greater success with students. These teachers noticed the connection between the tasks and student work. They noticed their own role and could see if they were dominating or if students have a chance to explore the material in fruitful ways. They could compare their actual teaching to their theories of learning to

see if their own methods match what they believe to be true.

This burgeoning body of research helps educators understand that through video teachers begin, literally, to *see* their teaching in a new light.

There are a number of activities that video groups can undertake:

Analyzing the strategy for its basis in learning. Watch the *Tootie Ta!* videotape (www.learningchannel.com). On initial viewing, the strategy this teacher uses just seems cute and sweet. When teachers working in small groups discuss the videotape to determine what dimensions of learning that this film addresses, they come up with the following list, which is academically substantial: ability to listen for directions; ability to follow directions; ability to do more than one activity at a time — indicating motor skill coordination; engaging; engaging in movement between seat-time activities, and the list goes on. Knowing the educational value of the strategy is the first step that leads teachers to want to use it to expand their own repertoire.

Translating pedagogical strategies to different grade levels and subject matters. Most educators believe that they learn best from teachers at their own grade level, from teachers who teach students just like theirs, and from those who teach their discipline. This isn't necessarily so, and such a stance substantially limits how and from whom teachers can learn. Many pedagogical strategies are translatable to other disciplines and grade levels. Teachers can analyze videos to identify the pedagogical strategies in use and then think about how they would need to change or adapt the strategy for their own grade level, discipline and student community.

Consider the following example: Leah Alcala is a middle school teacher in Berkeley, California. In *My Favorite No* (www.learningchannel.com), Leah uses a "checking for understanding" strategy with her students that has literally changed the way she teaches because she works with her students to determine what they understand and what they still find confusing. She did that by asking them to do a math problem at the beginning of class on a note card. She collected these and could tell in a few minutes who got the problem right and who was still confused. She looked for her favorite no — or her favorite wrong answer. She picked an answer that demonstrated that some of the students got some part of the equation right but had some part wrong. She then had the whole class work through what was right in the equation and what was wrong. They concluded with the steps needed to turn the "Favorite No" into a correct answer. This all takes a matter of minutes but gives Ms. Alcala a lot of information about how thoroughly her students understand the mathematical procedures she wants them to learn.

Benetrice Lucas, a first grade teacher at the Academy for Urban School Leadership (AUSL) in Chicago, thought the strategy looked promising and described how she worked to translate the strategy. When she first described the approach to her students, they were very excited that the teacher would be looking for mistakes, and — because first graders really want to please their teacher — every one of them made mistakes on the math problem she gave them. So, she changed the name to "My Favorite Fix" and told the students to do everything they could to get the answer right. With that adjustment, she had a workable strategy for first graders. She believes that the strategy works just as well in the 1st grade as it does in 6th grade. Believing that instructional strategies *can* travel from one grade level or subject to another, teachers find that they can open a big door to a large pool of strategies and a more sophisticated repertoire.

Using protocols. Many teachers use protocols and work in Critical Friends Groups (CFGs). A new version of a book that explicates the use of protocols gives a number of different procedures for engaging in collaborative review of each other's work on line entitled, *Going Online with Protocols: New Tools for Teaching and Learning* (McDonald, Zydney, Dichter, & McDonald, 2012; see "Chapter 17: Online Protocols" in this book). A video of teachers at a New Tech Network High School, Tech Valley in Rensselaer, New York, demonstrates how they help each other get better by using a protocol when they meet on a regular basis in a CFG (see "Chapter 7: Critical Friends Groups" in this book). They use protocols to make it easier for teachers to both give and receive feedback.

What viewers see in this video is a group of teachers who know that their work is good, but could be better. They review a project, the assignment, and the way it is chunked out; they examine samples of student's work and then make recommendations to strengthen everything. The teacher whose work is reviewed feels empowered by the feedback as she knows that the next time she tries this project, she will be able to help students achieve at a higher level. Other participants have learned something to apply in their own

classrooms. While this is a face-to-face group, the same work can be done online.

Reaching common ground on high quality teaching. Most states and districts are building new teacher evaluation systems based on rubrics that identify the characteristics of high quality teaching. Most of the video providers in the US have aligned their films to these rubrics. Principals can use the films to discuss with their teachers whether their strategies match their definition of some aspect of the rubric. Take, for example, the requirement for teachers to enable students to understand how words change. Sarah Wessling's activity *Vocabulary Paint Chips* (www.teachingchannel.org) which meets CCSS ELA-Literacy standard L.11–12.4B, is a good video to use for that discussion. Principals can ask teachers in small groups to talk about whether this activity is likely to enable students to build the skills they need to meet the standards. Teachers can critique the moves Sarah makes, suggest other approaches for meeting this standard, or rank the approaches for rigor, so that they create a range of activities for meeting the requirements of the Charlotte Danielson rubric (1996) and the Common Core State Standards. Building a shared understanding of what constitutes great teaching is key to enabling teachers to be successful with the new evaluation systems and to meeting the demands of the Common Core.

Analyzing user-generated classroom videos

Analyzing one's own video takes some practice. Initially, teachers who watch themselves on video notice all the superfluous things: "I look so . . ." It takes time to enable teachers to back up from their initial feelings in order to become analysts of their own work. Video provides teachers with an actual record of what *really* happened so that they and their colleagues can see how students were reacting, see the actual directions teachers give, and watch how teachers guide and support individual learning. There are a number of ways teachers can help others by sharing clips taped in their own classrooms.

Coaching new teachers. The Academy for School Leadership (AUSL) in Chicago runs a residency program that annually prepares some 160 teachers to work in low-performing schools. Mentor teachers videotape their mentees in action, annotate the films and send them to their mentees who are working on Teaching Channel's Teams platform. The mentees watch the clip, do their own annotations, offering insights about what they were attempting to do and noticing what was actually happening. Together mentors and mentees determine what the mentees might do differently to boost their success in working with young people.

Subject matter groups. Teachers can form subject matter groups to study videos of their teaching. For example, a group of math teachers from Kentucky has been working on Teaching Channel's Teams platform with math consultant Ann Shannon to understand the new requirements of the Common Core around ratio and proportion. First, the group considered the mathematics. Working online asynchronously, they began to compare how they would approach the material. Together they determined that teaching ratios and proportions required a different approach than those they had used in their classrooms.

The next step was to construct a new approach, try it in their own classrooms, videotape themselves in action, and send these video clips to each other for comment. Because they were teaching the new content for the first time, they discovered what needed to be clearer, tasks that needed more scaffolding, and directions that made better sense. They coached themselves to a higher level of performance and simultaneously improved their capacity to enable students to master the standards.

Analyzing video with the principal. Another use for video is for teachers and their principals to explore whether they are seeing the same thing when evaluating a teacher's performance. When a principal and a teacher watch the same videotape of a class — either recorded by the principal or provided by the teacher — they do not need to rely on memory or interpretation.

To help their members calibrate their understanding of quality teaching, the National Association for Secondary School Principals uses Teaching Channel video with principals around the country. Further, Mel Riddle, NASSP, offers principals a whole playlist of films that they can use with their teachers in order to move whole school faculties forward toward a common understanding of high-quality instruction.

Standards-focused collaborative improvement groups. Every year, NBC hosts *Education Nation*. Its purpose is to inform the American public on numerous dimensions of the educational landscape. As part of this effort, news anchor

Brian Williams and his team host a teacher Town Hall where some 300 teachers talk about the issues dominating their aim to improve student achievement. In 2013, NBC invited a number of partner organizations to create a Common Core Institute for the 300 teachers who attended the teacher Town Hall. The purpose was to engage teachers in learning how to implement the Common Core State Standards that have been adopted in 48 states.

In three rooms at different grade levels and subject matters, nine teachers taught short lessons to their colleagues and then opened up the discussion about the lessons. Lively discussions ensued as participating teachers asked questions, made recommendations and shared their own experiences. These teachers were invited to continue to work on the implementation of the Common Core on a Teaching Channel Teams site sponsored by the Helmsley Charitable Trust. Out of the 300 teachers, some 160 continued to work collaboratively over the next month to videotape themselves and to submit those videos for collaborative analysis. Those who participated found the collaborative analysis of videos insightful and productive and made the commitment to collaborate with Student Achievement Partners' Teaching Fellows, who facilitated the group work.

Challenges and how to address them

As with any new approach, there are challenges. Learning to create a good quality videotape for collaborative analysis takes some doing. Teaching Channel has developed a set of "How to" Videos to help with getting the sound and equipment right.

Permission forms are an absolute necessity. Teachers must have signed permission forms from every one of their students in order to use the videos with other teachers. Getting these forms back can be a real challenge. Districts need to develop a standard form that goes out at the beginning of the year. When there are students whose parents are concerned for their privacy, teachers must figure out how to video without making the student leave the room or feel in any way that she or he has done anything problematic.

Finding an appropriate clip from a video of a full class period can be time consuming. Even though there are easy-to-use tools for editing, do not spend an inordinate amount of time editing and re-editing. Rather, find an interesting segment, a clip where students are interacting or when the teacher and student are interacting, so that colleagues can discuss what is happening. Educators do not have tos see the whole lesson to learn; they can learn plenty from a carefully selected clip.

Both giving and receiving feedback can be quite challenging. Some people love to give advice. Others can only see things that seem wrong and don't have the skill to couch their feedback in terms that make it easy to hear. Groups providing feedback on videos need good ground rules or norms and skilled facilitators to keep moving in a productive direction.

Conclusion

Educators have created good standards. Good assessments that match the standards are under development. If the problem of lifting student achievement rests on the shoulders of teachers, then education leaders must provide them with the tools they need to build a more sophisticated repertoire of teaching and learning strategies — so that they can help every child in their classroom to achieve at higher levels. To do that successfully, teachers need to see how many ways they can approach a particular standard. They need to be able to collaborate with their colleagues to engage in analysis about teaching and learning. They need to be able to video themselves in action for group analysis. They need a good deal more growth-oriented feedback so that they can see the discrepancies between what they believe they are doing and what they are actually doing. They need to work in groups to examine the student work that comes out of their attempts to try new strategies so that they are *always* linking student learning to teacher learning.

Right now, for example, the U.S. spends $14.9 billion a year in professional development opportunities for teachers. Much of that is descriptive: Teachers sit in an auditorium or a hotel conference room and listen to good and well-intentioned educators tell them about promising strategies. Then, teachers are sent on their ways and asked to try the strategy in their own classrooms, that is, to translate the practice from the demonstration to their kids and contexts, and perfect their ability to use that strategy without the benefit of any feedback.

ONLINE RESOURCES

22.1   The learning from video process

Imagine trying to learn tennis without trying it. Without having partners and coaches who can help you see what you are doing wrong or incompletely or well! Educators have known for years that this is an ineffective way to support teacher growth. So why do we persist?

Policymakers need to make one more major investment — in teacher learning. Teachers need tools to be successful and they need to be able to align their growth with goals for increased student achievement. If educational leaders make it possible for teachers to move beyond the working conditions that have, for over a century, prevented their growth, teachers will finally be able to demonstrate that they do have the capacity to elevate student learning and to reduce the achievement gap. Teachers want kids to succeed, and if teachers are finally given the tools they need, students might just prove to become what people dream of for their children.

References

Bill & Melinda Gates Foundation. (2013). *Ensuring fair and reliable measures of effective teaching: Culminating findings from the MET project's three-year study.* Available at www.metproject.org/downloads/MET_Ensuring_Fair_and_Reliable_Measures_Practitioner_Brief.pdf.

Borko, H., Jacobs, J., Eiteljorg, E., & Pittman, M.E. (2006). *Video as a tool for fostering productive discussions in mathematics professional development.* Available at https://cset.stanford.edu/sites/default/files/files/documents/publications/Borko-VideoAsToolFosteringProductiveDiscussionsInMathematicsProfessionalDevelopment.pdf.

Clark, R.W. & Wasley, P.A. (1999, April). *Renewing schools and smarter kids: Promises for democracy.* Phi Delta Kappan, 80(8), 590–596.

Danielson, C. (1996). *Enhancing professional practice: A framework for teaching.* Alexandria, VA: ASCD.

Donovan, S., Bransford, J., & Pellegrino, J. (Eds.). (1999). *How people learn: Bridging research and practice.* Washington, DC: National Academy Press.

Education Teacher Professional Assessment. (n.d.). Frequently asked questions. Available at http://edtpa.aacte.org/faq.

Erickson, F. (1982, November). Audiovisual records as a primary data source. *Sociological Methods & Research, 11*(2), 213–232.

Goodlad, J. (1990). *Teachers for our nation's schools.* San Francisco, CA: Jossey-Bass.

Kersting, N.B., Givvin, K.B., Sotelo, F.L. & Stigler, J.W. (2010). Teachers' analyses of classroom video predict student learning of mathematics: Further explorations of a novel measure of teacher knowledge. *Journal of Teacher Education, 61*(1–2), 172–181.

Lampert, M. & Ball, D.L. (1998). *Teaching, multimedia, and mathematics.* New York, NY: Teachers College Press.

Learning Forward. (2011). *Standards for Professional Learning.* Oxford, OH: Author.

Lortie, D. (1975). *Schoolteacher: A sociological study.* Chicago, IL: University of Chicago Press.

McDonald, J., Zydney, J.M., Dichter, A., & McDonald, E.C. (2012). *Going online with protocols: New tools for teaching and learning.* New York, NY: Teachers College Press.

Sherin, M.G. (2004). New perspectives on the role of video in teacher education. In J. Brophy (Ed.), *Using video in teacher education* (pp. 1–27). New York, NY: Elsevier Science.

Sherin, M.G. (2007). The development of teachers' professional vision in video clubs. In R. Goldman, R. Pea, B. Barron, & S. J. Derry (Eds.), *Video research in the learning sciences* (pp. 383–395). Mahwah, NJ: Erlbaum.

Sherin, M.G. & Sherin, B.L. (2007). Research on how people learn with and from video. In S. Derry (Ed.), *Guidelines for video research in education: Recommendations from an expert panel* (pp. 47–58). Chicago, IL: Data Research and Development Center. Available at http://drdc.uchicago.edu/what/video-research-guidelines.pdf.

Sherin, M.G., Jacobs, V.R., & Philipp, R.A. (2010). *Mathematics teacher noticing: Seeing through teachers' eyes.* New York, NY: Routledge.

Wasley, P. (1994). *Stirring the chalkdust: Tales of teachers changing classroom practice.* New York, NY: Teachers College Press.

Wasley, P., Hampel, R., & Clark, R. (1996, April). *Collaborative inquiry: A method for the reform-minded.* Paper presented at the annual meeting of the American Educational Research Association, New York, NY.

Wasley, P., Hampel, R., & Clark, R. (1997). *Kids and school reform.* San Francisco, CA: Jossey-Bass.

CHAPTER 23

Visual Dialogue

Visual dialogue is a process of integrating words, images, and shapes into a single unit for communication.

By Suzanne Bailey and Lois Brown Easton

Carolina Blair is making last-minute changes to the room. She wants to get it just right for the delegates to City School District's Planning Retreat. She nudges a chair here, straightens a piece of butcher paper there, and watches for the arrival of the first participants. She's a little nervous. Her district has never tried visual dialogue before. But she has participated in the process and is sure the result will be a very different kind of meeting.

Late every spring (after state test scores have been released), the district engages in strategic planning, re-visiting the current plan, revising it if necessary, and setting the direction for the district for the next three years. This process has not, however, been very satisfactory. Even the president of the school board has acknowledged that it has felt like just going through a process. A few district-level staff members and a board member have advocated for more meaningful planning.

Carolina worked with a design team made up of several colleagues from the district office and two principals, authorized by the superintendent. The superintendent was a little reluctant to try this process rather than traditional strategic planning, so Carolina and the design team feel pressured to have a successful outcome.

Carolina and her design team know that the district needs to take a serious look at what is expected of educators. Test scores, for one thing, have not gone up.

The design team carefully considered the meeting's purpose: to have an accurate and current picture of the district and a plan to move the district forward so that all students learn at a high level. The secondary goal is to have retreat participants engage in real learning — professional learning — together.

The team considered who should be invited, and the group is intentionally mixed: every building principal;

enough teachers to make up a third of the group; the superintendent; the area superintendents; the district's curriculum, professional development, and special programs coordinators; the board of education members; the head of the union; the head of the parent-teacher association; active parents; active community members. In retrospect, Carolina wishes they had invited students.

As the participants enter the room, Carolina greets them and hands each one a nametag with a number representing a subgroup printed on it. She and her design team decided previously to break people into subgroups of five or six each, and they were unwilling to leave the mix of the groups to chance, fearing that people who were used to working together would join the same subgroup.

Carolina welcomes the group and says with a bright smile, "This will be a meeting like no other. The process we're going to follow today will yield incredible results, results that reveal our common agenda. You are all needed to create the current reality of the district. You'll learn from each other and from other groups. Then, this afternoon, you'll create a picture of the district you want. At the end of the day, we will leave the room with a common vision and a set of actions for what we need to do to improve education for all students in City School District. Are you ready?"

She explains that the numbers on the nametags correspond to the numbers on the 3 by 5 feet copies of the template posted on the walls. Participants turn to see the templates, which are the same: a diagram of a tree (see sidebar, Steps to create a template on p. 337; see also Online Resource 23.1: *The Impact of accumulated change*). Carolina invites the crowd to move, saying, "When you get to your wall chart, introduce yourselves to others who have the same number. You'll find directions on one of the chairs; one of you can read them aloud. And, then — just start!"

The participants seek their places in chairs arranged in horseshoe fashion in front of each wall chart. The groups examine the template and find the directions, which call on them to list all of the district's initiatives.

As she walks around listening, Carolina notices some groups are slow to start and some are moving faster. But eventually all groups are taking care of their own processes. They first write their own sticky notes, one for each district initiative with which they are familiar. They place these on the left side of the template. When they decide they have

accounted for all of the district's initiatives, they place each sticky note on the tree according to its status in the district: *bud, blossom, full flower,* or *withering flower.* Some sticky notes go into a *compost pile* or the *trashcan* beneath the tree. A few people make sticky notes to represent *new seeds* — initiatives that are on the horizon for the district. The noise in the room as people negotiate the placement of the sticky notes representing initiatives attests to their diligence.

Midway through, Carolina calls for a process check. Using the microphone and a bell, she gets most groups' attention. Carolina asks the groups to take three minutes to discuss their own processes. "Talk among yourselves. How are you doing? Are you following the norms? Are you rotating facilitator, recorder, and timekeeper duties?" The room buzzes for a few minutes, then becomes quieter as participants refocus on their task. Later, she interrupts the groups again to check whether they need more time. The show of hands leads her to provide seven more minutes for working on the template.

After the time is up, she helps the groups reorganize for a gallery tour. She explains the process, has them count off within their subgroups, and then has them begin to move in their new groups from chart to chart, listening and explaining the work done on each template.

Eventually, group members sit down and begin to list what they have seen on other charts, as well as what was on their own — the common elements. For example, most groups noticed that the district's assessment program needed to be composted.

Carolina brings all the groups back to the center of the room, away from their charts. She notices that the subgroups sit together, rather than returning to the seats they had taken when they entered the room. "Interesting," she thinks to herself. When she gathers the whole group together again and asks for common elements from the wall charts, she is pleasantly surprised at how similar the diverse groups are in naming initiatives, programs, and special projects and in placing them on the tree template. The groups have almost universally agreed on what should be discarded and what is a new seed blowing into the district.

Carolina's job isn't finished, however. She needs commitment to the master template. As they leave for lunch, she asks people to initial items that didn't make the list of common elements and that they think require additional study. Only a few do so.

During the working lunch, participants study questions prepared by the design team that are intended to move them to the next part of the process. These questions are, "What worked well in terms of this morning's process? What did not? What do you think we should do next?"

During lunch, Carolina and the design team meet to critique the morning's processes. They decide to proceed with the next step — another, simpler template. When participants return to the meeting room, the design team directs them to rejoin their gallery tour groups to work on the next template. The features of this template are simple:

Next steps	Who leads	Who helps	By when

These groups, different from the morning's groups, work hard on the new template. Meanwhile, Carolina meets with those who initialed items that were not on the common list. She helps them consider whether including these items will make district and school planning for the next three years more fruitful. In three cases, participants agree that their outlying item has been absorbed into another item or was not very important in the whole scheme. In two cases, participants and Carolina agree that "uncommon ideas" need to be considered. She provides time for the participants to make their cases before the whole group at the end of the meeting.

When the afternoon groups have completed their new templates — more traditional than the morning's templates — they take another gallery tour. By 4:30 p.m., participants are pleased. Several comment that they learned a great deal from each other, more about the way the district and its schools function, and what the future could be like. And, they note, they enjoyed their work and their colleagues more than they had expected to. One participant comments that she doubts they would have gotten as far or as deep as they did on the afternoon's planning if they hadn't worked on the morning's template. This is music to Carolina's ears.

Later, the design team meets at Carolina's condo to debrief. They are pleased with the visual dialogue process, wishing that more people could have gone through it.

Overview

Visual dialogue is the process of integrating words, images, and shapes into a single unit for communication. Its intent is to introduce a new way of collecting or packaging information so that people can understand complex ideas more easily and take action. Seeing thoughts expressed visually helps drive intense and meaningful dialogue.

Visual dialogue can lead to powerful meetings — and to powerful professional learning. It is useful when a group intends to create significant change. The tools associated with it help people bring out their ideas, discuss them, and visualize the system as a whole, whether it is a school, a district, a community, or the state educational system.

Uses of visual dialogue

The process can be used in a variety of groups with many outcomes. Carolina facilitated visual dialogue with a mixed-job group focused on planning the school district's future. The process also can be used to:

- Help map curriculum or plan interdisciplinary units (with teachers in the same or adjacent grade levels);
- Assess the impact of school programs and processes or identify indicators of success throughout the system (with school faculty);
- Create a classroom culture (with students);
- Assess a school's progress (with parents, community members, teachers, and students);
- Make connections (with cross-school teams);
- Understand differences in approaches to state reform initiatives (with cross-district teams).

Characteristics of visual dialogue

Visual dialogue has several characteristics.

Templates. The first characteristic is the use of a template. Templates represent complex concepts visually. They pull together diverse data on one large piece of paper. Creating these visualizations helps viewers work together to make connections and links from a systems perspective and detect patterns in order to answer questions about deeper issues and structures. The template represents the cognitive processes that a group goes through to co-create a product. It is an outline of the group's thought and collaboration.

Online Resources 23.1-23.10 are sample templates with directions for use. Readers may use these templates or design their own. The templates help groups:

- Find leaders among members;
- Discover what skills, experience, knowledge, and perspective each member brings to the group;

ADDITIONAL RESOURCES

Systems change

Art of the Long View: Planning for the Future in an Uncertain World, by Peter Schwartz. New York: Doubleday Currency, 1991.

Discovering Common Ground: How Future Search Conferences Bring People Together to Achieve Break-through Innovation, Empowerment, Shared Vision, and Collaborative Action, by Marvin Ross Weisbord and 35 co-authors. San Francisco, CA: Berrett-Koehler, 1992.

The Fifth Discipline: The Art and Practice of the Learning Organization, by Peter M. Senge. New York: Doubleday Currency, 1990.

Managing Transitions: Making the Most of Change, by William Bridges. New York: Addison Wesley, 1991.

Managing the Unknowable: Strategic Boundaries Between Order and Chaos in Organizations, by Ralph D. Stacey. San Francisco: Jossey-Bass, 1992.

Organizational development: Strategies and models, by Richard Beckhard. New York: Addison-Wesley. 1969.

Parzival's Briefcase: Six Practices and a New Philosophy for Healthy Organizational Change, by Tony Smith. New York: Chronicle Books, 1993.

Productive Workplaces: Organizing and Managing for Dignity, Meaning, and Community, by Marvin R. Weisbord. San Francisco: Jossey-Bass, 1987.

Reframing Organizations: Artistry, Choice, and Leadership, by Lee G. Bolman and Terrence E. Deal. San Francisco: Jossey-Bass, 2003.

Sculpting the Learning Organization: Lessons in the Art and Science of Systemic Change, by Karen E. Watkins and Victoria J. Marsick. San Francisco: Jossey-Bass, 1993.

Stewardship: Choosing Service Over Self-Interest, by Peter Block. San Francisco, CA: Berrett-Koehler, 1993.

Ten Steps to a Learning Organization, by Peter Kline and Bernard Saunders. Colton, CA: Great River Books, 1997.

Visual language

Envisioning Information, by Edward R. Tufte. Cheshire, CT: Graphics Press LLC, 1990.

Graphic Guide to Facilitation Principles/Practices, by David Sibbet. San Francisco, CA: The Grove Consultants International, 1994.

The Visual Display of Quantitative Information (2nd ed.), by Edward R. Tufte. Cheshire, CT: Graphic Press, 2001.

Visual Explanations — Images and Quantities, Evidence, and Narrative, by Edward R. Tufte. Cheshire, CT: Graphic Press, 1997.

Visual Language — Global Communication for the 21st Century, by Robert E. Horn. Bainbridge Island, WA: MacroVu, Inc. 1998.

Visual Leaders: New Tools for Visioning, Management, and Organization, by David Sibbet. New York: Wiley, 2013.

Visual Meetings: How Graphics, Sticky Notes and Idea Mapping Can Transform Group Productivity, by David Sibbet. New York: Wiley, 2013.

Visual Teams: Graphic Tools for Commitment, Innovation, and High Performance, by David Sibbet, New York: Wiley, 2011.

- Predict trends, directions, visions;
- Assess the current situation;
- Engage stakeholders; and
- Create communities of inquiry and practice.

Learning by constructing knowledge. The second characteristic of visual dialogue is reliance on the theory that people learn by constructing knowledge, a premise that goes back to the work of Lev Vygotsky (1978). The constructivist theory of learning addresses how people process information, asserting that the learner is "an active processor of information" (Mayer, 1997). Constructivism "assumes all knowledge is constructed from previous knowledge" (National Research Council, 2000).

A related theory proposes that people construct meaning socially; that is, they learn from one other. No single member of a group has all the information or skills needed for a task; all of them have some information and some skills that they offer to the whole group. Those who understand how meaning is built socially use a metaphor to describe what happens during the process: a scaffold. Before construction workers move to the next floor of the high rise they're building, they need to build the scaffolding that will support them in moving higher. Imagine people building scaffolds to help each other gain meaning. Scaffolding is the means by which people construct knowledge socially.

Visual learning. A third characteristic of visual dialogue is visual learning. Most people are used to processing ideas using language. People use language to learn and to communicate. The preferred learning style in schools and society is linguistic. But language can inhibit thought. It can prove inadequate for dealing with complexity. It is slower than thought. Visual processing opens up a new world for learning. Visual language uses symbols and pictographs, stars, bullets, arrows, different colors and shapes, and icons to communicate meaning and enhance learning.

Use of dialogue. The fourth characteristic of the process is the use of dialogue. Discussion and dialogue are counterparts, according to Peter Senge (1990). "In a discussion, different views are presented and defended, and … this may provide a useful analysis of the whole situation. In dialogue, different views are presented as a means toward discovering a new view." Robert J. Garmston and Bruce Wellman (1999) describe the phenomenon of group talk as a shared way of learning. They describe dialogue as a way to get to a shared understanding, while discussion is a way to get to a decision. Dialogue is convivial; discussion resembles a debate. (See "Chapter 10: Dialogue" in this book.)

Natural consensus building. The final characteristic of this powerful form of professional learning is natural consensus building. As people co-create knowledge, they naturally build consensus. They decide together what matters, recording their decisions on the chart paper in front of them. Then, through a mechanism related to visual dialogue — the gallery tour — separate groups build consensus for the whole group. At the end of the entire process, participants realize that they have naturally found common ground.

Initiating visual dialogue

Visual dialogue can be initiated informally or formally. Informally, any group of educators can initiate the process regarding almost any topic. Fourth-grade teachers can engage in visual dialogue as a way to understand their approaches to reading in the content areas. Vertical learning teams in a district, getting together over the summer, can use visual dialogue to plot how they are helping to teach writing. A principal can use visual dialogue with a small group to examine policies from within and outside the school that affect retention. These groups do not need to go through the formal process of a more systemic change. While they are engaged in important dialogue, they are probably not addressing systemic change beyond the school level.

The more formal way of initiating dialogue begins with a perceived need and has a goal of significant and systemic change. For example, someone notices the system is not working as well as it should and may believe a systems change is needed. Better, this person may discuss the concern with others until there is consensus to act. Those who perceive the need sponsor the effort or find someone with enough influence to authorize it.

Rationale

Nothing today is as simple as it once was. People work in a world of high technology, global business, and instant telecommunications. As the world becomes more complex, people need to solve problems faster. To solve problems, people need immediate access to the big picture, and simultaneously, to many levels of detail. Visual dialogue provides both.

Educators, in particular, need to help students address a different world: the glut of information, the complexity of problems and solutions, the effect of decisions over the long run, and rapid change. Educators need to address their world, too: the myriad reforms, innovations, responsibilities, and tasks; the diversity of students and communities; rapid changes in the world outside education.

The world becomes less chaotic when people think with the whole brain (Caine & Caine, 1997, 2004). When people combine words, images, and shapes, they bring more of their intelligence to their work. Thinking and learning are more powerful when they vary their tools and strategies according to brain research and theories of intelligence. Visual tools help people grow new neural pathways by forcing them to integrate right brain strategies into planning and collective thinking (The Institute for the Advancement of Research at AEL, 2003).

No one can change systems alone. Everyone is necessary, but everyone needs others to engage in systems change. New ways of working with others help people address complex work.

As important is the psychological effect of using visual dialogue. Even though these are clichés, visual dialogue levels the playing field, makes it an open stage, and puts topics up there for everyone to see. Visual dialogue helps people make their ideas transparent. It helps people uncover assumptions. It helps groups become insightful as they seek to understand (Covey, 2013).

Visual dialogue helps build trust. People negotiating what to put on a template have an immediate incentive to be honest. Visual dialogue is especially valuable as a professional learning strategy for groups that have known a toxic culture — one that is not trustworthy and that has betrayed them in the past. Visual dialogue is a way for people to venture past behavior and work with a clean slate.

Steps

The following steps make up the formal process of facilitating successful visual dialogue.

Step 1: Form a design team

The design team plans, and then helps the facilitator during sessions or meetings. Members provide feedback to the facilitator for midcourse corrections.

Form a group of four to six people. If the participating group is small, the entire group may be the design team. If selecting members from a large group, be sure the design team includes someone from each stakeholder group.

To plan, have the design team ask:

- **What:** What is it, generally, that we are trying to do (subject to approval of the whole group at the first meeting)?
- **Who:** Who should participate? If space allows, all of the people who will be affected by the work should be invited — they are the stakeholders. If space is limited, invite representatives of each stakeholder group. Because it's hard to think of all the people who should attend as well as all the roles that should be represented, ask this question: Who else needs to participate?
- **Why:** What's the rationale? Why should people devote considerable time and energy to this project? The design team should prepare at least a preliminary rationale, subject to the ideas of the whole group at the first meeting.
- **When/Where/How:** These are the logistics of the meeting. Good visual dialogue requires at least a half-day; Carolina Blair's process had two steps, each proceeding according to a different template, so her meeting required a full day. Remember food, time for reflection, time for movement, and time to socialize. If possible, the location should be away from the regular place of business. Make the appropriate arrangements.

Step 2: Prepare

Decide whether to use an existing template or to create one. Some templates created by the Bailey Alliance are included in the Online Resources 23. 1 – 23.9. These can be used or altered for various purposes. Templates help a group:

- Provide leadership;
- Use stories to predict future trends;
- Create communities of inquiry and practice;
- Create a common vision;
- Predict future trends, direction, and vision; and
- Assess the current situation.

Sometimes the work requires more than one template. The design team may create the template together, itself a professional learning experience (see sidebar Steps to

Steps to create a template

1. Determine the outcome. What do you want to accomplish by the end of the visual dialogue process? Write this in the center of a wall chart or piece of paper.

2. What big steps are necessary to achieve the outcome? List these along one side of the blank wall chart or an 8 1/2" x 11" paper.

3. What assumptions are likely to be operating in the dialogue? One example of an assumption is whether or not a group has decision-making authority. List these along another side of the chart or paper.

4. What time factors affect reaching the outcome? Describe these in a corner of the chart or paper. How are past, present, and future conditions likely to affect the outcome?

5. What points of view are likely to be represented within the proposed group? List these along another side of the wall chart or piece of paper.

6. What contextual factors are likely to influence the outcome? List these around the outcome in the center of the document.

7. Decide which of the thinking processes (described in Steps 2-6) the visual dialogue subgroups need to go through. Will time be a big factor? Will context profoundly influence the outcome? Will there be conflicting points of view? Circle the items written on the wall chart or paper that will be key to realizing the outcome.

8. Create the template by organizing the essential aspects of the process around the outcome. For example, if you think that conflicting points of view will affect the outcome, create a chart such as the one in Online Resource 23.1, *The impact of accumulated change.*

The impact of accumulated change: The template

Growing and pruning reform programs

This template will help groups analyze the current state of their organization, so having mixed role groups is ideal. Participants will understand what they need to keep, change, add and discard.

Radar screen of all improvement initiatives

New seeds

Blossoms

Full flowers

Buds

Withering flowers

Trash can

Compost pile

create a template). Draft a template on 8 1/2" x 11" paper and take it to a copy place to be enlarged and duplicated as a 3' x 5' (or larger) wall chart. If the group is large and will be divided, create one chart for each small group of five to six.

Step 3: Communicate with participants

Send an invitation to the designated participants outlining purpose and goals (the "What" and "Why") and giving the meeting date, time, and place. Let participants know that they will be using different processes to work together toward their goal. Ask them to think about the goal before they arrive.

Step 4: Prepare the room

Identify a room appropriate to the work. Some parts of visual dialogue require small groups to come together as a whole, such as when Carolina started the meeting and brought people together before and after lunch and at the end of the day. Even when the small groups are working on templates or taking gallery tours, they should be in the same large room, if at all possible, rather than separate breakout rooms.

Schedule a large room with long, flat, empty, smooth walls where templates can be taped or pinned for subgroups.

Have the room furnished with tables and movable chairs. Find a room with round tables, if possible.

Recommendations for facilitators

In the group meeting, the facilitator's job is to make sure all subgroups share their work with the whole group and that through sharing, the whole group achieves common ground. However, participants perform the real work of visual dialogue. A visual dialogue activity is not a sit-and-get activity. Facilitators should observe these recommendations:

- **Use the tools first yourself.** Before you use the tools with a group, try them, preferably with a design team. Get a feel for how the participants will work through the template. Anticipate questions and problems with the process.

- **Carefully consider the staging.** If using visual language is new to you or your organization, or new to you in your role, start small and let others warm up to the change in behavior. Carefully consider how you will introduce this new way of working.

- **Move beyond collecting data into creating meaning.** The point of visual dialogue is not just to fill in the blanks. The real work starts when the data are on the wall — the dialogue about the patterns in the data is where new meaning originates. Get to the dialogue.

- **Move beyond the usual cast of characters.** Include individuals who have different roles, backgrounds, styles, and points of view. Be strategic in inviting people from different teams, departments, and committees who can inform your work in critical ways. Remember: same people, same ideas, same ownership; new people, new ideas.

- **Distribute completed templates while they are fresh.** If a group works together on a template to set the wheels in motion, make sure group members receive a copy of the work afterward so they can follow through. After three working days, the data get cold and commitment wanes. Make sure you or someone else takes responsibility for quick turnaround.

- **Do something!** Use the templates as a road map to prompt and guide new behavior. A basketful of completed wall charts is not sufficient return on the time and energy invested in a meeting or two. Add value by supporting an improvement initiative in new ways.

- **Know when not to use visual dialogue.** Use your eyes, ears, and gut feelings to gauge when to proceed with plans to use one of the tools. Highly emotional situations demand intense listening, not charting. Or a group may move beyond the need for a specific template, even though its use was planned weeks ago.

Hang charts on the walls around the room far enough away from each other so that participants in subgroups can hear each other without disturbing other groups.

Arrange chairs in horseshoe style in front of each chart, with the open end of the horseshoe facing the template. Be sure participants can see and hear one another and can see the wall chart.

Place a flip chart near each wall chart to help participants park items that are not ready to go on the template.

Provide each group with dark colored, washable markers (as allowed by the owner of the facility). Color is a big part of visual dialogue, as are the graphics that participants create to connect, highlight, or illustrate items — lines, arrows, asterisks, and icons. Black, blue, purple, and brown can be used to record the main ideas. Brilliant colors such as red, orange, or yellow can be used to highlight items.

Decide whether to provide each subgroup with specific directions on how to proceed through the template — which should be as brief as possible as most groups are able to figure out what to do. Copy the instructions, if desired, and place a copy with each subgroup.

Step 5: Establish the visual dialogue groups

The design team may divide the whole group into subgroups before the meeting, including representatives of different roles in the system in each subgroup. Alternatively, mix people according to the way they usually contribute to group processes (some extroverts, some introverts, for example) or allow subgroups to form after the whole group has met at the beginning.

Form subgroups small enough that everyone has time to speak, but large enough to get diversity of opinion. A group of six to eight people gives a good range for visual dialogue groups.

Step 6: Have subgroups work concurrently on the templates to seek consensus within each group

You may want to encourage them to take full advantage of the size of the template by writing ideas on the margins; you might want them to write on sticky notes before they agree to put ideas on the template. You may want to ask them to park on a piece of chart paper to the side of the template ideas they are not ready to reach consensus on. Encourage them to take full advantage of the meaning of colors and various graphics (such as asterisks, lines, arrows, icons) that illustrate emphasis and relationships.

You also may want to address the issue of leadership: Your subgroups may find that they need a facilitator. This is the person who has volunteered, for part of the time only, to keep the group on track. Facilitation should change frequently so that everybody has a chance to be a participant.

You also may find that subgroups need a recorder and a timekeeper. Again, emphasize that these positions are temporary and do not convey any status in terms of ideas. Emphasize that the recorder has to be especially exacting about what is written on the template, checking with the entire group to be sure the idea has been agreed upon and is ready to go on the template and making sure that it is stated correctly.

Consider also suggesting some norms (see sidebar Suggested norms for group work). As subgroups work, circulate to pick up clues about how the process is going. Have you given groups enough time? Is one person dominating a group, not letting others speak? Is someone doing the work on his or her own, figuring it all out for the group?

If you detect problems, decide whether to bring these problems to the whole group or to the subgroup only. Your decision depends on whether the problems are widespread or isolated and whether the group members need to be protected from criticism. Generally, it is better not to interrupt the whole group unless the problem is pervasive. And, if the visual dialogue process is working well, most subgroups will ignore attempted interruptions in order to continue their work.

Step 7: Conduct a gallery tour for whole group consensus

Reserve at least 10 minutes per subgroup for a gallery tour. Have the original subgroups form new subgroups by

Suggested norms for group work on visual dialogue

- Work together to co-create parts of the template rather than dividing them up for individuals to do; do not figure out any part of the template on your own.

- Listen first to understand; build on each others' ideas.

- Look for commonalities but treat each idea with respect and look for its fit.

- Ensure that everybody has air time.

- Park ideas that are not yet fully developed or haven't been agreed upon on a separate piece of chart paper. Make sure to go back to those ideas during the process.

counting off in each template group. Counting off ensures that each new gallery group includes one representative from each template group. The number of people in the original template groups determines the size of the new gallery groups. For example, 50 people who divided up to work on seven templates will result in groups of about seven. Members in each subgroup number themselves one to seven. All the "Ones" then form a new subgroup, with each able to answer questions and gather comments as the group reaches the template that person helped create. The last person of the 50 can join any group (see Online Resource 23.10: *Directions for visual dialogue and directions for gallery tours* for a summary of these processes that you can share with participants).

Once groups are renumbered, before individuals move, explain the metaphor of gallery tour. Tell the group to imagine an art walk on Friday night. Say that you walk with others from gallery to gallery viewing the paintings, drawings, and sculptures. Imagine that at each gallery, you have a docent (often the owner of the gallery or the artist whose work is being displayed). This docent is available to answer questions and comment on the work as you view it.

Explain that the person or persons who worked on each template will be the docent(s) when the gallery tour stops in front of that template. The docent will explain what the template group did and why, answer questions, and listen to comments, recording them if possible to share when the template groups reform.

Have participants introduce themselves to one another and make sure the group has at least one person from each original template group. Tell the group that tour members are responsible for taking notes as they move from gallery to gallery. They should use the templates to ask questions, make comments, and record common elements that they see. They should also notice any outliers, items that they notice on no other template but that deserve consideration later.

Keep the gallery tours moving quickly from template to template, from five to seven minutes in front of each. Move them on by asking them to thank their docents and proceed to the next gallery.

When all tour groups have visited all templates, have them thank their tour companions and return to their own templates, where they can share what they heard and saw as they visited the others. Have each group prepare a consolidated list of commonalities to present to the whole group.

Step 8: Recognize common elements from the groups

If possible, have groups move from the space in front of their templates to the center of the room where they can hear and see one another. Using a round-robin strategy, have reporters from each template group call out one common element, something seen on several of the charts. Record these on a blank template. Reporters can pass if what they would call out already is recorded on the master template.

Once there are no more common elements to be added to the master template, invite participants to contribute items that were not common but that seem significant. Record these on a separate piece of chart paper to be discussed later.

Step 9: Address the common elements

In Carolina Blair's group, participants turned the common elements into action steps using this simple template:

Next steps	Who leads	Who helps	By when

One step participants can take is to return to the templates they worked on and modify them so that they represent the commonalities and outliers. Here are some other actions groups can take with the common elements:

- Ask committees to take one or more items and develop them in more depth, to be presented to the whole group at a future date;

- Have someone prepare a summary of the outcomes of the visual dialogue and gallery walk to be presented to a decision-making body, such as a board of education, for further action; or
- Have each template group appoint someone to describe that template and explain how and why it was developed the way it was. Collect written reports from each group and use them to build a model of the system that others, such as district administrators, can use as the basis for decisions in the future.

Variations

Different templates dictate differences in the visual dialogue process used by Carolina Blair. For the list of additional templates, see Online Resources for this chapter. Introductory comments for each template establish the overall goal and process for the visual dialogue. Steps for each template help the facilitator lead subgroups through the work they are to do.

The Future Search Conference, developed by Weisbord (1987, 1992) has its own structure. Many steps involve the use of a template for visual dialogue.

One of the major variations to consider is going online with visual dialogue. An easy way to do so is with Skype, WebEx, or other conference call or meeting devices that allow for visual as well as auditory connections. A more complex but feasible way to engage in visual dialogue is through a virtual gathering. Participants use graphic tablets that are loaded with the templates and electronically connected to the devices of other participants. One consideration for these online dialogues is parity. Everyone should be either online or in the same physical space; if some are online and some together in a room, the dialogue tends to be unbalanced.

One advantage to a digital visual dialogue is that, once the meeting is over, the digital record of it can be sent to all participants for further action. Participants have immediate access to their work; it doesn't get "cold" and action is more likely when participants don't have to wait for the official record of work.

Another variation with a slightly different purpose is visual or graphic recording of the proceedings of a group. The purpose of this variation is to create a group memory. Rather than begin with a template, groups contribute to a colorful map of their thoughts as they progress over time. Sometimes, a graphic recording takes the form of a story map that tells the story of an organization — what its vision is, what its ideas are, and what it hopes to do. Sometimes the graphic recorder is actually offsite but listening to and watching what occurs and representing proceedings visually. Others can watch what the recorder is doing from separate locations or together in the same room. Whatever is created during the meeting can be sent electronically to participants using a white board or SmartBoard, for example.

Technology, of course, is not fail-proof. Have paper and markers ready just in case technology fails. Also, be sure to allow sufficient time for introductions and a meaningful introductory activity, one that is connected to the work but also allows participants to connect.

Challenges and how to address them.

Sponsorship. One of the challenges to those participating in the generative process of visual dialogue is that their work goes nowhere. One solution is to get sponsorship beforehand. Getting sponsorship or a charter to proceed with systems analysis and possible change can be tricky. A group or individual must have enough information about the system so those in authority believe in the outcome and process. However, the group or individual does not need so much information that one of the chief purposes of visual dialogue — collecting information — becomes irrelevant. Visual dialogue does not always need a sponsor, such as when a cross-curricular team in a high school plans an interdisciplinary curriculum.

Facilitation. Visual dialogue does not just happen. Like verbal dialogue (see "Chapter 10: Dialogue" in this book), visual dialogue needs to be learned and practiced to be effective; furthermore, someone needs to prepare for the process.

Visual dialogue requires two facilitator roles. The first is the whole-group facilitator who, working with a design team, plans the purposes, rationale, and logistics of the meeting. This person usually runs the meeting, sets up the room, makes the templates, gathers other materials, greets the group, and sets people up for the work. This person also monitors progress, adjusts the process as necessary, and keeps the group on track, moving toward its purposes.

The other role for facilitation is within the subgroups.

Working at the templates, subgroups need volunteers to facilitate the small group work. The subgroup facilitator is not the person with all the ideas (everyone has ideas to contribute), but agrees to keep the subgroup on track. The facilitator role in subgroups should change frequently so that everybody has a chance to participate.

A design team. Any single person — no matter how knowledgeable, talented, and well placed in the organization — cannot represent the needs of all of the stakeholders in that organization. No matter how much the facilitator knows about a system, the people inside the system know more. A design team can help the facilitator choose the right people for the work, discover how these people work together, identify barriers and boosters, and create the right work for all of the participants. The facilitator uses the design team to check in on the process periodically during the actual work.

Whole group commitment. Engaging in visual dialogue is hard work; it is not a day away from work. Although there is some element of play in visual dialogue and gallery tours, participants need to be aware that the work of systems change using visual dialogue and gallery tours is demanding. The facilitator needs to get commitment from the whole group. Make meeting times and places as convenient as possible, but emphasize that participants need to be present at all meetings for the duration of the work. A group lacking or adding a member is, in fact, a brand new group.

Consensus. Even work that is facilitated through visual dialogue and gallery tours can be insular rather than systemic. Even though subgroups work as parts of a whole group — and everyone is involved — some work needs to have whole group consensus. The facilitator must ensure that key items are brought to the whole group for agreement.

Action. Groups that do a lot of work leading to no action can become so frustrated that they are cynical when asked, later, to do similar work. In fact, they may be cynical enough that they refuse to act at all. Be sure the tools lead to a desired action. Part of each meeting should be reserved for next steps. Each meeting should begin with follow-up on the previous meeting. Were the steps accomplished? Why or why not? After the meetings end, help the whole group remain active by having participants schedule follow-up themselves.

Conclusion

Carolina Blair and her design team planned and facilitated two more half-day meetings of the district, with Carolina cheerfully handing off the facilitator role to others on the design team. As a result of the meetings, the district developed a clear vision and a set of goals that everyone committed to, as well as a set of steps that they (and others) would take to achieve the vision and goals. The process had been successful.

What was even more exciting to Carolina, however, was how the strategy of visual dialogue spread throughout the district. Principals and teachers introduced it through meaningful work within their buildings and soon found that visual dialogue had become part of the repertoire of powerful professional learning designs used by all sorts of teacher teams. Community members shared the strategy with their colleagues, and soon groups outside the school system were using visual dialogue to help them learn together and take meaningful action. In some of its study groups, the board of education created templates that helped board members deal with complex issues.

Carolina had felt cautiously optimistic when she and the design team had introduced the design to district staff. She now felt completely optimistic about its power to transform professional learning.

References

Caine, R.N. & Caine, G. (1997). *Unleashing the power of perceptual change: The promise of brain-based teaching.* Alexandria, VA: ASCD.

Caine, R.N. & Caine, G. (2004). *Making connections: Teaching and the human brain.* Thousand Oaks, CA: Corwin Press.

Covey, S.R. (2013). *The 7 habits of highly effective people: Powerful lessons in personal change* (anniversary edition). New York: Simon & Schuster, Inc.

Garmston, R.J. & Wellman, B. (1999). *The adaptive school: A sourcebook for developing collaborative groups.* Norwood, MA: Christopher-Gordon.

Institute for the Advancement of Research in Education at AEL. (2003, July). *Graphic organizers: A review of scientifically based research.* Available at www.inspiration.com/sites/default/files/documents/Detailed-Summary.pdf.

Mayer, R.E. (1998). Cognitive theory for education: What teachers need to know. In N. M. Lambert & B. L. McCombs (Eds.), *How students learn: Reforming schools through learner-centered instruction.* Washington, DC: American Psychological Association.

National Research Council. (2000). *How people learn: Brain, mind, experience, and school.* Washington, DC: National Academy Press.

Senge, P.M. (1990). *The fifth discipline: The art and practice of the learning organization.* New York, NY: Doubleday Currency.

Vygotsky, L. (1978). *Mind in society: The development of higher psychological processes* (14th ed.). Cambridge, MA: Harvard University Press.

Weisbord, M.R. (1987). *Productive workplaces: Organizing and managing for dignity, meaning, and community.* San Francisco, CA: Jossey-Bass.

Weisbord, M.R., Schindler-Rainman, E., Lippitt, R., Emery, F., Baburoglu, O.N., Garr, III, M.A., . . . Burgess, M.S. (1992). *Discovering common ground: How future search conferences bring people together to achieve breakthrough innovation, empowerment, shared vision, and collaborative action.* San Francisco: Berrett-Koehler.

Webinars

Chris Dede: "Interactivity and individualization are central to learning, whether the experience is face to face or online." [1]

By Tom Manning

Joe was at a crossroads. The districtwide technology leadership team he'd been leading for more than three months had been exploring ways to incorporate technology into the district's professional learning program by studying and sharing best practices for technology use and trying new models of technology-based learning for adults.

During the team's time together it had explored a range of technology tools that could improve professional learning for its schools' PLCs and for the district as a whole, including producing online courses through a learning management system (LMS), implementing cameras in classrooms so teachers can share best instructional practices, and implementing an online coaching program.

But Joe was thinking that some of the work being done by individual PLCs across the district could be shared with other learning teams. He knew that across the district PLCs were looking at student data and devising solutions to meet diverse student needs. But those teams, even though they were doing good work, were operating in a bubble. There were no opportunities in place for cross-PLC sharing on a larger scale, where the work of one team could be shared with others throughout the district. What tools could his technology team explore that would bring all of this learning across the district's campuses together?

As the technology team gathered for the start of that afternoon's meeting, Darla, a school guidance counselor and member of the technology team, was telling a colleague that earlier in the week she attended a free webinar on

[1] Crow, 2010, p. 10.

effective teaching strategies for implementing Common Core standards. The webinar featured a national expert showcasing new instructional models through short videos and robust discussions among attendees.

Darla reported that she walked away with some new instructional strategies for implementing the standards that she gained from both the presenter and from participants who shared their own implementation success stories during the webinar. She was in the process of building activities for her next PLC meeting around what she learned during the webinar. Without ever leaving her school, Darla was able to draw from the expertise of a national expert while keeping her learning focused on specific actions her PLC could take based on what she had learned.

A lightbulb turned on for Joe. At the meeting, he asked Darla to share her webinar experience during check-in. While the topic was not an item on that day's agenda, Joe ended the meeting with a challenge for the following meeting: Explore whether the district could implement webinars to provide technology-based learning opportunities for teachers and other district personnel. How could the team develop and implement a plan for hosting regular webinars that feature the expertise residing within their schools? And how might they seek opportunities to engage outside experts who could share their expertise without having to come to the district?

Team members were excited to explore the possibility of implementing webinars as part of the district's professional learning plan. But where would they begin? What steps needed to be taken to begin producing webinars that would be engaging, interactive, and reflect best practices in adult learning?

Overview

Simply defined, a webinar is a live, interactive presentation or meeting that is broadcast to an audience over the Internet.

A typical webinar includes a single presenter or a small group of presenters delivering content in real time via presentation and multimedia tools, leading activities, and facilitating discussion, all within a webinar platform that allows participants to engage fully from wherever they are, either individually or in small groups.

The core component of a webinar is most often a slide presentation (specifically PowerPoint), although effective webinars incorporate numerous other features to engage attendees, including videos, interactive polling, and other tools.

For larger webinars, attendees generally listen to presenters over their computers, providing feedback and asking questions through a text chat feature that allows them to type comments to presenters and other attendees during the meeting. For webinars designed for smaller groups or learning teams, participants sometimes call into a phone line, allowing them to participate verbally as well as via text, or they can even participate via streaming audio and video directly through their computers.

While a series of webinars can constitute a more comprehensive learning opportunity or be "packaged" to create an asynchronous, on-demand learning experience, a webinar is generally considered to be a single event, lasting no more than an hour to 90 minutes.

A webinar or a series of webinars needs to be moderated. Webinars do not run themselves, and people in professional learning groups, such as PLCs, generally do not have the time to set them up and run them. While the webinar content presenter can also serve as the moderator, the ideal model is to divide responsibilities between a dedicated moderator who handles all technical components of the event and a presenter who focuses solely on delivering content and engaging participants in learning.

Businesses and organizations have traditionally used webinars both internally for professional learning and externally as an outreach tool for marketing to and educating their customers or members. States, school districts, and even learning teams within districts have in recent years turned to webinars as learning tools that provide educators with new opportunities to collaborate, as well as to bring in outside presenters to deliver content and lead online discussion.

Good webinars follow the same general structure as good face-to-face meetings: They have an agenda, norms, and opportunities for reflection and dialogue. They give participants a chance to engage in follow-up activities and discussions that build on their learning and help them incorporate it into their work. In fact, the principles of standards-based professional learning that guide face-to-face team meetings can be transferred effectively to online meetings. Many of those goals can be achieved by taking full advantage of the features available on most webinar platforms.

Knowing that you want to start hosting webinars does not mean your webinars will succeed. This chapter provides a process for not only creating effective webinars but also securing buy-in from team members by making them comfortable with the technology being used, establishing norms that promote collaborative online learning, and building additional learning opportunities around webinars that use Web 2.0 tools to create a more complete experience for team members.

Rationale

The most obvious attraction of webinars is that they allow people to participate in meetings and presentations from any location. This eliminates the need to coordinate (and pay for) travel, as well as the requirement that all participants be in the same place for a meeting. But beyond addressing logistical meeting concerns, webinars also provide learning opportunities that model effective use of Web 2.0 tools while still meeting standards for effective professional learning.

Learning Forward's Learning Design standard acknowledges the role technology can play in integrating theories, research, and models of human learning to increase educator effectiveness and results for students:

> Technology is rapidly enhancing and extending opportunities for professional learning. It particularly facilitates access to, sharing, construction, and analysis of information to enhance practice. Technology exponentially increases possibilities for personalizing, differentiating, and deepening learning, especially for educators who have limited access to on-site professional learning or who are eager to reach beyond the boundaries of their own work setting to join local or global networks to enrich their learning. (Learning Forward, 2011, p. 41)

It seems that there are countless tools available for educators to engage in online collaboration and expand both their knowledge base and their communities of practice to include colleagues from around the world striving to share their own expertise and absorb the work and expertise of others.

A typical educator can follow a variety of experts and organizations sharing their knowledge and expertise on Twitter; be connected with fellow educators around the world on Facebook; participate in an online community of people who teach their subjects and grade levels on Edmodo; subscribe to a service that provides users with endless video clips of great teaching to apply in their own learning; have numerous apps and RSS feeds that provide instant access to information; participate in an internal social network set up by the district to share news and learning opportunities; and take advantage of numerous additional opportunities to learn and collaborate at the click of a button. (See "Chapter 20: Social Media" in this book.)

Technology-integrated professional learning is an expectation for schools charged with producing educators who can teach 21st century skills and engage students for whom Web 2.0 technology is a way of life. The New Media Consortium (NMC) *2013 Horizon Report, K–12,* concludes that, "Ongoing (technology-based) professional development needs to be integrated into the culture of the school" (Johnson et al., 2013, p. 9).

Joellen Killion adds:

> Technology tools enable people to connect for learning-focused discussions and to explore ideas from multiple perspectives and in multiple presentation formats. When learners are able to interrogate information, ideas, positions, and people, they clarify, expand, and deepen learning. Technology brings learners closer to the source of ideas, information, and positions to promote higher levels of learning. (Killion, 2013, p. 23)

For many learners and learning teams, however, webinars are not part of this collaborative online learning experience. While businesses and organizations report that webinars are one of their most effective methods for getting information out to customers, clients, or members, webinars are not often part of an integrated professional learning plan for PLCs, schools, or districts.

In fact, some educators view the webinar as a tool that doesn't necessarily reflect effective professional learning or engage participants in extended collaboration at all. In the world of online learning, webinars are often viewed as the equivalent of a "one-stop workshop," something that users participate in for an hour, perhaps get a nugget or two of information that they can share with others or use in their work, and then never think about again. Those who plan, schedule, and moderate webinars see this first-hand when 200 people sign up for an online event, and 60 wind up attending.

Unlike many online learning options, webinars do not provide access to learning on the individual learner's time. An educator can receive an alert that someone has posted a new video or article in an online community and access it immediately. Posts that are made in discussion forums can be read throughout the day as people add to a discussion thread. Twitter feeds are checked dozens of times a day.

Webinars don't work that way. They are live, scheduled events that need to be planned for and for which other commitments may need to be shifted to accommodate. More importantly, they are often seen as more of a tool for an organization to promote something or to deliver content, as opposed to an opportunity to engage in true collaborative learning.

But those whose work involves developing online learning opportunities that reflect effective adult learning principles know that webinars can be an incredibly effective tool. Webinars allow the opportunity to learn from those who are doing great work in the field. They allow educators to share best practices and, according to Joni K. Falk and Brian Drayton, allow "teachers [to] become essential resources for one another's professional development. . . . learning with and from colleagues about the substance of their work" (Falk & Drayton, 2009, p. 3). Is there any doubt that the educators in Joe's school would benefit from having access to the expertise of their colleagues, share best practices, and learn from leaders in the field while engaging in learning opportunities that reflect effective use of Web 2.0 tools and 21st century learning?

Falk and Dayton suggest in their book, *Creating and Sustaining Online Professional Learning Communities,* that webinars, like many online learning opportunities, "evoke excitement, anger, boredom, dissent, and commitment — often all at the same time!" (p. ix). Prepare yourself for the uncommon journey.

Steps

What follows is not only a process for producing webinars that advance the Standards for Professional Learning but also a guide for integrating webinars into the structure of professional learning communities in ways that model effective use of technology and advance learning for educators and students.

Step 1: Choose the right technology

Webinar platforms, no matter how innovative, are simply tools for content delivery and collaboration and, on their own, do nothing to ensure either successful online meetings or that the meetings themselves are part of a larger, cohesive learning framework.

There are dozens of webinar platforms to choose from. Some are expensive — thousands of dollars a year. Others are far cheaper, with monthly fees of $100 or less for unlimited webinars, including pricing tiers based on participant limits. Still other platforms are free, although they usually require users to display advertisements during their meetings.

The vast majority of these platforms, regardless of price, offer features that enhance the learning experience far beyond forcing participants to watch a PowerPoint presentation while someone lectures them over their computers. Some key engagement tools that are standard on most webinar platforms include:

- Slides and other resource documents that display on screen and can also be downloaded by attendees during or after the meeting;
- Uploading video files to play during the meeting, or integration with video sites like YouTube or Vimeo that allow videos from those sites to play in the room;
- Instant polls that participants can complete on screen in real time;
- Note-taking features that allow presenters to write notes on pre-existing slides or create slides on the fly where notes can be taken on screen;
- Live streaming video of the presenter(s) during the meeting (and in some cases streaming video options for attendees as well when they want to ask a question or make a comment);
- Screen sharing, or the ability for presenters to share their

Criteria for choosing a webinar platform

- Cost
- Number of participants allowed
- Core features
- Internal technology limitations
- Audio/video capabilities
- Recording/archiving
- Ease of use for presenters/moderators
- Ease of use for attendees
- Customer support

desktops with attendees to walk through a website or document directly from their computers;

- Chat features that allow attendees to type in questions or comments that display to the group;

- Recording options that allow hosts to archive webinars and send attendees a web link to the recording after the live event; this feature also allows for the editing of webinar content to create short clips that can be used as learning tools; and

- The ability to send follow-up communications, such as evaluations or emails outlining next steps, immediately after the end of the meeting.

The majority of these features are standard on virtually all webinar platforms, with some variation on how the features work. An organization or PLC interested in using webinars as a professional learning tool should start by determining the features that will allow it to create the most effective learning experiences for team members based on the resources available to them, and choosing a platform accordingly.

The sidebar, Criteria for choosing a webinar platform, provides a guide for developing selection criteria. Note the item "Internal technology limitations." The team charged with evaluating and selecting a platform must keep in mind any technology limitations that may be in place for both participants and potential presenters. For example, many schools block access to YouTube. Therefore, a platform that allows videos to be shown only from YouTube will mean that many attendees will be staring at an error message while their colleagues are watching and then discussing the video.

Additionally, some webinar platforms require a

"plug-in"— a program specific to the webinar platform that presenters and attendees must download to their computers in order to launch the webinar. This could present an issue in some school districts that have restrictions on programs or tools downloaded from the Internet.

Thankfully, virtually all webinar providers allow potential customers to take demos that allow them to test the platform's features. Some go even further, providing potential customers with a free trial account, giving them access to the platform where they can set up test meetings and explore features on their own.

Step 2: Schedule the webinars

Let's say Joe and his team determined that a webinar is an effective tool for bringing campus-based teams together to share their learning, as well as learn from outside experts. They've chosen their platform, and Joe has taken on the role of moderator; he will be providing technical assistance during all webinars and online events the districts hosts. The next question to answer is, "When and how often are we going to host webinars, and who will present them?"

Setting aside regular time to participate ensures attendance at webinars or other online events and establishes the expectation that this form of professional learning is critical. If Joe's team determines that the district is going to host monthly webinars from September to May, alternating between a team sharing its work and an outside expert presenting information and new ideas, his team needs to get those events scheduled and present a complete schedule of events to participants as quickly as possible. Presenters often need to be scheduled well ahead of their presentations.

Setting the right time for an online event always creates stress for those who plan and facilitate webinars. Coming to consensus on a day and time that accommodates everyone works for small teams. A consistent schedule (e.g. the first Tuesday of each month at 2 p.m.) is obviously ideal.

Larger groups, of course, find it more difficult to accommodate individual schedules, but members need to be sensitive to the job responsibilities and schedules of participants and arrange for webinars at a time that creates as little disruption as possible. To ensure that those who miss a session can easily catch up and not feel left behind, the moderator makes sure the event is recorded and sends members a link to the recording as soon as possible after a webinar.

Technology questions

Technology Questions: Participants

- How do I log in?
- Do I need to install anything? How do I test that my computer is set up for this?
- How do I listen? Do I have to call a phone number?
- Will I be able to ask a question or make a comment? How?

Technology Questions: Presenters

- How do I log in? The same way as everyone else?
- Do I also have to call a phone number or do I speak directly through my computer? If I speak through my computer, do I need a headset? How do I do this?
- Will people see me on screen? If they do, where should I be so that I look okay?
- How will I be able to see or hear people's questions or comments?
- How do I move my PowerPoint slides? How do I show my video and launch my poll? Is someone else going to handle that for me?

Once a date and time for the webinar are decided, the moderator schedules the meeting on the webinar platform. This generates a web link that the moderator can send to attendees in and email announcing the event.

A good rule of thumb for a moderator is to provide attendees with an initial email with the link about the webinar a week before the meeting, including all of the technical requirements, and asking everyone to run appropriate tests on their computers. The moderator can send out a second reminder email the day before the event, including the bare essentials of how to participate and referencing the previous email if people have not done the preparation steps.

Step 3: Be explicit about technology requirements

Webinar participants need "the five W's" when preparing for a webinar: What is it? When is it? Who will be presenting? Where is it? (which can be translated as "What is the login link?"), and Why are we doing this? (i.e. What is the content/topic?).

Along with the five W's, webinar moderators, presenters

and attendees need to be able to answer a sixth crucial question: How?

Every webinar platform and every online meeting space is different. No matter how many webinars participants have attended or how technologically advanced people may seem, they still need to know exactly what is required to successfully navigate their way into a webinar room and to fully participate once they're in there.

Ensuring that all participants know what is expected and how to engage is particularly important if a team or organization is integrating webinars into its professional learning for the first time. Securing buy-in from all participants hinges on ensuring everyone is prepared to fully engage the technology and participate in a successful meeting.

The sidebar, Technology questions, gives a sample of questions that the moderator must be ready to answer from webinar attendees and presenters. Most platforms include a document that provides answers to these questions as well as a web link that runs a test on users' systems and alerts them if they need to do anything in order to participate in the webinar.

Nothing will derail a webinar faster and more completely than attendees not being comfortable with the technology and no one being on hand to anticipate and address their issues. Communicating these technical requirements early, asking all attendees to run appropriate tests to ensure they can successfully get into the webinar, and telling them how to contact the moderator if they have any problems will minimize the probability of technical assistance and troubleshooting that cuts into learning time during the event. It may even be wise to set up a test webinar that people can briefly join a few days before the event to make sure that everything works.

Of course, as a team gets more experienced using the webinar technology, these technical preparation steps will become second nature.

Step 4: Prepare a great webinar

Designing the content for a webinar requires the same attention to detail and understanding of the key principles of adult learning as designing a face-to-face presentation. "Interactivity and individualization are central to learning, whether the experience is face to face or online," says Chris Dede of the Harvard Graduate School of Education. "In face-to-face settings, you don't want to be just sitting in lectures, you want to have lively discussion where your voice is frequently heard, and online, you don't want to be just reading PDFs or watching streaming video, you want to be part of a lively, interpretive community that's sorting out different types of things" (Crow, 2010, p. 10).

As in face-to-face meetings (and probably even more so), the audience will tune out quickly if some key components are not built into an online meeting. Remember, "The design of learning influences its outcomes, particularly when the design incorporates core elements of effective learning" (Killion, 2013, p. 8).

As previously noted, webinar platforms make available a multitude of tools to help create an engaging and collaborative learning experience. Whether and how they are used can make or break a presentation.

The sample agenda of a PLC meeting presented in "Chapter 18: Professional Learning Communities" in this book is a great starting point for planning a webinar. Likewise, the sidebar, Sample webinar agenda, is an effective model for designing a well-paced, hour-long webinar that uses video, polling, reflection activities, and presentation slides to break the potential monotony of content delivery and provide multiple opportunities for engagement, reflection, and collaboration.

Here are a few details about the items on the list:

Norms. Establishing norms for a webinar is just as essential as establishing them for face-to-face meetings. Norms ensure that everyone knows when and how to share during the meeting. Can attendees type in questions or comments at any point (the usual norm), or should they wait until established reflection times? If people are on a phone line, do they need to mute their lines to avoid background noise? The answers to these and similar questions establish online norms that ensure all goes smoothly on the technical side once the meeting starts and require less time to establish as people become accustomed to webinars.

A set of meeting norms suggests how webinar participants should engage in the webinar. For example, here are the AEIOU norms for meeting online:

- **A**sk questions;
- **E**ngage fully;
- **I**ntegrate new information;
- **O**pen your mind to new views; and
- **U**tilize what you learn.

Sample webinar agenda

Welcome/Title Slide
1. Online norms
2. Meeting norms
3. Meeting agenda
4. Learning objectives (3)
5. Check-in/Opening activity
6. Poll (lead-in to content item #1)
7. Content item #1
   a. Lecture (4 slides)
   b. Video
   c. Reflection/Application
8. Poll (lead-in to content item #2)
9. Content Item #2
   a. Lecture (4 slides)
   b. Video
   c. Reflection/Application
10. Poll (lead-in to content item #3)
11. Content Item #3
    a. Lecture (4 slides)
    b. Activity
    c. Reflection/Application
12. Review of objectives and norms
    a. Poll
    b. Reflection/Application
13. Next steps
14. Details about next meeting
15. Closing activity/Check-Out

Objectives. Objectives outline the learning goals and key topics for the meeting. Typically, there should be no more than three distinct objectives for an hour-long webinar because only about three "big" pieces of content can be covered in an hour. Allowing time for reflection, questions and answers, and audience-member sharing, each key chunk of a presentation should take approximately 15 minutes. That means an hour-long webinar can cover establishing/reviewing norms and objectives at the start of the session, three chunks of key information, and discussion of next steps at the end.

Core content. This is the meat of the meeting. In the sidebar, Sample webinar agenda, each objective

Tips for presentation slides

- Use professional fonts that are easy to read.

- Make text large enough to read easily.

- The text color and font and the background color should complement each other, not compete with each other.

- Charts and graphs must be easy to read and quick to understand.

- Pictures and graphics can enhance content, but also distract from content. Use them wisely.

- The more words participants need to read on a slide, the greater the chance they aren't listening to the speaker.

- Good slides summarize and complement what the speaker is saying. Poor slides repeat what the speaker is saying or distract from what the speaker is saying.

- Don't use 20 words when 10 will do. Don't use three slides to make a point when one will do.

covered in the meeting includes the delivery of content, an engagement or multimedia piece, and processing and discussion time. Presenters can kick off reflection time by providing participants with reflection questions that are built into the presentation, or by allowing participants to ask questions on their own.

Next steps. While each section of the webinar is designed either to provide information or encourage collaboration and participation, the section devoted to next steps is perhaps the most important part of the meeting. One issue that arises among those who dismiss webinars as "quick hit" learning experiences is that participants can log into a meeting, give the webinar an hour of their time, and be done with it. Ensuring that webinars are simply one tool within a larger framework of professional learning means creating methods by which participants can expand on their learning and share with the group the challenges and successes that they are facing in implementing their learning. Setting a team norm

regarding follow-up communications and activities will ensure that the webinar is a jumping off point for a more comprehensive learning experience, not a stand-alone online meeting.

Step 5: Prepare slides

Numerous books, articles, and blog posts have been written on how to design effective presentation slides, and a quick web search of the term "designing Power-Point presentations" yields 1.7 million results. The fact is, there is no one way to design presentation slides that effectively communicate ideas during a webinar. Experienced webinar moderators can tell you, however, that there are rules that should guide the development of presentation slides. Some of those rules are presented in the sidebar Tips for presentation slides.

Slides can be powerful tools that visually enhance a presentation. They can also torpedo a webinar and distract those who attend it from engaging in actual learning during the presentation.

Step 6: Prepare everything else

This step may, of course, occur concurrently with Step 4. Notice in the sample agenda that, along with content being delivered with accompanying presentation slides, the webinar includes a video, two polls, activities, and time for reflection and discussion of how concepts can be applied to each attendee's work.

While a multitude of engagement tools are available during webinars, those planning content need to consider whether each piece is successfully advancing the goal of the meeting. For example, showing a video that provides an example that reinforces an objective of the meeting (such as a clip of a teacher implementing a strategy in her classroom) advances content.

Similarly, serious consideration must be given when planning reflection and discussion times. If the purpose of creating a stopping time for reflection is simply to allow a presenter to catch his or her breath, attendees are not going to focus their reflections and questions on learning and application of ideas.

Preparing content must include activities, but they must be meaningful activities. If they are not, no one will participate.

Step 7: Practice (show, don't tell)

It's one thing to **tell** webinar presenters how to log into the room, present their slides, and handle participants' questions and comments. It's another to **show** them. Without a practice run, no one's ready.

A good norm to establish when planning webinars is to do two practice runs with everyone who will be involved in delivering the presentation. The first should be a week in advance of the meeting, once the presentation is ready; the other should occur right before the actual event, in the meeting room itself.

There are three reasons to hold a practice meeting the week before the event:

1. To establish roles and responsibilities for "the real thing."
2. To make presenters comfortable with the technology they will be using and the support they will receive.
3. To run through content to make sure everything flows smoothly and will can be presented comfortably in the time allotted.

If problems occur regarding this third item, a week gives everyone plenty of time to adjust content.

During this practice run, everything that will be done during the actual meeting should be modeled. If presenters need to call a conference line, they should do it for the practice run. If videos will be shown or polls conducted during the meeting, they need to be practiced. Everyone involved in the practice session should go through each of their roles and responsibilities, testing the interactive components of the presentation, and doing an abbreviated (but timed) version of the actual presentation.

Establishing who will handle what during the live event gives confidence to presenters who may not be experienced in delivering webinars. They know their roles, and they know what will be handled for them by someone else. A good moderator builds trust with a presenter, allowing the presenter to focus on their content and feel confident that all other issues are being handled.

The moderator provides technical support for both presenters and attendees during the meeting. This person ensures that all of the presentation materials are properly loaded into the meeting room, engages attendees as they enter the room, and usually leads discussion of the online norms. The presenter provides the remainder of the content.

Even though a thorough practice has been run at least

a week before the actual event, having everyone who will be speaking or facilitating during the webinar enter the live room early on the day of the webinar is a valuable part of the process. If everyone logs in at least 15 minutes before the webinar, the moderator quickly re-establishes everyone's roles, allows those involved to double-check the technology, and possibly even go through a final dry run through the presentation. It may also be wise to ask individual attendees to log in early so they can get help with any small technological issues.

Step 8: The real thing: Conduct the webinar

True or false: Designing a quality presentation and conducting a thorough practice session with all involved ensures that everything will go well during your webinar.

Is an answer even required? No matter how prepared everyone is, successfully pulling off an online event is not guaranteed. From participants who haven't properly tested their systems and can't get into the room, to presenters on choppy phone lines, and participants on lines that aren't muted when they should be, to a wide range of other unforeseen issues, a moderator must be prepared to provide on-the-fly technical support while also fulfilling his or her responsibilities during the actual meeting.

Most webinar moderators have at some point experienced what they would refer to as a catastrophic event — something that goes wrong that causes a webinar to have to be canceled entirely. These events are rare, but they happen.

Avoiding common pitfalls

Pitfall #1: An attendee can't get into the room, hear properly, or view some portion or all of the presentation.

- *Preemptive solution:* Stress that all participants run appropriate system tests, and encourage them to enter the live meeting room early.

- *Live solution:* Provide offline assistance without disrupting the rest of the room (via email or instant message). Do not let any individual person delay the event with technical issues if everyone else is prepared and ready to begin.

Pitfall #2: The presenter is on a bad phone or Internet connection.

- *Preemptive solution:* Establish a norm requiring presenters to use a land line, and be on a wired Internet connection. Test all technology during the practice run and adjust if necessary.

- *Live solution:* Have a backup plan for delivering audio. Platforms have multiple ways presenters can be heard. Know and be ready to implement them. If a presenter loses Internet connection, a moderator can take over ensuring the presentation slides and other materials flow smoothly, and can share verbally any questions or comments that come in over the chat.

Pitfall #3: A video or other aspect of the presentation is not working.

- *Preemptive solution:* Test all components of the presentation during the practice run.

- *Live solution:* Don't use it. There will be ways to share it with attendees after the meeting. Do not waste learning time trying to make something work that isn't working.

Pitfall #4: Discussion amongst attendees is not focusing on the topic and is veering in multiple directions (a typical issue when attendees are familiar with one another).

- *Preemptive solution:* Set a norm that questions and comments must be directly related to content.

- *Live solution:* The moderator can either chat in or verbally redirect attendees to focus comments on the content.

Pitfall #5: Things are running behind schedule.

- *Preemptive solution:* Build time for each piece, particularly time set aside for reflection and sharing, into the event, and schedule them down to the minute.

- *Live solution:* As a moderator, send private chats to the presenter keeping him/her on schedule. Communicate to attendees that there will be additional *opportunities to share and ask questions following the meeting.*

Perhaps there is an emergency at the presenter's or the moderator's location, requiring them to leave the building. Or, most frustrating of all, something occurs with the webinar platform that prevents people from getting into a room, like a server crash. In these cases, if no other solution can be identified (e.g. just talking on a conference line and sending everyone the presentation materials to follow along), the last resort becomes a reality and the webinar needs to be canceled and rescheduled.

Barring those catastrophic events, there are common pitfalls that occur during webinars that experienced moderators learn to handle through trial and error. Read about several of them in the sidebar Avoiding common pitfalls. Some of these possible pitfalls can be addressed **before** they even occur, but some may have to be handled "live" during the webinar.

It is absolutely imperative, barring a catastrophic event, that a webinar begins on time, ends on time, and follows the online norms and agenda that have been established at the outset of the meeting. A moderator who can keep presenters and attendees on track and comfortable during the meeting has a greater chance of creating an effective learning opportunity for all involved. These basics are a particularly important outcome for attendees who are skeptical that a webinar can provide a quality learning experience.

Step 9: The webinar is over: Now what?

The most common activity webinar moderators engage in following the end of a successful online meeting is simply breathing a sigh of relief. But while a meeting may not have included any catastrophic events or even small technical glitches, that doesn't necessarily mean that it was effective *learning*. Only attendees can tell you that. Getting feedback from them following the end of the meeting is the best way to ensure that you make continuous improvement, and that participants will continue to value online learning events.

Smaller teams that meet online regularly may build in time to reflect on the successes and areas of improvement of a webinar at the end of the meeting itself. More commonly, the moderator can send attendees a quick survey following the end of the meeting that includes brief questions asking for feedback on what worked, what didn't, what could be improved, and any changes the team should make for future events. The sidebar, Webinar evaluation: Sample questions, provides a good basis for a post-webinar survey.

Providing participants with an opportunity to share feedback is a quick and effective way to get buy-in from participants and gather data on the effectiveness of both the technology and content of a webinar.

Step 10: The end is just the beginning

A common and previously mentioned misconception regarding webinars is that once they're over, they're over. This is only the case if webinar presenters, moderators, and attendees refuse to take full advantage of the learning opportunities available to them once their meeting ends.

Significant learning opportunities can be built around webinar content. If experts have been brought in to facilitate the webinar, what additional resources or discussion do they suggest to further the learning? Do they have websites that include additional resources?

Learning can be shared with others who did not attend the event in a variety of ways:

- By using social media to share key learning from the event;

Webinar evaluation: Sample questions

- Did you have any technical issues during the meeting?

- Did the meeting norms offer clear expectations for participation?

- What other norms could we add?

- Were the objectives of the meeting met?

- Did you feel there was enough time for you to ask questions and reflect on the content?

- What can we do better next time?

- What are two ways you or your team will apply your learning from today's session?

- By posting links to recorded webinars on the school or district website, or in an internal community that's been set up for educators;

- By pulling short clips from webinars and sending them to colleagues; and

- And, most importantly, by taking the knowledge and strategies gained from the meeting and sharing them with a professional learning community.

The end of a webinar is not the end, but is instead the beginning of an extended learning opportunity for the members of a professional learning community.

Variations

The type of webinar described in this chapter focuses primarily on the delivery of content. Even with reflection and discussion time built in, the majority of webinars do focus on providing content to a virtual audience. However, other effective models exist.

Since its inception in 2009, member schools in Learning Forward's Learning School Alliance (LSA) have engaged in monthly webinars throughout their year-long participation in the Alliance. A typical LSA cohort is made up of between ten and a dozen schools, each of which is represented by three to four members of the school's leadership teams. These team members participate in monthly webinars, then engage in follow-up discussion in an LSA community that has been set up for them in Learning Forward's online community. Leadership team members share their learning from the webinars and their discussion with members of PLCs in their schools.

Learning School Alliance webinars follow a format different from the ones that have been described in this chapter. Each month, a school presents a problem of practice that educators have been dealing with. The school's presentation is minimal — no more than 10 minutes, and rarely that long. The coordinator or facilitator sends supporting documents to fellow participants in advance, with the expectation that colleagues will study the documents and consider the problem of practice beforehand so they can use the majority of the time in the webinar to work through solutions.

Following a check-in activity and a review of norms and the agenda, the school presents its problem of practice. The facilitator then leads everyone through a protocol for feedback, which includes having colleagues from the other schools ask clarifying questions to ensure that they have a complete picture of the problem and provide "warm" and "cool" feedback." The vast majority of the time spent during the webinar is then spent assisting the presenting school by providing strategies and ideas to take back to their teams to address the problem.

This format has provided LSA members with an opportunity to take advantage of the expertise of colleagues from across North America to address issues specific to their learning teams. Follow-up questions and comments are then made asynchronously in the community following the event, creating an ongoing opportunity to reflect on and further address the issue. Each school has an opportunity to present its problem of practice during their time in LSA, with ongoing discussion for each taking place in the community throughout the groups' time together.

Another model for conducting a webinar is to treat it as a brainstorming session around a particular issue. Essentially the webinar platform is used as a tool to conduct a quick meeting, where people from different locations can gather to plan the content for an upcoming meeting with community members, for example. In this instance the platform becomes a tool for note-taking and recording, with a more informal process of guided discussion as opposed to the standard delivery of content.

Once a contract is signed or payment plan selected, virtually all webinar platforms allow for an unlimited number of events, which essentially allows school teams to use it for a variety of meeting types. Regardless of the goal or format of any webinar, however, it is important to establish and adhere to both online and meeting norms, outline objectives, and follow the other webinar best practices that have been outlined in this chapter.

Challenges and how to address them

In her *JSD* article, "Tapping Technology's Potential," Joellen Killion (2013) warns that

> Misuses of technology can occur in multiple ways, such as using technology as a substitute for all forms of professional learning; adding technology as a resource for professional learning without embedding it into a comprehensive plan for professional learning driven by a vision, definition, standards for all professional learning, and ongoing evaluation; and providing technology with no support for applying learning into practice or constructive feedback to refine practice over time. (Killion, p. 12)

This single statement encompasses many of the problems that can reduce (or completely eliminate) the effectiveness of webinars as tools for professional learning. Let's look at them individually:

Using technology as a substitute for learning. Obviously inviting participants into an empty webinar room with no presentation and no facilitator and telling them to learn is an over-simplified example of how technology is a vehicle for learning, not the learning itself. But there is a belief amongst some (even very skilled) presenters that the webinar technology will compensate for deficiencies in the design of a webinar. A lack of respect for the audience or the process of designing an effective online learning experience is difficult to recover from once a meeting has begun. The principles that guide effective collaborative team learning are the same for technology-based learning as they are with other formats.

Not applying feedback to refine practice over time. This can be translated to, "always be improving." Every online event is an opportunity to make the next online event better. Soliciting feedback on both the content and technology used in webinars is great; not implementing that feedback is malpractice.

Not embedding webinars into a comprehensive learning plan. The most frequent misuse of webinars as effective learning tools falls into this category. As covered previously, a webinar should be seen as a key component of a learning community, not the learning community itself. Eighty people attending a webinar do not represent a true learning community. Whether a team is conducting its own webinar or attending a webinar hosted by an external provider or organization, the end of the event should be seen as the beginning of the learning. The webinar is a starting point that provides the opportunity to design additional learning opportunities that build on the content and strategies learned during the event.

The single greatest challenge faced by those who develop and facilitate webinars is convincing potential participants that a live, online meeting is a valuable use of their time, given the myriad learning opportunities available to them to engage colleagues virtually and access resources in a matter of seconds. The following are excuses that run on a loop in the heads of those who coordinate webinars for their organizations:

"I had it on my schedule but forgot."

"Someone else watched (!) and summarized it for me."

"Can you just send me the PowerPoint?"

"I'll just watch the recording later."

Conclusion

Webinars can be true learning events. But like any valuable collaborative learning experience, webinars require planning and teamwork. Effective webinars push learning teams to increase their knowledge, launch further discussions, expand their resource portfolios, and extend their learning networks to include colleagues and experts they wouldn't have access to otherwise. To those who plan and execute webinars, the charge is simple. Make your webinars "can't miss" learning opportunities. Make them unforgettable.

References

Crow, T. (2010, February). Learning, no matter where you are: Q&A with Chris Dede. *JSD, 31*(1), 10–17.

Falk, J.K. & Drayton, B. (2009). *Creating and sustaining online professional learning communities.* New York, NY: Teachers College Press.

Johnson, L., Adams, S., Cummins, M., Estrada V., Freeman, A., & Ludgate, H. (2013). *NMC Horizon Report: 2013 K–12 Edition.* Austin, TX: The New Media Consortium.

Killion, J. (2013, February). Tapping technology's potential. *JSD, 34*(1), 10–14.

Killion, J. (2013). *Meet the promise of content standards: Tapping technology to enhance professional learning.* Oxford, OH: Learning Forward.

Learning Forward. (2011). *Standards for Professional Learning.* Oxford, OH: Author.

Author Biographies

Suzanne Bailey

Suzanne Bailey consults with leaders in school systems, business, industry, and government in the arena of whole systems change. Since 1980, she has helped organization leaders streamline and restructure services to improve results, conduct strategic future planning to provoke unprecedented action, and build internal capacity to implement complex, large-scale change. Business clients have included IBM, Hewlett Packard, Northern Telecom, Bank of Montreal, Kraft Foods, Shell Oil, and Scandinavian Airlines. Public sector clients have included the U.S. Army Corps of Engineers, Getty Museum, United Way, and President Clinton's Task Force on Sustainable Development. Education clients have included more than 40 school systems in the U.S. and Canada. In addition, Bailey has worked with indigenous cultures in creating long-range visions consistent with their cultures and beliefs. Now in semi-retirement, she enjoys shadow consulting and coaching other consultants and leaders. She resides in Northern California and enjoys a focus on celebrating health, a variety of outdoor activities, fine arts and her grandchildren. Contact her at suzannebailey77@gmail.com.

Victoria L. Bernhardt

Victoria L. Bernhardt is executive director of the *Education for the Future* Initiative whose mission is to build the capacity of learning organizations at all levels to gather, analyze, and use data to continuously improve learning for all students. She is also a research professor (currently on leave) in the College of Communication and Education at California State University, Chico. Bernhardt works with learning organizations all over the world to assist them with their continuous improvement

and data analysis. She is the author of 16 books on continuous school improvement and comprehensive data analysis. Contact her at *Education for the Future,* 530-898-4482, vbernhardt@csuchico.edu; website: http://eff.csuchico.edu.

Chris Bryan

Chris Bryan is a senior consultant with Learning Forward and an international consultant for school-based coaches in differentiated instruction and school improvement. Through the Center for Strategic Quality Professional Development, she has supported and facilitated schools' work to build and sustain change. Bryan has more than three decades of experience in education as a classroom teacher, learning specialist, mentor, staff developer, instructional coach, coach of coaches, and member of university partnership programs. She teaches and supervises student teachers at the University of Colorado Health Sciences Center and is an executive coach for principals in the Denver Public School District. Bryan is co-developer of the Learning Forward Coaches' Academy and of advanced coaching modules offered through Learning Forward. She is past president of Learning Forward Colorado and a current member of the Affiliate Leadership Committee. Contact her at bryan.chris48@gmail.com.

Cathy Caro-Bruce

Cathy Caro-Bruce is an educational consultant with the Wisconsin Department of Public Instruction, helping school districts build systems and strategies to improve learning outcomes for students. For 30 years, she was a staff and organization development specialist for the Madison Metropolitan School District, and for 15 years coordinated classroom action research as part of the district professional development program. Caro-Bruce was a co-author, with Mary Klehr, of *Creating Equitable Classrooms Through Action Research* (Corwin Press, 2007). She authored a book, *Action Research: Facilitator's Handbook,* published by the National Staff Development Council, to assist educators who lead and facilitate action research initiatives. She also co-authored a chapter, "A school district-based action research program in the United States" in the Sage *Handbook of Educational Action Research,* (S.E. Noffke and B. Somekh, 2009). With colleague Ken Zeichner of the University of Wisconsin-Madison, she received a grant from the Spencer and MacArthur Foundations to examine the impact of action research on teachers and students. In 1998, she was the recipient of the Best Non-Dissertation Award, awarded by the National Staff Development Council, for the report on findings from that study. Caro-Bruce also works with school districts around the country helping them implement action research based on principles that drive high-quality professional development initiatives. Contact her at ccarobru@wisc.edu.

Heather Clifton

Heather Clifton consults with schools, districts, state and municipal agencies, and nonprofit organizations in many aspects of professional learning and organizational reform. She has provided executive coaching to school principals and teachers at all levels and has facilitated the work of district and school leadership teams. She offers training and support for instructional coaches and their principals, and has experience as a teacher, principal, and central office curriculum and staff development specialist. She is co-developer of training modules for Learning Forward's Coaches' Academy, and was facilitator of the Community Learning Network, a project of the Anne E. Casey Foundation. She is past president of Learning Forward Colorado. She currently works as the implementation manager of a College Board School. Contact her at hlclifton@gmail.com.

Amy B. Colton

Amy B. Colton, executive director, Learning Forward Michigan, and senior consultant, Learning Forward, facilitates the effective design, implementation, and evaluation of standards-based professional learning to increase the capacity of educators to improve student learning. As a contractor with the American Institutes of Research's Great Lakes Regional Center, she supported the Michigan Department of Education in closing the African American achievement gap. She played a critical role in the adoption of the Michigan Professional Learning Policy and Standards. Colton served as an education teacher and district professional learning consultant early in her career. As teacher-in-residence of the National Board for Professional Teaching Standards, she helped coordinate the development of the Board's first teaching certificate. She holds a doctorate in education from the University of Michigan, and is a published author in *Journal of Teacher Education, Educational Leadership,* the Center on Great Teachers and Leaders at American Institutes for Research, and *JSD.* Contact her at acolton2@gmail.com.

Dan Condon

Dan Condon is an education activist and currently serves as the associate director of professional development at the Eagle Rock School & Professional Development Center, a corporate social responsibility initiative of the American Honda Education Corporation, a nonprofit subsidiary of the American Honda Motor Company. As the founding director of Public Allies in Colorado (holding the same position Michelle Obama held in Chicago), he prepared a new generation of innovative educators. He was selected as one of 20 young visionaries of 1996 by *Who Cares* Magazine, was named one of 40 under 40 by the *Boulder County Business Report* in 2010, received the inaugural CES Small Schools 'Commitment to Equity' award, and received the 2010 Governor's Commission on Community Service "Still Getting Things Done" award. He serves as a faculty member with Public Allies, Inc.'s Leadership Practice in collaboration with Northwestern University's Asset-Based Community Development Institute. He is a faculty member for the National Truancy Intervention & Prevention Center through the National Center for School Engagement. He serves as a leader with Opportunity Nation. Contact him at dcondon@eaglerockschool.org.

Kathleen Cushman

Kathleen Cushman is an educator and journalist who has focused on the lives and learning of youth for 25 years. In 2001 she co-founded What Kids Can Do (WKCD.org) with Barbara Cervone to bring the diverse perspectives of students to educators and policymakers. Her work there has resulted in nine book collaborations with students, including *Fires in the Bathroom: Advice for Teachers from High School Students* (New Press, 2003), *Fires in the Mind: What Kids Can Tell Us About Motivation and Mastery* (Jossey-Bass, 2010), and the multimedia e-book *The Motivation Equation* (motivationequation.org). In 2012 Cushman and Cervone co-authored "Teachers at Work," case studies of student-centered teaching practice in six high schools (Boston: JFF), followed in 2014 by "Learning by Heart: The Power of Social-Emotional Learning in Secondary Schools" (WKCD). Her mixed-media work for WKCD includes the YouTube video series "Just Listen: Youth Talk About Learning" and a series of "Case Studies of Practice" in which young people describe their experiences of getting to mastery. Cushman's work in school documentation and design for the Coalition of Essential Schools, the Annenberg Challenge, the Deeper Learning initiative, and others has given her a deep understanding of how school design, structures, and teaching practices can better support adolescent motivation, engagement, and mastery. She works with educators around the country. Contact her at kathleencushman@mac.com.

Ann Delehant

Ann Delehant is an experienced facilitator, learning leader, coach, and agent of system and school change. Her current work focuses on designing and facilitating professional learning programs; advancing the work of collaborative teams; supporting the work of teacher leaders, administrators and coaches; and coaching individuals and teams to establish and achieve great visions while meeting individual and group goals. A senior consultant for Learning Forward, Delehant also is a member of The Dolan Team, a management and labor-consulting firm that specializes in

trying to open, clarify, and improve relationships as a means of improving the work of the system. Earlier in her career, she worked for the City School District in Rochester, New York, as the director of staff development. She has notable state and national affiliations: She served as a Trustee of Learning Forward and was a founding member of Learning Forward New York. She received the NSDC Distinguished Service Award in 1996. She was a founding member of Coaching School Results. Delehant is the author of *Making Meetings Work* (co-published by Corwin and Learning Forward, 2006). Contact her at adelehant@gmail.com.

Alan Dichter

Alan Dichter is a former New York City teacher, principal, director of leadership and new school development, and local instructional superintendent. He helped create and oversee New York's Executive Leadership Academy, a program designed to help leaders develop and incorporate facilitative leadership practices. He is author of a number of articles on leadership and professional development as well as being co-author of *The Power of Protocols: An Educator's Guide to Better Practice* (Teachers College Press, 2003) and *Going Online with Protocols: New Tools for Teaching and Learning* (Teachers College Press, 2012). He has also worked as a coach/facilitator for the New York City Leadership Academy and most recently as director of leadership development for Portland, Oregon, public schools. He now does independent consulting and lives with his wife, Vivian and sons Ben and Jacob in Portland. Contact him at alan.dichter@gmail.com.

Eleanor Dougherty

Eleanor Dougherty is a consultant specializing in curriculum design and professional development. During her career, she has taught in public, private, and postsecondary institutions and worked in both practice and policy organizations, including the U.S. Department of Education and the Education Trust. Her work over the last two decades has focused on literacy and its role in the larger curriculum, particularly in the core subjects. Dougherty is the author of numerous articles and three education books, including *Assignments Matter: Making the Connections That Help Students Meet Standards* (ASCD, 2012). She is currently involved in developing a national literacy strategy to help teachers in the core subjects align their practice to the Common Core State Standards. Contact her at edthink.ecd.@gmail.com.

Carolyn J. Downey

Carolyn J. Downey is president of Palo Verde Associates, an educational consultant firm. She is also professor emeritus in the Educational Leadership Department, College of Education at San Diego State University. She formerly was the Superintendent for the Kyrene School District, Tempe, Arizona, and served over 30 years as an administrator in K–12 systems. Downey was a senior staff member in curriculum and staff development for the Ohio State Center for Vocational and Technical Education. She was also a staff member for the Southwest Regional Laboratory for Educational Research and Development for four years. Downey has written over 30 books and articles, including the book and multimedia kit, *Three-Minute Walk-Through* (Corwin Press, 2004); *Advancing the Three-Minute Walk-Through: Mastering Reflective Practice;* (Corwin Press, 2009) and *50 Ways to Close the Achievement Gap* (Corwin Press, 2008). She is also the lead author of several books about quality in systems and is the author of the series *Mentoring the Reflective Principal* by Curriculum Management Systems, Inc. (CMSi). She is a senior lead trainer, senior lead auditor and a board member of CMSi. Downey is an international consultant in several areas, including quality leadership, systems thinking, urban school district reform, organizational development and motivation, planning and the change process, working with low-performing schools and districts, instructional supervision, curriculum development, staff development, program evaluation, site-based management, and program budgeting. Contact her at cdowney@san.rr.com.

Lois Brown Easton

Lois Easton works as a consultant, coach, and author. She is particularly interested in learning designs — for adults and for students. She retired in 2005 as director of professional development at Eagle Rock School and Professional Development Center, Estes Park, Colorado. Prior to Eagle Rock, Easton was director of Re:Learning Systems at the Education Commission of the States (ECS); director of

curriculum and assessment planning, Arizona Department of Education; and English/Language arts coordinator, Arizona Department of Education. A middle school English teacher for 15 years, Easton earned her Ph.D. at the University of Arizona. Easton was co-chair of the 2001 NSDC Conference in Denver. She has been a frequent presenter at conferences and contributor to educational journals. Her books include *The Other Side of Curriculum: Lessons From Learners* (2002), *Powerful Designs for Professional Learning* (1st edition in 2004, 2nd edition in 2008, 3rd edition in 2015); *Protocols for Professional Learning* (2009), and *Professional Learning Communities By Design: Putting the Learning Back Into PLCs* (2011). Her book *Engaging the Disengaged: How Schools Can Help Struggling Students Succeed* (2008) won the Educational Book of the Year Award from Kappa Delta Gamma. She lives in Tucson, Arizona. Contact her at leastoners@aol.com.

Marcella Emberger

Marcella (Marcy) Emberger is the former director of the Maryland Assessment Consortium, a nonprofit organization created to support school improvement among Maryland school districts. She now serves as a consultant who specializes in building learning communities through examination of classroom assessments. She is a faculty member with the ASCD Understanding by Design cadre and a co-Teacher with the Differentiated Instruction cadre. She also is an adjunct professor at the University of New Brunswick where she teaches assessment. As an instructor at Johns Hopkins University School of Continuing Studies, she taught action research and teacher leadership courses. Her current interests include supporting curriculum and assessment for indigenous cultures. Her most recent publications include, "UbD and PYP: Complementary planning frameworks" with Jay McTighe and Steven Carber, *International School Journal,* Vol. XXVII, No.1, November 2008; "Helping Teachers Improve Classroom Assessments," *Principal Leadership,* May 2007; and "Helping Teachers Think Like Assessors," *Principal,* March/April 2006. Contact her at marcy@marcyemberger or through her website: www.marcyemberger.com.

Matthew Esterman

Matthew Esterman is a secondary (grades 7–12) history teacher in Sydney, Australia. He holds a teaching degree from Macquarie University, a Master of Learning Science and Technology degree from the University of Sydney and a Master of Arts in Modern History from Macquarie University. He is currently the elearning coordinator at St Scholastica's College, a Catholic independent girls' school where he is responsible for the development of staff pedagogical and technical skills in a range of contexts from individual training to whole-staff workshops. Esterman has been heavily involved in the TeachMeet Sydney movement, a growing group of keen educators who hold "teachmeets" to share ideas, build their personal learning networks (PLNs) and inspire each other. Esterman is also on the Board of the ICT Educators' Association of New South Wales (ICTENSW) that promotes the study of computer science and the use of ICT for learning. He is currently undertaking further study in the Master of Research course at Macquarie University looking to investigate the factors influencing teachers' self-efficacy with, and use of, technology in the classroom. Contact him at Learning.esterman@gmail.com.

Stacy Galiatsos

Stacy Galiatsos brings almost 20 years of experience in education. She began her career as a high school English teacher and then joined the staff of the Annenberg Foundation's Children Achieving Challenge in Philadelphia. From there, she served as a member of Superintendent Vicki Phillips' leadership team as the director of development and acting director of human resources at the School District of Lancaster (Pennsylvania). In Lancaster, she raised $35 million in competitive funding, which, most importantly, supported innovative curriculum design efforts and the improvement of teaching and learning across the district. Galiatsos then served as an education and development consultant to a variety of entities, including the Pennsylvania Department of Education, Portland Schools Foundation, New Visions for Public Schools, Expeditionary Learning, and others. Most recently, Galiatsos was the chief of staff at New Visions for Public Schools and then a design team member of the Literacy Design Collaborative. Galiatsos

graduated *cum laude* with honors in English from Colgate University and received a Master of Arts in English from Stanford University. Contact her at sgaliatsos@mac.com.

Oscar Graybill

Oscar Graybill is an independent educational consultant specializing in training, coaching, and consulting of school leaders in the art and practice of genuine dialogue. Over the last 37 years, Graybill has taught and coached at the secondary level and served as a central office administrator. In the classroom, he facilitated dialogue in the form of Socratic Seminars to engage students in thoughtful and rigorous conversations. As director of Socratic Seminars International, he works with scores of teachers and administrators throughout the United States in the art and practice of dialogue by providing training, coaching, and consulting in Socratic Seminar leadership skills. As director of dialogue leadership, Graybill brings genuine dialogue to school leadership by consulting with superintendents, principals, and school faculties in dialogue facilitation that promotes and supports professional learning communities. He also specializes in facilitating professional learning in cooperative learning, Socratic questioning, critical thinking and critical reading strategies that support teachers in addressing Common Core State Standards. Contact him at Oscar@DialogueLeadership.com or at www.SocraticSeminars.com.

Cindy Harrison

Cindy Harrison is an international education consultant in instructional coaching, leadership, organizational change, and professional learning. Harrison consults with school districts, professional groups, and organizations throughout the world providing training and on-site services in creating instructional coaching programs, teacher leader programs and evaluation systems for principals and teachers. Currently, she is working with state agencies and districts implementing the Common Core State Standards. She previously served as director of staff development in a large suburban school district with 32,000 students and 42 school sites, designing and delivering a variety of professional learning programs for administrators, teachers, and classified staff. She has been a middle school principal, teacher at all secondary levels, a curriculum writer, and a central office director. She is the co-author with Joellen Killion of *Taking the Lead: New Roles for Teachers and School-Based Coaches* (NSCD, 2006). Contact her at Harrison.cindy@gmail.com.

Lynmarie Hilt

Lynmarie Hilt is an instructional technology integrator and coach in the Eastern Lancaster County School District in Lancaster County, Pennsylvania, where she serves three elementary schools. Prior to her current position she served as elementary principal for five years in the same district. Hilt is an avid blogger and contributor to social networks such as Twitter, and has presented at various local, state, and national conferences on topics ranging from professional learning to networked educational leadership. She also teaches the uses of technology to support today's educational leader through online graduate courses for Powerful Learning Practice and as an adjunct instructor for Cabrini College. Hilt has contributed to various publications in print and online, including *The Connected Teacher: Powering Up* from Powerful Learning Practice and the Connected Principals blog. Her work and experiences have been featured in *Education Week, THE Journal, Personal Learning Networks: Using the Power of Connections to Transform Education* by Will Richardson and Rob Mancabelli, and Eric Sheninger's *Digital Leadership: Changing Paradigms for Changing Times*. Contact her at lynhilt@gmail.com, via her blog (lynhilt.com), and on Twitter @lynhilt.

Joellen Killion

Joellen Killion is senior advisor for Learning Forward, and formerly its deputy executive director. She is currently leading a seven-state initiative focused on transforming professional learning to support implementation of Common Core State Standards. Killion is a frequent contributor to *JSD*. Her books about what works in middle, elementary, and high schools summarized two-year studies she did of content-specific staff development. Her study of schools that have received the U.S. Department of Education's Model Professional Development Awards resulted in *Teachers Who Learn, Kids Who Achieve: A Look at Model Professional Development*. She has also published *E-Learning for Educators: Implementing the Standards* (NSDC and NICI, 2000); *Assessing Impact: Evaluating Staff Development, 2nd edition* (NSDC, 2008); *Collaborative Professional Learning Teams in School and Beyond: A Tool Kit for New Jersey Educators* (New Jersey Department of Education, the New Jersey Professional Teaching Standards Board, and NSDC, 2008); *Taking the Lead: New Roles for Teacher and School-Based Coaches* (NSDC, 2006; with Cindy Harrison); *The Learning Educator: A New Era in Professional Learning* (NSDC, 2007; with Stephanie Hirsh); *Becoming a Learning School* (NSDC, 2009; with Patricia Roy); *and Coaching Matters* (Learning Forward, 2012; with Cindy Harrison, Chris Bryan, and Heather Clifton). Contact her at joellen.killion@learningforward.org.

Mary Klehr

Mary Klehr holds a joint Madison Metropolitan School District/ University of Wisconsin-Madison appointment as clinical supervisor for the Midvale-Lincoln Elementary Professional Development School Partnership in teacher education, which prepares skilled and caring teachers who are committed to working in culturally diverse, urban public school districts. Klehr was a 4th-grade teacher when she first learned about action research, and it entirely changed her understanding of how and by whom pedagogical knowledge is constructed. She currently coordinates the Madison District's Classroom Action Research program and facilitates research groups. She recently completed her doctoral dissertation featuring K–12 teachers who use aesthetic research methods to study classroom life. Klehr has contributed to a number of articles about the power and importance of teacher voice in educational research, and co-authored *Creating Equitable Classrooms Through Action Research* (Corwin Press, 2007) with Cathy Caro-Bruce. She worked in educational theater before becoming an elementary teacher, and has degrees from Brown University and UW-Madison. Contact her at mklehr@madison.k12.wi.us

Georgea M. Langer

Georgea M. Langer has a long history of work with teachers' professional learning. In her 24 years with the Eastern Michigan University Department of Teacher Education, she led several initiatives to improve teacher preparation and assessment. At the same time, Langer joined Amy Colton to study and develop classroom teachers' ability to define, assess, analyze, and reflect upon their pupils' learning as displayed in student work samples. This work culminated in the 2003 ASCD bestseller, *Collaborative Analysis of Student Work: Improving Teaching and Learning.* The second edition will be published in 2015 by Corwin Press. Since receiving her doctorate in educational psychology (Research on Teaching) at Stanford University, Langer has published extensively in the areas of staff development (as Georgea M. Sparks), teacher education, and teachers' reflective inquiry in journals such as the *Journal of Educational Psychology, Educational Leadership, The Journal of Teacher Education,* and *JSD.* She has presented workshops on these topics nationally and internationally with the Association for Supervision and Curriculum Development (ASCD), Phi Delta Kappa, and numerous states, counties, districts, and schools. She is the co-author of two preservice methods textbooks. Contact her at glanger1@att.net.

Anne C. Lewis

Anne C. Lewis is an education policy writer specializing in documentation, narration and analysis of education change and development. As a journalist, she has focused on making education research and initiatives accessible to wide audiences. She wrote the national affairs commentary in *Phi Delta Kappan* for more than 20 years, prepared reports on education investments for several national foundations, consulted for and wrote reports for most major national and state policy groups in education, and was the editorial consultant for the Literacy Design Collaborative for five years. For 10 years, Lewis was editor of the weekly *Education USA.* She received awards for her newspaper reporting and is a past president of the Education Writers Association. She resides most of the time in Mexico. Contact her at anneclewis@earthlink.net.

Catherine C. Lewis

Currently a distinguished research scholar at Mills College, Catherine Lewis comes from three generations of public school teachers. Fluent in Japanese, she has conducted research in Japanese and U.S. schools for 35 years. Many U.S. educators have been introduced to lesson study through her book *Lesson Study Step by Step: How Teacher Learning Communities Improve Instruction* (Heinemann, 2011, co-authored with Jackie Hurd) and videos "Can You Lift 100 Kilograms?" and "How Many Seats?: A U.S. Lesson Study Cycle." Lewis has been principal investigator for projects funded by the National Science Foundation and the U.S. Department of Education, including a randomized, controlled trial of lesson study with mathematical resource kits that significantly increased in both teachers' and students' knowledge of fractions. The study, conducted with Rebecca Perry, was identified by the What Works Clearinghouse as one of only two studies (of 634 reviewed) of mathematics professional learning that demonstrated impact on students' mathematical proficiency and met scientific criteria. Lewis is author of more than 40 publications on elementary education and child development, including the award-winning book *Educating Hearts and Minds: Reflections on Japanese Preschool and Elementary Education* (Cambridge University Press, 1995). Videos and articles available at www.lessonresearch.net. Contact her at clewis@mills.edu.

Tom Manning

Tom Manning is the associate director of e-learning for Learning Forward. He has directed the implementation of a wide range of e-learning projects in the organization, including the launch of the Learning Exchange online community of practice, virtual conferences, and e-learning programs focused on key issues for educators. He works with Learning Forward authors and other leaders in the field to provide online learning experiences that reflect Learning Forward's Standards for Professional Learning. Before joining Learning Forward, Manning worked with a number of universities to develop online graduate programs. He served as a case writer for the Center for Reform of School Systems, and reported on education issues for the *Houston Chronicle* and *Austin American Statesman*. His work has been published in the *Journal of Cases in Educational Leadership*. Contact him at tom.manning@learningforward.org.

Jay McTighe

Jay McTighe is an accomplished author, having published articles in a number of leading educational journals. He has co-authored thirteen books, including the best-selling *Understanding By Design* series with Grant Wiggins. McTighe has an extensive background in professional learning and is a featured speaker at national, state, and district conferences and workshops. He has made presentations in 47 states within the United States, in 7 Canadian provinces, and internationally in 19 countries on six continents. He received his undergraduate degree from the College of William and Mary, earned a master's degree from the University of Maryland and completed postgraduate studies at the Johns Hopkins University. He was selected to participate in the Educational Policy Fellowship Program through the Institute for Educational Leadership in Washington, D.C., and served as a member of the National Assessment Forum. Since education is a "learning" profession McTighe set a learning goal when he was 57 years of age to be surfing by 60. He did it! Contact him at jmctigh@aol.com.

David Niguidula

David Niguidula is founder of Ideas Consulting, an educational technology and consulting firm based in Providence, Rhode Island, and developer of the Richer Picture software. He has been involved in research in educational technology since the 1980s, and led the first research project on digital portfolios while at the Coalition of Essential Schools and Annenberg Institute for School Reform at Brown University. Through Ideas Consulting, Nguidula has led professional learning workshops to help schools throughout the U.S. successfully implement portfolios in their own settings. He has also led development of additional software tools for authentic assessment, calibration, data dashboards and tracking progress toward graduation. He works with policymakers and educators on statewide implementation of portfolios, including the use of portfolios as a graduation requirement. His most recent work helps

schools connect portfolios to other initiatives, including curriculum mapping, individual learning plans and personal literacy plans. Nguidula received two bachelors' degrees (in computer science and education) from Brown University and his doctorate in Instructional Technology and Media from Teachers College, Columbia University. Contact him at david@richerpicture.com; website: www.richerpicture.com.

Colin Packard

Colin Packard completed his role as the professional development fellow at Eagle Rock School & Professional Development Center in 2013, part of which involved him in managing the Professional Development Center and working with visiting educators from around the world. In 2010, Packard and two former undergraduate classmates traveled to India to produce a documentary, called "Talim," on grassroots innovation, sustainable development, and education. While there, he started on his path into rethinking education and community development. While living in Chicago, he moved into a position with Public Allies Chicago and worked with the National Runaway Safeline (formerly the National Runaway Switchboard), providing mediation and crisis intervention to runaway and homeless youth and their families. At Public Allies, Packard and a small team founded a partnership between students at the City Colleges of Chicago and the directing staff of the Peace School to facilitate peaceful communities among campuses across the city. Currently, he is the community programs manager and chief storyteller at FoodLab Detroit (www. foodlabdetroit.com), where he designs, organizes, and manages communications to facilitate a network of local food entrepreneurs, partner organizations, and key community players. Contact him at colinmichael36@gmail.com or colin@foodlabdetroit.com.

Cameron Paterson

Cameron Paterson is a history teacher and the mentor of learning and teaching, responsible for the strategic leadership of learning and teaching and promoting excellence in teaching practice at Shore School in Australia. He has recently worked at Harvard as a teacher education program advisor (2010–2011), and a fellow at the Project

Zero Classroom and the Future of Learning Institute (2013). He holds postgraduate degrees in education (Harvard), history (University of Sydney), philosophy of education, (University of New England) and educational administration (University of New England). He has received an Australian Davos Connection Future Summit Leadership Award, a Premier's History Scholarship, and a New South Wales Minister's Quality Teaching Award. Contact him at cpaterso@shore.nsw.edu.au.

Kay Psencik

Kay Psencik is a senior consultant with Learning Forward, designing professional learning for principals including establishing effective coaching approaches. She has a bachelor's degree from the University of Mary Hardin-Baylor, master's in educational administration from Texas State, and a doctorate from Baylor University. She has been a preconference and conference presenter and has published several articles: "Site Planning in a Strategic Context," *Educational Leadership,* ASCD, April 1991; "Orchestrating Resources for Students at Austin ISD," *Insights,* Texas Association of School Administrators, 1996; "Building Facilities to Equalize Opportunities for Kids," *Insights,* Texas Association of School Administrators, 1997; and "Instruction First: A Process for Facility Planning," *The School Administrator,* 1997. She and Stephanie Hirsh, executive director of Learning Forward, co-authored *Transforming Schools through Powerful Planning* (Learning Forward, 2004). She also published *Accelerating Student and Staff Learning, Purposeful Curriculum Collaboration* (Corwin Press, 2009). *The Coach's Craft* was published by Learning Forward in 2011. With Hirsh and Fred Brown, deputy executive director of Learning Forward, Psencik authored *Becoming a Learning System,* published in 2014. Contact her at kay.psencik@outlook.com.

Stevi Quate

From the time she was a young girl, Stevi Quate knew she wanted to teach. With her friends seated on the floor, she would stand in front of the chalkboard in her playroom, make up lessons on the spot, and charge her friends two cents. Years later when she taught secondary students, she learned to avoid impromptu teaching. After teaching for

nearly 30 years, she moved to the Colorado Department of Education as the state's literacy coordinator. Missing the classroom, she returned to teaching at the University of Colorado at Denver (UCD) where she worked with pre-service teachers and teachers working on their graduate degrees. At UCD, she launched Colorado Critical Friends. Over the years, she has been the director of Colorado Writing Project, president of Colorado Language Arts Society and Colorado Council of International Reading, and co-editor of the *Colorado Reading Journal.* Along with John McDermott, she is the author of *Clock Watchers: Six Steps to Motivating and Engaging Disengaged Students Across the Content Areas* (Heinemann, 2009) and *The Just-Right Challenge* (Heinemann, 2013). Currently, she consults across nationally and internationally. Contact her at steviq@gmail.com.

John D. Ross

John Ross has spent more than 15 years helping educators understand how technology integration enhances school improvement efforts. Formerly the director of the Institute for the Advancement of Emerging Technologies in Education and the director of technology for the Appalachia Regional Comprehensive Center (ARCC), he currently works as an independent educational consultant. He spearheaded the launch of a regional online professional learning environment in 2004 and has since designed and facilitated online professional learning with thousands of educators, also connecting with others across the nation through podcasts, webcasts, webconferences, social networks, dabbling in Second Life, and his blog. His book, *Online Professional Development: Design, Deliver, Succeed!* (Corwin, 2011) was selected as book-of-the-month for July 2011 by Learning Forward and was a publisher's bestseller in its first year of publication. He taught an online graduate class based on the textbook he co-authored with Katherine Cennamo from Virginia Tech and Peg Ertmer from Purdue, *Technology Integration for Meaningful Classroom Use: A Standards-Based Approach* (Cengage Learning, 2009), and was a classroom teacher for 10 years. Ross holds a doctorate in curriculum and instruction and instructional technology from Virginia Tech. You can find out more about him on his website TeachLearnTech.com. Contact him at JR@TeachLearnTech.com.

Michael Soguero

Michael Soguero was a founding member of the Eagle Rock School and Professional Development Center development team in Estes Park, Colorado, which was created as a laboratory for reengaging students who did not expect to graduate from high school. This formative experience laid the groundwork for leadership in New York City's burgeoning high school reform movement. Soguero became the co-Director of the School for the Physical City and later the founder and director of the Bronx Guild, recognized by Teachers College for "Excellence in Teaching." He served as mentor to other aspiring principals and partnered for teacher training with the Teachers College at Columbia University. This experience led him to become a lead facilitator for the Scaffolded Apprenticeship program within the New York City Leadership Academy where he sharpened his facilitation skills, his broad understanding of urban school reform, and the power of dynamic leadership as a means to reform schools and change the lives of students. After nearly 10 years in New York City, Soguero returned to Eagle Rock as the director of professional development. He is an avid reader and passionate about the latest organizational development theories and facilitation practices. Contact him at msoguero@eaglerockschool.org.

Lee Teitel

Lee Teitel teaches courses at the Harvard Graduate School of Education on leadership development, on partnership and networking, and on understanding organizations and how to improve them. He directs the Masters'-level School Leadership Program. He was the founding director and then faculty senior associate of the Executive Leadership Program for Educators, a five-year collaboration of Harvard's Graduate School of Education, Business School, and Kennedy School of Government that focused on bringing high-quality teaching and learning to scale in urban and high-need districts. As a consultant, Teitel works frequently with superintendents, central office staff, union leaders, principals, and teacher leaders to support school and district improvement efforts. Teitel is coauthor (with Liz City, Richard Elmore, and Sarah Fiarman) of *Instructional Rounds in Education: A Network Approach to Improving Teaching and Learning* (Harvard Education Press, 2009). He has facilitated or helped launch instructional rounds networks in 10 states in the United States and in Australia, Canada, and Sweden. His most recent book is *School-Based Instructional Rounds: Improving Teaching and Learning Across Classrooms* (Harvard Education Press, 2013). Contact him at Lee_Teitel@Harvard.edu.

Patricia A. Wasley

Currently the chief executive officer at Teaching Channel (Tch), Patricia Wasley oversees this nonprofit organization that aims to revolutionize the way teachers learn so that they can improve their ability to lift student achievement. The Tch seeks to affect adult learning through a PBS-quality video library of teachers working with children in classrooms across the U.S., three seasons of the PBS show, Teaching Channel Presents, the Teams group collaboration platform, and Tch's newest product, Learning Labs. Previously, she served as the dean of the College of Education at the University of Washington where she was the co-PI on "Teachers for a New Era" and instrumental in building local and national partnerships as well as partnerships with institutions in China, South Africa, and England. Before that, she was the dean of the Graduate School of Education at Bank Street College in New York City. She began her education career as a public school teacher and administrator and then served as senior researcher for school change with the Coalition of Essential Schools and at the Annenberg Institute for School Reform at Brown University. She has accumulated a substantial record of action-based research on the improvement of teachers' capacity to serve the students they teach. Wasley is the author of numerous articles and several books on school reform, including *Teachers Who Lead* (Teachers College Press, 1991) and *Stirring the Chalkdust* (Teachers College Press, 1994), and and co-author of *Kids and School Reform* (Jossey-Bass, 1997). Contact her at pwasley@teachingchannel.org.

Janet Mannheimer Zydney

Janet Mannheimer Zydney is an associate professor in Curriculum and Instruction at University of Cincinnati's College of Education, Criminal Justice, and Human